THE BOY MECHANIC

BOOK TWO — 1915

1000 Things for Boys to Do

Lindsay Publications Inc

The Boy Mechanic
Book 2

Originally published by
Popular Mechanics Press
Chicago

Reprinted by
Lindsay Publications Inc
Bradley IL 60915

paper edition: ISBN 1-55918-067-6
cloth edition: ISBN 1-55918-068-4

1 2 3 4 5 6 7 8 9 0

1991

THE BOY MECHANIC

BOOK 2

Printed in U. S. A.

See Page 24

THE BOY MECHANIC

BOOK 2

1000 THINGS FOR BOYS TO DO

HOW TO CONSTRUCT

DEVICES FOR WINTER SPORTS, MOTION-PICTURE CAMERA, INDOOR GAMES, REED FURNITURE, ELECTRICAL NOVELTIES, BOATS, FISHING RODS, CAMPS AND CAMP APPLIANCES, KITES AND GLIDERS, PUSHMOBILES, ROLLER COASTER, FERRIS WHEEL

AND

HUNDREDS OF OTHER THINGS WHICH DELIGHT EVERY BOY

WITH 995 ILLUSTRATIONS

POPULAR MECHANICS PRESS
CHICAGO

After the First Station has been Selected, It is Marked by a Pile of Stones, a Stake, or, If Precise Work is to be Done, a Tack in the Top of a Stake. The Table is Then Set Up over This Station Point and Leveled So That the Surface of the Paper will Be Truly Horizontal

The Boy Surveyor

Plane-Table Surveying

by

HAROLD G. McGEE

[In the training of a boy for a trade or profession there is none so profitable for outdoor work as that of a surveyor. This article sets forth how to accomplish surveying and the making of simple maps with the use of commonplace tools that any boy can make.—Editor.]

Surveying and map making have always been two of the most interesting things a civil engineer has had to do. And, like George Washington, many of the men we look up to today as successes in different lines worked as surveyors in their younger days. Surveying takes one out of doors, and is apt to lead him into the unknown and unexplored byways of the earth.

Though modern surveyors often use precise and expensive instruments, creditable surveys can be made with simple and inexpensive apparatus. Of such apparatus, two of the simplest are the plane table and the camera. Since one must know the principles of plane-table surveying before he can do camera surveying, this paper will describe the plane table alone, leaving the camera for another chapter.

A plane table is simply a drawing board mounted on a tripod so that it can be set up and worked upon in the field. One kind of plane table, which is used in the army for reconnaissance, does not even have a tripod; it is simply strapped to the arm of the man who is using it.

Plane-table maps vary greatly in scale and the area they represent. Landscape artists' plans may show only single city lots, while some topographic maps cover hundreds of square miles on a single sheet. For maps of a small farm, a park, or a residence block in the city, a plane table is almost ideal, since plane-table maps are made with rather simple apparatus and do not require much actual measuring on the ground. Most objects are located without ever going to them, or even sending a rodman to them.

Just a Few Weeks After George Washington's Sixteenth Birthday, in 1748, Lord Fairfax, Owner of a Large Estate in Virginia, Took Him into His Employ as a Surveyor

Besides the plane table itself and a sheet of paper, only a small carpenter's level, a tape to measure a few distances with, and some spikes for markers, a hard lead pencil, a ruler, and a few needles are absolutely necessary for this sort of a map.

To start a plane-table map, a station must first be selected from which as many as possible of the objects to be located on the finished map can be seen. Ordinarily, the objects one would locate are corners of buildings, fence corners, intersections of roads, corners of lots, banks of streams, possibly trees, and section and quarter-section corners in the country. A railroad, a lake, a mountain, or anything which forms a noticeable landmark in any particular locality, ought to be on the map. In mapping a territory which has never been surveyed before, the first surveyor may name the hills and streams.

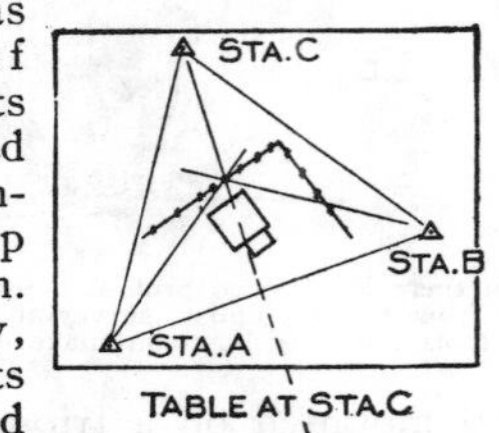

TABLE AT STA.C

Three Stations are Used for Setting the Plane Table in Succession to Locate the Various Objects

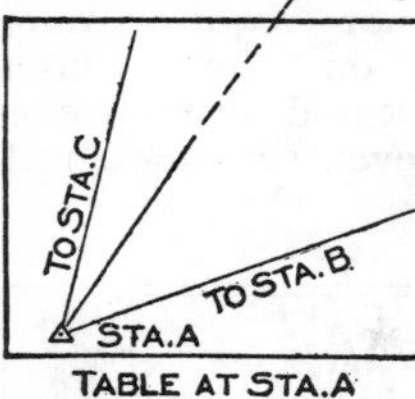

TABLE AT STA.A

After the first station has been selected, it is marked by a pile of stones, a stake, or, if precise work is to be done, a tack in the top of a stake. The table is then set up over this station point and leveled so that the surface of the paper will be truly horizontal. Generally, too, the board is "oriented," that is, placed so that two of its edges point north and south and two east and west. It is then clamped so that it will not move while working on it.

To begin the map, a point on the table is chosen to represent the station on the ground over which the table is set. This point is marked by sticking a fine needle into the paper, vertically. A small triangle should be drawn around the needle hole in the paper and labeled "Sta. A," so that it will not be lost in the maze of points which will soon cover the sheet. By sighting past this needle toward some object which is wanted on the map, like the corner of a house, its direction can be marked by setting another needle on the far side of the table, in line with the first and the given object. Then, if a ruler or straightedge be placed against these two needles and a fine line drawn connecting them, this line will show the exact direction of the object from Sta. A. All the other objects which are wanted on the finished map and can be seen from Sta. A are located by direction in the same way.

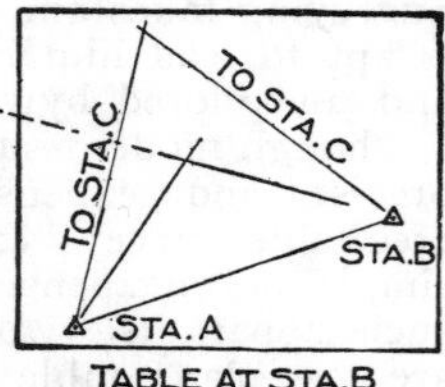

TABLE AT STA.B

The first points to have their direction thus marked ought to be the next stations to be occupied. If all the objects to be located can be seen from three stations, or even two of three stations, three stations will be sufficient. The distance to one of them from Sta. A should be carefully measured and laid off to scale along its direction line on the map. Its place on the map should be marked exactly as the first station was, substituting B for A. It is wise, after every few sights at other objects, to take a sight along the line AB to make sure that the board has not turned. A good map is impossible if the board twists.

To measure the distance between

stations, a 50 or 100-ft. tape, or some accurate substitute, is necessary. An ordinary piece of iron telegraph wire, 105 ft. long, is a good substitute. A point, about 2½ ft. from one end, is marked with a little lump of solder. A chisel dent in this solder will mark one end of the 100-ft. section. Then, with a borrowed tape or a good rule, measure off and mark every 10 ft., just as the first point was marked, until the entire 100 ft. have been laid off. The last 10 ft. should be divided into feet. In all this measuring and marking, the wire must be stretched out taut and straight. The extra 2½ ft. at each end are used for making handles. By estimating the tenths of a foot, measurements can be made with such a tape, or "chain," as an old-time surveyor might call it, just as accurately as they can be laid off on the map.

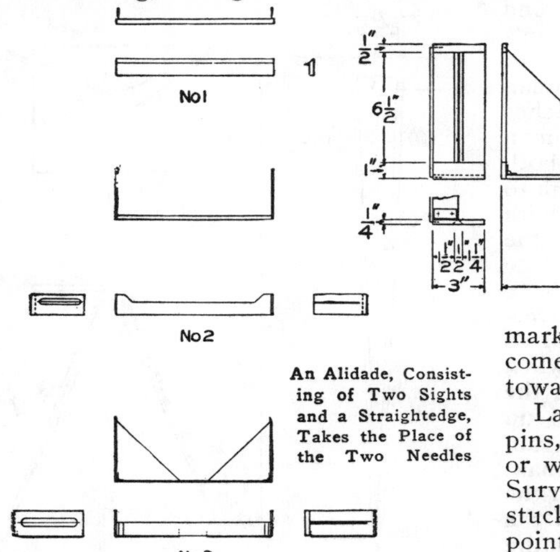

An Alidade, Consisting of Two Sights and a Straightedge, Takes the Place of the Two Needles

Two men are required for measuring, or "chaining," a head and a rear chainman. The rear chainman holds the 100-ft. end of the tape on the station point, while the head chainman takes his end forward toward the station to which they are measuring. When he has gone nearly the length of the tape, the rear chainman calls "halt." The head chainman stops and draws the tape up tight, while the rear chainman holds his division end on the starting point. Then the head chainman sticks a spike into the ground to mark the place where his division end comes, calls out "stuck," and starts on toward the object point.

Large spikes make good marking pins, especially if they have little red or white strips of cloth tied to them. Surveyors use 11 markers. One is stuck into the ground at the starting point and is carried forward by the rear chainman, who also picks up the markers at each 100-ft. point as soon as the head chainman calls "stuck." In this way, the number of markers which the rear chainman has in his hand is always the same as the number of hundreds of feet which the last set marker is from the starting point.

In measuring between two points, care must be taken to draw the tape out taut and straight, its two ends must be level with each other, and it must be exactly in line with the two points between which the measurement is being made. In measuring downhill, one end may have to be held up high, and the point on the ground where the end division would come, found by dropping a stone from the place where it is in the air and watching for the spot where the rock strikes the ground. A surer way to do this is to hold a plumb-bob string on the last division and carefully let the bob down until it touches the ground. A rod with a red or white flag on it ought to be placed at or just beyond the point to which the measurement is to be made so that the rear chainman can easily line in the head chainman. The latter, before he places his marker, looks back to the rear chainman to be told whether or not he is "on line" with the object point. If he is not, and ought to go to the rear chainman's right to get "on," the latter holds out his right arm and the head chainman moves accordingly. When he reaches the right point, the rear chainman signals "all right" by holding out both of his arms and then dropping them to his side; the marker is stuck, and both move up a hundred feet and repeat the process.

After all the points possible have been located from Sta. A, and the direction lines labeled lightly in pencil so that they can be distinguished when the board has been removed from the station, the plane table is picked up and carried to Sta. B. Here it is again set up, leveled, and oriented by making the direction of the line AB on the paper exactly the same as that of the line from Sta. A to Sta. B on the ground. This is done by placing needles at points A and B on the table and then turning the board until the two needles and Sta. A are in line. Sights are taken on the same objects which were "shot" at Sta. A, and to objects which were not visible from Sta. A. The intersection of the lines of sight toward a given object from A and from B marks the location on the paper of that object. If the two ends of a straight fence have been located in this way, a straight line joining the points will show the location of the fence on the map. By exactly similar methods, every other object is located on the paper.

In order to avoid errors, it is an excellent scheme to locate three stations near the outside edges of the area to be mapped, and locate all objects possible by sights from each of the three stations. If, instead of all three crossing each other at a point, the lines of sight from the three stations form a triangle, something is wrong. If the triangle is very small, it may be safe to use its center as the correct point; if not, the work must be repeated and checked. Locating even a few points by this method may prevent some bad blunders. The three stations ought to form as nearly as possible, an equilateral triangle; and the distances between all of them should be measured and laid out accurately on the plane table.

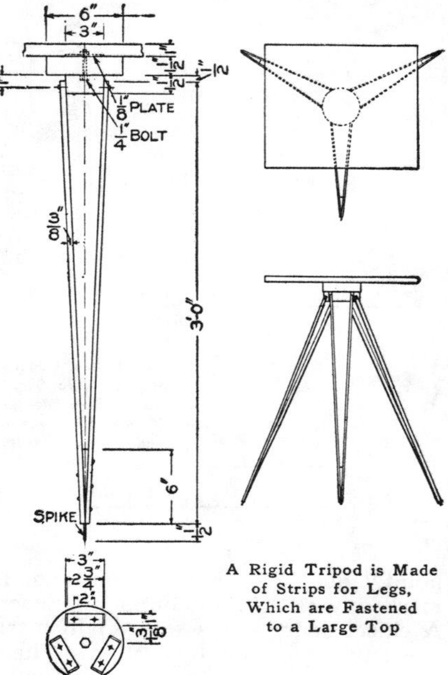

A Rigid Tripod is Made of Strips for Legs, Which are Fastened to a Large Top

There are two ways in which the map may be finished, inked, or traced. By drawing in the "culture," that is, the things built by man, like the houses, the fences, the roads, and the railroads, in black ink; the topography, that is, the hills and valleys, in brown; the water, in blue, and then erasing all the construction lines, a very neat map can be made. Another way is to get some "onion-skin" paper, or some tracing cloth, tack it over the penciled map, and trace the lines right through, using black India ink. This tracing can be blueprinted, just as a photographic film. A plain, neat title, describing location of map; who made it and when; the scale used; why it was made, if it was made for a special purpose, and the direction of the north point, ought to be on every map. The topographic sheets published by the United States Geological Survey are

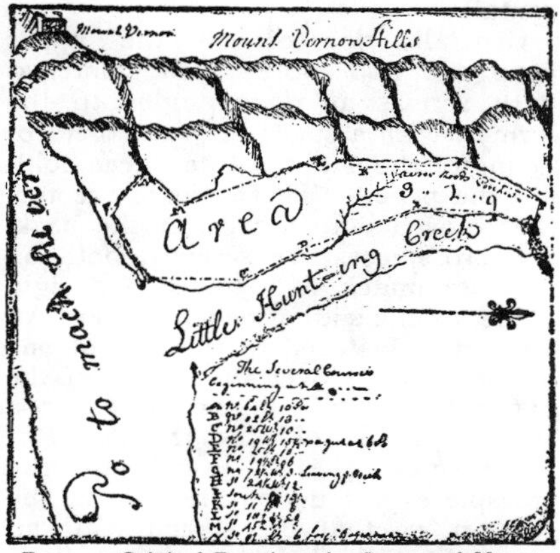

From an Original Drawing of a Survey of Mount Vernon, Made by George Washington at the Age of 14

good samples to follow. They have been published for a great many places all over the country, and single copies can be obtained by sending 10 cents to the Director, United States Geological Survey, Washington, D. C.

Plane tables are almost as easily made as they are bought. If there is no old drawing board around the house, a new bread board from the ten-cent store will serve. For ordinary work, a table which is 15 or 20 in. square will do very well. The board must be mounted on a tripod so that it will be rigid while it is being worked upon and yet can be unclamped and oriented. A brass plate, with a hole in it and a nut soldered over the hole, screwed to the bottom of the board will permit the board and tripod to be bolted together in good shape. Another method, which is not nearly as good, is to drill a hole clear through the board, countersink it on top for a bolt head, and bolt the board and tripod head directly together. With the brass plate and nut, the camera tripod can be pressed into service if a nut of the proper size has been used. The camera tripod is, however, apt to be wabbly with a drawing board on top; a much more satisfactory tripod can be built as shown in the accompanying drawings. Each leg is made of two strips of wood, 3/4 by 3/8 in. and 3 ft. long. These strips are screwed together at their lower ends, gripping a spike between them which will prevent the legs from slipping on the ground. The tops of the strips are spread apart and screwed to the opposite ends of an oak or maple cleat. This cleat is, in turn, screwed to the under side of the circular tripod head.

In place of the two needles and the ruler described for marking the line of sight, most plane-table men use an alidade, which is a combination of two sights and a straightedge. A very simple alidade may be made by mounting two needles on a ruler. The straight edge of the ruler is placed against the needle which marks the station at which the plane table is set up. Then, by swinging the ruler around this needle until its two sighting needles come in line with some object, the line of sight can be drawn directly on the paper along the edge of the ruler. A surveyor in India once made an alidade out of a piece of straightedge and two sights made of native coins hammered out by a native blacksmith. Two pieces of cigar box, one with a fine vertical saw slit in it, and the other with a vertical slot and a piece of fine wire or silk thread stretched down the center, glued to a well planed, straight, flat piece of wood, make a fine alidade. A careful worker may be able to put his sights on hinges so that they will fold down when not in use.

More than anything else, map making rewards care and accuracy, and shows up slipshod workmanship. If the pencils are sharp, the lines fine, and if the work is checked often, beautiful maps can be made with very simple apparatus.

¶White marks on waxed surfaces may be removed by rubbing lightly with a soft rag moistened in alcohol, after which rub with raw linseed oil.

Machine for Sketching Pictures

An ordinary drawing board, with the attachments shown, provides an easy way to sketch pictures, even if

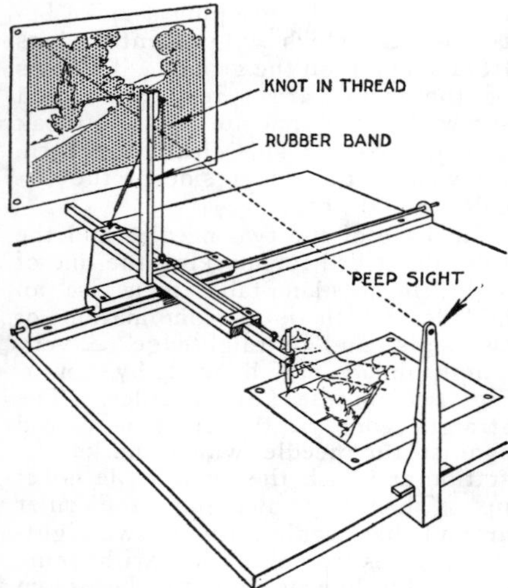

This Machine Aids a Person in Drawing the True Outline of a Picture

one is not proficient in this line of work. It is only necessary to look through the sight and move the pencil about so that the knot in the thread follows the outline of the landscape or object being drawn.

The size of the machine depends on the one building it, but a fair-sized drawing board is sufficient for the beginner. A strip of wood is fastened to the board, near one edge, which has a metal piece on each end, fastened to the under side and bent up over the end to form an extension for the rod to support the moving parts. The strip of wood should be ¾ in. wide and ¼ in. thick, and the sliding arm, holding the pencil, ½ in. wide and ¼ in. thick. A like strip, but much shorter than the one fastened to the board, is also fitted with metal pieces in an inverted position so the projections will be downward. A $\frac{3}{16}$-in. rod is run through holes in the metal pieces of the strips at both ends, and soldered to those on the strip fastened to the board. This will make a hinged joint, as well as one that will allow the upper strip to slide horizontally.

Centrally located on the upper strip are two more strips, fastened with screws at right angles to the former, with a space between them of ½ in. for the sliding center piece holding the pencil. These pieces are further braced with a wire at the back, and crosspieces are screwed both on top and under side, to make a rigid guide for the sliding pencil holder. An upright is fastened to the side of one of these pieces over the center of the upper horizontal sliding piece for a screw eye to hold the thread. Another screw eye is turned into the crosspiece just under the one on the support, so that the thread will run perpendicularly between them. Two more screw eyes are fastened, one into the upper surface of the rear crosspiece, and the other in the end of the pencil holder, near the pencil. By connecting these screw eyes, as shown, with a thread, having a rubber band fastened in the rear end and a knot tied in it near the screw eye in the upper end of the vertical stick, a means for following the outlines of the picture is provided.

A vertical stick is fastened to the front edge of the board by means of a notch and wedge. In the upper end of this stick a very small hole is bored for a sight, similar to a peep sight on a rifle.

To use the machine, set the board on a table, or tripod, and level it up in front of the object to be drawn. Look through the sight at the front of the board and move the pencil about to keep the knot of the thread on the outlines of the picture to be drawn.—Contributed by Wm. C. Coppess, Union City, Ind.

¶A walnut filler is made of 3 lb. burnt Turkey umber, 1 lb. of burnt Italian sienna, both ground in oil, then mixed to a paste with 1 qt. of turpentine and 1 pt. of japan drier.

THE BOY SURVEYOR
Camera Surveying
by Harold G. McGee

[This article explains the preparation of the camera for taking the pictures at each of the three stations, after which the plates are developed, printed and kept until a convenient time may be had for plotting the ground. The succeeding article will give in detail the making of the map from the photographs.—Editor.]

CAMERA surveying is simply plane-table surveying in which the landscape has been photographically picked up and carried indoors. It has the enormous advantage that one can obtain a record of the utmost fidelity in a small fraction of the time taken to do the field work of even a sketchy plane-table survey, and that plotting can be done in the comfort and with the conveniences of a drafting room. When the hours one can work are short or the periods of clear, dry weather are few and far between, a camera is an ideal surveying instrument. It sees and records with the click of the shutter.

Surveying by camera was proposed early in the infant days of photography; but not until the eighties were photographic surveys commenced in earnest. With the extensive surveys of the Canadian Rockies by the Canadian government within the past decade and the topographic surveys of the Alps, the camera has very recently indeed achieved the dignity of being known as a "sure-enough" surveying instrument. Even today, few surveyors have ever used photography for making surveys, even though for mountain topography or any survey which includes a large number of distinctive, inaccessible landmarks, the camera asks no odds of either the plane table or the stadia transit.

A camera survey taken of the summer cottage or the camping ground will be a source of great delight while it is being plotted up of winter evenings. There is something weird in watching each tent and dock slip into its place with naught but a pair of dividers and a few pictures to do the trick. And when the map is done, there are all the data to tell just where a tennis court can go or a walk ought to be built.

In making surveys, a plate camera will do more accurate work than will a film camera; and a fixed focus is a big help in plotting. In spite of the special and expensive instruments which have been designed solely for surveying work, a little ingenuity on the part of the owner of most any kind of a camera, be it big or little, film or plate, box or folding, will do wonders toward producing good results.

To be used for surveying, a camera

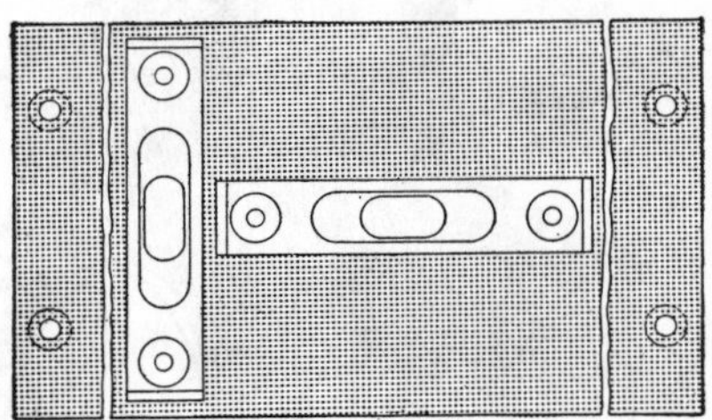

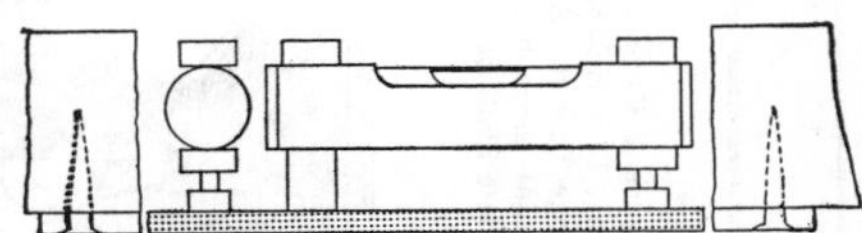

A T-Shaped Level with Adjusting Nuts is Located on the Camera Box, or on the Bed of the Folding Camera

must be fitted with a spirit level and some arrangement for cross hairs. A T-shaped level on the bed or the box, carefully adjusted, will show when the

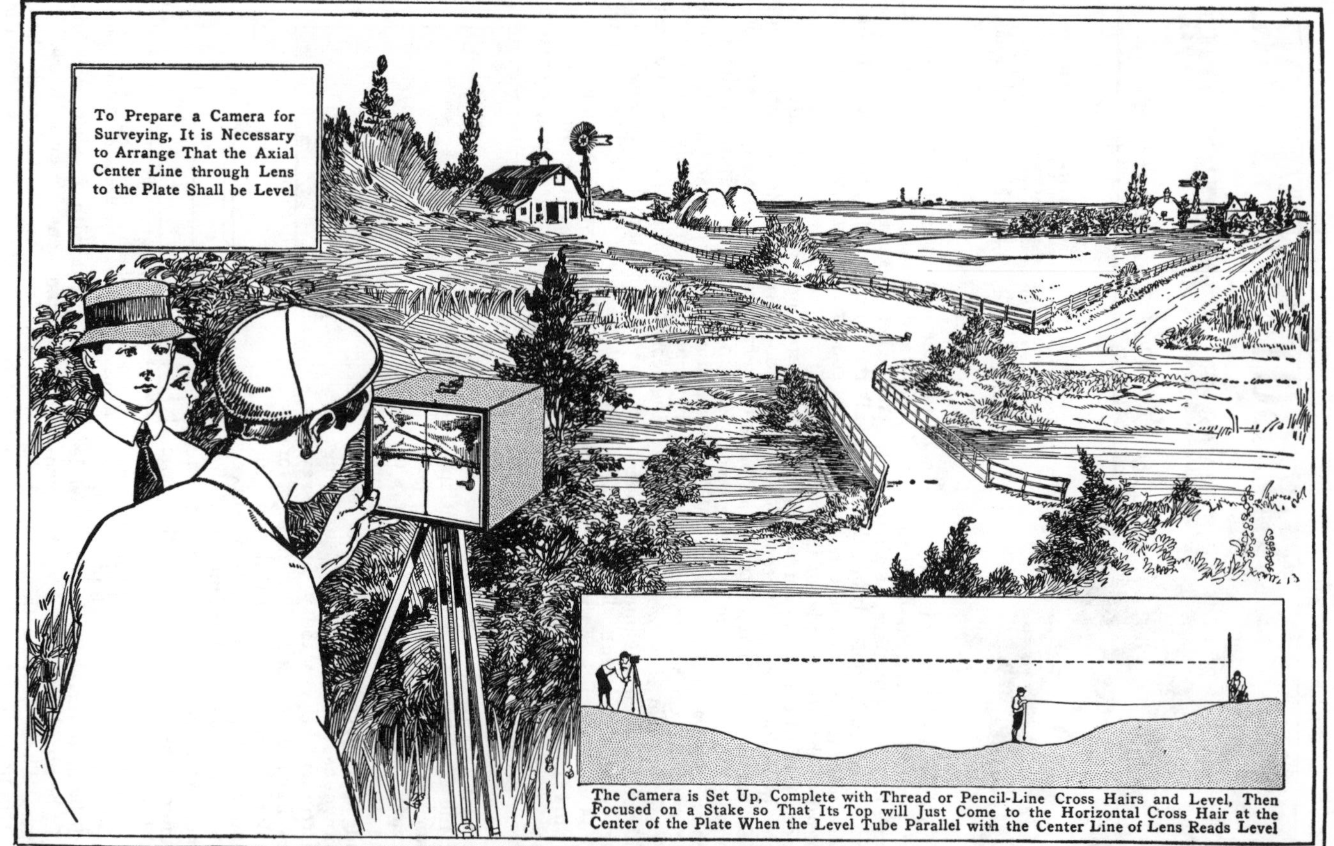

To Prepare a Camera for Surveying, It is Necessary to Arrange That the Axial Center Line through Lens to the Plate Shall be Level

The Camera is Set Up, Complete with Thread or Pencil-Line Cross Hairs and Level, Then Focused on a Stake so That Its Top will Just Come to the Horizontal Cross Hair at the Center of the Plate When the Level Tube Parallel with the Center Line of Lens Reads Level

plate is vertical and when the perpendicular line from the center of the plate to the center of the lens is horizontal. Actual cross hairs in the camera are not as good as four tiny points of V's, one projecting from the middle of each side, top, and bottom of the camera box, just in front of the plate holder. How the level is to be adjusted so that a line between the upper and lower points will be truly vertical, and one through the die-side points truly horizontal and on a level with the center of the lens when the bubbles are in the center of the spirit level, will be described later.

Camera Preparation

To prepare a camera for surveying, it is necessary to arrange that the axial center line through the lens to the plate shall be level, and that the location of the horizontal and vertical center lines shall be indicated on the plate. A spirit level is the best solution of the first problem, and indicated center points of the second.

The spirit level preferably may be of the T-form, with two level tubes, or of the "universal" circular form, with which some hand cameras are equipped. However, ordinary hand-camera levels are generally too rough and difficult of adjustment to insure accurate work. On a view camera, the level may be conveniently located on the bed which carries the lens board. If it is screwed to the under side of the arms it will be convenient for use and out of the way. The bed is likewise a good location for the level on a folding hand camera, while the top of the box is about the only possible location with a box-type instrument.

The cross hairs or center-line indicators should be placed on the back of the camera, just in front of the plate. If indicators are used, fine-thread cross hairs or pencil lines drawn on the ground glass must be used temporarily for making adjustments. Generally, the two cross hairs will divide the plate vertically and horizontally into four equal parts and the hairs or indicators will join the center point of the sides and top and bottom of the opening immediately in front of the plate. But it is essential that the cross hairs have their intersection in a line per-

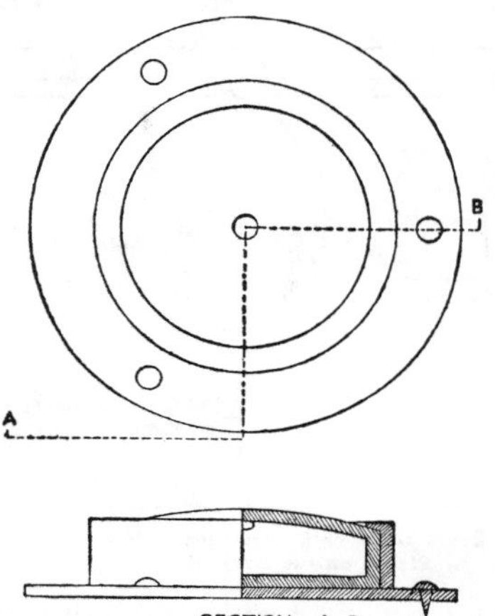

The Ordinary Round Level may be Used, but It Is Not so Good as the T-Level

pendicular to the plate and passing through the center of the lens. Thus in a camera in which the lens is not placed in the center of the plate, or in which the rising and sliding front has placed the lens off center, either or both of the cross hairs may be off center with regard to the plate.

After the cross-hair indicators and the level have been attached to the camera, adjustments are necessary. Surveyors distinguish between permanent and temporary adjustments, permanent adjustments being those for which the instrument maker is responsible, and temporary adjustments being those which can be and are made in the field. The principal permanent or maker's adjustments of the surveying camera are those which insure the center line through the lens, or axial center line, or line of collimation, being perpendicular to the plate, the intersection of the cross hairs being on this line, and that the cross hairs themselves are mutually perpendicular. Temporary or field adjustments must be so made that one tube of the spirit level shall be parallel with the axial center line through the lens and the other parallel with the horizontal cross hair.

The first field adjustment is made in the following manner. The camera is

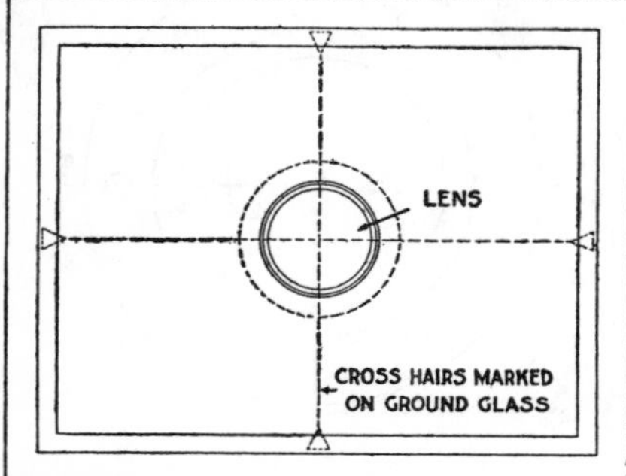

The Cross Hairs or Center-Line Indicators should be Placed on the Back of the Camera

set up, complete with thread or pencil-line cross hairs and level, and focused on a stake whose top shall just come to the horizontal cross hair at the center of the plate, when the level tube parallel with the center line of the lens reads level. This stake may be driven to the required elevation or a rod may be held on it and the point where, in the image on the ground glass, it is intersected by the cross hair marked with pencil on the rod as it is held vertically on the stake. The distance to this stake is measured from the camera and another similar stake set at the same elevation by the same method, but in an opposite direction and at the same distance from the camera. The two stakes or the mark on the vertical rod which is held on these stakes in turn will be level with each other, though they may not be level with the camera. The camera is then moved to a point very much closer to one stake than to the other and again leveled. The vertical distance from one stake-top or mark on the rod is measured and the camera then focused on the second stake. If the level is actually in adjustment, the distance from the second stake top or mark will be exactly the same as it was on the first. If not, the difference, or "error," is found between the two vertical distances from the cross hair to the two stake tops. Half this error is corrected by raising or lowering one end of the level tube by means of the threaded nuts which are placed on it for the purpose. The whole process is then repeated until the vertical distances from the horizontal cross hair at the center to the two level stakes, one close to and one distant from the camera, are identical. The axial center line of the lens, or the line of collimation, is then in adjustment with the level. All that remains is to make the horizontal cross hair parallel with the cross level.

This is done by using one marked stake. The camera is leveled as far as the "fore-and-aft" level is concerned and the horizontal cross-hair point at the center marked on the stake. The camera is then swung round until the stake just shows on one edge of the ground glass, the fore-and-aft or longitudinal level being checked to make sure its bubble is still in the center. Then the bubble in the cross or transverse level tube is brought to the center by means of the threaded adjusting nuts, and the camera is thrown hard over so that the stake appears along the opposite

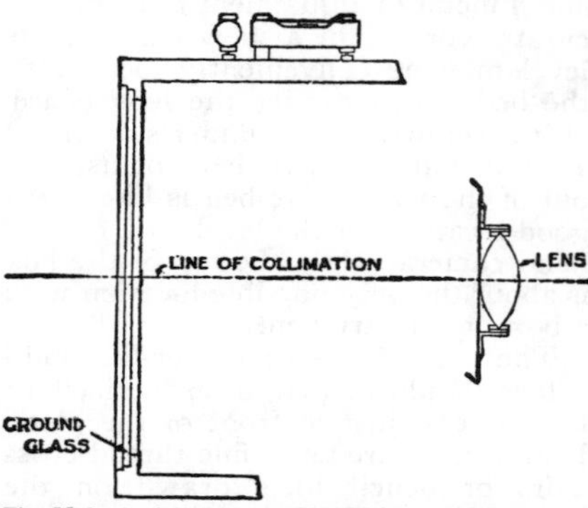

The Maker's Adjustments Should Insure the Line of Collimation being Perpendicular to the Plate

edge of the plate. This time, the bubble of the longitudinal level being kept in the center, half the error introduced by turning from one edge to the other is corrected. All of the adjustments are then rechecked, and if they are found correct the instrument is ready for use. If a circular level be used, the method of adjustment is exactly the same, the swing of the bubble along the axis of the camera and transverse to it being used to determine the longitudinal and transverse adjustments. Slips of paper may be used for lifting one side in place of the adjustment nuts of the T-level.

A leveling head or ball-and-socket joint on the top of the tripod will be found of material aid in leveling the instrument.

No great mechanical genius is necessary to prepare a camera for or to make a successful camera survey. But if a boy have not patience and an infinite desire for accuracy, camera surveying, or indeed any sort of surveying, will be a source of neither pleasure, satisfaction, nor profit.

To Make Transparent Paper

Transparent paper of parchmentlike appearance and strength, which can be dyed with almost all kinds of aniline dyes and assumes much more brilliant hues than ordinary colored glass, can be made in the following manner: Procure a white paper, made of cotton or linen rags, and put it in soak in a saturated solution of camphor in alcohol. When dry, the paper so treated can be cut up into any forms suitable for parts of lamp shades, etc.

Toasting Bread over an Open Fire

Having experienced some difficulty in obtaining good toast over a gas or open fire I tried the following plan with good results: An old tin pan was placed over the flame and the ordinary wire bread toaster clasping the slice of bread was held about ½ in. from the pan. In a few minutes the toast was crisp and ready to serve.—Contributed by Katy Doherty, New York City.

Adjustable Stilts

The beginner with stilts always selects short sticks so that he will not be very far from the ground, but as he becomes more experienced, the longer the sticks the better. Then, too, the small boy and the large boy require different lengths of sticks. The device shown makes a pair of sticks universal for use of beginners or a boy of any age or height.

To make the stilts, procure two long hardwood sticks of even length, and smooth up the edges; then begin at a point 1 ft. from one end and bore 12 holes, ⅜ in. in diameter and 2 in. apart from center to center. If there is no diestock at hand, have a blacksmith, or mechanic, make a thread on both ends of a ⅜-in. rod, 12 in. long. Bend the rod in the shape shown, so that the two threaded ends will be just 2 in. apart from center to center. The thread on the straight horizontal end should be so long that a nut can be placed on both sides of the stick. A piece of a garden hose or small rubber hose, slipped on the rod, will keep the shoe sole from slipping. The steps can be set in any two adjacent holes to give the desired height.—Contributed by Walter Veene, San Diego, Cal.

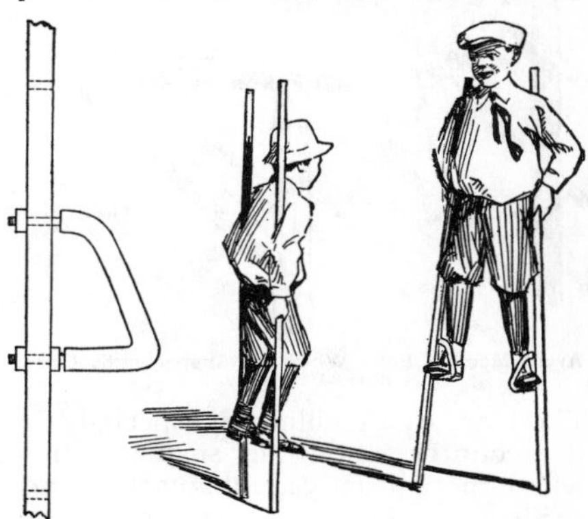

Stilts Having Stirrups That can be Set at Any Desired Height

Grape Arbor Built of Poles

In building outdoor structures, such as grape arbors, pergolas, or arches, it is not necessary to use sawed lumber, as they can be built as substantial, and frequently more artistic and cheap, of poles.

Arbor Made of Poles Which are Supported by One Row of Uprights

These are easily obtained, especially in the country or in the smaller cities where there usually are many trees and gardens.

The illustrated grape arbor consists of but one row of uprights. Across the top of each is placed a horizontal support for the roof poles, as shown in Fig. 1, which is carried near its outer end by an inclined brace. The brace should be connected at each end with a toe joint, as shown in Fig. 2. The upper end of the upright is beveled off on both sides, to form a double-splayed joint with the crosspiece. In order to securely bind the roof of the arbor, the long poles, or roof beams, should be notched near each end to fit over the supports. Similar notches in the poles forming the side of the arbor are to fit the uprights, thereby binding them together and preventing toppling over. Each set of long poles connecting two uprights should have the end notches the same distance apart, one pole being used as a gauge. All the joints and notches may be cut with a sharp hatchet.

In setting the arbor, the uprights should first be assembled complete with braces and roof supports, and placed in the ground a distance apart corresponding to that of the notches on the long poles. The uprights being set, the long poles are placed and fastened with nails.—Contributed by W. E. Crane, Cleveland, Ohio.

Forcing Fruit Blossoms for Decorations

Twigs trimmed from the fruit trees rather late in the season had quite large buds on them, and we experimented with them in this way: A large box was filled with wet sand, and the twigs were stuck in it and the box set in the warmest corner of the yard. The buds soon swelled and burst into bloom. We then arranged a smaller box of sand and put the blooming twigs into it, and took it into the house where they remained fresh for several days.—Contributed by A. Louise Culver, Oakland, Cal.

Corner Cleaner Attached to a Scrubbing Brush

Dirt will accumulate and harden in the corners of a floor and the baseboard just because the end of the scrubbing brush will not enter them. The water gets in with the dirt and leaves a hard crust. This may be easily cleaned out if a metal point is attached to the end of the brush handle, as shown in the illustration. It is used as a scraper to break up the crust and clean it out where the bristles will not enter.—Contributed by L. E. Turner, New York City.

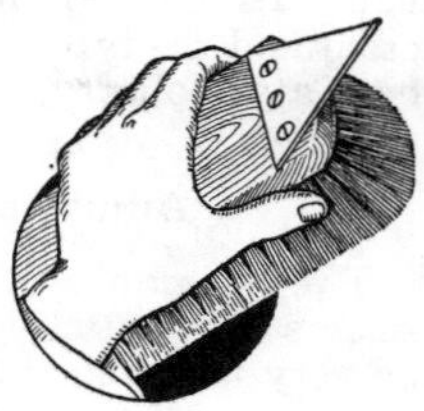

THE BOY SURVEYOR
Plotting a Camera Survey
by
Harold G. McGee

[The camera records pictures that can be taken in camp or on a vacation trip and kept until more leisure may be had in winter for plotting the ground.—Editor.]

A PREVIOUSLY measured base triangle with "stations" at each corner is necessary for making a camera survey, just as it is for the plane-table survey. It is preferable to have each of the three sides measured independently, though if one side has been accurately chained, the other two may be less satisfactorily determined by the use of the plane table. If the camera has a fixed focus, it is possible to make an entire survey from the two ends of a single base line; but this method has no check and should be used only when and where the triangle method is impossible. With an adjustable focus, it will rarely give good results.

Once the triangle has been laid out, the fieldwork is very simple. The camera is set up at one station, carefully leveled, and then a series of pictures is taken, each single plate overlapping the last so as to form a panorama of the area to be mapped. The focus of the lens must not be changed during a series, and plotting is facilitated by keeping the focus constant during all the exposures which make up a survey. To secure good depth of focus, a small stop is generally used, since it is necessary to use a tripod to keep the camera level. If contours are to be drawn, the height of the lens above the ground at the station should be measured and recorded. After a series has been taken at each station, the fieldwork is complete. It is an excellent plan to keep a record of the plate numbers, and the order in which and the station from which the exposures were made, so

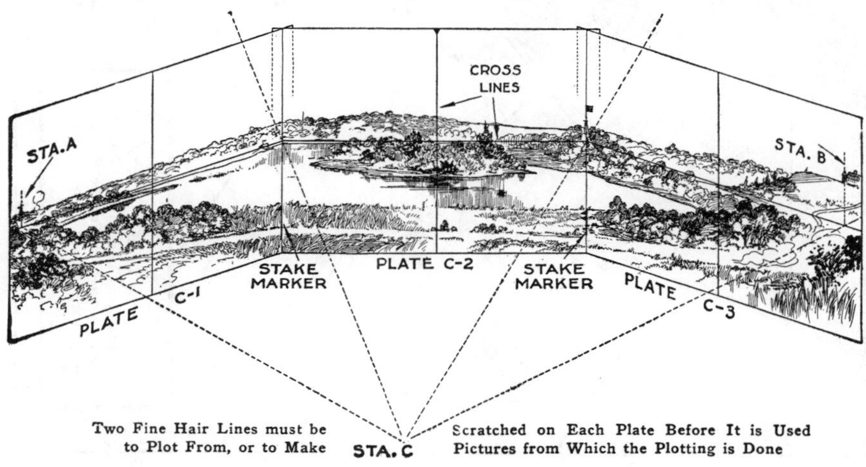

Two Fine Hair Lines must be Scratched on Each Plate Before It is Used to Plot From, or to Make Pictures from Which the Plotting is Done

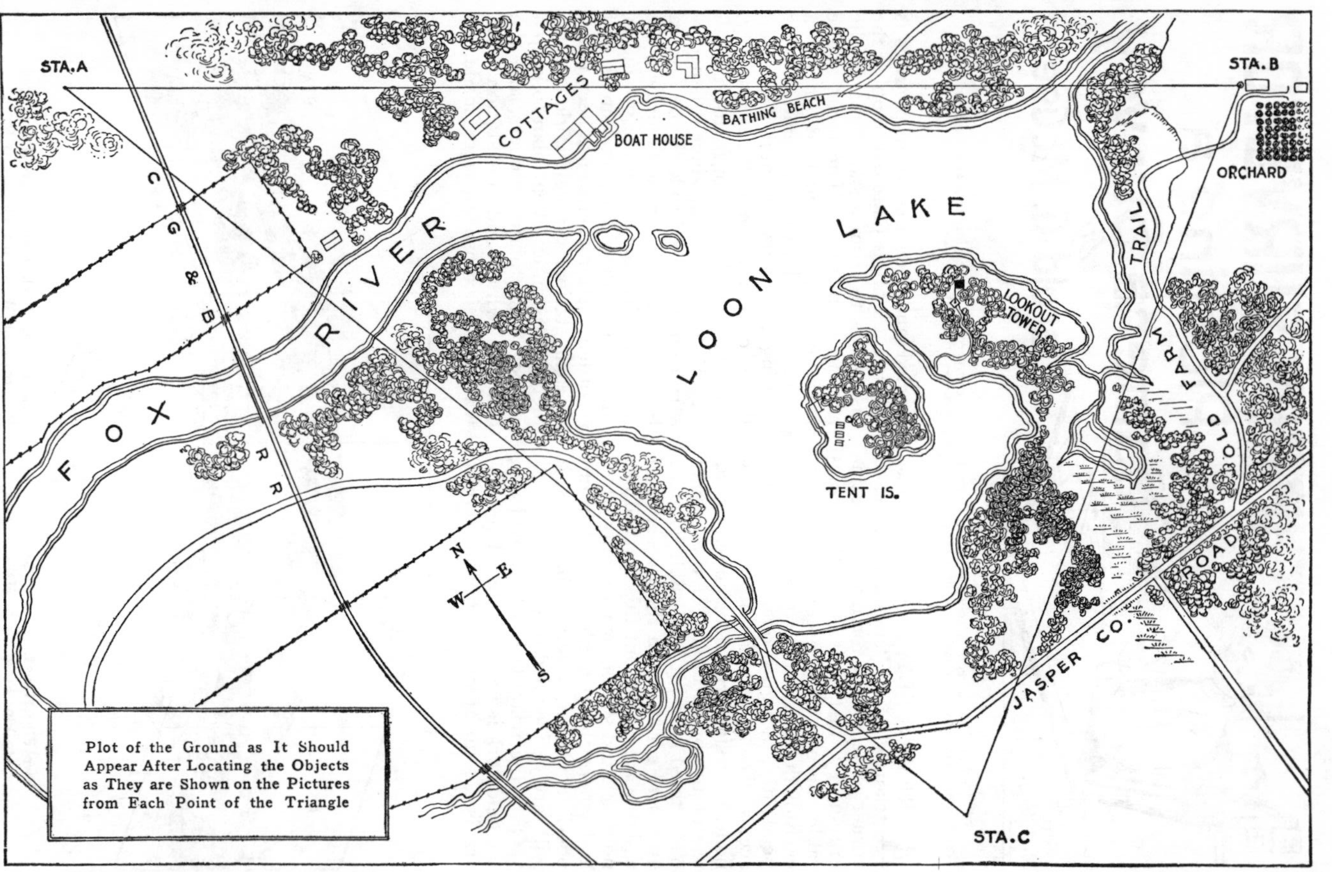

Plot of the Ground as It Should Appear After Locating the Objects as They are Shown on the Pictures from Each Point of the Triangle that the 10 or 12 plates which a small survey will comprise may not get hopelessly mixed up. If the camera is turned each time to the right, clockwise, and the plates are numbered A-1, A-2, B-4, etc., indicating by A-1, for example, the leftmost plate taken at Sta. A; by A-2, the plate just to the right of A-1, just as II is to the right of I on the clock dial, and by B-4, the fourth to the right taken at Sta. B, there ought to be no difficulty in identifying the plates after the exact details of the ground are forgotten.

While the pictures are being taken, "flags" of white wood or with white-cloth streamers tied to them must be stuck in the ground or held at the other stations in order that their exact location can be readily and certainly found on the plates. A few distinctive stakes, some with one and some with two or three strips of cloth tied to them, placed at important points on the ground will help immensely in the location of knolls and shore lines.

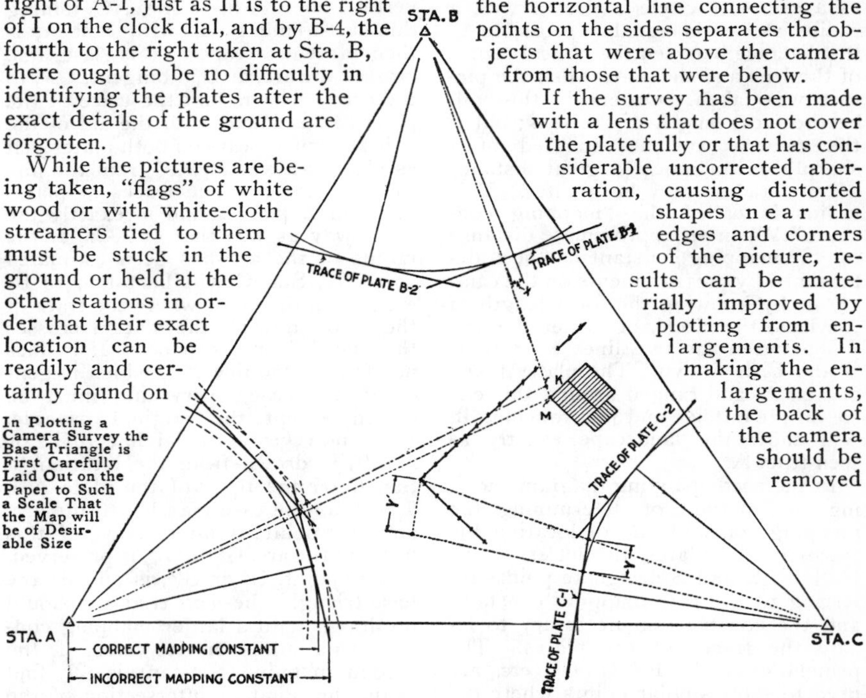

In plotting a camera survey, either the original plates, the prints, or enlargements may be used. The plates are the most accurate if a corrected lens has been used; and the enlargements made back through the lens will be best if the images on the plates are distorted. In any case, two fine hair lines must be scratched on each plate before it is used to plot from, or to make the prints from which the plotting is to be done. One of these lines should connect the points at the top and bottom of the plate, and the other, the points at the sides. The vertical line divides the objects which were on the right of the center of the camera from those that were on the left, and the horizontal line connecting the points on the sides separates the objects that were above the camera from those that were below.

If the survey has been made with a lens that does not cover the plate fully or that has considerable uncorrected aberration, causing distorted shapes near the edges and corners of the picture, results can be materially improved by plotting from enlargements. In making the enlargements, the back of the camera should be removed and the light should be allowed to pass through the plate and the lens in the reverse order and direction of that in which it passed when the negative was made. In this way, the errors which were made by the lens originally will be straightened out, and the resulting enlargements will be free from distortion. To make successful enlargements for surveying work, the easel on which the bromide paper is tacked must be square with the camera, and the paper itself should be flat and smooth. It is just as necessary to keep the easel at a constant distance from the camera during the enlarging

STA. B
TRACE OF PLATE B-2
TRACE OF PLATE B-1
TRACE OF PLATE C-2
TRACE OF PLATE C-1
STA. A
STA. C
CORRECT MAPPING CONSTANT
INCORRECT MAPPING CONSTANT

In Plotting a Camera Survey the Base Triangle is First Carefully Laid Out on the Paper to Such a Scale That the Map will be of Desirable Size

as it was to keep the same focus while the original negatives were being made.

In plotting a camera survey the base triangle is first carefully laid out on the paper to such a scale that the map will be of a desirable size. With the apex of the triangle representing Sta. A, say, as a center, a circle is drawn with a radius as nearly equal as possible to the distance between the optical center of the lens and the plate when the picture was taken. Ordinarily this will be the focal length of the lens; but if the camera was not focused most sharply on an object a great distance off, the radius may be greater. This radius is called the "mapping constant." When an approximate distance for the mapping constant has been determined by measurements on the camera or by knowing the focal length of the lens, the circle, or rather the arc, FG between the two lines to stations B and C, is drawn. The plates taken at Sta. A, and ranged around this circle on the outside and just touching it, will show the landscape exactly as seen from A.

In the accompanying diagram showing the method of determining the mapping constant and of locating the traces of the plates, the letters F, G, H, J, P, R and S designate points referring to the true mapping constant, and the construction necessary to locate the traces of the plates. The primed letters F′, F″, G′, G″, etc., are used to show similar points where the trial mapping constant is either too long or too short. The following description refers equally to the construction necessary with true or trial-mapping constants.

Next, a line FH is drawn perpendicular to the line AB of the triangle at the point F where the arc intersects it. On this line is laid off, in the proper direction, a distance equal to the distance on the plate or print from Sta. B to the center vertical line. From this point is drawn a light line, HJ, toward the center of the arc. Where this line crosses the arc, at J, a tangent, KJM, is drawn, which will show the location of the plate A-1 on the drawing. This line is called the trace of the plate. An object which appears both on plate A-1 and A-2 is next picked out and its location on the trace of plate A-1 determined by measuring the distance JN equal to the distance on the plate from the image of the object to the center vertical line. A light line, NO, joining this last-found point with Sta. A, is then drawn. Where this last line crosses the arc, at O, a tangent, OP, to the arc is drawn, and the trace of the plate A-2 is found with the aid of the point which appears on both plates just as plate A-1 was located from the picture of Sta. B. The traces of plates A-3 and A-4 are found in exactly the same way as was that of A-2. If the radius of the arc has been estimated correctly, Sta. C will be found to be exactly on the point where the trace of the plate showing the station crosses the line AC on the paper. If it does not fall on the line AC, which is generally the case, everything must be erased except the original triangle. First, however, a radial line S′G′, or S″G″, is drawn from the location of Sta. C on the trace of the plate A-2, 3 or 4, as the case may be, to the arc, and the point of intersection of this line and the arc, G′ or G″, is preserved. If this point, G′ or G″, is outside the base triangle, the next trial arc should be drawn with a larger mapping constant as a radius, or vice versa. If the second mapping constant is off, find again the point of intersection of the radial line through the new location of Sta. C on the newly located trace of the last plate and the new arc. Join this point and the one found previously, in the same manner, with a straight line, G′G″. The point G where this last drawn line intersects the line AC of the base triangle, will be the point through which the arc, with the correct mapping constant as radius, ought to pass, provided the first two approximations were not too far in error. This third trial ought to make the location of the traces of the plates exactly correct. If, however, the focus of the camera was changed between exposures at one station, the traces of the plates will not all be at an equal distance from the station point, and their location will be an almost impossible task. The traces of the plates taken at stations B and C are found in exactly the same manner as were those for Sta. A. After the traces have all been located, it is a good plan to ink them in lightly and erase the pencil construction lines which would otherwise form an impenetrable maze. The traces located, the difficult and tiresome part of the plotting is over; the landscape, brought indoors photographically, is located as with the plane table; all that remains to be done is to take the sights and find the points on the paper which show where the objects were on the ground.

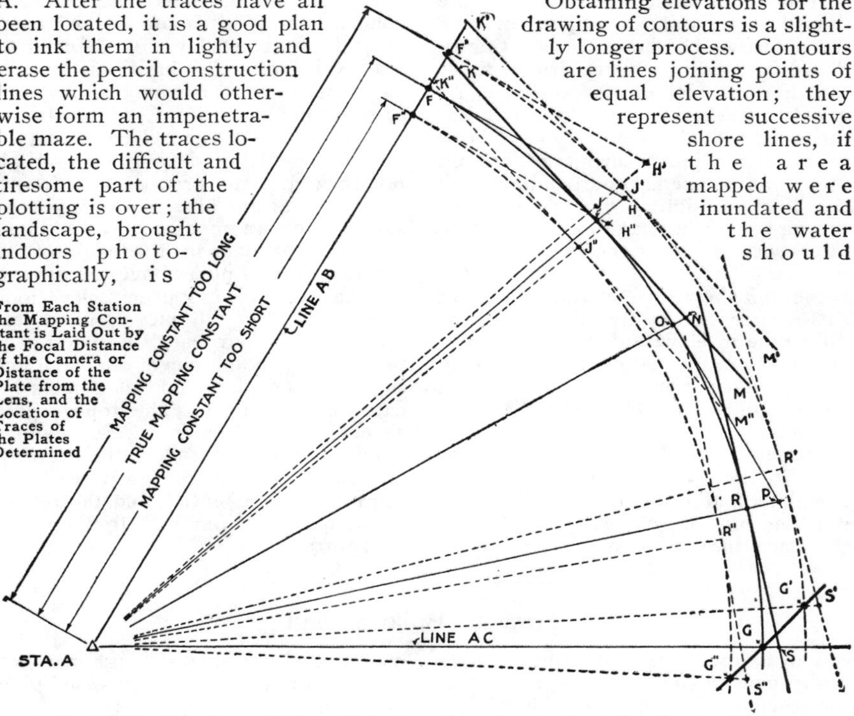

From Each Station the Mapping Constant is Laid Out by the Focal Distance of the Camera or Distance of the Plate from the Lens, and the Location of Traces of the Plates Determined

This taking the sights is a simple matter. With a pair of dividers, the distance from a given object from the center line of the plate is measured. This distance is laid off on the proper side of the point marking the center line of the trace of the same plate; a radial line is drawn through the trace at the given distance from the center-line point and the station at which the given plate is taken; this is one line of sight to the object. The same object is located from another station in the same way; as on the plane table, the intersection of the two lines to the same object marks the location of the point which represents the object on the map.

Obtaining elevations for the drawing of contours is a slightly longer process. Contours are lines joining points of equal elevation; they represent successive shore lines, if the area mapped were inundated and the water should rise slowly foot by foot. If the contours are close together, the ground represented has a steep slope, and vice versa. If, on a map, a number of points are of known elevation, it is simply a question of judgment and practice to tell where contour lines go.

Before contours can be drawn the elevations of a considerable number of points must be known. If the elevation of any one of them is known and the difference between that one and any other can be found, determining the elevation of the second point is simply a problem in addition or subtraction. If it be desired to find, for instance, the difference in elevation between Sta. C and the corner of the fence, as shown in the sketch, two solutions are possible, as follows:

First: Perpendicular to the line of sight from Sta. C to the fence corner, two lines are drawn, one at the intersection of the trace of the plate by the line of sight, and one at the point on the paper which shows the location of the fence corner. On the first of these two lines is laid off the distance Y′, equal to the distance of the ground at the fence post above or below the horizontal center line on the plate. Through this point, on the first perpendicular on the line of sight, is drawn a line through the Sta. C and extended to an intersection with the second drawn perpendicular. The distance from the corner of the fence, on the paper, to this intersection is the distance Y, the difference in elevation from the center of the camera at Sta. C to the ground at the fence post. This solution is longer and less desirable than the second.

Second: In place of perpendicular lines to the line of sight, the trace of the plate, and a line, through the point representing the object, parallel with the trace, may be used.

A datum plane, or reference surface, from which all elevations are measured up to the ground surface must be assumed. The United States Geological Survey uses mean, or average, sea level for the datum in all its topographic sheets. Generally, unless there is a United States Geological Survey "bench mark," a monument of carefully determined elevation referred to sea level, within the limits of the survey, it is better to assume the elevation of some point, as Sta. C, at 100 ft., or greater if necessary to place the datum plane below the ground level at all points within the area to be mapped. Other elevations are figured from the assumed elevation of Sta. C. Allowance must be made for the height of the center of the camera above the ground at Sta. C in computing elevations above Sta. C. All elevations determined for the purpose of drawing contours are ground elevations and not the elevation of the top of objects located on the map. The topographic sheets of the Geological Survey are good examples to follow, in drawing contours. For many purposes, contours are not essential, and the refinements necessary for their drawing may be omitted.

How to Build a Skiff

The following is a description of an easily constructed 12-ft. skiff, suitable for rowing and paddling. This is the type used by many duck hunters, as it may be easily pushed through marshes. It is constructed of ¾-in. dressed pine, or cypress.

The sides consist of planks, 14 in.

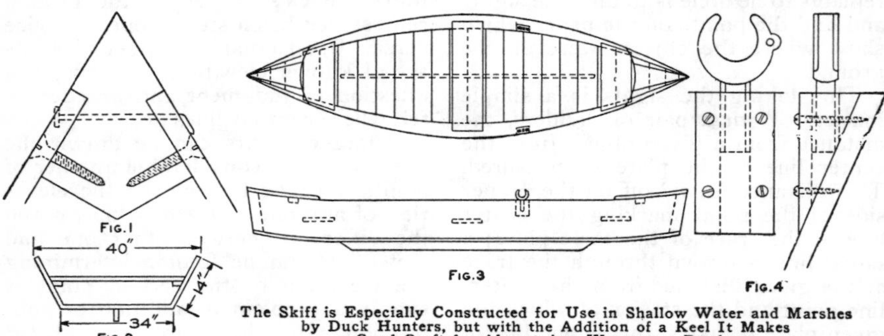

The Skiff is Especially Constructed for Use in Shallow Water and Marshes by Duck Hunters, but with the Addition of a Keel It Makes a Good Craft for Almost Any Water as a Rowboat

wide, but 12-in. planks may be used, the length being 12 ft. 4 in. Two stem pieces are constructed as shown in Fig. 1, and the plank ends are fastened to them with screws. Nail a crosspiece on the plank edges in the exact center, so as to space the planks 34 in. apart, as shown in Fig. 2; then turn it over and nail another crosspiece in the center of the planks for width, and make the spacing of the other edges 40 in. Plane the lower edges so that, in placing a board across them, the surfaces will be level. The floor boards are 6 in. wide and fastened on crosswise, being careful to apply plenty of red lead between all joints and using galvanized nails, 2 in. long.

A deck, 18 in. long, is fastened on each end, as shown in Fig. 3. It is made of strips fastened to a crosspiece. The seats, or thwarts, consist of 10-in. boards, and are placed on short strips fastened to the side planks about 5 in. from the bottom. The oarlocks are held in a wedge-shaped piece of wood, having a piece of gas pipe in them for a bushing, the whole being fastened at the upper edge of the side planks with screws, as shown in Fig. 4. The location of these must be determined by the builder.

Some calking may be required between the bottom, or floor, boards, if they are not nailed tightly against one another. The calking material may be loosely woven cotton cord, which is well forced into the seams. The first coat of paint should be of red lead mixed with raw linseed oil, and when dry any color may be applied for the second coat.

While, for use in shallow water, these boats are not built with a keel, one can be attached to prevent the boat from "sliding off" in a side wind or when turning around. When one is attached, it should be ¾ in. thick, 3 in. wide, and about 8 ft. long.—Contributed by B. Francis Dashiell, Baltimore, Md.

¶An aniline color soluble in alcohol, by adding a little carbolic acid, will hold fast on celluloid.

Double-Swing Gate with Common Hinge

Ordinary hinges can be easily bent and so placed on posts that a gate can be swung in either direction. As

The Post and Gate are Cut Away Back of the Hinge to Allow the Latter to Swing Back

shown in the illustration, hinges can be made to fit either round or square posts. The gate half of the hinge is fastened in the usual way. The post half is bent and so placed that the hinge pin will approximately be on a line between the centers of the posts. The gate and post should be beveled off to permit a full-open gateway.—Contributed by R. R. Schmitz, Birmingham, Ala.

Testing Out Induction Coils

While winding an induction coil, I found it necessary to test the sections for continuity. Having no galvanometer, I connected a battery and low-resistance telephone receiver in series with the section and battery. The battery and telephone receiver may also be used for testing out the secondary of an induction coil, to determine if it is burnt out.—Contributed by John M. Wells, Moosomin, Can.

How to Make a Surveyor's Transit

By BENNETT BLACKLIDGE

A boy who likes to do the things that "grown ups" do can derive considerable pleasure from the making of a transit, which will enable him to start in surveying railroads, laying off town sites, and doing lots of kindred work. It is necessary to have a compass, and one, 1¾ in. in diameter, can be purchased at a reasonable price. A hole is bored with an expansive bit into a board, ⅞ in. in thickness, just deep enough to admit the compass snugly, then a circle, A, 4½ in. in diameter, is drawn, having the same center as the compass hole, and the disk is cut out with a compass or scroll saw. A ring, B, is cut in the same manner from the same material, its inside diameter being such that the ring just fits around the disk A, and the outside diameter, 6¾ in. Another block, 5½ in. in diameter, is glued to the bottom of the small disk A. This will appear as shown at C. A small hole is bored in the center of the bottom block on the under side to receive the threaded end of the screw on a camera tripod. By careful adjustment the threads in the wood will hold the transit firmly. A plumb bob must be attached exactly in the center of the tripod head. This can be easily done if the head is wood, but in case the top is of metal, the line can be attached to the screw with a double loop, as shown at D, so that the bob will hang centrally. Two standards are made as shown at E, each about 5 in. high, and fastened to the ring B in the positions shown in the drawing of the complete instrument. An arc of a circle is marked on one of the standards, as shown, to designate angles, the markings being laid out with a bevel protractor. The pointer is a hand from an old alarm clock.

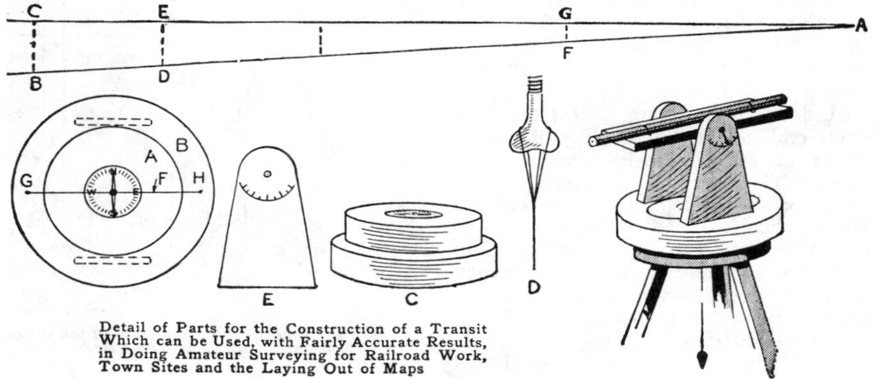

Detail of Parts for the Construction of a Transit Which can be Used, with Fairly Accurate Results, in Doing Amateur Surveying for Railroad Work, Town Sites and the Laying Out of Maps

The telescope arrangement consists of a piece of pasteboard tubing, about 1¼ in. in diameter, one end being covered with a piece of black paper with a pinhole in the exact center, and the other equipped with "cross hairs." Four small notches are cut in the latter end of the tube, exactly quartering it, and two silk threads as fine as can be obtained, are stretched across in these notches. The tube is fastened to a block of wood, 5 in. wide and 7 in. long, with small tacks and two pieces of fine copper wire. This block is pinioned between the standards with two nails. The hand is secured to the nail in such a position that it will point straight down when the tube is level.

The instrument is adjusted in the following manner: It is set up where a lone tree can be seen, about one mile distant, and the center of the cross hairs is carefully set on the tree. Then a very fine wire is stretched across the compass, as shown at F, and while keeping it directly over the center of the compass it is also placed on a direct line pointing to the tree. Very small brass nails, driven in at G and H, serve to fasten it in the position thus found. When this adjustment has been made the telescope can be turned to sight any object, after first placing the instrument so that the needle points to the N on the dial, and a glance at the wire will show the exact direction in which the object is located.

The instrument is then taken to a level stretch of road and set up, and a stick is placed on end and marked at the height of the telescope. The stick is taken along the road about 200 yd., the telescope sighted on it, and the hand set. This makes the instrument level enough for all practical purposes. The plumb bob is then dropped, a distance of 20 ft. measured from it on the road, and a mark made. The telescope is sighted on this mark, and a mark is made on the standard at the point of the arc, to which the hand points. Another 20 ft. is measured, or 40 ft. from the bob, and another mark made. The telescope is sighted on it, and the location of the hand again marked. This works well up to about 300 ft., then the marks begin to come very close together. This method is used for laying out town sites. The instrument is set up directly over a stake from which to work, and the telescope is turned down until the 20-ft. mark is indicated, when the operator looks through the telescope and tells his helper where to set the stake. Then another is driven at the next point, and so on, until the limit of the instrument is reached.

When doing railroad surveying several start out together, one with an ax to cut away brush; one to carry pegs; two to measure, or chain, the distance between stakes, and one to do the sighting. In this manner a line can be run that comes very near being perfectly straight for three miles.

A concrete example of how the transit was used to lay out a map of a ranch will now be given. The start was made on an east and west fence. The instrument was set 5 ft. from the fence at one point, and at the other end of the fence the stick was set at a point 5 ft. from the fence. When the stick was sighted, the wire cut the E and W on the compass, thus showing that the fence was set on a line, due east and west. The distance was measured from the fence to the house, which was 1/4 mile, and this was noted in a book. This operation was repeated on the rear, and the distance found to be 780 ft. while the compass showed the direction to be 4 deg. west of south. The next line ran 427 ft. and 1 deg. east of south. This was kept up all the way around. After these notes had been obtained, it was an easy matter to take a piece of plain paper and strike a line representing north and south and lay off the directions. A bevel protractor was used to find the degrees. The transit was set on the posts of the corrals and this saved the measuring out from the inclosure. The creek was surveyed in the same manner. So many feet southwest, so many feet west, so many feet 5 deg. south of west, and so on, until its length was run.

The transit can also be used for finding distances without measuring. A line from A to B is sighted, and F represents a point 1/2 mile distant, the line from F to G being 100 ft. A line is now sighted from A, through G to C. A person standing at D is directed to move toward the point E and he is stopped as soon as sighted in the telescope. He then measures the distance from D to E. Suppose this distance is 250 ft. As each 100 ft. means 1/2 mile, and the 50 ft., 1/4 mile, the point E is 1 1/4 miles from the transit. This method can be used quite extensively and distances obtained are fairly accurate.

¶A small whisk broom makes a handy cleaner to brush the caked grease and lint from pulleys and gear wheels where waste and rags are useless.

To Enlarge or Reduce Plots

Sometimes it is necessary to enlarge or reduce a plot to a different scale. This can be easily and quickly accomplished without resorting to the slow process of protracting the angles and scaling the individual lines.

Enlarging and Reducing Plots by Radial Lines from a Common Point Located Properly

Take any point, P, and from it draw light pencil lines through each of the corners of the plot. On any one of these lines, as AP, lay off with dividers AC equal to CP. Place a triangle on the line AB and with a straightedge, or another triangle, laid on the line AP, slide the former to the point C, then draw line CD parallel with AB until it intersects the radial line PB. In the same manner draw line DE parallel with BF, and so on, all about the plot. A test of accuracy will be in striking the point C with the last line. If the original plot has a scale of 40 ft. to the inch the reduced plot would be 80 ft. to the inch. If it is required to enlarge the plot to 20 ft. to the inch, make AG equal to AP, and proceed as in the first case, using G as the starting point.

The location of the point P is arbitrary and may be outside of the boundary of the plot or figure to be enlarged or reduced, but should be so located, if possible, that the radial line to any corner does not parallel either of the plot lines to that corner. If the point cannot be so located for all the lines, it may be necessary to scale the lines. A little practice in picking out the best location for the point will give gratifying results. — Contributed by Junius D. McCabe, Pittsburgh, Pa.

A Lathe Bench

While working at a bench, or foot-power lathe, it is quite convenient to have some sort of a seat to sit on while at work, or between operations. In making such a seat, I used a board, 27 in. long and 12 in. wide, for the top, and two boards, 19 in. long and 12 in. wide, for the supports. These boards were 3/4 in. thick. The supports were squared at the ends and securely fastened to the top with nails, their positions being 3 in. in from the ends of the top board. These were well braced, as shown, and a cross board

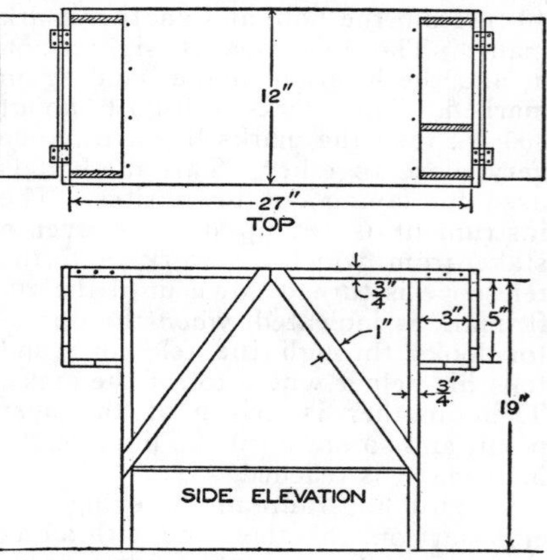

The Bench Provides a Seat for the Worker in Doing Operations on a Small Foot Lathe

was placed between them, near the lower ends.

The projecting ends of the top were cut out, and a box, 5 in. deep, constructed against the supports. A covering was made to fit in each of the openings in the top board and hinged to the outer edge of the box. The boxes made a convenient place for the tools used in the turning work.—Contributed by Harold R. Harvey, Buhl, Idaho.

Cleaning and Polishing Shoes

In using the polishes now on the market for tan shoes, I found that the leather cracked in an unreasonably short time. The following was suggested and tried out with good results. Wash the shoes with castile soap and water by applying the mixture with a dauber. Work up a little lather and then rub dry with a cloth, without rinsing. The leather will be cleaned without becoming dark, and it will not crack. A higher polish may be obtained by using some paste polish in the usual manner. — Contributed by George Bliss, Washington, D. C.

Shaving Cabinet Mounted on an Adjustable Pedestal

The illustration represents a shaving cabinet mounted on an adjustable pedestal, whose style and size are such that it may easily be moved about or set away without requiring much room. The material required for its construction is as follows:

1 framed mirror, 8 by 10 in.
1 square-head bolt and wing nut, ½ by 4 in.
2 cabinet sides, ½ by 7 by 15 in.
2 partitions and shelf, ½ by 6 by 6 in.
1 cabinet top, ½ by 7 by 10½ in.
1 cabinet bottom, ½ by 6 by 10½ in.
2 cabinet backs and doors, ½ by 6½ by 10½ in.
4 cabinet moldings, 1 by 4 by 4 in.
1 cabinet support, 2 by 2 by 26 in.
4 pedestal moldings, 1 by 1 by 6 in.
4 pedestal frames, 1 by 3 by 36 in.
1 base, 2 by 12 by 12 in.
Screws, nails, and varnish.

The sidepieces of the cabinet are extended at one corner, thereby forming the supports for the mirror. The door fits in between the sides and may be attached either by hinges or two wood screws, one on each side, holes being bored in the sides forming a loose fit for the screw so they can freely turn with the door. The pedestal consists of a 4-in. square box resting on the base block, and secured in place by means of molding strips. The sliding support for the cabinet consists of a 2-in. square piece secured to the bot-

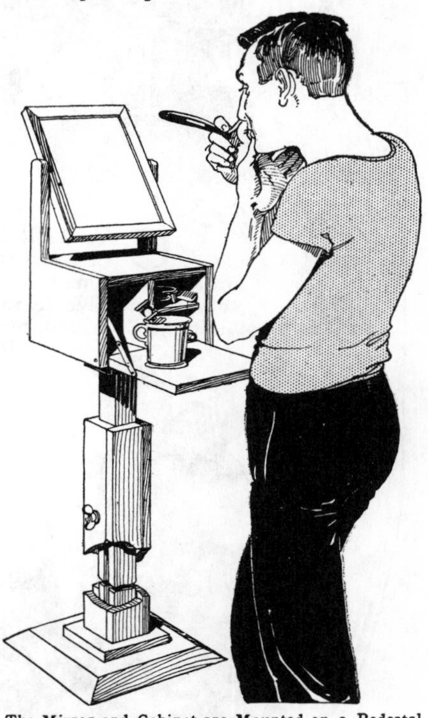

The Mirror and Cabinet are Mounted on a Pedestal That can be Moved as Desired

tom of the cabinet by means of molding, and provided with a slot so the support can freely slide over the clamp bolt, which fastens it in place by clamping it against the pedestal. If it is desired to conceal the head of the bolt, a recess should be made in the pedestal frame for it, as shown, so the support will freely slide over it. Before assembling the pedestal it will be necessary to drill a hole in the front side in line with the recess of the back side, and insert the bolt. If this precaution is not taken, it will not be possible to insert the bolt, unless a hole be made for the head either through the back side or front side.—Contributed by D. Toppan, Watervliet, N. Y.

Four-Passenger Coasting Bobsled

By R. H. ALLEN

COASTER bobs usually have about the same form of construction, and only slight changes from the ordinary are made to satisfy the builder. The one shown has some distinctive features which make it a sled of luxury, and the builder will pride himself in the making. A list of the materials required is given on the opposite page. Any wood may be used for the sled, except for the runners, which should be made of ash.

Shape the runners all alike by cutting one out and using it as a pattern to make the others. After cutting them to the proper shape, a groove is formed on the under edge to admit the curve of a 5/8-in. round iron rod about 1/4 in. deep. The iron rods are then shaped to fit over the runner in the groove and extend up the back part of the runner and over the top at the front end. The extensions should be flattened so that two holes can be drilled in them for two wood screws at each end. If the builder does not have the necessary equipment for flattening these ends, a local blacksmith can do it at a nominal price. After the irons are fitted, they are fastened in place.

The top edges of the runners are notched for the crosspieces so that the top surfaces of these pieces will come flush with the upper edges of the runners. The location of these pieces is not essential, but should be near the ends of the runners, and the notches of each pair of runners should coin-

Coasting Is One of the Best Sports a Boy Enjoys during Winter, and a Sled of Luxury Is Something to Be Proud of among Others on a Hill or Toboggan Slide

cide. When the notches are cut, fit in the pieces snugly, and fasten them with long, slim wood screws. Small metal braces are then fastened to the runners and crosspiece on the inside, to stiffen the joint.

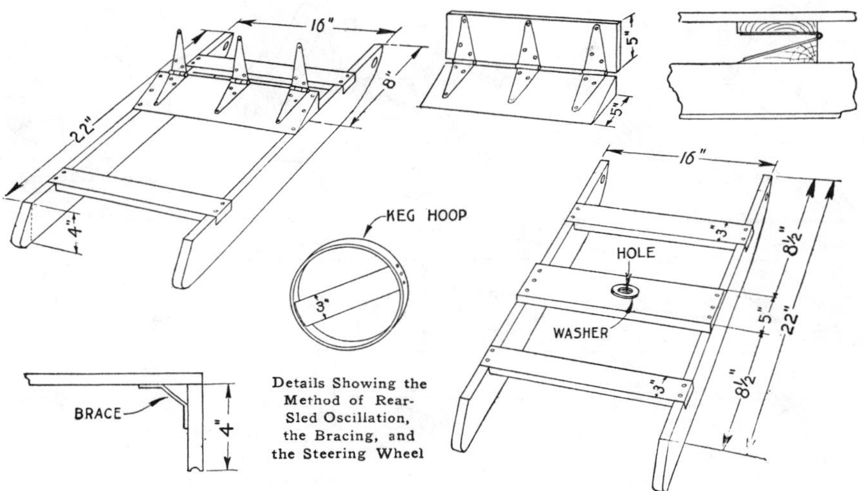

Details Showing the Method of Rear-Sled Oscillation, the Bracing, and the Steering Wheel

As the rear sled must oscillate some, means must be provided for this tilting motion while at the same time preventing sidewise turning. The construction used for this purpose is a hinged joint. The heavy 2 by 5-in. crosspiece is cut sloping on the width so that it remains 2 in. thick at one edge and tapers down to a feather edge at the opposite side. This makes a wedge-shaped piece, to which surface the three large hinges are attached. The piece is then solidly fastened to the upper edges of the runners that are to be used for the rear sled, and so located that the center of the piece will be 8 in. from the front end of the runners.

The supporting crosspiece on the front sled is fastened on top of the runners, at a place where its center will be 11 in. from the front end of the runners.

The top board is prepared by making both ends rounding and planing the surfaces smooth. On the under side, the two crosspieces are placed, which should have two ½-in. holes bored through the width of each, near the ends, to receive the eyebolts. They are placed, one with its center 12 in. from the end to be used for the rear, and the other with its center 8 in. from the front end, and securely fastened with screws. The shore is placed in the center of the board, and wires are run over it connecting the eyebolts. The eyebolts are then drawn up tightly to make the wire taut over the shore. This will prevent the long board from sagging.

On the upper side of the board and

LIST OF MATERIALS

1 top, 6½ ft. long, 16 in. wide, and 1¼ in. thick.
4 runners, 22 in. long, 4 in. wide, and 1 in. thick.
4 crosspieces, 16 in. long, 3 in. wide, and 1 in. thick.
3 pieces, 16 in. long, 5 in. wide, and 2 in. thick.
1 piece, 16 in. long, 5 in. wide, and 1 in. thick.
1 shore, 16 in. long, 3 in. wide, and 1 in. thick.
4 seat backs, 12 in. long, 16 in. wide, and 1 in. thick.
1 dowel, 3 ft. long, and 1 in. in diameter.
4 rods, ⅝ in. in diameter, and 30 in. long.
4 eyebolts, ½ in. by 6 in. long.
3 hinges, 5-in. strap.
8 hinges, 3-in. strap.

beginning at the rear end, the backs are fastened at intervals of 18 in. They are first prepared by rounding the corners on the ends used for the tops, and the opposite ends are cut slightly on an angle to give the back a slant. They are then fastened with the small hinges to the top board. On the edges of the top board, 1-in. holes are bored about 1 in. deep, and pins driven for foot rests. These are located 18 in. apart, beginning about 5 in. from the front end. The dowel is used for the pins, which are made 4 in. long.

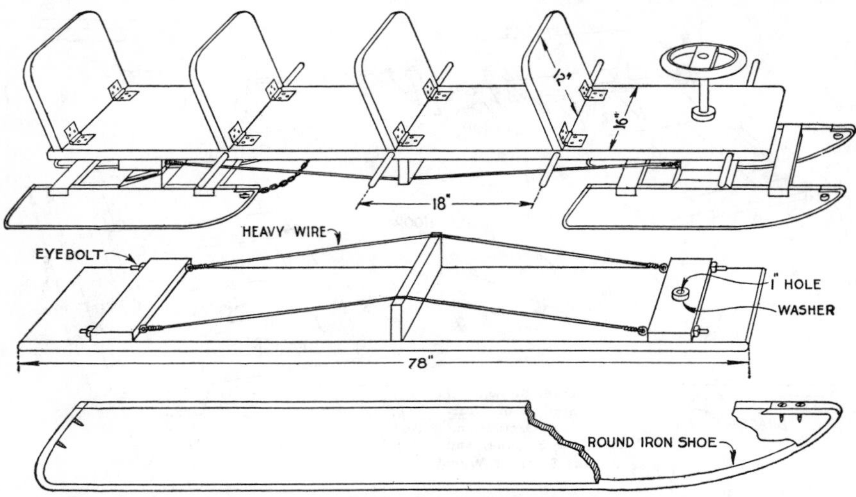

The Top Board is Well Braced on the Under Side and Fitted with Four Backs on Top to Make It a Luxurious Riding Sled, and the Runners are Provided with Metal Shoes for Speed

The steering device consists of a broom handle, cut to 18 in. in length, with one end fastened in a hole bored centrally in the 5-in. crosspiece of the front sled. A hole is bored in the top board through the center of the crosspiece fastened to the under side for the steering post. The broomstick is run through this hole after first placing two metal washers on it. After running the stick through, a hardwood collar is fastened to it just above the top board, so that the top cannot be raised away from the sled. At the upper end of the broomstick a steering wheel is attached, made from a nail-keg hoop. A piece of wood is fastened across its diameter, and the hoop is covered with a piece of garden hose and wrapped with twine. In the center of the crosspiece, a hole is bored to snugly fit on the broom handle, which is then fastened with screws.

The rear sled is fastened to the top board with screws through the extending wings of the hinges and into the crosspiece. Holes are bored in the front ends of all runners, and a chain or rope is attached in them, the loop end of the rear one being attached to the under side of the top board, and the one in the front used for drawing the sled.

To Prevent Drill from Catching As It Passes through Metal

The regular slope of a drill will cause the cutting edge to catch as it breaks through the metal on the opposite side of the piece being drilled. But if a twist drill is ground more flat like a flat drill, it will not "grab" into the metal as it passes through.—Contributed by James H. Beebee, Rochester, N. Y.

An Ice Boat and Catamaran

By ROBERT K. PATTERSON

THIS combination is produced by using the regular type of ice boat and substituting boats for the runners, to make the catamaran.

In constructing the ice boat, use two poles, or timbers, one 16 ft. and the other 10½ ft. long, crossed at a point 2½ ft. from one end of the longer timber. The crossed pieces are firmly braced with wires, as shown.

The mast, which should be about 12 ft. long, is set into a mortise cut in the long timber, 15 in. from the front end, and is further stabilized by wires, as shown. A jib boom, about 6 ft. long, as well as a main boom, which is 11½ ft. long, are hung on the mast in the usual manner.

The Ice Boat Provides an Ideal Outing in Winter Where There Is a Body of Water Large Enough for Sailing

The front runners consist of band-iron strips, 18 in. long, 3 in. wide, and ⅛ in. thick, with one edge ground like the edge of a skate, and the ends rounding, which are fastened with bolts to the sides of wood pieces, 18 in. long, 6 in. wide, and 2 in. thick, allowing the ground edge to project about 1 inch.

When the ice-boat frame is made of poles, the runners are attached to a piece of wood, 12 in. long, shaped as shown and fastened at right angles with bolts running through the shouldered part diagonally. This makes a surface on which the pole end rests and where it is securely fastened with bolts. If squared timbers are used, the runners can be fastened directly to them. The rear, or guiding, runner is fastened between two pieces of wood, so that its edge projects; then it is clamped in a bicycle fork, which should be cut down so that about 3 in. of the forks remain. A hole is bored through the rear end of the long pole to receive the fork head, the upper end of which is supplied with a lever. The lever is attached to the fork head by

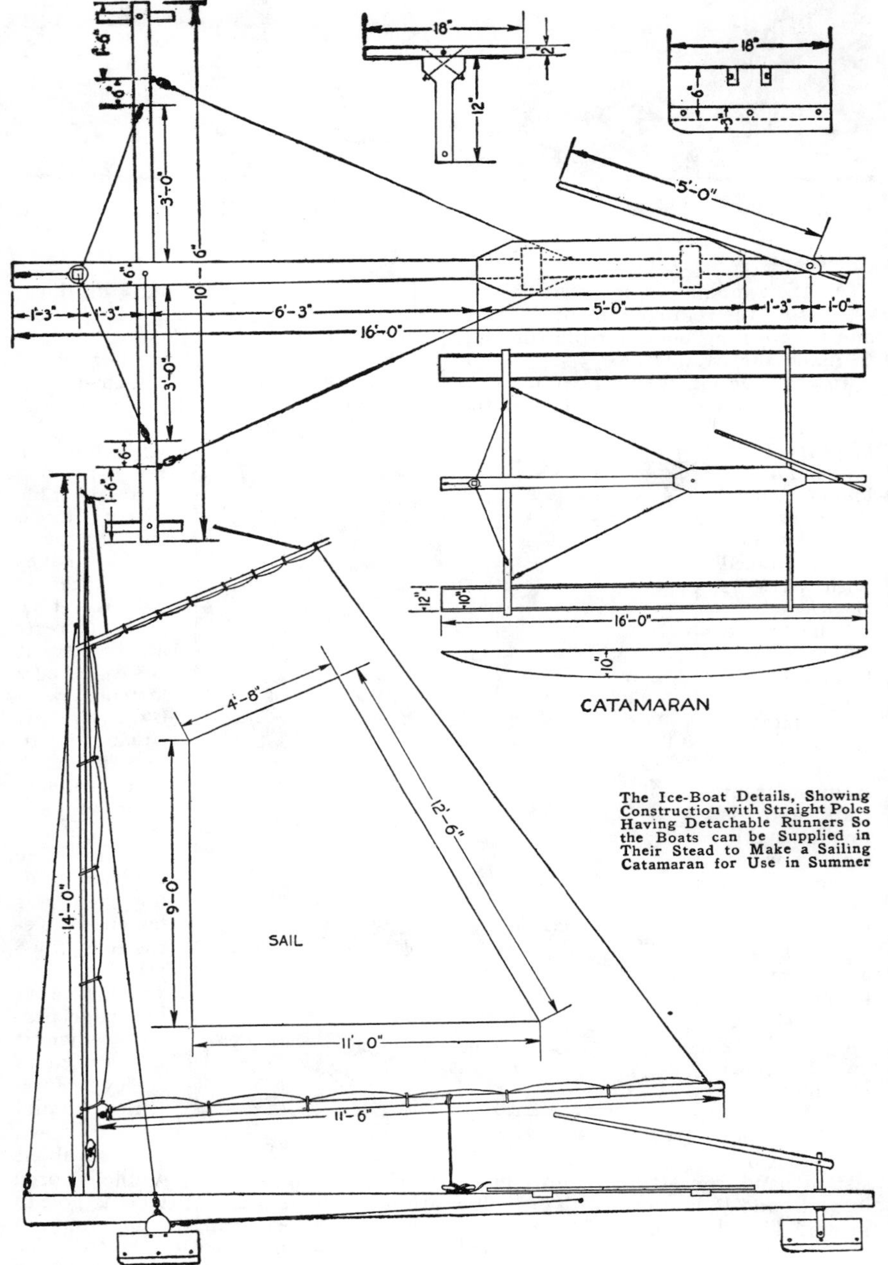

The Ice-Boat Details, Showing Construction with Straight Poles Having Detachable Runners So the Boats can be Supplied in Their Stead to Make a Sailing Catamaran for Use in Summer

boring a hole through the lever end at a slight angle to fit the head, allowing sufficient end to be slotted, whereupon a hole is bored through the width of the handle, and a bolt inserted, to act as a clamp.

A board is fastened on two crosspieces mortised in the upper part of the pole, for a place to sit on when driving the boat. The sail can be constructed of any good material to the dimensions given.

To rig up the ice boat for use as a catamaran, place a pole across the stern, the length of the pole being equal to the one used on the front part of the ice boat. Two water-tight boats are constructed, 16 ft. long, 12 in. wide, and 10 in. deep at the center. To make these two boats procure six boards, 16 ft. long, 10 in. wide, and 1 in. thick. Three boards are used to make each boat. Bend one board so that it will be in an arc of a circle, then nail on the two side boards, after which the edges of the sides are cut away to the shape of the bent board. The runners are removed from the ice boat, and the boats fastened to the pole ends. A rudder is attached in the place of the rear, or guiding, runner. The tops of the boats, or floats, can be covered and made water-tight.

Mind-Reading Effect with Cards

Five cards are shown, and some one person is asked to think of two cards in the lot, after which the performer places the cards behind his back and removes any two cards, then shows the remaining three and asks if the two cards in mind have been removed. The answer is always yes, as it cannot be otherwise.

To prepare the cards, take any 10 cards from the pack and paste the back of one card to another, making five double cards. Removing any two cards behind the performer's back reduces the number of cards to three, and when these are turned over they will not have the same faces so that the ones first seen cannot be shown the second time even though all five cards were turned over and shown.

An Air Pencil to Make Embossed Letters

The device illustrated is for making embossed letters on show cards, signs, post cards, etc. A small bulb, such as

The Oilcan Spout Is the Reservoir to Hold the Paint, and the Bulb Produces the Air Pressure

used on cameras, is procured, also the spout from a small oilcan. The bulb is fastened to the spout as shown.

The material for use in the pencil is quick-drying mucilage thickened with flake white. If some special color is desired, tint the mixture with aniline. Fill the spout with the mixture and attach the bulb. Squeeze the bulb gently while forming the letters, then dust over with bronze, and allow to dry.

An Endless Dish or Floor Mop

A good way to use up cord that collects about the house, is to make an endless dish or floor mop of it. Procure a thin board that will make a good length and wind the cord around it, then remove it from the board and tie the bunch together in the center.

Combination Tie Rack and Collar Holder

An unusual though simple tie rack can be made by supporting the tie bar in the center. By this arrangement the ties can be placed on it from either end, thus avoiding the tedious threading through, required on the ordinary rack supported at each end. Collars may be hung on a peg placed above the tie bar.

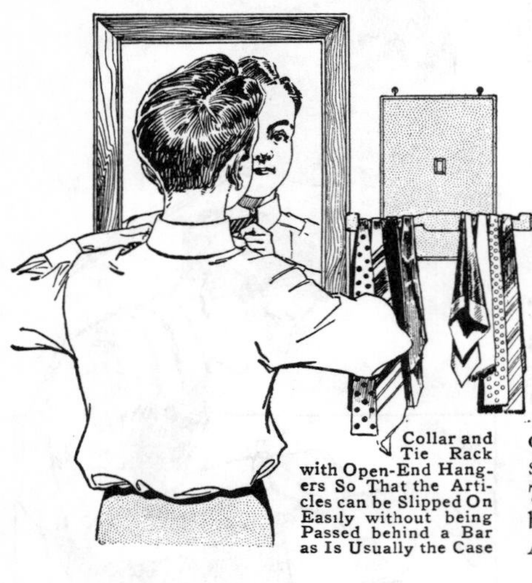

Collar and Tie Rack with Open-End Hangers So That the Articles can be Slipped On Easily without being Passed behind a Bar as Is Usually the Case

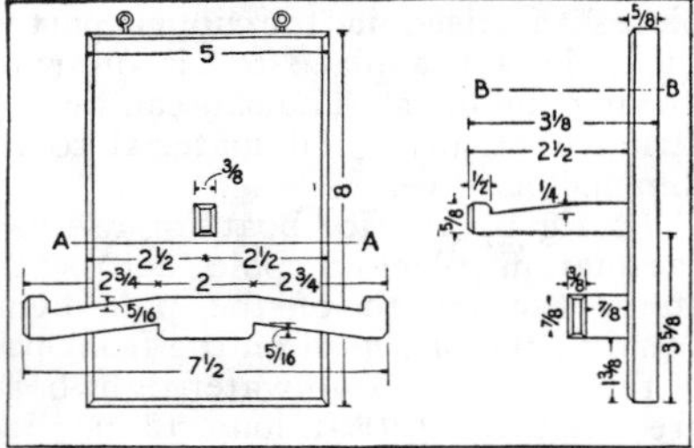

The pieces can be glued together and a good finish given in the usual way. The rack can be hung up by two screw eyes. The material required consists of four pieces, dimensioned ⅝ by 5 by 8 in., ⅜ by ⅞ by 7½ in., ⅜ by ⅝ by 3⅛ in., and ⅞ by ⅞ by 2 in. respectively.—Contributed by Arthur C. Vener, Dallas, Texas.

Skates Made of Wood

Skates that will take the place of the usual steel-runner kind and which will prevent spraining of the ankles, can be made of a few pieces of ½-in. hardwood boards.

Four runners are cut out, 2 in. wide at the back and 1½ in. wide at the front, the length to be 2 in. longer than the shoe. The top edges of a pair of runners are then nailed to the under side of a board 4 in. wide, at its edges.

A piece of board, or block, 2 in. wide is fastened between the runners at the rear, and one 1 in. wide, in front. Two bolts are run through holes bored in the runners, one just back of the front board, or block, and the other in front of the rear one.

Four triangular pieces are fastened, one on each corner, so that the heel and toe of the shoe will fit between them, and, if desired, a crosspiece can be nailed in front of the heel. Straps are attached to the sides for attaching

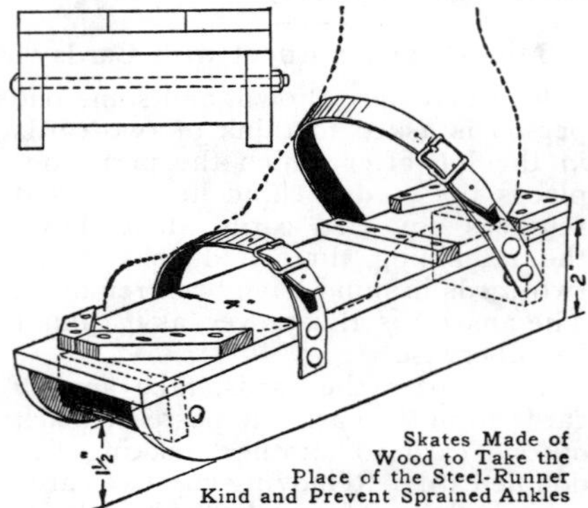

Skates Made of Wood to Take the Place of the Steel-Runner Kind and Prevent Sprained Ankles

the skate to the shoe. Both skates are made alike.—Contributed by F. E. Kennar, Hennessey, Okla.

¶The best paint for paper roofing is asphaltum varnish.

An Ice Glider

By MILDRED E. THOMAS

THE enthusiastic pushmobilist need not put aside his hobby during the winter, as an amusement device for use on ice, which will surpass the very best pushmobile, can be easily made as shown in the illustration.

Similar to an ice yacht, only a great deal smaller, the ice glider will require three ordinary skates, two of which are fastened to the ends of the front crosspiece, so that their blades will stand at an angle of about 30 deg. with their edges outward. To get this angle tapering block are fastened to the crosspiece ends, as shown. The skates are then fastened to these blocks.

The Glider is Pushed over the Ice Similarly to a Pushmobile, and the Speed That can be Attained is Much Greater

The crosspiece is 30 in. long and about 8 in. wide. In the center of this piece an upright is constructed, 26 in. high. The edges of the front crosspiece are cut on a slant so that a piece nailed to its front and back edge will stand sloping toward the rear. A handle, 24 in. long, is fastened between the two uprights at the upper end. The rear part is made of a board, 8 in. wide and 40 in. long. The remaining skate is fastened in a perfectly straight position on the rear end. The skates may be attached with screws run through holes drilled in the top plates, or with straps. The front end of the rear board has a hole for a bolt to attach it to the center of the front crosspiece, so that the latter will turn to guide the glider.

A pusher is prepared from a block of wood, into which nails are driven with their ends projecting on the under side. The block is strapped to one shoe, as shown.

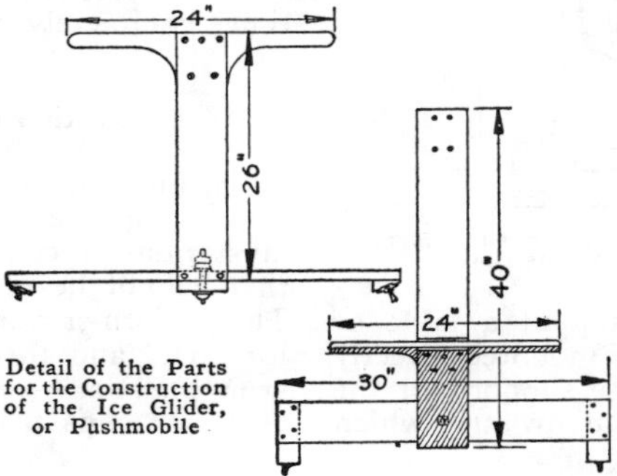

Detail of the Parts for the Construction of the Ice Glider, or Pushmobile

The glider is used in the same manner as a pushmobile.

The pusher can be made in another way by using sole leather instead of the block. Small slots are cut in the sides for the straps. Nails are driven through the leather so that the points project. Either kind of pusher is especially adapted for the pushmobile to prevent wear on the shoe.

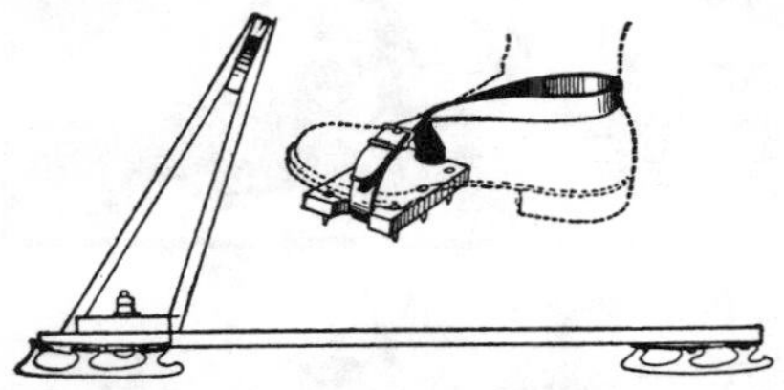

The Block of Wood with Protecting Nails to Fasten on the Shoe That Does the Pushing

Prony Brake for Testing Small Motors

The ordinary prony brake is not, as a rule, sensitive enough to make an accurate test on small motors, such as those used in driving sewing machines, washing machines, vacuum cleaners, etc. The arrangement shown in the accompanying sketch has been used for this purpose with good results and was very accurate. The operation of the brake is exceedingly simple.

A pulley without a crown face is attached to the shaft of the motor, which is fastened to the top of a table or bench, and a balance mounted directly over the pulley. The support for the balance should be a narrow strip, which in turn is supported on two upright pieces, as shown. A light rope is put under the pulley, and the ends are looped over the platforms of the balance so that it does not interfere with the operation of the balance. The ends of the rope should be vertical and parallel. The piece upon which the balance rests is raised by inserting wedges, thus increasing the tension in the rope. The resulting friction of the rope on the pulley increases the load.

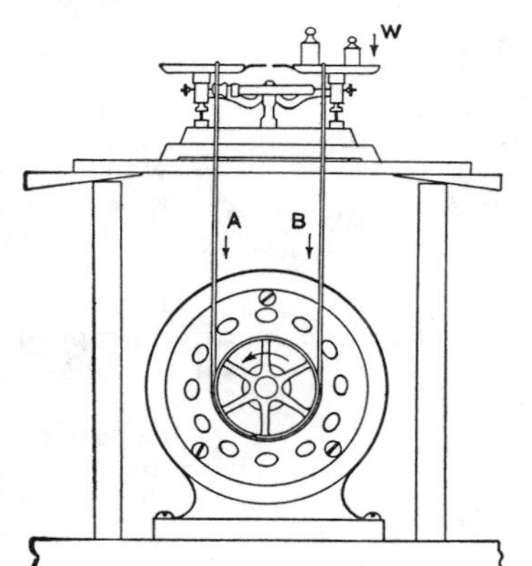

Prony Brake Used in Connection with a Small Balance to Find the Horsepower

If the motor is running in the direction indicated by the arrow on the pulley, the tension in the left-hand end of the rope will be greater than in the right-hand end and a weight must be placed on the right-hand platform of the balance. When the weight W is adjusted so that the two pointers on the platforms are exactly opposite each other, the value of the weight W, in pounds, will represent the difference in pull, in pounds, between A and B. If the value of the weight W is known and also the speed of the machine when the weight was determined, the horsepower output can be computed by means of the following equation:

$$\text{Hp.} = \frac{6.2832 \times L \times W \times \text{R.P.M.}}{33{,}000 \times 12}$$

In this equation, L is the distance in inches from the center of the pulley to the center of the rope. Two ordinary spring balances may be substituted for the beam balance and the difference in their readings taken for the value W. For best results, the tension in the slack end of the rope should be as small as possible, and it may be necessary to wrap the rope one or more times completely around the pulley.

A Mystic Fortune Teller

Fortune telling by means of weights striking glasses or bottles is quite mysterious if controlled in a manner that cannot be seen by the audience. The performer can arrange two strikes for "no," and three for "yes" to answer questions. Any kind of bottles, glass, or cups may be used. In the bottles the pendulum can be suspended from the cork, and in the glasses from small tripods set on the table.

The secret of the trick is as follows: A rubber tube with a bulb attached to each end is placed under a rug, one bulb being located under one table leg and the other near the chair of the performer set at some distance from the table where it can be pressed with the foot. Some one selects a pendulum; the performer gazes intently at it, and presses the bulb under his foot lightly at first; then, by watching the swaying of the pendulum selected, he will know when to give the second impulse, and continue until the weight strikes the glass. As the pendulums are of different lengths they must necessarily swing at different rates per second. The impulses must be given at the proper time or else the pendulum will be retarded instead of increased in amplitude. A table with four legs is best to use, and the leg diagonally opposite that with the bulb beneath it must not touch the carpet or floor. This can be arranged by placing pieces of cardboard under the other two legs. —Contributed by James J. McIntyre.

The Rocking of the Table is Caused by the Pressure of Air in the Bulb under the Foot, the Movement Causing the Pendulum to Swing and Strike the Glass

Holding Prints in a Liquid-Filled Tray

After having considerable trouble in keeping my paper prints in the hypo fixing bath from curling, which would force the edges out of the liquid, I found the plan here illustrated a success. I procured a piece of wood, the size of a postcard, and stuck four glass push pins into one surface, one at each corner, and fastened a handle to the center of the upper side. The papers are first placed in the bath, then the board is set over them with the pins down. This holds the prints under the liquid but does not press them tightly together.—Contributed by J. J. Kolar, Maywood, Ill.

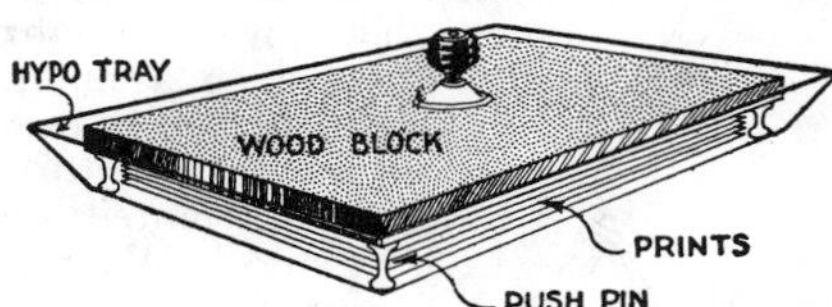

Push Pins on the Under Side of the Board Raise It and Provide a Space for the Prints in the Liquid

---

¶A piece of an old gunny sack will polish brass work very nicely.

Cellar-Door Holder

A cellar door that opened up against a wall required a catch of some kind to keep it open at times. As I did not want a catch to show on the wall, I devised a holder as shown. Three pieces of wood were nailed to the under side of the door in such positions that they formed a recess in which a fourth piece, 2 in. wide and 1 in. thick, would slide endways. A knob was attached to the upper end of the slide, which served the double purpose of a handle and a stop for the slide. The manner of using the holder is clearly shown.—Contributed by H. T. Smith, Topeka, Kansas.

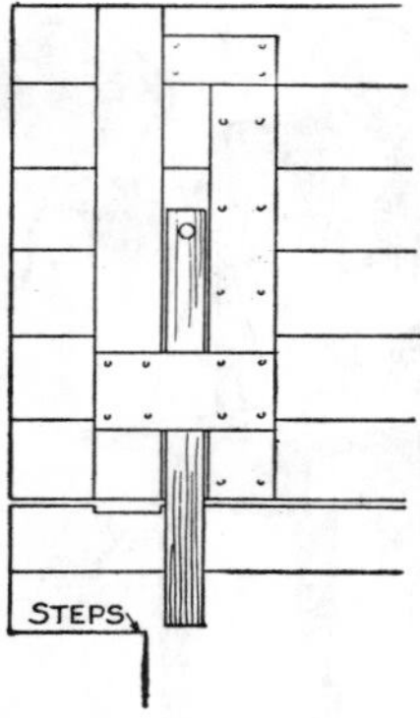

An Emergency Pencil Compass

The need of a compass when none was at hand caused me to quickly devise a substitute for the work. A piece of stiff wire, about the length of the pencil, was procured, and several turns were made around the pencil, as shown. The lower straight end was filed to a point. The wire can be bent to obtain the radius distance.—Contributed by Preston Ware, Rome, Ga.

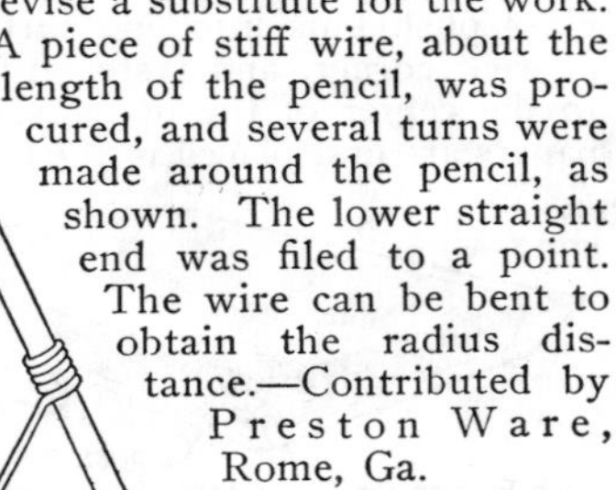

¶A very effective dip for brass and copper articles, that will leave a clean and bright finish, is 2 qt. of aqua fortis, 1 gal. of sulphuric acid, 1 pt. of water and a pinch of salt.

Renewing Carbon Paper

When carbon paper has been used several times, the preparation becomes almost worn off on some parts, while other parts of the paper are as good as new. The process of renewing is very simple and it can be done by anyone without special apparatus. All that is necessary is to hold the paper in front of a fire or over a radiator a few seconds. The heat will cause the preparation to dissolve and spread over the paper, so that when it is dry the paper will have a new coating. This can be repeated, and in some cases will double the life of the carbon paper.—Contributed by Chester M. Kearney, Danville, Quebec.

How to Clinch a Finishing Nail

A wire or finishing nail may be clinched as nicely as a wrought nail, if a nail punch or piece of iron is placed along the side of it, as shown at A, and the nail hammered into an arched form, as at B. The punch or rod is then withdrawn and the arch driven into the wood.—Contributed by James M. Kane, Doylestown, Pa.

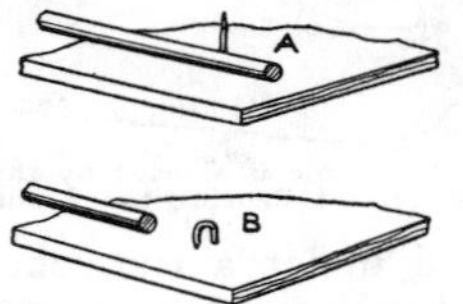

To Prevent Washbasin Bottom from Wearing Out

The ears from some sirup buckets were removed and three of them soldered, at equal distances apart, on the bottom of the washbasin near the outside edge of the lower part. These prevented the wear from coming on the bottom of the basin, and it lasted several times as long as ordinarily.—Contributed by A. A. Ashley, Blanket, Texas.

¶To curl feathers, heat slightly before a fire, then stroke with something like the back of a case knife.

PART I—Shapes of Snowshoes

TO the inventive mind of the North American Indian we owe the snowshoe, and its conception was doubtless brought about through that prolific source of invention—necessity. The first models were crude web-footed affairs, but improvements in model and manner of filling the frames were gradually added until the perfected and graceful shoe of the present was finally reached. The first snowshoes were made by the Indians, and the Indians of Maine and Canada continue to fashion the finest models today.

The snowshoe is a necessity for the sportsman and trapper whose pleasure or business leads him out in the open during the winter season, when roads and trails are heavily blanketed by a deep fall of powdery snow. But the use of the web shoe is by no means confined to the dweller in the wilderness, since the charm of wintry wood and plain beckons many lovers of the outdoors to participate in this invigorating sport, and snowshoe tramps are fast growing in popularity in and about our cities and towns.

All the modern snowshoes are constructed upon practically the same general lines, although the types of frames differ considerably in size as well as in shape, and the filling of hide is often woven in many varied and intricate patterns. The frame or bow—usually made of ash in order to get strength with light weight—is bent in many shapes, but the one shown in the diagram is a typical general-purpose shoe, and may be called standard. The frame is held in shape by means of two wooden cross braces, neatly mortised into the frame. These braces are spaced some 15 or 16 in. apart, and so divide the shoe into three sections, known as the toe, center, and heel. The filling is woven into a lanyard, which is a light strip of hide firmly laced to the frame through a double row of holes drilled in the wood. The center filling is woven of heavy strands of rawhide, in a fairly coarse mesh, because this part of the shoe must bear the weight of the body and the brunt of wear. The end fillers for toe and heel are woven of lighter strands of hide, and the mesh is, of course, smaller.

As may be noted by referring to the drawing, a center opening or "toe hole" is provided, and as the greater strain on the filling lies directly under the ball of the foot, the shoe is reinforced at this point by the "toe cord" running across, and the "toe-cord stays," which are tied in on each side of the toe hole—one end being fastened to the toe cord and the other lashed over the wooden cross bar of the frame. These reinforcing cords are formed of several strands of hide, the stays being again wound with finer strands.

To prevent slipping and to secure a good foothold while walking, the manner of attaching the foot to the shoe is of importance, and this is done by making use of a toe strap, which will allow the toe to push down through the toe opening as the heel of the foot is lifted in the act of walking. A second strap, or thong, leading from the top around the foot, above the curve of the heel, is needed to lend additional support in lifting the snowshoe, to effect the easy shambling stride characteristic of the snowshoer.

There are, of course, a great number of models or styles, some one style being popular in one locality, while an altogether different style is preferred in another part of the country. The most representative types are well shown in the illustrations, and a brief description will point out their practical advantages, because each model possesses certain merits—one model being designed for fast traveling in the open, another better adapted for brush travel, while others are more convenient for use in a hilly country where much climbing is done, and so on.

Style A is regarded by snowshoe experts as an extreme style, for it is long and narrow. It is designed for fast traveling over smooth and level country, and over loose, powdery snow. This style is much used by the Cree Indians, and is usually made 12 in. wide by 60 in. long, with a deeply upcurved toe. It is a good shoe for cross-country work, but is somewhat difficult to manage on broken trails, when the snow is packed, and also affords rather slippery footing when crossing ice. Owing to the stout construction of the frame and reinforcement needed to retain the high, curved toe, style A is more difficult to manage than the more conservative models, and its stiffness of frame makes it more fatiguing to wear, while its use is a decided handicap in mountainous districts, because a curved toe always makes hill climbing more difficult.

Style B may be considered the ordinary eastern model, and a common style best adapted for all-around use. It is a neat and gracefully designed frame, about 12 in. wide and 42 in. long, and is usually made with a slightly upcurving toe, about 2 in. turn at the toe being correct. When made by the Indians of Maine, this model is fashioned with a rather heavy heel, which is an advantage for fast walking, while it increases the difficulty in quick turning.

Style C is a favorite model among the hunters and woodsmen of New England. This is a splendid style for general purposes in this section of the country, since the full, round toe keeps the toe up near the surface, and lets the heel cut down more than the narrow-toe models. Style C is an easy shoe to wear, and while not so fast as the long, narrow frame, its full shape is more convenient for use in the woods. It is usually made with about 1 to 1½-in. turn at the toe.

Style D is the familiar "bear's paw," a model originating with the northeastern trapper. This model is well adapted for short tramps in the brush, and having a flat toe, is likewise a good shoe for mountain climbing. For tramping about in thick brush, a short, full shoe enables one to take a shorter stride and turn more quickly, but it is a slow shoe for straight-ahead traveling.

When purchasing a pair of snowshoes, some few important considerations should be kept in mind, and the size and model will depend upon the man to some extent, since a large, heavy man will require a larger snowshoe than would suffice for a person of lighter weight. Height also enters into the choice, and while a small person can travel faster and with less fatigue when equipped with a proportionately small shoe, a tall man will naturally pick out a larger-sized snowshoe for his use. For a country where deep snows prevail, larger sizes are best, but in localities where the snow packs solidly and there is considerable ice, and in mountainous districts, or for rough-country traveling, the smaller sizes will give more satisfaction and prove more durable also. For a wet-snow locality, the center filling should be strung in rather coarse mesh, while for soft, powdery snow, a finer mesh will be the logical choice.

There are snowshoes and snowshoes, and while there are fine models regularly stocked by a few of the better sporting-goods firms, there is likewise a deal of poorly made snowshoes on the market. It is well to pay a fair price and secure a dependable handmade article, for the cheaper snowshoes—often filled with seine twine and the cheapest hide (commonly known in the trade as "gut")—will warp and twist in the frame, and the shoddy filling will soon become loosened up and "bag" after a little use. The best snowshoes that the writer is acquainted with are made by the Indians, and the filling is ordinarily made of neat's hide; cowhide for the center filling, and calfskin for the toe and heel. A first-class pair of snowshoes may be had for about $6 to $7.50, and when possible to do so, it is best to have them made to order. This plan is, of course, necessary in case one wishes to incorporate any little wrinkles of his own into their making, or desires a flatter toe, lighter heel, or a different mesh from the usual stock models.

Where but one pair of snowshoes is purchased, style B will probably prove the best selection, and should be ordered with the flat toe, or a turn not greater than 1 in. The frame may be in either one or two pieces, depending upon the size of the shoe and the ideas of the Indian maker, but it is well to specify white ash for the frames in the order. No Indian maker would be guilty of using screws or other metal fastenings, but many of the cheap and poorly fashioned snowshoes are fastened at the heel with screws, thus making this a decidedly weak point, since the wood is quite certain to split after a little rough service. In contrast to the poor workmanship of these low-priced snowshoes, the Indian-made article is fashioned from sound and properly seasoned wood; the cross bars are snugly fitted by mortising to the frame; the filling is tightly woven, and the heel is properly fastened by lacing with a rawhide

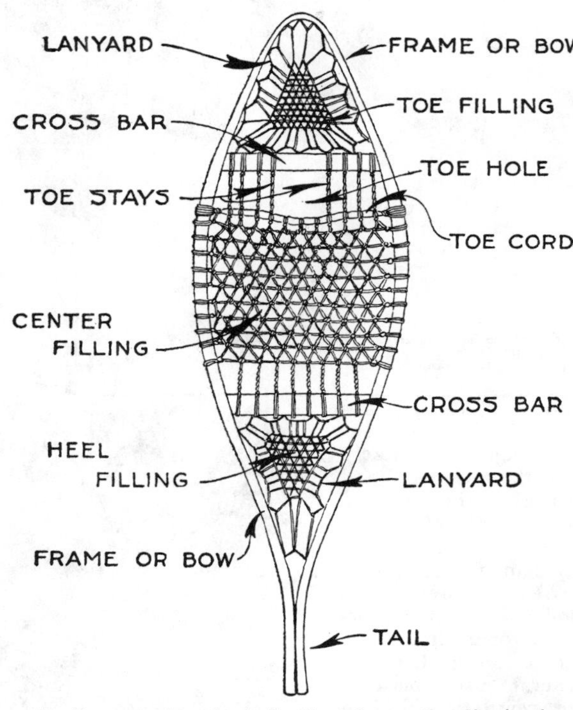

The Frame of a Snowshoe in Its Usual Construction, Showing the Crosspieces with Their Laced Fillings of Hide and the Different Parts Named, for a Ready Reference

Snowshoe Experts Regard This as an Extreme Style, for It is Long and Narrow

it is a good idea to select a filling of good heavy weight and with a firmly woven and open mesh, say, about ¾ in. The toe and heel sections will, of course, be of finer-cut hide and smaller mesh, and it is wise to avoid those shoes employing seine twine for the end filling. Some factory-made snowshoes are given a coat or two of varnish, but this, while serving to make them partly waterproof, makes them rather slippery when crossing logs and ice. Most woodsmen prefer to leave both frame and filling in their natural condition.

The Indian-made snowshoe is always

thong. However, Indian makers are likely to make the toe small and leave the wood to form a rather heavy heel. Some few woodsmen and sportsmen may prefer this model, but the majority favor a fuller toe and a lighter heel for general use, because the regulation Indian model, cutting down at toe and heel equally deep, increases the difficulty of easy traveling over soft snow, although it is a good shoe when used over broken trails.

When buying snowshoes at the store, see that the frames are stoutly and well made, and for all-around use,

This Snowshoe is Considered the Ordinary Eastern Model and One Best Adapted for All-Around Use

provided with a generously large toe hole, so that ample foot covering may be used. This point is generally overlooked in the machine-made product, and the toe cords are also frequently roughly formed, thus chafing the feet and making them sore. These details may or may not prove a handicap for short tramps near town, but for long trips through the woods, they are important considerations.

The Indian manner of tying the snowshoe to the foot by means of a single twisted and knotted thong is a good method of attachment, in that, if the thong is properly adjusted to the requisite snugness in the first place, the shoes may be quickly removed by a simple twist of the ankle. A better fastening is secured by using a fairly wide (¾ in.) toe strap and a long thong. The toe strap is placed over the toes, immediately over the ball of the foot, and secured against slipping by weaving the ends in and out between the meshes of the filling until it reaches the frame on either side. This grips the toe strap firmly and does away with the necessity of tying a knot. A narrow thong, about 4 ft. long, is now doubled, the center placed just

The Style Illustrated Here is Splendid for General Purposes and is a Favorite among Hunters and Woodsmen

This is the Familiar "Bear's-Paw" Model, Originated by the Northeastern Trapper for Use on Short Tramps and in Brush

above the heel of the foot, and the ends passed under the toe cord, just outside of the toe-cord stays on each side. The thong is then brought up and across the toes, one end passing over and the other under the toe strap. Each end of the thong is now looped around the crossed thong, on either side, and then carried back over the back of the heel and knotted with a common square or reef knot. Calfskin makes a good flexible foot binding, or a suitable strip of folded cloth or canvas may be used.

The regulation snowshoe harness, consisting of a leather stirrup for the toe and an instep and heel strap, will be found more comfortable than the thong, and when once adjusted snugly to the foot, the shoes may be quickly taken off and put on again by pushing the heel strap down, when the foot may be slipped out of the toe stirrup.

The use of heavy leather shoes is of course undesirable, and the only correct footwear for snowshoeing is a pair of high-cut moccasins, cut roomy enough to allow one or more pairs of heavy woolen stockings to be worn. The heavy and long German socks, extending halfway to the knee, drawn on over the trouser legs, are by far the most comfortable for cold-weather wear. The feet, thus shod, will not only be warm in the coldest weather, but the free use of the toes is not interfered with. Leather shoes are cold and stiff, and the heavy soles and heels, chafing against the snowshoes, will soon ruin the filling.

Soldering and Riveting

By JOHN D. ADAMS

There are two simple processes that every experimenter should master: soldering and riveting. The large soldering copper will find only a very restricted use with the amateur on account not only of its clumsiness, but of the fact that it requires a fire, which is often impracticable to obtain. The experimenter should therefore construct a small alcohol lamp, which, after a little experience, will reveal the following advantages: It may be brought into instant use at any place; it will make a more perfect connection; with a small blowpipe places may be reached that are entirely inaccessible to the large iron; several small pieces may be set in position and soldered without disturbing them, which is quite impossible with the large iron.

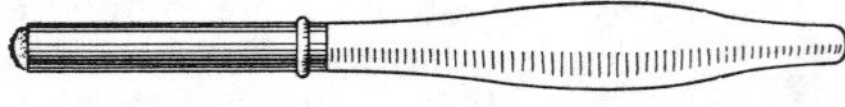

A Small Torch Made of a Penholder is Handy to Use in Soldering Electrical Apparatus

To make such a lamp, procure a small wide-mouthed bottle so that very little alcohol will be necessary and the lamp may be tipped at any desired angle. A short piece of seamless brass tubing should be procured, or, preferably, one of those capped brass cylinders for holding pencil leads, the button of which should be sawn off and the cap used to keep the alcohol from evaporating. A good, sound cork is next in order, and in cutting the central hole, use the brass tube, which should be sharpened around the lower end. Proceed with a rotary motion, and a clean core will be removed. If an ordinary lamp wick is not at hand, soft cotton string may be bundled up as a substitute. Such a lamp is safe, odorless and will not blacken the work in the least as in the case of kerosene or gasoline.

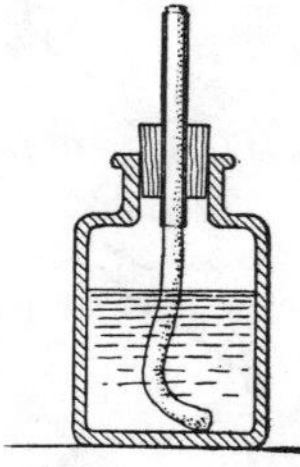

There are many good soldering fluxes on the market, but that obtained by dissolving as much scrap of zinc as possible in muriatic acid will solder practically everything that may be necessary, provided, of course, the surfaces are filed or scraped bright. Wire solder is usually the most convenient, as small pieces can be readily cut off and placed directly on the work where required. A small blowpipe is often a valuable adjunct, as it makes possible a long, narrow flame that may be directed in almost any direction.

Where numerous small connections are to be made, as is often the case with electrical apparatus, the small torch illustrated will be found very convenient. It is simply an old penholder with the wood portion shortened somewhat and the metal end filed off square and cleaned out. This is then filled with wicking, and it is only necessary to dip it in alcohol in order to soak up enough to solder an ordinary connection.

The second simple process, of which many fail to appreciate the usefulness in experimental work, is that of riveting—particularly when done on a small scale. Very often the material in hand is tempered steel and cannot, therefore, be soldered to advantage, or it may be a case where subsequent heating makes a heat-proof connection imperative. Then, again, the joint may require the combined strength of both solder and rivet.

When properly set, the strength of the ordinary brass pin, when used as a rivet, is quite great. Should the work require a particularly soft rivet, it is only necessary to hold the pin for a moment in the flame of a match. A somewhat larger and stronger rivet may be made by softening and cutting to the required length the small flat-headed nails used in making cigar boxes. The ordinary shingle nail is also of a suitable shape after the burrs have been filed off under the head.

In setting these small rivets, it is absolutely necessary that they closely fit the holes, as at A, otherwise the result will be as indicated at B in the sketch. Be careful not to leave too great a length for rounding over on the metal. This extra length should approximately equal the diameter of the rivet and must be filed flat on the top before riveting. In case of pins, it will be found easier to cut them off to the proper length after they are inserted. Use the smallest hammer available, striking many light blows rather than a few heavy ones.

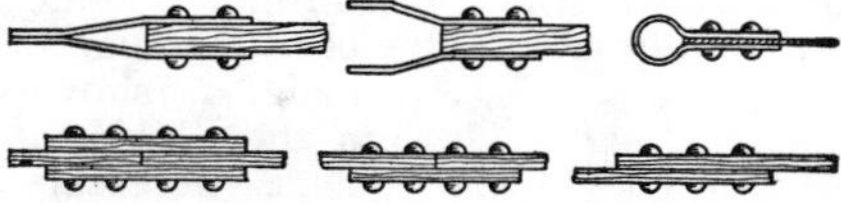

A Few Joints Where Rivets are Used to Hold the Parts Solidly Together

A Whistle

Cut a circular piece of tin any convenient size, preferably 3 in. in diameter, and bend it across the diameter so that it will be in a narrow U-shape. Then drill or punch a hole through both parts as shown. Place it in the mouth with the open edges out, being sure to press the lips on the metal tightly on both upper and lower pieces outside of the holes and to rest the tongue against the edge of the tin, even with the holes, and blow.

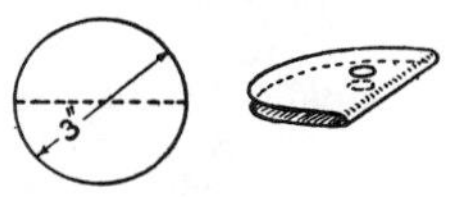

The result of the first attempt may not be a sound, but with a little practice any familiar tune may be whistled. —Contributed by Chas. C. Bradley, W. Toledo, O.

Card-and-Coin Trick

If a card is balanced on the finger and a coin placed on the card directly over the finger, one would not think that the card could be flipped out leaving the coin on the finger end. This is easily accomplished, if care is taken to snap the card sharply and squarely.—Contributed by R. Neland, Minneapolis, Minn.

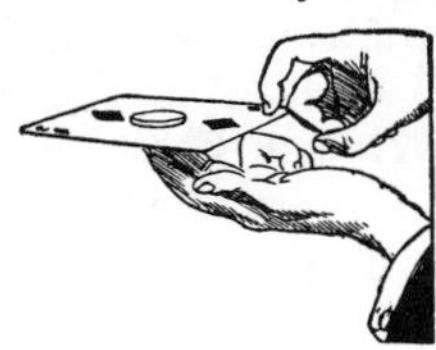

How to Make a Costumer

With but little skill, and such tools as are ordinarily found around a home, a plain but serviceable costumer can be made, as shown in the sketch. The necessary materials for it are: One main post, 1½ in. square and about 6½ ft. long; four legs, or foot brackets, ¾ by 6 by 9 in.; four brass clothes hooks, and the necessary screws and varnish for assembling and finishing.

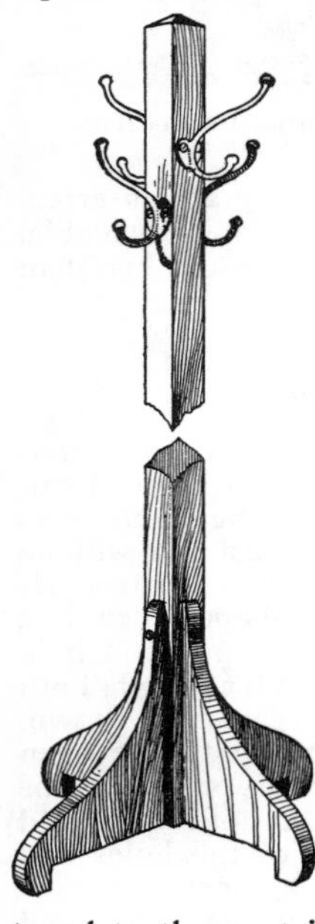

The center post should be chamfered at the top to relieve the abruptness. The four legs should all be made alike and in some shape that allows them to be fastened to the post in a simple manner. In the sketch, the legs are fastened to the post by one visible screw at the top and one put in on an incline through the bottom edge of the leg. The clothes hooks are fastened to the post in pairs at different heights, thereby preventing the screws of adjacent hooks from running into one another. The finish of the costumer should be such as to match the woodwork of its surroundings.—Contributed by Harry A. Packard, Norway, Maine.

Window Catch Used for Locking an Extension Table

To prevent the two ends of an extension table from pulling apart when not desired, an ordinary window catch can be fastened and locked in place to the under side of the table top with one part on each end of the table. If but one catch is used and fastened in the center, it is best to mark it off first, and then pull the table ends apart to fasten the catch more easily. It may be desired to use two catches for a very heavy table, in which case it would be best to place one on either side of the center.—Contributed by F. M. Griswold, New York, N. Y.

Relieving Pressure on Heated Canned Foods for Opening

In opening a can of food that has been heated, the instant the cover is punctured the steam will force out a part of the contents, which is very annoying. To avoid this, pour a little cold water on the cover and allow it to remain a few seconds, then turn it off and immediately puncture the cover. This will counteract the interior force, and the can may be opened without trouble.—Contributed by Joseph Kohlbecher, Jr., San Francisco, Cal.

Clothespin Bag

Clothespins are usually kept in a bag, and the one our home possessed had a draw string which would always stick and hold the bag shut. The remedy for this, and a time saver also, was to remove the draw string and insert instead a piece of wire, which was afterward shaped to a circle with an eyelet at the joint. The bag can be hung on a nail and the mouth is always open to its fullest extent, yet lies flat against the wall.—Contributed by Jas. A. Hart, Philadelphia, Pa.

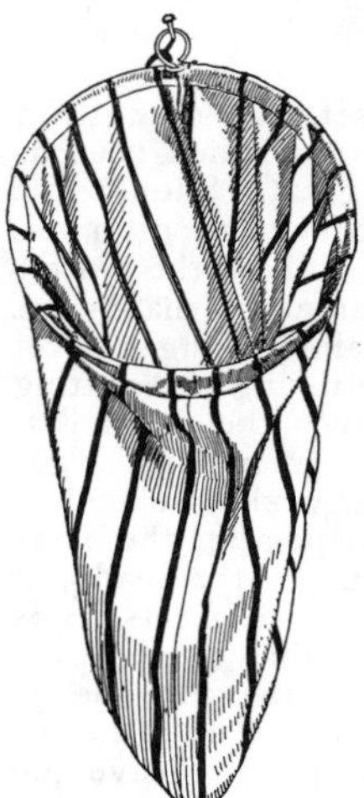

SNOWSHOES

HOW TO MAKE AND USE THEM

By Stillman Taylor

PART II—Making the Shoe

[In making the snowshoe it may be necessary to refer to the previous chapter to select the style, or to locate the name of the parts used in the description.—Editor.]

SNOWSHOE making is an art, and while few, if any, white men can equal the Indian in weaving the intricate patterns which they prefer to employ for filling the frames, it is not very difficult to fashion a good solid frame and then fill it by making use of a simple and open system of meshing. For the frames, white ash is much the best wood, but hickory and white birch are dependable substitutes, if the former cannot be obtained. Birch is perhaps the best wood to use when the sportsman wishes to cut and split up his own wood, but as suitable material for the frames may be readily purchased for a small sum, probably the majority of the readers will elect to buy the material. Any lumber dealer will be able to supply white ash, and it is a simple matter to saw out the frames from the board. The sawed-out frame is inferior to the hand-split bow, but if good, selected material can be obtained, there will be little, if any, difference for ordinary use.

When dry and well-seasoned lumber is used, the frame may be made to the proper dimensions, but when green wood is selected, the frame must be made somewhat heavier, to allow for the usual shrinkage in seasoning. For a stout snowshoe frame, the width should be about $1\frac{1}{16}$ in.; thickness at toe, $\frac{7}{16}$ in., and thickness at heel, $\frac{9}{16}$ in. The frame should be cut 2 in. longer

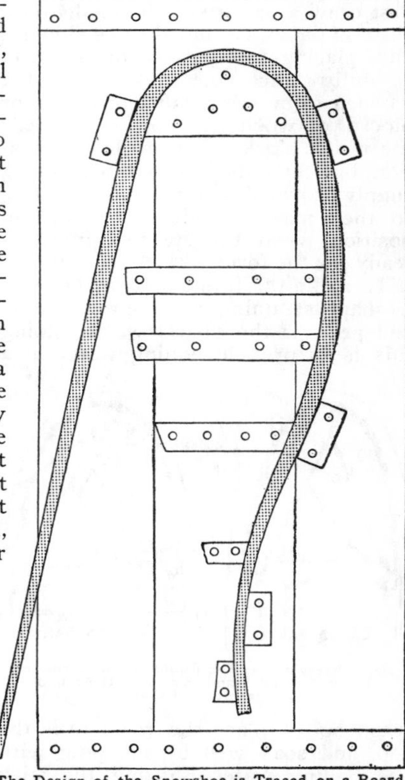

The Design of the Snowshoe is Traced on a Board, and Blocks are Used to Shape the Frame or Bow

than the finished length desired, and in working the wood, remember that the toe of the finished frame will be the center of the stick; the heel, the end of the stick, and the center of the shoe will lie halfway between the heel and toe.

Locate the Cross Bars by Balancing the Frame, Then Fit the Ends in Shallow Mortises

After the frames have been finished, the dry wood must be steamed before it can be safely bent to the required shape, and before doing this, a wooden bending form must be made. An easy way to make this form is to first draw a pattern of the model on a sheet of paper, cut out the pencil mark, and, placing this pattern on a board, carefully trace the design on the wooden form. A number of cleats, or blocks, of wood will now be needed; the inside blocks being nailed in position, but the outside stay blocks being simply provided with nails in the holes, so they may be quickly fastened in position when the steamed frame is ready for the form.

To make the frame soft for bending to shape, steaming must be resorted to, and perhaps the easiest way of doing this is to provide boiling water in a

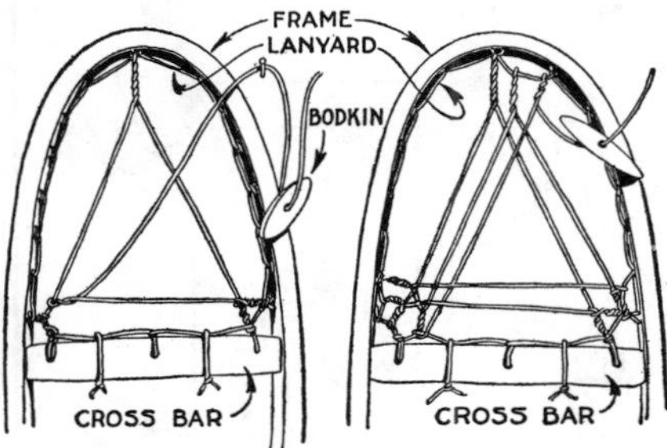

Begin Weaving the Toe Filling at the Corner of Cross Bar and Frame, Carrying It Around in a Triangle until Complete

wash boiler, place the wood over the top, and soak well by mopping with the boiling water, shifting the stick about until the fibers have become soft and pliable. After 10 or 15 minutes of the hot-water treatment, wrap the stick with cloth and bend it back and forth to render it more and more pliable, then use the hot-water treatment, and repeat the process until the wood is sufficiently soft to bend easily without splintering. The toe being the greatest curve, must be well softened before putting on the form, otherwise the fibers are likely to splinter off at this point. When the frame is well softened, place it on the bending form while hot, slowly bend it against the wooden inside blocks, and nail on the outside blocks to hold it to the proper curve. Begin with the toe, and after fastening the outside blocks to hold this end, finish one side, then bend the other half to shape. The bent frame should be allowed to dry on the form for at least a week; if removed before the wood has become thoroughly dry and has taken a permanent set, the frame will not retain its shape. The same bending form may be used for both frames, but if one is in a hurry to finish the shoes, two forms should be made, and considerable pains must be taken to make them exactly alike in every way.

When the frames are dry, secure the tail end of the frame by boring three holes about 4 in. from the end, and fasten with rawhide. The work of fitting the two cross bars may now be undertaken, and the balance of the snowshoe depends upon fitting these bars in their proper places. Before cutting the mortise, spring the two bars in the frame about 15 in. apart, and balance the shoe in the center by holding it in the hands. When the frame exactly balances, move the bars sufficiently to make the heel about 3 oz. heavier than the toe, and mark the place where the mortises are to be cut. The cross bars and mortise must be a good tight fit, and a small, sharp chisel will enable the builder to make a neat job. It is not necessary to cut the mortise very deep; 1/4 in. is ample to afford a firm and snug mortised joint.

The lanyard to which the filling is woven is next put in, by boring pairs of small holes in the toe and heel sections, and lacing a narrow rawhide thong through the obliquely drilled holes. Three holes are then bored in the cross bar—one on each side about 1½ in. from the frame, and the third in the center of the bar; the lanyard being carried through these holes in the cross bar.

Begin the toe filling first, by making an eye in one end of the thong, put the end through the lanyard loop and then through the eye, thus making a slipknot. Start to weave at the corner where the bar and frame are mortised, carry the strand up and twist it around the lanyards in the middle of the toe, then carry it down and make a like twist around the lanyard loop in the opposite corner. The thong is now looped around the next lanyard (No. 2 from the cross-bar lanyard) and fastened with the twisted loop knot illustrated. Continue the strand across the width of toe space and make a similar loop knot on No. 2 lanyard on the starting side, twist it around the strand first made and loop it under the next cross-bar lanyard loop, then carry it up and twist it around the lanyard loop in the toe of the frame, continuing in the same manner until the last lanyard of the toe is reached, when the space is finished by making the twisted loop knot until the space is entirely filled. It is a difficult matter to describe by text, but the illustrations will point out the correct way, and show the manner of making an endless thong by eye-splicing, as well as illustrating the wooden bodkin or needle used in pulling the woven strands taut. This bodkin is easily made from a small piece of wood, about ¼ in. thick, and about 2 in. long.

An Endless Thong is Made with Eyes Cut in the Ends of the Leather, and Each Part is Run through the Eye of the Other

To simplify matters, the heel may be filled in the same manner as the toe.

For the center, which must be woven strong and tight, a heavier strand of hide must be used. Begin with the toe cord first, and to make this amply strong, carry the strand across the frame five or six times, finishing with a half-hitch knot, as shown, then carry

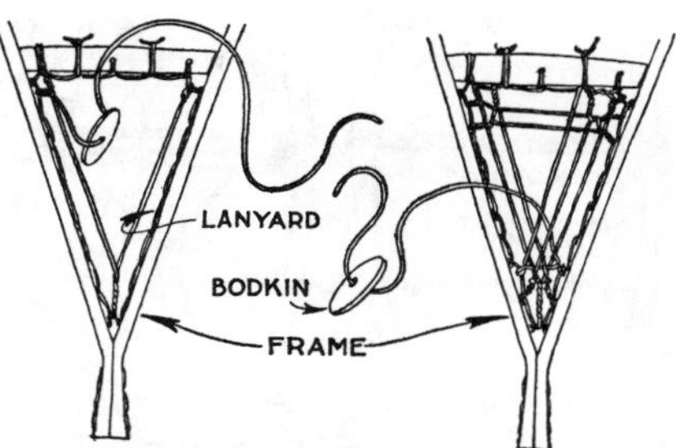

The Heel Filling is Woven by Making the Connection with the Lanyard in the Same Manner as for the Toe Filling

it up and twist it around the cross bar to form the first toe-cord stay.

As may be noted, the center section is filled by looping back and twisting the strands as when filling the toe. However, the filling is looped around the frame instead of a lanyard, and a clove hitch is used. A toe hole, 4 in. wide, must be provided for, and when enough of the filling has been woven in to make this opening, the thong is no longer looped around the cross bar, but woven through the toe cord. As the filling ends in the toe cord, it should be woven in and out at this point several times, finishing the toe hole by looping a strand around the cross bar at the side of the toe hole, then passing it down the toe-cord stay by twisting around it; then twisted around the toe cord along the filling to the other side of the toe hole, where it is twisted around the toe-cord stay on the opposite side, looped around the frame and ended in a clove hitch.

At the first reading, it will doubtless appear difficult, but a careful examination of the illustrations will soon show how the trick is done, and indeed it is really a very simple matter, being one of those things which are easier to do than it is to tell how to do them. The method of filling has been purposely made simple, but the majority of shoes are filled in practically the same manner, which answers quite as well as the more intricate Indian design.

The knack of using the snowshoe is quickly mastered, providing the shoes are properly attached, to allow the toe

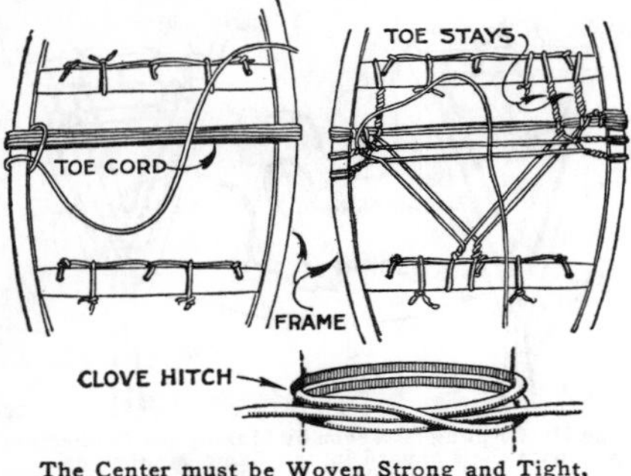

The Center must be Woven Strong and Tight, and for This Reason a Heavier Strand of Hide must be Used

ample freedom to work down through the toe hole as each foot is lifted. The shoe is, of course, not actually lifted in the air, but rather slid along the surface, half the width of one shoe covering the other when it is lifted in the act of walking. At first the novice may be inclined to think snowshoes a bit cumbersome and unwieldy, and doubt his ability to penetrate the brush. However, as the snowshoer becomes accustomed to their use, he will experience little if any difficulty in traveling where he wills. When making a trail in a more or less open country, it is a good plan to blaze it thoroughly, thus enabling one to return over the same trail, in case a fall of snow should occur in the meantime, or drifting snow fill up and obliterate the trail first made. When the trail is first broken by traveling over it once by snowshoe, the snow is packed well and forms a solid foundation, and even should a heavy fall of snow cover it, the blaze marks on tree and bush will point out the trail, which will afford faster and easier traveling than breaking a new trail each time one journeys in the same direction.

A well-made pair of snowshoes will stand a couple of seasons' hard use, or last for a year or two longer for general wear. To keep them in good shape, they should be dried out after use, although it is never advisable to place them close to a hot fire, or the hide filling will be injured. Jumping puts severe strain on the frame of the shoe, and while damage may not occur when so used in deep, soft snow, it is well to avoid the possibility of breakage. Accidents will now and then happen, to be sure, and as a thong may snap at some unexpected moment, keep a strand or two of rawhide on hand, to meet this emergency.

Combination Settee Rocker and Cradle

By fastening a frame with hinges to the front of a settee rocker, a combination piece of furniture can be made, which may be used either as a regular settee or as a cradle. For this purpose, a covered frame should be provided, being sufficiently long to extend across the front between the arm supports and having such a width that it will easily fit under the arms when hinged to the seat, as shown in the illustration. To keep the frame in position while serving as a cradle front, or when turned down for regular use, screw hooks are placed at each end, so that, in the former case, the frame, when swung up, can be secured in place by attaching the hooks to screw eyes fastened under the arm supports; while, for regular use, the frame is secured in its swung-down position by fastening the hooks into screw eyes properly placed in the front legs.—Contributed by Maurice Baudier, New Orleans, La.

A Settee Rocker with a Front Attachment to Make It into a Cradle When Desired

A Snowball Thrower

By ALBERT BATES, Jr.

The snow fort with its infantry is not complete without the artillery. A set of mortars, or cannon, placed in the fort to hurl snowballs at the entrenched enemy makes the battle more real. A device to substitute the cannon or a mortar can be easily constructed by any boy, and a few of them set in a snow fort will add greatly to the interest of the conflict.

The substitute, which is called a snowball thrower, consists of a base, A, with a standard, B, which stops the arm C, controlled by the bar D, when the trigger E is released. The tripping of the trigger is accomplished by the sloping end of D on the slanting end of the upright F. Sides, G, are fastened on the piece F, with their upper ends extending above the bar D, to

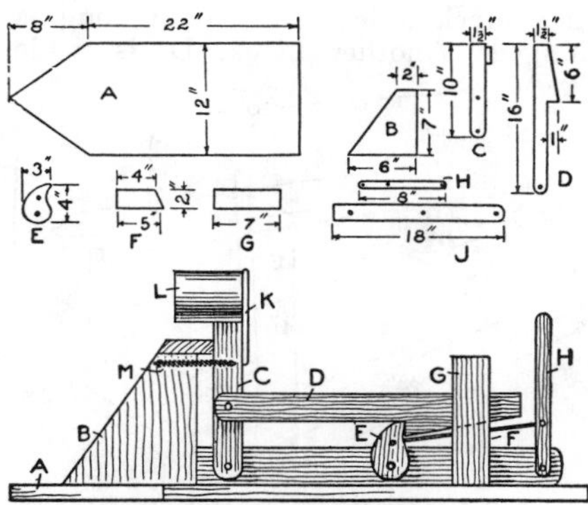

The Dimensioned Parts and the Detail of the Completed Snowball Thrower

prevent the latter from jumping out when it is released by the trigger.

The trigger E is tripped with the handle H, connected to the piece J, on which all the working parts are mounted. The upper end of the arm C has a piece, K, to which is attached a

Cannonading a Snow Fort with the Use of a Snowball Thrower

tin can, L, for holding the snowball to be thrown. A set of door springs, M, furnishes the force to throw the snowball.

All the parts are given dimensions, and if cut properly, they will fit together to make the thrower as illustrated.

Springs on the Chains of a Porch Swing

Two coil springs of medium strength placed in the chains of a porch swing will make it ride easier and also take up any unpleasant jars and rattles occasioned when a person sits heavily in the swing. If the swing is provided with a four-chain suspension, the springs should be used on the two rear chains to get the best results.—Contributed by E. K. Marshall, Oak Park, Illinois.

Homemade Water Meter

Where it is necessary to measure water in large quantities the meter illustrated will serve the purpose as well

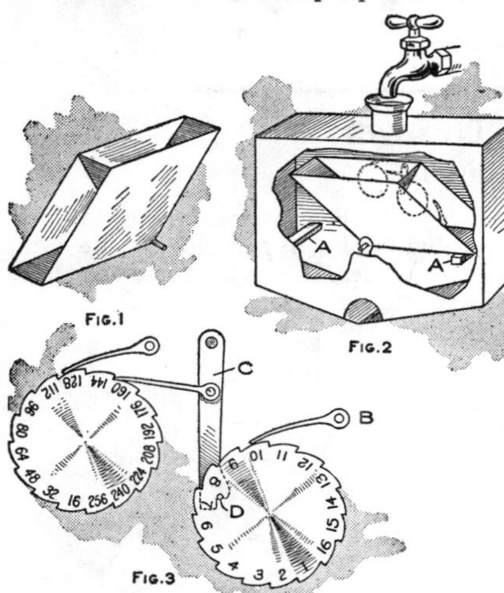

When a Bucket is Filled to the Proper Amount It is Turned Out by the Weight

as an expensive one, and can be made cheaply. The vessel, or bucket, for measuring the water is made diamond-shaped, as shown in Fig. 1, with a partition in the center to make two pockets of a triangular shape, each holding 2 qt., or any amount of sufficient size to take care of the flow of water.

The part forming the pockets is swung on an axis fastened to the lower part, which engages into bearings fastened to the sides of the casing, as shown in Fig. 2. Stops, A, are placed in the casing at the right places for each pocket to spill when exactly 2 qt. of water has run into it. It is obvious that when one pocket is filled, the weight will tip it over and bring the other one up under the flow of water.

The registering device consists of one or more wheels worked with pawls and ratchets, the first wheel being turned a notch at a time by the pawl B, Fig. 3. If each pocket holds 2 qt., the wheel is marked as shown, as each pocket must discharge to cause the wheel to turn one notch. The second wheel is worked by the lever and pawl C, which is driven with a pin D located in the first wheel. Any number of wheels can be made to turn in a like manner.—Contributed by F. A. Porter, Oderville, Utah.

A Snowball Maker

Snowball making is slow when carried on by hand, and where a thrower is employed in a snow fort it becomes necessary to have a number of assistants in making the snowballs. The time of making these balls can be greatly reduced by the use of the snowball maker shown in the illustration.

The base consists of a board, 24 in. long, 6½ in. wide, and 1 in. thick. A block of wood, A, is hollowed out in the center to make a depression in the shape of a hemisphere, 2½ in. in diameter and 1¼ in. deep. This block is nailed to the base about 1 in. from one end. To make the dimensions come out right, fasten a block, B, 6 in. high, made of one or more pieces, at the other end of the base with its back edge 14½ in. from the center of the hemispherical depression. On top of this block a lever, C, 20 in. long is hinged. Another block, D, is made

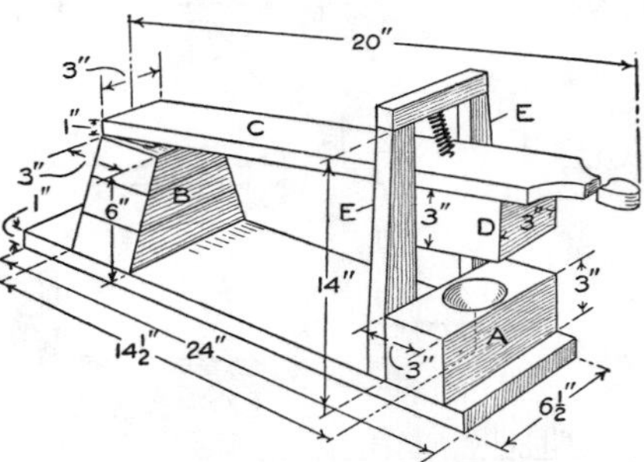

A Device for Making Snowballs Quickly and Perfectly Spherical in Shape

with a hemispherical depression like the block A, and fastened to the under side of the lever, so that the depressions in both blocks will coincide. The lever end is shaped into a handle.

Two uprights, E, are fastened to the back side of the block A as guides for the lever C. A piece is fastened across their tops, and a spring is attached between it and the lever. A curtain-roller spring will be suitable.

In making the balls a bunch of snow is thrown into the lower depression and the lever brought down with considerable force.—Contributed by Abbott W. France, Chester, Pa.

An Inexpensive Bobsled

Any boy who can drive a nail and bore a hole can have a bobsled on short notice. The materials necessary are four good, solid barrel staves; four blocks of wood, 4 in. long, 4 in. wide, and 2 in. thick; two pieces, 12 in. long, 4 in. wide, and 1 in. thick; one piece, 12 in. long, 2 in. wide, and 1¾ in. thick; and a good board, 4 ft. long, 12 in. wide, and 1 in. thick.

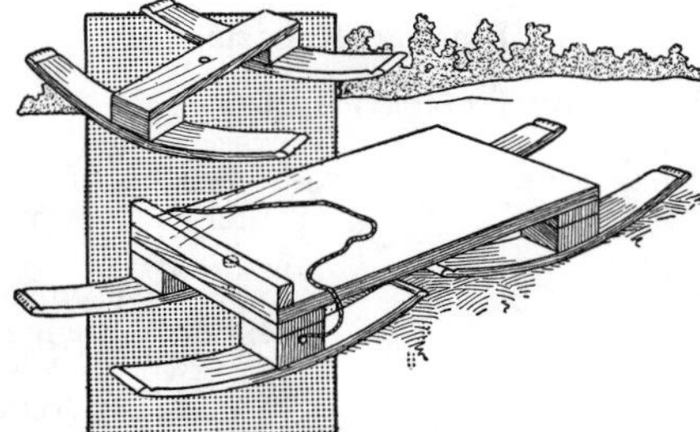

A Bobsled of Simple Construction Using Ordinary Barrel Staves for the Runners

The crosspieces and knees are made with the blocks and the 1-in. pieces, 12 in. long, as shown; to which the staves are nailed for runners. One of these pieces with the runners is fastened to one end of the board, the other is attached with a bolt in the center. The 1¾ by 2-in. piece, 12 in. long, is fastened across the top of the board at the front end. A rope fastened to the knees of the front runners provides a means of steering the sled.

The sled can be quickly made, and it will serve the purpose well when an expensive one cannot be had.—Contributed by H. J. Blacklidge, San Rafael, Cal.

Motor Made of Candles

A tube of tin, or cardboard, having an inside diameter to receive a candle snugly, is hung on an axle in the center that turns in bearings made of wood.

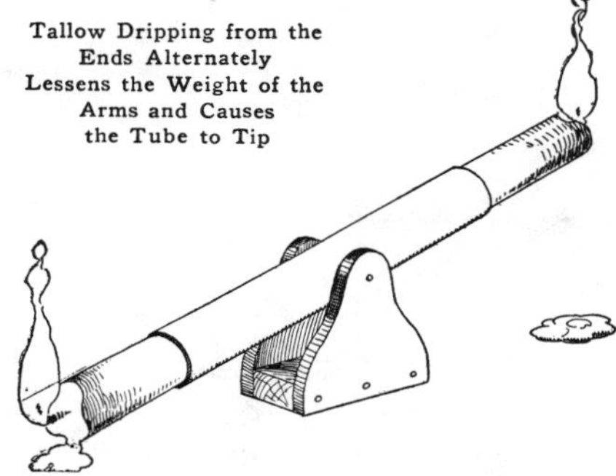

Tallow Dripping from the Ends Alternately Lessens the Weight of the Arms and Causes the Tube to Tip

The construction of the bearings is simple, and they can be made from three pieces of wood as shown. The tube should be well balanced. Pieces of candle are then inserted in the ends, also well balanced. If one is heavier than the other, light it and allow the tallow to run off until it rises; then light the other end. The alternate dripping from the candles will cause the tube to tip back and forth like a walking beam. It will keep going automatically until the candles are entirely consumed.—Contributed by Geo. Jaques, Chicago.

Kettle-Handle Support

The handle of a kettle lying on the kettle rim will become so hot that it cannot be held in the bare hand. To keep the handle fairly cool it must be supported in an upright position. To do this, form a piece of spring wire in the shape shown, and slip it over the kettle rim. The shape of the extending end will hold the handle upright and away from the heat.

How to Make a Monorail Sled

A monorail sled, having a simple tandem arrangement of the runners, is very easily constructed as follows: The runners are cut from 1-in. plank

An Exhilarating Glide Accompanied by a Buoyant Sense of Freedom Only Obtained in the Monorail Type

of the size and shape given in the sketch, and are shod with strap iron, 1 in. wide and 1/4 in. thick. Round iron or half-round iron should not be used, as these are liable to skid. The square, sharp edges of the strap iron prevent this and grip the surface just as a skate.

The top is a board 6 ft. long and 1 in. thick, securely fastened to the runners as follows: Blocks are nailed, or bolted, on either side of the upper edge of the rear runner and the top is fastened to them with screws. The runner is also braced with strap iron, as shown. The same method applies to the front runner, except that only one pair of blocks are used at the center and a thin piece of wood fastened to their tops to serve as the fifth wheel.

The hole for the steering post should

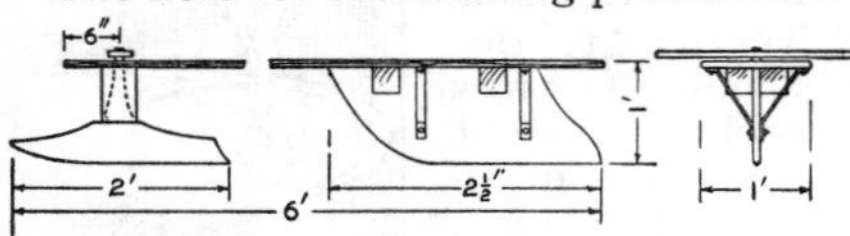

The Construction is Much More Simple Than Making a Double-Runner Bobsled

be 6 in. from the front end and a little larger in diameter than the steering post. The latter should be rounded where it passes through the hole, but square on the upper end to receive the steering bar, which must be tightly fitted in place.

In coasting, the rider lies full length on the board with his hands on the steering bar. This makes the center of gravity so low that there is no necessity for lateral steadying runners, and aside from the exhilarating glide of the ordinary sled, the rider experiences a buoyant sense of freedom and a zest peculiar to the monorail type. Then, too, the steering is effected much more easily. Instead of dragging the feet, a slight turn of the front runner with a corresponding movement of the body is sufficient to change the direction or to restore the balance. This latter is, of course, maintained quite mechanically, as everyone who rides a bicycle well knows.—Contributed by Harry Hardy, Whitby, Ont.

Binding Magazines

To bind magazines for rough service, proceed as follows: Place the magazines carefully one on top of the other in order, and space the upper one, near the back edge, for two rivets, marking off

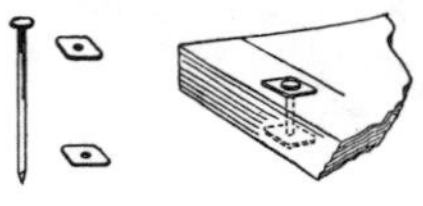

three equal distances, or, perhaps, the center space longer than the other two. Make two holes through all the magazines on the marks with an awl, or drill, then drive nails of the right length through them. Use small washers on both ends of the nails under the head and at the point, which is cut off and riveted over. This makes a good, serviceable binding for rough use.—Contributed by Carl W. Lindgreen, Los Angeles, Cal.

A Shellac Cement

As shellac is the basis of almost all cements, a good cement can be made by thickening shellac varnish with dry white lead. The two may be worked together on a piece of glass with a putty knife.

A Blackboard for Children

Take a wide window shade and attach it to a roller as if hanging it to a window. Cut it to about 3 ft. in length, hem the lower edge and insert in the slot in the usual manner. Procure some black slate paint and cover the shade on one side, giving it two coats. Allow sufficient time for the first coat to dry before applying the second coat.

A blackboard of this kind is strong, and if attached to the wall with the shade fixtures, it can be rolled out of the way when not in use.—Contributed by Elizabeth Motz Rossoter, Colorado Springs, Col.

How to Make a Ski Staff

A ski staff will greatly assist progress over level stretches and is an aid to the ski runner in preserving his balance. A homemade staff that is easy to construct is shown in Fig. 1. At the upper end is a narrow leather loop for the wrist; at the extreme lower end a spike is placed for use on icy ground, and just above this spike is a disk, or stop, which, in deep snow, prevents the staff from sinking in too far and gives the necessary leverage for steering, propelling or righting oneself as needed.

The staff is made of a piece of bamboo pole, 1¼ or 1½ in. in diameter, and 4½ ft. long. The leather for the loop can be made from an old strap, shaved down thinner and cut to a width of about ½ in. The stop is a disk of wood, ½ in. thick and 5 in. in diameter. This material should be well-seasoned white pine or spruce and coated with shellac. A hole is bored through the center of the disk to let it pass upward on the staff about 6 in. Here it is fastened with two pieces of heavy wire, A and B, Fig. 2. In this diagram, C is the staff, and D, the stop or disk. The wire A passes through the staff below the wire B and at right angles to it, wherefore the wire B must be bent as shown. Both wires are fastened to the stop with staples.

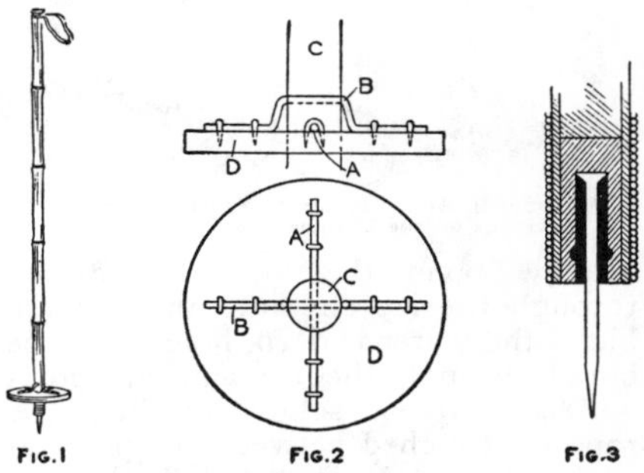

The Staff, being Made of a Bamboo Pole, is Strong as Well as Light

The lower end of the staff, as shown in Fig. 3, is plugged with hard wood, which is bored part way through its center to admit a wire spike. Slight recesses are made in the sides of this hole to anchor the lead which is poured in around the spike. The point of the latter is sharpened and then the bamboo wound with waxed twine, or fine wire, to prevent its splitting.

¶Fine emery cloth, glued to both sides of a piece of bristol board, makes a handy tool for cleaning the platinum points of a vibrator.

A Game Played on the Ice

A novel and interesting winter game for young and old, described as a novelty by a Swedish paper, is played as follows:

Two poles of convenient height are erected on the ice; if skating on a shallow pond they may be driven through the ice and into the ground, but if the water is deep, holes must be bored through the ice and the poles will soon freeze solidly in them. A rope is stretched between the poles at such a height as is suited to the size of the players, or as agreed on to make the game more or less difficult, and on this are strung a number of pieces of board, A, each having a ring of spring steel, B, attached to its lower end. The purpose of the game is to run at good speed between the poles and catch a ring on a spear, each player being entitled to make a certain number of runs, and the winner being the one who can catch the most rings.

A Player in Action Ready to Spear a Ring that Hangs on the Line between the Poles

The spears may be made of broom handles tapered toward one end, and with a shield made of tin and attached at a suitable distance from the thicker end (Pattern C). The line is fastened at the top of one pole and run through a pulley, D, at the top of the other, thence to a weight or line fastener. Each player should start from the same base line and pass between the poles at such a speed that he will glide at least 100 ft. on the other side of the poles without pushing himself forward by the aid of the skates. Twenty runs are usually allowed each player, or 10 players may divide into two parties, playing one against the other, etc. An umpire will be needed to see that fair play is maintained and settle any disputes that may arise.

An Electric Display for a Show Window

A novel window display that is very attractive, yet simple in construction and operation, can be made in the following manner: First, make a small watertight chamber, A, as long as the focal length of the lens to be used, and having a glass window, B, at one end, and a small round opening, C, at the other. In this opening is placed a cork through which a glass tube about 2 in. long is inserted. The tube makes a smooth passage for the stream of water flowing out of the box. Water from any source of supply enters the chamber through the tube D, which may be a pipe or hose, whichever is most convenient. The interior is painted a dull black.

A convenient and compact light is placed at the window end of the box. A very good light can be made by placing an electric light with a reflector in a closed box and fastening a biconvex lens, F, in the side facing the window of the water box. When the electric light and the water are turned on, the light is focused at the point where the water is issuing from the box, and follows the course of the stream of water, illuminating it in a pleasing manner.

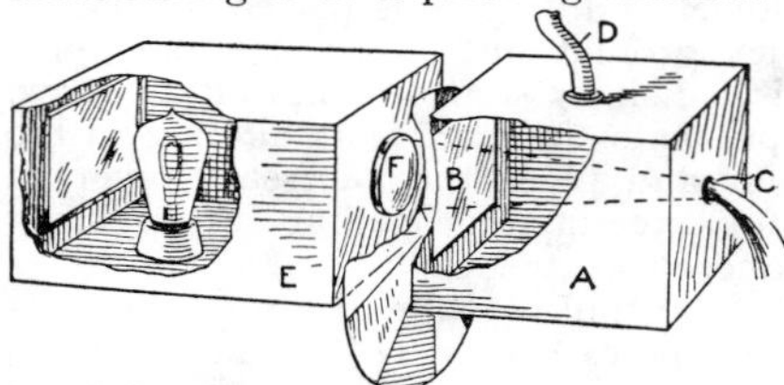

The Arrangement of the Boxes Showing the Path of the Light Rays through the Water

A still better effect can be obtained by passing colored plates between the lens F and the window B. A glass disk with sectors of different colors may be revolved by any source of power, such as a small electric motor or even a waterwheel turned by the flowing water.

Two or three streams of water flowing in different colors make a very pretty display and may be produced by using two or more boxes made up in the same manner. The apparatus should be concealed and nothing but the box end or tube with the flowing water shown.—Contributed by Grant Linton, Whitby, Ont.

Strainer for a Milk Pail

Even though a milker may be careful, small particles of dirt, hairs, etc., will fall into the milk pail. It is true that the milk is strained afterward, but a large percentage of the dirt dissolves and passes through the strainer along with the milk.

The best plan to prevent this dirt from falling into the milk is to put a piece of cheesecloth over the pail opening, securing it there by slipping an open wire ring, A, over the rim. The milk will readily pass through the cloth without spattering.—Contributed by W. A. Jaquythe, Richmond, Cal.

Baking Bread in Hot Sand

A driving crew on the river wanted to move camp, but the cook objected as he had started to bake. One of the party suggested using a modified form of the method of baking in vogue more than a century ago, which was to place the dough in the hot earth where a fire had been burning. So, to help the cook out, a barrel was sawed in half and the bread, after being properly protected, was placed in each half barrel and covered with hot sand. Two of the men carried the half barrels on their backs. When the new camp was reached the bread was done.—Contributed by F. B. Ripley, Eau Claire, Wis.

How to Make Small Cams

In making models of machinery or toy machines, cams are very often required. A simple way of making these

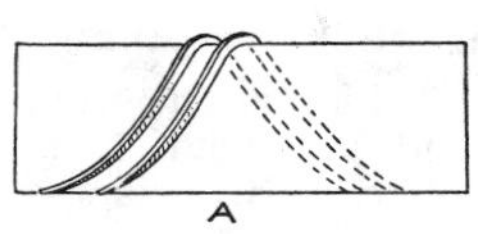

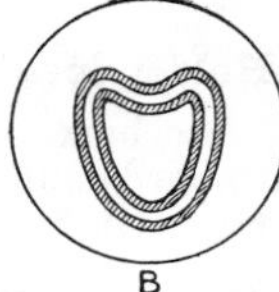

Channels of the Cams Formed with Strips of Brass Soldered to the Drum or Disk

is to lay out the cam plate, or drum, and then bend pieces of brass to the correct shape and solder them in place, whereupon they may be smoothed up with a file or scraper. A cam of this sort on a drum is shown in the sketch at A, and on a faceplate, at B. The method is not quite as accurate as milling, but answers the purpose in most cases.—Contributed by Chas. Hattenberger, Buffalo, N. Y.

Display Holder for Coins

If the luster of coins fresh from the mint is to be preserved, they must be immediately placed so as to be protected against contact with the hands. A good holder that will display both sides of a coin can be made of two pieces of glass, BB, between which is placed a cardboard cut as shown at A. The cardboard should be about the same thickness as the coins. The glass may be framed by using strips

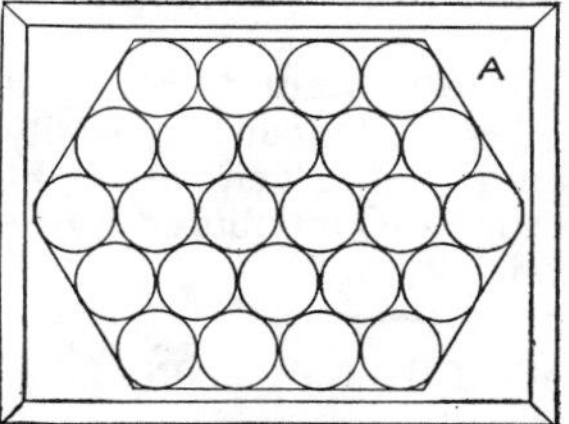

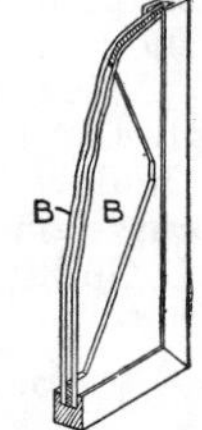

Two Pieces of Glass Inclosing between Them Coins of the Same Size and Thickness

of wood rabbeted to receive the edges of both pieces; or their edges may be bound with passe-partout tape. Even when a frame is used, it is best to bind the edges as this will prevent tarnish from the air. Old negative glass is suitable for making the holder.—Contributed by R. B. Cole, New Haven, Conn.

Holder for Skates while Sharpening

The base of the holder is cut from a board and should be about 3 in. longer than the skate. Two clamps

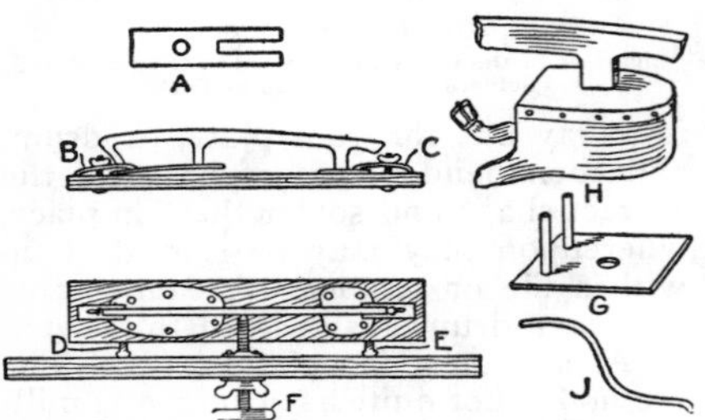

The Holder Provides a Way to Grind a Slight Curve in the Edge of a Skate Blade

are cut as shown at A, from metal of sufficient thickness to hold the skate firmly, then bent to shape and attached to the baseboard with bolts having wing nuts, as shown at B and C.

One edge of the board is provided with two pins, D and E, solidly fastened, which are of sufficient height to bring the center of the blade on a level with the grinder axle. An adjusting screw, F, is provided for the grinder base to adjust the skate blade accurately. The support G is for use on baseboards where skates with strap heels, H, are to be sharpened. The shape of the clamp for this support is shown at J.

When the skate is securely clamped to the base the blade can be easily "hollow ground" or given a slight curve on the edge.—Contributed by C. G. Smith, Brooklyn, N. Y.

A Homemade Direct-View Finder for Cameras

Every hand camera and most of the tripod cameras are equipped with finders of one type or another, and usually one in which the image of the field is reflected upward on a small ground glass—being, in fact, a miniature camera obscura. The later and generally more approved style of finder has a small concave lens conveniently set on the outer edge of the camera. When this direct-vision type of finder is used, the camera is held so that the finder is at the height of the eye, a condition that is particularly desirable. When in a crowd, of course, the professional and many amateurs are familiar with the method of holding the camera inverted over the head and looking up into the finder to determine the range of the field. Even this method is inconvenient, often impractical.

The up-to-date newspaper photographer insists on having his camera equipped with direct finders, as it saves him much trouble and many failures. Anyone with a little ingenuity can change one of the old-type finders into a combination device, either direct or indirect. The sketches are self-explanatory, but it may be said that Fig. 1 represents a box camera with a regulation finder set in one corner of the box. To make it a direct finder, a small brass hinge is used. Cut off part of one wing, leaving a stub just long

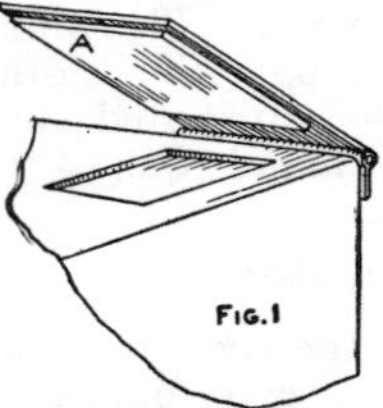

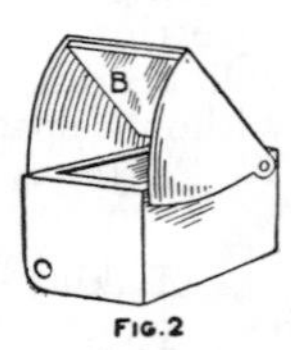

Two Types of Ordinary View Finders and Methods of Converting Them into Direct-View Finders

enough to be attached to the front of the camera directly above the lens of the finder and so as not to interfere with it, and high enough to permit the other wing to be turned down on the ground glass, with space allowed for the thin glass mirror A, that is to be glued to the under side of the long wing. The joint of the hinge should work quite stiffly in order to keep it from jarring out of any position in which it may be set.

If the wing is turned upward at an angle of 45 deg., the finder can be used as a direct-vision instrument when held at the height of the eyes. The image reflected from the small mirror is inverted, but this is no disadvantage to the photographer. The small pocket mirror given out for advertising purposes serves very well for making the reflecting mirror.

The finder shown in Fig. 2 is another very common kind, and one that is readily converted into the direct type by inserting a close-fitting mirror, B, on the inside of the shield to be used as a reflector of the finder image. If the mirror is too thick, it may interfere with the closing of the shield, though in many cases this is not essential, but if it should be necessary to close down the shield in order to fold the camera, it can usually be readjusted to accommodate the mirror.

A Non-Rolling Spool

Bend a piece of wire in the shape shown in the illustration and attach it to a spool of thread. The ends of the wire should clamp the spool slightly and the loop in the wire will keep it from rolling. Place the end of the thread through the loop in the wire and it will not become tangled.—Contributed by J. V. Loeffler, Evansville, Ind.

How to Make a Cartridge Belt

Procure a leather belt, about 2½ in. wide and long enough to reach about the waist, also a piece of leather, 1 in. wide and twice as long as the belt. Attach a buckle to one end of the belt and rivet one end of the narrow piece to the belt near the buckle. Cut two slits in the belt, a distance apart equal to the diameter of the cartridge. Pass the narrow leather piece through one slit and back through the other, thus forming a loop on the belt to receive a cartridge. About ¼ in. from the first loop form another by cutting two more slits and passing the leather through them as described, and so on, until the belt has loops along its whole length.

Two Pieces of Leather of Different Widths Forming a Belt for Holding Cartridges

The end of the narrow leather can be riveted to the belt or used in the buckle as desired, the latter way providing an adjustment for cartridges of different sizes.—Contributed by Robert Pound, Lavina, Mont.

Removing Iodine Stains

A good way to chemically remove iodine stains from the hands or linen is to wash the stains in a strong solution of hyposulphite of sodium, known as "hypo," which is procurable at any photographic-supply dealer's or drug store.

There is no danger of using too strong a solution, but the best results are obtained with a mixture of 1 oz. of hypo to 2 oz. of water.

Bed-Cover Fasteners

The arrangement shown in the sketch is easily made and will keep the bed covers in place. The covers are provided with eyelets, either sewed, A, or brass eyelets, B, 6 or 8 in. apart along the edge. A wood strip, C, 3 by 1½ in., is cut as long as the width of the bed and fastened to the frame with wire, bolts, or wedges. Screwhooks, about 1¼ in. long, are turned into the strip so that they will match with the eyelets placed in the covers. Thus the covers will be kept in place when the bed is occupied, and the bed is also easily made up.—Contributed by Warren E. Crane, Cleveland, O.

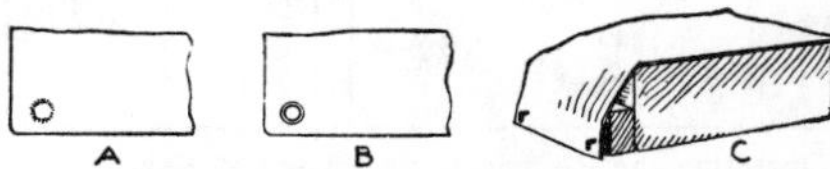

The Hooks Prevent the Covers from Slipping Off the Sleeper and Keep Them Straight on the Bed

Collar Fasteners

An excellent fastener to be used on soft collars can be assembled from an ordinary paper fastener and two shoe buttons of the desired color. This device keeps the soft collar in good shape at the front, and serves the purpose just as well as a more expensive collar fastener. The illustration shows how it is used.—Contributed by B. E. Ahlport, Oakland, Cal.

Operating a Bathroom Light Automatically

A device for automatically turning an electric light on and off when entering and leaving the room is illustrated in the sketch. A pull-chain lamp socket is placed upon the wall or ceiling, and is connected to a screw hook in the door by a cord and several rubber bands, as shown.

When the door is opened, the lamp is lit, and when leaving the room the opening of the door again turns it out. The hook should be placed quite close to the edge of the door, to reduce the length of the movement, and even then it is too much for the length of the pull required to operate the switch, hence the need of the rubber bands.

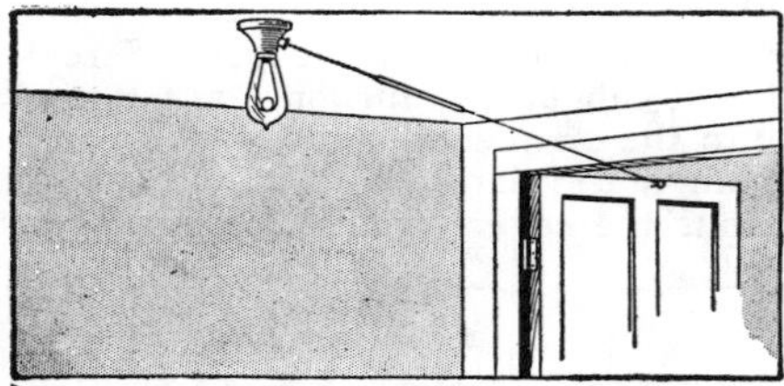

Operating the Electric Lamp Switch or Key by the Opening of the Door

The lamp chain pulls out just 1 in., and consequently the lamp is lit when the door is opened part way; and swinging the door farther only stretches the rubber. This is an advantage, however, because the lamp is sure to light regardless of the swing of the door. If no rubber were used, the door would have to open just a certain distance each time.

If the cord is connected to the hook with a loop or a ring, it may be easily disconnected during the day when not needed. A light coil spring may be used in place of the rubbers.—Contributed by C. M. Rogers, Ann Arbor, Michigan.

A Finger-Ring Trick

A coin soldered to some inexpensive ring, or a piece of brass cut from tubing, will make an interesting surprise coin for friends. The ring when placed on the middle finger with the coin in the palm makes the trick complete. Ask some one if he has ever seen such a coin, or say it is a very old one, as the date is almost worn away. He will try to pick it up, but will find it fast to the finger.—Contributed by Wm. Jenkins, New York City.

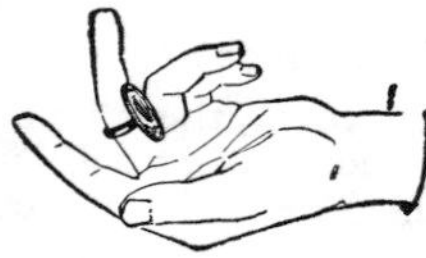

Preventing Marks from Basting Threads on Wool

In making up woolen garments it is necessary to press portions of them before removing the basting threads. Sometimes the marks of the basting threads show after the pressing. This can be avoided by using silk thread for basting instead of the usual cotton thread. The silk thread will not leave any marks.—Contributed by L. Alberta Norrell, Gainesville, Ga.

¶Cranberries will keep fresh for weeks if placed in water in a cool place.

Skating Merry-Go-Round

By HENRY BURICH

After once making and using the ice merry-go-round as illustrated, no pond will be complete unless it has one or more of these devices. To construct an amusement device of this kind, select a good pole that will reach to the bottom of the pond. The measurement can be obtained by cutting a hole in the ice at the desired place and dropping in a line weighted on one end. A sufficient length of the pole should be driven into the bottom of the pond to make it solid and allow the upper end to project above the surface of the ice at least 4 feet.

A turning crosspiece for the upper end of the pole is made as follows: First prepare the end of the pole by sawing it off level, then cutting off the bark and making it round for a metal ring which should be driven on tightly. A pin, about ¾ in. in diameter, is then driven into a hole bored in the end of the pole. The crosspiece is made of 2 by 6-in. material, at least 18 ft. long. A hole is bored in the center to receive the pin in the pole end.

Skaters Holding the Rope Ends are Drawn Around in a Circle Rapidly by the Revolving Crosspiece, Turned near the Center by Other Skaters

The crosspiece is easily pushed around the pole and the faster it goes the closer to the center the pushers can travel. Ropes can be tied to the ends of the crosspiece for the skaters to hold on to as they are propelled around in a circle.

Relieving Air Pressure When Closing Record Boxes

The ordinary pasteboard boxes for holding phonograph records are very hard to close, due to the air pressure on the inside. I overcome this difficulty by making three small holes in the cover with a pin.—Contributed by Robert Bandul, New Orleans, La.

A Steering Sled

An ordinary hand sled can be easily converted into a sled that can be guided like a bobsled by the addition of one extra runner. To attach this runner, a piece of wood is fastened to the under side and in the center at the front end of the sled top. A runner with a crosspiece on top is pivoted to the extending wood piece, which should be of a length to make the position comfortable when the coaster, sitting on the sled top, has his feet on the ends of the crosspiece. Careful

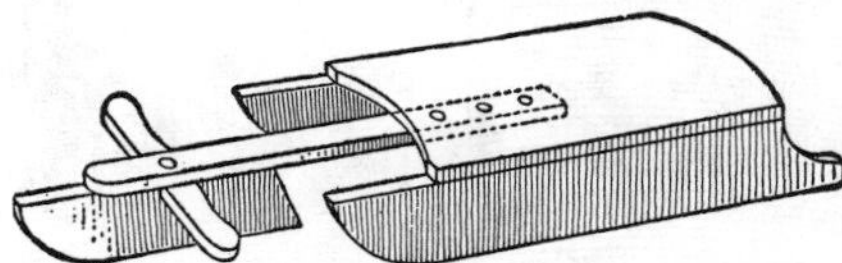

The Extra Runner in Front is Pivoted, and When Turned, Guides the Sled

measurements should be made to have the lower edge of the runner on a level with or a little lower than the sled runners.

To Hold a Straw Hat on the Head

On windy days it is almost impossible to make a straw hat stay on the head. To avoid this trouble, place

The Rubber Bands are Linked Like a Lock Stitch and Fastened in the Band

rubber bands through the sweatband. Before inserting, make them into loops, as shown, and draw enough to be comfortable to the head. This device will save a good many steps when the wind blows.—Contributed by T. D. Hall, Fort Worth, Texas.

Carrying Fishhooks in a Cane Pole

The person using a cane pole for fishing can easily provide a place for the hooks and sinkers in the first large joint of the pole. Cut the cane off just above the first large joint, and it will leave a space, 4 or 5 in. long, which can be used for the hooks and sinkers. A cork is fitted in the end, to hold them in place.—Contributed by Victor E. Carpenter, South Bend, Ind.

Drying Small Laundered Articles

Where mechanical drying is not in use it takes considerable time to hang out a number of handkerchiefs, laces, collars, etc., and very often the wind will blow away many of them. The task of drying these articles is made light by using a bag of mosquito netting with the articles placed in it and hung on a line. The air can pass through the netting and when the articles are dry it does not take long to take them out.—Contributed by Edward P. Braun, Philadelphia, Pa.

Decorative Wood Panels

Procure an unplaned board that is deeply scored by the teeth of the saw and mark an outline of the desired figure on its surface. Sandpaper the background lightly, cut in a moon and smooth down the tree trunks. The background can be smoothed with a sharp chisel, or large portions planed, but in all cases leave the foliage rough.

Finish the surfaces with oils or stains, applying colors to suit the parts; a piece of dried red cedar, oiled, will produce a warm red, and a green red cedar, oiled, becomes soft yellow, each producing a very pretty effect. These panels offer unlimited opportunity for originality in design and color finishing of different woods.—Contributed by Mrs. Wm. Donovan, Seattle, Wash.

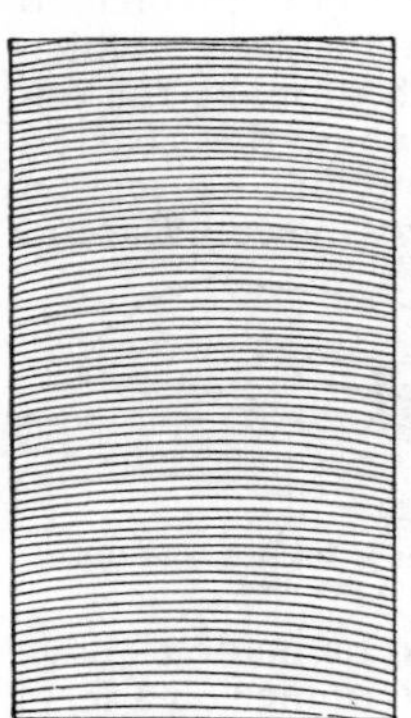

The Designs are Worked into the Unfinished Surface of Boards with Sandpaper, Sharp Chisels and a Plane, and Then Colored with Dyes to Produce the Desired Effect

Fishing-Rod Making and Angling

By STILLMAN TAYLOR

PART I—A One-Piece Casting Rod

THE pleasures of outdoor life are most keenly enjoyed by those sportsmen who are familiar with all the little tricks—the "ins and outs"—of the open. It is the active participation in any chosen sport which makes the sport well worth while, for the enjoyment gleaned from little journeys to forest and stream largely rests with the outer's own knowledge of his sport. Not all of the fun of fishing lies in the catching of the fish, since the satisfaction which comes through handling a well-balanced rod and tackle must be reckoned the chief contributor to the outing. In other words, the pleasures of fishing do not depend so much upon the number of fish caught, as the manner in which the person fishes for them. The rod is naturally the first and important consideration in the angler's kit, and it is the purpose of these articles to set forth, at first, a few hints which my own long experience leads me to think may be of some assistance to those anglers who enjoy making and repairing their own rods and tackle, to be followed, later, by some suggestions on the art of angling generally. The hints given are merely my own methods, and while they may not be the best way of accomplishing the desired end, a good fishing rod may be constructed. Like the majority of amateurs, I have achieved the desired results with a few common tools, namely, a saw, plane, jackknife, file, and sandpaper. These simple tools are really all that is needed to turn out a serviceable and well-finished rod of excellent action.

Kind of Material

The great elasticity and durability of the split-cane or split-bamboo rod cannot be easily disputed. The handmade split bamboo is unquestionably the best rod for every kind of fishing, but it is also the most expensive and the most difficult material for the amateur to work. In making the first rod or two, the beginner will be better satisfied with the results in making a good solid-wood rod. Of course, glued-up split-bamboo butts, joints, and tip stock may be purchased, and if the angler is determined to have only bamboo, it is advisable to purchase these built-up sections rather than to risk certain failure by attempting to glue the cane. However, there are several good woods particularly well adapted for rod making, and while slightly inferior to the finest bamboo in elasticity and spring, the carefully made solid-wood rod is good enough for any angler and will probably suit the average fisherman as well as any rod that can be purchased.

Bethabara, or washaba, a native wood of British Guinea, makes a fine rod, but it is a heavy wood, very hard, and for this reason is perhaps less desirable than all other woods. With the single exception of snakewood it is the heaviest wood for rod making and is only used for short bait-casting rods. Possessing considerable strength Bethabara can be worked quite slender, and a 5-ft. casting tip can be safely made of 5 oz. weight.

Greenheart, a South American wood, is popular alike with manufacturers and amateur rod makers, and 90 per cent of the better class of solid-wood rods are made of this material. It resembles Bethabara in color, but is lighter in weight, although it apparently possesses about the same strength and elasticity. In point of fact, there is little, if any, choice between these woods, and providing sound and well-selected wood is used, the merits of a rod made of Bethabara or greenheart are more likely to be due to the careful workmanship of the maker than to the variety of the wood used.

Dagame, or dagama, a native of the forests of Cuba, is in many respects the ideal material for rod making, as it has strength and elasticity. This wood is straight-grained and free from knots, which makes it easily worked; it polishes well and is durable. While there is always more or less difficulty about procuring first-class Bethabara

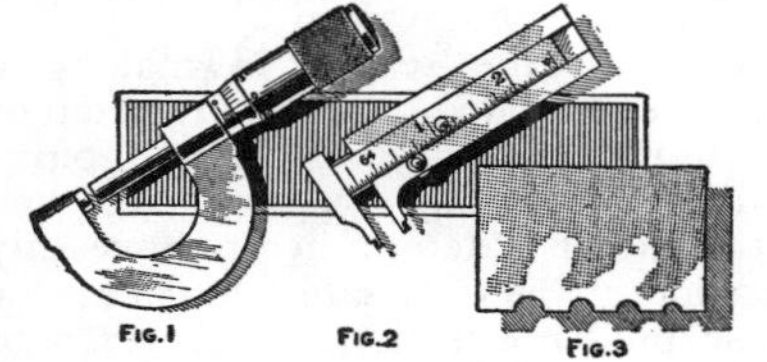

Two Tools for Gauging the Diameter of the Rods, and a Homemade Scraper

and greenheart, dagame of good quality is easily obtained.

Lancewood is much used in turning out the cheaper grades of fishing rods, but it is somewhat soft and has a marked tendency to take set under the strain of fishing and warp out of shape. It is less expensive than the other woods, and while it has a straight and even grain, there are numerous small knots present which make this material less satisfactory to work than the other woods. For heavy sea rods, lancewood may serve the purpose fairly well, but for the smaller fishing tools this material is inferior to Bethabara, greenheart, and dagame. Other woods are often used, and while a good rod may be frequently made from almost any of them, the three mentioned are held in the highest esteem by the angling fraternity. For the first rod, the amateur will make no mistake in selecting dagame, whether the slender fly rod or the more easily constructed short bait-casting tool is to be made.

The Necessary Tools

The construction of a thoroughly well-made and nicely balanced rod is more a matter of careful work than outfit, but a few suitable tools will greatly facilitate the labor. A good firm workbench, or table, 4 ft. or more in length, will be needed. A regulation bench vise will come in handy, but one of the small iron vises will do very well. A couple of iron planes, one of medium size for rough planing-up work, and a small 4-in. block plane for finishing, will be required. As the cutters of the planes must be kept as sharp as possible to do good work, a small oilstone—preferably one in a wood case with cover to keep out dust—will be needed; a coarse single-cut mill file about 16 in. long; a few sheets of No. 1 and No. 0 sandpaper; a sheet or two of fine emery cloth; a small thin "back" or other saw, and a steel cabinet scraper.

A caliper of some kind is a necessity, and while the best is a micrometer, Fig. 1, registering to a thousandth part of an inch, as well as indicating 8ths, 16ths, 32ds, and 64ths, this tool is somewhat expensive, but a very good caliper may be had in the sliding-arm type, Fig. 2, with the scale graduated to 64ths and taking work up to 2 in. in diameter. Cheaper measuring gauges are to be had in plenty, but as the brass and boxwood scales are provided only with coarse graduations, the better quality of mechanics' tools will give better satisfaction.

The set of grooved planes used by the professional rod makers are rather expensive, although they are most convenient for quickly rounding up the rod to the desired diameter. However, the beginner may dispense with the planes by making the tool illustrated in Fig. 3. To make this handy little tool purchase a steel wood scraper, such as cabinetmakers use, and file a series of grooves along the edges with a round file. File at right angles to the steel, finishing up with a finer file to give a sharp cutting edge. The tool thus made is very handy for scraping the rod after it has been roughly rounded with the plane. Its use will be mentioned later on in the description.

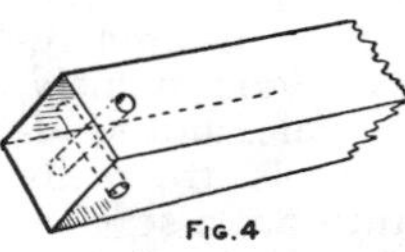

Five-Foot Bait-Casting Rod

The short one-piece bait-casting rod with but one ferrule is the easiest rod to make, and for this reason the beginner will do well to select this popular type for the first attempt. As the total length of the rod is to measure

5 ft., exclusive of the agate tip, the wood should be 1 or 2 in. longer to allow for cutting down to 60 inches.

Having selected a good strip of

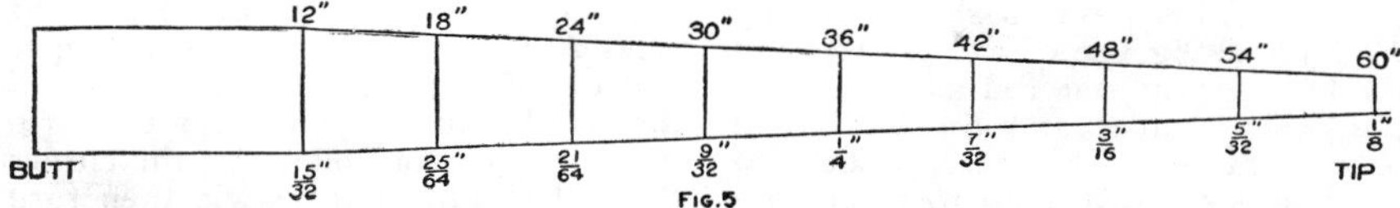

Fig. 5

Diagram or Layout for a One-Piece Bait-Casting Rod, Showing Calipered Dimensions for Each Six Inches of Length. A Paper Pattern of Any Rod may be Drawn Up, Providing the Amateur Rod Maker Has a Rod to Use for a Pattern, or Possesses the Exact Diameter of the Rod at Intervals of Six Inches along Its Length

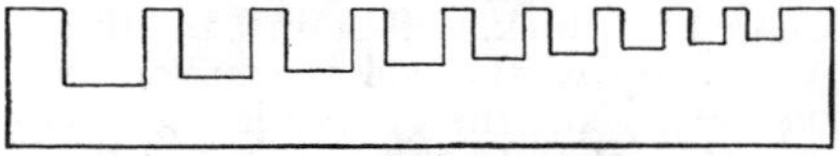

dagame, 5/8 in. square, run the plane along each side and from both ends. This will determine the direction in which the grain runs. Drill two holes at the end decided upon for the butt, spacing them about 1/4 in. from the end, as shown in Fig. 4. Drive a stout brad in the corner of the bench top and hook the butt end over the nail. By rigging the stick up in this manner it will be securely held, and planing may be done with the grain with greater ease and accuracy than when the end of the stick is butted up against a cleat nailed to the bench top.

The wood should be planed straight and true from end to end and calipered until it is 1/2 in. square. It may appear crooked, but this need not trouble one at this stage of the work, since it may be made perfectly straight later on. Overlook any kinks, and do not attempt to straighten the stick by planing more from one side than the other. The chief thing to be done is to fashion a square stick, and when the caliper shows the approximate diameter, draw crosslines at the ends to find the center.

The length of the hand grasp should be marked out. If a double grasp is wanted, allow 12 in. from the butt end. This will afford an 11-in. hand grasp after sawing off the end in which the holes were drilled. For a single hand grasp make an allowance of 11 in. However, the double grasp—with cork above and below the reel seat—is preferred by most anglers because it affords a better grip for the hand when reeling in the line. Mark the handgrasp distance by running a knife mark around the rod 12 in. from the butt end.

Lay out a diagram showing the full length of the rod by placing a strip of paper—the unprinted back of a strip of wall paper is just the thing—on the bench and drawing two lines from the diameter of the butt to that of the tip. While the caliber of casting rods differs somewhat, the dimensions given will suit the average angler, and I would advise the beginner to make the rod to these measurements. For the butt, draw a line, exactly 1/2 in. long, across the paper and from the center of this line run a straight pencil mark at right angles to the tip end, or 60 in. distant, at which point another crossline is drawn, exactly 1/8 in. long, to represent the diameter. Connect the ends of these two crosslines to make a long tapering form. Divide this pattern into eight equal parts, beginning at 12 in. from the butt end, marking a crossline at every 6 in. This layout is shown exaggerated in Fig. 5. If it is desired to copy a certain rod, find the diameter at the several 6-in. stations with the caliper and write them down at the corresponding sections of the paper diagram. However, if a splendid all-around casting

Fig. 6

Gauge Made of Sheet Brass Having Slots Corresponding in Length and Width with the Caliper-Layout Measurements

rod is desired, it is perfectly safe to follow the dimensions given in Fig. 5, which show the manner of dividing the paper pattern into the equal parts and the final diameter of the rod at each 6-in. station, or line.

Procure a small strip of thin brass, or zinc, and file nine slots on one edge to correspond in diameter with the width of the horizontal lines which indicate the diameter of the rod on the pattern. This piece is shown in Fig. 6. By making use of the pattern and the brass gauge, the rod may be given the desired taper and the work will proceed more quickly than if the caliper is alone relied upon to repeatedly check up the work.

When a good layout of the work is thus made, the next step is to carefully plane the stick so that it will be evenly tapered in the square. Plane with the grain and from the butt toward the tip end, and make frequent tests with caliper and gauge, noting the diameter every 6 in. Mark all the thick spots with a pencil, and plane lightly to reduce the wood to the proper diameter. Reduce the stick in this manner until all sides have an even taper from the butt to the tip. The stick should now be perfectly square with a nice, even taper. Test it by resting the tip end on the floor and bending it from the butt end. Note the arch it takes and see if it resumes its original shape when the pressure is released. If it does, the elasticity of the material is as it should be, but if it remains bent or takes "set," the wood is very likely to be imperfectly seasoned and the rod should be hung up in a warm closet, or near the kitchen stove, for a few weeks, to season.

To facilitate the work of planing the stick to shape, a length of pine board with a groove in one edge will be found handy. A 5-ft. length of the ordinary tongue-and-groove board, about 1 in. thick, will be just the thing. As the tip of the rod is smaller than the butt, plane the groove in the board to make it gradually shallower to correspond to the taper of the rod. Nail this board, with the groove uppermost, to the edge of the workbench, and place the rod in the groove with one of the square corners up, which can be easily taken off with the finely set plane. Plane off the other three corners in a like manner, transforming the square stick into one of octagon form. This part of the work should be carefully done, and the stick frequently calipered at each 6-in. mark, to obtain the proper taper. It is important to make each of the eight sides as nearly uniform as the caliper and eye can do it. Set the cutter of the small plane very fine, lay the strip in the groove and plane off the corner the full length of the stick, then turn another corner uppermost and plane it off, and so on, until the stick is almost round and tapering gradually from the mark of the hand grasp to the tip.

To make the rod perfectly round, use the steel scraper in which the grooves were filed and scrape the whole rod to remove any flat or uneven spots, and finish up by sandpapering it down smooth.

The action of the rod differs with the material used, and in trying out the action, it is well to tie on the tip and guides and affix the reel by a string in order to try a few casts. If the action seems about right, give the rod a final smoothing down with No. 0 sandpaper.

For the hand grasp nothing is so good as solid cork, and while hand grasps may be purchased assembled, it is a simple matter to make them. In Fig. 7 are shown four kinds of handles, namely, a wood sleeve, or core, A, bored to fit the butt of the rod and shaped for winding the fishing cord; a built-up cork grasp, B, made by cementing cork washers over a wood sleeve, or directly to the butt of the rod; a cane-wound grip, C, mostly used for salt-water fishing, and the double-wound grip, D, made in one piece, then sawed apart in the center, the forward grip being glued in place after the reel seat is in position.

To make a grip, select a number of cork washers, which may be obtained from dealers in the wholesale drug trade, or from any large fishing-tackle dealer. Make a tool for cutting a hole in their centers from a piece of tubing, or an old ferrule of the required diameter, by filing one edge sharp, then covering the other end with several thicknesses of cloth. Turn this tube around in the cork like a wad cutter. If the cutter is sharp, a nice clean cut will result, but the opposite will likely occur if an attempt is made to hammer the tube through the cork.

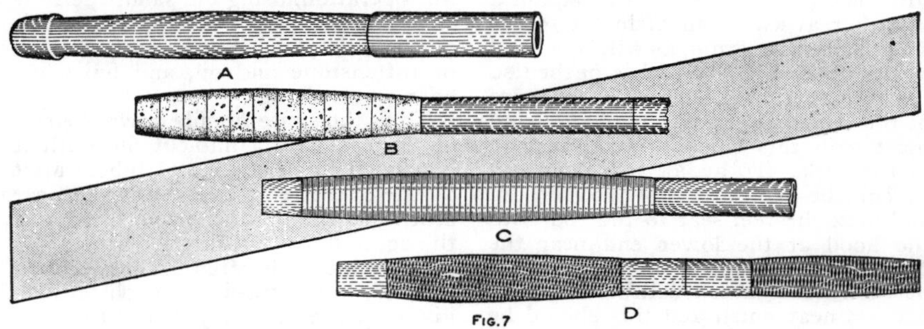

The Four Different Types of Hand Grasps Are a Wood Sleeve Bored to Fit the Butt of the Rod; the Built-Up Cork over a Wood Sleeve; a Cane-Wound Grasp, and the Double Cord-Wound Grasps with a Reel Seat between Them

Having cut the butt end of the rod off square, about 1 in. from the end, or enough to remove the holes, smear a little hot glue on the end, drop a cork washer over the tip of the rod and work it down to the butt. Cut another cork, give the first one a coat of glue, slip the former over the tip and press the two together, and so on, until about 10 corks have been glued together in position. This will give a hand grasp a trifle over 5 in. long.

A sleeve will be needed for the reel seat to slip over, and a soft-wood core of this sort can be purchased from any dealer in rod-making materials, or it can be made at home. For the material procure a piece of white pine, about $\frac{3}{4}$ in. in diameter and 5 in. long. A section sawed from a discarded curtain roller will serve the purpose well. Bore a $\frac{15}{32}$-in. hole through the piece and plane down the outside until it slips inside the reel seat. It should be well made and a good fit, and one end tapered to fit the taper of the reel seat, while the opposite end should be about $\frac{1}{4}$ in. shorter than the reel seat. Slide this wood sleeve down the rod, as shown in Fig. 8, coat the rod and the upper part of the last cork with glue and force the sleeve tightly in place. A day or two should be allowed for the glue to set and thoroughly dry, before giving the hand grasp the final touches.

If a lathe is at hand, the hand grasp may be turned to any desired shape, but most anglers prefer a cylindrical-shaped grip, leaving the top cork untrimmed to form a kind of shoulder when the metal reel seat is pressed into the cork. If corks of $1\frac{1}{4}$-in. diameter are purchased, but little trimming will be necessary to work the hand grasp down to $1\frac{1}{16}$ in. in diameter. This size seems to fit the average hand about right. The lower corks will need a little trimming to fit the taper of the butt cap so that it may fit snugly in place. Cement the butt cap in place by heating the cap moderately hot, then rub a little of the melted ferrule cement inside the cap, and force it over the cork butt. When the cement has hardened, drive a small brass pin or

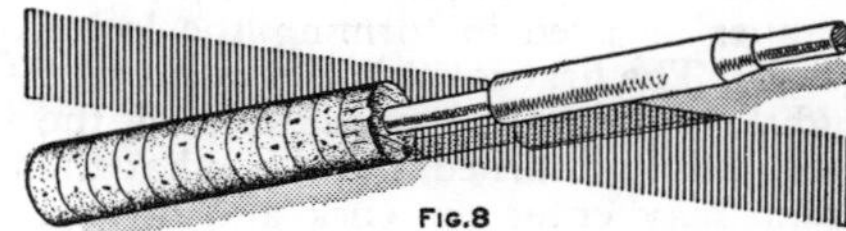

The Corks Glued in Place on the Butt and the Wood Sleeve, or Reel-Seat Core, Ready to Slide Down and Glue in Position

brad through the cap, and file the ends off flush with the metal surface. All the guides, ferrules, and reel seat are shown in Fig. 9.

The regulation metal reel seat is about 4½ in. long, and in fitting it to the old type of bait rod, the covered hood is affixed to the upper end of the reel seat. This arrangement is satisfactory enough for the 9-ft. bait rod, but it is rather awkward in fitting it to the short bait-casting rod, as with the hood at the upper end the reel is pushed so far forward that it leaves 1 in. or more of the reel seat exposed, and the hand must grip this smooth metal instead of the cork. To avoid this, it is best to cut the reel seat down to 3⅞ in. and affix the reel seat to the rod with the hood at the lower end near the hand. For a single hand grasp, a tapered winding check will be needed to make a neat finish and this should be ordered of the correct diameter to fit the reel seat at the lower end and the diameter of the rod at the other. In the double hand grasp the winding check is used to finish off the upper end of the cork, which is tapering to fit the rod at this point.

In assembling the reel seat, push it with the hooded end well down and work it into the cork to make a tight waterproof joint. Push the reel seat up the rod, coat the sleeve with cement and push the reel seat home. Drive a small pin through the hooded end and reel seat to make the whole rigid. This pin should not be driven through the rod or it will weaken it at this point. Just let it enter the wood a short distance to prevent the reel seat from turning.

The upper or double grasp is fashioned after the reel seat is in position, and the corks are cemented on and pushed tightly together in the same manner as used in forming the lower grasp. The first cork should be pressed tightly against the upper end of the reel seat and turned about so that the metal may enter the cork and form a tight joint. As many corks as are required to form a grip of proper length are in turn cemented to each other and the rod. After the glue has become dry, the cork may be worked down and tapered to make a smooth, swelled grasp. The winding check is now cemented on, to make a neat finish between the upper grip and the rod.

Before affixing the guides, go over the rod with fine sandpaper, then wet the wood to raise the grain, and repeat this operation, using old sandpaper. If an extra-fine polish is wanted, rub it down with powdered pumice and oil, or rottenstone and oil, and finish off with an oiled rag.

To fit the agate tip, file down the end of the rod with a fine-cut file until it is a good fit in the metal tube. Melt a little of the ferrule cement and smear a little on the tip of the rod, then push the agate down in place.

Spar varnish is often used to protect the rod, but extra-light coach varnish gives a better gloss, and it is as durable and waterproof as any varnish. It is only necessary to purchase a quarter pint of the varnish, as a very small quantity is used. The final varnishing is, of course, done after the rod has been wound and the guides are permanently whipped in position. However, it is an excellent idea to fill the pores of the wood by rubbing it over with a cloth saturated in the varnish before the silk whippings are put on. Merely fill the cells of the wood and wipe off all surplus, leaving the rod clean and smooth.

The guides may now be fastened in place, and for the 5-ft. rod, but two of them are necessary. The first guide should be placed 19½ in. from the metal taper which finishes off the upper hand grasp, and the second guide spaced 15½ in. from the first. By spacing the guides in this manner, the line will run through them with the least possible friction.

Winding, or Whipping, the Rod

Before whipping on the guides, take a fine file and round off the sharp edges of the base to prevent the possibility of the silk being cut. Measure off the required distances at which the guides are to be affixed, and fasten them in position by winding with a few turns of common thread. Ordinary silk of No. A size may be used, but No. 00 is the best for small rods. Most anglers agree that the size of the silk to use for the whippings should be in proportion to the size of the rod—heavy silk from the spool and tuck the end under the whipping by pulling on the ends of the waxed loop, as shown at G.

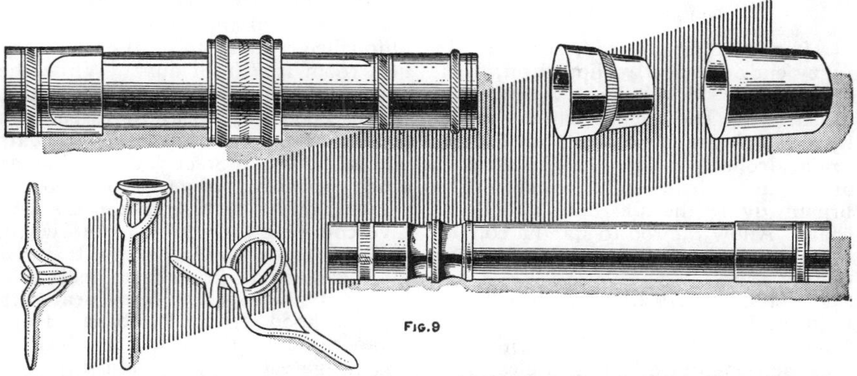

The Mountings Used on a Bait-Casting Rod Consist of a Reel Seat, Butt Cap, Taper Sleeve, Narrow Agate Guide, Agate Offset Top, One Ring Guide, and a Welted, Shouldered Ferrule

for the heavy rod, and fine silk for the small rod. Size A is the finest silk commonly stocked in the stores, but one or more spools of No. 00 and No. 0 may be ordered from any large dealer in fishing tackle. As a rule, size 0 gives a more workmanlike finish to the butt and joints of fly and bait rods, while No. 00 is about right to use for winding the tips. In fact, all rods weighing up to 6 oz. may be whipped with No. 00 size.

In whipping the rod, the so-called invisible knot is used. Begin the whipping, as shown at E, Fig. 10, by tucking the end under the first coil and holding it with the left thumb. The spool of silk is held in the right hand and the rod is turned to the left, sufficient tension being kept on the silk so that it can be evenly coiled with each strand tightly against the other. A loop of silk, some 4 in. long, is well waxed and placed so that its end will project a short distance beyond the last coil which finishes the whipping. This detail is shown at F. In whipping on guides, begin the whipping at the base and work over the pointed end of the flange, winding on sufficient silk to extend about ⅛ in. beyond the pointed flange of the guide base. When the last coil is made, cut off the thread

Cut off the ends neatly with a sharp knife.

For colors, bright red and a medium shade of apple green are the best, since these colors keep their original tint after varnishing, and are less likely to fade than the more delicate shades. Red finished off with a narrow circle of green always looks well, and red with yellow is likewise a good combination. Narrow windings look much better than wide whippings, and a dozen turns make about as wide a winding as the angler desires. For edgings, three or four turns of silk are about

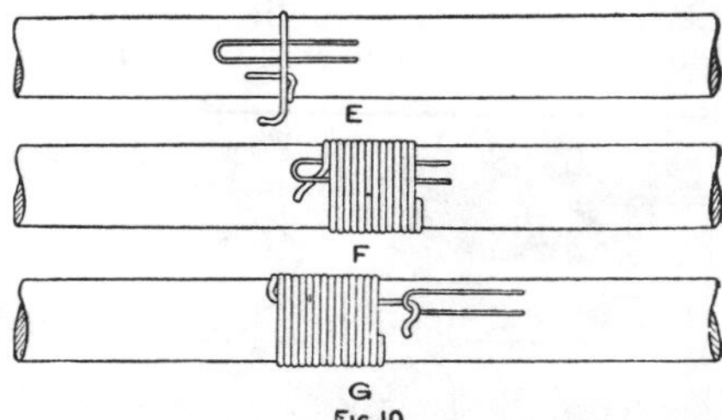

Both Ends of the Silk Thread are Placed under the Winding to Form an Invisible Knot

right, and these should be put on after the wider windings have been whipped on and in the same manner, although it is best to tuck the ends of the edging beneath the wider winding when pulling the end through to make the invisible knot.

Varnishing the Rod

After winding the rod, see that all fuzzy ends are neatly clipped off, then go over the silk windings with a coat of shellac. The shellac can be made by dissolving a little white shellac in grain alcohol. Warm the shellac and apply it with a small camel's-hair brush, giving the silk only two light coats. Allow the rod to stand a couple of days for the shellac to become thoroughly dry.

A small camel's-hair brush will be required for the varnishing—one about ½ in. wide will do. If the varnishing is to be done out of doors, a clear and warm day should be selected, and the can of coach varnish should be placed in a pot of hot water for five minutes, so that the varnish will spread evenly. A temperature of about 75 deg. is best for this work, as the varnish will not spread if cold or in a cold place. The varnish should be evenly brushed on, and care taken that no spots are left untouched. Hang up by the tip to dry in a room free from dust. While the varnish will set in four or five hours, it is a good plan to allow three days for drying between coats. Two coats will suffice to protect the rod, but as coach varnish, properly applied, is rather thin in body, three coats will give complete protection to the wood.

The materials required for this rod are, 1 dagame or greenheart stick, 5 ft. long and ⅝ in. square; 1 reel seat with straight hood, ¾ in.; 1 butt cap, 1 in.; 1 taper, small end $\frac{15}{32}$ in.; 1 offset, or angle, agate top, $\frac{3}{32}$ in., and 2 narrow agate guides, ½ in., all in German silver; 2 doz. corks, 1¼ by 1⅛ in., and two 50-yd. spools of silk, red and green, 00 size.

Automatic Watering System for Poultry Yards

Where a large number of poultry is cared for, the annoyance and attention necessary to furnish a constant water supply can be overcome by using the system shown in the illustration. For this purpose a storage tank must be provided. This may be some old toilet flush tank, or any open reservoir that will hold sufficient water to keep all the drinking pans supplied. A float is provided and connected with a stop valve, so that when the float drops below a certain level, the valve will be turned open, and a fresh supply of water will enter the storage tank, thereby again raising the float and closing the valve.

Each drinking pan should be about 10 in. in diameter by 4 in. deep, and is drilled for a ⅞-in. hole to fit a ½-in. pipe. At the pan end, the pipe is threaded so that a lock nut and leather washer can be attached on each side of the pan bottom, to provide a watertight joint; at the other end, the pipe

Simple Arrangement of a Flush Tank in Connection with a System of Pipes to Supply One or More Pans of Water for the Poultry Yard

is screwed into a tee in the ½-in. main line which connects with the storage tank.

In using the system, sufficient water is run into the tank to fill the pans about three-quarters full. The float may then be adjusted to a shut-off position for the inlet valve. All pans are automatically kept at one level, even though several may be used considerably more than others. When the general water level has dropped sufficiently, the float, dropping with it, will open the stop valve, and cause the water to enter the tank and pans until the original level is again restored.—Contributed by D. E. Hall, Hadlyme, Connecticut.

Changing Pip on a Card

Cut out the center pip on the five-spot of spades with a sharp knife. Cut a slot centrally in another card, about ⅜ in. wide and 1¼ in. long. Glue the surfaces of both cards together near the edges to form a pocket for a slide, which is cut from another card and has one-half of its surface colored black. A drop of sealing wax attached to the back of the sliding part, so that it projects through the slot, provides a means of moving the slide in the pocket. A lightning change can be made from a five-spot to a four-spot while swinging the card.

To Make a Special Envelope

Any size of envelope for mailing special papers or documents can be made as follows: All envelopes are of the same shape as shown in Fig. 1; the size for the papers to be inclosed is represented by the dotted lines in Fig. 2. The projections A are coated with paste, and the flap B is folded over them. The envelope is then ready for the inclosure. The flap C is pasted and folded over as with an ordinary envelope.—Contributed by L. E. Turner, New York City.

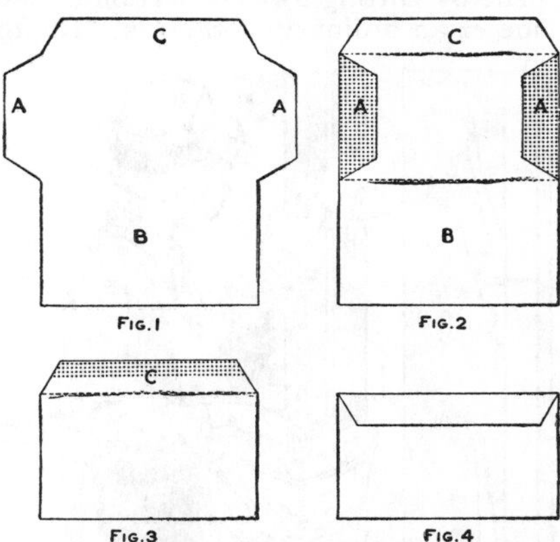

Various Stages in the Forming of an Envelope to Make Any Size for Special Papers

Automatically Extinguishing a Candle

Candles can be easily fitted with attachments to extinguish the light at a set time. To determine the length of time, it is necessary to mark a candle of the size used and time how long a certain length of it will burn. Then it is sufficient to suspend a small metal dome, or cap, to which a string is attached, directly over the flame, and run the opposite end of the string over nails or through screw eyes, so that it can be tied around the candle such a distance from the flame end, that the part between the flame and the string will be consumed in the time desired for the light to burn. When this point is reached, the string slips off the candle, and the cap drops on the flame.

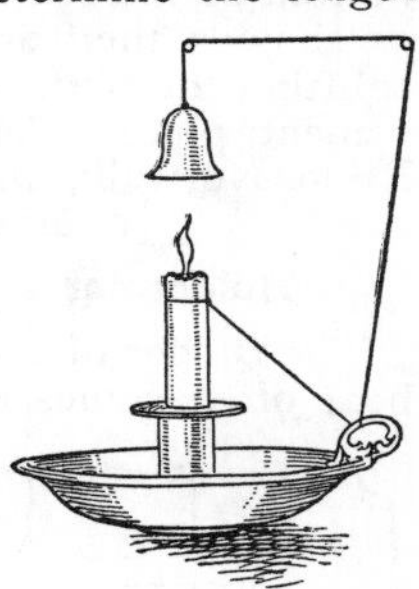

Clothespin Newspaper Holder

A simple newspaper holder can be made by cutting away a portion of one side of an ordinary clothespin, drilling

Shaping a Clothespin Head and Fastening It to a Wall Provides a Holder for Newspapers

a hole through the thick end for a screw or nail, and fastening it in place where desired. Another way is to split off one side of a clothespin and cut the bottom of the remaining part tapering as shown; then drill a hole to avoid splitting the piece and fasten in a convenient place.—Contributed by J. P. Rupp, Norwalk, O.

Holder for a Dory Rudder

The rudder of a sailing dory or rowboat often comes off in rough water,

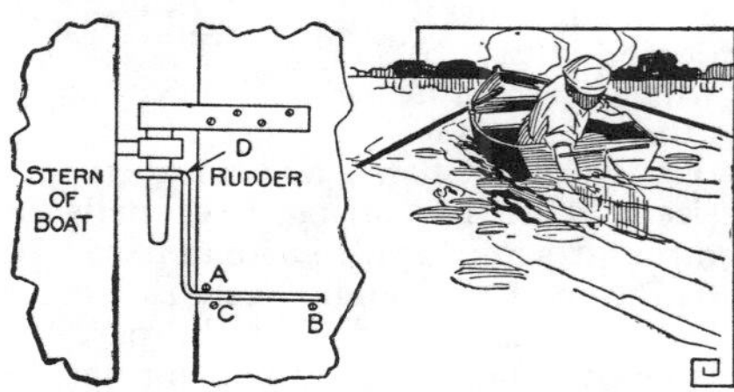

The Loop on the Iron Rod Holds the Pin of the Rudder in the Eye

and in order to keep it in place and yet have it easily detachable at will, the following method is useful: Procure a 10-in. length of soft-iron rod and bend one end of it into a loop large enough to fit around the rudder pin after the latter is inserted in the eyelet. Insert screws at A, B and C, letting them project about ½ in. from the surface. Bend the rod at D and A in the shape shown, and with a little adjustment it will easily snap into position. It will prevent the rudder from riding up out of the eyelets, but can be detached instantly. The device should be applied to the upper pin so as to be within easy reach.—Contributed by B. A. Thresher, Lakeville, Connecticut.

Trimming Photographs

In trimming small photograph prints I experienced some difficulty in getting them square, and I did not care to invest in a trimming board. By following a line drawn around the print with a triangle, it was impossible to make a perfect rectangle. In the place of a trimming board I now use a piece of glass cut a little smaller than the desired print. The edges of the glass are smoothed by filing or grinding them. In making a glass, be sure to have the corners cut at perfect right angles and the edges ground straight.

The glass is easily located over the print, and by holding the two tightly together the edges of the print can be trimmed with a pair of shears.—Contributed by E. Leslie McFarlane, Nashwaaksis, N. B.

A Metal Polish

A metal polish that is safe to use about the home is composed of 30 parts alcohol, 3 parts ammonia water, 45 parts water, 6½ parts carbon tetrachloride, 8 parts kieselguhr, 4 parts white bole, and 8 parts of chalk. These substances can be purchased at a local drug store and should be mixed in the order named. Any grease on metal will be dissolved by this solution.—Contributed by Loren Ward, Des Moines, Iowa.

Fishing-Rod Making and Angling

By STILLMAN TAYLOR

PART II—Various Two and Three-Piece Rods

WHILE the action of the one-piece rod is undeniably better than when the rod is made in two or three pieces, it is less compact to carry. To make a 5-ft. two-piece bait-casting rod, the same dimensions as given for the one-piece rod will make a very fine fishing tool. It is well to make two tips in view of a possible breakage. The rod may consist of two pieces of equal length, but a rod of better action is secured by making the butt section somewhat shorter with a relatively longer tip. By making the butt section about 23 in. long, exclusive of ferrule and butt cap, and the tip section 32½ in. long, a splendid little rod is obtained which will fit any of the regulation rod cases of 35-in. length. To make a 6½-oz. rod of this kind with a cork hand grasp, caliper it in the same manner as the one-piece rod, making the butt section 32½ in. long, tapering from 15/32 in. at the upper end of the hand grasp to 19/64 in. at the ferrule. The tip is made 33 in. long, tapering from 17/64 in. to 7/64 in. By making the tip and butt to these lengths, both parts will be of equal length when the ferrules and the tops are added. The material list is as follows, the attachments being made of german silver: Dagame or greenheart butt, 5/8 in. by 3 ft. long; two tips 3/8 in. by 3 ft. long; one 3/4-in. reel seat with straight hood; one 1-in. butt cap; one taper, 15/32 in. at the small end; two 3/32-in. offset agate tops; two ½-in. narrow agate guides; two No. 1 size one-ring casting guides; one 17/64-in. welted and shouldered ferrule, with two closed-end centers, one for each tip; two dozen cork washers, 1¼ in. in diameter, and two spools of winding silk.

The Making of a Rod Not Only Affords Much Pleasure, but the Rod can be Constructed as Desired

The three-piece rod should be made up to 6 ft. in length to secure the best action, but even if so made, the use of the extra ferrules makes the rod less resilient and elastic than the rod of one or two-piece construction. The best action is obtained only when the rod bends to a uniform curve, and since the ferrules cannot conform to this curve, or arc, the more joints incorporated in a rod, the less satisfactory it will be from an angling standpoint.

Convenience in packing and carrying are the sole merits which the many-jointed rod possesses. Complete specifications for making a three-piece bait-casting rod, together with a material list, is as follows: A rod, about $5\frac{1}{2}$ ft. long with a single or double hand grasp made of cork, will weigh about 7 oz. Caliper the butt so that it will taper from $\frac{15}{32}$ in. to $\frac{11}{32}$ in. at the cap of the ferrule, making it $21\frac{1}{2}$ in. long. The middle joint is tapered from $\frac{21}{64}$ in. to $\frac{15}{64}$ in., and is $21\frac{3}{4}$ in. long. The tips are 21 in. long and are tapered from $\frac{13}{64}$ in. to $\frac{7}{64}$ in. Dagame or greenheart is used for the butt, joint, and tips, and german silver for the fittings. All pieces are 2 ft. long, the butt is $\frac{5}{8}$ in., the joint and tips, $\frac{3}{8}$ in. One $\frac{3}{4}$-in. reel seat with straight hood; one 1-in. butt cap; one taper, small end $\frac{15}{32}$ in.; one $\frac{21}{64}$-in. welted and shouldered ferrule; one $\frac{15}{64}$-in. welted and shouldered ferrule with two closed centers, one for each tip; two $\frac{3}{32}$-in. offset agate tops; two $\frac{1}{2}$-in. narrow agate guides; two No. 1 size one-ring casting guides; two dozen cork washers, and winding silk, size 00 or 0.

Fly Rods for Trout and Bass

Having made a good bait-casting rod, the amateur will find little trouble in making a rod with a number of joints, and no special instructions need be given, since the work of planing and smoothing up the wood, and finishing and mounting the rod, is the same as has been described in detail before. For fly fishing for trout, accuracy and delicacy are of more importance than length of cast, and the rod best suited to this phase of angling differs greatly from that used in bait casting. A stiff, heavy rod is entirely unsuited for fly casting, and while it is, of course, possible to make a rod too willowy for the sport, the amateur, working by rule of thumb, is more likely to err on the other side and make the fly rods of too stout a caliber. The idea is simply to help the amateur over the hard part by giving a list of dimensions of a representative trout and a bass fly rod. To make a 9-ft. trout fly rod, with a cork grasp having a length of 9 in. above the reel seat, caliper the material as follows: The butt is tapered from $\frac{7}{16}$ in. to $\frac{25}{64}$ in. at 1 ft. from the butt end; $1\frac{1}{2}$ ft., $\frac{11}{32}$ in.; 2 ft., $\frac{21}{64}$ in.; $2\frac{1}{2}$ ft., $\frac{5}{16}$ in., and 3 ft., $\frac{19}{64}$ in. The first 6 in. of the middle joint is calipered to $\frac{9}{32}$ in.; 1 ft., $\frac{17}{64}$ in.; $1\frac{1}{2}$ ft., $\frac{15}{64}$ in.; 2 ft., $\frac{7}{32}$ in.; $2\frac{1}{2}$ ft., $\frac{13}{64}$ in., and 3 ft., $\frac{3}{16}$ in. The first 6 in. of the tips are calipered to $\frac{11}{64}$ in.; 1 ft., $\frac{5}{32}$ in.; $1\frac{1}{2}$ ft., $\frac{1}{8}$ in.; 2 ft., $\frac{7}{64}$ in.; $2\frac{1}{2}$ ft., $\frac{3}{32}$ in., and 3 ft., $\frac{5}{64}$ in. All joints are made $36\frac{1}{2}$ in. long. The material used is dagame, or greenheart, the butt being $\frac{5}{8}$ in. by 4 ft., the joint $\frac{3}{8}$ in. by 4 ft., and the tips $\frac{3}{8}$ in. by 4 ft. The attachments, of german silver, are: One $\frac{3}{4}$-in. reel seat, fly-rod type with butt cap; one taper, $\frac{33}{64}$ in. at the small end; one $\frac{9}{32}$-in. welted and shouldered ferrule; one $\frac{11}{64}$-in. welted and shouldered ferrule with two closed-end centers, one for each tip; two No. 4 snake guides for the butt joint; three No. 3 snake guides for the middle joint, and six No. 2 snake guides, three for each tip section; two No. 7 agate angle fly tops, the kind to wind on; one dozen cork washers, and two 10-yd. spools of winding silk, 00 size.

A bass fly rod $9\frac{1}{2}$ ft. long, weighing $7\frac{1}{2}$ oz., with a cork grasp, $9\frac{1}{2}$ in. above the reel seat, is calipered as follows: The butt is tapered from $\frac{13}{32}$ in. to $\frac{25}{64}$ in. 1 ft. from the end; $1\frac{1}{2}$ ft. from butt, $\frac{23}{64}$ in.; 2 ft., $\frac{11}{32}$ in.; $2\frac{1}{2}$ ft., $\frac{21}{64}$ in., and 3 ft., $\frac{19}{64}$ in. The first 6 in. of the middle joint is $\frac{19}{64}$ in.; 1 ft., $\frac{9}{32}$ in.; $1\frac{1}{2}$ ft., $\frac{17}{64}$ in.; 2 ft., $\frac{15}{64}$ in.; $2\frac{1}{2}$ ft., $\frac{7}{32}$ in., and 3 ft., $\frac{13}{64}$ in. The first 6 in. of the tips, $\frac{11}{64}$ in.; 1 ft., $\frac{5}{32}$ in.; $1\frac{1}{2}$ ft., $\frac{9}{64}$ in.; 2 ft., $\frac{1}{8}$ in.; $2\frac{1}{2}$ ft., $\frac{7}{64}$ in., and 3 ft., $\frac{5}{64}$ in. The joints are $36\frac{1}{2}$ in. long. The mountings are the same as for the trout fly rod. Dagame, or greenheart, wood is used, the butt being $\frac{5}{8}$ in. by 4 ft., the joint $\frac{3}{8}$ in. by 4 ft. and the tips $\frac{3}{8}$ in. by 4 feet.

The two-piece salt-water rod with an 18-in. double cork hand grasp, the whole being $6\frac{1}{2}$ ft. long, is made to weigh about 13 oz., with the following caliperings: A uniform taper of $\frac{35}{64}$ in. to $\frac{29}{64}$ in., from the cork grasp to the ferrule, is given to the butt. The first 6 in. of the tips is 13/32 in.; 1 ft., 25/64 in.; 1½ ft., 11/32 in.; 2 ft., 21/64 in.; 2½ ft., 9/32 in., and to tip, 15/64 in. The

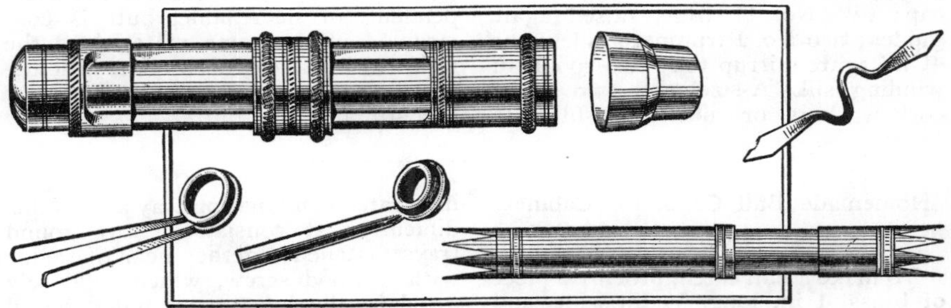

The Mountings for a Fly Rod Consist of a Reel Seat with a Straight Hood, a Taper, Snake Guide, Agate Angle Top, and Serrated Ferrule. The Toothed Ends are Wound with Silk to Afford Additional Strength

joints are made 36¾ in. long. Dagame, or greenheart, is used with german-silver mountings. Both pieces of wood are 4 ft. long, the butt being of ¾-in. and the tip of ½-in. material. One ⅞-in. reel seat with straight hood, one 1-in. butt cap, one 7/16-in. ferrule, one taper with small end 35/64 in.; one 10/32-in. stirrup-tube agate top; two No. 3 bell guides; two dozen cork washers, and two spools, size A, winding silk.

The Independent-Butt Rod

The independent-butt rod, in which the hand grasp contains the ferrule and the tip is made in one piece, is a favorite type with many of the best fishermen. This mode of construction may be used with all classes of rods, the light fly and bait-casting rods, and the heavier caliber rods used in salt-water angling. In rods of this type, it is only necessary to use the same size ferrule to make as many tips as desired to fit the one butt. Tips of several calibers and weights may thus be fashioned to fit the one butt, and if the single-piece tip is too long for some special use, one tip may be made a jointed one for ease in carrying.

The independent butt, or hand grasp, is made by fitting the ferrule directly on a length of dagame, or greenheart, which has been rounded so that the seated ferrule will not touch the wood. The ferrule is then cemented and riveted in place, and a soft-pine sleeve is fitted over the wood core and the ferrule. The forward end of the sleeve is, of course, tapered to fit the taper of the reel seat, and when properly fitted, its lower end will project about ¼ in. beyond the pine sleeve. Glue the sleeve on this wood core, cement the reel seat to the sleeve, and rivet the reel seat in place.

The cork washers are glued in position, working the first one into the metal edge of the reel seat, to make a nice, tight joint at this point. The other corks are then glued in place until the hand grasp is of the desired length. The projecting end of the wood core is then cut off flush with the last cork, and the rod is mounted in the usual manner.

In making a double hand grasp, the forward grasp may be fitted over the wood core in the fashion already described in making the hand grasp for the one-piece bait-casting rod, or the forward grasp may be fitted to the tip, just above the ferrule, as preferred. Both methods are commonly used, the only difference being in the manner of finishing up the forward grasp. If the forward grip is affixed to the ferruled end of the tip, two tapered thimbles will be required to make a nice finish.

The heavy-surf, or tarpon, rod is made up of an independent, detachable butt, 20 in. long, having a solid-cork or cord-wound hand grasp, and a one-piece tip, 5½ ft. long, altogether weighing 23½ oz. It is uniformly calipered to taper from 29/32 in. to 5/16 in. One piece of dagame, or greenheart, 1 in. by 6½ ft., will be required. One 1-in. reel seat for detachable butt, including one ¾-in. male ferrule; one 1⅛-in. butt cap; two No. 11 wide, raised agate guides; two No. 1 trumpet guides; one ⅜-in. agate stirrup top; two spools of winding silk, A-size, and two dozen cork washers, or sufficient fishline to cord the butt. The guides are whipped on double, the first set spaced 10 in. from the top, and the second, 26 in. from the reel. The core of the independent, or detachable, butt is constructed of the same material as the rod, which makes the hand grasp somewhat elastic and very much superior to a stiff and rigid butt.

Homemade Ball Catch for Cabinet Doors

To make a ball catch, procure a piece of brass, 1 in. long, ½ in. wide, and about 1/16 in. thick, and an old gas burner having a diameter of ⅜ in. As described by Work, London, the threaded part of the burner is cut off, which forms a contracted end that will hold a steel ball 5/16 in. in diameter and allow it to project ⅛ in. A hole is drilled in the center of the brass plate, and the barrel soldered in place. A piece of spiral spring is inserted behind the ball. The stiffness of the spring will depend on the use of the catch. The barrel is cut to length and plugged. Another plate of brass is fitted with screw holes and a hole in the center to receive the projecting ball part, for the strike.

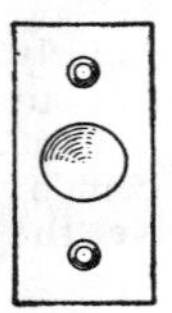

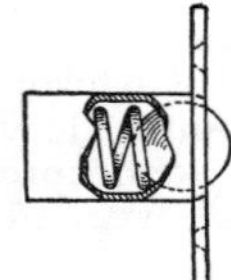

Combination Needle and Thread Tray

When any attempt is made to keep sewing material, such as needles, spools, or buttons, separate, each of the articles is usually kept in some special drawer, or by itself, and when necessary to use one, the others must be found, frequently necessitating many extra steps or much lost time in hunting up the various articles. The illustrated combination tray avoids this difficulty. It consists of two round trays fastened together near one edge with a wood screw, which is loosely fitted in the lower tray but screwed into the upper to permit them being swung apart. Extra thickness and weight should be given the bottom piece so no tipping will result when the top is swung out to expose the buttons in the lower section. The thread spools are placed on pegs set in the upper tray, and the cushion in the center is provided for the pins and needles.—Contributed by J. Harger, Honolulu, Hawaiian Islands.

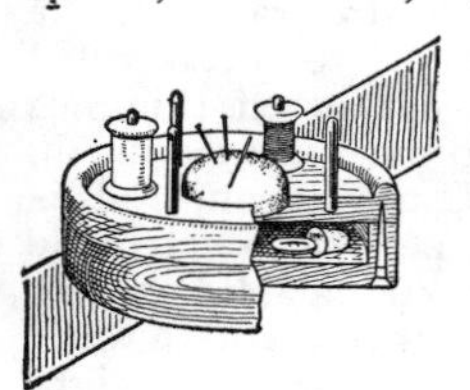

Repairing Worn Escapement Wheel of a Clock

When the ordinary clock has served its usefulness and is apparently worn out, the jeweler's price to overhaul it frequently amounts to almost as much as the original purchase price. One weak place in the clock is the escapement wheel. The points soon wear down, thereby producing a greater escapement and pendulum movement, resulting in an increased strain and wear of the clock. If the tips of the teeth on the wheel are bent up slightly with a pair of pliers, the swing of the pendulum will be reduced, thereby increasing the life of the clock. Many of the grandfather's clocks can be put in order in this manner so as to serve as a timepiece as well as a cherished ornament.—Contributed by C. F. Spaulding, Chicago, Ill.

¶A piece of work should never be fingered while filing it in a lathe.

Fishing-Rod Making and Angling

BY STILLMAN TAYLOR

PART III—Trout Fishing with Fly and Bait

If He would Take Full Advantage of Any Sport and Reap the Greatest Pleasure from a Day Spent in the Open, the Sportsman should Get Together a Good Outfit

THE art of angling is generally viewed as one of the world's greatest recreations, and while each and every phase of fishing may be said to possess certain charms of its own, fly fishing for trout is regarded by most well-informed sportsmen as the alpha and omega of the angler's art. This is so because the trout family are uncommonly wary and game fish, and the tackle used for their capture is of finer balance and less clumsy than any employed in angling for the coarser game fishes. If he would take full advantage of any sport and reap the greatest pleasure from a day spent in the open, it is really necessary for the sportsman to get together a good outfit. It is not essential to have a very expensive one, but it should be good of its kind, well proportioned for the purpose for which it is to be used. The beginner, who buys without good knowledge of the articles required, or fails to use careful discrimination, is almost certain to accumulate a varied assortment of junk, attractive enough in appearance, perhaps, but well-nigh useless when it is tested out on the stream. A good representative outfit, then, is of the first importance; it means making a good beginning by initiating the novice in the sport under the most favorable conditions. Let us then consider the selection of a good fishing kit, a well-balanced rod, the kind of a reel to use with it, the right sort of a line, flies, and the other few items found in the kit of the practical and experienced trout fisherman.

Selecting a Good Fly Rod

The ordinary fishing pole may be bought offhand at almost any hardware store, but a well-balanced rod for fly fishing should be well tested out beforehand. The requirements call for a rod of comparatively light weight, a rod that is elastic and resilient, and yet strong enough to prove durable under the continued strain of much fishing. If the angler has made his own rod, as suggested in former chapters, he will have a good dependable fly rod, but the large majority of anglers who are about to purchase their first fishing kit should carefully consider the selection of the rod. At the outset it must be understood that good tackle is simply a matter of price, the finest rods and reels are necessarily high in price, and the same thing may be said of lines and flies. Providing the angler has no objection to paying $15, or more, for a rod, the choice will naturally fall upon the handmade split bamboo. For this amount of money a fair quality fly rod may be purchased, the finer split bamboos costing anywhere up to $50, but under $15 it is very doubtful whether the angler can procure a built-up rod that is in every way satisfactory. The question may arise, Is a split-bamboo rod necessary? The writer's own long experience says that it is not, and that a finely made solid-wood rod, of greenheart or dagame, is quite as satisfactory in the hands of the average angler as the most expensive split bamboo. A good rod of this sort may be had for $10, and with reasonable care ought to last a lifetime.

The points to look for in a fly rod, whether the material is split bamboo or solid wood, is an even taper from the butt to the tip; that is, the rod should register a uniform curve, or arc, the entire length. For general fly casting 9 ft. is a handy length, and a rod of 6½ oz. weight will prove more durable than a lighter tool. A good elastic rod is wanted for fly casting, but a too willowy or whippy action had best be avoided. However, for small-brook fishing, where the overgrown banks prohibit long casts, a somewhat shorter and stiffer rod will be more useful. For casting in large northern streams, where the current is swift and the trout run to a larger size, a 9½ or 10-ft. rod of 8 oz. weight is often preferred. Of course, the veteran angler can safely use a much lighter rod than the beginner, and one occasionally meets a man on the stream that uses a 5-oz. rod for pretty heavy fishing. To be on the safe side, the novice will make no mistake in choosing a rod of fair length and conservative weight.

When selecting a rod in the tackle shop, do not rest content with a mere examination of the appearance, but have the dealer affix a reel of the weight and size intended to be used with it. By reeling on a short length of line and reeving it through the guides and then fastening the end to a weight lying upon the floor, a very good idea of the rod's behavior may be gained, since by reeling in the line and putting tension on the rod its elasticity and curve may be seen and felt as well as in actual fishing. To give the utmost satisfaction, the rod should fit its owner, and several rods should be tried until one is found that most fully meets the angler's idea of what a rod should be. If one happens to have a good fly reel, by all means take it along and attach it to the rod while making the tests. It is practically impossible to gauge the balance of a rod without affixing the reel, and many a finely balanced tool will appear badly balanced until the proper-weight reel is affixed to it.

The Proper Kind of Reel

For fly fishing nothing is so good as the English style of click reel, which is made with a one-piece revolving side plate and with the handle affixed directly to it. Any kind of a balanced-handle reel is an out-and-out nuisance on the fly rod, because it has no advantage in quickly recovering the line, and the projecting handle is forever catching the line while casting. In fly casting, the length of cast is regulated by the amount of line taken from the reel before the cast is made, and it is while "pumping" this slack line through the guides, in making the actual cast, that the balanced or projecting handle is very apt to foul the line. A good reel that is smooth-running like a watch will cost about $10, but a very good one may be had for $5, and cheaper ones, while not so durable, may be

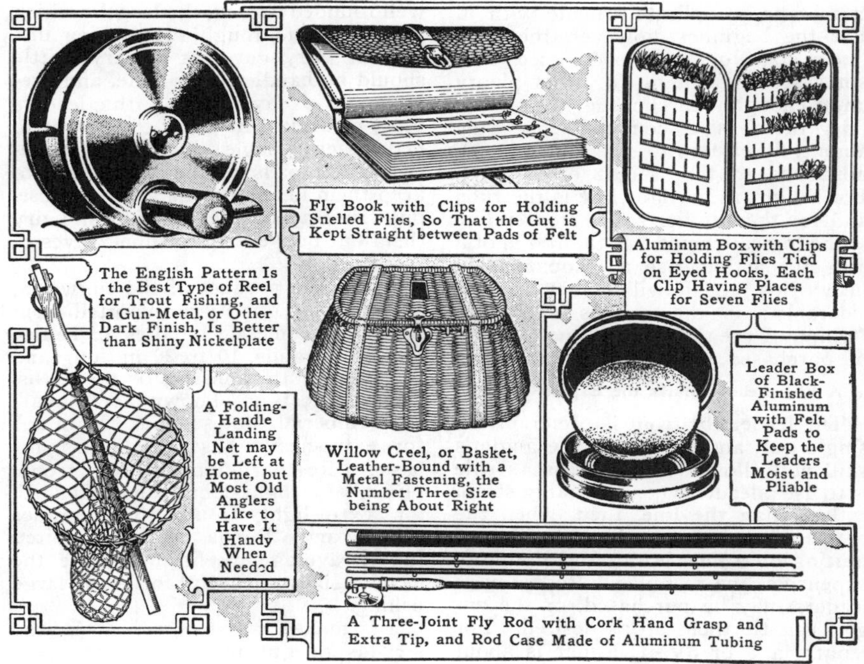

The English Pattern Is the Best Type of Reel for Trout Fishing, and a Gun-Metal, or Other Dark Finish, Is Better than Shiny Nickelplate

Fly Book with Clips for Holding Snelled Flies, So That the Gut is Kept Straight between Pads of Felt

Aluminum Box with Clips for Holding Flies Tied on Eyed Hooks, Each Clip Having Places for Seven Flies

A Folding-Handle Landing Net may be Left at Home, but Most Old Anglers Like to Have It Handy When Needed

Willow Creel, or Basket, Leather-Bound with a Metal Fastening, the Number Three Size being About Right

Leader Box of Black-Finished Aluminum with Felt Pads to Keep the Leaders Moist and Pliable

A Three-Joint Fly Rod with Cork Hand Grasp and Extra Tip, and Rod Case Made of Aluminum Tubing

used with fair satisfaction. The heavier multiplying reels, so essential for bait casting from a free reel, are altogether unsuited for the fly rod, being too heavy when placed below the hand, which is the only proper position for the reel when fly casting. The single-action click reel, having a comparatively large diameter, but being quite narrow between the plates, is the one to use, and hard rubber, or vulcanite, is a good material for the side plates, while the trimmings may be of german silver or aluminum. The all-metal reel is of about equal merit, but whatever the material, the most useful size is one holding about 40 yd. of No. E size waterproof line. A reel of this capacity will measure about 3 in. in diameter and have a width of about 7/8 in. between plates. A narrow-spooled reel of this type enables the fisherman to reel in the line plenty fast enough. Owing to the fact that the reel is placed below the grip on fly rods, a rather light-weight instrument is needed to balance the rod. Of the two extremes, it is better to err on the side of lightness, because a heavy reel makes a butt-heavy rod and, throwing extra weight on the wrist and arm, makes casting increasingly difficult after an hour's fishing. An old hand at the game will appreciate this point better than the novice.

The Kind of Line to Use

The fly-casting line used by a veteran is generally of silk, enameled and having a double taper; that is, the line is thickest in the center and gradually tapers to a smaller diameter at each end. Single-tapered lines are likewise extensively used, and while they cost less, they are tapered at one end only and cannot be reversed to equalize the wear caused by casting. The level line, which has the same diameter throughout its entire length, is the line most generally used, but the cast cannot be so delicately made with it. For the beginner, however, the level line in size No. E is a good choice. For small-brook fishing, No. F is plenty large enough. In choosing the size of line, there is a common-sense rule among fly casters to select a line proportioned to the weight of the rod. For a light rod a light line is the rule, and for the heavier rod a stouter line is the logical choice. If the rod is of a too stiff action, use a comparatively heavy line, and it will limber up considerably; if the rod is extremely "whippy," use the lightest line that can be purchased, and used with safety.

A Fine Leader Marks the Expert Caster

The leader for trout is preferably of single gut, and as fine as the angler's skill will allow. The fly caster's rule is to use a leader whose breaking strain is less than the line, then, when the tackle parts, it is simply a question of putting on a new leader and the more expensive line is saved. Ready-made leaders may be purchased, or the angler can tie them up as desired. For length, a 3 or 3½-ft. leader is about right for average fishing. Longer leaders are used, and while they sometimes are of advantage, the 3-ft. length is more useful. A longer leader is awkward to handle because the loop is apt to catch in the top of the rod when reeling in the line to bring the fish close to the landing net. Leaders may be had with a loop at each end, or with loops tied in, for using a cast of two or three flies. For all average casting, the two-fly cast is the best, but the expert angler uses the single-fly very often. For lake fishing, the single large fly is generally preferred. For using two flies, the leader is provided with three loops, one at the top, another at the bottom, and an extra loop tied in about 15 in. from the lower loop. In fly casting, the first, or upper, fly is known as the "dropper," and the lower one as the "tail" fly. For the single-fly cast but two loops are required.

Gut used for leaders should be carefully selected, and only those lengths which are of uniform diameter and well rounded chosen, the lengths which show flat and rough spots being discarded. Dry gut that is very brittle should be handled very little, and previous to a day's fishing the leaders must be soaked in water over night to make them pliable, then coiled in between felt pads of the leader box to keep them in fishing shape. After use, put the frayed leaders aside and dry them out between the flannel leaves of the fly book.

Gut is the product of the silkworm, and the best quality is imported from Spain. It comes in bundles, or hanks, of 1,000 strands, 10 to 20 in. long and in different thicknesses, or strengths. The heaviest are known as "Royal" and "Imperial," for salmon; "Marana," for extra-heavy bass; "Padron," for bass; "Regular," for heavy trout; "Fina," for light trout, and "Refina," for extra-light trout. The grades "Fina" and "Refina" are well suited for all average fly fishing, while the heavier sizes are useful for heavy large fishing.

To make the leaders, soak the strands of gut in warm water over night until they are soft and pliable. Select the strands for each leader of the desired thickness and length so that the finished leader will have a slight taper to one end only. By using the "Fina" gut for the upper length and tying in two lengths of "Refina" gut, a nicely tapered leader of light weight is obtained. Begin the leader by uniting the strands together to make it the correct length, three 12-in. strands being about right for average casting. The "single water knot" is the strongest and neatest to use. Make it by taking the thick end of the strand and doubling it back enough to tie in a common knot just large enough for the line to pass through and drawing it up tightly. Tie a single loose knot in the other end of the strand, about ⅛ in. in diameter and close to the end; take the next thickest strand of gut, thread the thicker end through the loose knot and tie a second square knot around the strand, as shown at A. By pulling on the two long ends the loops can be drawn up tightly, and the two knots will slide together and make a neat and very strong knot. Repeat this operation until as many strands of gut are knotted together as required to make the leader of the desired length. For making the loop at the ends, a double-bighted knot, tied as shown at B, is used. If a dropper fly is desired, do not pull the water knot tightly, but first insert a short length of gut with a common knot at the end and a loop in the other, then draw the water knot up tightly, and a short snell will be made for attaching the fly as usually.

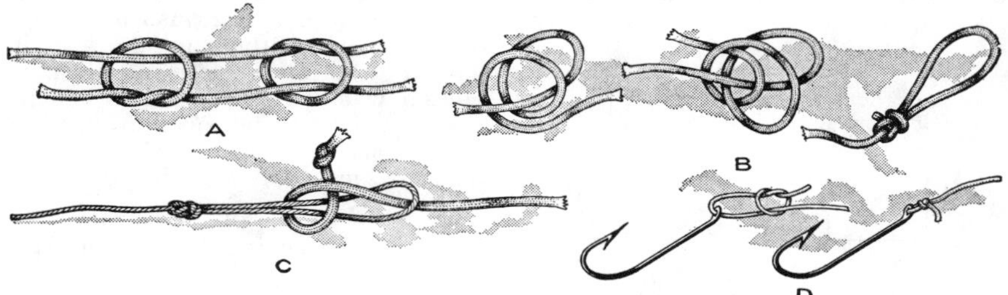

The Single Water Knot Used in Tying Leaders; a Good Knot for Making the Loop at the End of the Leaders; an Angler's Knot Used for Attaching the Line to the Leader, and a Jam Knot for Attaching Eyed Flies, or Hooks, to the Leader or Snell

Flies for Trout Fishing

The standard selection of artificial flies numbers about 60, but the average fisherman will find about 24 selected patterns to answer every need. For making up the most "killing" flies for the trout season, the following can be recommended: Use red ibis, stone fly, cinnamon, red spinner, and parchmenee belle, for April; turkey brown, yellow dun, iron blue, spinner, montreal and red fox, for May; spider, black gnat, silver doctor, gray drake, orange dun, and green drake, for June; July dun, grizzly king, pale evening dun, red ant, and brown palmer, for July; Seth green, coachman, shad, governor, August dun, and royal coachman, for August, and black palmer, willow, whirling dun, queen of the water, and blue bottle, for September.

To attach a line to the leader the well-known "angler's knot" is mostly used. This knot is shown at C. The snelled fly is attached by passing the loop over the loop of the leader and inserting the fly through the leader loop. When eyed flies are used they are often attached direct to the leader, or a looped snell may be used as in the ordinary American-tied fly. To attach the eyed fly direct to the leader, the common "jam knot," shown at D, is mostly used, and when the slipknot is drawn up tightly and the extra end cut off it makes a small, neat knot, not apt to slip.

Catch to Hold Two Joining Doors Open

Where two open doors meet, a catch to keep them open can be made of a piece of wire, shaped as shown. The hooks at the ends of the wire are slipped over the shanks of the knobs.—Contributed by W. A. Saul, Lexington, Mass.

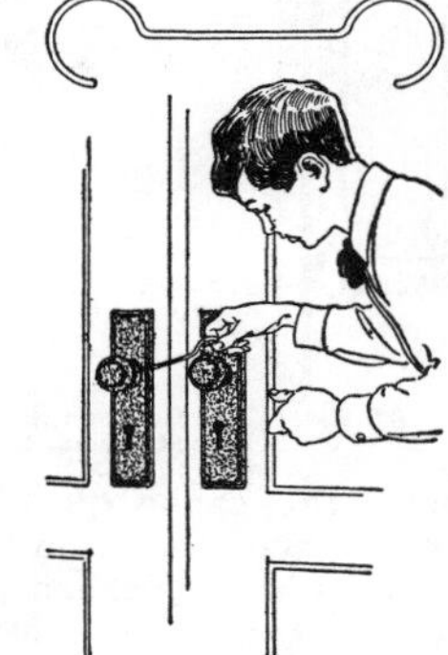

¶Strips cut from wood dishes used by grocers for butter, thoroughly soaked in warm water, will make excellent repair pieces for market baskets.

Bicycle Oil Lamp Changed to Electric Light

The desire for an electric light for my bicycle caused me to change a fine oil lamp, too good to be thrown away,

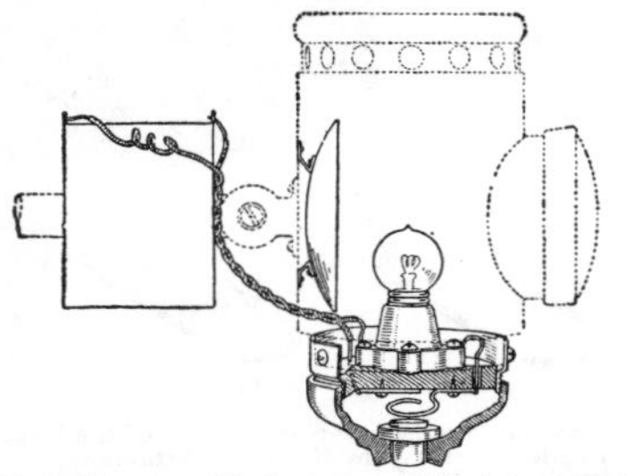

A Push Button with Socket and Miniature Globe Used in an Oil Lamp for Electric Light

so that an electric globe could be used in it. The oil cup of the lamp was removed, and a wood push button fastened in its place with three screws. Before fastening the push button, a porcelain socket was attached to its bottom, and connections were made between socket and push button, ends being left protruding for connection to the battery. A small flash-light battery was fastened to the lamp bracket. A small rubber washer was placed between the head of the push button on the switch and the cap, so that in screwing the cap up, a permanent connection was made. The lamp can be used as a lantern when removed from the bicycle. — Contributed by Lee Baker, Chicago.

Lifter for Removing Eggs from Hot Water

An improvement over the customary way of removing eggs from hot water with a tablespoon, is to use an old-fashioned coffee strainer. This brings up the eggs without carrying hot water with them.—Contributed by L. E. Turner, New York, N. Y.

¶Genuine oxalic acid may be used for removing stains from all woods except mahogany.

Double Top for a Table

The need of two tables in a kitchen where there was space for only one,

An Extra Top Covers the Table When It is Placed against the Wall

was the cause of devising the arrangement shown in the illustration. An ordinary kitchen table was mounted on trunk casters or domes so that it could be moved easily, whereupon a zinc top was put on it with raised edges. The table was then placed against the wall where it was to be used, and an extra, plain top fitted to it and hinged to the wall.

When it was desired to wash dishes on the zinc top, the table was pulled out without disturbing the articles on the hinged top. After drying the dishes, they are removed from the zinc top to the hinged part, and the

The Table When Drawn Out Uncovers the Zinc Tray, Fastened on Top

table is pushed back against the wall. —Contributed by Louis Drummond, Philadelphia, Pa.

As a General Thing, the Veteran Fly Fisherman Prefers to Wade with the Current, and Fishes the Water in Front of Him by Making Diagonal Casts across the Stream

Fishing-Rod Making and Angling

By STILLMAN TAYLOR

PART IV—Trout Fishing with Fly and Bait

How to Cast the Fly

TO be able to cast the artificial fly a distance of 50 ft., or more, and let the feathered lure alight upon the desired bit of water as lightly as a falling leaf is no small accomplishment, for fly casting is an art, and to become an expert, much practice is necessary. The personal assistance of a skillful caster is not often available, but if the angler will follow the suggestions outlined, a beginner will soon grasp the knack of handling the fly rod, and the casting will steadily improve with practice. As the knack of handling a gun is best gained—not in the field, shooting live game, but through shooting at targets—so may the art of fly casting be more quickly acquired by intelligent practice conducted away from the stream, in the back yard, or any other place roomy enough to swing the rod and a moderately long line. By practicing in this way, the angler's attention is focused upon the cast and is not partly occupied with the excitement of fishing. To make a good beginning, let the reel contain about 25 yd. of common, braided, linen line (size E is about right) and instead of a fly, or hook, affix a small split shot to the end of the line. It is well to begin with a cheap rod and save a good outfit, and if the angler learns how to make a fairly long and accurate cast with a common rod, he may feel assured that he can even do better with a first-rate outfit.

The first point to observe in making the cast is to grip the rod correctly, and this is done by grasping the rod at the right point where it balances best. By shifting the hand about, this point of balance is quickly found, for at no other point will the rod "hang" well in the hand. In casting, the reel is turned to the under side of the rod with the thumb extended along the top of the grip, as shown in Fig. 1. Taking up an easy casting position, with the left foot slightly advanced, pull from the reel about 25 yd. of line and let this slack line fall in coils upon the ground in front; bring the rod up slightly above the horizontal, as shown in Fig. 2, and with a quick snap of the wrist, avoiding shoulder or body movement, throw the tip upward, checking it sharply as

Fig. 1—The Proper Way to Take Hold of the Handle with the Reel on the Under Side

soon as the tip is carried over the shoulder about 25° beyond the vertical plane as in Fig. 3. This snappy upstroke of the rod makes the "back cast," by projecting the line high in the air, and carries it well behind the angler. Before the line has fully straightened out behind, and before it has an opportunity to fall much below the caster's shoulders, the rod is snapped forward with a quick wrist-and-forearm movement, which throws the line forward in front of the fisherman and in the direction he is facing, which finishes the cast with the rod in the position shown in Fig. 4.

Long and accurate fly casting is much more a matter of skill than muscle, and while some fly fishermen cast directly from the shoulder and upper arm, and thus use a considerable amount of muscular force in making the cast, this cannot be regarded as the best method of casting. The great elasticity of the fly rod ought to be taken full advantage of by the caster, and if this is done, casting will be naturally accomplished by the wrist and forearm. To make strenuous efforts to hurl the fly through the air, using an arm or body movement, is extremely tiring after an hour or so of fishing, while if the cast is made from the wrist, aided by the forearm, the snap of the rod may be depended upon to project the fly to greater length of line and allow it to fall close to the desired spot, lightly and without splashing.

Fig. 2—Begin the Cast with the Rod in a Position Just above the Horizontal Plane

Timing the back cast is the most difficult detail of fly casting, because the line is behind the angler and the eye cannot aid the hand. The novice will soon acquire the knack of casting, however, if he will remember to keep the elbow close to the side, and to keep the line well up in the air when making the back cast, and to begin the forward movement before the line has fully straightened out behind him. After a little practice, the hand will feel the slight tension communicated to the rod as the line begins to straighten out, and this should be taken advantage of to correctly time the forward movement. Counting "one" for the upstroke, "two and" for the interval required for the line to straighten out in the rear, and "three" for the forward movement, is also a good way to time the cast.

At the beginning the caster should make no attempt to secure distance. Accuracy and delicacy in placing the fly on the water is of much more importance than length of cast in trout fishing, and to attain this end, it is a good plan to place a newspaper about 25 ft. distant and try to drop the end of the line on this mark. When the caster can drop the line on the target lightly and with reasonable accuracy, he may feel justified in lengthening his cast. Other casts than the overhead cast just described are occasionally used, as the Spey, switch, wind, and flip casts, but the overhead cast is mostly used, although it is much more difficult to master.

To make the Spey cast, the angler requires a rapid stream which will carry the line downstream until it is straight and taut, the tip of the rod being held as long as possible to accomplish this end. The rod is then raised high in the air with a quick wrist movement, which lifts the line from the water to the extreme end, then without pausing the rod is carried upstream with just sufficient force to let the fly fall just above the angler. The line is now on the reverse, or upper, side of the fisherman, when with a sweep of the rod the line is projected over the water's surface—not along the surface—in the manner used in making the overhead cast.

Fig. 3—The Rod is Quickly Checked When It is Carried over the Shoulder About 25 Degrees

The switch cast is sometimes useful when trees or rocks are immediately back of the fisherman, thus preventing the line from extending far enough backward to make the overhead cast. In making this cast the line is not lifted from the water, but merely to the surface by raising the tip of the rod. The line is dragged through the water by carrying the tip in the direction one is standing until it is as far in the rear as the obstructions will permit. By a quick downward sweep of the rod the line is projected with sufficient force to roll it forward in a large coil or loop, much as a wheel rolls on a track.

The wind cast is a modification of the switch cast, but easier to make. The caster brings his line almost to his feet, and with a quick downward motion of the rod the line is thrown in a long loop against the wind. The underhand and the flip casts are so simple that it seems almost unnecessary to describe them. Both are short casts and are only used when the angler is fishing in an overgrown stream. The underhand cast is really a side cast, inasmuch as the short line is lifted from the water in a loop and propelled in the desired direction by a side sweep of the rod. The flip cast is made by holding the fly between the thumb and finger and with a few coils of line in the right hand. Bend the rod like a bow, release the fly suddenly, and the snap of the rod will project it in the desired direction and allow it to drop lightly like a fly.

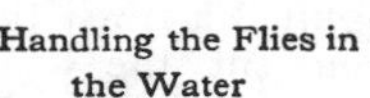

Handling the Flies in the Water

As a general thing the veteran fly fisherman prefers to wade with the current and fishes the water in front of him by making diagonal casts across the stream. A good fisherman will systematically cover every inch of good water and little will be left to chance. The novice is inclined to fish his flies in a contrary manner, he casts more or less at random, and is as likely to splash the flies recklessly about in the most impossible places as he is to drop them in a favorable riffle or pool. To be able to pick out fishable water, the angler should know something about the habits of the trout, their characteristics at the several seasons of the fishing year, and their habits, which differ greatly in different streams. A fishing knowledge of the stream to be visited is of much value, but if the angler knows how to make a fair cast and possesses average skill in handling flies on water, there should be no question but that he will creel a fair number of trout even though he casts in strange waters.

To imitate the action of the natural insect is the most successful manner of fishing the flies, and as the natural fly will struggle more or less when borne down with the current, the fisherman endeavors to duplicate this movement by making his artificial fly wriggle about. This motion must not be overdone, for if the flies are twitched and skipped about, or pulled against the current, the wary trout will refuse to fall for any such obvious deceit. A gentle motion of the wrist will cause the fly to move somewhat as the natural insect will struggle.

Fig. 4—The Cast is Finished by Throwing the Line Forward with a Quick Wrist-and-Forearm Movement

In making the cast do not cast directly down or upstream, but across the current at an angle. Let the flies fall upon the water as lightly as possible, so that the water will carry them downstream over the likely places where the trout are hiding. Keep the line as taut as possible by drawing the slack in with the left hand. The flies should not be allowed to soak in the water, neither should they be retrieved in haste. The experienced fly caster will invariably fish with a wet line, that is to say, with a slightly submerged fly, and will let the flies drag over as much water as possible before making a second cast. Owing to the fact that trout lie with their noses pointing upstream awaiting their food carried down by the current, the caster will naturally take pains to float his flies downstream with the leader fairly taut. To neglect this detail and allow the leader to float in a wide loop near or before the flies is slovenly fishing, and few trout will strike a fly presented in this amateurish fashion.

Early in the fishing season, and when the stream is flooded and discolored after a heavy rain, it is a good plan to fish the flies below the surface. Fishing in this manner makes it more difficult to tell when to strike a fish, and some little practice is needed to determine the opportune moment by feeling the slight tension on the line. Many fish will be pricked to be sure, but some trout will be creeled, and fishing with the submerged fly is sometimes the only way trout can be taken.

On fair days and in smooth water, better luck may be expected when the fly is kept upon the surface, and this is easily managed by keeping the tip of the rod well in the air. Often the fisherman can take advantage of a bit of floating foam, and if the fly is cast upon it and allowed to float with it downstream, the ruse will often prove effective.

The trout is a hard striker and it is not unusual to have a trout rush ahead of the fly in his attempt to mouth it. In rapid water the savage rush of the fish is sufficient to hook it securely, but when casting in quiet pools, the hook is imbedded by a snap of the wrist. At what exact moment to strike, as well as the amount of force to use, depends upon circumstances. When fishing in small streams and brooks where the trout run small, much less force is necessary to hook the fish, but in quiet water and in larger streams where 2 or 3-lb. trout are not uncommon, the fish may be struck with a smart upward jerk of the forearm and wrist. So far as my experience goes, the matter of striking is governed by the temperament as well as the judgment of the angler. The deliberate thinking man is likely to strike too late, while the nervous individual, striking too early, is apt to prick the trout and roll him over.

The best time to fish for trout is when they are feeding on the surface; and in the early days of spring, when there are few flies about, the warmer part of the day, say, from 10 in the morning to 5 in the afternoon, will prove to be the most successful time. Later on, when flies are numerous, good luck may be expected at an early hour in the morning, and in the hot summer months the cooler hours of the day may be chosen. Of course, there are many exceptions, since there are many cool days in summer, as well as exceptionally warm days in spring, and these changes of weather should be considered. However, extremes are not likely to make good fishing, and the trout will not rise as freely on cold, windy days, nor will they fight as gamely. On hot days, too, not so much luck can be expected during the hours of the greatest heat—12 to 4—but a good basket of trout may be creeled early in the morning or late in the afternoon of summer. A bright, clear day is usually the best for fly fishing, because the sun brings out more flies, but a warm rain, or even a fog, is also considered good fishing weather.

Among the live baits available for trout fishing are the minnow, white grub, cricket, grasshopper, and other insects, and last, but by no means least, the common angle or earthworm. The minnow is beyond a doubt the most enticing morsel that can be offered to a hungry trout, and a minnow may be reckoned to secure a rise when other baits fail. The inconvenience of transporting this bait is a great drawback, and as minnows are delicate fish, a minnow bucket is necessary for their preservation. This means a lot of trouble, as the water must be frequently changed or aerated, and this labor, together with the difficulty of carrying a bulky pail through the brush, makes this desirable bait almost impossible for stream and brook fishing. The salt-water minnow, known as a "shiner" or "mummychug," is a topnotch trout bait, and being much tougher than the fresh-water minnow, makes a bait often used by anglers residing near the seacoast.

The white grub, or larvae of the so-called May beetle, is a good bait available for early-season fishing, and may be obtained in the early spring months by spading up grass land. The grub is about 1 in. long, and of a creamy yellow color with a darker head. It may be kept a month, or more, by putting it in a box with a number of pieces of fresh turf.

Crickets, grasshoppers, and many other insects, make good baits, while the earthworm is a good all-around bait for trout. A supply dug some days before and kept by packing in fresh moss and slightly moistening with milk and water will prove more attractive in appearance and the worms will be tougher and cleaner to handle than when carried in earth.

Other good baits include the fin of a trout, and if this is used in combination with the eye of the same fish, it forms an attractive lure. In using this bait, do not puncture the eyeball, but hook through the thin flexible skin surrounding the eye. A fat piece of salt pork, cut into pieces 1 in. long and 1/4 in. wide, makes a fairly good bait. Spoons and other spinning baits are presumably attractive, but few sportsmen use them when angling for so fine a fish as trout.

A Nonagon-Shaped Shelter Provided a Splendid Inclosure for a Peanut Stand

A Bark-Inclosed House Made an Excellent Home in All Kinds of Weather

This Building was Used by a Band in Giving Concerts Evenings and on Any Special Holiday

A Commodious Shelter Where Ice Cream and Other Refreshments were Served

[In this article descriptions are given of several shelters suitable for a resort, but the reader may select any one of them that answers his needs and build a camp house, or fit up a more substantial one to make living quarters for the whole year.—Editor.]

BEING forced to take the open-air treatment to regain health, a person adopted the plan of building a pole house in the woods, and the scheme was so successful that it was decided to make a resort grounds, to attract crowds during holidays, by which an income could be realized for living expenses. All the pavilions, stands, furniture, and amusement devices were constructed of straight poles cut from young growth of timber with the bark remaining on them. Outside of boards for flooring and roofing material, the entire construction of the buildings and fences consisted of poles.

A level spot was selected and a house built having three rooms. The location was in a grove of young timbers, most of it being straight, and 13 trees were easily found that would make posts 12 ft. long, required for the sides, and two poles 16 ft. long, for the center of the ends, so that they would reach to the ridge. The plot was laid out rectangular and marked for the poles, which were set in the ground for a depth of 4 ft., at distances of 6 ft. apart. This made the house 8 ft. high at the eaves with a square pitch roof; that is, the ridge was 3 ft. high in the center from the plate surfaces for this width of a house. The rule for finding this height is to take one-quarter of the width of

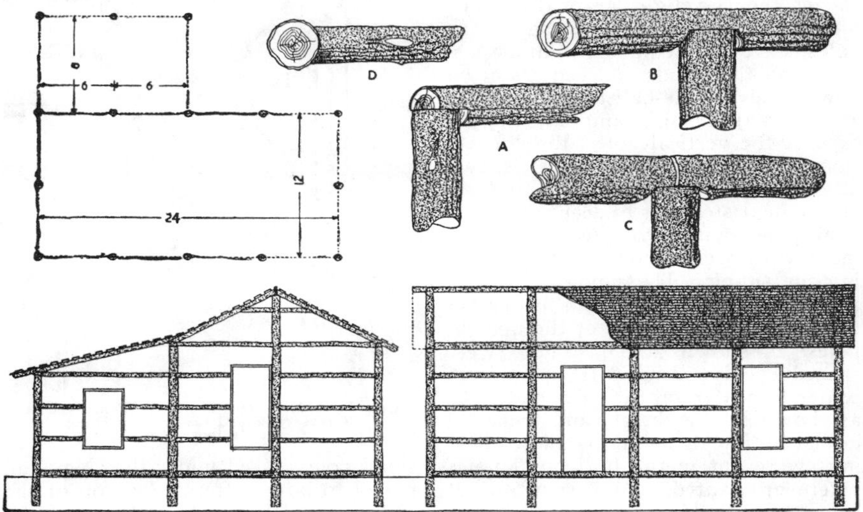

The Frame Construction of the House Made Entirely of Rough Poles, the Verticals being Set in the Ground, Plumbed, and Sighted to Make a Perfect Rectangle of the Desired Proportions

the house for the height in the center from the plate.

The corner poles were carefully lo-

The Steps are Supported on Pairs of Vertical Poles Set in the Ground to Make Different Levels

cated to make the size 12 by 24 ft., with a lean-to 8 by 12 ft., and then plumbed to get them straight vertically. The plates for the sides, consisting of five poles, were selected as straight as possible and their ends and centers hewn down to about one-half their thickness, as shown at A and B, and nailed to the tops of the vertical poles, the connection for center poles being as shown at C.

The next step was to secure the vertical poles with crosspieces between them which were used later for supporting the siding. These poles were cut about 6 ft. long, their ends being cut concave to fit the curve of the upright poles, as shown at D. These were spaced evenly, about 2 ft. apart from center to center, on the sides and ends, as shown in the sketch, and toenailed in place. The doors and window openings were cut in the horizontal poles wherever wanted, and casements set in and nailed. The first row of horizontal poles was placed close to the ground and used both as support for the lower ends of the siding and to nail the ends of the flooring boards to, which were fastened in the center to poles laid on stones, or, better still, placed on top of short blocks, 5 ft. long, set in the ground. These poles for the floor should be placed not over 2 ft. apart to make the flooring solid.

A lean-to was built by setting three poles at a distance of 8 ft. from one side, beginning at the center and extending to the end of the main building. These poles were about 6 ft. long above the ground. The rafter poles for this part were about 9½ ft. long, notched at both ends for the plates, the ends of the house rafters being sawed off even with the outside of the plate along this edge. The rafter poles for the house were 10 in all, 8 ft. long, and were laid off and cut to fit a ridge made of a board. These poles were notched about 15 in. from their lower ends to fit over the rounding edge of the plate pole, and were then placed directly over each vertical wall pole. They were nailed both to the plate and to the ridge, also further strengthened by a brace made of a piece of board or a

Gate Openings were Made in the Fence Where Necessary, and Gates of Poles Hung in the Ordinary Manner

small pole, placed under the ridge and nailed to both rafters. On top of the rafters boards were placed horizontally, spaced about 1 ft. apart, but this is optional with the builder, as other roofing material can be used. In this instance metal roofing was used, and it only required fastening at intervals, and to prevent rusting out, it was well painted on the under side before laying it and coated on the outside when fastened in place. If a more substantial shelter is wanted, it is best to lay the roof solid with boards, then cover it with the regular prepared roofing material.

All Furniture, Together with the Large Lawn Swings, Took on the General Appearance of the Woodland, and As the Pieces were Made Up of the Same Material As the Houses, the Cost Was Only the Labor and a Few Nails

Some large trees were selected and felled, then cut into 4-ft. lengths and the bark removed, or if desired, the bark removed in 4-ft. lengths, and nailed on the outside of the poles, beginning at the bottom in the same manner as laying shingles, to form the siding of the house. If a more substantial house is wanted, boards can be nailed on the poles, then the bark fastened to the boards; also, the interior can be finished in wall board.

The same general construction is used for the porch, with horizontal poles latticed, as shown, to form the railing. It is very easy to make ornamental parts, such as shown, on the eave of the porch, by splitting sticks and nailing them on closely together to make a frieze. Floors are laid on the porch and in the house, and doors hung and window sash fitted in the same manner as in an ordinary house.

A band stand was constructed on sloping ground, and after setting the poles, the floor horizontals were placed about 2 ft. above the ground, on the upper side, and 4 ft. on the lower side. The poles used were about 18 ft. long. Instead of having the horizontals 2 ft. apart, the first was placed 1 ft. above the floor, the next at about one-half the distance from the lower one to the plate at the top, and the space between was ornamented with cross poles, as shown. A balcony or bay was constructed at one end, and a fancy roof was made of poles whose ends rested on a curved pole attached to the vertical pieces. Steps were formed of several straight poles, hewn down on their ends to make a level place to rest on horizontal pieces attached to stakes at the ends. A pair of stakes were used at each end of a step, and these were fastened to a slanting piece at the top, their lower ends being set into the ground. The manner of bracing and crossing with horizontals makes a rigid form of construction, and if choice poles are selected for the step pieces, they will be comparatively level and of sufficient strength to hold up all the load put on them. The roof of this building was made for a sun

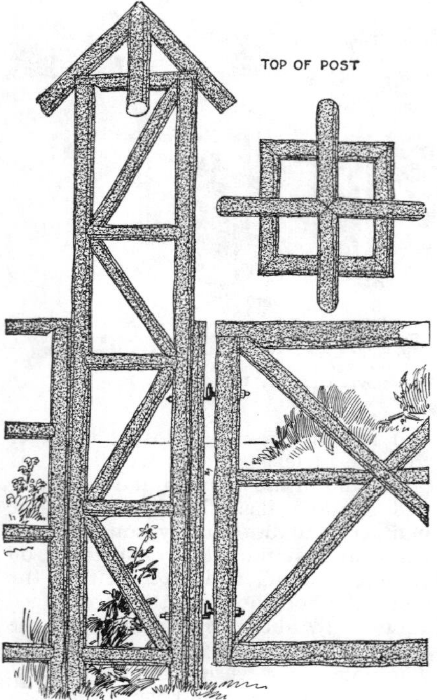

The Entrance to the Grounds was Given an Inviting Appearance with Large Posts and Swinging Gates

shade only and consisted of boards nailed closely together on the rafters.

An ice-cream parlor was built on the same plan, but without any board floor; the ground, being level, was used instead. There were five vertical poles used for each end with a space left between the two poles at the center, on both sides, for an entrance. This building was covered with prepared roofing, so that the things kept for sale could be protected in case of a shower.

A peanut stand was also built without a floor, and to make it with nine sides, nine poles were set in the ground to form a perfect nonagon and joined at their tops with latticed horizontals. Then a rafter was run from the top of each post to the center, and boards were fitted on each pair of rafters over the V-shaped openings. The boards were then covered with prepared roofing. A railing was formed of horizontals set in notches, cut in the posts, and then ornamented in the same manner as for the other buildings.

Fences were constructed about the grounds, made of pole posts with horizontals on top, hewn down and fitted as the plates for the house; and the lower pieces were set in the same as for making the house railing. Gates were made of two vertical pieces, the height of the posts, and two horizontals, then braced with a piece running from the lower corner at the hinge side to the upper opposite corner, the other cross brace being joined to the sides of the former, whereupon two short horizontals were fitted in the center. A blacksmith formed some hinges of rods and strap iron, as shown, and these were fastened in holes bored in the post and the gate vertical. A latch was made by boring a hole through the gate vertical and into the end of the short piece. Then a slot was cut in the side to receive a pin inserted in a shaft made to fit the horizontal hole. A keeper was made in the post by boring a hole to receive the end of the latch.

Large posts were constructed at the entrance to the grounds, and on these double swing gates, made up in the same manner as the small one, were attached. These large posts were built up of four slender poles and were considerably higher than the fence poles. The poles were set in a perfect square, having sides about 18 in. long, and a square top put on by mitering the corners, whereupon four small rafters were fitted on top. The gates were swung on hinges made like those for the small gate.

Among the best and most enjoyed amusement devices on the grounds were the swings. Several of these were built, with and without tables. Four poles, about 20 ft. long, were set in the ground at an angle, and each pair of side poles was joined with two horizontals, about 12 ft. long, spreaders being fastened between the two horizontals to keep the tops of the poles evenly spaced. The distance apart of the poles will depend on the size of the swing and the number of persons to be seated. Each pair of side poles are further strengthened with crossed poles, as shown. If no table is to be used in the swing, the poles may be set closer together, so that the top horizontals will be about 8 ft. long. The platform for the swinging part consists of two poles, 12 ft. long, which are swung on six vertical poles, about 14 ft. long. These poles are attached to the top horizontals with long bolts, or rods, running through both, the bottom being attached in the same manner. Poles are nailed across the platform horizontals at the bottom for a floor, and a table with seats at the ends is formed of poles. The construction is obvious.

A short space between two trees can be made into a seat by fastening two horizontals, one on each tree, with the ends supported by braces. Poles are nailed on the upper surface for a seat.

Other furniture for the house and grounds was made of poles in the manner illustrated. Tables were built for picnickers by setting four or six poles in the ground and making a top of poles or boards. Horizontals were placed across the legs with extending ends, on which seats were made for the tables. Chairs and settees were built in the same manner, poles being used for the entire construction.

An Electric Water Heater

Procure the barrel and cap from a hand bicycle pump and prepare them as follows: Make a tube of paper, about double the thickness of a postal card, to fit snugly in the pump barrel and oil it slightly before slipping it into place. Procure some resistance wire of the proper length and size to heat quickly. The wire can be tested out by coiling it on some nonconducting material, such as an earthen jug or glazed tile, and connecting one end to the current supply and running the other wire of the supply over the coil until it heats properly. Cut the resistance at this point and temporarily coil it to fit into the bottom of the pump barrel, allowing one end to extend up through the space in the center with sufficient length to make a connection to supply wires.

Mix some dental plaster to the consistency of thick cream and, while keeping the wire in the center of the pump barrel, pour in the mixture until it is filled to within 1½ in. of the top. Allow the plaster to set for about a day, then remove it from the barrel and take off the paper roll. The coil of wire at the bottom is now straightened out and wound in a coil over the outside of the plaster core, allowing sufficient end for connecting to the supply wires.

Cut two or three disks of mica to fit snugly in the bottom of the pump barrel, also cut a mica sheet to make a covering tube over the coil on the plaster core and insert the whole into the barrel. The two terminals are connected to the ends of a flexible cord which has a plug attached to the opposite end. Be sure to insulate the ends of the wire where they connect to the flexible cord inside of the pump barrel under the cap. In winding the resistance wire on the core, be sure that one turn does not touch the other. The heater when connected to a current supply and placed in 1 qt. of water will bring it to a boil quickly.—Contributed by A. H. Waychoff, Lyons, Colo.

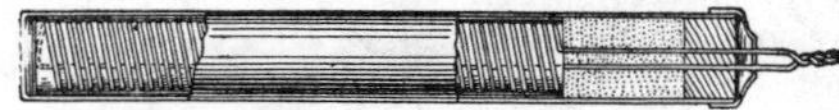

An Electric Heating Coil Made of Resistance Wire Placed in a Bicycle-Pump Barrel for Boiling Water

Camps

By F. S. CHARLES

A good site, pure water in abundance, and a convenient fuel supply, are the features of a temporary camp that should be given first consideration when starting out to enjoy a vacation in the woods. The site should be high and dry, level enough for the tent and camp fire, and with surrounding ground sloping enough to insure proper drainage. A sufficient fuel supply is an important factor, and a spot should be chosen where great effort is not required to collect it and get it into proper shape for the fire.

When locating near streams of water be careful to select a spot above high water mark so the ground will not be overflowed by a sudden rise of the stream. Do not select the site of an old camp, as the surroundings are usually stripped of all fuel, and the grounds are unclean.

Wall Tent

Lean-To of Boughs

Division of Work

Clear the selected spot and lay out the lines for the tent, camp fire, etc. If the camping party consists of more than two persons, each one should do the part allotted to him, and the work will be speedily accomplished. Remember that discipline brings efficiency, and do not be slack about a camp just because it is pleasure. One of the party should attend to the camp fire and prepare the meals while another secures the fuel and water. The tent can be unpacked and the ground cleared by the other members of the party, and when ready, all should assist in raising the tent, especially if it is a large one.

Tents

An ordinary A or wedge tent is sufficient for one or two campers. Where you do not wish to locate permanently, this tent can be set up and taken down quickly. It should have a ring fastened to the cloth in each peak through which to pass a rope or line to take the place of a ridge pole. Such a tent can be pitched be-

Log Cabin

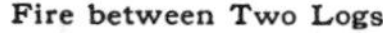

Fire between Two Logs

Fire Built against a Log

tween two trees or saplings, and, after tying the rope to the trees, it can be tightened with a long forked stick, placed under one end of the rope. If two trees are not conveniently located, then two poles crossed and tied together will make supports for one or both ends, the ridge line running over them and staked to the ground.

On a chilly night, the A tent is quite advantageous. The stakes can be pulled on one side and the cloth doubled to make a lean-to, open on the side away from the wind. A fire can be built in front and the deflected heat on the sleeper will keep him comfortable and warm.

For larger parties, the wall tent with a fly is recommended. These tents can be purchased in various sizes. The fly is an extra covering stretched over the top to make an open air space between the two roofs. It keeps the interior of the tent delightfully cool in hot summer weather and provides a better protection from rain. The fly can be made extra long, to extend over the end of the tent, making a shady retreat which can be used for lounging or a dining place.

Protection from Insects

Where mosquitoes and other insects are numerous, it is well to make a second tent of cheesecloth with binding tape along the top to tie it to the ridge pole of the regular tent. The sides should be made somewhat longer than the regular tent so that there will be plenty of cloth to weight it down at the bottom. This second tent should be made without any opening whatever. The occupant must crawl under the edge to enter. The cheesecloth tent is used inside of the ordinary tent, and when not in use it is pushed aside.

Two camps are illustrated showing the construction of a lean-to for a temporary one-season camp, and a log cabin which makes a permanent place from year to year. (A more elaborate and more expensive camp was described in the May issue of this magazine.) The construction of these camps are very simple. The first is made of poles cut in the woods. A ridge pole is placed between two trees or held in place with poles of sufficient

Forked Sticks Supporting Cooking Utensils

length, set in the ground. Poles are placed on this at an angle of about 45 deg., forming a lean-to that will be entirely open in front when finished. The poles are covered, beginning at the bottom, with pine boughs, laid in layers so as to make a roof that will shed water. A large fire, built a short distance from the open front will make a warm place to sleep, the heat being reflected down the same as described for the A tent.

A Permanent Camp

A good permanent camp is a log cabin. This can be constructed of materials found in the woods. Trees may be felled, cut to length, and notched to join the ends together at each corner so as to leave little or no space between the logs. The roof is constructed of long clapboards, split from blocks of wood. The builder can finish such a camp as elaborately as he chooses, and for this reason the site should be selected with great care.

Camp Fires

There is no better way to make a camp fire than to have a large log or two against which to start a fire with small boughs. Larger sticks can be placed over the logs in such a way as to hold a pot of water or to set a frying pan. Forked sticks can be laid on the log and weighted on the lower end with a stone, using the upper end to hang a cooking vessel over the flames. Two logs placed parallel, with space enough between for the smaller sticks, make one of the best camp cooking arrangements. Two forked sticks, one at each end of the logs, may be set in the ground and a pole placed in the forks lengthwise of the fire. This makes a convenient place for hanging the cooking utensils with bent wires.

Food Supplies

The conditions in various localities make a difference in the camper's appetite and in consequence no special list of food can be recommended, but the amount needed by the average person in a vacation camp for two weeks, is about as follows:

Bacon	15 lb.	Baking Powder	½ lb.
Ham	5 "	Sugar	5 "
Flour	20 "	Beans	4 "
Corn Meal	5 "	Salt	2 "
Rice	5 "	Lard	3 "
Coffee	3 lb.		

A number of small things must be added to this list, such as pepper, olive oil, sage, nutmeg and vinegar. If the weight is not to be considered, canned goods, preserves, jam and marmalade, also vegetables and dried fruits may be added. Do not forget soap and matches.

Food can be kept cool in a box or a box-like arrangement made of straight sticks over which burlap is hung and kept wet. This is accomplished by setting a pan on top of the box and fixing wicks of cloth over the edges. The wicks will siphon the water out evenly and keep the burlap wet.

A Drinking Tube

When on a walking tour through the woods or country, it might be well to provide a way to procure water for drinking purposes. Take with you several feet of small rubber tubing and a few inches of hollow cane of the size to fit the tube.

In one end insert the cane for a mouthpiece, and allow the other end to reach into the water. Exhaust the air from the tube and the water will rush up to your lips.—Contributed by L. Alberta Norrell, Augusta, Ga.

Washing Photographic Prints

The usual way of washing photographic prints is to place them in a shallow tray in which they will become stuck together in bunches, if they are not often separated. A French magazine suggests that a deep tank be used instead, and that each print be attached to a cork by means of a pin stuck through one corner, the cork thus becoming a float which keeps the print suspended vertically, and at the same time prevents contact with its nearest neighbor.

Camp Furnishings

By CHELSEA CURTIS FRASER

When on a camping trip nothing should be carried but the necessities, and the furnishings should be made up from materials found in the woods. A good spring bed can be made up in the following manner: Cut two stringers from small, straight trees, about 4 in. in diameter, and make them about 6 ft. long. All branches are trimmed off smooth and a trench is dug in the ground for each piece, the trenches being 24 in. apart. Small saplings, about 1 in. in diameter, and as straight as can be found, are cut and trimmed of all branches, and nailed across the stringers for the springs. Knots, bulges, etc., should be turned downward as far as possible. The ends of each piece are flattened as shown at A, Fig. 1, to give it a good seat on the stringers.

A larger sapling is cut, flattened, and nailed at the head of the bed across the stringers, and to it a number of head-stay saplings, B, are nailed. These head-stay pieces are cut about 12 in. long, sharpened on one end and driven a little way into the ground, after which they are nailed to the head crosspiece.

In the absence of an empty mattress tick and pillow cover which can be filled with straw, boughs of fir may be used. These boughs should not be larger than a match and crooked stems should be turned down. Begin at the head of the bed and lay a row of boughs

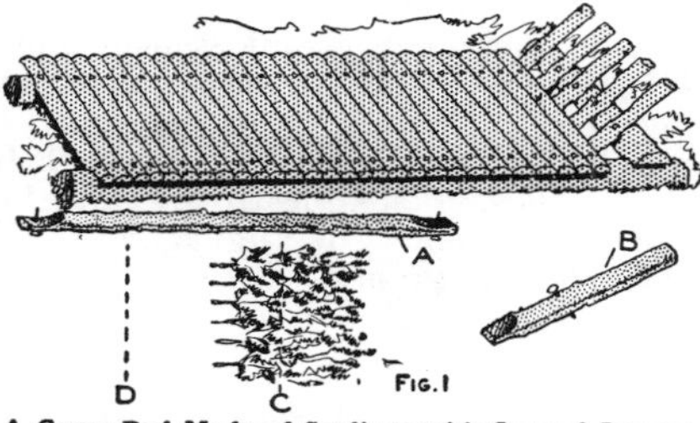

A Camp Bed Made of Saplings with Several Layers of Boughs for the Mattress

with the stems pointing toward the foot. Over this row, and half-lapping it, place another row so that the tops of the boughs lie on the line C and their stems on the line D. This process is continued until the crosspiece springs are entirely covered, and then another layer is laid in the same manner on top

A Table Made of Packing-Box Material and a Wash Basin Stand of Three Stakes

of these, and so on, until a depth of 6 or 8 in. is obtained. This will make a good substitute for a mattress. A pillow can be made by filling a meal bag with boughs or leaves.

A good and serviceable table can be constructed from a few fence boards, or boards taken from a packing box. The table and chairs are made in one piece, the construction being clearly shown in Fig. 2. The height of the ends should be about 29 in., and the seats about 17 in. from the ground. The other dimensions will be governed by the material at hand and the number of campers.

A wash-basin support can be made of three stakes, cut from saplings and driven in the ground, as shown in Fig. 3. The basin is hung by its rim between the ends of the stakes.

Wherever a suitable tree is handy, a seat can be constructed as shown in Fig. 4. Bore two 1-in. holes, 8 in. apart, in the trunk, 15 in. above the ground, and drive two pins, about 12 in. long, cut from a sapling into them. The extending ends are supported on legs of the same material. The seat is made of a slab with the rounding side down.

A clothes hanger for the tent ridge

pole can be made as shown in Fig. 5. The hanger consists of a piece, 7 in. long, cut from a 2-in. sapling, nails be-

A Seat Against the Trunk of a Tree, and a Clothes Hanger for the Tent Ridge Pole

ing driven into its sides for hooks. The upper end is fitted with a rope which is tied over the ridge pole of the tent.

A Fruit Stemmer

In the berry season the stemmer shown in the sketch is a very handy article for the kitchen. It is made of spring steel and tempered, the length being about 2½ in. The end

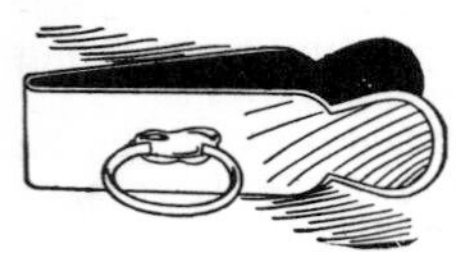

used for removing the stem is ground from the outside edge after tempering. A ring large enough to admit the second finger is soldered at a convenient distance from the end on one leg.—Contributed by H. F. Reams, Nashville, Tennessee.

A Homemade Fountain Pen

A very serviceable fountain pen can be made from two 38-72 rifle cartridges and a steel pen. Clean out the cartridges, fit a hardwood plug tightly in

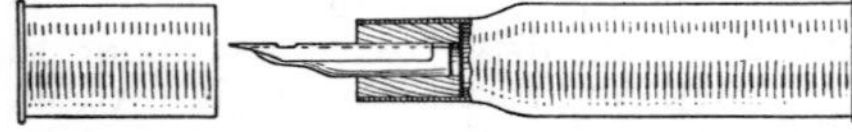

One Cartridge Shell Makes the Fountain Part of the Pen, and the Other the Cap

the end of one shell, and cut it off smooth with the end of the metal. Drill a $\frac{3}{16}$-in. hole in the center of the wood plug and fit another plug into this hole with sufficient end projecting to be shaped for the length of the steel pen to be used. The shank of the pen and the plug must enter the hole together. One side of the projecting end of the plug should be shaped to fit the inside surface of the pen and then cut off at a point a little farther out than the eye in the pen. On the surface that is to lie against the pen a groove is cut in the plug extending from near the point to the back end where it is to enter the hole in the first plug. The under side of the plug is shaped about as shown.

The other cartridge is cut off at such a point that it will fit on the tapering end of the first one, and is used for a cap. The cartridge being filled with ink and the plug inserted, the ink will flow down the small groove in the feeder plug and supply the pen with ink. Care must be taken that the surface of the smaller plug fits the pen snugly and that the groove is not cut through to the point end. This will keep the ink from flooding, and only that which is used for writing will be able to get through or leak out.—Contributed by Edwin N. Harnish, Ceylon, Canada.

Destroying Caterpillars on Grapevines

The grapes in my back yard were being destroyed by caterpillars which could be found under all the large leaves. The vine was almost dead when I began to cut off all the large leaves and those eaten by the caterpillars, which allowed the sun's rays to reach the grapes. This destroyed all the caterpillars and the light and heat ripened the grapes.—Contributed by Wm. Singer, Rahway, N. J.

¶It will require 1 gal. of ordinary mixed calcimine to cover 270 sq. ft. of plastered surface, 180 sq. ft. of brickwork and 225 sq. ft. of average woodwork.

A Camp Provision Box

While on a camping and canoeing trip recently, I used a device which added a touch of completeness to our outfit and made camp life really enjoyable. This useful device is none other than a provision or "grub" box.

From experience campers know that the first important factor in having a successful trip is compactness of outfit. When undertaking an outing of this kind it is most desirable to have as few bundles to carry as possible, especially if one is going to be on the move part of the time. This device eliminates an unnecessary amount of bundles, thus making the trip easier for the campers, and doubly so if they intend canoeing part of the time; and, apart from its usefulness as a provision container, it affords a general repository for the small articles which mean so much to the camper's welfare.

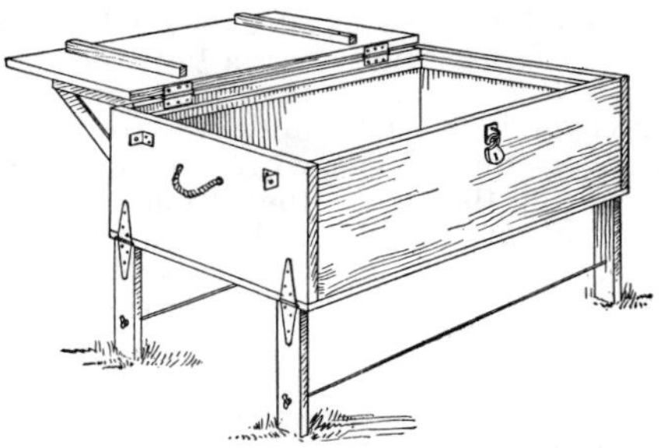

The Provision Box Ready for Use in Camp, the Cover Turned Back on the Brackets and the Legs Extended

The box proper may be made of any convenient size, so long as it is not too cumbersome for two people to handle. The dimensions given are for a box I used on a canoe trip of several hundred miles; and from experience I know it to be of a suitable size for canoeists. If the camper is going to have a fixed camp and have his luggage hauled, a larger box is much to be preferred. A glance at the figures will show the general proportions of the box. It may be possible, in some cases, to secure a strong packing box near the required dimensions, thus doing away with the trouble of constructing it. The distinguishing features of this box are the hinged cover, the folding legs, and the folding brackets. The brackets, upon which the top rests when open, fold in against the back of the box when not in use. The same may be said of the legs. They fold up alongside the box and are held there by spring-brass clips.

On our trips we carry an alcohol stove on which we do all of our cooking. The inner side of the top is covered with a sheet of asbestos, this side being uppermost when the hinged top is opened and resting on the folding brackets. The stove rested on this asbestos, thus making everything safe. The cover is large enough to do all the cooking on, and the box is so high that the cooking can be attended to without stooping over, which is much more pleasant than squatting before a camp fire getting the eyes full of smoke. The legs are hinged to the box in such a manner that all of the weight of the box

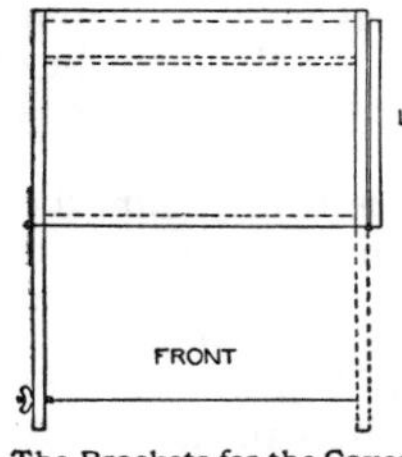

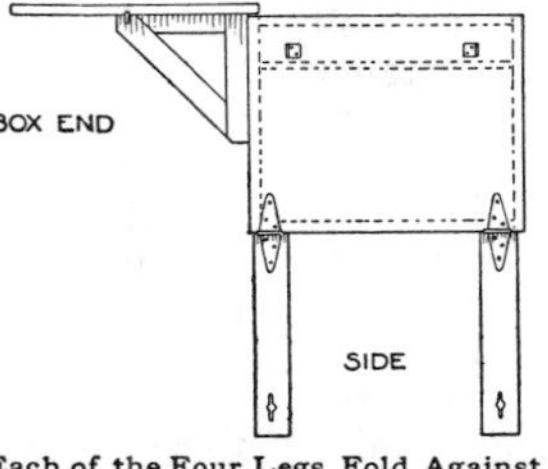

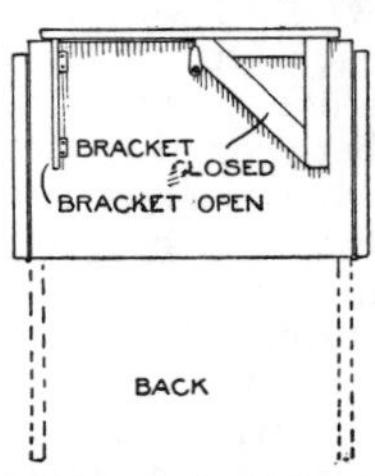

The Brackets for the Cover as Well as Each of the Four Legs Fold Against the Sides of the Box in Such a Manner as to be Out of the Way, Making the Box Easy to Carry and Store Away in a Small Space

rests on the legs rather than on the hinges, and are kept from spreading apart by wire turnbuckles. These, being just bolts and wire, may be tucked inside the box when on the move. The

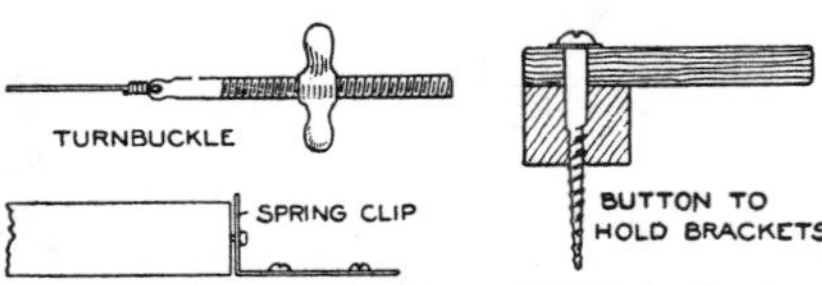

Detail of the Turnbuckle, Button to Hold the Brackets, and the Spring Clip for Holding the Legs on the Side of the Box

top is fitted with unexposed hinges and with a lock to make it a safe place for storing valuables.

In constructing the cover it is well to make it so that it covers the joints of the sides, thus making the box waterproof from the top, if rain should fall on it. A partition can be made in one end to hold odds and ends. A tray could be installed, like the tray in a trunk, to hold knives, forks, spoons, etc., while the perishable supplies are kept underneath the tray. Give the box two coats of lead paint, and shellac the inside.

The wire braces for the legs are made as follows. Procure four machine bolts, about 1/4 in. in diameter and 2 in. long—any thread will do—with wing nuts and washers to fit. Saw or file off the heads and drill a small hole in one end of each bolt, large enough to receive a No. 16 galvanized iron wire. Two inches from the bottom of each leg drill a hole to take the bolt loosely. Determine the exact distance between the outside edges of the legs when the box is resting on them. Make the wire braces 1 in. longer than this distance so that the bolts will protrude through the holes in the legs and allow for putting on the nuts and washers. Screwing up on the nuts draws the wire taut, thus holding the legs firm.

The size of the top determines the dimensions of the folding brackets which support it when open. These brackets may be solid blocks of wood, but a lighter and more serviceable bracket is constructed as follows. If the top is 20 in. wide and 30 in. long, make the brackets 10 by 13 in. Constructing the brackets so that their combined length is 4 in. shorter than the total length of the box, facilitates their folding against the back of the box when not in use. This point is clearly shown in the drawing. Our brackets were made of 1/2-in. oak, 1 1/2 in. wide, and the joints halved together. They are hinged to the back of the box as shown; and when folded are held in place by a simple catch. The weight of the lid is sufficient to hold the brackets in place when open, but to make sure they will not creep when in use insert a 1/4-in. dowel in the end of each so that it protrudes 1/4 in. Drill two holes in the top to the depth of 1/4 in., so that when the top rests on the brackets, these holes engage with the dowels. In hinging the brackets to the back see that they are high enough to support the lid at right angles to the box.

The box here shown is made of 7/8 in. white pine throughout. The legs are 7/8 by 2 1/2 by 18 in. They are fastened to the box with ordinary strap hinges. When folded up against the box they do not come quite to the top so that the box should be at least 19 in. high for 18-in. legs. About 2 in. from the bottom of the legs drive in a brad so it protrudes 1/8 in. as shown. This brad engages in a hole in the spring-brass clip when folded up as shown in the illustration.

If in a fixed camp, it is a good idea to stand the legs in tomato cans partly full of water. This prevents ants from crawling up the legs into the box, but it necessitates placing the wire braces higher on the legs.

Our box cost us nothing but the hardware, as we knocked some old packing boxes to pieces and planed up enough boards to make the sides. Of course, the builder need not adhere to these dimensions, for he can make the size to suit his requirements, while the finish is a matter of personal taste.

¶A blue writing ink is easily made of 1 oz. Prussian blue, 1 1/2 oz. oxalic acid and 1 pt. of soft water. Shake and allow it to stand until dissolved.

Wall Pockets in a Tent

When camping I find a few wall pockets sewed to the tent walls at the back end provide a convenient means to hold the soap, mirror, razor and other small articles liable to be lost. The pockets can be made of the same material as the tent and sewed on as a patch pocket.—Contributed by A. M. Barnes, Atlanta, Ga.

Camp Stoves

The camp stoves illustrated are different forms of the same idea. Both can be taken apart and laid flat for packing. Iron rods, 1/2 in. in diameter, are used for the legs. They are sharpened at the lower end so that they may be easily driven into the ground. The rods of the one shown in the first illustration are bent in the form of a hook at the upper end, and two pieces of light tire iron, with holes in either end, are hung on these

Camp-Stove Top, Either Solid or Pieced, Supported on Rods at the Corners

hooks. Across these supports are laid other pieces of the tire iron. In the other stove, the rods have a large head and are slipped through holes in the four corners of the piece of heavy sheet iron used for the top. A cotter is slipped through a hole in each rod just below the top, to hold the latter in place.—Contributed by Mrs. Lelia Munsell, Herington, Kansas.

Attractor for Game Fish

A piece of light wood, shaped as shown and with four small screweyes attached, makes a practical attractor for game fish, such as bass, etc., by its action when drawn through the water or carried by the flow of a stream. Hooks are attached to three of the screweyes and the fourth one, on the

A Device for Attracting Game Fish Which is Used in Place of Bait

sloping surface, is used for the line.—Contributed by Arthur Vogel, Indianapolis, Ind.

Simple Photographic-Print Washer

The ordinary washbowl supplied with a faucet may be easily converted into a washing tray for photographic prints or film negatives. Procure a medicine dropper from a druggist, and attach it to the faucet end with a short piece of rubber tubing. Be sure to procure a dropper that has the point turned at right angles to the body.

The Whirling Motion Set Up by the Forced Stream at an Angle Thoroughly Washes Prints

When the water is turned on it is forced through the small opening in the dropper in such a manner that the water in the bowl is kept in a constant whirling motion. This will keep the prints on the move, which is necessary for a thorough washing.

How to Make an Electric Fishing Signal

A unique electric fishing signal, which may be rigged up on a wharf or pier, and the electric circuit so ar-

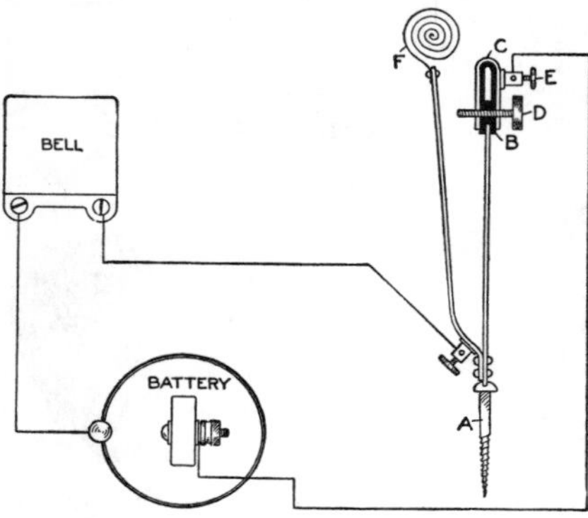

Construction of the Parts to Make the Contact Points and the Electric Connections

ranged as to operate an electric bell or buzzer, located in the fisherman's cottage, or any other convenient place, may be constructed as follows: Obtain two pieces of $\frac{1}{16}$-in. spring brass, one 6 in. long and ¾ in. wide, and the other 7 in. long and ½ in. wide. Mount a 2-in. brass wood screw, A, in one end of the 6-in. piece as shown.

Place over the end of the 6-in. piece a thin sheet of insulating fiber, B, allowing it to extend down on each side about 1 in. Then bend a piece of $\frac{1}{16}$-in. brass, C, over the insulating fiber, allowing it to extend down on each side the same distance as the insulating fiber. Drill a small hole through the lower ends of the U-shaped piece of brass, C, the insulation, B, and the 6-in. piece, while they are all in place. Remove the insulation and the U-shaped brass piece, and tap the holes in the brass for a machine screw, D. Enlarge the hole in the 6-in piece, and provide an insulating bushing for it with an opening of the same diameter as the brass machine screw. Mount a small binding post, E, on one side of the U-shaped piece of brass, and the parts may then be put together and held in place by means of the brass screw.

Drill two holes in the other end of the 6-in piece, also two holes in one end of the 7-in piece, and rivet them together with two small rivets. The 7-in. piece should project beyond the end of the 6-in. piece. A piece of thin spring brass should be made into the form of a spiral, F, and fastened to the upper end of the 7-in. piece. Provision should be made for attaching the fishline to the inside end of the brass spiral. A small binding post should be soldered to either the 6-in. or 7-in. piece, at the bottom.

If the device is set up with the head of the brass adjusting screw in the top of the 6-in. piece, pointing in the direction the line to the fishing hook is to run, and if a fish pulls upon the line, the 7-in. piece is pulled over and touches the point of the adjusting screw. If a battery and bell, or buzzer, is connected as shown, the circuit will be completed when the 7-in. piece comes in contact with the adjusting screw, and the bell will ring.

A Chair Swing

A comfortable porch or lawn swing can be easily and quickly made with a chair as a seat, as follows. Procure some rope of sufficient strength to bear

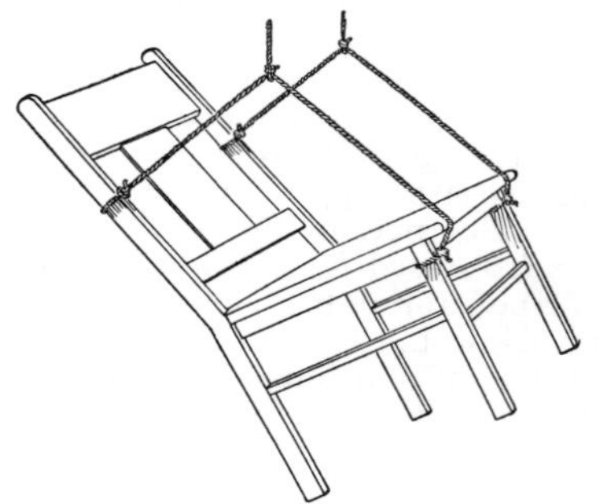

The Ropes are Tied to the Chair so That It will be Held in a Reclining Position

the weight of the person, and fasten one end securely to one of the front legs of the chair and the other end to the same side of the back as shown in the illustration, allowing enough slack to form a right angle. Another piece of rope, of the same length, is then attached to the other side of the chair. The supporting ropes are tied to these ropes and to the joist or holding piece overhead.—Contributed by Wm. A. Robinson, Waynesboro, Pa.

Another Broom Holder

Of the many homemade devices for holding a broom this is one of the simplest, and one that any handy boy can make.

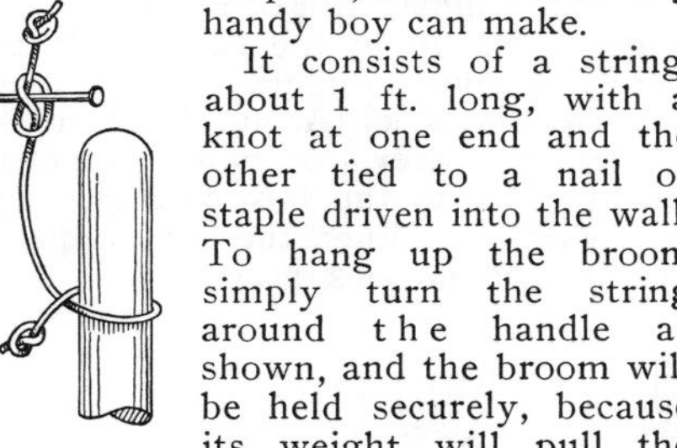

It consists of a string, about 1 ft. long, with a knot at one end and the other tied to a nail or staple driven into the wall. To hang up the broom simply turn the string around the handle as shown, and the broom will be held securely, because its weight will pull the string taut and the knot at the end will prevent the string from running off the handle.—Contributed by Jef De Vries, Antwerp, Belgium.

Squaring Wood Stock

The device shown in the sketch is a great help to the maker of mission furniture as a guide on short cuts. It

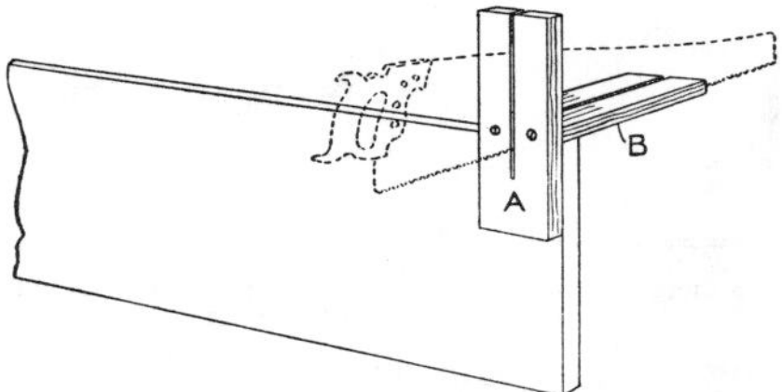

The Saw Teeth Edge can be Run through Both Pieces, the Stock being in the Corner

consists of two pieces of wood, A and B, preferably of oak, fastened together at right angles by two large flat-head screws. The pieces should be placed exactly at right angles.

A cut is then made through both pieces. The cut on B should be exactly at right angles to the surface of piece A. This device can be either clamped on a board or merely held by hand, and will insure a true cut.—Contributed by F. W. Pumphrey, Owensboro, Ky.

A Wind Vane

A novelty in wind vanes is shown in the accompanying sketch. The vane can be made of sheet metal or carved from light wood. The wings are so set on the body as to cause the dragon to rise when the wind strikes them. The dragon is pivoted on a shaft running through its center of gravity, so it will readily turn with the wind. The tail part may also be made to revolve as the propeller of an aeroplane.

The length and size of the shaft will depend on the dimensions of the dragon, and similarly, the location of the weights on the chains will be determined by its size and weight. Upon these circumstances and the varying velocities of the wind will depend how high the dragon will rise on its shaft, and the height reached by it will thus serve to indicate—in a relative manner only—the velocity of the wind, but it is also possible to arrange the weights at such distances apart that the dragon will rise to A in a 20-mile wind, to B in a 30-mile wind, to C in a 40-mile gale, and so on, with as many weights as desired. This can be done with the aid of an anemometer, if one can be borrowed for some time, or the device may be taken to the nearest weather bureau to be set.—Contributed by H. J. Holden, Ontario, Cal.

Never rock a file—push it straight on filing work.

How to Make a Flutter Ring

The flutter ring is for inclosing in an envelope and to surprise the person opening it by the revolving of the

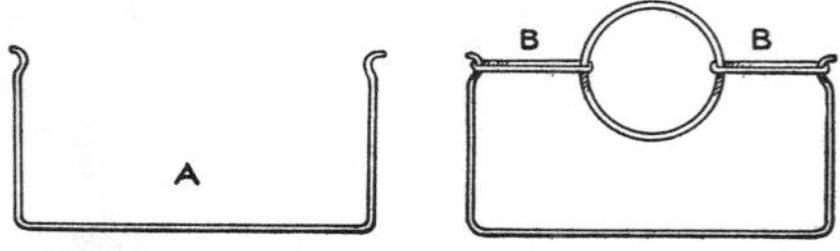

The Shape of the Wire and Manner of Attaching the Rubber Bands to the Ring

ring. The main part is made of a piece of wire, A, bent so that the depth will be about 2 in. and the length 4 in. Procure or make a ring, 2 in. in diameter. The ring should be open like a key ring. Use two rubber bands, BB, in connecting the ring to the wire.

To use it, turn the ring over repeatedly, until the rubber bands are twisted tightly, then lay it flat in a paper folded like a letter. Hand it to someone in this shape or after first putting it into an envelope. When the paper is opened up, the ring will do the rest.—Contributed by D. Andrew McComb, Toledo, O.

A Kitchen Utensil Hanger

Every cook knows how troublesome it is to have several things hanging on one nail. When one of the articles is wanted it is usually at the back, and the others must be removed to secure it. A revolving rack for hanging a can opener, egg beater and cooking spoons, etc., takes up less

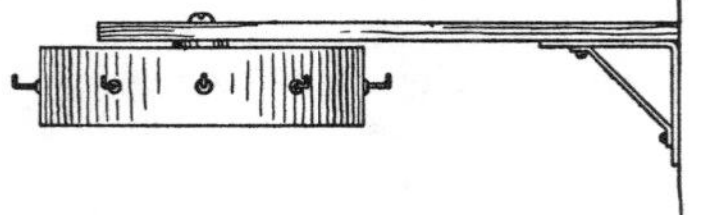

The Hook Support Revolves so as to Make Each One Readily Accessible for Hanging Utensils

space than several nails, and places every article within easy reach as well as providing individual hooks for all the pieces.

The rack is easily made of a block of wood, 2½ in. in diameter and 1 in. thick; an arm, ¾ in. wide, ¼ in. thick and 6 in. long, and a metal bracket. The arm is fastened to the bracket and the bracket to the wall. A screw is turned through a loose-fitting hole bored in the end of the arm and into the disk. Screw hooks are placed around the edge of the dish as hangers.—Contributed by A. R. Moore, Toronto, Can.

Homemade Hinges for Boxes

A very simple form of hinge can be made as shown in the sketch. It is merely a matter of cutting out two pieces of flat steel, A, punching holes in them for screws or nails, and fastening them to the box corners, one on each side. When the box is open, the lid swings back clear and is out

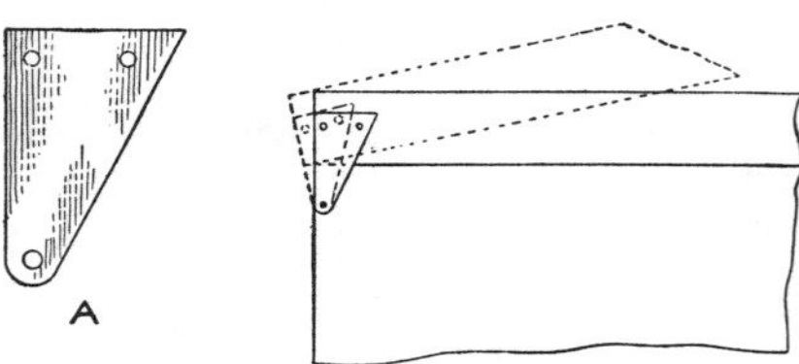

Hinge Parts Made of Sheet Metal and Their Use on a Box Cover

of the way. A hinge of this kind is very strong. For a light box, the parts can be cut from tin.—Contributed by Chas. Homewood, Waterloo, Iowa.

To Remove Odors from Ice Boxes

An easy way to prevent odors in an ice box is to place a can of coke in the box. This will take up all gases and prevent milk from tasting of onions or vegetables which may be kept in the box.

In factories where bad odors are apt to spoil the men's lunches put up in pails or baskets, a box can be constructed to hold these receptacles and a large pail of coke placed in it. Anything placed in this box will remain free from odors, and fresh.—Contributed by Loren Ward, Des Moines, Iowa.

Preventing Window Sash from Freezing to the Sill

When it is cold enough to cause the window sash to freeze fast in the bathroom and bedrooms not having double sash, much discomfort will be experienced and the health may even be menaced. I have discovered a simple method to overcome this difficulty. Lay on the outside sill, close up against the window frame, a thin, narrow strip of wood, on which the window can rest when down. This gives a continual current of fresh air between the sashes at the center, but no unpleasant draft below, and no amount of dripping and freezing will fasten the window sash upon it.—Contributed by Mary Murry, Amherst, Nova Scotia.

A Hanger for the Camp

A garment, or utensil, hanger can be easily made for the camp in the following manner: Procure a long strap, about $1\frac{1}{4}$ in. wide, and attach hooks made of wire to it. Each hook should be about 4 in. long and of about No. 9 gauge wire. Bend a ring on one end of the wire and stick the other end through a hole punched in the center of the belt. The ring will prevent the wire from passing through the leather, and it should be bent in such a manner that the hook end of the wire will hang downward when the width of the belt is vertical. These hooks are placed about 2 in. apart for the length of the belt, allowing sufficient ends for a buckle and holes. The strap can be buckled around a tree or tent pole.—Contributed by W. C. Loy, Rochester, Ind.

¶Never stand in a direct line of a swiftly revolving object, such as an emery wheel.

Locking Several Drawers with One Lock

A lock for a number of drawers in a bench or cabinet may be applied with a strip of wood hinged to the cabinet edge so that it will overlap the drawer fronts, as shown. A hasp and staple complete the arrangement for use with a padlock.—Contributed by H. W. Hahn, Chicago.

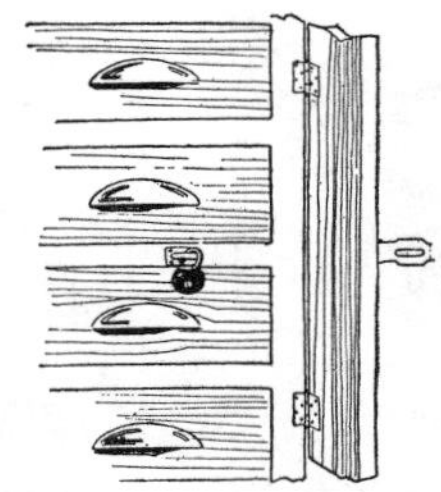

A Lightning-Calculation Trick

By means of a simple arrangement of numbers, a calculation can be made which will easily puzzle any unsuspecting person. If the two numbers 41,096 and 83 be written out in multiplication form, very few will endeavor to write down the answer directly without first going through the regular work. By placing the 3 in front of the 4 and the 8 back of the 6, the answer is obtained at once, thus: 41,096×83=3,410,968. A larger number which can be treated in the same way is the following: 4,109,589,041,096×83=341,095,890,410,968.

An Adjustable Nutcracker

The advantage of the nutcracker shown in the illustration is that it can be adjusted to various-sized nuts. The handles are similar to those usually found on nutcrackers except that they are slotted at the cracking end to receive a special bar. This bar is 2 in. long, $\frac{1}{2}$ in. wide, and $\frac{1}{8}$ in. thick, with $\frac{1}{8}$-in. holes drilled in it at intervals to allow for adjustment. Cotters are used in the holes as pins.

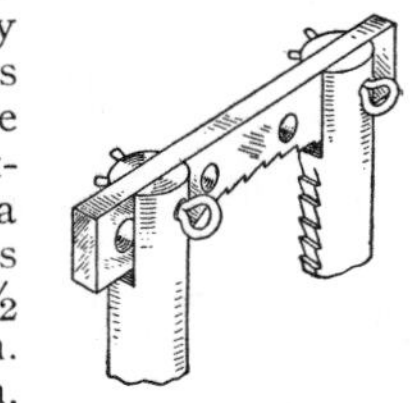

Substitute for a Rubber Stamp

A large number of coupons had to be marked, and having no suitable rubber stamp at hand, I selected a

Initials Cut in a Cork Served the Purpose in the Absence of a Rubber Stamp

cork with a smooth end and cut the initials in it. I found that it worked as well, not to say better, than a rubber stamp. An ordinary rubber-stamp pad was used for inking. Angular letters will cut better than curved ones, as the cork quickly dulls the edge of any cutting tool.—Contributed by James M. Kane, Doylestown, Pa.

A Furniture Polish

A good pastelike furniture polish, which is very cheap and keeps indefinitely, can be made as follows: Mix 3 oz. of white wax, 2 oz. of pearlash, commonly known as potassium carbonate, and 6 oz. of water. Heat the mixture until it becomes dissolved, then add 4 oz. of boiled linseed oil and 5 oz. of turpentine. Stir well and pour into cans to cool. Apply with a cloth and rub to a polish. The paste is nonpoisonous.

A Hanging Vase

A very neat and attractive hanging corner vase can be made of a colored bottle. The bottom is broken out or cut off as desired and a wire hanger attached as shown. The opening in the neck of the bottle is well corked. Rectangular shaped bottles fitted with hangers can be used on walls.—Contributed by A. D. Tanaka, Jujiya, Kioto, Japan.

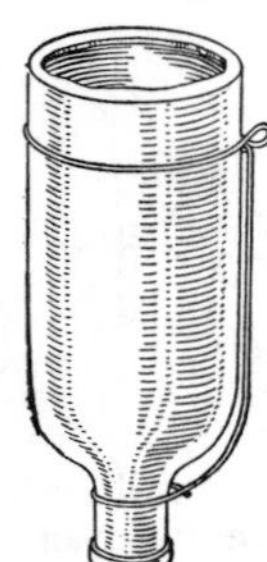

Filing Soft Metals

It is well known to mechanics that when lead, tin, soft solder or aluminum are filed, the file is soon filled with the metal and it will not cut. It cannot be cleaned like the wood rasp by dipping it into hot water or pouring boiling water over it, but if the file and the work are kept wet with water, there will be no trouble whatever. Both file and work must be kept thoroughly wet at all times.—Contributed by J. H. Beebee, Rochester, N. Y.

Locking Screws in Door Hinges

When screws once work loose in hinges of doors they will never again hold firmly in the same hole. This trouble can be avoided if the screws are securely locked when they are first put on the door. The sketch shows a

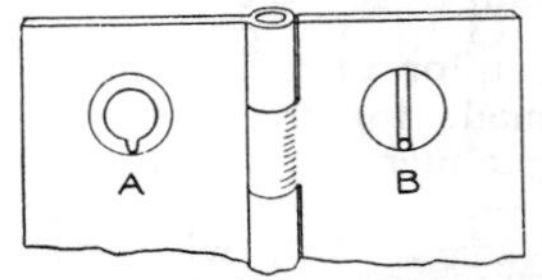

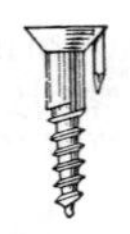

The Screw is Permanently Locked with a Small Nail Driven into the Slot Prepared for It

very successful way to lock the screws. The hole in the hinge for the screw is filed to produce a notch, as shown at A, deep enough to receive a small wire nail or brad, which is driven through the slot in the screw head at one side, as shown at B.

To Remove Grease from Clothing

Equal parts of ether, ammonia and alcohol make a solution that will readily remove grease from clothing. The solution must be kept away from fire, and should be contained in corked bottles as it evaporates quickly, but can be used without danger. It removes grease spots from the finest fabrics and is harmless to the texture.

¶Jeweler's rouge rubbed well into chamois skin is handy to polish gold and silver articles with.

Stove Made of an Old Oilcan with Extending Sides and Weighted with Sand for Use on a Fishing Boat Holds the Cooking Vessel Safely in a Sea

A Canoe Stove

By F. V. WILLIAMS

Limited space and the rocking motion of salmon-fishing boats in a heavy sea on the Pacific coast brought about the construction of the canoe stove shown in the illustration. It is made of a discarded kerosene can whose form is square. A draft hole is cut in one side of the can, 4 or 5 in. from the bottom, and a layer of sand placed on the bottom. Two holes are punched through opposite sides, parallel with the draft hole and about 3 in. from the top edge. Rods are run through these holes to provide a support for the cooking utensil. The smoke from the fire passes out at the corners around the vessel.

The main reason for making the stove in this manner is to hold the cooking vessel within the sides extending above the rods. No amount of rocking can cause the vessel to slide from the stove top, and as the stove is weighted with the sand, it cannot be easily moved from the place where it is set in the canoe.

The use of such a stove in a canoe has the advantage that the stove can be cleaned quickly, as the ashes and fire can be dumped into the water and the stove used for a storage box. The whole thing may be tossed overboard and a new one made for another trip.

To Prevent Washboard from Slipping in Tub

The modern stationary washtubs are box-shaped, with one side set at an outward angle or slope. The washboard, when used in these tubs, will slide up and down against the sloping part of the tub while the clothes are rubbed against them. This annoying trouble can be avoided by tacking, on the top edge of the board, strips of rubber cut from a discarded bicycle tire, placing the rubber side out. The friction of the rubber prevents any motion of the board.—Contributed by Jas. A. Hart, Philadelphia, Pa.

¶To print on celluloid, use a good gloss ink and old rollers.

Clips to Hold Magazine Pages Together

When a magazine is placed in a bookcase the outer pages are liable to turn back if it is inserted with the back on the outside. To overcome this difficulty I made clips for each magazine to hold the open pages together. Each clip was made of wire, about 8 in. long, shaped as shown. The width of the clip is made equal to the thickness of the magazine and the extending ends are

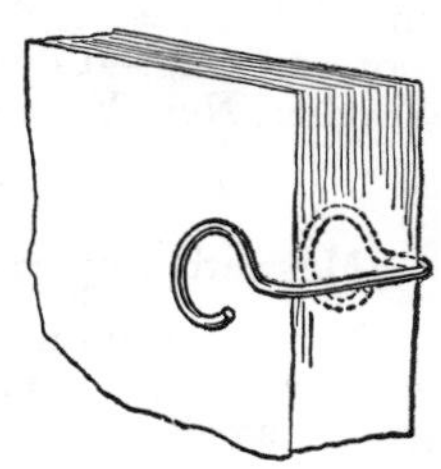

slightly pressed together so that they will spring and grip the pages.—Contributed by W. A. Saul, E. Lexington, Massachusetts.

Slide-Opening Cover for a Plate Holder

The length of time required for the slide of a plate holder to be removed

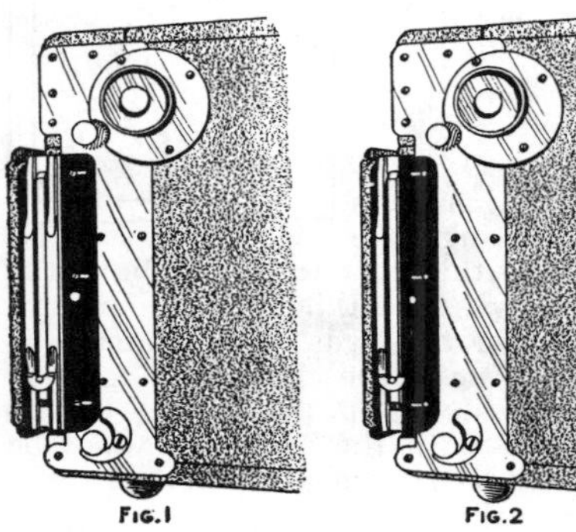

The Two Positions Occupied by the Slide-Opening Cover as It is Used on a Camera

on a reflecting camera spoiled many of my plates, because strong light would enter the unprotected slot when the camera was in certain positions. To protect this slot so that the slide could be left out indefinitely, I made a cover of a piece of sheet metal having three slots, to admit screws turned into the camera. A knob was attached at the center. The illustration shows the application of this cover. In Fig. 1 the plate holder is shown slipped in with the cover back, and Fig. 2 shows the slide drawn and the cover over the slot opening.—Contributed by B. J. Weeber, New York City.

Magnetic-Suspension Pendulum

When a pendulum is not periodically supplied with energy its amplitude grows smaller and finally the motion ceases, due to the resistance of the air and the friction at the point of suspension. Usually the suspension is in the form of a knife edge bearing against plates of agate; sometimes the pendulum rod is simply attached to a very slender and flexible spring without any bearings. But the minimum of friction is obtained by means of magnetic suspension, as the following experiment will prove.

If the rod of a pendulum about 12 in. long, beating half seconds, is sharpened to a needle point and suspended from one of the poles of a magnet, it will be found that, if set into motion, it will continue to swing 15 times as long as the ordinary knife-edge suspended pendulum, and it will not stop until after about 16 hours, while one working on agate plates will stop in from 50 to 60 minutes. Similarly a top, provided with a fine-pointed axis of iron, will spin much longer when suspended from a magnet.

Magnetic suspension is used in precision instruments; for example, the minute mirrors which are used in certain telegraph systems to register writing photographically at the receiving end.

Use for Pencil Stubs

In mechanical drawings cast iron is indicated by a series of straight lines across the parts made of this material. These lines can be quickly made with the usually discarded pencil stubs, if these are saved and sharpened in the following manner: The point is filed flat, as shown at A; then a slot is filed in the center of the lead with a knife file, as shown at B, and the points sharpened as in C. In this way two lines are drawn at one stroke neatly and in half the time.—Contributed by J. Kolar, Maywood, Ill.

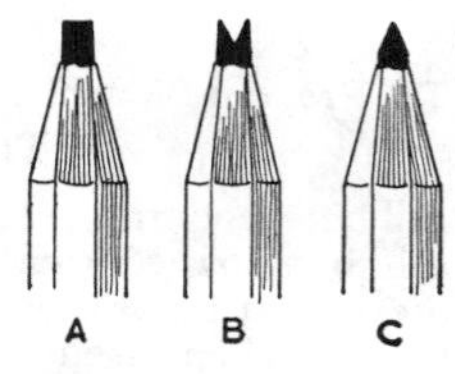

¶To sharpen a carving knife draw the edge through and against the open edge of a pair of shears.

How to Build a Paddle-Wheel Boat

By P. A. BAUMEISTER

THE paddle-wheel boat, illustrated herewith, was built in the spare time I had on rainy afternoons and Saturdays, and the enjoyment I derived from it at my summer camp more than repaid me for the time spent in the building. The materials used in its construction were:

- 2 side boards, 14 ft. long, 10 in. wide and ⅞ in. thick.
- 2 side boards, 14 ft. long, 5 in. wide and ⅞ in. thick.
- 1 outside keel board, 14 ft. long, 8 in. wide and ⅞ in. thick.
- 1 inside keel board, 14 ft. long, 10 in. wide and ⅞ in. thick.
- 120 sq. ft. of tongue-and-groove boards, ¾ in. thick, for bottom and wheel boxes.
- 1 piece, 2 in. square and 18 in. long.
- 4 washers.
- 2 iron cranks.
- 10 screweyes.
- 30 ft. of rope.
- Nails.

The dimensions given in the drawing will be found satisfactory, but these may be altered to suit the conditions. The first step will be to cut and make the sides. Nail the two pieces forming each side together and then cut the end boards and nail them to the sides. Lay this framework, bottom side up, on a level surface and proceed to nail on the bottom boards across the sides. The ends of these boards are sawed off flush with the outside surface of the sides after they are nailed in place. The material list calls for tongue-and-groove boards for the bottom, but plain boards can be used, although it is then difficult to make the joint water-tight. When the tongue-and-groove boards are used a piece of string, well soaked in white lead or paint and placed in the groove of each board, will be sufficient to make a tight joint.

Having finished the sides and bottom, the next step will be to fasten on the bottom keel. Adjust the board to its position and nail it in the center part where it lies flat on the bottom boards, then work toward the ends, gradually drawing it down over the turn and nailing it down. If the keel board cannot be bent easily, it is best to soak it in hot water where the bend takes place and the wood can then be nailed down without the fibers breaking. The inside keel is put on in the same manner, but reversed.

The Boat As It Appears without the Spring and Running Board and Used as a Pleasure Craft or for Carrying Freight, the Operator Facing in the Direction of the Boat's Travel

The next procedure is to make the paddle wheels. The hub for each

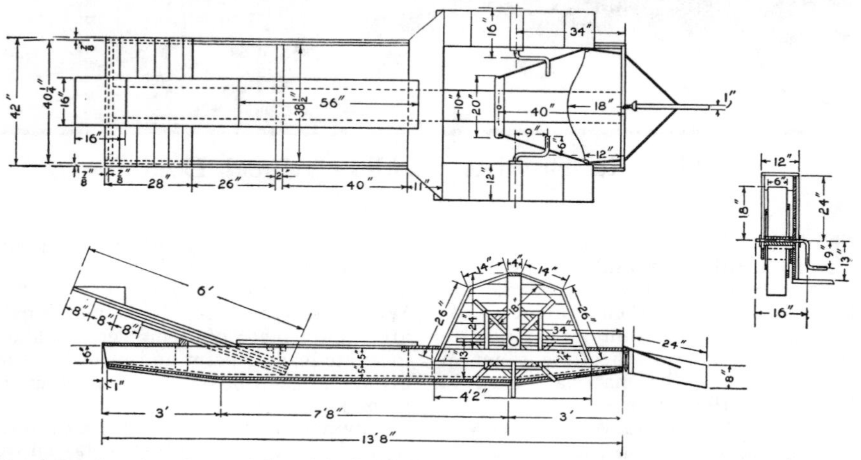

Detail Drawing of the Boat and One of the Paddle Wheels. All the Material Required for the Construction is Such That can be Cut and Shaped with Ordinary Tools Found in the Home Workshop

wheel is made of a 2-in. square piece of timber, 9 in. long. Trim off the corners to make 8 sides to the piece, then bore a ¾-in. hole through its center. The 8 blades of each wheel, 16 in all, are 17 in. long, 6 in. wide and ¾ in. thick. One end of each blade is nailed to one side of the hub, then it is braced as shown to strengthen the wheel.

The cranks are made of round iron, ¾ in. in diameter, and they are keyed to the wheels with large nails in the manner shown. I had a blacksmith shape the cranks for me, but if one has a forge, the work can be done at home without that expense. The bearings for the crankshafts consist of wood, although it is preferable to use for this purpose two large iron washers, having a hole slightly larger than the diameter of the shaft, and drill holes in their rims so that they can be screwed to the wheel-box upright as shown. The bearings thus made are lubricated with a little lard or grease.

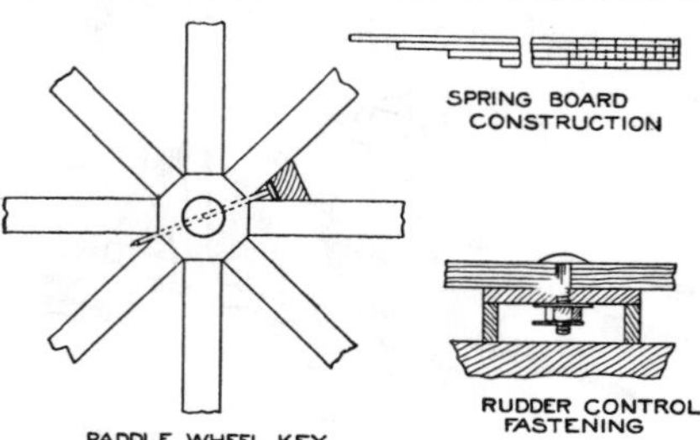

Detail of Paddle-Wheel Fastening, the Springboard Construction and the Fastening for the Rudder Control

The paddle-wheel boxes are built over the wheels with the dimensions given in the drawing, to prevent the splashing of water on the occupants of the boat.

The trimmings for the boat consist of three seats, a running board and a springboard. The drawings show the location of the seats. The springboard is built up of 4 boards, ¾ in. thick, as shown, only nailing them together at the back end. This construction allows the boards to slide over each other when a person's weight is on the outer end. The action of the boards is the same as of a spring on a vehicle.

It is necessary to have a good brace across the boat for the back end of the springboard to catch on—a 2 by 4-in. timber being none too large. At the point where the springboard rests on the front seat there should be another good-sized crosspiece. The board can be held in place by a cleat and a few short pieces of rope, the cleat being placed across the board back of the brace. A little diving platform is attached on the outer end of the springboard and a strip of old carpet or gunny sack placed on it to prevent slivers from running into the flesh. In making the spring and running board, it is advisable to make them removable so that the boat can be used for other purposes.

The boat is steered with a foot-operated lever, the construction of which is clearly shown. For the tiller-rope guides, large screweyes are used and also for the rudder hinges, the pin of the hinge being a large nail. The hull can be further strengthened by putting a few angle-iron braces either on the in or outside.

To make the boat water-tight will require calking by filling the cracks with twine and white lead or thick paint. The necessary tools are a broad, dull chisel and a mallet. A couple of coats of good paint, well brushed into the cracks, will help to make it water-tight as well as shipshape. The boat may leak a little when it is first put into the water, but after a few hours of soaking, the boards will swell and close the openings.

This boat was used for carrying trunks, firewood, rocks, sand, and for fishing, and last, but not least, for swimming. The boat is capable of carrying a load of three-quarters of a ton. It draws very little water, thereby allowing its use in shallow water. It has the further advantage that the operator faces in the direction the boat is going, furnishing the power with his hands and steering with his feet.

A Camp Loom

The camper who desires to "rough it" as much as possible and to carry only the necessities will find it quite a comfort to construct the bedding from grass or moss by weaving it in the manner of making a rag carpet, using heavy twine or small rope as the warp. Two stakes are set the width of the bed or mattress to be made, and a cross stick is attached to their tops. Several stakes are set parallel with the cross

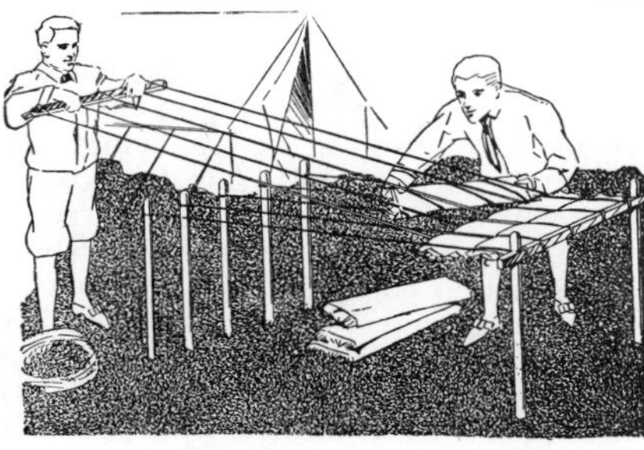

Loom Constructed of Sticks for Weaving Grass or Moss into a Camp Mattress

stick and at a distance to make the length of the mattress. The warp is tied between the tops of the stakes and the cross stick. An equal number of cords are then attached to the cross stick and to another loose cross stick which is used to move the cords up and down while the grass or moss is placed in for the woof. The ends of the warp are then tied to hold it together. When breaking up camp the cords can be removed and carried to the next camp.—Contributed by W. P. Shaw, Bloor West, Can.

A Milk-Bottle Carrier

Carrying a milk bottle by the rim is tiresome work for the fingers, so I constructed a handle, as shown in the sketch, from a piece of wire. The carrier can be easily placed in the pocket.

The part fitting under the rim of the bottle neck is bent to form two semicircles, one hooking permanently at A, while the other is hooked at B

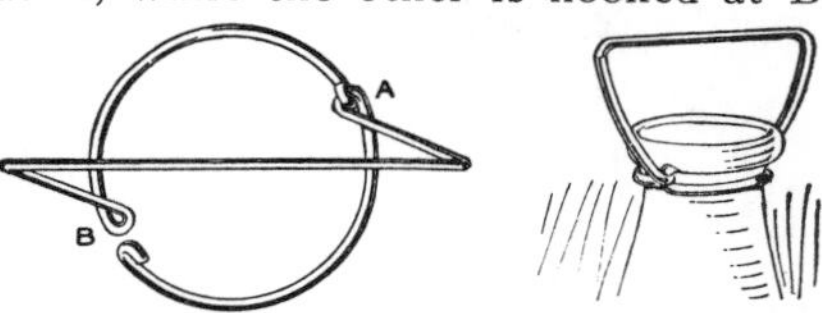

A Carrier Made of Wire to Quickly Attach on a Milk-Bottle Neck

after it is sprung around the neck of the bottle.—Contributed by Lawrence B. Robbins, Harwich, Mass.

How to Make a War Kite

By PARK SNYDER

The material required for the making of a war kite is three pine sticks, each 60 in. long, one stick 54 in. long, one stick 18 in. long, all ½ in. square; 4 yd. of cambric; a box of tacks; some linen thread, and 16 ft. of stout twine.

Place two 60-in. sticks parallel with each other and 18 in. apart, then lay the 54-in. piece across at right angles to them 18 in. from the upper ends, as shown in Fig. 1, and fasten the joints with brads. At a point 21 in. below this crosspiece, attach the 18-in. crosspiece.

The extending ends of all the three long pieces are notched, Fig. 2, and the line is stretched taut around them, as shown by the dotted lines.

If the cambric is not of sufficient size to cover the frame, two pieces must be sewed together, then a piece cut out to the shape of the string, allowing 1 in. to project all around for a lap. The cambric is sewn fast to the string with the linen thread. Fasten the cloth to the frame part with the tacks, spacing them 1 in. apart. The space in the center, between the sticks, is cut out. Make two pieces of the remaining goods, one 36 in. by 18 in., and the other 36 in. by 21 in. The remaining 60-in. stick is fastened to these pieces of cambric, as shown in Fig. 3, and the whole is fastened to the main frame so as to make a V-shaped projection. The bridle strings, for giving the proper distribution of pull on the line to the kite, are fastened, one to the upper end of the long stick in the V-shaped piece attached to the kite, and the other to the lower end, as shown in Fig. 4. The inclination can be varied to suit the builder by changing the point of attachment of the kite line to the bridle. If it is desired to fly the kite directly overhead, attach the line above the regular point and for low flying make the connection below this point. The regular point is found by trial flights with the line fastened temporarily to the bridle, after which the fastening is made permanent.

The Line should be a Very Strong One, Then Banners can be Flown on It

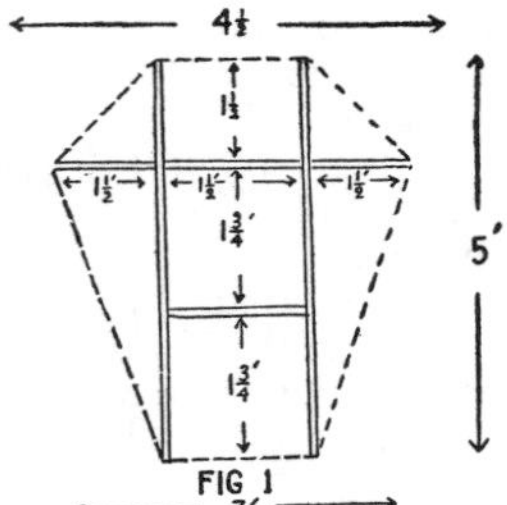

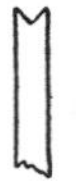

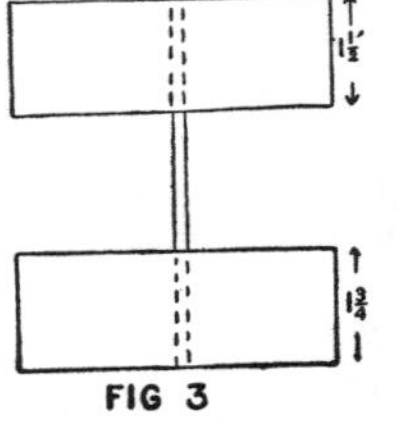

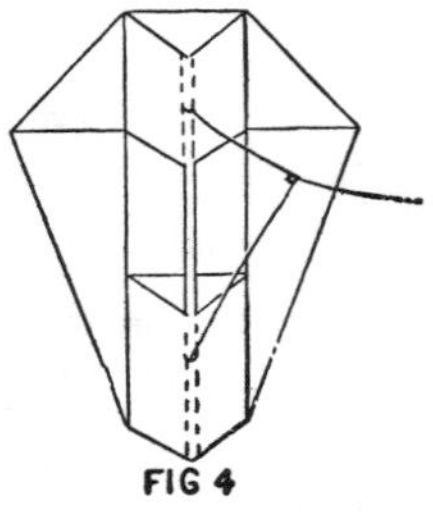

The Sticks are Fastened Solidly with Brads, and the Cloth Sewed to the String around Their Ends

Paper Glider That Loops the Loop

By C. A. THOMPSON

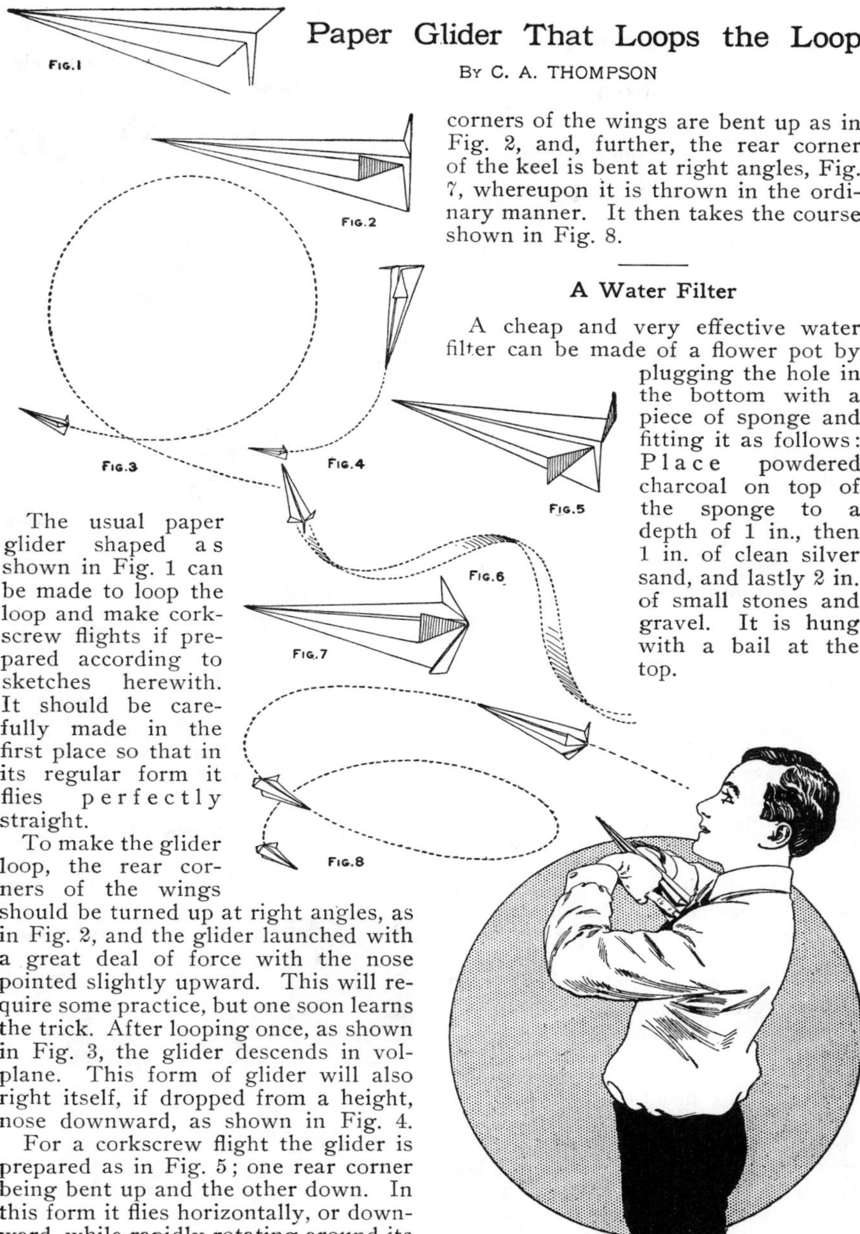

Ordinary Paper Glider and the Manner of Throwing It to Make the Different Flights

The usual paper glider shaped as shown in Fig. 1 can be made to loop the loop and make corkscrew flights if prepared according to sketches herewith. It should be carefully made in the first place so that in its regular form it flies perfectly straight.

To make the glider loop, the rear corners of the wings should be turned up at right angles, as in Fig. 2, and the glider launched with a great deal of force with the nose pointed slightly upward. This will require some practice, but one soon learns the trick. After looping once, as shown in Fig. 3, the glider descends in volplane. This form of glider will also right itself, if dropped from a height, nose downward, as shown in Fig. 4.

For a corkscrew flight the glider is prepared as in Fig. 5; one rear corner being bent up and the other down. In this form it flies horizontally, or downward, while rapidly rotating around its longitudinal axis, as shown in Fig. 6.

To make a spiral descent, the rear corners of the wings are bent up as in Fig. 2, and, further, the rear corner of the keel is bent at right angles, Fig. 7, whereupon it is thrown in the ordinary manner. It then takes the course shown in Fig. 8.

A Water Filter

A cheap and very effective water filter can be made of a flower pot by plugging the hole in the bottom with a piece of sponge and fitting it as follows: Place powdered charcoal on top of the sponge to a depth of 1 in., then 1 in. of clean silver sand, and lastly 2 in. of small stones and gravel. It is hung with a bail at the top.

A Combination Electrically Operated Door Lock

The illustration shows a very useful application of an ordinary electric door lock in the construction of a combination lock and alarm to be operated from the outside of the building.

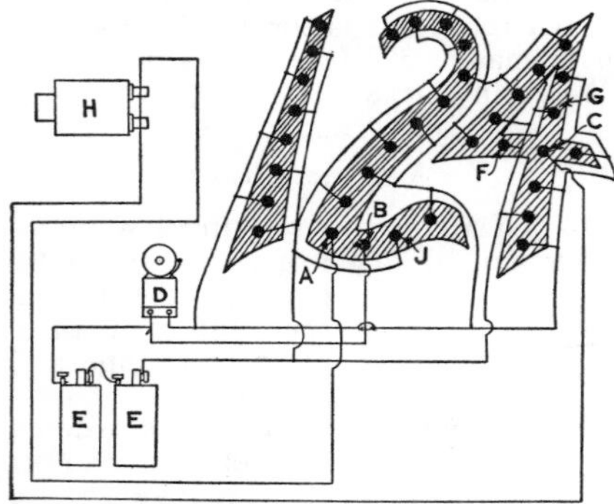

The Brass-Tack Heads Holding the Numerals in Place Constitute the Combination Points

The three numerals, 1, 2, and 4, or any other combination of numbers constituting the house number on a door, are made of some kind of insulating material and fastened in place on a base of insulating fiber, or wood, about 1/4 in. thick, by means of ordinary brass-headed tacks, as indicated by the black dots. The tacks will extend through the base a short distance so the electrical connections may be made by soldering wires to them, as shown by the diagram, alternate tacks being connected together with the exception of three; for instance, A, B, and C.

The terminals of the leads that are connected to alternate tacks are in turn connected to the terminals of a circuit composed of an ordinary vibrating bell, D, and battery, E. If any two adjacent tack heads be connected together, except tacks A, B, and C, the bell circuit will be completed and the bell ring, which will serve as an indication that some one is tampering with the circuit. The person knowing the combination, connects the tack heads A and B, and at the same time connects the tack head C with F or G, or any other tack head that is connected to the plus side of the battery, whereby a circuit will be completed through the lock H and the door is opened. Any metallic substance, such as a knife, key, or finger ring, may be used in making the above indicated connection, and there will be no need of carrying a key for this particular door so long as the combination is known.

The base upon which the numbers are mounted and through which the points of the tacks protrude, should be mounted on a second base that has a recess cut in its surface to accommodate the wires and points of the tacks.

The combination may be made more or less complicated, as desired, by connecting the tacks in different ways, and by using a separate battery for the bell and lock. The circuit leading to the door lock, if there is one already installed, may be used and then no extra circuit is needed.

Such a device has been used on a private-desk drawer with entire satisfaction. The battery was placed in the back end of the drawer, and if it happened to fail, a new one could be connected to the points B and J so that the drawer could be opened and a new battery put in.

Lock for a Fancy Hairpin

To avoid losing a fancy hairpin, bend one leg of the pin as shown in the illustration. The hair caught in the notch formed by the bend will prevent the pin from dropping out.—Contributed by W. C. Loy, Rochester, Ind.

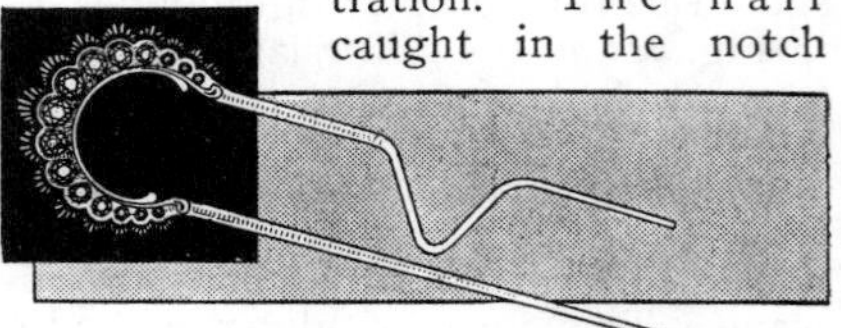

The Bend in the Pin will Hold in the Hair and Prevent the Loss of the Pin

---

¶A metal surface polished with oil will keep clean longer than when polished dry.

An Aeroplane Kite

By W. A. REICH

After building a number of kites from a recent description in Amateur Mechanics I branched out and constructed the aeroplane kite shown in the illustration, which has excited considerable comment in the neighborhood on account of its appearance and behavior in the air.

The main frame consists of a centerstick, A, 31 in. long, and two crosssticks, of which one, B, is 31 in. long and the other, C, 15½ in. long. The location of the crosspieces on the centerpiece A is shown in the sketch, the front piece B being 1¾ in. from the end, and the rear piece C, 2¼ in. from the other end. The ends of the sticks have small notches cut to receive a string, D, which is run around the outside to make the outline of the frame and to brace the parts. Two cross-strings are placed at E and F, 7 in. from either end of the centerpiece A, other brace strings being crossed, as shown at G, and then tied to the cross-string F on both sides, as at H.

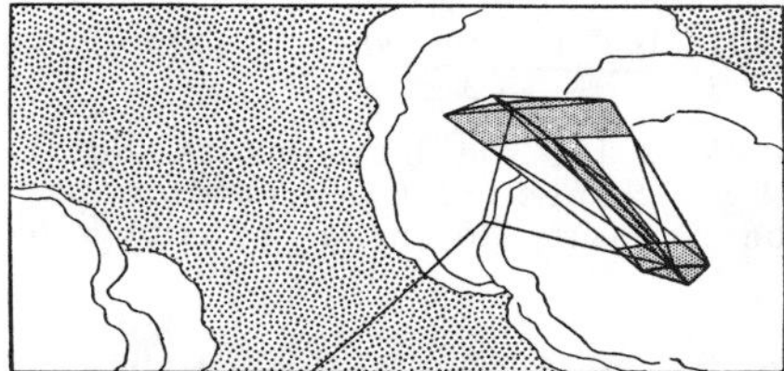

The Kite Being Tailless Rides the Air Waves Like an Aeroplane in a Steady Breeze

The long crosspiece B is curved upward to form a bow, the center of which should be 3¼ in. above the string by which its ends are tied together. The shorter crosspiece is bent and tied in the same manner to make the curve 2½ in., and the centerpiece to curve 1¾ in., both upward. The front and rear parts, between the end and the cross-strings E and F, are covered with yellow tissue paper, which is pasted to the crosspieces and strings. The small wings L are purple tissue paper, 4 in. wide at M and tapering to a point at N.

The bridle string is attached on the centerpiece A at the junction of the crosspieces B and C, and must be adjusted for the size and weight of the kite. The kite is tailless and requires a steady breeze to make it float in the air currents like an aeroplane.

The bridle string and the bending of the sticks must be adjusted until the desired results are obtained. The bridle string should be tied so that it will about center under the cross-stick B for the best results, but a slight change from this location may be necessary to make the kite ride the air currents properly. The center of gravity will not be the same in the construction of each kite and the string can be located only by trial, after which it is permanently fastened.

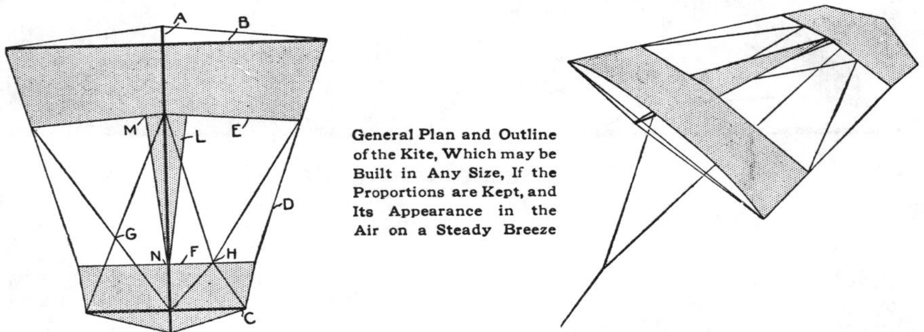

General Plan and Outline of the Kite, Which may be Built in Any Size, If the Proportions are Kept, and Its Appearance in the Air on a Steady Breeze

---

Distilling Apparatus for Water

Pure water, free from all foreign substances, is frequently wanted for making up photographic solutions and many other purposes. An apparatus for distilling water can be very easily made from galvanized pipe fittings. The outer cooling jacket A is a piece of 1-in. pipe, 2 ft. long, threaded on both ends, and bored and tapped for ½-in. pipe at B and C. A hole is bored and tapped for ½-in. pipe in each of the two caps used on the ends of the pipe A, and a piece of ½-in. pipe, D, 2 ft. 8 in. long, is run through the holes as shown. The joints are soldered to make them water-tight. Two ½-in. nipples, 4 in. long, are screwed in at B and C. The retort, or boiler, E, in which the impure water is boiled may be made of any suitable vessel and heated with a Bunsen or gas burner. A beaker, or other vessel, F, is placed below the lower end of the small pipe. The cold water from the faucet, which flows into the outer jacket at C and out at B, condenses the steam in the small pipe D, turning it into water which falls into the beaker in large drops. The water is often distilled a second time to remove any impurities which it might still contain.—Contributed by O. E. Tronnes, Evanston, Ill.

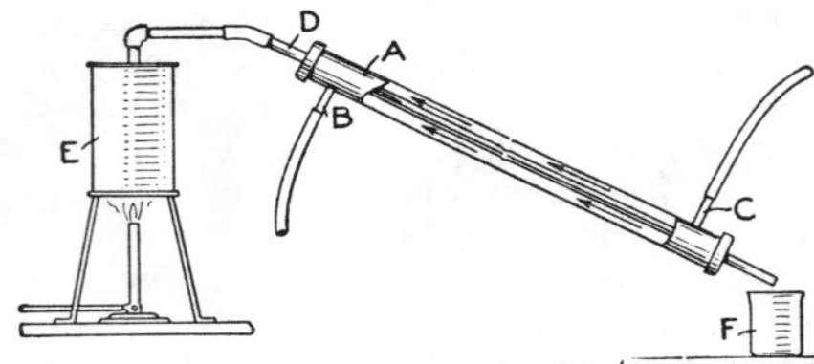

Homemade Still for Removing the Impurities in Water That is Used in Mixing Chemicals

---

Telephone Stand for a Sloping Desk

Having a sloping-top desk and being compelled to use the telephone quite frequently, I devised a support for the telephone so that it might stand level and not fall off. The sides of the stand were cut on the same slope as the desk top, and their under edges were provided with rubber strips to prevent slipping.—Contributed by J. M. Kane, Doylestown, Pa.

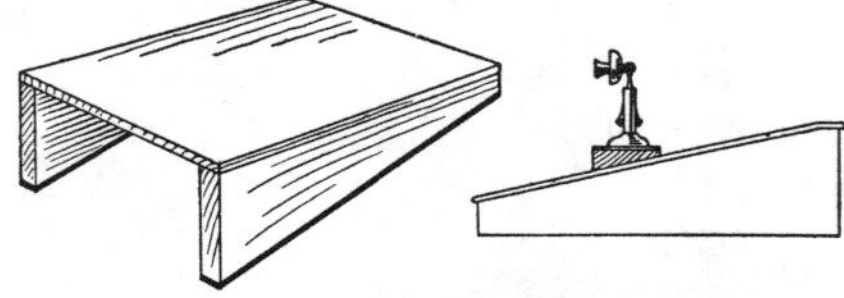

Stand with a Level Surface for a Desk Telephone to be Used on a Sloping Desk Top

Tandem Monoplane Glider

By GEORGE F. MACE

The monoplane glider illustrated has better fore-and-aft stability than the biplane, is lighter in proportion to the supporting surface, simpler to build, and requires very little time to assemble or take apart. The material list is as follows:

FRAME

4 pieces of bamboo, 14 ft. long, tapering from 1½ to 1 in.
8 pieces of spruce, ½ in. thick, 1 in. wide, and 3 ft. long.
8 pieces of spruce, ½ in. thick, 1 in. wide, and 2 ft. long.

WINGS

4 main-wing bars, spruce, ¾ in. thick, 1¼ in. wide, and 18 ft. long.
8 wing crosspieces, spruce, ¾ in. square, and 4 ft. long.
36 wing ribs, poplar or spruce, ¼ in. thick, ¾ in. wide, and 64 in. long.

The first thing to do is to make the main frame which is composed of the four bamboo poles. The poles take the corners of a 2-ft. square space and are supported with the pieces of spruce that are 2 ft. and 3 ft. long, the shorter lengths running horizontally and the longer upright, so that each upright piece extends 1 ft. above the two upper poles. All joints should be fastened with $\frac{3}{16}$-in. stove bolts. The wire used to truss the glider is No. 16 gauge piano wire. The trussing is done in all directions, crossing the wires between the frame parts, except in the center or space between the four poles.

The Start of the Glide should be Made from the Top of a Hill, Then a Little Run will Carry the Airman Several Hundred Feet through the Air

The framework of the main wings is put together by bolting one of the crosspieces at each end of two wing bars, then another 4 ft. from each end, whereupon the wing bars are bolted to the main frame. The frame is then braced diagonally between these pieces. The ribs, spaced 1 ft. apart, are fastened to this frame with 1-in. brads. The ribs are so bent that the highest part will be 5 or 6 in. above the horizontal. The bending must be uniform and is done when fastening them in place.

The material used to cover the wings and rudders is strong muslin. The cloth is first tacked to the front wing bar, then to the ribs, and sewed to a wire which is fastened between the ends of the ribs. Large brass-head tacks should be used through a strip of tape to fasten the cloth to the ribs. The rear wings are constructed in a similar manner. After the cloth is in place it is coated with starch or varnish.

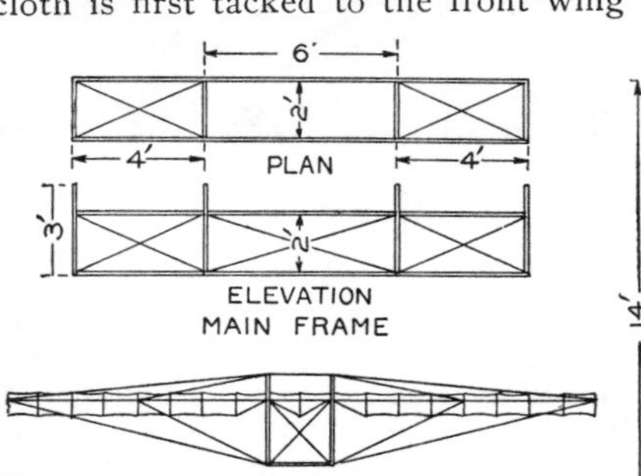

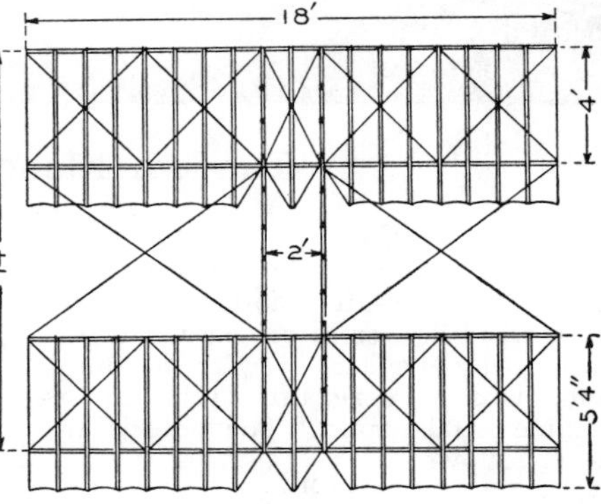

Details of Tandem Monoplane Glider, Showing the Main Frame and Wing Construction, and the Manner of Placing the Crossed Bracing Wires Between the Parts and to the Wing Ends

The two vertical rectangular spaces in the main frame, just under the rear wings, are covered with cloth to act as a rudder. The upper and lower bracing wires for the wings are attached with snaps and rings so that the glider can be easily taken apart.

It is best not to use the glider in a wind greater than 30 miles an hour. It is started from the top of a hill in the usual manner. Glides can be made running from 60 to several hundred feet.

Carrier for a Suitcase

Where it is necessary to carry a well filled and heavy suitcase the light truck shown in the sketch will be a great assistance. The truck is constructed on the folding plan, similar to a go-cart, and can be carried on the side of the case. The wheels are those used on a go-cart, with rubber tires and about 6 in. in diameter. These are fitted to standards carrying a hinged top piece, the upper ends of the standards being hinged in a like manner. The standards should be cut to the proper length for the person carrying the suitcase.—Contributed by Mrs. Harriet M. S. Kerbaugh, Allentown, Pa.

The Small Truck will Greatly Assist the Carrying of a Heavily Loaded Suitcase

Light in a Keyhole

Remove the lock and cut the mortise deep enough to admit a 3-volt battery lamp with a suitable socket attached. The lamp is then connected to wires which are concealed and run to a battery of three dry cells in the basement or other convenient place. A small push button is attached in the line and placed near the knob on the door. A small recess must be cut in the mortise so that the light from the lamp will shine directly on the inside of the plate over the keyhole.—Contributed by Armand F. Lamarre, St. Remi, Can.

How to Make a Monoplane Glider

By WILLIAM GROTZINGER

A simple glider of the monoplane type can be easily constructed in a small workshop; the cost of materials is not great and the building does not require skilled workmen. Select the material with care and see that the wood is straight-grained and free from knots. The following list of spruce pieces is required:

4 main wing spars, ¾ by 1¼ in. by 17 ft.
2 rudder spars, ¾ by 1 in. by 8 ft.
8 wing crosspieces, ¾ by ¾ in. by 4 ft.
4 rudder crosspieces, ½ by ½ in. by 2 ft.
1 piece for main-frame crosspieces, ½ by 1 in. by 12 ft.
2 arm pieces, 1½ by 2 in. by 3½ ft.

The following list of poplar pieces is required in making the supports for the cloth covering on the wings and rudders.

34 main-wing ribs, ¼ by ¾ by 64 in.
8 rudder ribs, ¼ by ½ by 36 in.
5 rudder ribs, ¼ by ¾ by 48 in.

The following list of oak pieces is needed:

1 piece, ⅝ by 1¼ in. by 12 ft.
1 piece, ⅝ by 1¼ in. by 6 ft.
1 piece, ¾ by ¾ in. by 3½ ft.
2 pieces, ⅝ by 1½ in. by 5 ft.
4 pieces, ¾ by 1 by 28 in.

In addition to the lists given, four pieces of bamboo, 16 ft. long, tapering from 1 or 1¼ in. at the large end to ¾ in. at the small end, are used for the main frame.

Construction

The first part to make is the main frame A which is constructed of the four bamboo poles. They are made into a rectangular frame with crossbars marked B cut to the right length from the 12-ft. piece of spruce, ½ in. by 1 in. The bars C and D are of oak

Monoplane Glider in Flight

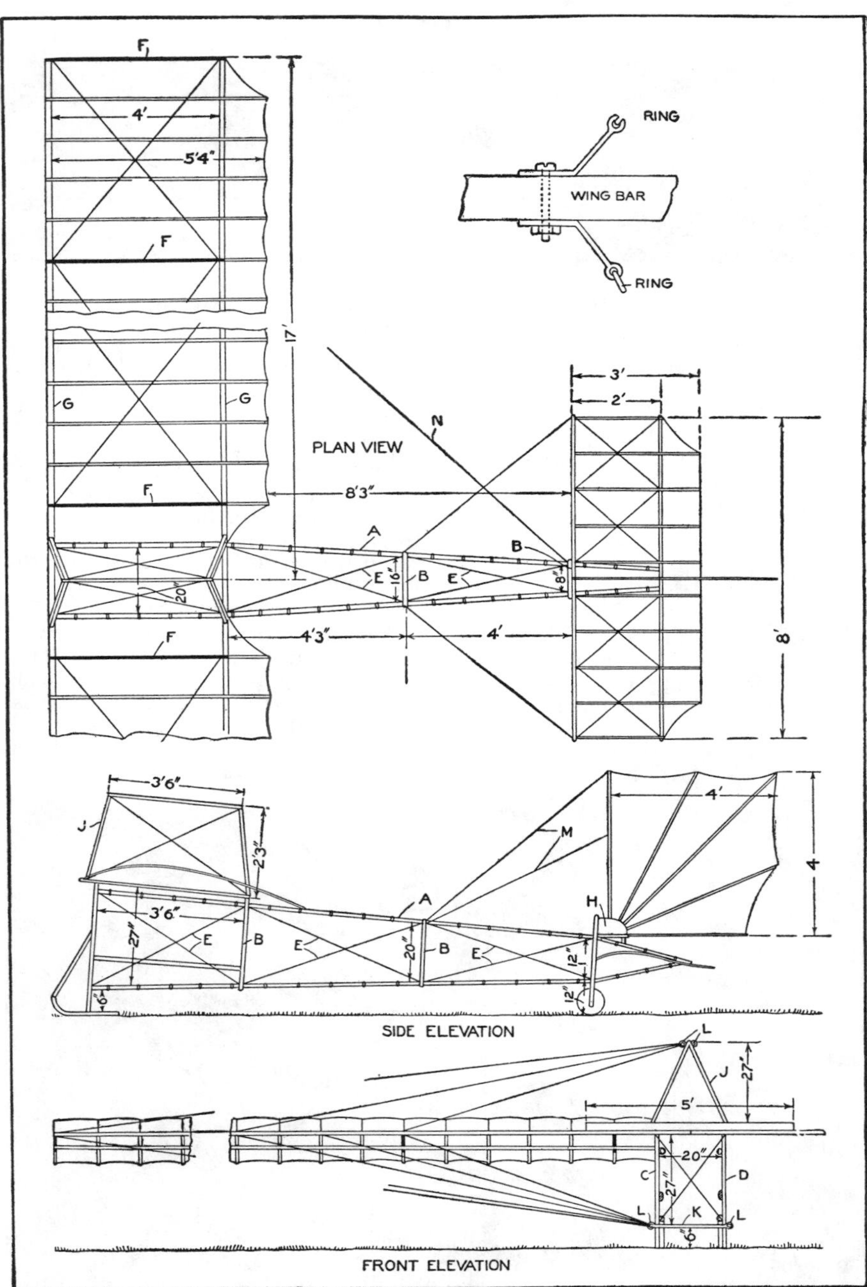

Details of Monoplane Glider

cut from the 6-ft. piece, 5/8 in. by 1 1/4 in. All of these crossbars are fastened together in rectangular form by means of stove bolts. The bamboo poles are then bolted to the inner corners of the frames with 3/16-in. bolts. Place the bolts through the bamboo close to a joint to prevent splitting. The frame is then rigidly trussed by diagonal wires marked E crossing all rectangles. The wire used for trussing all the parts throughout the glider is piano wire, 16 gauge. The arm pieces are bolted to the sides of the rectangular frames beneath the wings.

The framework of the main wings or planes should be put together by bolting the cross struts F at regular intervals on the under side of the main spars G. Brace the frame diagonally with the piano wire. The ribs are nailed to the main spars by using 1-in. brads. The ribs are spaced 1 ft. apart, and curved so that the highest part will be 5 in. from the horizontal. Each rib extends 15 in. back of the rear spar. The rudder is made in the same manner.

The vertical rudder is made to fold. A small pocket arrangement H is made from which the rigs of the vertical rudder diverge.

The covering of the wings and rudders should be a good quality of muslin or some light aeronautical goods. The cloth should be tacked to the front spar, to the ribs, and then sewn to a wire which connects the ends of the ribs.

Construct the triangular arrangement marked J to which the wings are braced. The wing bar supports are shown in the illustration. The bottom wires are braced to the crossbar K shown in the front elevation.

The bracing wires are all fastened to a snaphook which can be snapped into the rings at the places marked L. This method will allow one quickly to assemble or take apart the plane and store it in a small place. The vertical rudder should be braced from each rib to the front spar of the horizontal rudder and then braced by the wires M to hold the rudder from falling back. The rudder is then braced to the main frame and the main frame is braced by the wires N to the wings. This will hold the plane rigid. Use snaphooks and eyebolts wherever possible so that the plane can be quickly assembled.

Assembling

The triangular arrangement J is bolted to the wings and the top wires put in place. The wings are then put on the main frame and bolted to the bars marked C and D, after which the bottom wires are fixed in place.

Gliding

Take the glider to the top of a hill, step into the center of the main frame just a little back of the center of the wings. Put your arms around the arm pieces, face the wind and run a few steps. You will be lifted off the ground and carried down the slope. The balancing is done by shifting the legs. The glides should be short at first, but by daily practice, and, as the operator gains skill, glides can be made up to a length of several hundred feet. Do not attempt to fly in a wind having a velocity of more than 15 miles an hour.

Exerciser for a Chained Dog

The exerciser consists of a disk, 5 ft. in diameter, pivoted in the ground near the kennel. The disk revolves on a 5/8-in. pin set in a post made of a 4 by 4-in. piece of timber. The disk is made of common lumber fastened together with battens on the under side. Our dog seems to enjoy this kind of exercise.—Contributed by Hazel Duncan, Denver, Colo.

Revolving Disk Exerciser

A Laboratory Gas Generator

The sketch illustrates a gas generator designed for laboratories where gases are needed in large quantities

Gas Generator of Large Capacity That will Work Automatically as the Gas is Removed

and frequently. The shelf holding the large inverted bottle is of thick wood, and to reinforce the whole apparatus, a 1-in. copper strip is placed around the bottle tightly and fastened with screws turned into the woodwork. The shelf above is attached last, and upon it rests the bottle of commercial acid required in the gas generation. The pump shown is for use in starting the siphon.

The large bottle used as a generator may be either a 3 or 5-gal. size, and after it is placed in the position shown, a sufficient amount of the solid reagent needed in gas generating is placed in the mouth before the exit tube, leading away below, is fixed in position. If sulphureted hydrogen is required, ferrous sulphide is used; if hydrogen is required, zinc is placed within; and to make a carbon dioxide, marble, or its equivalent, is inserted. Whatever gas is required, a sufficient quantity of the solid material is put in to last for some time in order not to disturb the fastenings.

When all is ready, the pump is used gently to start the acid over the siphon and into the generator from below. The gas generated by the action of the acid on the solid soon fills the bottle. The screw clamp on the exit tube is loosened and the gas passes into the bottle of water and charges it, in the case when sulphureted hydrogen is required. In the other cases, when sufficient gas has been generated, the screw clamp is tightened, and the gas soon attains considerable pressure which forces the acid back out of the generator and into the acid bottle above. The whole apparatus now comes to an equilibrium, and the gas in the generator is ready for another use.—Contributed by W. M. Mills, Bakersfield, Cal.

Holding Small Armatures for Winding

Procure a strip of sheet metal, 6 in. long, 1 in. wide, or as wide as the armature core is long, and $\frac{3}{32}$ in. thick. Bend this into a U-shape, as shown, and file each end similar to the barb on a fishhook. Drill two holes for a bolt to pass through the sheet-metal ends. Fasten a screw or bolt in the center of the bend, to be used for gripping in a chuck

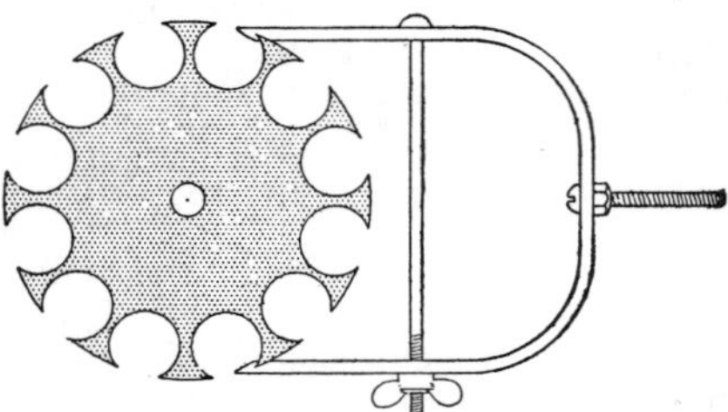

Armature Cores are Easily Revolved to Fill the Core Openings with Insulated Wire

or polishing head. Core segments can be quickly wound with this device.—Contributed by Geo. B. Schulz, Austin, Illinois.

Footstool for Cement Floors

A clerk finding the cement floor of the office uncomfortably cold to the feet, devised a footstool in the following manner: A shallow box was procured, and four small truck casters were fastened to the bottom. A piece of carpet was laid on the inside of the bottom and some old newspapers placed on top of it. When seated at the desk, he placed his feet inside the box on the papers. The casters elevated the box from the cement, just high enough to avoid dampness and cold, and permitted an easy change of position.—Contributed by L. Alberta Norrell, Gainesville, Ga.

Homemade Telegraph Sounder

The material required to construct a telegraph sounder, like the one shown in the sketch, consists of two binding posts, magnets, a piece of sheet metal, and a rubber band. These are arranged as shown, on a wood base or, better still, on a metal box. In using a metal-box base, be sure to insulate the connections at the magnet coils and binding posts.

This instrument will be found by

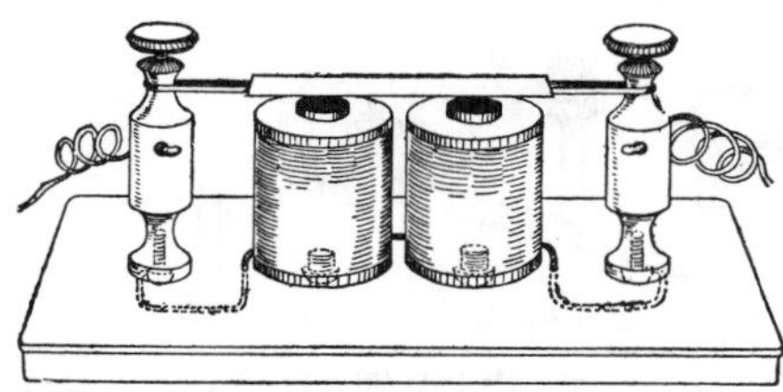

An Inexpensive and Homemade Sounder for Use in Learning the Telegraph Codes

those studying the telegraph codes to give good results, equal to any of the expensive outfits sold for this purpose.—Contributed by Chas. J. La Prille, Flushing, N. Y.

Laboratory Force Filter

The sketch represents a force filter which is well adapted for use in small laboratories. The water is turned on

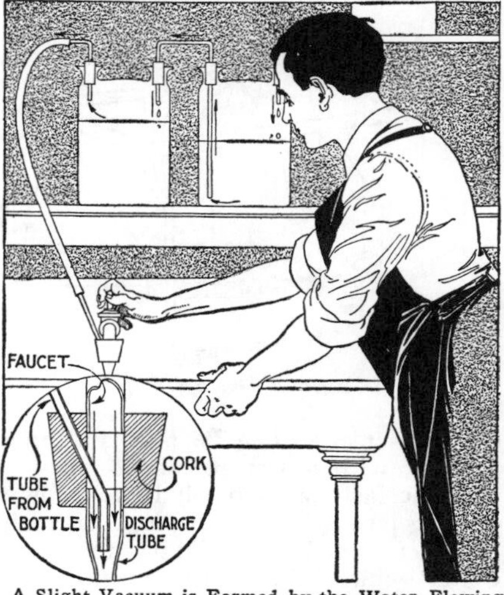

A Slight Vacuum is Formed by the Water Flowing through the Cork, Which Forces the Filter

at the faucet and draws the air through the side tube by suction, which in turn draws the air in a steady stream through the Wolff bottles. The tubes may be attached to a filter inserted in a filter bottle and filtering thus greatly facilitated. The connection to the faucet can be made, as shown in the detailed sketch, out of a long cork, by boring a hole large enough to fit the faucet through the cork and another slanting hole, joining the central hole, on the side for a pipe or tube. At the lower end of the cork a tube is also fitted, which may be drawn out to increase the suction. The inclined tube should be slightly bent at the lower end.—Contributed by W. M. Mills, Bakersfield, Cal.

Beginner's Helper for Roller Skating

One of the most amusing as well as useful devices for a beginner on roller skates is shown in the sketch. The

Beginner Cannot Fall

device is made of ¾-in. pipe and pipe fittings, with a strip of sheet metal 1 in. wide fastened about half way down on the legs. On the bottom of each leg is fastened an ordinary furniture caster which allows the machine to roll easily on the floor. The rear is left open to allow the beginner to enter, then by grasping the top rail he is able to move about on the floor at ease, without fear of falling.—Contributed by J. H. Harris, Berkeley, Cal.

Atmospheric Thermo-Engine

The device illustrated has for its object the production of power in small quantities with little attention and no expense. All that is needed to produce the power is common ordinary water, and the device will continue to operate until the amount of water placed in the receptacle has evaporated.

The device consists of a rectangular vessel provided with legs and a cover. Each end of the vessel is provided with an opening, A, adapted to receive and hold in place plaster-of-paris cups, B. The part extending into the tank is provided with a wick, C, which reaches to the bottom of the vessel. A glass tube, D, is provided with a bulb on each end and partly filled with alcohol, the remaining space being exhausted of air. The glass tube is secured to a hanger which is pivoted to the bottom of the vessel.

After a quantity of water has been poured into the vessel and the device allowed to stand undisturbed for a few minutes, the tube will begin to move with an oscillating motion. Some of the water in the vessel has been conducted by means of the wicks C to the bent plaster cups, from the surface of which it evaporates, thus absorbing latent heat and producing a lower temperature in the cups than that of the surrounding atmosphere. The bulb in contact with the cup thus acquires a lower temperature than the one at the end D, which will result in condensation of the alcohol vapor within the former. The pressure of the vapor in the lower bulb will then force the alcohol up the inclined tube into the higher bulb, the evaporation in the lower bulb maintaining the pressure therein.

When a sufficient quantity of alco-

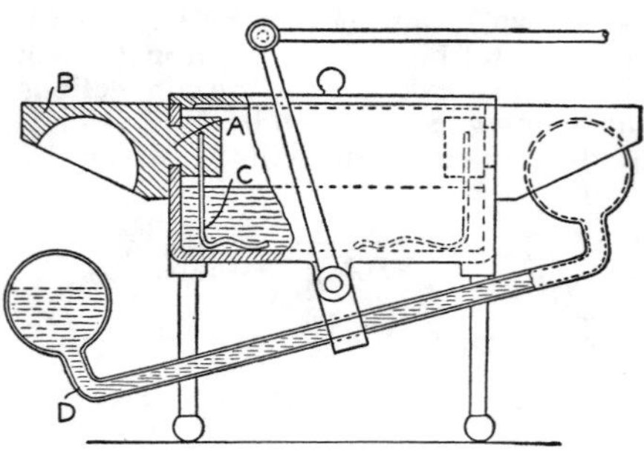

Details of the Engine

hol has been forced into the upper bulb, it will descend, and thus elevate the other bulb into its cup. The phenomena just described will be repeated in this bulb and the oscillation will continue until the water in the vessel has been absorbed and evaporated.—Contributed by E. W. Davis, Chicago.

A Mirror an Aid in Rowing a Boat

The young oarsman is apt to experience difficulty in keeping a straight course until he has had some practice. Rowing a boat in a narrow channel calls for considerable skill to hold a course in mid-stream. A variation of force in pulling the oars almost instantly results in the rowboat making a landfall on one or the other of the banks.

The skilled oarsman does not need an appliance that the beginner might welcome. With the aid of a mirror

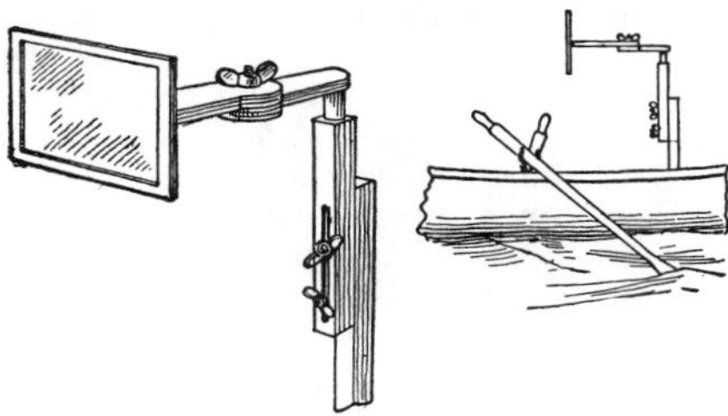

The Mirror Attached to a Boat

conveniently supported at a suitable angle and height before the oarsman's face, the water, the shores and approaching boats may be seen with distinctness. The mirror may be set directly in front or a little distance to one side as shown in the sketch.—Contributed by Thaleon Blake, Sidney, O.

Developing Tray Made of a Tin Can

Obtain a tomato or other can, 5 or 6 in. long and 4 in. in diameter, which should be secured before it has been opened, says Camera Craft. Cut both ends exactly half way around, keeping close to the edge, as shown in the first sketch, and slit it lengthwise to open the side. Trim off the end pieces to within 1 in. of the center and cut off the surplus tin of the sides of the can, leaving enough to bend over and form the ends of the tank as shown in the second sketch.

The support, as shown in the last sketch, is made by screwing together

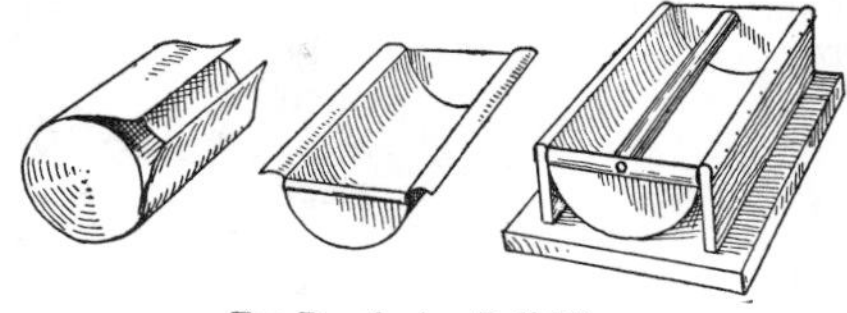

For Developing Roll Films

three pieces of wood, the base piece being 6½ in. square and thick enough to make the tank solid and heavy. Bend the sides of the can over the edges of the two uprights and tack them firmly to the sides, bending the tin so as to have a rounded surface that will not scratch the films. The ends of the can are bent over sharply to form the sides of the tank. Procure a round wood stick, the length of the tank, place in position, and fasten with a screw through the tin at both ends. Give the whole tank two coats of black asphaltum varnish to protect it from the action of the developer.

White Rubber on Croquet Arches

A white cloth is usually tied to croquet arches when the game is played late in the evening. A much better plan is to slip a piece of white rubber tubing about 1 ft. long on the arch. This tubing can be purchased at any local drug store.

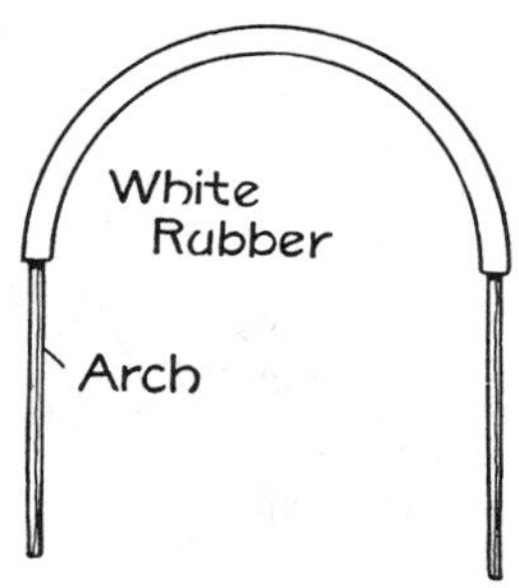

This makes the top part of the arch conspicuous so that it may be plainly seen in the dark, and, when the tubing becomes soiled it can be cleaned off with a damp cloth.—Contributed by John Blake, Franklyn, Mass.

Illuminating an Outside Thermometer

During the season of furnace fires the thermometer outside the north window becomes of added interest and usefulness in helping one to judge the proper draft adjustments of the furnace for the night. A pocket electric flashlamp is convenient for examining the thermometer after dark, but it is not always at hand, matches are dangerous when lace curtains are at the window, and besides, the reflection from the glass of both matches and flashlamp on the inside makes it very difficult to read the thermometer.

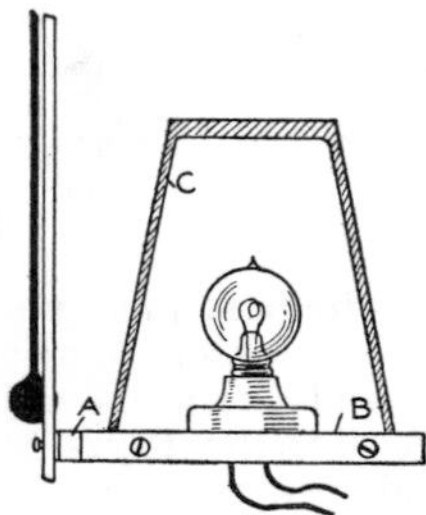

To avoid these difficulties I attached to my thermometer the device shown herewith, which consists of a miniature battery lamp placed at the back of the translucent-glass thermometer and operated by a battery within the house, the light being turned on by an ordinary push button placed conveniently inside of the window.

A strip of brass, A, 3/8 in. wide by 1/16 in. thick, was riveted (soldering will do) to the lower support of the thermometer. The free end of this brass strip was bent around a disk of hardwood, B, and fastened to it by three or four small screws in such a manner that the disk made a circular platform just behind the thermometer scale. This disk was slightly larger than the mouth of a small, thin tumbler. On the upper surface of this disk was fastened with shellac and small nails close to the periphery, a disk of cork, 1/4 in. thick, this cork disk being a close fit for the mouth of the tumbler. A miniature porcelain electric-lamp socket was fastened with screws on the cork of the base. Wires were then run from the lamp socket through the cork and wood disks and the whole painted with melted paraffin to close all apertures and keep out moisture. Good rubber-covered electric-light wire will do nicely for the wiring outside the house, although, if it can be obtained, a piece of lead-covered paired wire is preferable. These wires must be only long enough to reach inside the house, where they may be joined to the ordinary sort of wire used in electric-bell work for connecting with push button and battery.

A 4-volt lamp of about 2 cp. will be sufficient to illuminate the thermometer and allow the scale and mercury column to be distinctly seen. It may be found necessary to make some adjustment by bending the brass strip in order to bring the lamp centrally behind the scale and at the proper height to give the best lighting on the range of from 10 to 40 deg. Over the lamp is placed the tumbler for protection from the weather, and, if desired, half of the tumbler may be painted as a reflector on the inside with white enamel paint, although, in practice, I have not found this necessary.

Within the house the push button should be placed at the window where it can be most conveniently reached when viewing the thermometer, and connections may be made to the battery regularly used for ringing the house bells, or to a separate battery of, say, 4 dry cells, placed in some location, as a closet, near the thermometer. —Contributed by C. F. A. Siedhof, Winchester, Mass.

How to Make an Automobile Robe

When driving an automobile in cold weather, it is impossible to have a robe come down over the feet without being in the way so that it is inconvenient in working the pedals. Procure a common heavy robe and cut two holes in it about 5 in. from the bottom just large enough for the toe of the shoes to slip through and bind the edges with cloth or fur. The 5 in. of robe below the holes should come back under the feet so that no wind can enter. Make the holes far enough apart so that both outside pedals can be reached easily and you will have no trouble with your feet. This robe, with the use of overshoes, will insure comfort in driving a car.—Contributed by Earl R. Hastings, Corinth, Vt.

Locating a Droplight in the Dark

It is very hard to locate an electric-light globe in a dark room. Anyone trying to find one by striking the air in its vicinity with one hand, usually finds that the globe is not there, although the hand may have passed within ½ in. of the globe.

The best way to locate a globe is to approach the proximity of the drop with thumbs touching and fingers extended as shown in the sketch, in which manner the hands will cover a radius of about 14 in. and offer a better chance of locating the light quickly than if

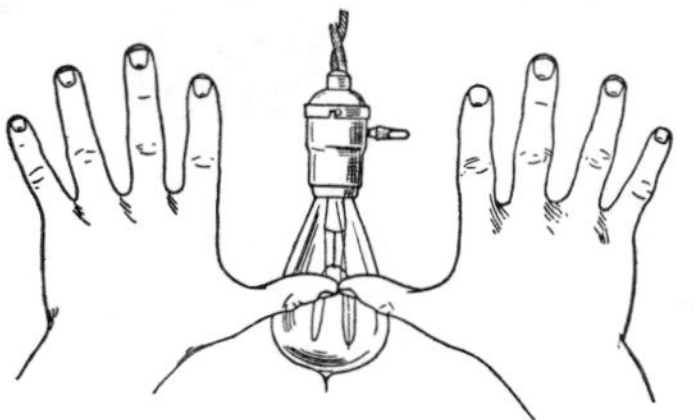

Covering a Wide Range

one groped about with one hand extended.—Contributed by Victor Labadie, Dallas, Tex.

Lighting a Room for Making Photographs

When it becomes too cold for the amateur photographer to take pictures outdoors, he generally lays aside his camera and thinks no more about it until the coming of another spring or summer. While some winter scenes would make up an interesting part of anyone's collection, it is not always pleasant to go out to take them.

Some derive pleasure from making groups and portraits, but this is very difficult, if the room is not well lighted. Overhead light is the best for this work and few residences are constructed to furnish this kind of light.

I find a very good way to get a light

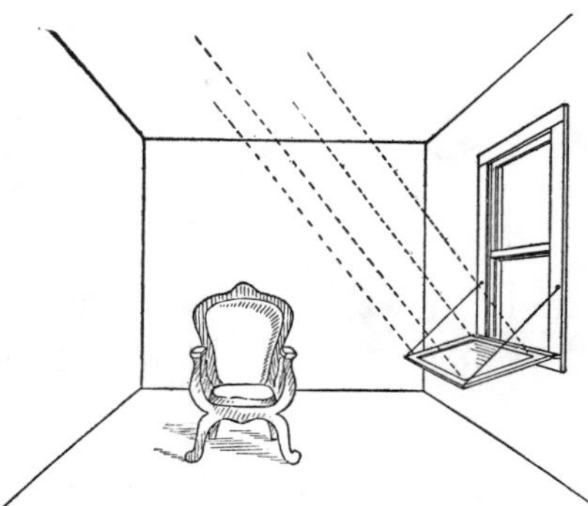

Light Reflected on Ceiling

overhead is to take a large mirror—one from an ordinary dresser will do—and place it in the window in such a position that the reflection will strike the ceiling just above the subject. The result will be a soft but very strong light, almost equal to a north skylight. Splendid portraits can be made in this way.—Contributed by Chas. Piper, Kokomo, Ind.

Detachable Hinged Cover for Kettles

A kettle cover equipped with the hinge shown in Fig. 1 will not fall off when in place, and can be raised or removed entirely when desired.

One wing of an ordinary hinge is soldered or riveted to the cover and wire clasps soldered to the other wing.

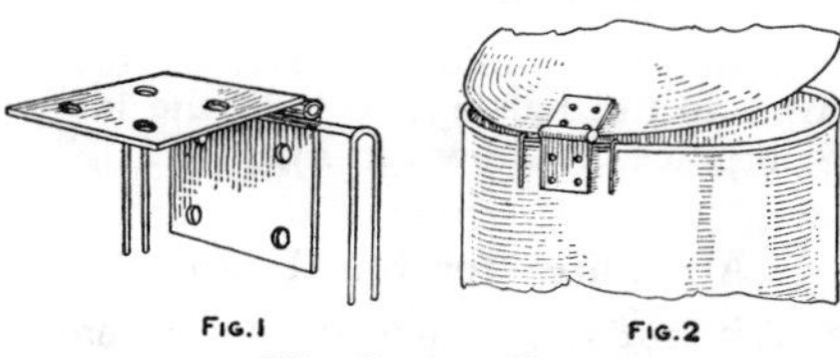

Wire Clasps on Hinge

It is slipped on the kettle as shown in Fig. 2. The cover is interchangeable and can be placed on almost any kettle.

A Use for Discarded Wafer Razor Blades

A paper trimmer and mat cutter can be made from a wafer razor blade. As a paper trimmer, place the blade C over the part A of the razor, as shown, with only two of the holes engaging in one post and the center screw. Then place the part B in position and clamp with the handle. This will allow about ½ in. of the blade to project at one end. If a part of the extending blade is cut or broken off, it will be more easily handled. The cutter is guided along the straightedge as shown in Fig. 1.

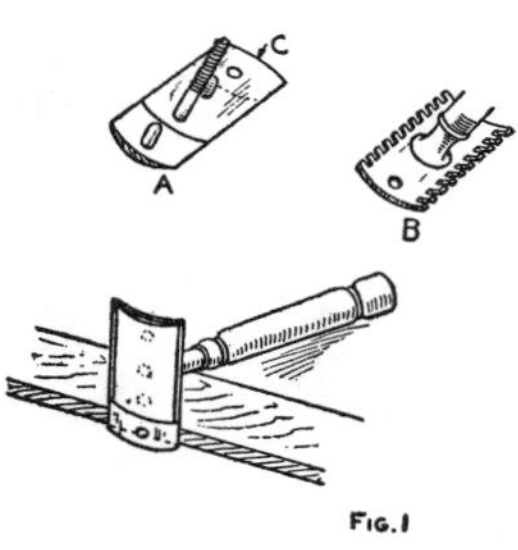

If it is desired to make a more permanent form of instrument, or if no holder is at hand and only a castoff wafer blade, a handle, C, may be cut from a piece of wood and fitted with two or three binding-posts, A, taken from an old battery, to hold the blade B in place, as shown in Fig. 2.

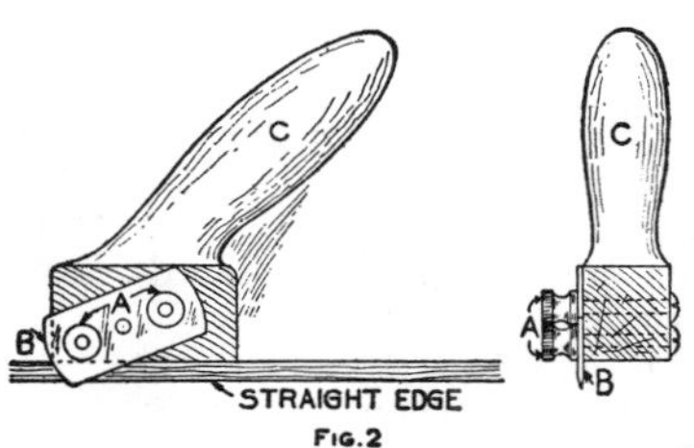

Blade Attached to Handle

Armatures for Small Motors

Without the proper tools and material, the amateur electrician will find it quite difficult to construct a small armature for a battery motor that will run true, without vibration and have a neat appearance. Ordinary cast-iron gears or pinions, as shown in Fig. 1, make excellent cores for armatures on small motors. A gear of any number of teeth can be used for an armature with a smaller number of coils by cutting out a certain number of teeth. For example, a gear with 12 teeth will take 12 coils, but if every other tooth is cut out, it will take only 6 coils, etc. The teeth can be easily chipped out with a cold chisel.

Larger armatures can be made from gears with spokes, the spokes being cut out, if a ring armature is desired. The gear, when wound, can be mounted on a hub made of empty thread spools. The spool can be turned at one end to insert it in the armature, and if too long, one end will serve for the core of the commutator, as shown in Fig. 2.

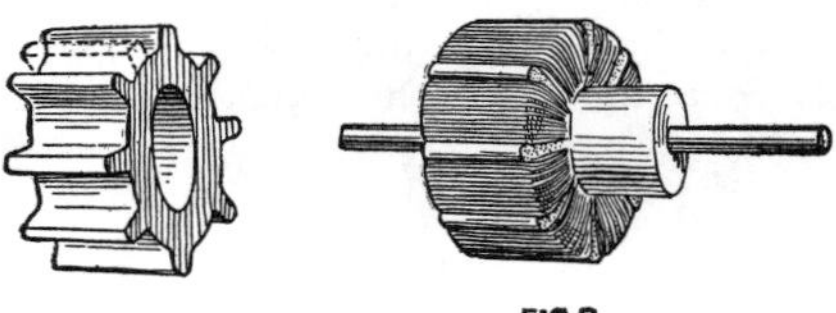

Gear Used as a Core

This combination will make a neat, efficient little armature, which will run quite free from vibration. Only simple tools, such as a hammer, cold chisel, file, jackknife and a vise, are required.—Contributed by R. J. Nault, Hartford, Conn.

Ice Creeper for Shoe Heels

Many persons, young and old, have falls every winter on the ice or snow which can be avoided if their shoes are fitted with ice creepers. A very efficient device of this kind, which any boy can make at home in a short time, is shown in the sketch. These ice creepers need not be removed from the shoes or boots until the winter is past, for they may be worn indoors without injuring the finest floor.

The two plates A may be made from either iron or steel—preferably the latter. An all-steel scraper, or a piece of a saw blade, makes good creepers. Draw the temper by heating the steel to a cherry red and then letting it cool slowly. It may then be sawn with a hacksaw, cut with a cold chisel, or filed into plates of the proper shape, as shown. The teeth are filed to points. The two L-shaped slots are made by drilling $\frac{3}{16}$-in. holes through the plates, and then sawing, filing or chiseling out the metal between the holes. The projections at the ends are then bent out at right angles with heavy pliers or the claws of a hammer, and finally the plates bent to fit the curve of the heel.

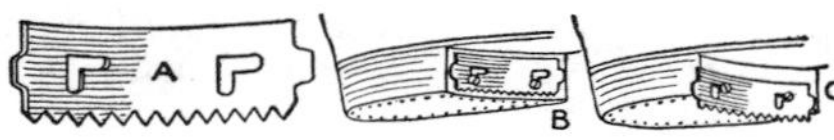

Creeper Attached to Heel

The creepers are attached by means of round-head wood screws turned into the leather. In this operation place the teeth of the plates just below the bottom of the heel and turn the screws into the ends of the upright slots until the heads just bind. The plate as set when indoors or else not needed is shown at B. To place the plate so it will grip the ice, slide it to the right, which will bring the screws into the horizontal slots, as shown at C.—Contributed by Chelsea C. Fraser, Saginaw, Mich.

Opening Screw-Top Fruit Jars

Screw-top fruit jars may be easily opened in the following manner: Secure a strap with a buckle and place it around the top as if it were to be buckled, but instead draw the loose end back and hold it with the thumb as shown. Turn cover and strap while held in this position and it will easily turn from the jar.—Contributed by Chas. A. Bickert, Clinton, Iowa.

Lamp-Chimney Cleaner

Lamp chimneys of various makes are very difficult to clean quickly and thoroughly. The simple device shown

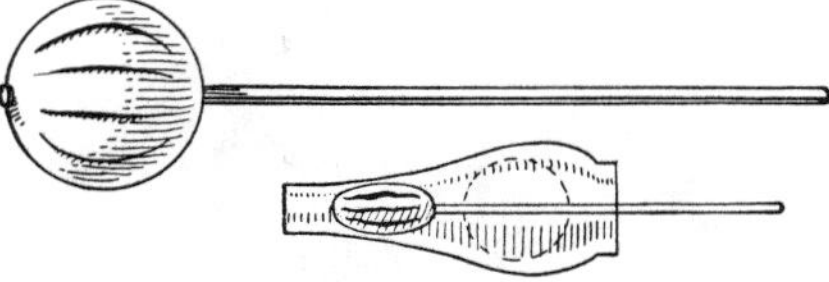
Rubber Ball on Stick

in the sketch makes the cleaning process a simple matter. The cleaner is made of a round rubber ball with slits cut in it as shown and then fastened to the end of a stick. When a cloth is placed over the ball it presses evenly against the curved surfaces of the glass. There is no danger of breaking a chimney with this cleaner.

A Pop-Corn Popper

The accompanying sketch shows the construction of a pop-corn popper for thoroughly flavoring the corn with the hot butter or lard, and at the same time mixing it with the necessary amount of salt. Procure a metal bucket that just fits the bottom of the frying pan. The stirring device is made of heavy wire bent as shown and provided with an empty spool for a handle. A brace is made of tin bent in the shape shown and riveted to the bottom of the bucket.—Contributed by F. A. Wirth, Farwell, Texas.

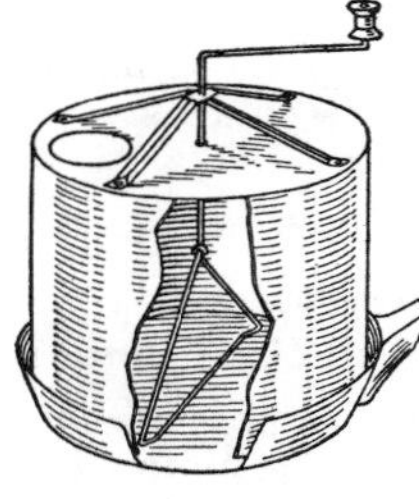

A Homemade Floor Polisher

An efficient and cheap floor polisher may be readily constructed in the following manner: Make a box about 4 by 6 by 12 in., or the exact size may be determined by building it around the household flatirons as these are used to give weight and pressure. The handle, which is attached as shown, should be at least 2½ in. wide

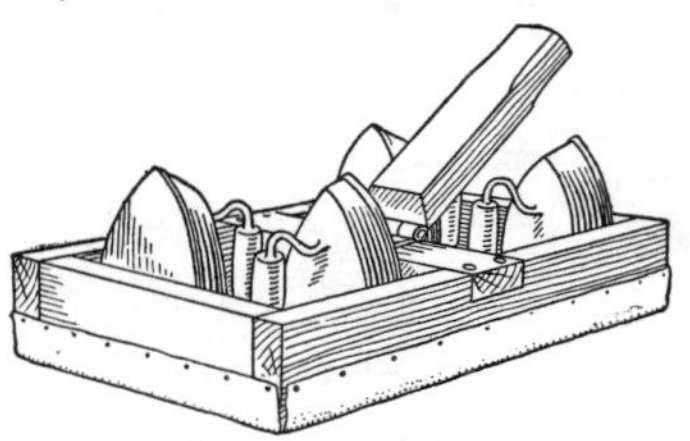

Flatirons in the Box

at the hinged end and should be sandpapered where it is grasped by the hands. A half-strap hinge is preferable, with the strap part fastened to the handle. The bottom of the polisher is covered with a piece of Brussels carpet.

In use, it is well to set the polisher on a soft piece of cotton or flannel cloth, which may be readily renewed when badly soiled.

A more sightly polisher may be made by filling the box with pieces of old iron or lead, tightly packed with paper to prevent rattling, and attaching a cover over the top. The handle may be hinged directly to this cover by means of a full-strap hinge.—Contributed by B. O. Longyear, Ft. Collins, Colo.

Simple Way to Mark Poison Bottles

A way to prevent any possible mistake of taking bottles containing poisons is to mark them as shown in the sketch. This method provides a way to designate a poison bottle in the dark.

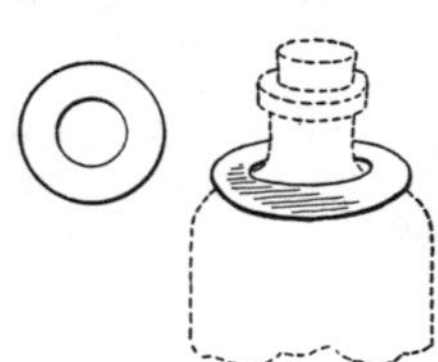

The marker is made of a circle of heavy cardboard with a hole in the center so as to fit tightly over the neck of the bottle. No matter how dark it may be or how much of a hurry a person may be in, one cannot fail to note the character of the contents of the bottle as soon as the hand touches the cardboard marker.—Contributed by Katharine D. Morse, Syracuse, N. Y.

Removing Varnish

A good and easy way to remove varnish from old furniture is to wash the surface thoroughly with 95-percent alcohol. This dissolves the varnish and the wood can then be cleaned with a strong solution of soap, or weak lye. If lye is used, it should be washed off quickly and the wood dried with flannel cloth. When the wood is thoroughly dry it will take a fine finish. —Contributed by Loren Ward, Des Moines, Iowa.

Curling-Iron Heater

The curling-iron holder shown in the sketch can be made of metal tubing

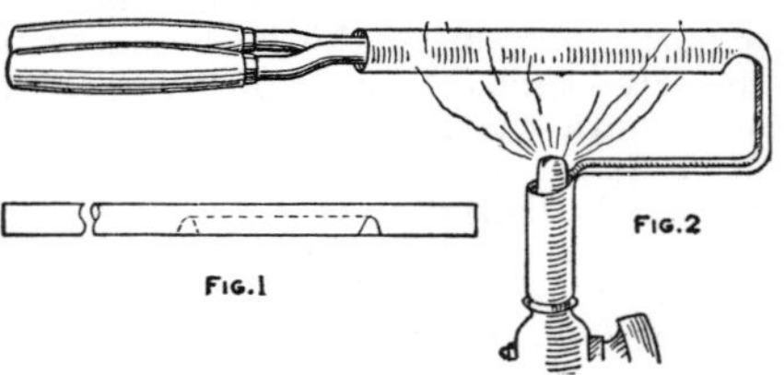

Heater on Gas Jet

having the size to fit both iron and gas jet. One-half of the tubing for a portion of its length is removed, as shown in Fig. 1. The remaining part is bent as in Fig. 2 and set on the burner of the gas jet.

The tube prevents the curling iron from becoming black with soot. The position on the jet may be changed. The tube can be placed on the jet and removed with the curling iron.—Contributed by W. A. Jaquythe, Richmond, Cal.

¶A whisk broom is the best cleaner for a gas stove. It will clean dirt from nickel parts as well as from the burner, grates, ovens and sheet-metal bottoms.

Preserving Flowers in Color and Form

One of the most distressing sides of botanical study is the short life of the colors in flowers. Those who have found the usual method of preserving plants by pressure between paper unsatisfactory will be interested to learn of a treatment whereby many kinds of flowers may be dried so that they retain a great deal of their natural form and color.

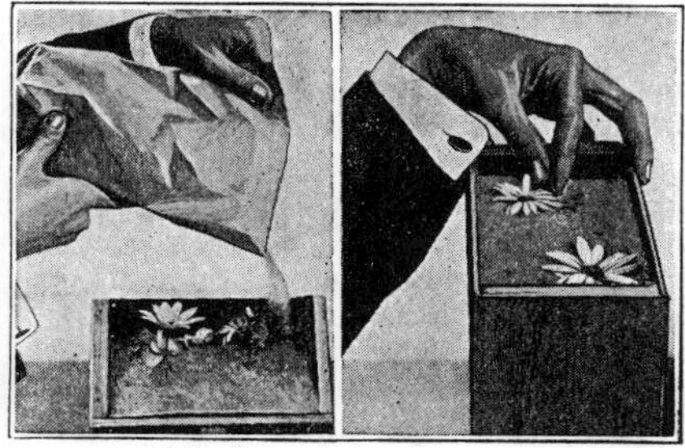

Placing the Flowers on the Steel Pins and Pouring the Dry Sand around Them

The flowers should be gathered as soon as the blossoms have fully opened. It is important that they should be quite dry, and in order to free them of drops of rain or dew, they may be suspended with heads downward for a few hours in a warm place. It is well to begin with some simple form of flower.

A large, strongly made wooden box —one of tin is better—will be necessary, together with a sufficient amount of sand to fill it. If possible, the sand should be of the kind known as "silver sand," which is very fine. The best that can be procured will be found far from clean, and it must, therefore, be thoroughly washed. The sand should be poured into a bowl of clean water. Much of the dirt will float on the surface. This is skimmed off and thrown away, and clean water added. The sand should be washed in this manner at least a dozen times, or until nothing remains but pure white grains of sand. The clean sand is spread out to dry on a cloth in a thin layer. When thoroughly dry, it should be placed in a heavy earthenware vessel and further dried in a hot oven. Allow it to remain in the oven for some time until it is completely warmed through so that one can scarcely hold the bare hands in it.

Obtain a piece of heavy cardboard and cut it to fit easily in the bottom of the box. Through the bottom of the cardboard insert a number of steel pins, one for each of the flowers to be preserved. Take the dry blossoms and press the stalk of each on a steel pin so that it is held in an upright position. When the cardboard is thus filled, place it in the box.

The warm sand is put in a bag or some other receptacle from which it can be easily poured. Pour the sand into the box gently, allowing it to trickle slowly in so that it spreads

The Dried Flowers

evenly. Keep on pouring sand until the heads of the flowers are reached, taking care that all of them stand in a vertical position. The utmost care must be taken, when the heads are reached, to see that all the petals are in their right order. Remember that any crumpled flowers will be pressed into any position they may assume by the weight of the sand. When the box is filled it should be covered and set aside in a dry place.

The box should be allowed to stand at least 48 hours. After the first day, if only a small amount of sand has been used, the material may have cooled off to some extent, and the box must be set in a moderately heated oven for a short time, but no great amount of warmth is advisable. After 48 hours the box may be uncovered and the sand carefully poured off. As the flowers are now in a very brittle condition, any rough handling will cause serious damage. When all the sand has been emptied, the cardboard should be removed from the box and each blossom taken from its pin. In the case of succulent specimens, the stems will have shrunk considerably, but the thinner petals will be in an almost natural condition. The colors will be bright and attractive. Some tints will have kept better than others, but most of the results will be surprisingly good. Whatever state the flowers are in when they are taken from the box, if the drying process has been thorough, they will keep almost indefinitely.

Flowers preserved in this manner are admirable for the decoration of homes. If they are exposed to light, care should be taken to see that the direct sunshine does not strike them, as it will fade the colors. Sprigs with leaves attached may be dried in this way, but it has been found that much of the intensity of the green is lost in the process.

Reading Pulse Beats with the Sun's Rays

The pulse beats may be counted by this unusual method. On a clear day, when the sun is shining brightly, darken a room and select one window toward the sunlight, which should be prepared as follows: Draw the curtain part way down and cover the rest of the window with a heavy cardboard. Cut a small hole in the cardboard to admit a beam of light. Set a bowl of water on a table in the path of the beam so as to deflect it to the ceiling as shown by the dotted lines in the sketch.

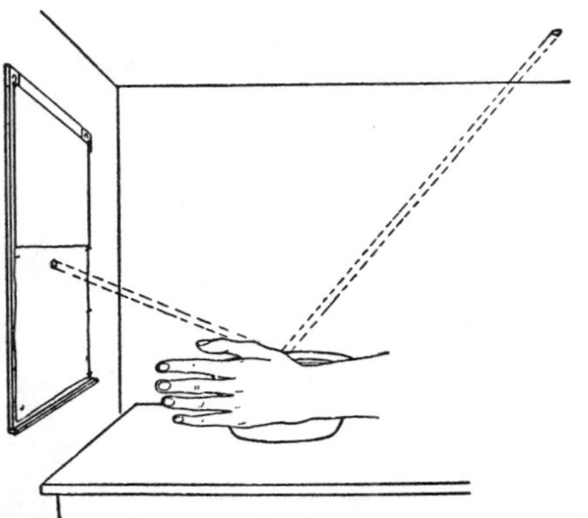

Sun's Rays Deflected to the Ceiling

It is now a simple matter to show the pulse beats. Place the wrist against the edge of the bowl as shown, and the beam of light directed to the ceiling will record every beat of the pulse by short, abrupt movements.

Artistic Wood Turning

Some very odd and beautiful effects can be obtained in lathe work by making up the stock from several pieces of various kinds of wood glued together. The pieces can be arranged in many pleasing combinations, and if good joints are made and a good quality of glue used, the built-up stock is just as durable as a solid piece.

Candlesticks turned from built-up

stock are especially attractive, parts of the various light and dark woods appearing here and there in all manner of odd shapes and proportions. If the stock is placed off center in the lathe, a still greater variety of effects will be produced.

The application of a potassium-bichromate solution to the finished work turns each piece a different color. This solution can be made in any depth of color by varying the amounts of potassium salt and water. Maple or birch treated with this solution are colored to a rich Osage orange which cannot be surpassed in beauty. Mahogany is turned a deep reddish brown, and walnut is darkened a great deal. The solution is applied as evenly as possible with a camel's-hair brush while the wood is turning in the lathe. The grain of the wood is somewhat roughened

Vase Made of Different Woods

by this process, but it can be dressed down again with very fine sandpaper.

In polishing the work, only the best shellac should be used, and several thin coats applied rather than one or two heavy ones. Each coat, with the exception of the last, should be sandpapered slightly. Powdered pumice stone on a cloth held in the palm of the hand can be used to apply a beautiful luster. Some suggestions as to the manner of combining various woods, and a simple candlestick of mahogany and maple are shown in the sketch.—Contributed by Olaf Tronnes, Wilmette, Ill.

A Variable Condenser

A simple variable condenser for receiving in wireless, which will give good results, was made by a correspondent of Modern Electrics as follows: Each clip on the switch was made of ribbon brass or copper in the shape shown at A, the first one from the joint of the knife switch being the longest and each succeeding one shorter. The handle was taken from a single-pole switch. The case was

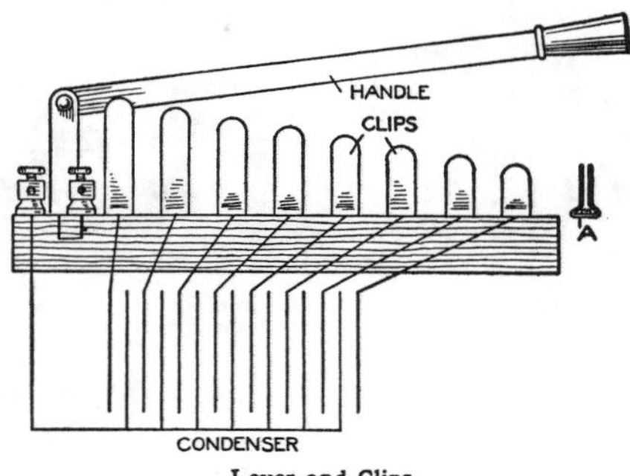

Lever and Clips

made of oak and varnished and the condenser was made of tinfoil and thin sheets of mica, 2 by 3 in. in size. After placing the condenser in the case, hot paraffin was poured around it.

Adjustable Baking-Pan Shoes

At times bread, meat, or other food, placed in ordinary baking pans in the oven becomes burned on the bottom. If the detachable metal strips shown in the sketch are placed on the pan, this will not happen, as the pan does not come in direct contact with the oven floor.

The attachment can be placed on agate ware or sheet-iron pans of any length. The shoes are made from light

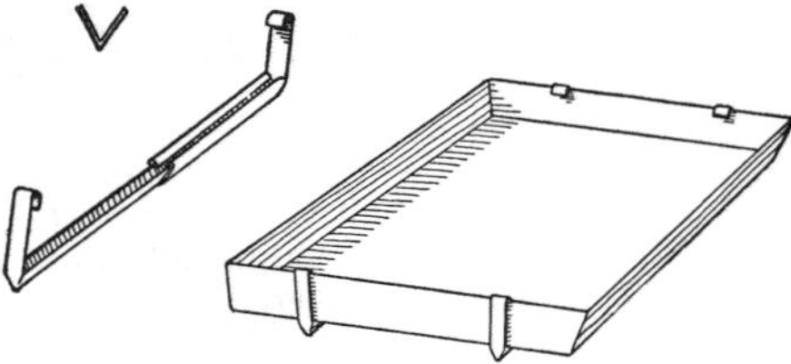

Shoe and How It is Attached to the Pan

V-shaped metal strips and in two parts, as shown, with the edges of one part lapped over so that the other strip will slide in it.

Cars Lined Up Ready for the Start and the Course Patrolled by the Boy Scouts, All Traffic being Halted for the Race and the Roadway Made Clear for the Entire Half Mile of Track

A Pushmobile Race

Pending the time set for a 500-mile international automobile race that was scheduled to take place several weeks later, a number of boys in the sixth and seventh grades of a public school were enthusiastic over the idea of building for themselves, in the school shops, pushmobiles and having a race meet similar to the large one advertised.

The pushmobiles were made and the race run as an opening feature of a field meet held in the city. The course was about a half mile long, and was chosen to give the contestants plenty of curves, a part of the run being over brick streets and the final quarter on the regular track where the field meet was held.

Interest was added to the event by petitioning the mayor of the city for a permit to run the race, and the Boy Scouts patrolled the route, while the city policemen cleared the streets, and during the race all traffic was halted.

Two of the requirements for entering the race were that the car had to be made in the school shops and that it must have a certain kind of a wheel, which in this case was one condemned by a local factory, thus making the wheels and wheel base of all cars alike. Two boys to a car constituted a racing team, and during the race they could exchange positions at their pleasure. The necessity of "nursing" their cars down the steep grades and around difficult corners developed into an important factor. All cars were named and numbered.

The car that finished first was disqualified for the reason that it took on a fresh pusher along the course.

The Cars Winning the First, Second and Third Prizes Respectively, the "Hoosier" being Penalized 10 Yards at the Starting Tape for Having Larger and Better-Grade Wheels

The cars were constructed under the supervision of the regular shop instructor, and a drawing was furnished each boy making a car. The design of the hood and the arrangement of the seat and steering gear was left for each boy to settle as he desired. The matter of expense was watched closely by each one. Most of the hoods and seats were constructed of empty dry-goods boxes.

With the aid of the sketch any boy can make a car as strong as the "Peugeot" that won the race. The side rails of the main frame were made of cypress, 58 in. long and 2 in. square.

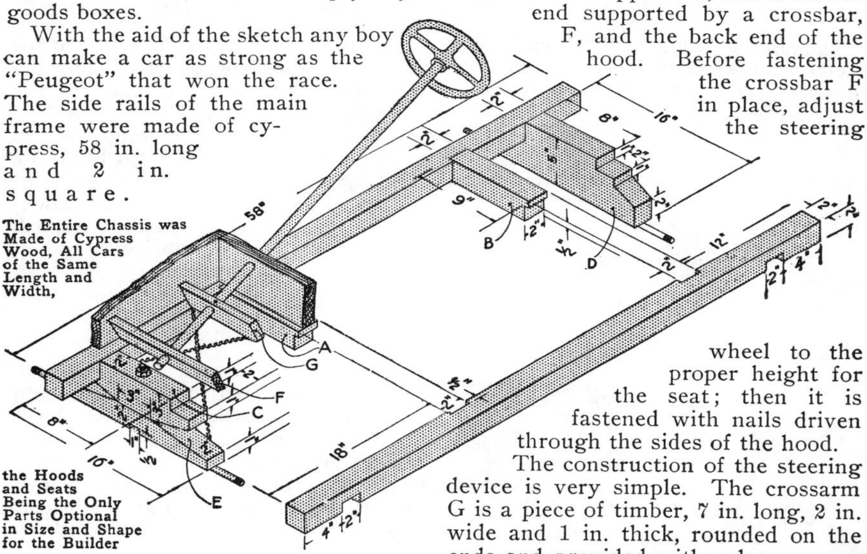

The Entire Chassis was Made of Cypress Wood, All Cars of the Same Length and Width, the Hoods and Seats Being the Only Parts Optional in Size and Shape for the Builder

The location of the crossbars A and B is very important, as they give rigidity to the frame and reinforce the two bolsters C and D. The size of the hood and the location of the seat determine where they should be set into the rail, after which they are fastened with large wood screws. The three bolsters C, D, and E are cut from regular 2 by 4-in. stock. Be careful to get a uniform distance between the rails when they are framed together. If desired, the dimensions can be increased, but do not reduce them, as this will narrow the tread too much. The bolt connecting the bolsters C and E is a common carriage bolt, 5 in. long and ½ in. in diameter. A washer is placed between the pieces C and E, to make the turning easy.

Two pieces of ½-in. soft-steel rod were used for the axles, a hole being drilled near each end for a cotter, to hold the wheels in place, and also holes through the diameter between the wheels, for 1½-in. screws to fasten the axles to the bolsters.

The steering wheel is constructed of a broom handle with a small wheel fastened to its upper end, and the lower end supported by a crossbar, F, and the back end of the hood. Before fastening the crossbar F in place, adjust the steering wheel to the proper height for the seat; then it is fastened with nails driven through the sides of the hood.

The construction of the steering device is very simple. The crossarm G is a piece of timber, 7 in. long, 2 in. wide and 1 in. thick, rounded on the ends and provided with a large screw eye near each end on the under side to which are fastened the ends of two small-linked chains. The chains are then crossed and fastened to the bottom bolster in front and as near the wheels as practical. The connection is made with a screw eye similar to the one used in the crossarm. Another type of steering device may be made by building on the rod a 5-in. drum which takes the place of the steering arm. It is a more positive appliance, but is somewhat harder to make and adjust.

The making of the hood and the seat completes the car. Decide upon the shape and size of the hood, but, in any case and irrespective of the size, it will require a front and back end. These are made first and then secured at the proper distance apart with two side rails. These two ends are nailed on the ends of the connecting rails. It is then well to fasten the hood skeleton to the car frame and cover it after the steering device is in place.

The seat bottom is cut the shape desired, and fastened to the rear bolster and crosspiece, first placing a piece of the proper thickness under the front edge, to give it the desired slant backward. The back curved part can be formed of a piece of sheet metal and lined on the inside with wood pieces, or with cloth or leather, padded to resemble the regular cushion.

Pencil Rack

The simple pencil rack shown in the sketch can be easily made from any suitable strip of metal, preferably

A Strip of Sheet Metal Cut and Clips Formed to Make a Pencil Rack

brass of about No. 15 gauge. Mark off a number of rectangles corresponding to the number of pencil holders desired. With a sharp chisel, cut through the metal on three sides of each rectangle, leaving one of the short sides untouched. The loose laps can then be bent to a shape suited to hold a pencil. The rack can be fastened in place with nails or screws through holes pierced at each end. —Contributed by Mark Gluckman, Jersey City, N. J.

¶Indistinct but not entirely worn-off dates on coins may be read by heating slightly.

Reducing Size of a Hat Sweatband

Very often a hat has been worn for some time and it becomes too loose on the head, then paper is used in the sweatband to reduce the size. A better, easier, and neater method, as well as one that will be cooler for the head, is to insert a flat lamp wick inside of the sweatband. Wicks of all thicknesses and widths are easily obtained. —Contributed by Maurice Bandier, New Orleans, La.

A Catapult

The catapult shown in the sketch is one I constructed some time ago and found to be amusing and very inexpensive. The catapult consists of a small piece of dowel or pine, whittled into the shape of a handle, a screweye, an elastic band and an arrow. It is surprising how a well-balanced arrow will fly into the sky until lost to sight when propelled through the eye of the screw with a medium-strong elastic. A number of forms of this

The Eye of the Screw Serves as a Guide for the Arrow

simple gun were made, but the one shown is the simplest and most effective.—Contributed by C. A. Needham, New York, N. Y.

Growing Clean Strawberries

A very good method of growing individual strawberry plants that will produce large clean berries is to provide a covering constructed from a board 10 in. square with a 3-in. hole bored in the center. This covering is placed over the plant, as shown in the sketch, to keep down weeds, retain moisture, and to make a base for the ripening berries. A shower cannot spatter dirt and sand on the growing fruit. The rays of the sun beating on the surface of the board will aid in the ripening.

If a log can be obtained, the boards can be made better and more quickly. Disks about 1 in. thick are sawed from the log and holes in their centers either cut with a chisel or bored, as desired.

Growing Strawberries on the Surface of a Board Where They will Ripen Fast and Keep Clean

The grain of the wood will be vertical and no warping will take place—Contributed by Johnny Banholster, Gresham, Oregon

A Magic Change Card

Procure two cards, the "5" of diamonds and the "5" of spades, for example. Bend each exactly in the center, with the face of the cards in, and then paste any card on the back, with its face against the two ends of the bent cards. The two opposite ends will then have their backs together, and these are also pasted. The illustration clearly shows this arrangement.

To perform the trick pick up this card, which is placed in the pack beforehand, and show to the audience both the front and back of the card, being sure to keep the center part flat against one end or the other, then pass the hand over the card, and in

A Card Having Two Faces, Either of Which can be Shown to the Audience Instantly

doing so catch the center part and turn it over. The card can be changed back again in the same manner.—Contributed by R. Bennett, Pittsburgh, Pa.

Cleaning Pearl Articles

A good way to clean pearl articles or ornaments is to moisten them with alcohol and then dry in magnesia powder or French chalk. These last two articles may be purchased at any drug store and the process of cleaning is absolutely harmless. It also polishes the pearl and will not bleach delicate colors.

Bed for a Camp

A quickly made bed for a camp is shown in the illustration. The corner posts consist of four forked stakes driven in the earth so that the crotches are on a level and about 1 ft. from

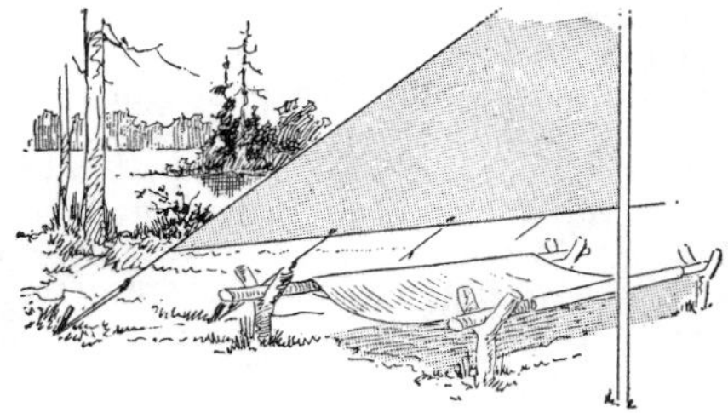

Canvas Bed Made on Two Poles Laid in the Crotches of Forked Stakes

the ground. Poles are laid in the crotches, lengthwise of the bed, and canvas covering double-lapped over them. If desired, the canvas can be stitched along the inside of the poles. —Contributed by Thomas Simpson, Pawtucket, R. I.

Sail for a Boy's Wagon

Every boy, who loves a boat and has only a wagon, can make a combination affair in which he can sail even though

The Sail Wagon will Travel at a Good Speed in a Stiff Breeze

there is no water for miles around. One boy accomplished this as shown in the illustration, and the only assistance he had was in making the sails.

The box of the wagon is removed and the boat deck bolted in its place. The deck is 14 in. wide and 5 ft. long. The mast consists of an old rake handle, 6 ft. long; the boom and gaff are broomsticks, and the tiller is connected with wire to the front axle, which gives perfect control of the steering. The sails are made of drilling.

On a brick pavement the sail wagon can draw two other wagons with two boys in each, making in all five boys. Of course a good wind must be blowing. With two boys it has made a mile in five minutes on pavement.—Contributed by Arthur Carruthers, Oberlin, Ohio.

Extracting a Broken Screw

A screw will often break off in a piece of work in such a manner that it is quite impossible to remove it by using a pair of pliers or a wrench. In this case the following method is very efficient and expedient.

Drill a small hole in the screw as near the center as possible. Roughen the edges on the tang of a file with a cold chisel, and drive the tang into the hole with a mallet. The roughened edges of the tang exert enough friction on the metal to remove the screw by turning the file in the proper direction.

Keeping Out Dampness

A good way to keep a bed from becoming damp, if left for any length of time, is to place a blanket on the top after it is made up. Take the blanket off before using and the bed covers will be quite dry, as the blanket absorbs the moisture.—Contributed by G. Nordyke, Lexington, Ore.

A Double-Claw Hammer for Pulling Nails Straight

A nail pulled with an ordinary claw hammer will be bent in the operation, and for this reason the double claw is used to draw the nail straight out of the wood. An ordinary claw hammer can be easily converted into a double-claw by filing out one of the claws as shown. The notch is filed only large enough to slip under the head of an average-size nail. After drawing the nail a short distance in the

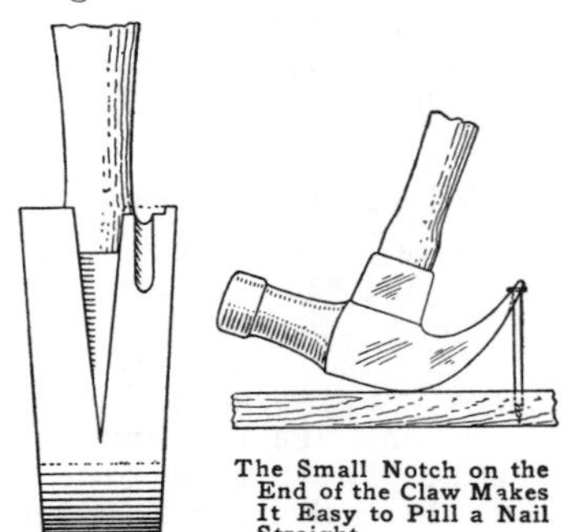

The Small Notch on the End of the Claw Makes It Easy to Pull a Nail Straight

usual manner the small notch is set under the head of the nail which is then pulled out straight.—Contributed by J. V. Loeffler, Evansville, Ind.

A Cyclemobile

By FRANK PFEFFERLE

The cyclemobile is of the three-wheeled type and can be easily constructed in the home workshop with ordinary tools. The main frame is built up of two sidepieces, AA, Fig. 1, each 2 in. thick, 4 in. wide, and 7 ft. long, joined together at the front end with a crosspiece, B, of the same material, 17 in. long. The sides are placed slightly tapering so that the rear ends are 11 in. apart at the point where they are joined together with the blocks and rear-wheel attachments. A crosspiece, C, 13 in. long, is fastened in the center of the frame.

The place for the seat is cut out of each sidepiece, as shown by the notches at D, which are 2 ft. from the rear ends. Two strips of wood, E, ½ in. thick, 4 in. wide, and 22 in. long, are fastened with nails to the rear ends of the sides, as shown. The rear wheel

Three-Wheeled Cyclemobile Propelled Like a Bicycle and Steered as an Automobile

is a bicycle wheel, which can be taken from an old bicycle, or a wheel may be purchased cheaply at a bicycle store. It is held in place with two pieces of strap iron, F, shaped similar to the rear forks on a bicycle, and each piece is bolted to a block of wood 3 in. thick, 4 in. wide, and 6 in. long, which is fastened to the sidepiece with the same bolts that hold the strap iron in place. The blocks are located 20 in. from the rear ends of the sidepieces.

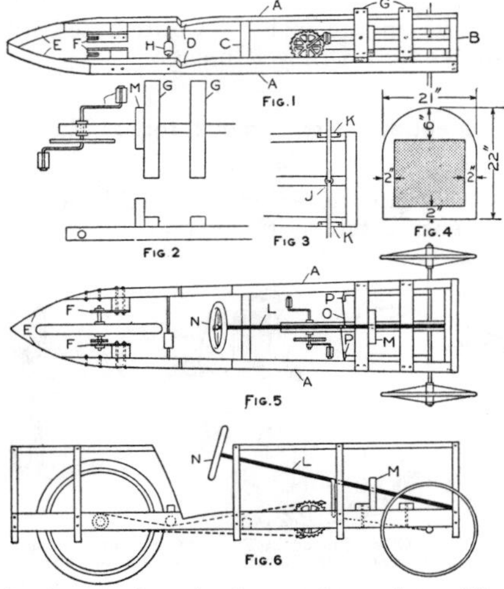

Detail of the Parts for Constructing an Automobile-Type Foot-Power Car

The pedal arrangement, Fig. 2, consists of an ordinary bicycle hanger, with cranks and sprocket wheel set into the end of a piece of wood, 2 in. thick, 4 in. wide and 33 in. long, at a point 4 in. from one end. The pieces GG are nailed on across the frame at the front end of the car, to hold the hanger piece in the center between the sidepieces, as shown in Fig. 1. A small pulley, H, is made to run loosely on a shaft fastened between the sidepieces. This is used as an idler to keep the upper part of the chain below the seat.

The front axle is 30 in. long, pivoted as shown at J, Fig. 3, 6 in. from the front end of the main frame. Two small brass plates, KK, are fastened with screws on the under edge of each sidepiece, as shown, to provide a bearing for the axle. The front wheels are taken from a discarded baby carriage and are about 21 in. in diameter.

A good imitation radiator can be made by cutting a board to the dimensions given in Fig. 4. A large-mesh screen is fastened to the rear side to imitate the water cells.

The steering gear L, Fig. 5, is made of a broom handle, one end of which passes through the support M and fits into a hole bored into the lower part of the imitation radiator board. A steering wheel, N, is attached to the upper end of the broom handle. The center part of a rope, O, is given a few turns around the broom handle, and the ends are passed through the openings in screweyes, PP, turned into the inner surfaces of the sidepieces AA, and tied to the front axle.

The seat is constructed of ½-in. lumber and is built in the notches cut in the main frame shown at D, Fig. 1. The body frame is made of lath, or other thin strips of wood, that can be bent in the shape of the radiator and nailed to the sidepieces, as shown in Fig. 6. These are braced at the top with a longitudinal strip. The frame is then covered with canvas and painted as desired.

How to Make a Humidor

The humidor is an ideal gift for any person who smokes. The wood for making one, as shown in the illustra-

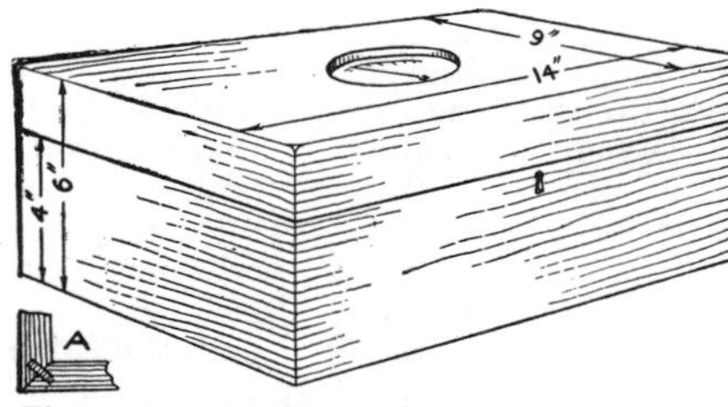

The Amount of Moisture within the Box is Shown on the Dial in the Cover

tion, may be of Spanish cedar, mahogany, or quartered oak, as the builder desires. The box and cover are made and glued together in one piece, then the cover is sawed off to insure a perfect fit. A strong corner connection is shown at A. A piece of a strawberry box or peach basket makes a good key to glue in the grooves. Care must be taken to run the grain with the width and not with the length of the strip.

Finish the outside of the box with two coats of the desired stain, then cover with a coat of wax, shellac, or varnish. The inside should be finished with one coat of white lead and two or three coats of white enamel, to make the wood impervious to moisture.

In the center of the cover top is set a piece of glass and to the under side of the latter a hygrometer is attached with a little glue. This instrument tells the relative humidity, or the amount of moisture, in the air within. The moisture may be regulated by adding a few drops of water, as needed, to a piece of ordinary blotting paper placed on the inside.—Contributed by James T. Gaffney, Chicago.

Telephoto Attachment for a Hand Camera

It is not necessary to purchase an expensive telephoto lens for a box or hand camera if the owner has a pair of

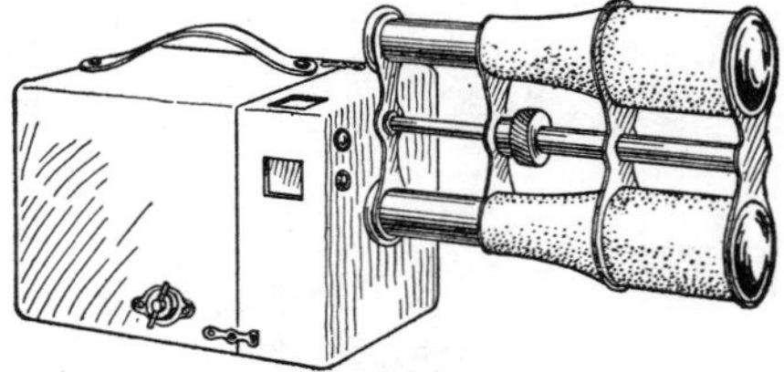

A Field Glass Placed in Front of a Camera Lens will Increase the Diameter of the Photograph

opera or field glasses. First focus the glasses on the distant object to be photographed and then set the camera. One of the glasses is placed directly in line with and in front of the camera lens, as shown in the sketch. If the camera is of the focusing type, it is focused in the ordinary manner. Box and other cameras are set as usual.

The glasses should be well supported in front of the camera lens, as any slight move will be quite perceptible on the ground glass. As the light rays are largely reduced in passing through the field glass and camera lens, it is necessary to give a much longer exposure. This can only be determined by trying it out, as lenses have different speeds.—Contributed by Charles Leonard, St. John, Can.

A Turn Feeding Table for Birds

Never in the past has the public at large taken so great an interest in protecting and furthering the well-being of birds as at present. In addition to protective legislation, clubs everywhere are organizing to promote bird life and many citizens, old and young, are making bird houses and feeding tables.

One of the best forms of feeding tables which I have ever seen is shown in the sketch. It possesses a great advantage over the average table in being turned automatically, whirling about by the action of the winds and always keeping its open front on the lee or protected quarter. This is a good feature especially in the fall and winter, the very time when birds need and seek protection from storms and cold winds.

To make such a feed table almost any kind of boards can be utilized. The shelter may be of any shape or size to suit the tastes of the maker, but one constructed to the dimensions given will be found to work well in most localities. Along the center of the roof is attached a wing, A, which is an active aid in causing the wind to keep the open front turned away. The shelter turns upon a wood or iron rod which passes from the end of a post up through the central bottom and central roof of the structure. If wood is used for the rod, it should be about 1 in. in diameter and of hard

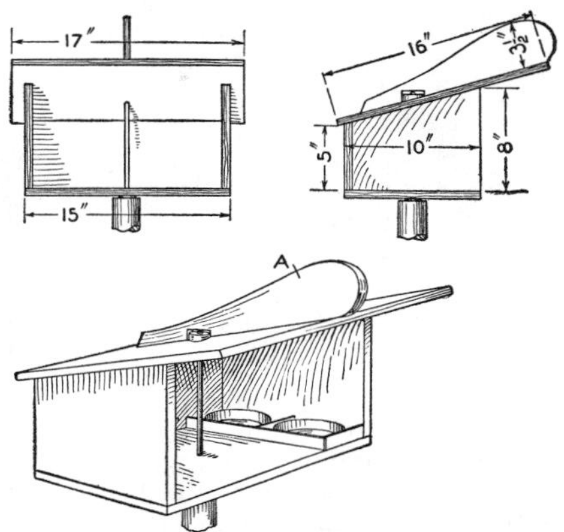

A Feeding Table for Birds That will Keep Its Open Side Protected from the Storms

stock. An iron rod may be somewhat smaller. Keep the holes well greased.

The house should be given a couple of coats of white, red, or green paint, and the post painted to correspond. Feed and water are placed in shallow dishes on the floor and they should be blocked to keep them from sliding out. —Contributed by C. C. Fraser, Saginaw, Mich.

A Sack Holder

An old granite kettle or tin pail with the bottom cut out and three 8-penny wire nails bent and fastened on with rivets, as shown at A, makes as good a sack holder as one could desire. A chain attached to the handle makes it conveniently adjustable to the proper height for the sack.

A Granite Kettle Forms a Holder That Makes It Easy to Fill the Sack

Time Indicator for Medicine Bottles

The time to give a patient the next dose of medicine can be set on the indicator, as shown in the sketch, and retained without fear of its being changed until the dose is again given. The indicator consists of a strip of paper which will reach around the bottle neck and is divided into 24 equal parts representing hours and half hours. The paper is then pasted to the bottle neck. An ordinary pin is then pushed into the cork as shown. After a dose of medicine is given to the patient the cork is replaced so that the head of the pin will indicate the time for the next dose. By this method, an accidental shifting of the indicator is almost impossible.

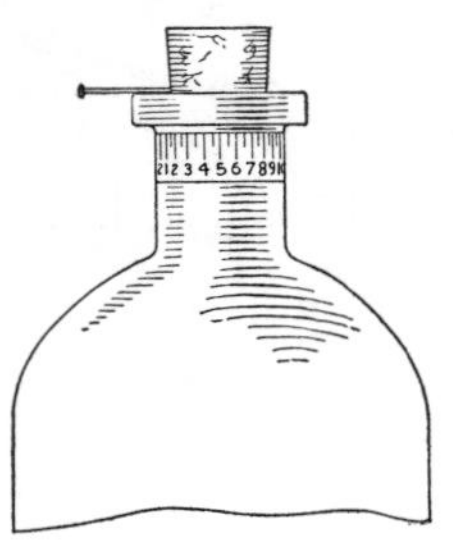

A Washtub Stand

Usually two old chairs or an old box makes the stand for the washtub, and these are not always the right height. A stand, like that shown in the illustration and having the proper height for the one who does the washing, can be easily made of 2 by 4-in. material and a few boards. As it is shown, the wringer is fastened on top of the back and may remain there all the time, it being out of the way, always in its proper place, and held very firmly.

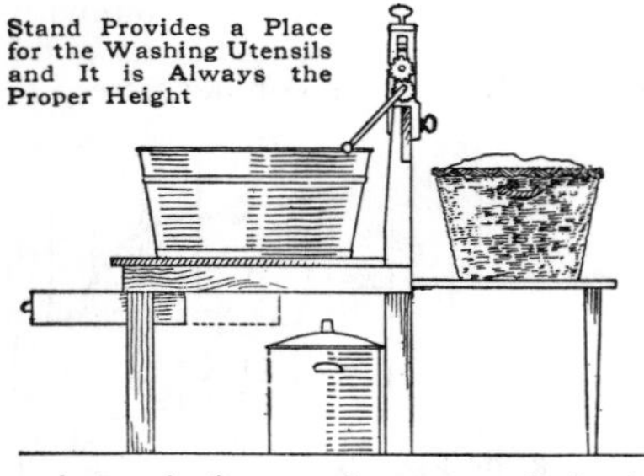

Stand Provides a Place for the Washing Utensils and It is Always the Proper Height

A light bracket, on which to set the clothes basket, can be made and fastened on the back of the stand, connected with two hinges and supported by a leg hinged to the bracket, the lower end of the leg resting on the floor back of the stand.

A small drawer may also be provided in the front, in which to put away the soap and brushes, and the wash boiler can be set underneath. When one is through washing, the bracket at the back is let down, the washstand set up against the wall out of the way, and everything is then in its place, ready for the next wash day.—Contributed by Chas. Homewood, Waterloo, Ia.

Pipe Used as a Leather Punch

The sketch shows how a very cheap and serviceable leather punch can be made of an old pipe nipple. Pieces of pipe of almost any size can be found around a shop, and it is, therefore, usually possible to quickly make a punch of the required size. The cutter end can be ground very thin to prevent an overcut, while a small slot cut a little above it will allow the removal of the leather slugs. For its purpose, this homemade tool is all that can be desired in cheapness and utility.

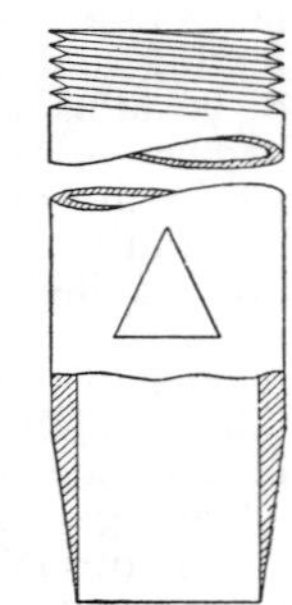

To Prevent Oilcloth from Cracking

A good method to prevent oilcloth from cracking, when it is used on shop tables or counters, is to first cut a paper cover for the table on which to place the oilcloth and prepare it as follows: The paper should be well oiled with common machine oil and placed smoothly on the table to be covered. The oilcloth is then smoothed out on top of the paper and stretched tightly. The oiled paper tends to keep the under side of the cloth moist, which prevents cracking. The cloth wears much longer because the paper acts as a pad

How to Make a Flymobile

By EDWARD SIEJA

The boy owning a pushmobile, or even a power-driven auto car, is often very much disappointed because motion soon stops when the power is not applied. The car illustrated is of a little different type, being equipped with a flywheel that will propel the car and carry the rider a considerable distance after stopping the pedaling. The flywheel also aids the operator, as it will steady the motion and help him over a rough place or a bump in the road.

The main frame of the flymobile is made up of a few pieces of 2 by 4-in. timbers. The pieces A are 6 ft. 4 in. long, and the end crosspieces B, 24 in. long. These are jointed, glued and screwed together, as shown in Fig. 1. The frame that supports the driving parts consists of a piece, C, 6 ft. 2 in. long, and a piece D, 2 ft. 11 in. long. These are fitted in the main frame and securely fastened to the end crosspieces B. Two other crosspieces, E and F, are used to strengthen the driving-parts frame.

The entire hanger G, with its bearings, cranks and pedals, can be procured from a discarded bicycle and fastened to the piece C; the barrel holding the bearings being snugly fitted into a hole bored in the piece with an expansive bit. The location will depend on the builder and should be marked as follows: Place the hanger on top of the piece C, then put a box or board on the frame where the seat is to be and set the hanger where it will be in a comfortable position for pedaling. Mark this location and bore the hole.

The transmission H consists of a bicycle coaster-brake hub, shown in detail in Fig. 2. A split pulley, J, 6 in. in diameter, is bored out to fit over the center of the hub between the spoke flanges. The halves of the pulley are then clamped on the hub with two bolts, run through the holes in opposite directions. Their heads and nuts are let into countersunk holes so that no part will extend above the surface of the pulley. The supports for the hub axle consist of two pieces of bar iron, 4 in. long, drilled to admit the axle ends, and screws for fastening them to the frame pieces C and D. This construction is clearly shown in Fig. 2.

The Flymobile is a Miniature Automobile in Appearance and is Propelled by Foot Power

The arrangement of the coaster-brake hub produces the same effect as a coaster brake on a bicycle. The one propelling the flymobile may stop the foot-power work without interfering with the travel of the machine, and, besides, a little back pressure on the pedals will apply the brake in the same manner.

The flywheel K should be about 18 in. in diameter with a 2-in. rim, or face. Such a wheel can be purchased cheaply from any junk dealer. The flywheel is set on a shaft, turning between the pieces C and D and back of the coaster-brake wheel H. Two pulleys, L, about 3 in. in diameter, are fastened to turn with the flywheel on the shaft and are fitted with flanges to separate the belts. The ends of the shaft should run in good bearings, well oiled.

Another pulley, M, 6 in. in diameter, is made of wood and fastened to the rear axle. An idler wheel, shown in Fig. 3, is constructed of a small pulley, or a large spool, attached to an L-shaped piece of metal, which in turn is fastened on the end of a shaft controlled by the lever N. The function of this idler is to tighten up the belt or release it, thus changing the speed in the same manner as on a motorcycle.

The elevation of the flymobile is given in Fig. 4, which shows the arrangement of the belting. The size of the pulleys on the flywheel shaft causes it to turn rapidly, and, for this reason, the weight of the wheel will run the car a considerable distance when the coaster hub is released.

The rear axle revolves in bearings, half of which is recessed in the under edges of the pieces A while the other half is fastened to a block, screwed on fastening them to the pieces P and Q, as shown. These pieces are hinged with strap iron, R, at one end, the other end of the piece P being fastened to the crosspiece F, Fig. 1, of the main frame. The lower piece Q is worked by the lever S and side bars, T. A small spring, U, keeps the ends of the pieces apart and allows the free turning of the axle until the brake lever is drawn. The lever S is connected by a long bar to the hand lever V.

The steering apparatus W, Figs. 1 and 4, is constructed of a piece of gas pipe, 3 ft. 4 in. long, with a wheel at one end and a cord, X, at the other. The center part of the cord is wound several times around the pipe and the ends are passed through screweyes in the main frame pieces A and attached to the front axle, which is pivoted in the center under the block Y. The lower end of the pipe turns in a hole bored slanting in the block. A turn of the steering wheel causes one end of the cord to wind and the other to unwind, which turns the axle on the center pivot.

The wheels are bicycle wheels, and the ends of the front axle are turned to

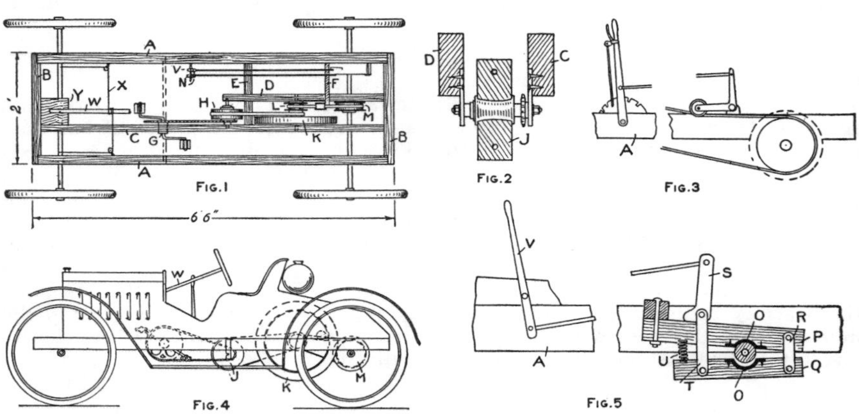

Plan and Elevation of the Flymobile, Showing the Location of the Working Parts, to Which, with a Few Changes, a Motorcycle Engine can be Attached to Make It a Cyclecar; Also Details of the Brakes, Belt Tightener and Coaster-Brake Hub

over the axle. A simple brake is made as shown in Fig. 5. Two metal pieces, O, preferably brass, are shaped to fit over the shaft with extending ends for receive the cones and nuts, instead of using the regular hub axles. The ends of the rear axle are turned to closely fit the hubs after the ball cups have been removed. A large washer and nut clamp each wheel to the axle so that it will turn with it.

The body can be made up as desired, from sheet metal, wood, or cloth stretched over ribs of wood, and painted in the manner of an automobile. A tank and tires can be placed on the back to add to the appearance. Fenders and a running board can be attached to the main frame.

With the addition of some crosspieces in the main frame at the front and a motorcycle engine fastened to them so that the driving sprocket will be in line with the sprocket on the coaster hub, the builder will have a real cyclecar.

The Die-and-Box Trick

The die-and-box trick, so often performed on the stage, is a very interesting and mystifying one. The apparatus, however, is simple, consisting of a box, die, a piece of tin in the form of three adjacent sides of the die, and a hat. The die and box are constructed entirely of wood, 1/8 in. thick, and the piece of tin can be cut from any large coffee can. The box is closed by four doors, as shown in Fig. 1, two of which are 2 3/4 in. square, and the others, 3 1/8 in. by 3 1/4 in. The first two are the front doors and are preferably hinged with cloth to the two uprights A and B. Small pieces of tin are fastened on the doors at C and D, to provide a means to open them. The other doors are placed on top and are hinged to the back, as shown.

The die is 3 in. square on all sides, and is constructed of two pieces, 3 in. square; two pieces, 2 3/4 in. by 3 in., and two pieces, 2 3/4 in. square. These are fastened together with 1/2-in. brads. The tin, forming the false die, is cut out as shown in Fig. 2, and is then bent on the dotted lines and soldered together on the joint formed by the two edges E and F. All parts should be painted a dull black with white spots on the die and false die.

The trick is performed as follows: Procure a hat from some one in the audience and place in it the die with the tin false die covering three sides of the block, at the same time telling the audience that the block will be caused to pass from the hat into the

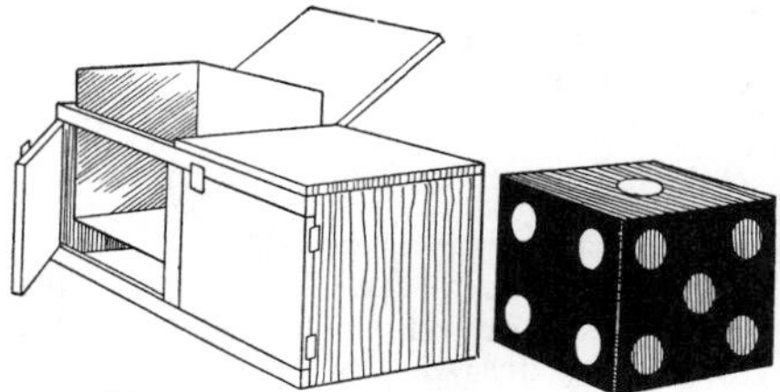

With the False Die in Place It Appears as If the Box Were Empty

box, the latter being placed some distance away. Inform the audience that it would be more difficult for the die to pass from the box into the hat. Remove the tin piece from the hat and leave the die, holding the surfaces of the false die toward the audience. This will give the impression that the die has been removed. Set the hat on the table above the level of the eyes of the audience. With the back of the box toward the audience, open one top door and insert the tin piece in the right-hand compartment so that one side touches the back, another the

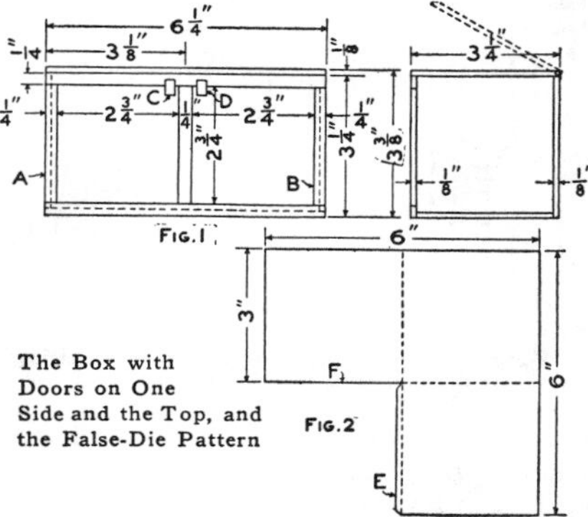

The Box with Doors on One Side and the Top, and the False-Die Pattern

side and the other the bottom of the box. Close the door and open the two doors of the opposite compartment which, when shown, will appear to be empty. Tilt the box to this side and open the doors of the side opposite to the one just opened, which, of course, will be empty. This should be done several times until some one asks that all doors be opened at the same time. After a few more reversals and openings as given, open all doors and show it empty, then take the die from the hat.—Contributed by Harold L. Groesbeck, Salt Lake City, Utah.

Homemade Pantograph

The pantograph consists of four pieces of wood, the dimensions depending somewhat on the size of the work to be drawn. A convenient size for ordinary drawing and enlarging is

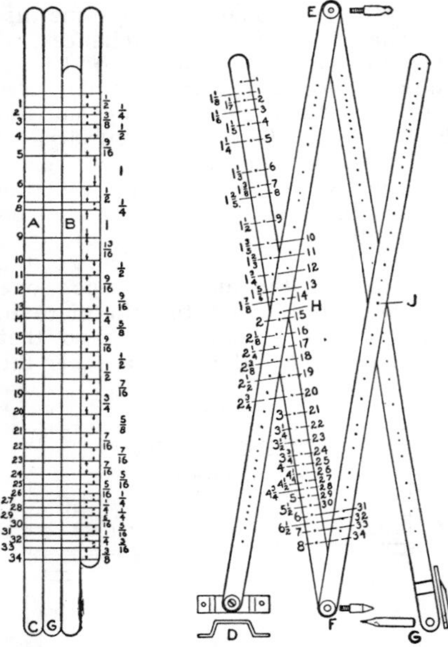

A Picture can be Enlarged or Reduced by Setting the Screweyes in the Holes Designated

constructed of four pieces of hardwood, preferably maple, $\frac{3}{16}$ in. thick and 5/8 in. wide, two of them 20¾ in. in length and the other two, 18¾ in. long. These are planed and sandpapered and the ends cut round.

All four pieces are laid flat on a level board or bench top with their edges together so that the edges of the two longer pieces make right angles with a line drawn tangent to their ends. One end of one short piece is placed flush with the lower ends of the two long pieces, and one end of the other short piece flush with the upper ends, as shown. They should be clamped down solidly to keep them from moving while laying off the divisions. Light lines are drawn across their faces as designated by the dimensions. On these lines and exactly in the center of the pieces make small marks with a pencil point. Through the pieces A and B holes are drilled to snugly receive the body of a small screweye. The other two pieces are drilled with a smaller drill so that the threads of the screweye will take hold in the wood.

The end C of the piece A has a metal stand made of brass as shown at D. This is fastened to the end of the wood with a small bolt. The hole should be a snug fit over the body of the bolt. The lower ends of the brass are drilled to admit thumb tacks for holding it to the drawing board.

The joint at E is made of a suitable binding post that can be procured at an electrical shop, the shank below the two joined pieces to be the same length as the height of the metal stand D. The end should be filed round and polished so that it will slip over the board or paper easily.

The stylus or tracing point F is made of another binding post, in the same manner, but instead of a rounding end a slightly blunt, pointed end is filed on it. The end of the piece G is strengthened by gluing a small block of the same material on both upper and under side. A hole is then made through them to receive a pencil rather tightly.

The holes, as will be seen, are numbered from 1 to 34. At the crossing of each pair, H and J, the screweyes must be set in the holes numbered alike on both pieces of each pair. This will insure the proper working of the parts. The other numbers designate how much the instrument will enlarge a picture or reduce it. On the pair not numbered in the sketch the numbers run in the opposite direction.

The end C is fastened to the left side of the drawing board, the picture to be enlarged is placed under the stylus or tracer point, and the paper under the pencil point G. Move the tracing point over the general outline of the picture without making any line before starting, so as to make sure that the paper and picture are located right. It is then only necessary to take hold of the pencil and move it over the paper while watching the tracer point to keep it following the lines of the picture. To make a reduced picture, the original is placed under G, the tracer point changed to G and the pencil to F.

Trapping Mosquitoes

Mosquitoes that light on the ceiling may be easily destroyed with the instrument shown in the sketch. It consists of a cover, such as used on jelly glasses, nailed to the end of an old broom handle. A little kerosene oil is placed in the cover and the device is passed closely beneath the location of the mosquitoes. They will be overcome by the fumes and drop into the fluid as soon as it comes under them. —Contributed by J. J. Kolar, Maywood, Ill.

Pen Rack on an Ink Bottle

A piece of wire, about 1 ft. long, is bent into the shape shown and slipped over the neck of the ink bottle. The ends forming the loop around the neck should fit tightly. The upper part of the wire is shaped to hold the penholder.—Contributed by W. A. Saul, E. Lexington, Mass.

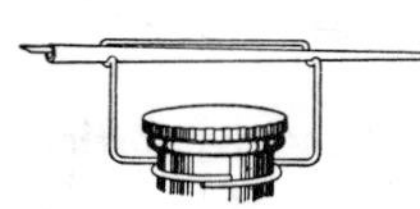

Substitute for a Broken Bench-Vise Nut

It is frequently the case that the nut on a bench-vise screw breaks from being subjected to a too violent strain. If one is working in a place where a new nut cannot be obtained, the broken part may be replaced by the substitute shown in the sketch. Any piece of strap iron may be used, and with a round file and a drill the two pieces can soon be made and attached to the bench with screws or bolts. A slight twist of the shaped ends is necessary to make them fit the angle of the thread. —Contributed by Oscar M. Waddell, Lamedeer, Mont.

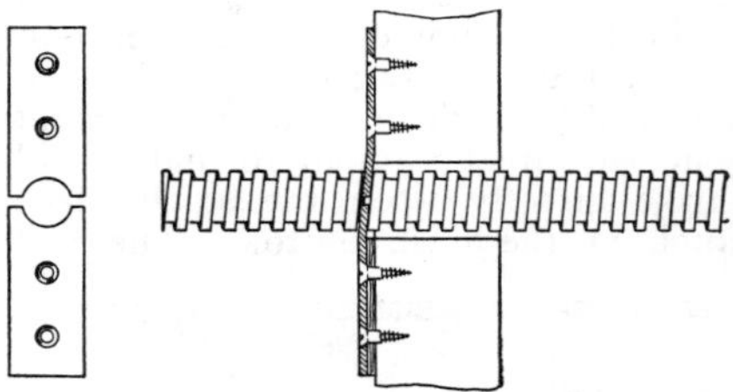

Two Pieces of Strap Iron Shaped to Fit the Square Thread Make a Good Substitute Nut

Scissors Sharpener

Procure an ordinary wood clothespin and drill a 1/8-in. hole through its blades, then insert a piece of hardened 1/8-in. drill rod, which should be a driving fit. In using this device, take the scissors and attempt to cut the steel rod. Do this three or four times and a good cutting edge will be obtained.—Contributed by Wm. J. Tolson, Lyons, Iowa.

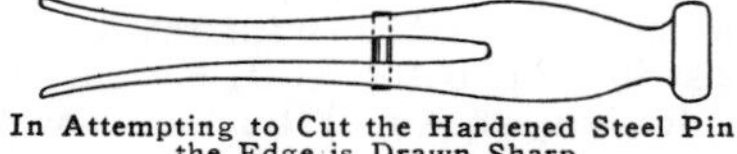

In Attempting to Cut the Hardened Steel Pin the Edge is Drawn Sharp

¶An imitation-gold color may be made with flake white, ground in varnish and tinted with a touch of vermilion. When striping or lettering is done with this, it will have the appearance of real gilding work.

Floor Push Button

An ordinary electric push button can be used for a floor push button by placing it on a bracket or shelf attached to a joist, as shown, and using a nail for the extension push. A ¼-in. hole is bored through the floor, also through a small piece of wood fastened beneath the floor, at the right place to direct the nail so that it will strike directly upon the small black knob of the push button. The nail

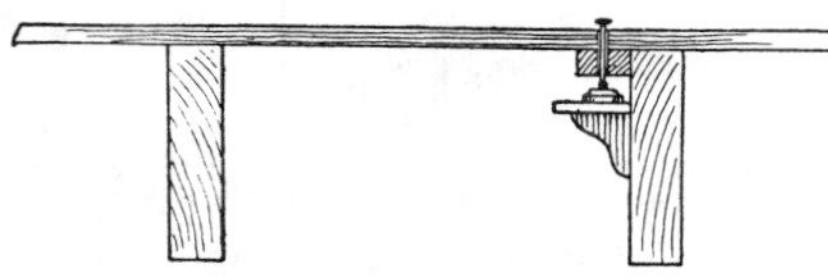

Push Button on Joist

should be just long enough to rest lightly on the knob.—Contributed by Reginald R. Insole, Hamilton, Can.

A Wrist Brace

To strengthen a weak wrist, take a piece of leather, preferably white oak tanned, 2 in. wide and 14 in. long, and carefully shave it down with a sharp knife, until it is $\frac{1}{16}$ in. thick. Then cut it as shown in Fig. 1, the wide part or body being 7 in. long, and the narrow part or neck, 6 in. long and 1 in. wide. Cut a semicircular hole, 1 in. from the extreme end of the body, ½ in. wide and 1¼ in. long, to allow the neck to slip through, then punch three holes in each end and lace with rawhide or shoestring, or, better still, if you happen to have a small buckle, sew it neatly to the body. It looks better

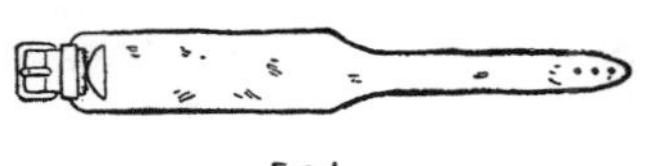

Fig. 1 Fig. 2

Brace Made of Leather

and saves time in adjusting. When complete and on the wrist, it will appear as in Fig. 2.—Contributed by J. H. Harris, Berkeley, Cal.

Protecting a Kettle Handle from Heat

The wood handle of a kettle or cooking utensil when not in use usually comes in contact with the side of the vessel and it will absorb enough heat each time to finally char and crack the wood.

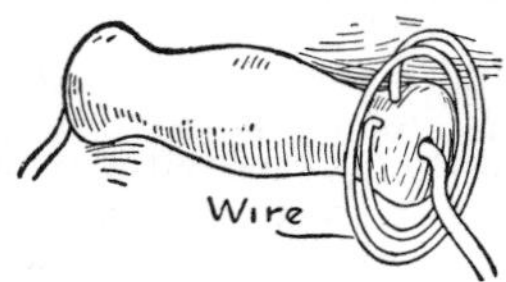

The heat of the handle at times is so intense that it often results in a burned hand. The spiral metal handle provides a way for cooling by exposing a considerable surface to the air, yet the metal retains the heat so that many times it is too hot to handle. If a wood handle is provided with a coil of wire as shown in the accompanying sketch, the wood cannot come in contact with the side of the heated vessel and the air encircling the wood prevents it from getting too hot to handle. The spiral can be attached to a metal handle with solder.

Tin Can Used for Watering Chickens

An ordinary discarded tomato can makes a good watering vessel for young chickens. Care must be taken in opening the can to cut the tin so the cover will hinge. Cut the tin about 1½ in. from the bottom so that it will form a U-shaped piece as shown in the

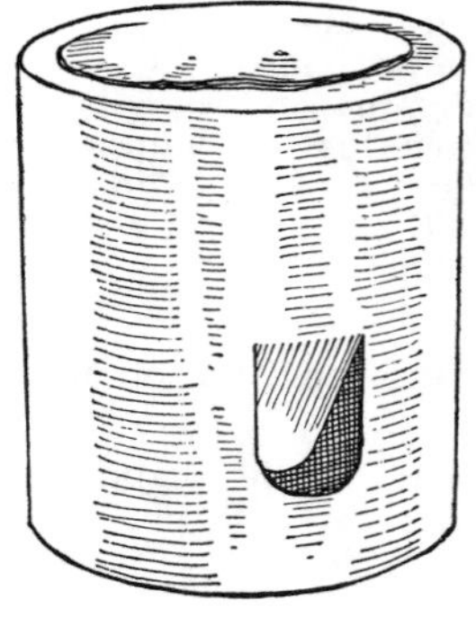

sketch and push the hanging portion in the can. Fill the can up to the opening with water, close the cover and set it in the coop.—Contributed by L. Alberta Norrell, Augusta, Ga.

How to Make a Hurdle

The hurdle consists of two standards, a reach, and a swing. The swing is first made in the shape of a rectangle of four pieces of wood, about 7/8 in. thick and 1 1/2 in. wide, of which two are 36 in. and the others 18 in. long. These pieces are nailed together in the manner shown.

Each standard is made of three pieces of wood, 7/8 in. thick, 3 in. wide, and 18 in. long. Nail the pieces firmly together, as shown, and connect their bases with another piece of the same material, 36 in. long. When this is finished, connect the swing to the standards with long nails, A, at the ends slightly off center. Before inserting the nails, make the holes in each standard to receive them large enough to permit the nails to turn freely without allowing the heads to pass through. Thus the frame will swing freely at the slightest touch of the jumper's foot, and right itself immediately. — Contributed by C. C. Fraser, Saginaw, Mich.

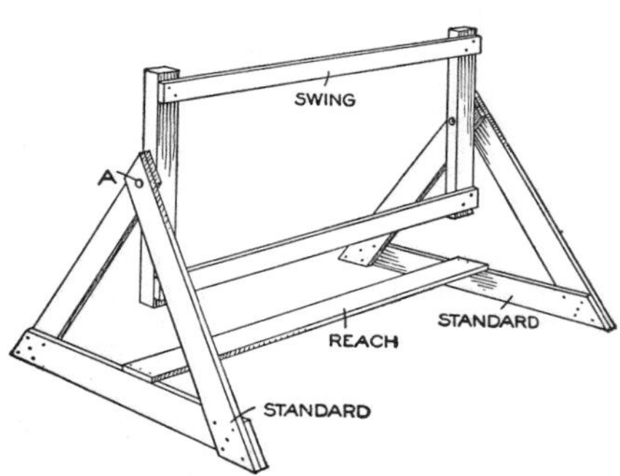

The Swing of the Hurdle will Turn When Slightly Touched and Right Itself Again

Oil Burner for a Cook Stove

The parts of the burner consist of ordinary gas pipe and fittings. The pipe in which the kerosene oil is converted into gas is 1/2 in. in diameter and is connected to a supply tank of oil with 1/4-in. pipe.

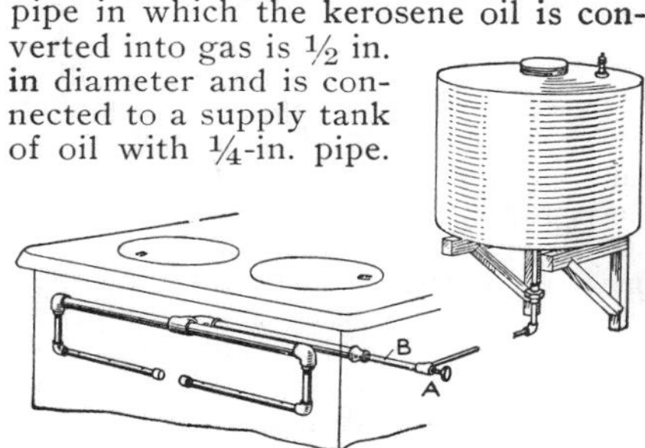

A Very Cheap Grade of Kerosene Oil can be Used in This Burner with Success

The burner part is also constructed of 1/4-in. pipe having three 1/16-in. holes drilled in each end for the gas to escape where it burns. These burners are located just beneath the large pipe so that the flames will heat it and convert the oil into gas. A needle valve, A, is used to control the flow of oil. The burner is placed in the fire box of the stove, and the pipes connected through a hole drilled in the stove door, at B.

The tank may be rectangular or round and should be of sufficient strength to withstand 5 or 10 lb. of pressure. The top of the tank has a pet cock where a connecting hose from an air pump may be attached. The tank is filled about half full and just a little pressure of air is put on the oil. To start the burner, run a little oil in a pan or fire shovel and light it so that the flames will convert the oil into gas in the large pipe, then turn the valve A and regulate the flame.—Contributed by Robert Hays, Siloam Springs, Ark.

A Fish Stringer

The illustration shows a very simple and inexpensive device for the angler to string and carry fish. It is

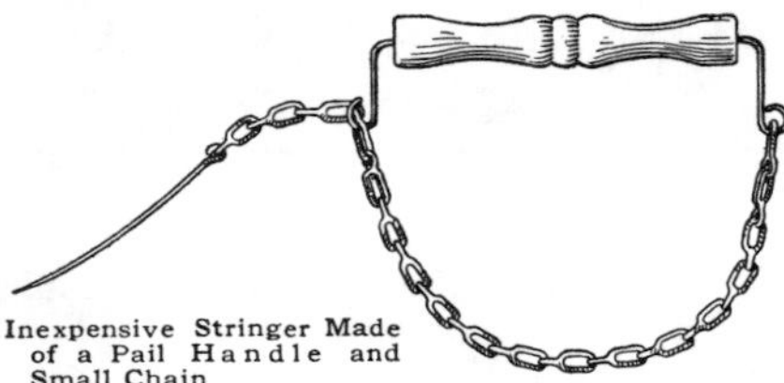

Inexpensive Stringer Made of a Pail Handle and Small Chain

made of a pail handle through which is passed a piece of soft wire, having sufficient length for bends or loops at each end, and a piece of chain. A chain 18 in. long is sufficient. One end of the chain is fastened in the loop at one end of the handle, and the other has a piece of wire attached for pushing through the gills of the fish. The other end of the wire through the handle is arranged in a hook to catch into the links of the chain.—Contributed by G. O. Reed, Stratford, Canada.

Substitutes for Drawing Instruments

Three of the most used draftsman's instruments are the compass, ruler and square or triangle. When it is necessary to make a rough drawing and no instruments are at hand, common and easily obtainable things can be used as substitutes.

A sheet of heavy paper folded as

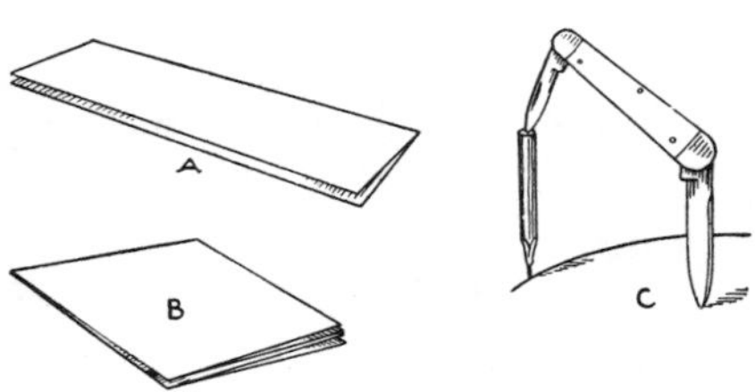

A Compass, Ruler and Square Made of Ordinary Things at Hand

shown at A will serve as a ruler, and the same sheet given another fold will make the square B. If given another fold diagonally, a 45-deg. triangle is formed. A substitute compass is readily made of a short pencil and a pocket knife, as shown at C.—Contributed by Jas. J. Joyce, Olongopo, Philippine Islands.

How to Make an Aspirator

A simple aspirator that may be used for a number of different purposes, such as accelerating the process of filtering, emptying water from tubs, producing a partial vacuum in vessels in which coils are being boiled in paraffin, etc., may be constructed as follows: Obtain two pieces of brass tubing of the following dimensions: one 7 in. long and 3/4 in. outside diameter, and the other, 3 in. long and 1/4 in. outside diameter. Drill a hole in one side of the large tube, about 3 in. from one end, of such a diameter that

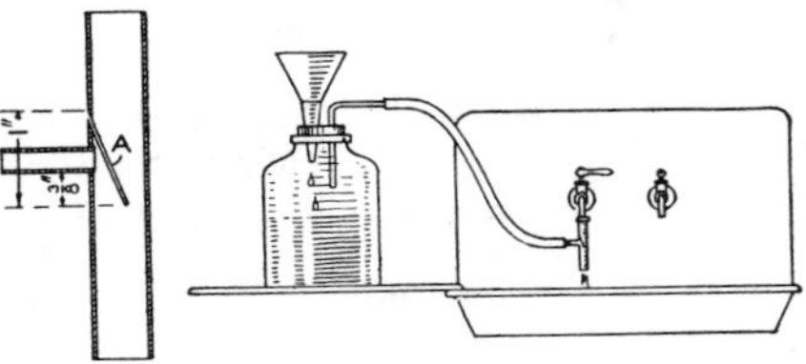

Detail of the Aspirator and Its Connections to a Faucet, for Increasing the Speed of Filtration

the small brass tube will fit it very tightly. Take an ordinary hacksaw and cut a slot in the side of the large piece, as shown at A. This slot is sawed diagonally across the tube and extends from one side to the center. Obtain a piece of sheet brass that will fit into this slot tightly, and then solder it and the small tube into the large tube. The slot and hole for the small tube should be so located with respect to each other that the small tube will empty into the larger one directly against the piece of sheet brass soldered in the slot.

The upper end of the large tube should be threaded inside to fit over the threads on the faucet, or an attachment soldered to it similar to those on the end of an ordinary garden hose. A rubber hose should be attached to the small tube and connected, as shown, to a piece of glass tubing that is sealed in the cork in the top of the large bottle. The funnel holding the filter paper is also sealed into the cork. Melted paraffin may be used in sealing the glass tube, funnel and cork in place, the object being to make them airtight. The filter paper should be folded so that it sticks tightly against the sides of the funnel when the liquid is poured in, thus preventing any air from entering the bottle between the paper and the funnel. Turn on the faucet, and it will be found that the time required to filter any liquid will be greatly reduced. Be careful, however, not to turn on too much water, as the suction may then be too strong and the filter paper become punctured.

A Key-Holder Hook

A good hook for hanging keys, toothbrushes and other small articles can be made from ordinary wire staples, as shown at A. One leg of the staple is cut away as shown at B and the other leg driven into the board as shown at C. These will answer the purpose as well as screw-hooks.—Contributed by W. C. Heidt, Chicago.

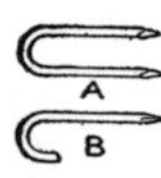

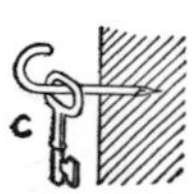

A Hand Hoe

A hand hoe, especially adapted for weeding or cultivating small truck, particularly onions, can be made of a piece of hard wood, 7/8 by 1 3/4 in. by 4 ft. long, and a piece of old bucksaw blade. A blade, 18 in. long and 2 in. wide, bent into a loop is attached with bolts to the handle.—Contributed by Geo. H. Miller, Iowa City, Iowa.

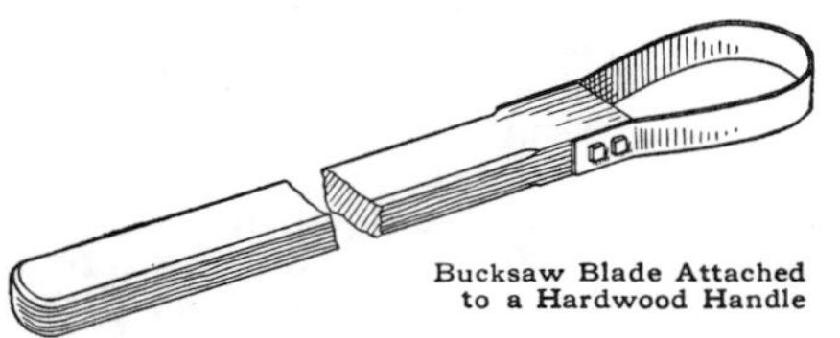

Bucksaw Blade Attached to a Hardwood Handle

Seed Receptacle for Bird-Cages

A handy seed and water container for a bird-cage can be made of a common spice tin. The receptacle can be filled without removal by simply taking off the cover. Thus the seed will not be scattered.

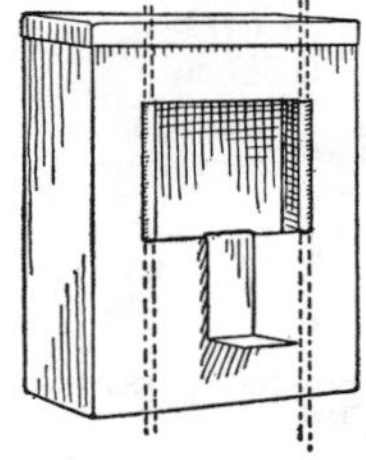

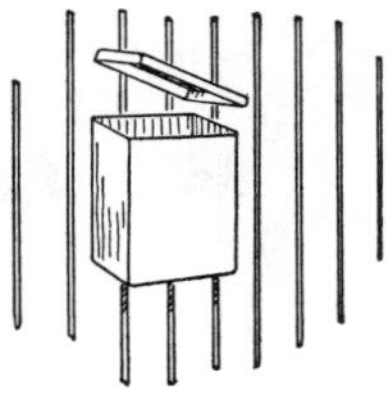

Spice Tin Attached to the Wires of a Bird-Cage for a Water or Seed Receptacle

The tin is attached by cutting a hole in the back as shown, and bending the side edges to fit over the wires to hold it in place. The bottom strip is a support which rests on the floor of the cage and prevents the tin from slipping down on the wires.

Kitchen-Utensil Scraper

A flexible utensil scraper is one of the most useful articles I have in my kitchen. It covers such a large surface in scraping pans, kettles, etc., that this most disagreeable part of the kitchen work is quickly and easily accomplished.

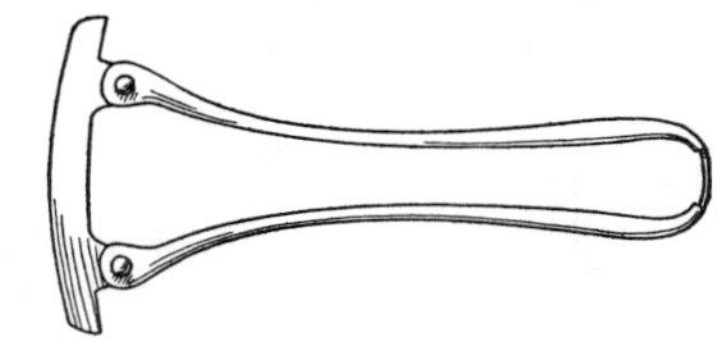

The Blade is Flexible so It can Readily Shape Itself to the Curves of a Kettle

The flexible blade is attached to the tin handles with small rivets. The blade should be thin and narrow enough to allow it to bend. When the handles are pressed together, the blade curves to the shape of the utensil's surface.—Contributed by Mrs. Della Schempp, Brodhead, Wis.

Anchor Posts for a Lawn Swing

A very substantial and convenient base for a lawn swing can be made by using four anchor posts of cement, as

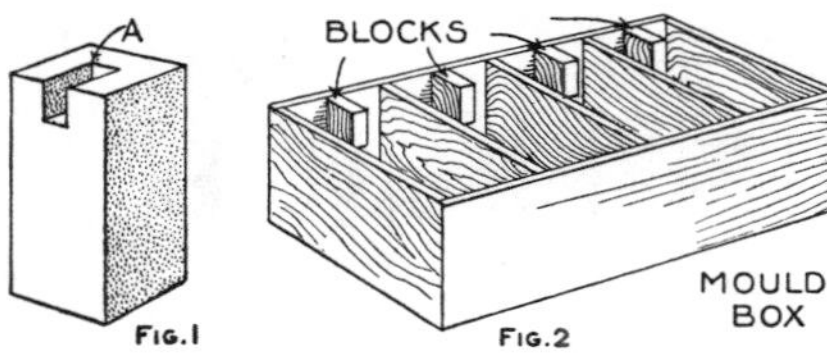

An Anchor Post of Cement and a Mold Box for Shaping Four Posts at a Time

shown in Fig. 1. The posts are made with a recess, A, to receive the legs of the swing, and of any suitable size. They may be placed with the upper face on a level with the lawn, or higher if desired.

A rough mold box, Fig. 2, lined with paper, will do for making the posts. The box does not require any top or bottom; it is simply placed on a board and lifted away when the blocks are thoroughly dried. If the blocks are leveled when placed in the earth, the swing may be taken down and erected again without the usual leveling and bracing.—Contributed by James M. Kane, Doylestown, Pa.

Automatic Filter

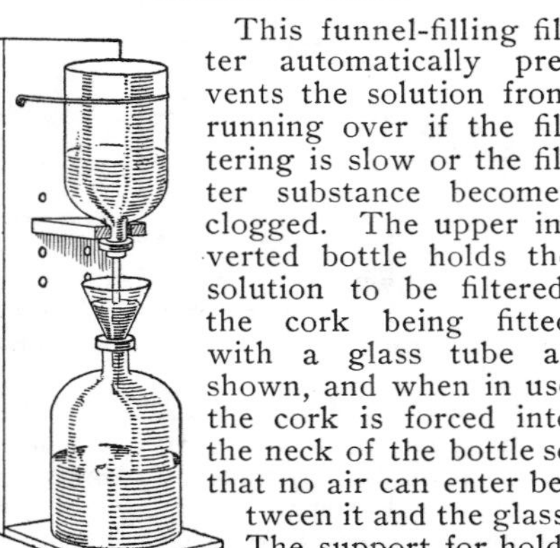

This funnel-filling filter automatically prevents the solution from running over if the filtering is slow or the filter substance becomes clogged. The upper inverted bottle holds the solution to be filtered, the cork being fitted with a glass tube as shown, and when in use the cork is forced into the neck of the bottle so that no air can enter between it and the glass. The support for holding the bottles has two brackets, one to fit the neck of the upper bottle and the other used as a shelf for the receiving bottle. In operation, the solution runs from the upper bottle into the funnel, holding the filter paper, but it cannot fill the funnel completely, because the end of the glass tube is lower than the edge of the funnel, and as soon as the liquid in the funnel covers the end of the tube, all inflow of air into the upper bottle is stopped, and, thereby, further flow of the solution into the funnel prevented, until enough has filtered through to uncover the end of the tube and thus permit air to again enter the upper bottle.—Contributed by G. Simons, Chicago.

Grinding Scissors

Whether a pair of scissors be ground or filed, the marks or scratches left from the contact with the abrasive should all extend across the bevel in

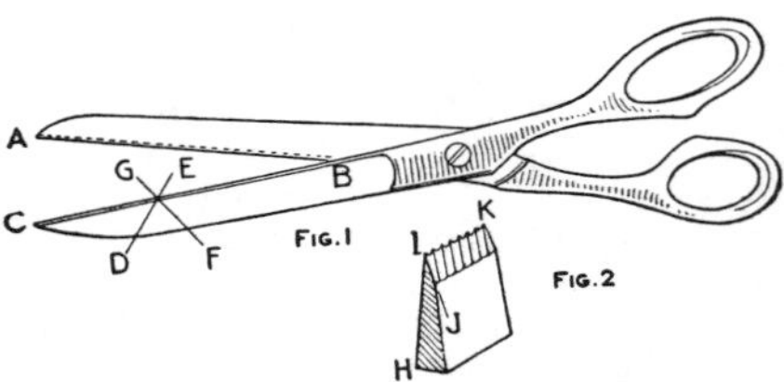

The Direction of the Grinding Tool should be Slightly Sloping Toward the Handles

the direction of the line ED, Fig. 1, and never in the direction of the line GF. If the cutting edge be examined under a magnifying glass, the tool marks or scratches left by the sharpening process will be very plainly seen, and where these scratches intersect with the face HI, Fig. 2, of the blade, they will appear as teeth along the cutting edge IK.

As a pair of scissors close, the natural tendency is to thrust the material to be cut out of the angle ABC, Fig. 1, but if these small teeth formed on the cutting edge point in the direction of the line ED, this slipping action is prevented or retarded because the fibrous material adheres to the fine teeth on the cutting edge of the blades.

Wet paper, silks, mohair cloths, etc., can be sheared with perfect ease and dispatch, when scissors are sharpened in this manner. The same principle holds good for metal snips.

The angle HIJ, Fig. 2, varies according to the material to be cut, and the type of shear. A greater angle is required on metal shears than on shears for domestic uses.—Contributed by A. Clifton, Chicago.

To Repair a Leak in a Canoe

After striking some rocks with our canoe, it sprung three very bad leaks. These were effectively patched with pieces of cheesecloth, well soaked in liquid shellac, which were pasted on the outside of the leak. After allowing this to set for a few hours, it will be almost impossible to remove the patch. This is an inexpensive and almost invariably a sure remedy for leaks. When the cloth is dry, paint it over with the same color as the boat, and the repair can scarcely be seen.—Contributed by William B. Smith, New York City.

Holder for Loose Window Glass

When the putty becomes loose and the glazing points work out on window glass, temporary repairs may be made by using a small piece of tin or sheet iron bent as shown in the sketch. The clip is inserted under the edge of the glass and hooked over the back of the sash parts. This will hold the glass firmly in place and also prevent rattling.

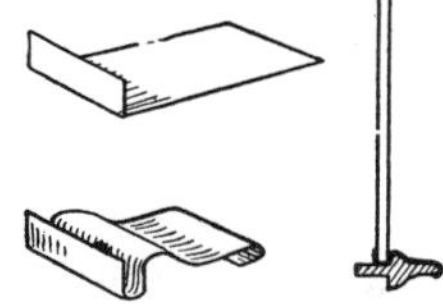

A Homemade Bench Vise

A form of a bench vise that can be easily made and attached to a workbench is shown in the illustration. This vise requires no screw, and the parts can be made from scrap material.

The substitute A for the screw is a rectangular piece of wood and is fastened with a tenon in a mortise cut in the vise jaw B. The clamping arrangement consists of a strap, C, attached to the piece A, then run over a pulley, D, and fastened to a foot pedal, E. The foot pedal is fulcrumed on a crosspiece of the bench and has a ratchet so as to hold it when the vise is set. The lower end of the vise is fitted with the usual form of device for parallel adjustment. A coil spring is located in the center for use in quickly opening the vise when the foot pedal is released.—Contributed by A. C. Westby, Porter, Minn.

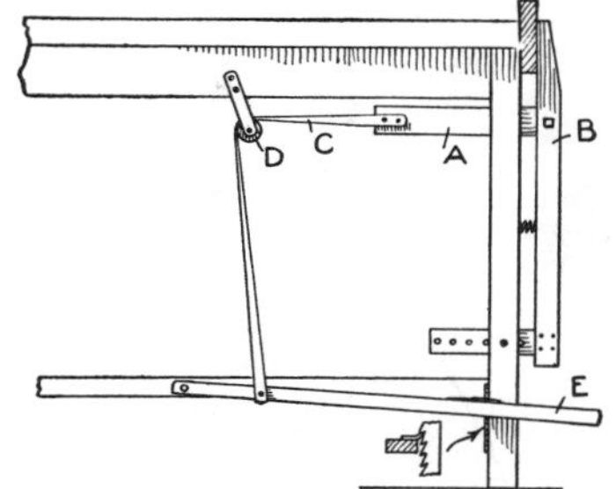

The Vise Jaw as It is Attached to the Bench and the Substitute Screw Arrangement

A Cover Strainer

Quite frequently the cook or housewife wishes to pour the hot water or liquid from boiling vegetables or other foods without removing the solids from the kettle. This is easily accomplished, if small holes are drilled in the cover as shown in the sketch. The saucepan or kettle can be tilted and the liquid drains through the holes. Further, the steam from cooking food can readily escape through the holes, thus preventing the cover from vibrating, or the liquids from boiling over.

A Sufficient Number of Holes are Drilled in the Edge of the Cover to Make a Strainer

Homemade Corn Sheller

Where there is but a small quantity of corn to be shelled a sheller can be made of a few scraps of wood usually

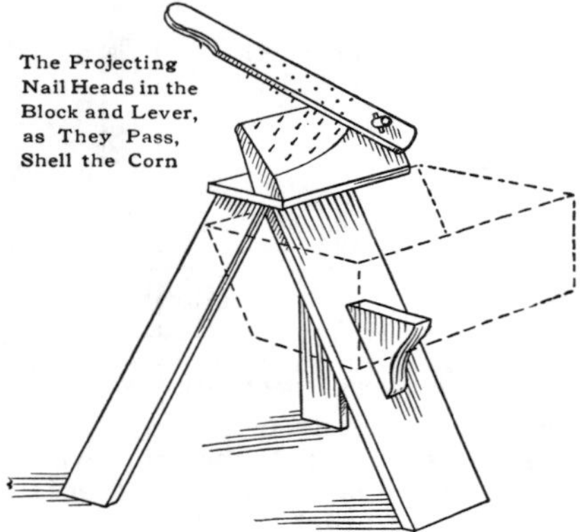

The Projecting Nail Heads in the Block and Lever, as They Pass, Shell the Corn

found on a farm. A block of wood having a sloping notch cut from one end is mounted on three legs as shown. The notched part as well as the lever is thickly filled with spikes driven in so that their heads protrude about ½ in.

The ear of corn is placed in the notched part and the lever pressed down. Two or three strokes of the lever will remove all the kernels from the cob. A box is provided and conveniently located on one leg to catch the shelled corn.—Contributed by A. S. Thomas, Gordon, Ont.

An Ornamental Metal Flatiron Holder

This antique iron holder or stand can be easily constructed by the amateur bent-iron worker. A strip of iron is bent over at the ends to form the side legs, and the front leg is formed of another piece, welded in the center.

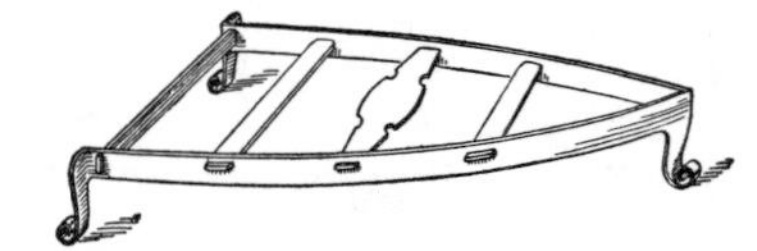

Ornamental Stand Made of Either Strap Iron or Sheet Metal to Hold a Flatiron

Openings for the crosspieces are then cut, the legs bent into a scroll shape, and the crosspieces inserted and fastened by spreading or upsetting the ends.

Instead of using strap iron, the stand can be cut from good sheet metal. This would save the trouble of welding on the front leg.

How to Make a Watch Demagnetizer

A watch demagnetizer that will give excellent satisfaction may be made as follows:

Procure a sheet of $\frac{1}{16}$-in. brass, 3¼ in. by 7 in. Bend this piece of brass around a piece of hard wood having a rectangular cross section of 2½ in. by 1 in. The joint between the two ends should be made on one side, and the edges should lack about ⅛ in. of touching. Next obtain two pieces of ⅛-in. brass, 3¾ in. by 3 in., and cut an opening in each of these, 2⅝ in. by 1⅛ in., as shown in the sketch. Bend one edge of each of these pieces over at right angles to the main portion of the piece. Solder these two pieces on the ends of the rectangular

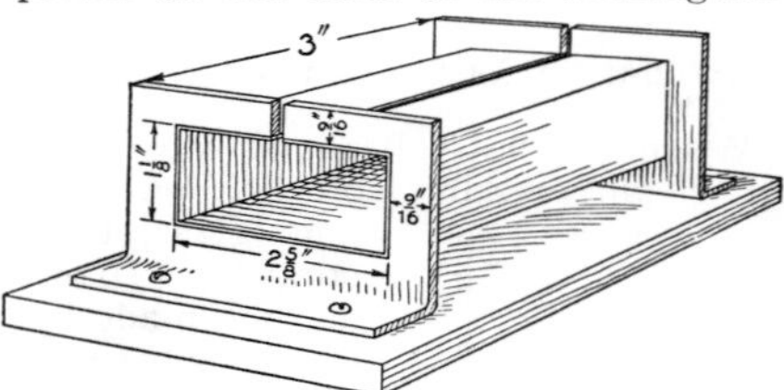

Dimensioned Parts for the Construction of the Core over Which the Insulated Wire is Wound

tube of brass and cut a slot in each of them to correspond to the one in the rectangular tube. Place the rectangular piece of wood back in the tube and you are ready for the winding. Use No. 18 gauge single cotton-covered copper wire and fill the winding space. Several layers of paper should be placed on the brass tube and between the layers of wire, to serve as an insulation. Holes may be drilled in the projecting portions on the ends and the coil can then be mounted on a wooden base. Mount two binding posts on this base and connect the terminals of the winding to them.

To use the demagnetizer, connect it to a 110-volt alternating-current circuit with a rheostat in circuit of such a form that the current will not exceed three amperes and that it may be reduced to practically zero in value by increasing the resistance of the rheostat. The magnetic field inside the coil is rapidly changing in direction and will tend to destroy any permanent magnetism that may be possessed by an object placed inside of it. The full current of three amperes should be allowed to pass through the winding for a few minutes after the object to be demagnetized is inserted, and then gradually reduced, and the object removed.

Remodeling a Talking Machine

Having a talking machine of an old model with a tapered horn I decided to change it into a more modern type, and this was accomplished as follows: An auxiliary base was constructed of ½-in. wood on which to set the part which revolves the disks. The inside of this base is so constructed as to form a horn or sounding box. The two sides and sloping bottom of the horn-part are made of ¼-in. wood. The form of this box is shown in Fig. 1. The dimensions should be determined according to the size of the talking machine.

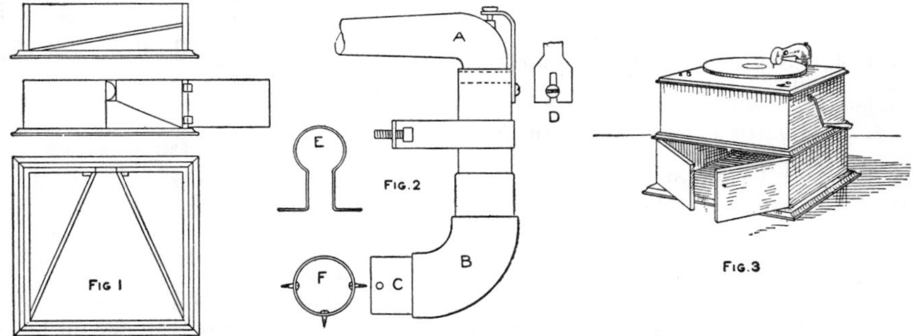

The Horn or Sounding Box is Constructed in the Auxiliary Base and the Part for Connecting the Sounding Tube to the Box Consists of Ordinary Gas Pipe Fastened with a Clip at the Back

The connecting parts to the original horn were turned downward, as shown at A, Fig. 2, with the opening entering a piece of ordinary gas pipe of sufficient length to allow an elbow with a nipple to enter the auxiliary base. The pivot-holding device for connection A is shown at D. The parts are attached to the box with a clasp, E, and with three screws in the nipple C, the end view of which is shown at F. The talking machine is placed on the auxiliary base as shown in Fig. 3. This construction produces a talking machine on the order of a cabinet machine without the tapering horn.—Contributed by H. W. J. Lomglatz, Harrisburg, Pa.

Needle for Sewing Burlap

A needle for sewing burlap can be easily made of the ordinary opener that comes with sardine cans. All that is necessary to convert this tool into a needle is to grind the blunt end to a sharp point, as shown in the sketch.—Contributed by G. C. Beven, Sault Ste. Marie, Ont.

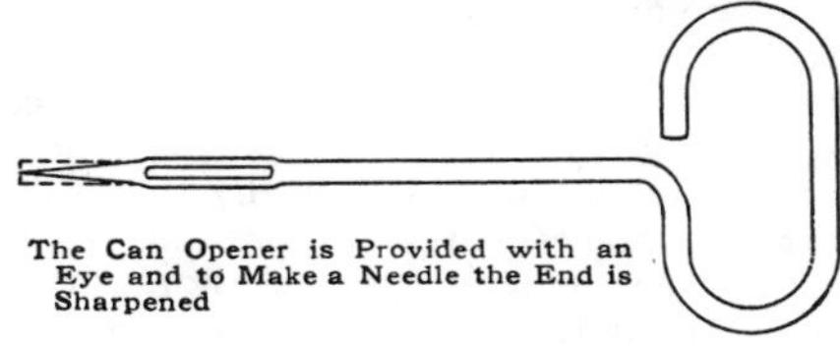
The Can Opener is Provided with an Eye and to Make a Needle the End is Sharpened

A Mysterious Revolving Wheel

The mystery of this wheel is that it seems to revolve automatically without any visible external power. It is at the same time an amusing trick and an instructive experiment. The apparatus required is very simple and can be made at home.

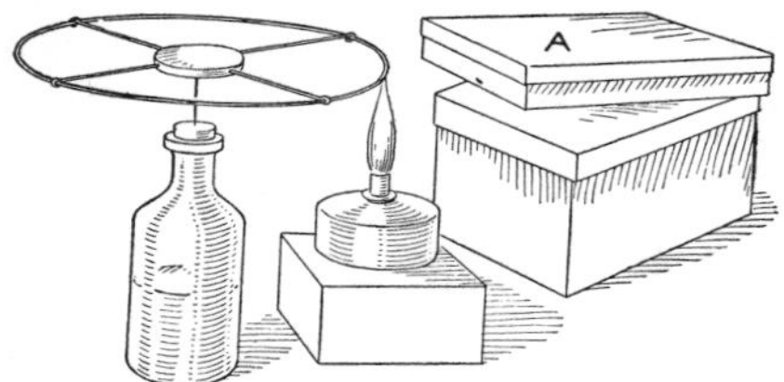

The Wheel as It is Mounted on a Needle, and Lamp and Box Containing Magnet to Make It Turn

A glass bottle is half filled with sand and water, so that it will stand securely, and a cork placed in the neck. Into this cork a needle should be inserted so that it projects perpendicularly, which is most easily done by heating one end of the needle to a red heat and then pushing it into the cork as deeply as possible. Into a disk of cork of suitable thickness and at four points on its side, at equal distances apart, are inserted four pieces of copper wire of the same length, each bent at the outer end to form a hook—these copper wires thus forming the spokes of the wheel. The rim is made of a small iron wire bent in a circular shape and held in the hooks on the ends of the copper wires. The now completed wheel is balanced on the free point on the needle, so that it can turn easily.

Place an alcohol lamp in such a position that when it is lighted the tip of the flame will just reach the rim of the wheel. (Any other flame that will not soot the rim may be used.) In the box A, placed with its bottom level with the wheel, put a horseshoe magnet so that the flame is opposite one of its poles. After the lamp has been lighted for a few seconds, the wheel will begin to revolve, seemingly without cause. Why does it do so? Because the magnet magnetizes or attracts the part of the ring nearest it while cold, but not when it is glowing. Instead, it will attract the cooler part of the ring nearest behind the flame and so on, the wheel thus spinning round, faster in the same proportion as the magnet is stronger and the iron rim smaller.

If this experiment is shown before spectators as a trick, the performer may say to the audience that he alone can make the wheel spin around without touching it. Should some one accept his challenge, he may, in a careless way, move the box containing the magnet away or turn it around so that it will not influence the iron ring and then, of course, the wheel will remain immovable.

How to Make a Rabbet Plane

A rabbet plane is very little used by mechanics, but when it is wanted for a piece of work, it is wanted badly. While doing an unusual piece of work I needed a rabbet plane, and having none, I made a plane as shown in the sketch in less time than it would have taken to go out and borrow one.

The body of the plane was made of a piece of 2 by 4-in. pine, 1 ft. long. A 1-in. chisel was used for the bit. A place was marked on one side of the wood to be cut out for the chisel, and a 1-in. hole bored through, the narrow way, so that one edge of the bit cut through the bottom, forming a slit for the edge of the chisel. After cutting a groove for the chisel blade and turning in a long wood screw as shown,

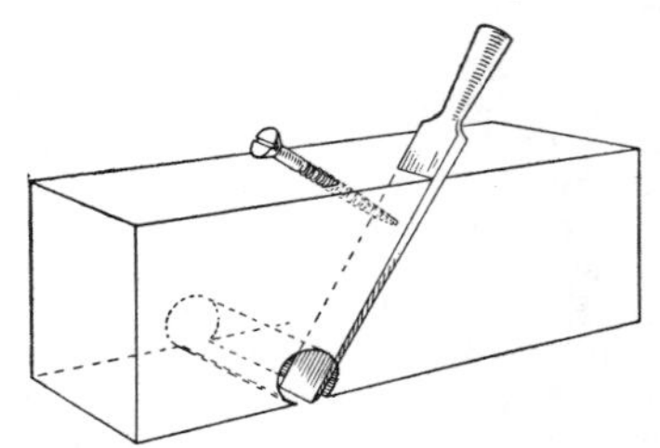

A Plane Made of a Piece of 2 by 4-In. Pine, a Chisel and a Large Wood Screw

to hold the chisel in place, I had as good a rabbet plane as could be purchased.—Contributed by W. H. Young, Thompson, Ga.

Eye Shield for a Microscope

The difficulty and discomfort amateurs experience in learning to use a microscope with both eyes open, or in trying to keep one eye shut, can be easily overcome by attaching a piece of cardboard, similar in shape to the one shown in the sketch, to the barrel of the microscope. The hole A should be of sufficient diameter to allow the cardboard to slide freely up and down on the barrel to the proper adjustment. This simple arrangement will relieve a great deal of the eye strain and will

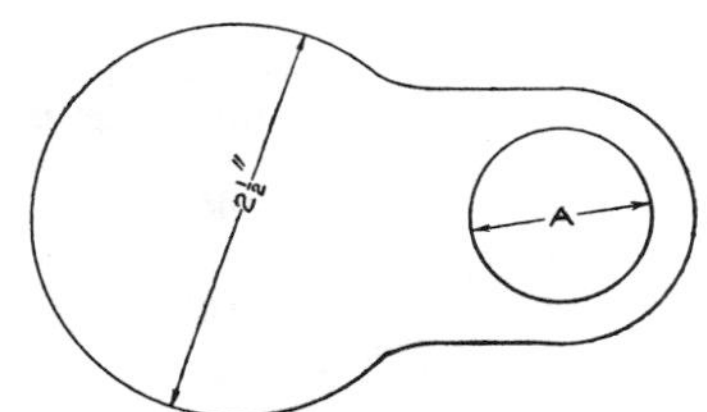

Shield to Cover the Eye That is Not Used When Looking into a Microscope

be of assistance to the most experienced users of microscopes.—Contributed by G. B. Fenton, Charleston, W. Virginia.

Transferring Magazine Pictures

Select pictures from newly printed papers and magazines. Rub wax from a paraffin candle over a sheet of clean white paper, covering a space as large as the picture to be copied. Place the paper, waxed side down, on the picture and while holding it firmly with the fingers of one hand, rub the back thoroughly with some hard substance until all parts of the picture have been gone over. Remove the paper and a perfect copy of the picture will be found upon the waxed side.—Contributed by Kenneth G. Merlin, Brooklyn, N. Y.

A Homemade Egg Separator

Secure some small wire and a very large can. Cut the wire into several pieces and bend them as shown at A,

The Contents of the Egg is Placed on the Wires Which will Separate the Yolk from the White

cut the can and bend the side down as shown and punch holes to receive the upper ends of the wires. Make the holes so that the wires will be about 5/16 in. apart.

A Glue-Spreader Holder

The spreader that is supplied with bottles of liquid glue should not be placed on any surface, as it will soon stick to it. A holder that will keep the spreader in a safe place can be made of a piece of wire which is twisted about the neck of the bottle, as shown in the sketch, and the ends bent up to receive the spreader.

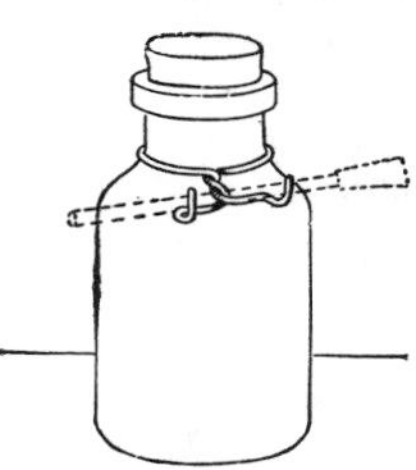

Stop on a Chair Rocker for a Baby

For a baby, too small to rock without tipping the chair over, a small willow or other suitable rocking chair

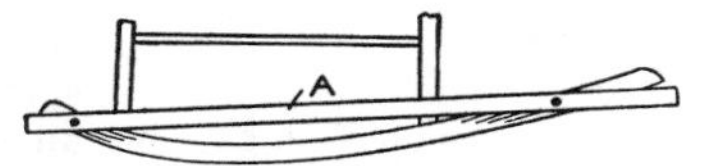

The Strip on the Rocker Prevents the Child Tipping the Chair Too Far Either Way

may be made safe in the following manner:

A strip, A, is fastened on the outside of the rocker with small screws so that it may be removed without injuring the chair. A rubber-covered tack driven in on the under side at each end of the strip modifies the shock and the baby can rock to its heart's content without danger of turning over.—Contributed by Mrs. G. W. Coplin, Bay City, Mich.

Homemade Countersink for Wood

A round or flat-head bolt can be made into a good rosebit or reamer for countersinking holes for screw heads.

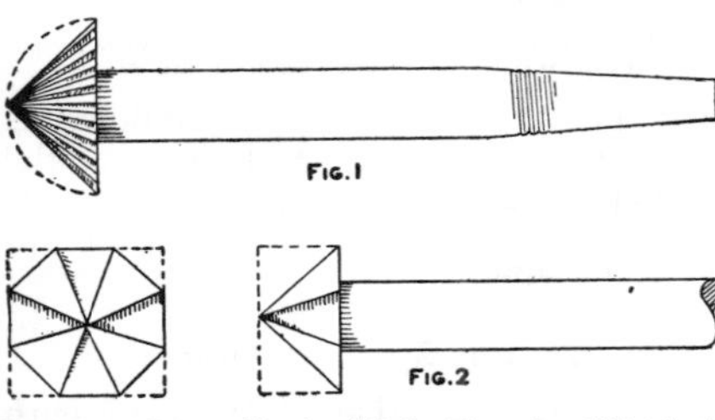

Round and Square Heads of Bolts Shaped and Notched to Make Countersinks

In the illustration, Fig. 1 shows a reamer made of a round-head bolt, and Fig. 2, one made of a square-head bolt. The round-head makes the best reamer as more cutters can be filed in the surface and less work is required to file it into shape.

To Maintain a Constant Level of Liquids in Vessels

It is frequently desirable in laboratory experiments, and in practical work as well, to maintain a constant level in a tank without allowing it to become full. In many cases an outlet pipe at a certain height in the side of the tank is not desirable, and in laboratory experiments with beakers or crocks is, of course, impossible.

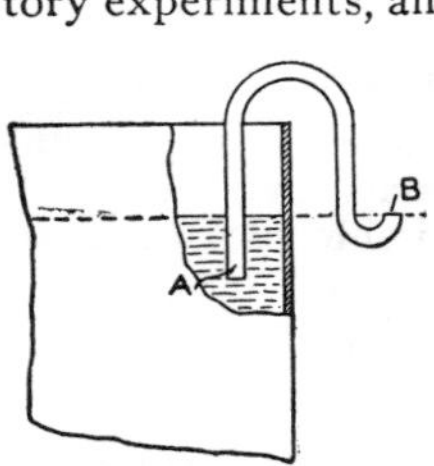

The diagram shows a simple but effective constant-level device. The outer end of the inverted U-tube is curved upward so that it never empties. If desired, the upward curve may be omitted and the straight end immersed in a small vessel of water. All that is necessary now for the successful working of the device is that the inner or tank end, A, of the tube be lower than the outer end—in other words, below the level of the end B—and the inner end below the level of the fluid. Of course, the U-tube must be first filled with liquid and will then act as an intermittent, never-breaking siphon. Should the tank fill above the end B, the siphon drains the fluid down to that level and no lower, even if the inner leg of the tube reach the bottom. To maintain this level against loss by evaporation some slight inflow is necessary.

It will be noted that if the inner end of the siphon were above the outer end, the siphon would break as soon as the liquid in the tank fell to the inner mouth.—Contributed by Harry N. Holmes, Richmond, Ind.

Homemade Electric Bed Warmer

The heat developed by a carbon-filament lamp is sufficiently high to allow its use as a heating element of, for instance, a bed warmer. There are a number of other small heaters which can be easily made and for which lamps form very suitable heating elements, but the bed warmer is probably the best example. All that is required is a tin covering which can be made of an old can about 3½ in. in diameter. The top is cut out and the edge filed smooth. The lamp-socket end of the flexible cord is inserted in the can and the shade holder gripped over the opening. A small lamp of about five candlepower will do the heating.

A flannel bag, large enough to slip over the tin can and provided with a neck that can be drawn together by means of a cord, gives the heater a more finished appearance, as well as making it more pleasant to the touch.

A Flash-Light Telegraph on a Kite Line

An ordinary pocket flash lamp is prepared in the following manner: A brass spring, as shown in the sketch, is bound tightly to the flash lamp with a cord, and two wires, one at each end, are twisted around the lamp's body, forming two loops at the top. The kite string is run through the loops and over the spring. The lamp is then placed near the kite. The ordinary pull on the kite string does not close the spring, but a sharp jerk will pull the string in contact with the push button and its slight pressure

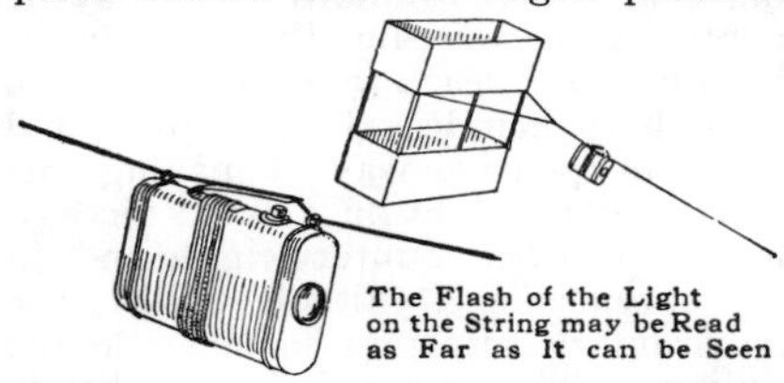

The Flash of the Light on the String may be Read as Far as It can be Seen

causes an instant flash of the light. By this method words may be spelled out in the telegraph code.—Contributed by Joe V. Romig, Allentown, Pa.

Hangers for Barn Tools

Means should be provided to have a place for all the tools used in and about a barn. The forks and shovels are usually stood up in a corner, but they can be more conveniently taken care of by making a hanger for them. The illustration shows how a hanger can be easily made and screwed to the wall of a barn. The hanger is cut from a piece of board and has a hole bored into it the size of the handle on the fork or shovel, then a notch is sawn into the hole to pass the handle through. The board may contain one

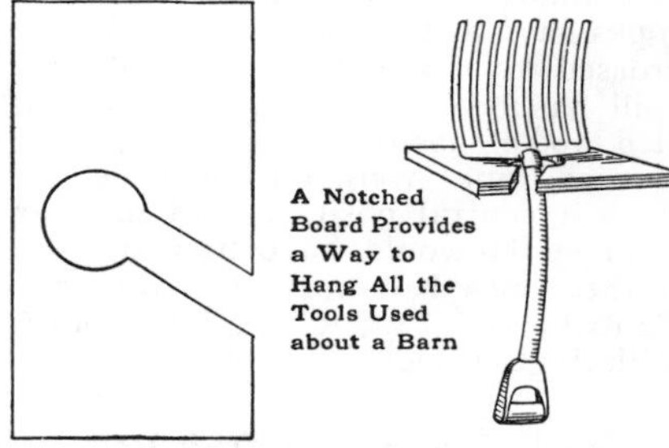

A Notched Board Provides a Way to Hang All the Tools Used about a Barn

or as many notches as there are forks and shovels to be hung on it. The implements are hung with the fork or shovel end upward.—Contributed by R. Snyder, Glidden, Ia.

Guide Ropes on a Bobsled

The sketch shows the front end of a bobsled or double runner made of a plank bolted upon two sleds. The front sled is so pivoted on the bolt A that it may be turned to steer the bob, and to accomplish this result the steersman ordinarily sits with his feet braced against the projecting ends of

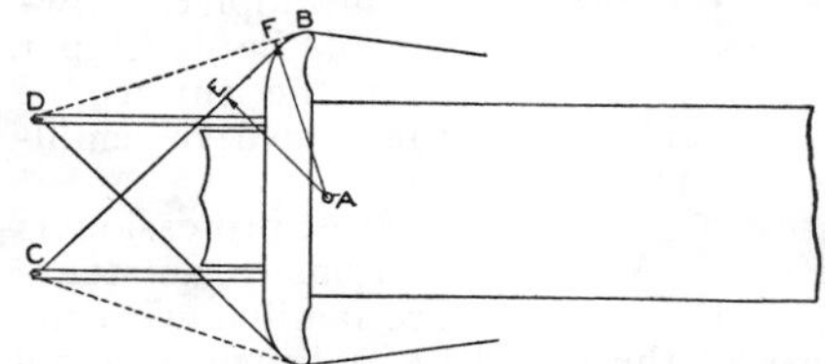

The Most Efficient Way of Attaching Ropes to the Guiding Runners of a Bobsled

the crosspiece and passes the steering ropes outside of his feet, with the ropes crossed as shown. The crossing of the ropes is supposed to add leverage, but that is quite wrong.

The rope, running from B to C, has a lever arm from A to E. If the ropes were not crossed, the rope would lie along the dotted line BD, whose lever arm is the distance AF, which is always greater than AE, therefore the uncrossed ropes have more leverage.

Observe what takes place when the sled is steered to the left: The distance AE decreases much more rapidly than AF, and when the crossed ropes have lost all their power, the uncrossed ropes are still useful. Many a spill has been caused by turning the sled to a position from which the crossed ropes were unable to restore it to a central position, and most of such spills would have been avoided if the ropes had not been crossed.—Contributed by R. R. Raymond, Wilmington, Del.

Brush Hanger for a Dark Room

Necessity may be the mother of invention, but it is also the grandmother of application, and application is the practical side of invention. Both the amateur and the professional photographer have been bothered by spotting and unequal development of negatives and prints in tray development, due to various causes, and sometimes by the presence of dirt particles or the unequal or incomplete flowing of the developer over the surface of the sensitive emulsion.

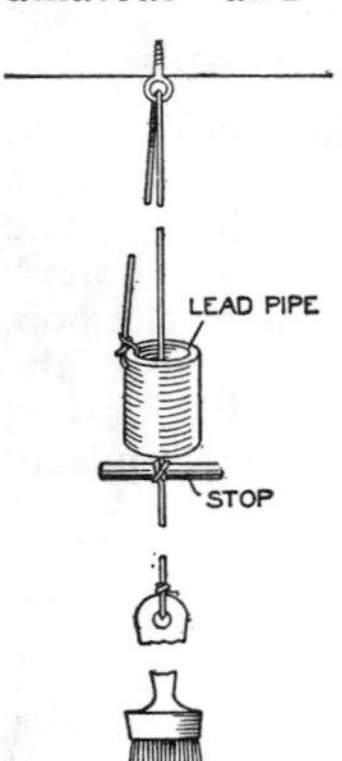

Most professionals and many amateurs are familiar with the use of the camel's-hair brush to avoid failures of this character, and many of them use a brush for local development in certain cases where it is necessary or desirable. Usually the brush is kept in a small glass cup, somewhere close at hand, but it is often in the way when not wanted and misplaced when most needed. The brush can be kept within reach and handy for the operator by arranging a light counterweight and pulley with a string attached to the brush, so that, normally, the brush will hang from the ceiling directly over the developing tray and can be obtained for use when desired.

The detail of this brush-string and counterweight combination was deliberately appropriated from the old plan of suspending the piece of chalk over a billiard table, so that the players could easily reach it, when needed, while, when released, it would be pulled out of the way by the counterweight. The developing brush thus suspended is always ready, never misplaced, nor in the way for other operations. This arrangement is particularly convenient where a bathroom is used as a dark room, and the shelf space is limited.

This same manner of counterweighting chalk on the billiard table may be applied to a stove-lid lifter, to keep it within easy reach and always cool enough to handle. The simplest and most inexpensive way of making this apparatus is to cut off a small piece of lead pipe for a counterweight, and, in the absence of a suitable pulley, use an ordinary screweye fastened in the ceiling. The latter is really better than a pulley because the string cannot run off the screweye. The arrangement is better understood by referring to the sketch.

Lighting a Basement Light

There was no switch at the basement door and it was difficult to find the droplight in the dark. Instead of going to the expense of placing a switch, the contrivance illustrated and described was rigged up and proved equal to the requirements.

A 7/8-in. piece of wood was cut about 6 in. long by 2 in. wide and a recess made at one end for the socket, as shown. A 1/8-in. hole was drilled in the center, about 2 in. from one end, and another, large enough to receive the projection from a pull socket, about 2 in. from the other end, or the end to be used as the bottom of the block. A clamp made of spring brass, as shown, was screwed securely to the board, to clamp the socket firmly. A wire was passed through the small hole and stretched across the room from the door at a height to bring the light about 6 ft. from the floor. Then the socket was clamped to the strip with the chain passed through the hole cut for it. The cord attached to the chain was run to the door casing, passed through a screweye and weighted with a nut or some light object, to keep it taut. To light the lamp or put it out only a pull on the string was necessary.

The light can be slid along on the wire from one end of the room to the

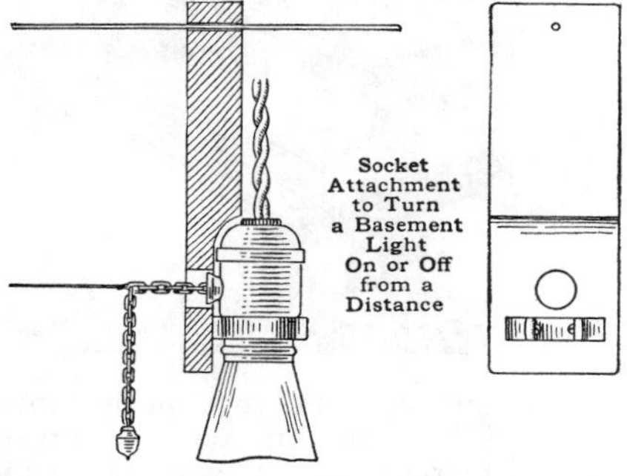
Socket Attachment to Turn a Basement Light On or Off from a Distance

other, or can be detached from the strip when desired by unhooking the cord from the chain and taking the socket from the clamp. If more desirable, the block can be fastened permanently to some object instead of being on the wire.—Contributed by L. M. Eifel, Chicago.

Projecting Protractor Readings

A simple and efficient means of projecting protractor readings to a larger size is shown in Fig. 1. One point of the compass is placed at the center of the protractor and an elastic band is looped between the points. Then the points are spread to the radius desired, and the protractor is read where the elastic band crosses its scale. A light band should be used, and

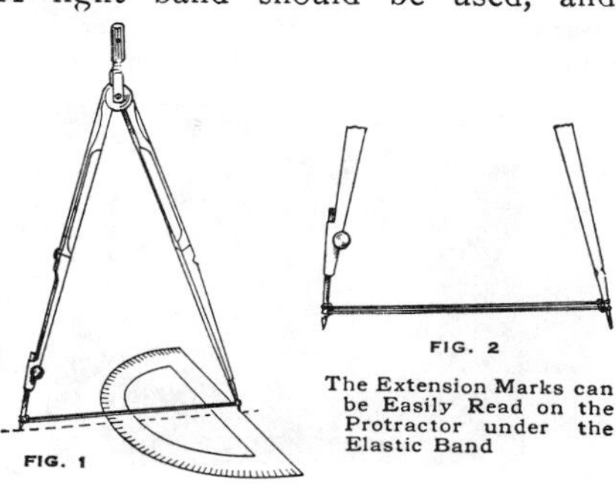

The Extension Marks can be Easily Read on the Protractor under the Elastic Band

looped as shown in Fig. 2. In this way a circle of any size may be quickly divided, if a pencil mark is made each time the band comes over the proper figure.—Contributed by Thos. L. Parker, Wibaux, Mont.

Removing Grease from Paint

When removing grease from paint by using ordinary cleaners, the paint is liable to come off in the washing. A good and cheaply applied method is to rub the painted surface with a paste of ordinary whiting. This is allowed to dry and when it is rubbed off with a cloth the dirt and grease is taken away with it. The whiting is cheap and can be purchased at any drug store.

A Door Stop

A very good door stop can be easily made of a piece of metal as shown in the sketch. The metal is bent and fastened with screws to the wall against which the door swings. The extending end fits under the door knob and prevents it from striking the wall.—Contributed by C. R. Poole, Los Angeles, California.

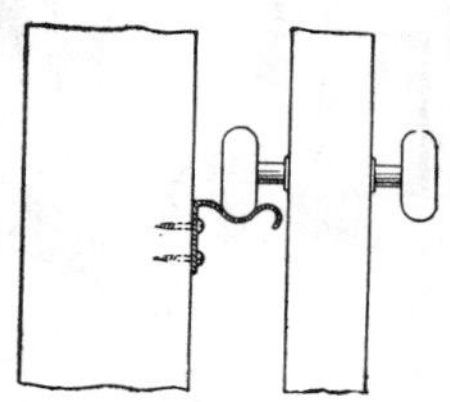

Stretching a Curtain without a Frame

A good way to avoid using the ordinary four-pole curtain stretcher is to make use of the following method.

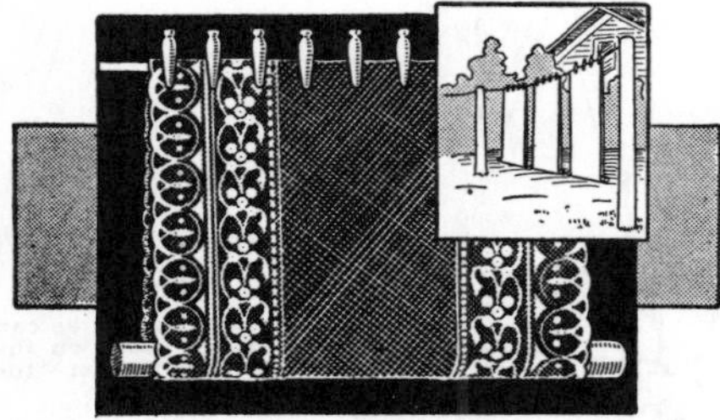

A Lace Curtain Hung Double on a Line with a Pole Inserted in the Fold

Take the lace curtain and fold it once lengthwise; then pin it up on a tightly stretched line with a large number of clothespins, and slip a clean pole between the two sides to keep it taut. This method not only stretches the curtain satisfactorily, but saves considerable time otherwise required in pinning the curtain to the four-sided frame.—Contributed by H. Wynning, Chicago, Ill.

Welding Small Resistance-Wire Connections

In making connections, especially in electrical heating devices subject to high temperatures, it is out of the question to use solder, since the temperature reached in the device would cause

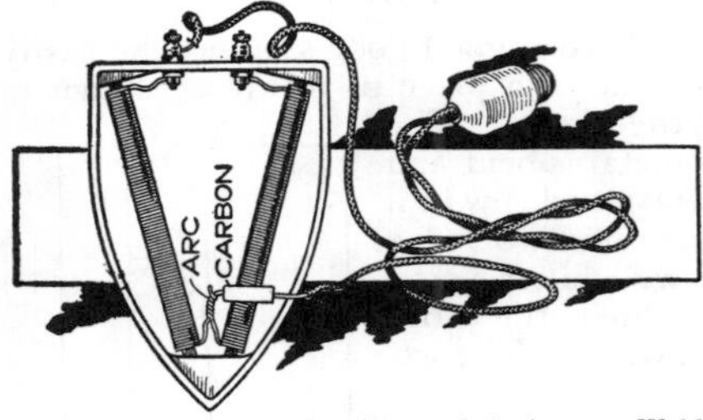

An Arc is Formed with a Piece of Carbon, to Weld the Twisted Ends of Wire Together

the solder to melt and run out. A convenient arrangement for welding the connections of flatirons, or any other fine wires, is shown in the illustration. The ends of the wires to be welded are twisted together, and the weld is completed by forming an arc, one electrode of which is the twisted connection and the other a piece of carbon. The resistance of the heating unit in the iron is sufficient to limit the amount of the current flow so that a short circuit does not result.—Contributed by G. Irving Davis, Albany, N. Y.

Bench with Folding Seats

To provide a bench with seats, or shelves, which cannot easily be taken away unless the table is brought along, hinged brackets are attached to stationary crosspieces, which are fastened

Bench, or Table, with a Seat on Each Side That can be Folded for Carrying Purposes

on the extended end braces of the table. When in use, the brackets are turned down, thereby providing a rigid support for anything that may be put on them. If it is desirable to have the brackets out of the way, as when carrying the bench, it is only necessary to fold them up.—Contributed by J. M. Kane, Doylestown, Pa.

Rim of Wire Wastebasket Wrapped with Felt

In offices where wire wastebaskets are used, the finish of the desks is often marred by the top rim of the baskets rubbing against them. This can be overcome by wrapping strips of felt around the rim to form a buffer.—Contributed by Miss F. D. Schweiger, Kansas City, Mo.

A Homemade Roller Coaster

By J. H. SANFORD

THE popular roller coaster that furnishes untold amusement for the multitudes that patronize amusement parks during the summer can be easily duplicated in a smaller way on a vacant lot or back yard for the children of the home; or the boys of a neighborhood could contribute to a fund and construct quite an elaborate affair, on the same lines as described, for the combined use of the owners. The one described was built with a track, 90 ft. long, 5 ft. high at one end and 3 ft. at the other, the track between being placed on the ground. In coasting from the high end to the low one, the coaster will run up on the incline, then drift back to within 24 ft. of the starting end. The car was built to seat four children or two adults. The cost of all the materials for building this roller coaster did not exceed $10.

Inexpensive Back-Yard Roller Coaster, Suitable for the Enjoyment of the Young as Well as the Older Persons

The track is of simple construction and requires but little description. It is necessary to have it straight and nailed firmly to the crossties on the ground and to the trestles where it is elevated. The ties and trestles are placed about 6 ft. apart. The two trestles for the starting platform should be set so that there is a slant to the track of about 6 in. for starting the car without pushing it. The car can be carried back for starting by adults, but for children a small rope can be used over the platform to draw it back on the track, or a small windlass may be arranged for the purpose.

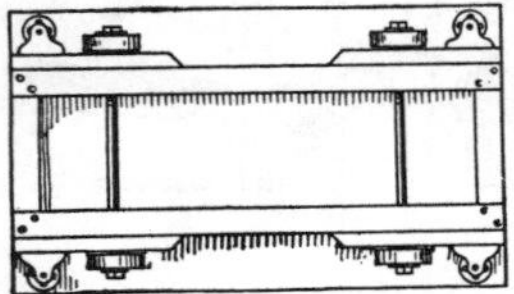

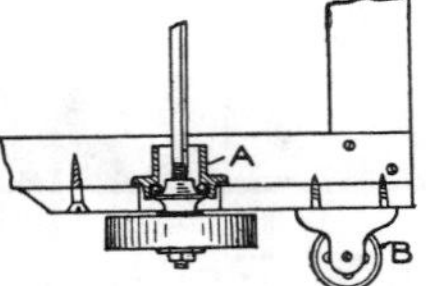

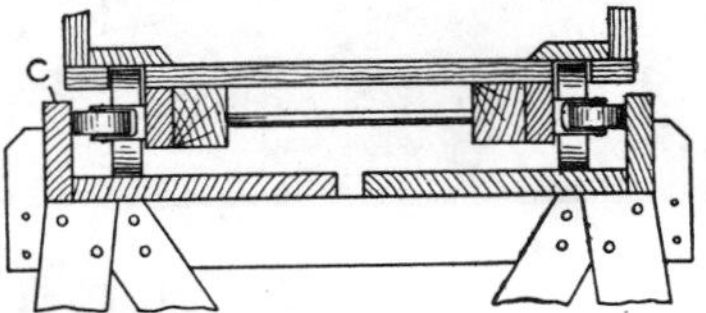

Detail of the Car, Wheels and the Trestle, Which is Attached to a Tie

The main frame of the car is 3 ft. long and about 13 in. wide, firmly fastened at the corners. The axles for the wheels are machine steel, 19 in. long, turned up on the ends and threaded in the manner of a bicycle axle to fit parts of bicycle hubs, attached to the main frame as shown at A. The wheels are solid, 4 in. in diameter and 1 in. thick, and are set on the bicycle cone of the ball cup, after they are properly adjusted, and securely fastened between washers with a nut on the end of the axle. Guide wheels, B, are placed on the sides in the manner shown. These wheels are ordinary truck casters, not the revolving kind, 2 in. in diameter.

About ½-in. clearance should be provided between the guide wheels B and the guard rail C, on the track. When the car is made in this manner it runs close to the track and there is no place where a child can get a foot or hand injured under or at the sides of the car. The one described has been used by all the children, large and small, for a year without accident.

Door-Bell Alarm

A simple door-bell alarm for informing one when the door of a shop or dwelling is opened is shown in the accompanying sketch. It consists of a piece of spring brass, A, bent into a circle in the center so that it may be clamped on the doorknob bar by means of a small bolt or screw. The two ends of this piece should be separated as shown and a second piece, B, mounted on the door so that its outwardly projecting end is between the ends of the piece A. One terminal of an ordinary vibrating bell circuit is then connected under the head of the clamp screw, and the other terminal under one of the screws holding the piece B in place on the door. It is now obvious that the bell circuit will be completed and the alarm sounded when the knob is turned. Make sure that the piece A is bent so that the circuit is completed before the latch has moved a sufficient amount to allow the door to open.

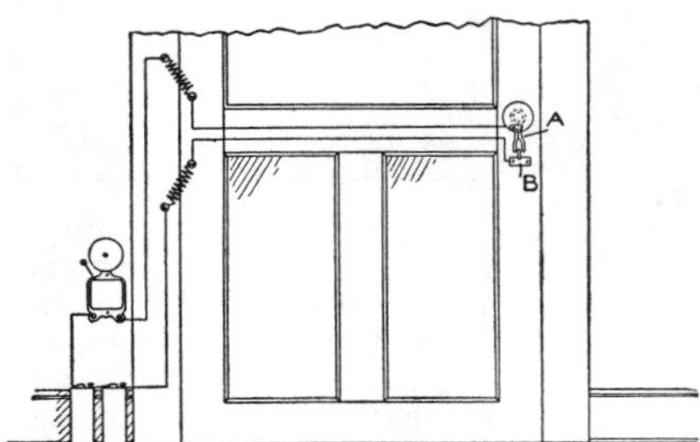

Wiring Diagram and Connections to an Electric Bell That Rings When a Door Knob is Turned

The circuit leading to and from the switch may be completed through the hinges of the door, but it would be better to use small coil springs as shown. There would then be no likelihood of the circuit being open at any time, which might occur if the hinges were used.

¶Discolored coffee and teapots may be restored to their original brightness by boiling them a few minutes in a solution of borax water.

A Playground Ferris Wheel

The whole wheel is carried on two uprights, each 3 by 4 in., by 10 ft. long. In the upper ends of these pieces, A, a half circle is cut out to receive the main shaft B. The end of the uprights are sunk 3 ft. into the earth and about 4 ft. apart, then braced as shown. They are further braced by wires attached to rings which are secured with staples near the top. The bearings should each have a cap to keep the shaft in place. These can be made of blocks of wood with a semicircle cut out, the blocks being nailed over the shaft, while it is in place, the nails entering the ends of the uprights.

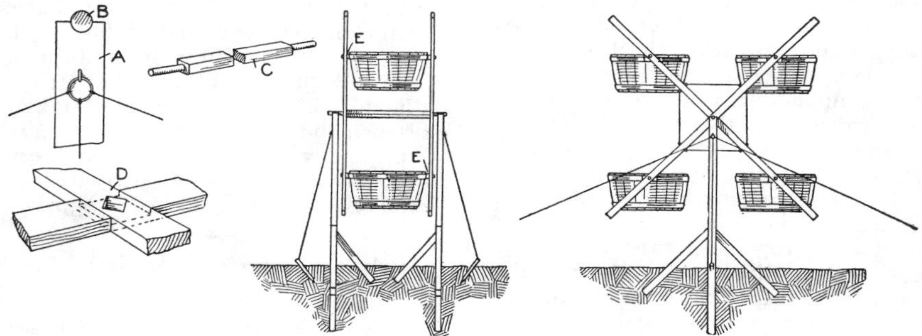

Detail of the Uprights, Axle and Spokes, and the End and Side Elevations of the Completed Wheel, Showing Braces and Cars Attached

The main shaft C is made of a 2½-in. square piece of good material, 4 ft. long. The ends are made round to serve as bearings, and the square part is fitted with the spokes or car carriers. These consist of 4 pieces, each 1 in. thick, 4 in. wide and 13 ft. long. In the center of each piece cut a notch one-half the thickness so that when each pair of pieces is crossed they will fit together with the surfaces smooth, as shown at D. A square hole is cut through the pieces as shown to fit on the square part of the main axle. While it is not shown in the illustration, it is best to strengthen this joint with another piece of wood, cut to fit on the axle and securely attached to the spokes.

The cars or carriers are made of two sugar barrels cut in half. The hoops are then securely nailed, both inside and outside; a block of wood, E, securely attached to the half barrel on the outside, and another block on the inside opposite the outside block. Holes are bored 2½ ft. from the ends of the spokes and a bolt run through them and through the blocks on the edges of the half barrels. The extending ends of the spokes are used to propel the wheel. Four children can ride in the wheel at one time.—Contributed by Maurice Baudier, New Orleans, La.

A Merry-Go-Round Pole

An inexpensive merry-go-round can be made of a single pole set in the ground where there is sufficient vacant

The Ropes being Tied to the Wheel Rim will Easily Turn around the Pole

space for the turning of the ropes. The pole may be of gas pipe or wood, long enough to extend about 12 ft. above the ground. An iron wheel is attached on the upper end so that it will revolve easily on an axle, which may be an iron pin driven into the post. A few iron washers placed on the pin under the wheel will reduce the friction.

Ropes of varying lengths are tied to the rim of the wheel. The rider takes hold of a rope and runs around the pole to start the wheel in motion, then he swings clear of the ground. Streamers of different colors and flowers for special occasions may be attached to make a pretty display.—Contributed by J. Bert Mitchell, Wichita, Kans.

A Theatrical Night Scene with the Appearance of Fireflies

Use small shining Christmas-tree balls, about the size of a hickory nut, strung on strong black linen threads. The thread is put loosely over a hook at the back of the stage among the evergreens that are used for the background. The ends of the threads are brought, like a pair of reins, to the front of the stage, diagonally, and there manipulated by some one in a wing near the front, standing high enough to prevent the threads from touching the heads of the actors. These bright little particles darting back and forth among the trees appear very lifelike, and with the addition of a crescent moon just peeping through the trees, the likeness to a summer night is quite striking.

The moon effect is made by using a piece of dark cardboard, about 2 ft. square, covered thickly with small green boughs, and by cutting a crescent-shaped opening in the center, covering it with yellow tissue paper. This cardboard is placed well back in the trees and a lantern hung behind it.—Contributed by Miss S. E. Jocelyn, New Haven, Conn.

Hulling Walnuts

Procure a barrel that is water-tight and mount it on a shaft so that it runs between standards like a barrel churn. Fill the barrel about half full of walnuts, cover them with water and throw in a small quantity of gravel as grinding material. Close the opening tightly and turn the barrel for about 20 minutes. The walnuts will come out clean and smooth as glass.—Contributed by Arthur Seufert, The Dalles, Oregon.

Stick for Lowering Top Sash of a Window

To make it easy to raise and lower the upper sash of a bathroom window which is behind the bathtub I devised

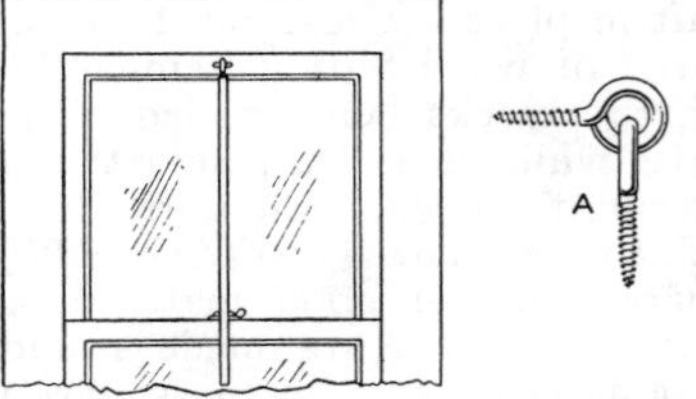

The Stick is Fastened to the Window Sash with Screw-eyes and is Always Ready for Use

the following: Procuring two screw-eyes I opened one sufficiently to slip it into the other as shown at A. Then one was screwed into the top rail of the sash and the other into the end of a light stick a little longer than the length of upper sash.

The device is left on the window permanently and affords a ready means of handling the sash without stepping into the bathtub, which would otherwise be necessary.—Contributed by W. E. Morey, Chicago.

An Adjustable Hacksaw Frame

The frame is constructed of cold-rolled steel, 1/4 in. in diameter and 17 1/2 in. long, bent into the shape shown and then cut in two parts at A. Starting at a point about 5/16 in. from the ends made by the cut, drill 1/8-in. holes, then space three other holes 1 in. between centers and drill them 1/8 in. in diameter.

A piece of steel tubing, 1/4 in. in inside diameter and 6 3/4 in. long, is notched on the ends to receive the pins B and C. Slots are cut in the ends D and E, to admit the blade of a saw,

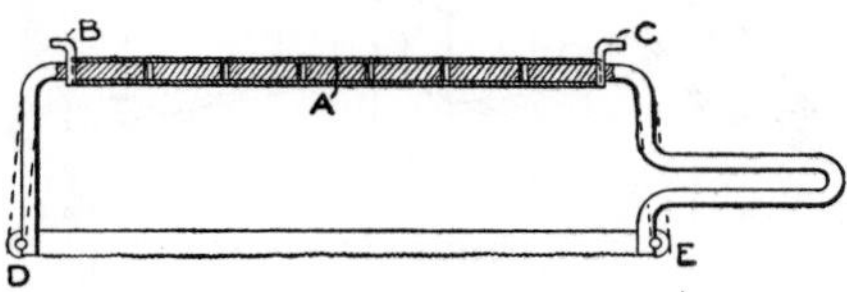

The Frame is Shaped of Cold-Rolled Steel and Made Adjustable with a Piece of Steel Tubing

and half-round notches filed on the outside surface for holding pins used in the hole of the saw blade. The spring of the steel will be sufficient to keep the saw blade in place. The 1/8-in. holes in the frame will permit adjustment for different lengths of blades.—Contributed by Clarence B. Hanson, Fitchburg, Mass.

A Bedroom Cabinet

The cabinet shown in the illustration can be made an ornament with a little care in workmanship and a choice selection of materials. The cabinet may be either fastened to the head or foot of the bed, facing in either of two directions.

The size of the cabinet will depend on the choice of the maker, and if the bed is brass, the wood can be finished

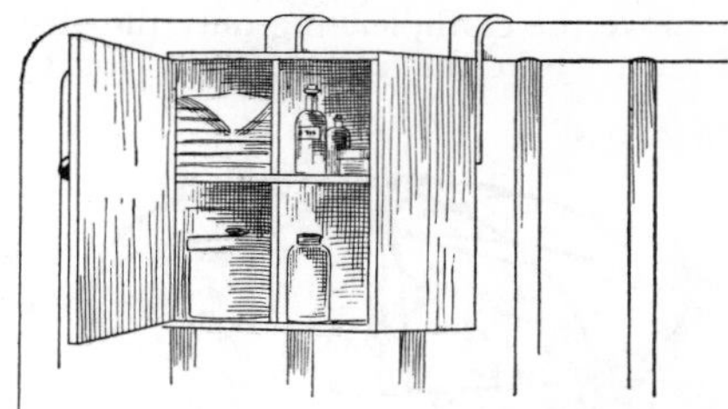

The Cabinet Makes a Handy Place to Keep Necessary Articles for a Sick Person

natural and fitted with brass bands for brackets and holding clips.—Contributed by W. E. Crane, Cleveland, O.

A Dull Black for Cameras

Such parts of a camera that are apt to reflect light must be covered with a dull black. A mixture for this purpose is made of lampblack, about a teaspoonful, and enough gold size to make a paste as thick as putty. Add about twice the volume of turpentine and apply to the parts with a camel's-hair brush.

As the turpentine fumes are detrimental to the sensitive plate, the camera should be left open until these fumes have entirely disappeared.

A Door Fastener

Sometimes it is necessary to fasten a door in a manner to prevent children from opening it, yet so that it is easily opened from either side. This can be done by putting a screw or curtain hook on the inside of the door frame and using a piece of cord long enough to loop over both hooks. A person coming in or out can remove the loop from either side.—Contributed by John A. Cohalan, Philadelphia, Pa.

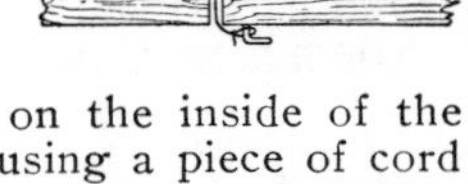

¶A floor wax can be made by melting 1 lb. of yellow beeswax in 1/2 pt. of hot, raw linseed oil; then adding 1 pt. of turpentine.

Umbrella Used as a Flower Trellis

Procure a discarded umbrella and remove the cloth, leaving only the steel frame. Join the ends of the ribs by

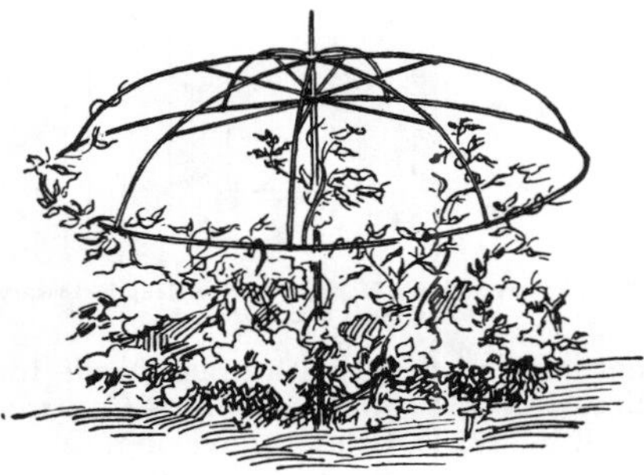

Frame Supporting a Vine

running a fine wire through the tip of each rib and giving it one turn around to hold them at equal distances apart. The handle is then inserted in the ground and some climbing vine planted beneath it. The plant will climb all over the steel frame and make a very attractive lawn piece.—Contributed by John F. Campbell, N. Somerville, Massachusetts.

Combined Shade and Awning

An ordinary window shade makes a good awning as well as a shade, if it is attached to the outside of the window with the device shown in the illustration. The shade and spring roller are put into a box for protection from the weather and the box is fastened in the window casing at the top.

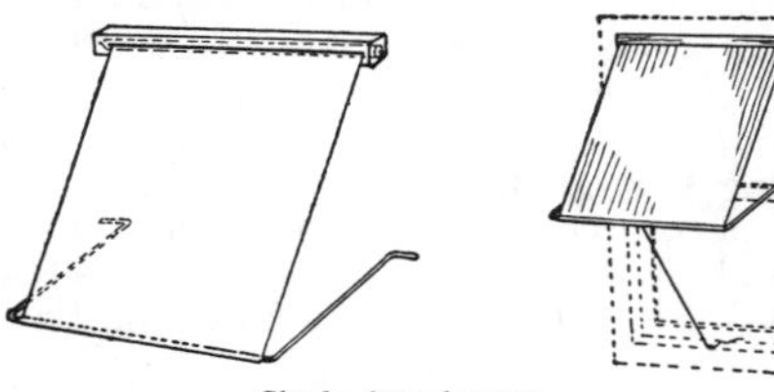

Shade Attachments

A narrow slit on the under side of the box permits the shade to be drawn out. The stick at the end is removed and a U-shaped wire inserted in the hem in its stead. The wire is bent so the ends may be inserted in holes in the window casing. As the shade is drawn out, it is extended outward by the wire in the position of an awning.—Contributed by Arthur Kesl, Chicago, Ill.

Vaulting-Pole Attachments

Some means must be provided on vaulting-pole standards to allow for the free release of the pole should the vaulter strike it in going over. One of the simplest of the many devices that can be used for this purpose is shown in Fig. 1. It is made of heavy wire, bent and slipped over the standard as shown in Fig. 2. The projection on the inside of the link is used similar to the tongue of a buckle in adjusting the height of the pole on the standards.

Each standard has a series of holes on its front side. These holes may be numbered for convenience. The pole

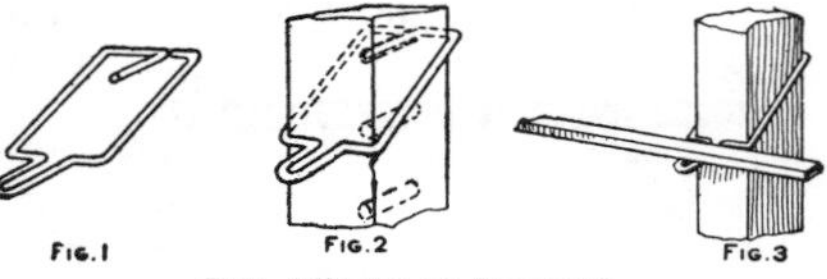

Pole Adjuster on Standard

in place is shown in Fig. 3.—Contributed by John Dunlap, Craghead, Tollcross, England.

Separating Drinking Glasses

When two thin glasses are put one into the other they often become stuck and cannot be removed. To separate them with ease, set the lower glass in warm (not hot) water and pour cold water in the upper one. The expansion of the lower and the contraction of the upper will make release an easy matter.—Contributed by Maurice Baudier, New Orleans, La.

¶ Bronze striping, when thoroughly dry, should be covered with a thin coat of white shellac to keep it from tarnishing.

A Magic String

Procure a few pieces of cotton string, each about 1½ ft. long, and fill them well with soap. Prepare a brine by dissolving three tablespoonfuls of salt in a cup of water. Place the strings in the brine and allow them to soak for two hours, or longer. It is necessary that they be thoroughly saturated with the brine.

When taken out of the brine and thoroughly dried, suspend one of them from a nail on a ledge, and hang a finger ring on its lower end. Apply a lighted match to the string and allow it to burn. The ring will not fall, but will hang by the ash.—Contributed by C. Frank Carber, Dorchester, Mass.

Edging Flower Beds

To improve the appearance of a flower bed, it must be edged evenly and quite often. As this became a tiresome task, I constructed an edger, as shown in the sketch. It consists of a wheel on a 4-ft. length of material, 2 by 4 in. in size, made tapering and having a cross handle, 18 in. long, attached to its end. The wheel is 8 in. in diameter, and the cutter is attached, as shown, across the center of the wheel axle, to make the edger turn easily on curves and corners. The cutter is 12 in. long and turned under 1½ in. It is pushed along in the same manner as a garden cultivator.—Contributed by A. S. Thomas, Amhurstburg, Can.

An Electric Stirring Machine

Desiring a stirring machine for mixing photographic chemicals, I set about to design the one shown in the illustration.

A Self-Contained Electric Stirring Machine for Use in Mixing Photographic Chemicals

The base and upright are made of pine, 1 in. thick, the former 8 in. wide and 10 in. long, the latter 8 in. wide and 16 in. long. A ⅜-in. slot, 12 in. long, is cut in the center of the upright, and two pieces of sheet metal or tin, 2 in. wide and 12 in. long, bent at right angles along the center of their length, are placed at equal distances, on each side of the slot, and fastened with screws. The distance between these pieces depends on the motor used, as its base should fit snugly between them.

A small battery motor is purchased,

An Edger, Similar to a Garden Plow, for Quickly Trimming the Sod around a Flower Bed

and its shaft is removed and replaced with one measuring 10 in. in length. To the end of the shaft is soldered a piece of wire, bent as shown in the sketch. A bolt is attached to the center of the motor base, so that its threaded end will pass through the slot in the upright, where it is held with a wing nut. The battery cells may be placed on the back of the upright and a small switch mounted at the top and in front. —Contributed by Ray F. Yates, Niagara Falls, N. Y.

A Clothes Rack

The rack is constructed of hard wood throughout, and as each piece is made, it should be sandpapered and varnished

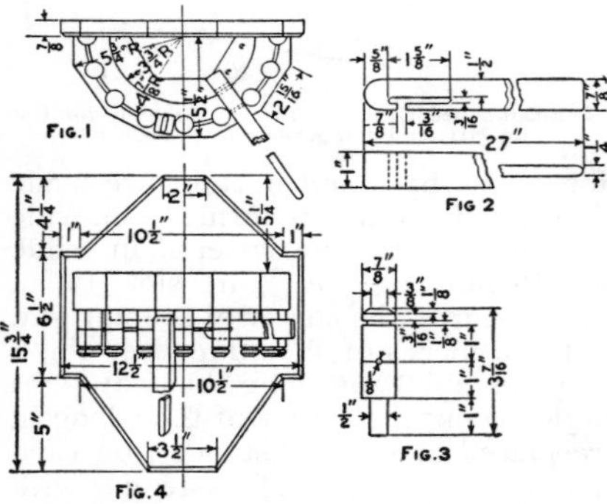

Any Number of Arms Up to Its Limit may be Used at a Time

or otherwise finished. The plan view is shown in Fig. 1; the construction of an arm, in Fig. 2; and the pin, in Fig. 3.

The base is ⅞ in. thick and of the dimensions shown in Fig 4. The projection on each side, measuring 6½ in. long and 1 in. wide, is made separately and glued to the main part after dressing and beveling the edges.

The shelf consists of material 2 in. thick and made in a semicircular form on a radius of 5¾ in. On this arc, lay off chords, as shown in Fig. 1; the first ones on each side being one-half the length of the others. Carefully square up the edges for appearance. To lay off the post holes, scribe an arc of a circle on a 4⅞-in. radius. Start at the edge on this arc and lay off eight chords of equal lengths, and bore ½-in. holes on the marks.

The posts are turned up, as shown by the detail, Fig. 3. This will require seven posts and two half posts. The half posts are secured to the base with small brads. The round part at the end is turned slightly tapering, so as to make a tight fit in the hole of the shelf. After stringing the posts on a piece of brass wire, ⅛ in. in diameter, and bending it in the proper shape, the posts are glued in the holes.

A T-shaped slot with a long top and a short leg is cut out with a scroll saw in one end of each arm. Make sure to have each slot exactly ½ in. from the upper side of each arm. All edges should be well rounded to prevent tearing of the clothes.

Make a semicircular platform for the arms to bear upon when extended. This may be either half of a turned disk or built up in the three segments, each fastened with screws to the base. If the brass wire is exactly 1 in. from the shelf and the thickness of the wood between the T-slot and the upper edge of the arm ½ in., the thickness of the platform should be slightly under ½ in. to make the arms rest horizontally when they are extended.

The shelf is fastened to the base with three or four 2-in. screws, and the ends of the brass wire are run through holes in the base and clinched on the back side. The rack may be fastened in place on the kitchen wall with two large wood screws, or, if the wall is brick, with expansion bolts. The fastening in either case must be secure to hold the heavy weight of wet clothes.—Contributed by D. A. Price, Wilmington, Del.

How to Make a Pair of Foot Boats

On ponds or small lakes not deep enough for a boat one can use the foot boats, as illustrated, for walking on the water. The boats are made of white wood, known as basswood, as this wood is easily bent when steamed, and the curved part should be shaped neatly.

Two sides are cut out, as shown, and the boards are nailed or, better still, screwed to them. Each straight part may consist of one piece, in which case there will be no joints to make waterproof, but if boards of sufficient size cannot be had, pieces can be used. In this instance the edges should be planed smooth, so that a good joint may be had, which can be made watertight with white lead.

It is best to make the bottom of one piece if possible, at least for the length of the curve. The wood is thoroughly steamed, then fastened in place on the curved part.

A strap of suitable length is fastened on the top for the toe, so that the boats can be controlled with the feet.

To propel the boats along easily, a web or wing should be attached to the under side, so that it will catch the

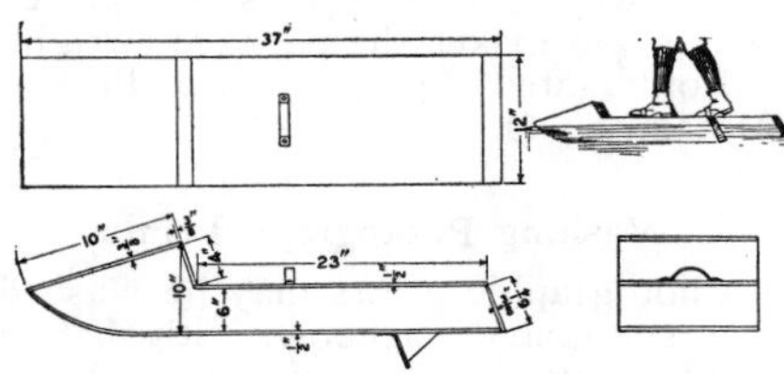

Foot Boats for Walking on Shallow Water Where a Boat cannot be Used

water on the back thrust while it will fold up when the boat is slid forward.—Contributed by Waldo Saul, Lexington, Mass.

A Green-Corn Holder

Neat and attractive green-corn holders for table use can be made of small-sized glass drawer knobs, having a bolt 1 in. in length. The bolt head is cut off with a hacksaw, and its body is filed to make four sides running to a taper, leaving enough threads to secure it in the knob. The threads are smeared with white lead, then it is screwed into the knob and sufficient time allowed for the lead to set before using it.

A pair of knobs are required for each ear of corn served. The square bolt end will hold the ear securely while the

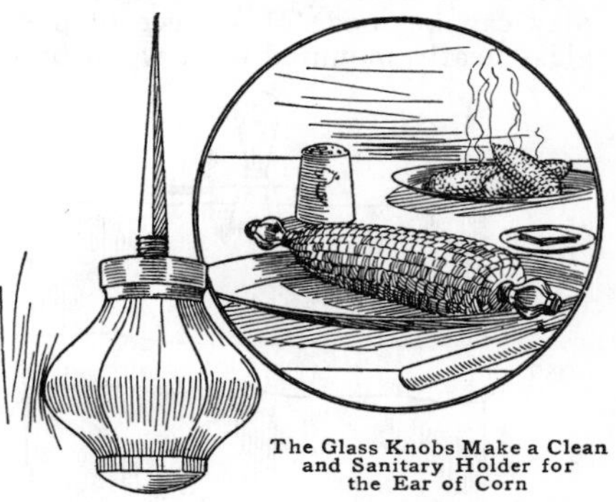

The Glass Knobs Make a Clean and Sanitary Holder for the Ear of Corn

kernels are eaten from the cob.—Contributed by Victor Labadie, Dallas, Texas.

Inflating Toy Balloons

The inflation of rubber balloons may be accomplished with manufactured gas by using the simple pipe arrangement shown in the sketch. The connection A is for the gas hose, which is similar to those used for a table lamp. The gas bag B is a football or punching bag connected to the pipe as shown. This receives the gas as it is let in by the valve A. The toy balloon C is connected to the pipe in the same manner and the valve D used to regulate the flow of gas. The gas is easily pressed out of the ball into the balloon.

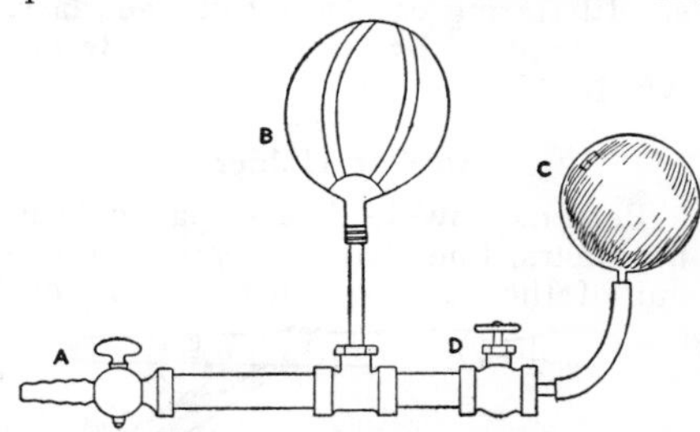

Pipe Arrangement, Punching Bag and Valves to Admit Gas to a Toy Rubber Balloon

As hydrogen gas is much better than the manufactured gas, it is best to use and can be put in the balloon in the same manner.

Electric-Light Mystery

A novel attraction for a window display can be made of a piece of plate glass neatly mounted on a wood base,

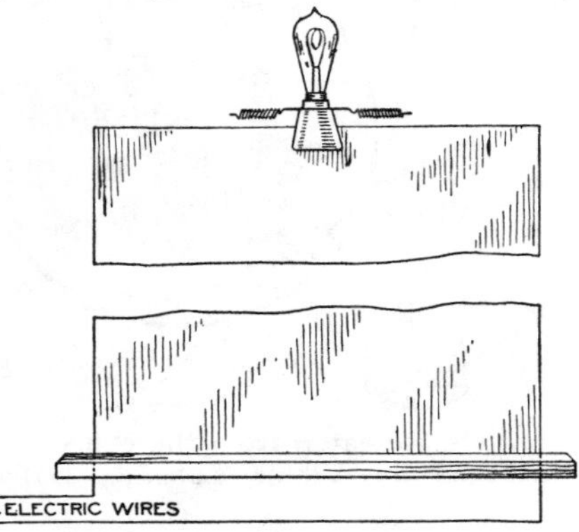

Electric Light Mounted on Top of a Plate Glass with Hidden Connections on the Glass Edge

and an electric light which is placed on the top edge and may be lighted apparently without any wire connections.

The method of concealing the connections is to paint the edges of the glass green, then, before the paint is quite dry, lay on a thin strip of copper, making the connections at the base on both sides, and to the lamp in the same manner. Another coat of paint is applied to cover the strip. The color should be an imitation of the greenish tint of glass edges. Any desired lettering can be put on the glass. —Contributed by O. Simonson, Brooklyn, N. Y.

An Oar Holder

Persons rowing boats, particularly beginners, find that the oars will slip out of the oarlocks, turn or fall into

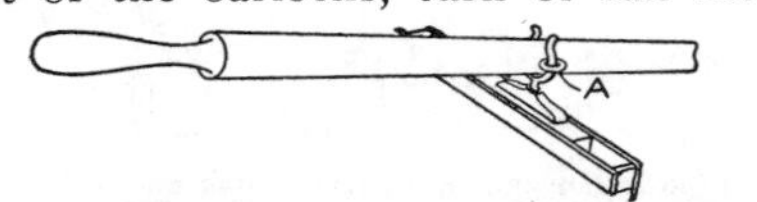

The Screweye in Position on the Oar and over One Prong of the Oarlock

the water. This may be avoided by turning a screweye of sufficient size to prevent binding on the lock into the oar and placing it over the lock as shown at A, so that the pull will be against the metal. The oars will never slip or jump out, will always be in the right position, and it is not necessary to pull them into the boat to prevent loss when not rowing. The locks will not wear the oars, as the pull is on the metal eye. Place the eye so it will have a horizontal position on the side of the oar when the blade is in its right position.

Cooking Food in Paper

A flat piece of paper is much more convenient to use than a paper sack in cooking, as it can be better fitted to the size of the article to be cooked. Wrap the article as a grocer wraps sugar, folding and refolding the two edges together until the package is of the proper size, then fasten with clips and proceed to close the ends in the same way. This avoids all pasted seams and makes the package airtight. —Contributed by J. J. A. Parker, Metamora, O.

Washing Photograph Prints

Photographic prints may be washed in a stationary washbowl with just as good results as if washed in a high-

A Medicine Dropper on a Faucet Produces a Whirling Motion of the Water in the Bowl

priced wash box, by cutting off the upper end of the rubber nipple on a bent glass medicine dropper and placing it on the faucet as shown in the illustration. This arrangement causes the water to whirl around in the bowl, which keeps the prints in constant motion, thus insuring a thorough washing.—Contributed by L. O. D. Sturgess, Arlington, Oregon.

Combination Lock for a Drawer

The principal parts of the combination lock are the five disks shown in Fig. 1. These are best made of sheet brass, about $\frac{1}{16}$ in. thick and $1\frac{1}{2}$ in. in diameter. The pins for turning the disks are each made a driving fit for a hole drilled through the metal at a point $\frac{15}{32}$ in. from the center. Notches are cut in the disks C, D and E, Fig. 1, to receive the latch end, and the disk B is made like a cam, its use being to raise the latch into its keeper when the handle is turned backward. The disk A is without a notch and has only a pin for turning the other disks.

The disks are mounted on the inside of the drawer front in a U-shaped piece of metal, F, Fig. 2, which carries a $\frac{1}{4}$-in. pin, G, as their bearing. The disks are placed on this pin with rubber washers, H, J, K, L and M, between them. These serve the purpose of preventing the disks from turning too freely. The disk A is fastened tightly to the end of the rod N, which is $\frac{1}{4}$ in. in diameter. The outer end of this rod is fitted with a handle or turning head as desired. That shown at O is made of two pieces of wood screwed together, with a pointer, P, placed between them. A washer, R, is placed between the drawer end and the handle to take up any looseness and to allow the free turning of the rod.

A dial, S, is made of paper and the division marks and numbers placed upon it. The latch T is fitted in a U-shaped piece of metal, U, which is fastened to the inside of the drawer end where its heel will rest on the edges of the disks. When the right combination is made by turning the handle first one way and then the other, the latch will drop into the notches of the disks as they will be all in one place.

When the drawer is to be locked, turn the handle back from the last turn made for the combination and the latch will be driven upward into its keeper and the notches scattered so that the latch will not drop until the combination is again set.

The numbers for the combination can be found after the disks are in place and by turning the handle until the notch comes up to the place for the

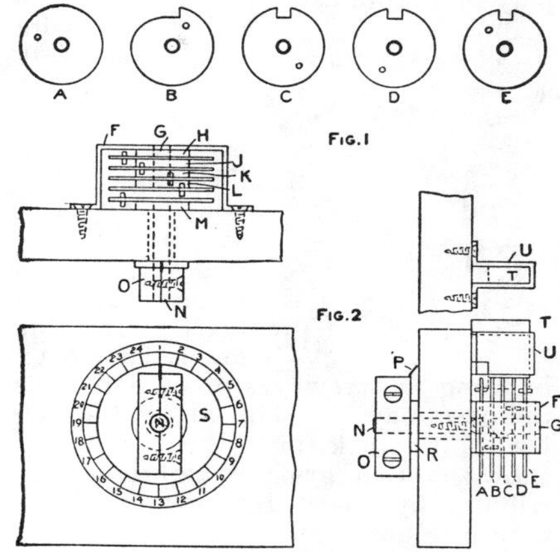

The Parts as They are Attached to a Drawer Front to Make a Combination Lock

heel of the latch. The number beneath the pointer is noted; then the next turned up in a like manner, all being done while the drawer is open and the disks in plain sight. The combination can be changed only by changing the location of the pins in the disks.—Contributed by C. B. Hanson, Fitchburg, Massachusetts.

How to Start Small Machine Screws

Small machine screws are sometimes very difficult to start, especially when used in parts of a machine that cannot be easily reached with the fingers. A good way to start them is by means of a piece of fine wire wound snugly around the screw under its head. They

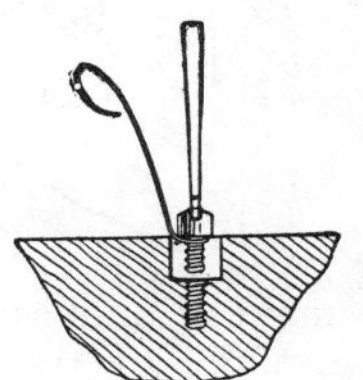

can be placed and started by means of the wire and when the first threads have caught the screw it can be held by the screwdriver while the wire is withdrawn.—Contributed by F. W. Bently, Huron, S. D.

An Umbrella Holder for Display Purposes

A holder that is especially adapted for use in hanging umbrellas for display in a store can be easily made of a piece of wire wound in a coil, as shown in the sketch, to fit over the end on the umbrella stick. The coil at one end of the spring is formed into a hook so that the umbrellas may be hung in screweyes or on a line, as the case may be. The end of the umbrella is stuck into the spring, as shown, which grips it tightly.—Contributed by Abner B. Shaw, N. Dartmouth, Mass.

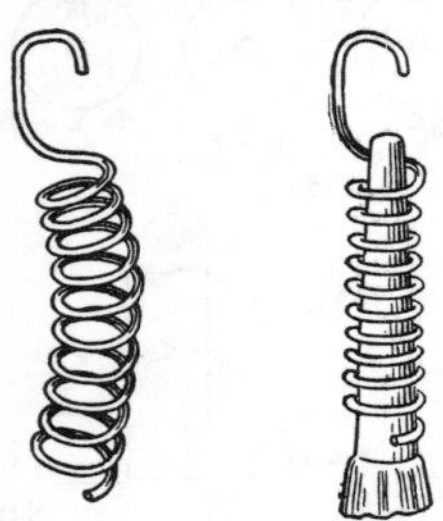

Holder for a Milk Card

It is the general practice of milkmen to furnish a monthly card on which the housewife marks the needs of the day and then hangs it outside of the door for the information of the driver. This card also serves as a record for checking the accounts of the milk delivered during the month, and therefore it is desirable to protect it from snow and sleet.

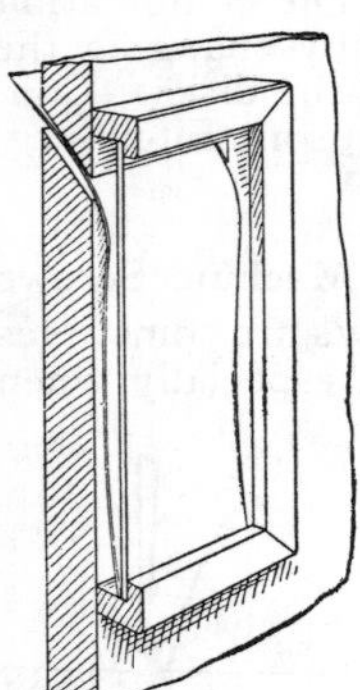

In order to furnish this protection and at the same time make it unnecessary for any one to go outside of the door to hang up the card on stormy days, one of our readers has submitted the following plan which he has used for some time.

On the outside of the kitchen door, where the milkman is to deliver his bottles, this man has fastened an ordinary picture frame with glass but no backing except the door. Through the door and just below the upper edge of the glass is cut a thin slot inclining downward and outward so that the milk card can be easily pushed through the slot and thus be displayed behind the glass in the frame. By this protection it is kept free from mud, snow and ice. It is not necessary to step outside to place the card in the frame.

Frame for Printing Post Cards from Negatives

As I desired to print only a portion of some of my 5 by 7-in. plates on post cards and the part wanted was near the edge of the plate, I cut out the printing frame, as shown at A in the sketch, to accommodate that part of the card I reserved for a margin. This permitted the card to be placed in the frame without making a bend.—Contributed by J. H. Maysilles, Rochelle, Ill.

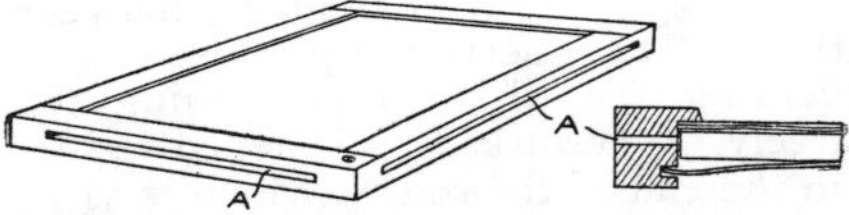

Slots Cut in the Frame to Receive the Post Cards without Bending Them

Finger Protection on Laboratory Vessels

A simple way of protecting the fingers against being burned by laboratory vessels in which liquids are boiling or chemical reactions producing great heat are going on, is shown in the sketch. A rather thick cord or yarn is wrapped around the neck of the vessel in the manner shown, the

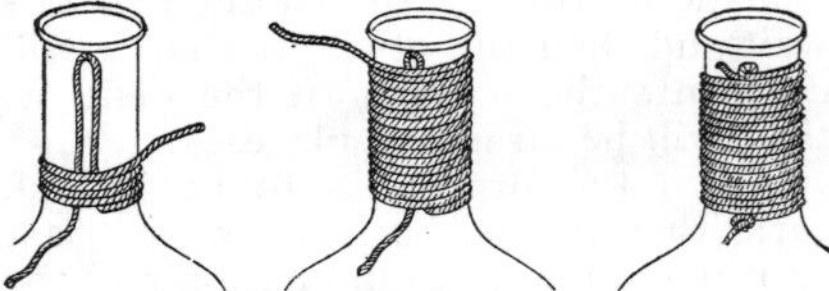
The Ends of the Cord are Held Tightly and the Winding Protects the Hands

upper end being drawn through the loop at the top and cut off, and the lower end then pulled out and a knot tied in it close to the windings of the yarn.

Inlaying Metals by Electroplating

Very pretty and artistic effects of silver or nickel inlay on bronze, copper, etc., or copper on dark oxidized metals, may be obtained by means of etching and electroplating.

The metal on which the inlay is to be used is first covered with a thin coating of wax and the design scratched through to the metal with a sharp, hard point of some kind. The design is then etched in slowly with well diluted nitric acid, allowing the etching to penetrate quite deeply. The metal is then taken out and after a thorough rinsing in water is hung in the plating bath.

As the wax has been left on, the plating will fill the lines of the design only, and will not touch the covered surface. When the etched lines are filled, the object is taken out of the bath and the wax removed.—Contributed by S. V. Cooke, Hamilton, Can.

A Novel Show-Window Attraction

This moving show-window attraction can be simply and cheaply made. The things necessary are a small battery motor, a large horseshoe magnet and a large polished steel ball, perfectly true and round, such as used in bearings. The other materials usually can be found in any store. Procure some thick cardboard and cut two disks, 8 in. in diameter, and two disks, 7½ in. in diameter. Glue these together to make the wheel A, the larger disks forming the flanges. Make a smaller wheel, B, the size of which will be governed by the speed of the motor used. The wheel A is mounted in a box to run with its surface close to the under side of the cover, which should be of a thin, stiff cardboard. The wheel B is mounted on an axle that runs in metal bearings. The magnet D is placed on the wheel A. The steel ball E is put on the thin cover of the box, and the magnet causes it to roll around as the wheel turns. The box

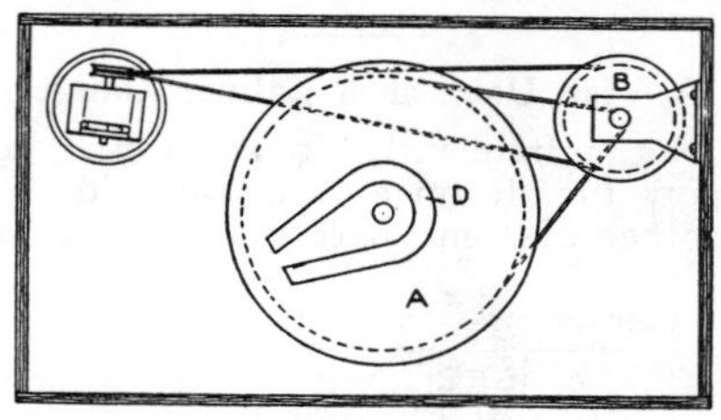

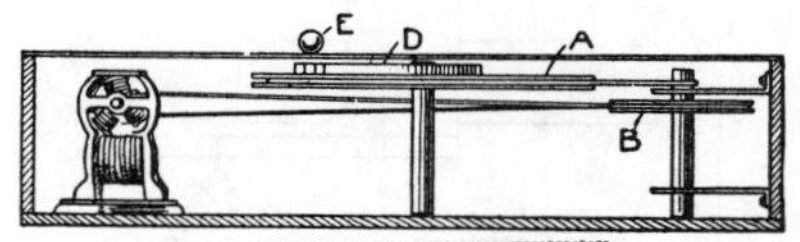

The Steel Ball is Caused to Roll Around on the Cover by the Moving Magnet

inclosing the mechanical parts should be placed out of sight when used in a window.—Contributed by Clarence Guse, Spokane, Wash.

How to Make a Mop Wringer

A mop wringer may be made and attached to an ordinary pail in the following manner: Two pieces of metal, A, are attached securely at opposite sides of the edge of the pail, holes being drilled in their upper ends to serve as bearings for the roller B. The piece of metal C, which is duplicated at the opposite side of the pail, is pivoted on a bolt. These pieces also carry a roller, E, at their upper ends,

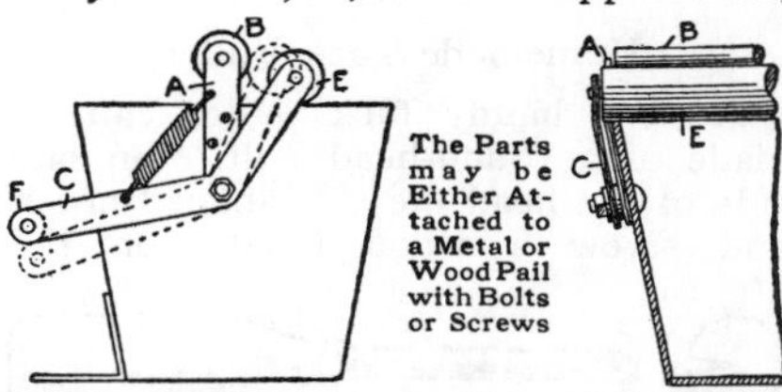

The Parts may be Either Attached to a Metal or Wood Pail with Bolts or Screws

and have a crosspiece, F, at their lower ends. Discarded wringer rollers can be used for B and E. A coil spring is attached as shown, to keep the rollers separate and in a position to receive the mop. When the mop is placed between the rollers they are brought together by a pressure of the foot on the crosspiece F.—Contributed by J. Dennis McKennon, New Britain, Conn.

A Vise Used as a Caliper Gauge

Not infrequently it is desired to know the distance from one side to another of some part that cannot be directly measured with a rule, and when no calipers are at hand. But with a vise handy, the measurement can be made with ease and with sufficient accuracy for all practical purposes if the vise is not too worn. This trick is particularly adapted for calipering threaded parts, as threads cannot be measured readily with ordinary calipers. How this may be done is shown in the sketch, which illustrates the method as applied to a screw. The work is gripped between the jaws of the vise and the opening then measured with a rule.—Contributed by Donald A. Hampson, Middletown, New York.

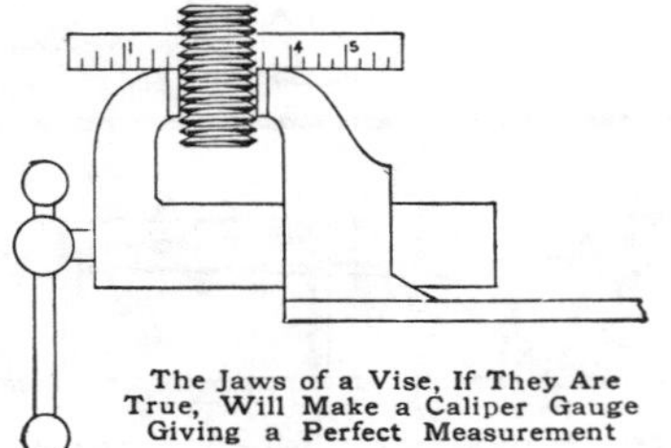

The Jaws of a Vise, If They Are True, Will Make a Caliper Gauge Giving a Perfect Measurement

Homemade Tack Puller

A very handy tack puller can be made of a round-head bolt. On one side of the head file a V-shaped notch and screw a wood handle on the threads. This makes a very powerful puller that will remove large tacks from hardwood easily.

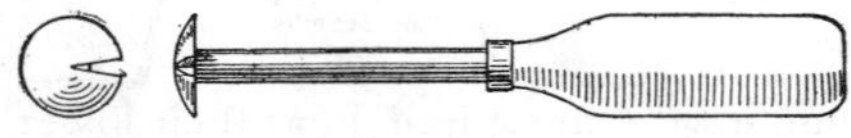

The Shape of the Head Permits a Leverage Action That Lifts the Tack Easily

How to Make a Radium Photograph

The radium rays, like the X-rays, affect the photographic plate, as is well known, but it would naturally be supposed that the enormous cost of radium would prevent the making of such a photograph by the amateur.

It is a fact, however, that a radium photograph can be made at home at practically no cost at all, provided the amateur has patience enough to gather the necessary material, which is nothing else but broken incandescent gas mantles. These (especially Welsbach mantles) contain a salt of the rare metal thorium, which is slightly radioactive. The thing to do, then, is to collect a sufficient quantity of broken mantles to cover the bottom of a small cardboard box—a dryplate box, for instance—with a layer of powdered mantle substance. Upon this layer and pressed tightly against it is placed a piece of cardboard; then some metal objects, a button, hairpin, a buckle, or the like, are laid on the cardboard and covered with a sensitized paper. This is again covered with a piece of cardboard and the box filled with crumpled paper to the top. The cover is then put on, the box tied up with a piece of string and set in some place where it is sure to be left undisturbed.

The radium rays from the powdered mantles readily penetrate the cardboard and paper, but not the metal articles. Being very weak, the rays must be given four weeks to accomplish their work. After that time, however, if the sensitive paper is taken out, pictures of the metal objects in white on a dark background will be found on it. These pictures will not be so sharp as ordinary photographs, because the rays are not focused, but they fairly represent the originals and the experiment is an interesting one.

¶A good imitation mahogany stain consists of 1 part Venetian red and 2 parts yellow lead, mixed with thin glue size, and is laid on with a woolen cloth.

Fountain for an Ordinary Pen

Fill the hollow end of an ordinary penholder with cotton—not too tightly—and one dip of the pen will hold enough ink to write a full page. The cotton should be changed each day. A small piece of sponge will answer the same purpose. It is necessary to dip the pen deeply into the ink.—Contributed by J. E. Noble, London Junction, Ontario.

Pulling Wire through Curved Electric Fixtures

To facilitate the running of electric wires through curved fixtures, nick a heavy shot, A, and fasten it on a cord,

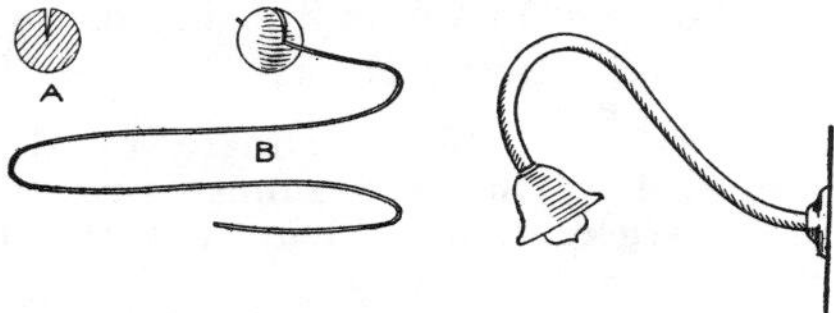

A Shot That will Pass through the Fixture Arm will Carry a Cord for Pulling in the Wires

B, in the same manner as a fishline is weighted. The shot will roll through the fixture tube, carrying the cord with it. A cord strong enough to pull the wires through can be easily drawn through the opening in this manner. The shot should, of course, not be so large that it can possibly bind in the tube.

An Automatically Closing Drawer

A very ingenious way to have a drawer close automatically is to attach a weight so that the rope or cord will pull on the rear end of the drawer. The sketch clearly shows the device which is an attachment similar to that used for closing gates. This can be

The Rope and Weight Attached to the Back End of the Drawer Pulls It Closed

applied to drawers that are frequently drawn out and in places where a person is liable to have the hands full.

A Cork Puller

The stopper of any ordinary bottle can be easily removed with a puller such as shown in the sketch. The puller is inserted between the stopper and the neck of the bottle until the hook end will pass under the bottom of the stopper, then given a quarter turn and pulled upward.

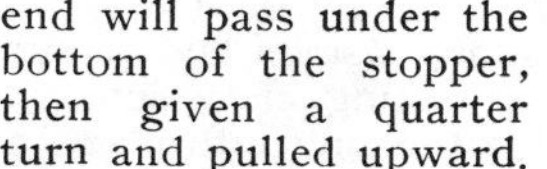

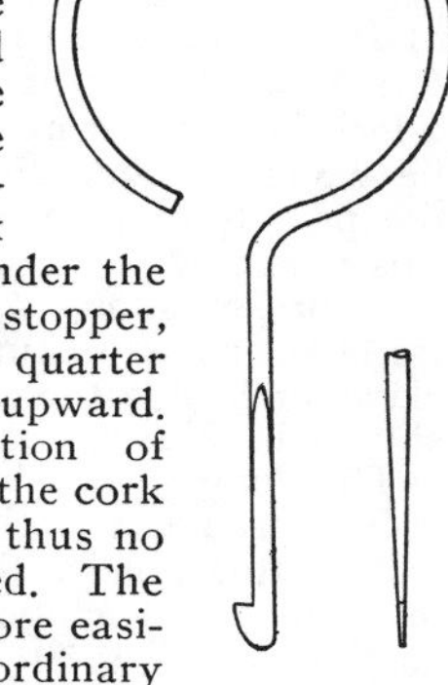

The construction of the puller vents the cork as it enters and thus no vacuum is created. The cork is pulled more easily than with an ordinary corkscrew, and there is no danger of tearing the cork to pieces.

Uses for a Bamboo Pole

Select a good bamboo pole, about 18 ft. long, and cut it into three lengths as follows: A piece from the top, $2\frac{1}{2}$ ft. long; the next length, $5\frac{1}{2}$ ft. long, and the remaining end of the pole, about 10 ft. long. The $2\frac{1}{2}$-ft. length is

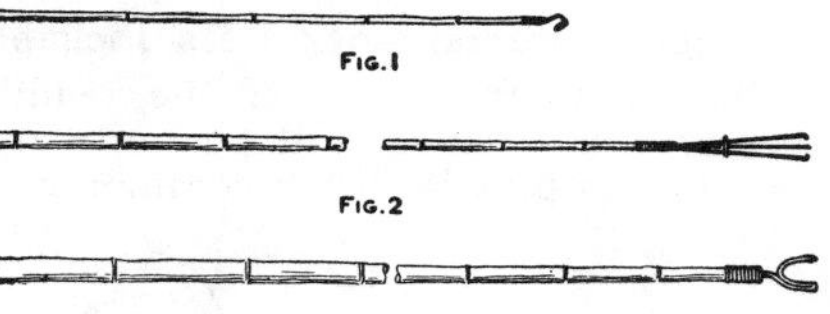

A Bamboo Pole Cut in Three Pieces Makes a Window-Shade Stick, Duster Holder and Clothesline Pole

equipped with a screw hook in the smaller end, as shown in Fig. 1. This stick is useful in lowering window shades that have a ring or screw eye attached to the lower part of the shade. When the stick is not in use, it is hung on the edge of the window casing.

The $5\frac{1}{2}$-ft. length makes the long handle for a duster. Procure an old-style lamp-chimney cleaner, wind a cord around the wires a few inches below the point where they begin to spread to keep them from coming apart, then cut or file the wires off 2 in. below the winding. This leaves a straight shank, over which a ferrule is slipped before it is inserted into the small end of the pole. Fill the remaining space in the pole end with plaster of Paris, and when it has set, slip the ferrule into place on the pole end. If a ferrule is not at hand, a fine wire can be wound around the end to prevent the pole from splitting. When using this pole to dust hardwood floors, tops of doors, window casings and picture frames, put a dusting cloth into the claws and slide the ring into place, as shown in Fig. 2.

The longer and larger end of the pole is used as a clothesline pole. One end of this pole is fitted with a yoke made of No. 6 gauge galvanized wire, as shown in Fig. 3. The wire for the yoke is 10 in. long, and after bending it in shape, the two upper ends should be 2 in. wide at the top and 2 in. deep. Insert the straight end of the wire into the smaller end of the pole and set it in firmly with plaster of Paris. The end of the pole should be securely wound with wire to keep the bamboo from splitting.—Contributed by Gertrude M. Bender, Utica, N. Y.

Making Common Lock Less Pickable

The ordinary lock can be readily changed so that it will be quite impossible to pick it with a common key.

The Small End Cut from the Key is Fastened on the Pin of the Lock

The way to do this is to cut off the small hollow portion of the key that fits over the pin. This part is placed on the pin of the lock and soldered, or fastened by any other means, so it cannot come out of the lock. This will prevent any ordinary key from entering the keyhole.—Contributed by A. J. Hamilton, Benton, Ark.

To Color Tan Leather Black

An inexpensive and effective way to blacken tan leather is as follows: The leather is first rubbed with a 10-percent solution of tannic acid, which may be purchased at any drug store. This treatment should be applied and the leather well dried. It should be rubbed with a cloth hard enough to produce a polish, then apply a 10-percent solution of iron sulphate. A chemical reaction takes place as the last solution is rubbed into the leather, making it black. After this is dry, the leather can be polished in the usual way.

To Prevent Corks Sticking in Bottle Necks

Corks will always adhere to the necks of bottles containing glue or other sticky liquids, with the result that it becomes necessary to cut or dig the cork into small pieces in order to remove the contents from the bottle.

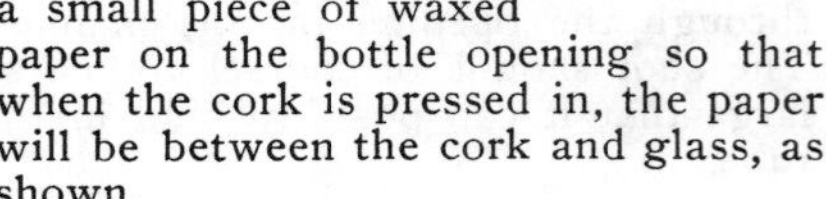

A simple and effective way to prevent a cork from sticking is to place a small piece of waxed paper on the bottle opening so that when the cork is pressed in, the paper will be between the cork and glass, as shown.

To Remove Rust Stains from Clothing

Many times when working around machinery, the clothes will come in contact with iron and get rust stains. These may be removed by using a weak solution of oxalic acid which must be applied carefully as it is highly poisonous. Sometimes the stain can be removed by washing the spot in buttermilk, in which case rubbing is necessary.

¶Small bits of onion placed in a room will absorb the disagreeable odors of paint and turpentine.

Eraser Holder

Any small piece of steel with a point, similar to that shown in the sketch, will make a good eraser holder. The saving of erasers is nothing compared to the convenience of having a small eraser with a chisel edge or point when delicate erasing is required. It is not clumsy as the usual chunk of rubber with a blunt point, for the person erasing can see what he is doing. I use a leg of an old pair of dividers and cut my erasers in four parts in shapes similar to that shown in the sketch by the dotted lines, and can use them easily until they are about

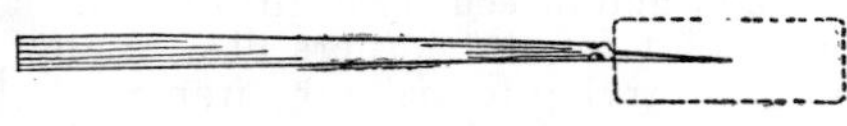

A Very Small Eraser can be Held on the Point and Used for Delicate Erasures

the size of a pea. The friction between the rubber and steel, after the point has been inserted into the rubber, holds the two together nicely.—Contributed by James F. Burke, Lakewood, O.

Bleaching Ivory

A good method to bleach ivory ornaments is to rub on a solution made of a small quantity of unslaked lime, bran and water. The mixture should be wiped off after the ivory has become sufficiently bleached, and the surface then rubbed with sawdust or magnesia, which gives it a brilliant polish.

A Soap Shake

To utilize scraps of soap, make a soap shake of a medium-size baking-powder can, as shown in the sketch. Punch holes in the can with an ice pick or some other sharp-pointed instrument, and attach a large wire to the center, twisting the ends to form a handle.—Contributed by Elizabeth P. Grant, Winchester, Virginia.

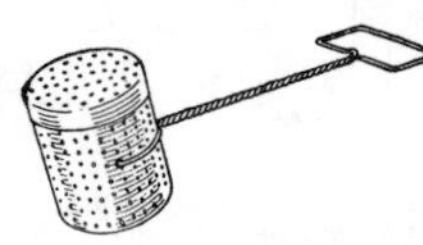

Ear Repair on a Bucket

A broken ear for a bail on a metal pail or bucket can be replaced with a window-shade fastener, such as shown at A in the sketch. The base of the fastener is turned down flat and attached with screw bolts or rivets, as shown at B.—Contributed by Harold Robinson, Suffern, N. Y.

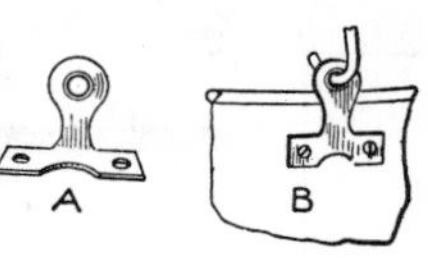

Cleaning Dirt from Tufts in Upholstering

A handy device for cleaning furniture upholstering and vehicle-seat tuftings may be easily made as follows: Take an ordinary round paintbrush and cut the handle off, leaving it about 1½ in. long, then saw a V-shaped notch in it, as shown in Fig. 1. Attach the brush to the ratchet screwdriver, Fig. 2, by inserting the screwdriver blade in the notch of the brush handle, and secure it by wrapping a strong cord around the handle. Place the brush in the tuft and work the screwdriver handle, as in turning a screw. A few quick turns of the brush will throw out the dirt which is impossible to remove with a straight brush.

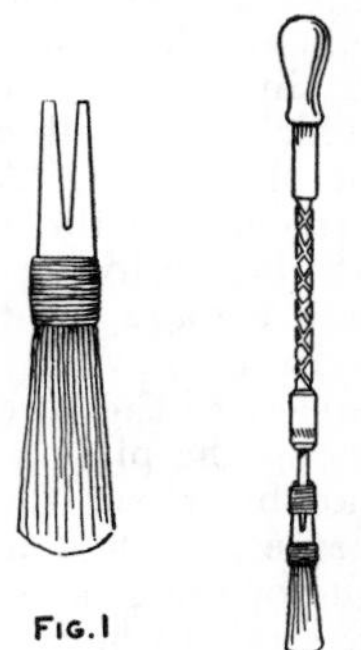

Painting Lead Pipe

The paint applied to lead pipes will chip and peel off, and to prevent this I first cover the lead surface with a thin coat of varnish, then apply the paint on the varnish. A lead pipe painted in this way will retain its coating.—Contributed by F. Schumacher, Brooklyn, N. Y.

Attaching a Vise Jaw to a Bench

Procure a toothed metal rail or rack, A, such as is used for small ladder tracks, and mount it on the lower

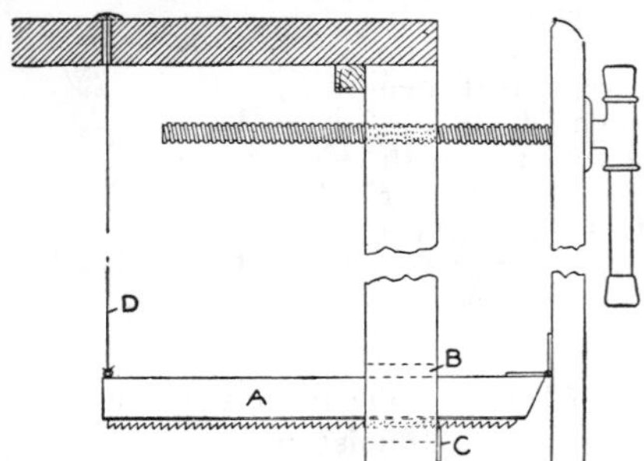

The Rack on the Lower Guide Rail Provides a Means to Keep the Vise Jaws Parallel

edge of the guide rail for the lower end of the vise jaw. Provide a slot, B, in the leg of the bench, through which the rail can run with plenty of play room. A beveled plate, C, is attached to the face of the bench leg at the bottom of the slot, so that it will engage the teeth of the rack.

In use, when opening the vise by means of the screw, the rack will drag along the plate, and stop and engage a notch when the opening operation ceases. When it is desired to reduce the opening, it is only necessary to lift the rail by means of the string D. A button is tied to the upper end of the string on top of the bench, to keep it handy for changing the jaw.—Contributed by Harry F. Lowe, Washington, District of Columbia.

Removing Vegetable Stains

To remove stains of vegetables or fruits of any kind from cloth or wood, the following method is very good: The stained piece is first moistened with water and then placed in a jar or pail that can be covered. A lump of sulphur is ignited and dropped into the jar. Place the sulphur on a fire shovel when lighting it to avoid burns. The burning sulphur should be placed in the receptacle on the side where the stain will be exposed to the fumes. The sulphur burns slowly so that the articles will not be harmed.

After the sulphur has burned away, the jar should be kept closed for a few minutes and when the articles are removed, the stains will be gone. This is harmless to try, and the cloth will not be injured if it is in a dry condition. The articles should be washed and dried as soon as they are taken out of the jar.

Picture-Frame Corner Joints

Very often the amateur craftsman comes across a picture which he would like to have framed, but the difficulty and insecurity of the ordinary miter joint for the corners discourage him from trying to make the frame. A very easy way to construct a rigid frame is shown in the illustration. The size of the frame must be determined by the picture to be framed. The width, A, of the pieces depends upon one's own taste.

Four pieces, the desired length and width and ½ in. thick, should be dressed out of the material intended for the frame. Four other pieces, ⅜ in. thick and ½ in. narrower than the first four pieces, are next made ready and fastened with glue and flat-head screws to the back of the first pieces, as shown. This allows ⅜ in. for glass, picture and backing, and ½ in. to lap over the front of the picture on all edges.

By arranging the pieces as shown in Fig. 1, a strong corner lap is secured.

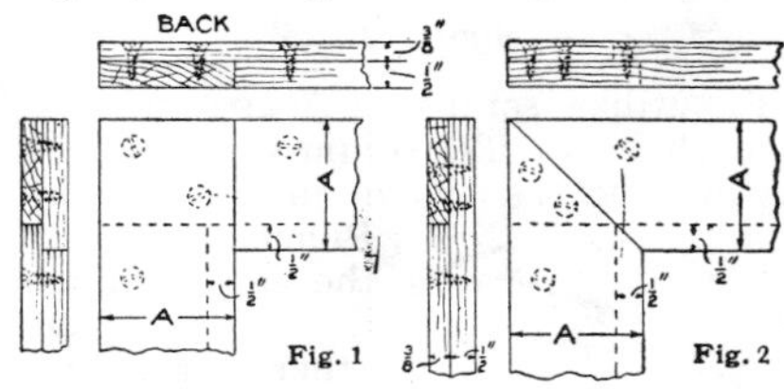

Square and Mitered Lap Joints for Making Rigid Picture Frames in Natural or Stained Woods

A miter lap joint which is not so strong is shown in Fig. 2. The latter gives a mitered-joint effect. This method does away with the use of the rabbeting plane and miter box, both of which are difficult to use with accuracy. Two screws should be used in each joint to reinforce the glue.—Contributed by James Gaffney, Chicago, Ill.

Hunting-Knife Handles

Very artistic handles for hunting knives and carving sets can be made by using disks of horn. Procure some cowhorns from a slaughter house and split them with a saw, using only the large portion of the horn. The split horn is then heated by dry heat—an oven is best—then pressed between two cold plates to a flat piece. If well heated, it is surprising how easily this can be done. The piece is then cut into squares of suitable size which are marked and perforated in the center, the hole being a trifle smaller than the tang of the blade. The tang should

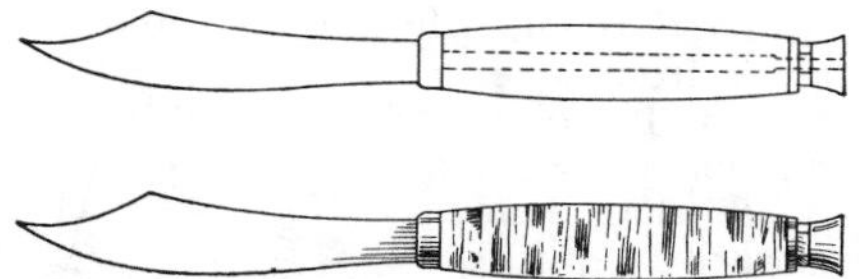

The Finished Handle, If the Work is Well Done, is Easily Mistaken for Agate

be flat and a little longer than the desired handle, with the end made round and threaded for a nut.

A suitable washer is placed on the tang, which is then heated sufficiently to burn its way through the pieces of horn as they are put on the metal. When a sufficient number of disks are on the tang a washer should be slipped on and followed by a round nut. Pressure is applied by turning the nut and repeated heatings of the disks will force them together to make perfect joints. Only a moderate pressure should be applied at a time.

The handle is now to be finished to the shape desired. If black and colored pieces of horn are interspersed, the finished handle will have the appearance of agate. The blade and handle can be lacquered and the ferrules nickelplated.—Contributed by James H. Beebee, Rochester, N. Y.

Holding Wood in a Sawbuck

Anyone who has used a sawbuck knows how inconvenient it is to have a stick roll or lift up as the saw blade

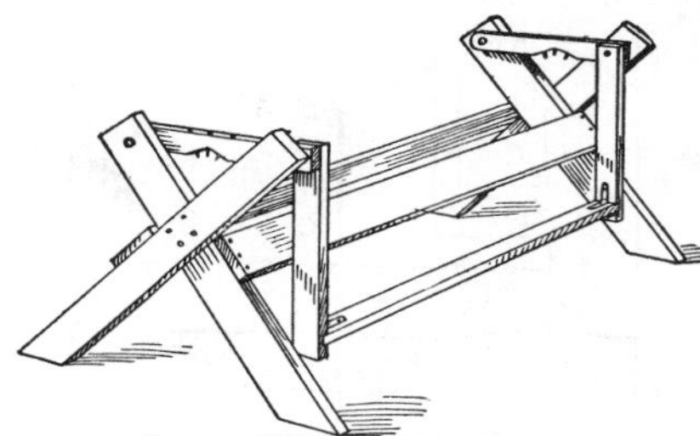

The Holding Attachment Easily Adjusts Itself to the Stick of Wood Placed in the Crotch

is pulled back for the next cut. With the supplementary device, shown in the sketch, which can be easily attached to the sawbuck, these troubles will be eliminated. It consists of two crosspieces hinged to the back uprights of the sawbuck and a foot-pressure stirrup fastened to their front ends as shown. Spikes are driven through the crosspieces so that their protruding ends will gouge into the stick of wood being sawed. The stirrup is easily thrown back for laying a piece of wood in the crotch.

A New Pail-Cover Handle

The handle of the cover, instead of being attached to the center, is placed near the edge and bail of the pail. On the bail and just above the handle of the cover there is formed a loop large enough to accommodate the thumb.

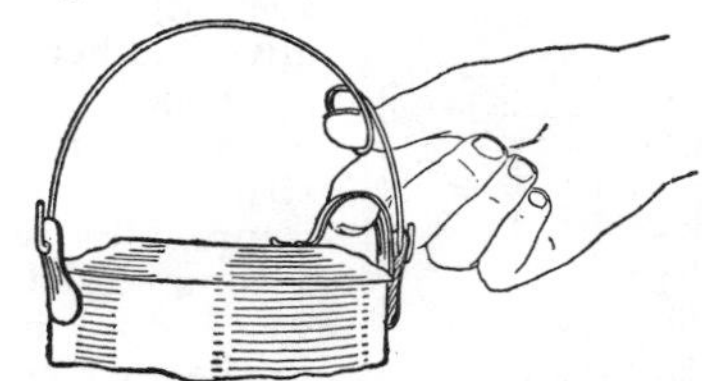

The Bail Loop and the Handle Make It Easy to Remove the Cover with One Hand

With this arrangement, the cover may be removed with the use of but one hand.

Drip-Pan Alarm

The trouble caused by overflowing of the drip pan for an ice box or refrigerator can be overcome by attaching a device that will sound an alarm when the water reaches a level safely below the overflow point. A device of this kind may be attached to the back of the refrigerator as shown in the sketch. A float, A, is attached to the lower end of a rod, B, which slides through staples CC. At the upper end of the rod, a V-shaped copper sheet, D, is soldered. This makes the contact points in the electric wiring. The battery E can be placed under or back of the refrigerator as desired. The method of wiring is clearly shown.

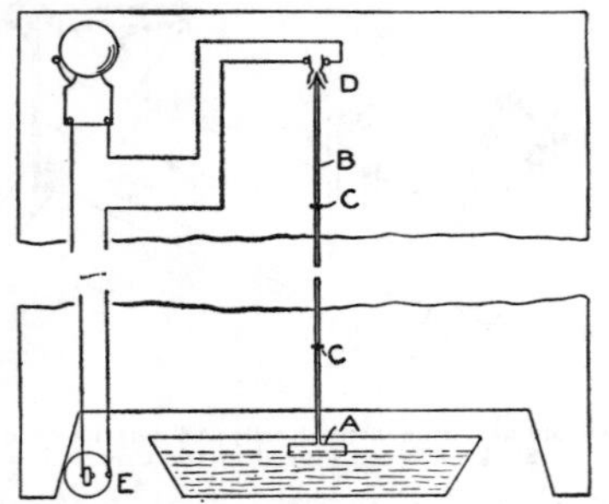

The Float in the Pan, and Contacts for Closing the Circuit to Ring the Bell

A Live-Bait Pail

Every fisherman knows that live bait will soon die if they do not receive sufficient air. I have succeeded in keeping bait alive and healthy by using a pail of my own construction, which is provided with a compressed-air space to force air to the surface of the water. The air space A takes up one-fifth of the interior at the bottom of the pail, and an ordinary hand bicycle pump is used to fill it through a bicycle-tire valve, B. The pipe C from the air space extends up along the side of the pail and the upper end is bent so that it just touches the surface of the water. The pipe contains a valve to regulate the flow of air.

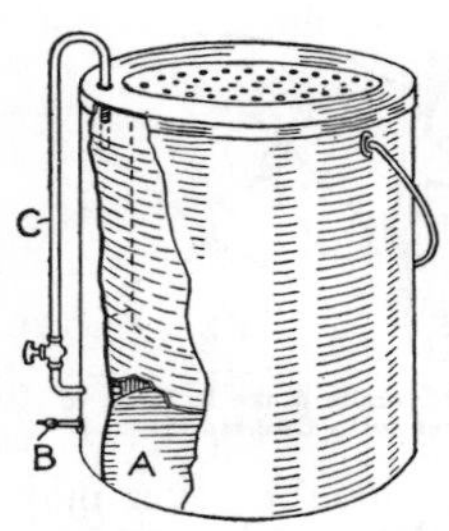

After the pail has been standing for an hour or more, the bait will rise to the top. The valve is then opened for a few minutes, and the minnows will soon swim around in the water as when this was fresh.—Contributed by T. Whelan, Paterson, N. J.

A Mouse Trap

After using various means to catch the mice in my pantry, I finally decided I could not catch them in the ordinary manner. Knowing that mice are not afraid of dishes but will run all over them, while they will stay away from other things, I took a dinner plate, a bowl that held about 1 qt., a thimble, filled with toasted cheese, and arranged the articles as shown in the sketch, balancing the bowl on the thimble. When the mouse nibbled the cheese, the bowl came down on it, making it a prisoner. The whole was then dropped in a pail of water. Scald the dish and bowl before using them again to remove all traces of the mouse.

Quickly Made Rheostat

A short time ago I found it necessary to melt some silver, and in setting up an arc light to obtain the heat I made a rheostat by winding wire around a large earthenware jar. As the jar is a non-conductor and would not burn, it served the purpose perfectly. In winding the wire, be careful to keep the coils from touching each other.—Contributed by P. D. Merrill, Chicago, Ill.

Sunlight Flasher for the Garden

By CLAUDE L. WOOLLEY

The following apparatus is likely to be novel, and certainly very striking when erected on country estates, particularly on high lands, hillsides, and along the seashore, where the flashes may be seen for many miles out at sea.

It is not unusual in country gardens to see a large hollow glass globe silvered on the inside, mounted on a pedestal, brilliantly reflecting the sunlight. The apparatus described is an elaboration of the idea. The drawing shows in diagram the general construction, exact measurements not being given. However, a convenient height is 3½ to 4 ft., and the circular frame, carrying the mirrors, may be 10 to 14 in. in diameter.

The supporting frame, of galvanized sheet iron or sheet copper, may be either circular or hexagonal in shape. Mounted upon a vertical shaft is a skeleton circular frame, carrying a double row of small mirrors, or ordinary flat mirror glass, mounted in grooves provided for them; the upper row inclined slightly upward, and the lower row slightly downward. If a greater number of angles of reflection are desired, the mirrors may be smaller, and arranged in four circular rows instead of two, each row being inclined at a slightly different angle.

The shaft is pointed at the lower end and rests in a bearing drilled with a V-shaped depression, the bearing being supported by soldering or riveting at each end to the inner sides of the pedestal shell. The upper portion of the shaft passes through a bearing which is also soldered or riveted at the ends, to the inner surfaces of the pedestal shell.

The mirrors, mounted on the shaft, thus are free to revolve vertically with very little friction. Upon the lower end of the shaft is fastened a light gear wheel of rather large diameter, and this in turn is geared to a smaller gear mounted on the end of the armature shaft of a small electric motor of the type that may be driven with a few dry cells; the relation of the sizes of the gears being such as will cause the mirrors to revolve slowly, when the motor is running at normal speed.

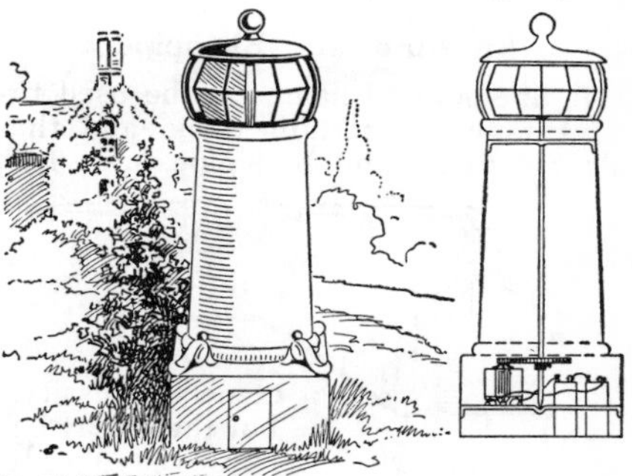

The Flasher as It Appears on the Stand and the Details of Its Construction

Connected to the motor are two or more dry, or other suitable batteries, a small door being provided on the side of the lower part of the pedestal to enable the batteries to be replaced, or turned off, and to give access to the motor. A circular shield is erected over the mirror carrier, surmounted by an ornamental ball, to protect from the weather and to provide a more finished appearance. A waterproof canvas cover may be slipped over the whole in rainy weather.

As new mirror faces at varying angles are constantly being presented to the sun, vivid flashes are constantly occurring when viewed from almost any angle or position on the side where the sun is shining. The circular shield on top is supported in position by four metal strips secured by soldering to the shield and the supporting pedestal.

Such a device may be constructed without much expense, producing a most brilliant effect over miles of territory. The small driving motor may be replaced with a suitable spring or weight-driven clockwork; or four hollow hemispherical metal cups may be mounted on arms, or placed at right angles, and the arms in turn mounted upon a vertical shaft and arranged above the mirror carrier and geared in such manner that the mirrors will revolve slowly, while the cups are revolving with comparatively high speed by the force of the wind.

The mounted revolving cups are similar in form to the apparatus used by the U. S. Weather Bureau for measuring the speed of the wind. They will respond to a good breeze from any point of the compass.

An Automatic Blowpipe

A fine-pointed flame can be used to advantage for certain work, and the alcohol flame and blowpipe have become a necessity, but these may be improved upon so as to make the apparatus automatic in action and more efficient in its work. A bottle or receptacle, A, having a large bottom to provide a sufficient heating surface, is supplied with a cork and a tube, B, bent at right angles. The receptacle, A, is supported on a stand so that it may be heated with a small lamp, C. The light D may be a candle, alcohol lamp, or any flame set at the right distance from the end of the tube B.

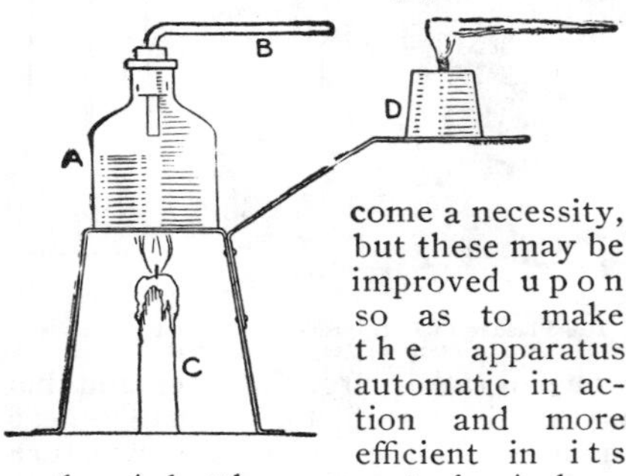

The receptacle A is partly filled with alcohol, and the heating lamp lit. The heat will turn the alcohol into gas and cause a pressure, driving it through the tube B, so that it is ignited by the flame from D. The flame will have a fine point with sufficient heat to melt glass.—Contributed by W. R. Sears, St. Paul, Minn.

Homemade Steam-Turbine Engine

Select a tomato can, or any can in which vegetables or fruit is sold, and carefully unsolder the small cap on the end when removing the contents. When the can is empty, clean it well and solder the cap in place again. Procure a strip of brass, bend it as shown at A and solder it to the can top in the center. Cut a piece of about No. 14 gauge wire, the length equal to the opening between the uprights of the U-shaped piece of brass, with about ½ in. added for a small pulley wheel. The uprights are punched or drilled at their upper ends to admit the wire which is then adjusted in place.

Two strips of tin are cut to fit in between the standards and are notched in the center, as shown at B, and slightly bent to fit over the wire shaft. These are soldered to the wire between the

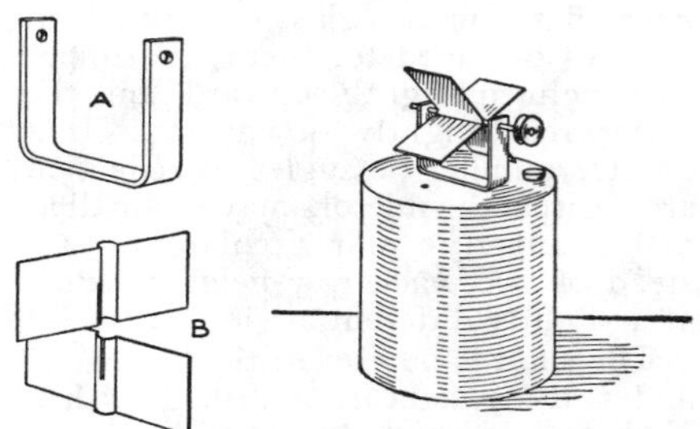

The Boiler is Made of a Fruit or Vegetable Can and the Turbine of Thin Metal Strips

uprights. A small hole is punched on one side in the top of the can so that it will center the paddle of the wheel. On the opposite side of the top another larger hole is punched and tightly fitted with a wood plug. This is the opening for filling the boiler with water. The can should be filled about two-thirds full and set on a stove. The steam, coming under pressure from the small hole, strikes the paddles of the wheel with considerable force and causes it to revolve rapidly. Be careful not to set the boiler on too hot a fire.

Electric Switch for Exposing Photographic Printing Papers

The proper time to expose a printing paper under a negative should be determined and the negative marked for future printing. When this time has been found some means should be provided for making the exposure exactly the same, then the prints will be perfect and of a good tone at all times. For this purpose the instrument shown in the illustration was designed and used with entire satisfaction.

The device consists of an ordinary cheap watch, a standard, or support, for an adjusting screw, a small coil, a movable armature, a knife switch, and a trip arrangement. A neat box or case, about 5 in. square and 3 in. high, is first constructed. A round recess, 1/8 in. deep, is cut in the center of the top, to admit the watch. The standard A is made of brass, 1/8 in. thick and 1/2 in. wide, bent as shown, and a 3/16-in. hole is drilled in the end of the long arm where it will exactly center over the pivot holding the watch hands. A 3/16-in. rod, B, is closely fitted in the hole and supplied with a knurled wheel, C, on the upper end, and an L-shaped arm, D, is fastened to the lower end. The end of this arm should be filed to a point, or a very thin piece of brass soldered to it, so that the end will just touch the minute hand of the watch. The tip end of the point should be bent slightly from the perpendicular toward the direction in which the watch hands are moving, so that, when it is set, the moving hand will easily break the contact.

The magnetic arrangement consists of a 3-ohm coil, E, mounted, as shown,

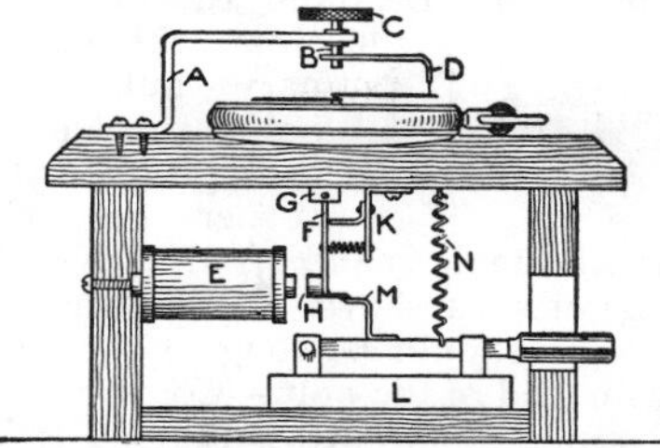

Time Switch for Operating an Electric Light in Printing Photographic Developing Papers

to one side of the case, where it operates the trip levers. The armature parts consist of an L-shaped piece of brass, F, pivoted at G, to which a square piece of soft iron, H, is attached. Two small parts, K, are bent and attached as shown, to furnish a limit stop for the piece F and a support for a spiral spring which holds the armature H away from the coil.

The knife switch L is fastened to the bottom of the case so that the handle will project through a slot in one side of the box. A trip piece, M, and a small eye for attaching a spiral spring, N, are soldered to the knife switch. These two attachments for the switch are insulated from the other parts.

Two binding posts are mounted on top, one being connected to one terminal of the coil E and the other to the watch case. The other terminal of the coil is connected to the standard A. The two binding posts are connected in series with one or two dry cells, and the switch L is connected in series with the lamp used for printing.

The operation is as follows: The arm D, being set for a certain time, the lever of the switch L is set and the light remains lit until the minute hand strikes the point on the arm D, when the battery circuit is closed causing the coil to draw the armature H and allowing the spring N to open the switch L. The lamp is then extinguished.—Contributed by James P. Lewis, Golden, Colorado.

How to Make a Wing Nut

Finding that I needed some wing nuts and not being able to purchase them in the size I wanted, I made them from the ordinary nuts. A hole was drilled through opposite corners of each nut and a staple made of wire riveted in the holes as shown in the sketch. The staple should be long enough to admit the end of the bolt.—Contributed by Clarence L. Orcutt, Buffalo, N. Y.

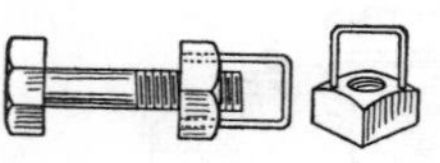

Cork-Covered Clothes Peg

When screws or nails are used to hang clothes or other articles on, run the nail or screw through a bottle cork as shown. The cork will prevent the nail or screw from tearing the article and also insure the cloth against rust marks, should the article be wet.

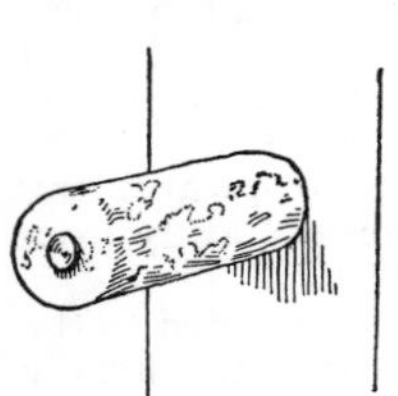

Shaping an Old Broom

A broom, having the straws bent and out of shape, yet not worn out, can be fixed up like new in the following manner: Slightly dampen the straw with water and wrap with heavy paper, then place a weight on it. After standing under pressure for several days the straw will be restored to the shape of

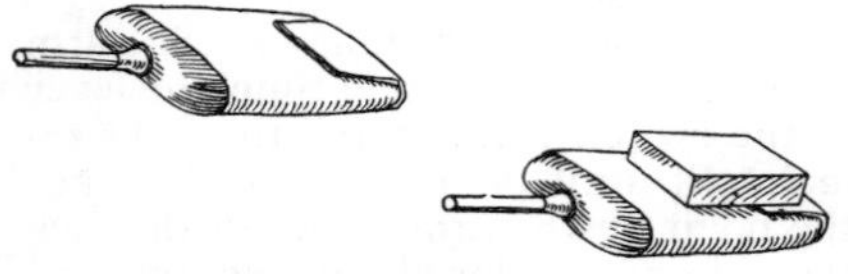

Method of Straightening the Straws

a new broom. Paint brushes can be treated in the same manner, but in that case linseed oil should be used instead of water.

How to Make a Bolster

The sketch shows a simple bed bolster which I have made and which can be constructed at very little cost. Three circular pieces of poplar or pine, 10½ in. in diameter, are required. These may be made in one cut by nailing the pieces together. Then nail on ten ⅜ by 2-in. strips, 52 in. long, or as long as the width of the bed, leaving about ½ in. space between the strips. These strips will thus go about two-thirds of the way around the circle, leaving room to insert the pillows when the bed is not in use. Cover the bolster with building paper or any other suitable material, and it is ready for the pillow shams.—Contributed by C. Martin, Jr., Chicago.

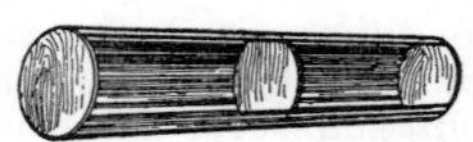

A Fish-Scaling Knife

A useful fish-scaling and skinning knife can be made of an old broken hacksaw blade. This must be at least 6 in. long and will make a knife with

Scaling Knife

a 3-in. blade. Grind the blade to the shape shown and make a handle for it by using two strips of maple, ¼ in. thick and 4 in. long. These are riveted together with 3 in. of the blade between them.—Contributed by John L. Waite, Cambridge, Mass.

To Prevent Moles from Damaging Growing Seeds

The food most liked by the ground mole is the sprouts of peas and corn. A way to protect these growing seeds is to dip them in kerosene just before planting. The mole will not touch the oil-covered seed, and the seeds are not injured in the least.—Contributed by J. W. Bauholster, Gresham, O.

The Heliograph as It is Used by Neighboring Boys to Send Messages on a Clear Day by Flashing the Sun's Rays from One to the Other, Which can be Read as Far as the Eye can See the Light

How to Make a Heliograph

By R. B. HUEY

The heliograph which is used in the army provides a good method of sending messages by the reflection of the sun's rays. In the mountains there are stations from which messages are sent by the heliograph for great distances, and guides carry them for use in case of trouble or accident. The wireless telegraph delivers messages by electricity through the air, but the heliograph sends them by flashes of light.

The main part of the instrument is the mirror, which should be about 4 in. square, set in a wood frame and swung on trunnions made of two square-head bolts, each 1/4 in. in diameter, and 1 in. long, which are firmly held to the frame with brass strips, 1/2 in. wide, and 3 in. long. The strips are drilled centrally to admit the bolts, and then drilled at each end for a screw to fasten them to the frame. This construction is clearly shown in Fig. 1.

A hole is cut centrally through the backing of the frame and a small hole, not over 1/8 in. in diameter, is scratched through the silvering on the glass. If the trunnions are centered properly, the small hole should be exactly in line with them and in the center.

A U-shaped support is made of wood strips, 3/8 in. thick and 1 in. wide, the length of the uprights being 3 1/2 in. and the crosspiece connecting their

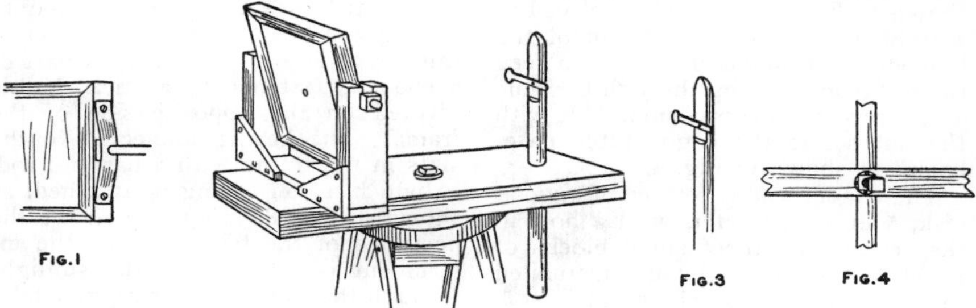

Detail of the Parts for Making the Mirror and Sight Rod Which are Placed on a Base Set on a Tripod Top, the Whole being Adjusted to Reflect the Sun's Rays in Any Direction Desired

lower ends a trifle longer than the width of the frame. These are put together, as shown in Fig. 2, with small upper unnailed ends are spread to slip over the blocks on the tripod top. These ends are bored to loosely fit over

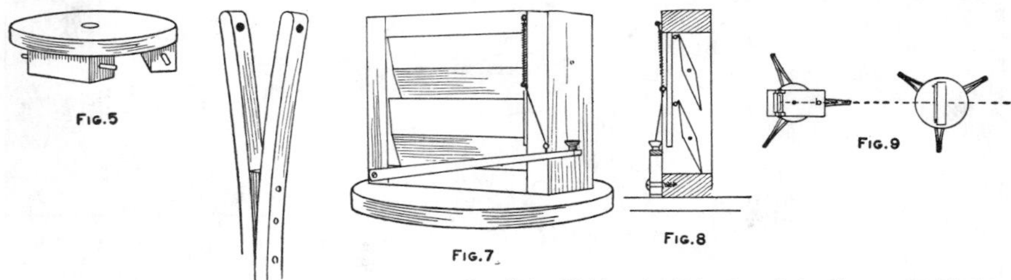

The Parts in Detail for Making the Tripods and the Shutter for Flashing the Light, and Diagram Showing the Location of the Tripods to Direct the Light through the Shutter

brackets at the corners. A slot, ½ in. deep and ¼ in. wide, is cut into the upper end of each upright to receive the trunnions on the mirror frame. Nuts are turned on the bolt ends tightly, to clamp the standard tops against the brass strips on the mirror frame. The cross strip at the bottom is clamped to the base by means of a bolt, 1½ in. long. The hole for this bolt should be exactly below the peephole in the mirror and run through one end of the baseboard, which is ¾ in. thick, 2 in. wide and 10 in. long.

At the opposite end of the base, place a sighting rod, which is made as follows: The rod is ½ in. in diameter and 8 in. long. The upper end is fitted with a piece of thick, white cardboard, cut ¼ in. in diameter and having a projecting shank 1 in. long, as shown in Fig. 3. The rod is placed in a ½-in. hole bored in the end of the baseboard, as shown in Fig. 2. To keep the rod from slipping through the hole a setscrew is made of a small bolt with the nut set in the edge of the baseboard, as shown in Fig. 4.

The tripod head is formed of a wood disk, 5 in. in diameter, with a hole in the center, and three small blocks of wood, 1 in. square and 2 in. long, nailed to the under side, as shown in Fig. 5. The tripod legs are made of light strips of wood, ⅜ in. thick, 1 in. wide and 5 ft. long. Two of these strips, nailed securely together to within 20 in. of the top, constitute one leg. The the headless nails driven part way into the block ends. One tripod leg is shown in Fig. 6.

The screen, or shutter, is mounted on a separate tripod and is shown in Fig. 7. Cut out two slats, ⅜ in. thick, 2½ in. wide and 6 in. long, from hard wood, and taper both edges of these slats down to $\frac{3}{16}$ in. Small nails are driven into the ends of the slats and the heads are filed off so that the projecting ends will form trunnions for the slats to turn on. Make a frame of wood pieces, ¾ in. thick and 2½ in. wide, the opening in the frame being 6 in. square. Before nailing the frame together bore holes in the side uprights for the trunnions of the slats to turn in. These holes are 1¾ in. apart. The frame is then nailed together and also nailed to the tripod top. The shutter is operated with a key very similar to a telegraph key. The construction of this key is shown in Fig. 7. A part of a spool is fastened to a stick that is pivoted on the opposite side of the frame. The key is connected to the slats in the frame with a bar and rod, to which a coil spring is attached, as shown in Fig. 8. Figure 9 shows the positions of the tripods when the instrument is set to flash the sunlight through the shutter. The regular telegraph code is used in flashing the light.

To set the instrument, first turn the cardboard disk down to uncover the point of the sight rod, then sight through the hole in the mirror and adjust the sight rod so that the tip end comes squarely in line with the receiving station. When the instrument is properly sighted, the shutter is set up directly in front of it and the cardboard disk is turned up to cover the end of the sight rod. The mirror is then turned so that it reflects a beam of light with a small shadow spot showing in the center made by the peephole in the mirror, which is directed to fall on the center of the cardboard sighting disk. It will be quite easy to direct this shadow spot to the disk by holding a sheet of paper 6 or 8 in. in front of the mirror and following the spot on the paper until it reaches the disk. The flashes are made by manipulating the key operating the shutter in the same manner as a telegraph key.

Twine Cutter for Use at a Wrapping Counter

A cutter for use at the wrapping counter in a drug or confectionery store may be easily made from a double-edged razor blade and a piece of thin board—a piece of cigar box will do. Cut the wood in the shape shown, with a protecting piece over the edge of the razor.

Screws are turned through the holes in the blade and into a support on the paper holder or any other convenient place.—Contributed by T. F. Managhan, Philadelphia, Pa.

Frosting Brass

A very fine ornamental finish, resembling brushed work, may be applied to brass articles by boiling them in a caustic-potash solution, then rinsing in clear water, whereupon they are dipped into dilute nitric acid until the oxide is removed, then rinsed quickly and dried in sawdust. The surface should be lacquered while the metal is hot.

A Cupboard-Door Spice-Box Shelf

To keep the spice boxes in a handy place where they would be together and not behind larger articles on the

The Shelf will Hold All the Spice Boxes and Keep Them Handy

cupboard shelves, I made a special spice-box shelf, as shown, to hang on the inside of the cupboard door. The shelf swings out with the door as it opens, and is made of two bracket ends to which a bottom board and front crosspiece is nailed. The size of the shelf and its capacity are only limited by the space on the door.—Contributed by Austin Miller, Santa Barbara, California.

Starting a Siphon

It is often necessary in a laboratory to siphon acids and poisonous liquids. If a pump is used there is always danger of the liquid entering the pump and damaging it, and, besides, a pump is not handy for this purpose. To fill a siphon by suction from the mouth, great care must be taken to keep

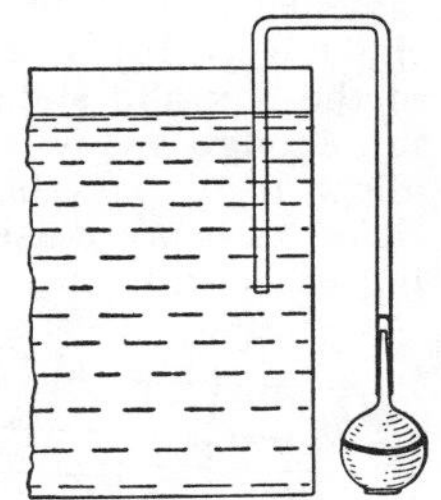

from drawing the liquid into the mouth. One of the best ways to fill a siphon is to procure a large dropper and having pressed all the air out of the bulb insert the end in the siphon. Releasing the pressure on the bulb will cause it to draw the liquid into the siphon.—Contributed by Bedell M. Neubert, Newtown, Conn.

A Window-Seat Sewing Box

The combined window seat and sewing box shown was made by using a shoe-packing box for the foundation.

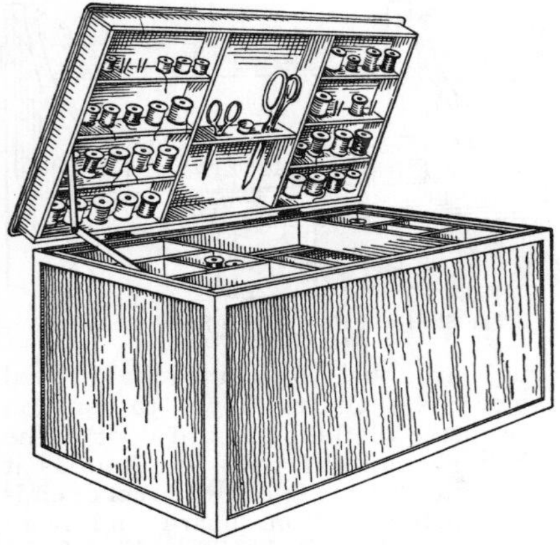

A Window-Seat Workbox for Sewing Materials, Made of an Ordinary Shoe-Packing Box

This was covered with matting and the edges and corners finished with wood strips, ½ in. thick and stained a dark red. Three trays were provided on the inside at the top part of the box, each of the two upper ones occupying one-fourth of the box opening and sliding on a pair of guides fastened to the sides of the box, while the lower tray is one-half the length of the box and slides on guides placed far enough below the upper trays to allow it to pass beneath these. The three trays were used for keeping sewing materials, such as buttons, hooks

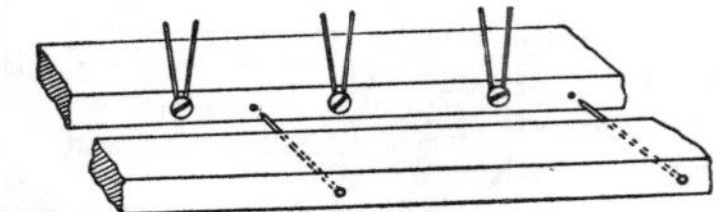

The Spindles for the Spools are Made of Cotters Fastened with Screws in the Shelves

and eyes, etc. When the trays are all moved to one end it gives access to the lower part of the box where the work or mending is kept out of sight.

The inside of the cover is 1½ in. deep and shelves are arranged for thread and silk spools on either side, the center space being used for the shears, thimbles and scissors. The little shelves are made of two pieces, each half as wide as the depth of the box cover. The first half of the shelf is fastened in place, then a row of cotters attached with wood screws, whereupon the other half of the shelf is put in place. The edges of the cover are rounded on the outside to make an attractive seat.

While no dimensions are necessary, as the box can be of any size to suit the maker, it may be mentioned that the one shown is 28 in. long, 12 in. wide and 16 in. deep.—Contributed by R. B. Thomas, Lowell, Mass.

Cutting a Glass Bottle

It is sometimes necessary to cut a heavy glass bottle or cylinder. Four methods are in use. A carborundum disk having a thin edge, if kept wet and rotated at a high speed, will cut heavy glass, but the cylinder must be fed against the wheel very gently. A better way is to make a file mark — clean, but not very deep—around the cylinder and heat it with a long slender flame while slowly rotating the cylinder all the time. It is very important that the gas flame should not spread over the surface of the glass, for it is only the file mark that should be heated. A mere glancing touch is sufficient. Usually the glass will crack off in a very clean cut.

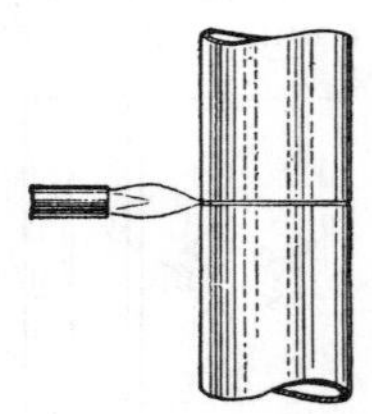

Sometimes a fine platinum wire is wound around in the file mark and heated by an electric current. Less common is the trick of wrapping a strand of yarn soaked in turpentine around the mark and burning it. The principle is the same in each case. The unequal heating of the glass causes it to break.—Contributed by Harry H. Holmes, Richmond, Ind.

To Clean Painted or Frescoed Walls

Use a paste made of vinegar and baking soda with a small amount of salt added. The ingredients should be mixed in a large dish and applied to the wall with a cloth. The grease and fly specks as well as the carbon deposits from kitchen smoke are quickly removed. The mixture is harmless. After the wall is thoroughly cleaned, it should be washed with warm water and soap, then dried with a cloth. The mixture works equally well on enameled baths and glass or white porcelain.

Securing Papers in a Mailing Tube

The illustrations show two methods of securing papers or photographs in a mailing tube. In Fig. 1 the mailing tube A is shown in cross section and the manner of running the string through the pasteboard walls illustrated. The ends of the string are drawn up and tied over or under the label. If the label is pasted over the string or string ends as they are tied, it makes a sealed package which is rated as first-class matter.

The second way is to run the cords in a cross form through holes near the ends, as in Fig. 2, then tie the knots as at BB. In each instance,

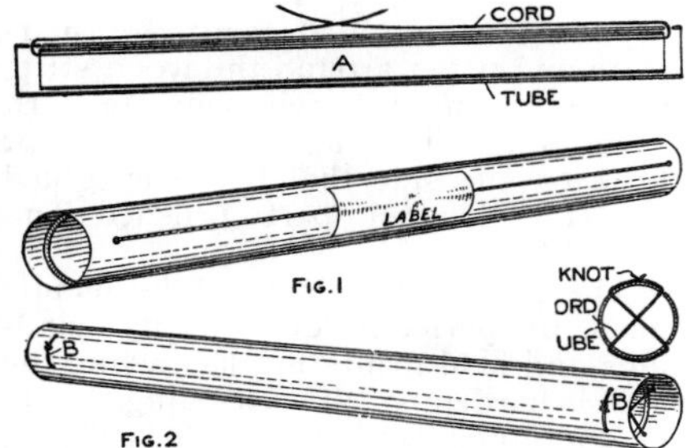

The String in Either Case Prevents the Papers from Slipping Out of the Mailing Tube

even if the papers fit the tube loosely, they will be held securely and can be easily extracted when the knots are untied.

Cooling Tube for a Laboratory Still

A simple and very effective device to replace the cumbersome cooling or condensation coil of a still for the

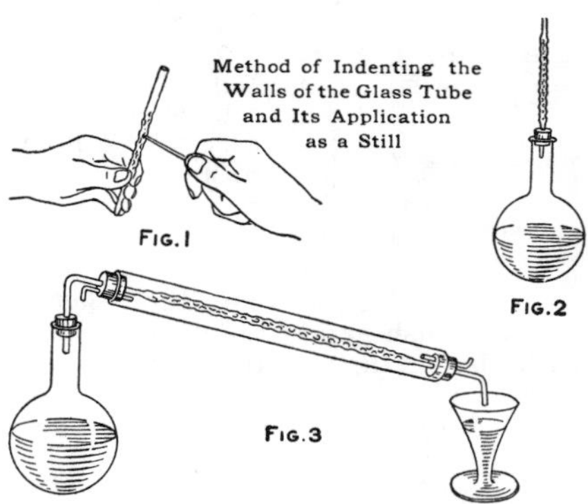

Method of Indenting the Walls of the Glass Tube and Its Application as a Still

amateur's laboratory can be easily made as follows:

Procure an ordinary straight glass tube of fairly large diameter and heat it in the flame of an alcohol lamp with the use of a blowpipe or in a Bunsen burner with a very reduced flame so that only a small spot of the tube is brought to a red heat at one time. Then, with a previously pointed and charred stick of wood—a penholder, for instance—produce a small recess in the wall by pushing the charred end gently into the glowing part of the tube. This procedure is repeated until the whole tube is thus provided with small recesses. The indentations should be made in spiral lines around the tube, thus increasing the surface that is in contact with the cooling water. The operation of making the recesses is shown in Fig. 1. The walls of the recesses should have a regular and uniform slant.

The tube thus produced can either be used as a rectifier (Fig. 2) above a vessel, for fractional distillation, because it will allow the most volatile parts to pass out first, or as a condenser (Fig. 3), the arrangement of which needs no explanation. The amateur will find it much easier to make this tube than to coil a very long one.

A Comb Cleaner

A good comb cleaner that does the work easily and quickly can be made from a worn-out varnish brush. The brush selected should not be over 2 in. wide; it should be thoroughly cleaned with benzine and the bristles cut to a bevel, as shown in the sketch. In use, brush across the comb parallel with the teeth, and the dirt between them will be easily removed.—Contributed by John V. Loeffler, Evansville, Ind.

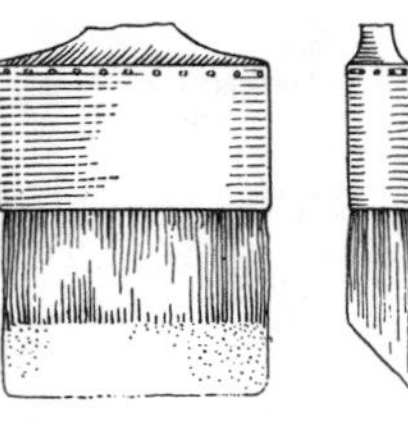

Scraping Off Surplus Water on a Grindstone

When using a grindstone, an ample flow of water is desirable in order to insure good cutting, and the objectionable spattering may be overcome by fastening a piece of leather to the grindstone frame so that its edge will bear lightly upon the stone just below the point where the work is held. This will scrape off all surplus water from the grinding surface and prevent spattering.—Contributed by Thos. L. Parker, Wibaux, Mont.

A Paper Drinking Cup

The cup is readily made of a piece of paper 8 in. square. Lay the paper on a flat surface, turn the point A over

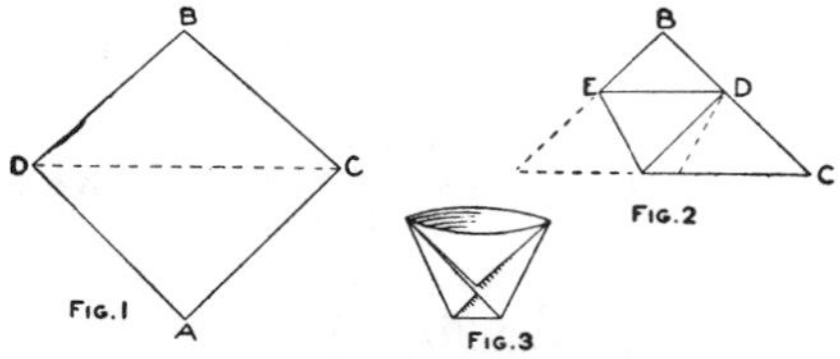

Several Cups can be Nested Together and Carried in the Pocket or Hand Bag

to meet the point B and crease on the dotted line CD, Fig. 1, then turn the corner D up to meet the line BC, Fig. 2, making sure that the new edge DE is parallel with the lower edge and crease. Turn the corner C in the same manner, that is, fold it over to the point E and crease. Fold the two corners at B outward and down, and crease, and the cup is complete as shown in Fig. 3.—Contributed by W. Douglas Matthews, Chappaqua, New York.

Homemade Brush for Cleaning Upholstered Furniture

A durable brush for cleaning upholstered furniture can be made in the following manner: Procure a piece of haircloth, which is made of horsehair woof and linen warp. Strips of haircloth, cut lengthwise and 1¾ in. wide, are laid out smooth on a table and a strip of wrapping paper, ½ in. wide, is firmly glued to one edge. When this has dried, take out the warp that is not covered by the paper. Brush the fringe of horsehair until it is straight and even, and before com-

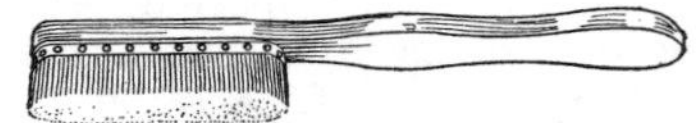

Brush Made of Strip of Upholsterers' Haircloth with the Warp Removed and Fastened to a Handle

mencing to wind, measure 6 in. from one end and glue this portion to the side of a strip of soft wood, 6 in. long, ⅝ in. wide and $\frac{1}{16}$ in. thick. When dry, wind the glued length of haircloth and paper around the wood strip, applying glue to each separate turn of winding. The turns should be kept flush on the side that has been glued and the fringed part brushed and straight.

The part to be glued to the handle must be perfectly even in its windings and held firmly in place while the glue is hardening. The winding should be continued until the brush is 1½ in. thick.

The handle is made of a piece of wood, 14 in. long, 1¾ in. wide and ½ in. thick. Wood that takes a cherry or mahogany stain is preferable. Shape it about as shown in the sketch and round off the edges. The part to which the brush is to be attached must be given a light coat of glue. When that has dried, glue the back of the brush to it, and after the glue has hardened, glue a piece of gimp around the brush part, then drive upholsterers' tacks into the gimp and wood, 3/4 in. apart. Stain and varnish the handle. The back of the handle can be used as a beater, and the brush for removing the dust.—Contributed by Gertrude M. Bender, Utica, N. Y.

Removing Calcium Deposits on Glass

A good way to clean glass vessels in which hard water is boiled is to use the following mixture to remove not only the calcium deposits, but also rust or sulphur stains that may be present. The solution is a mixture of ammonia water and a few ounces of salt. This should be placed in the glass vessel and boiled until the deposits disappear. The ammonia water may be made of any strength by diluting if necessary.

A Cold-Chisel Guide

When making long cuts with a cold chisel, it is almost impossible to guide the chisel edge along a line made with a scriber or pencil and have a straight cut. I find that it is much easier to use a guide, as shown in the sketch. The guide is made of a piece of wood, about 1 ft. long and 1½ in. wide. A slot is cut in the center, wide enough to receive the chisel edge snugly, and about 9 in. long. The guide is clamped

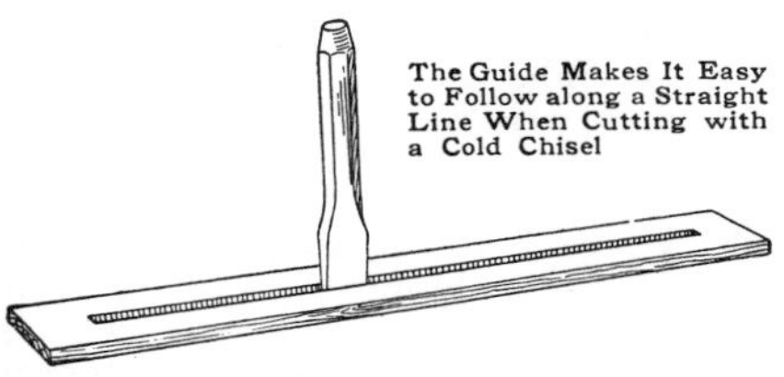

The Guide Makes It Easy to Follow along a Straight Line When Cutting with a Cold Chisel

to the work, and the cold chisel slipped along in the slot as it is successively hit with a hammer.—Contributed by G. H. Holter, Jasper, Minn.

Care of Paintbrushes

When laying aside paintbrushes, the usual custom is to place them in water and then forget all about them until needed again, with the result that the water usually is found more or less evaporated and the brushes hardened. If a quantity of oil, A, is poured on the water B, it will prevent this evaporation and keep the brushes in good shape.

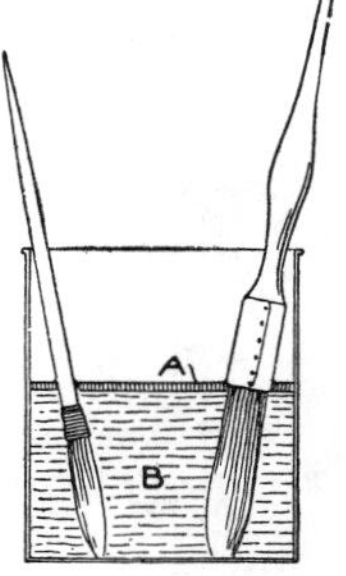

Filter in a Pump Spout

The sketch shows how to place an ordinary sponge in a pump spout, to filter out sand and dirt particles that may come up with the water as it is pumped. A wire is fastened in the sponge so that it can be easily taken out for washing. When washing the sponge give the pump handle a few strokes so that the dirt collected in the spout will be washed out. Do not press the sponge too tightly into the spout, as this will stop the flow of water.—Contributed by Chas. Homewood, Waterloo, Iowa.

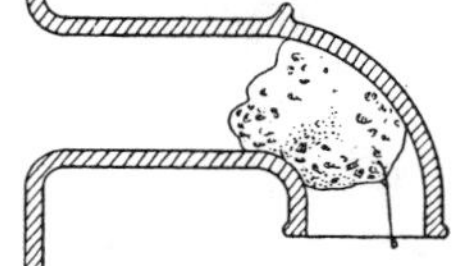

Brcwn Stain for Wood

Bichromate of potassium gives a lustrous, rich, light to dark brown stain on woods. The crystals are first dissolved into a saturated solution, which is then diluted with water. The stained surface needs no rubbing, as the stain leaves the wood perfectly clear for any desired finish. The satinlike appearance of wood treated by this stain cannot be produced with any of the pigment stains.—Contributed by August Meyer.

An Egg Boiler

In boiling eggs the usual method of dropping the eggs from a spoon into the boiling water often results in a burn, as well as in cracking of the eggs by the fall. In removing the eggs from the hot water and taking one out at a time, no two will be cooked alike. To overcome these difficulties I constructed an egg boiler as illustrated.

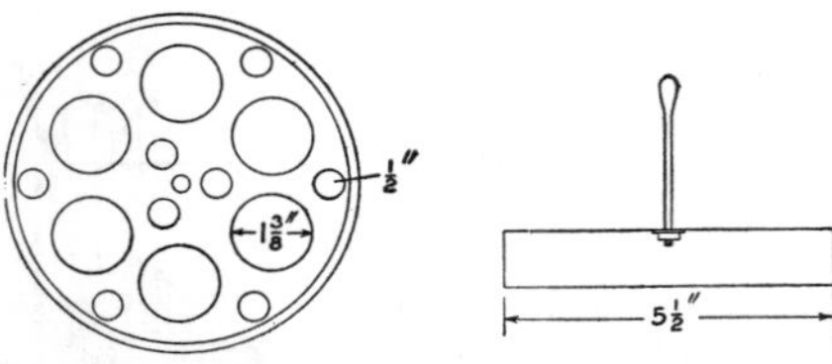

The Eggs are Prevented from Becoming Cracked and All are Easily Handled in One Operation

A pan was procured—tin or aluminum as desired—about 1 in. deep and 5½ in. in diameter, and holes were drilled in the bottom having dimensions as shown. A handle was attached to the center with washers and nuts. The small ends of the eggs are set in the 1⅜-in. holes and the whole pan set in a vessel of boiling water. When the boiling is completed, the entire lot of eggs are removed at the same time. As the device with its load of cooked eggs is quite pleasing in appearance, it may be set on a plate and the eggs served from it on the table.—Contributed by W. E. Crane, Cleveland, O.

Removing Black Deposit on Bathtubs

A good way to remove the black deposit left on bathtubs by the water is to use a strong solution of sulphuric acid. The acid should be poured on the discolored enameled surface and washed around with a cloth. The acid should not touch the hands so it is best to use a stick to move the cloth. Neither should it be allowed to touch the metal parts, but if this happens, no harm will result if it is quickly rubbed off with a cloth and water then applied.

In using this acid never pour water into the acid, but always pour the acid into the water.—Contributed by Loren Ward, Des Moines, Iowa.

A Stocking-Stretcher Form

A simple as well as inexpensive device for preventing the shrinking of stockings, more particularly those of children, after they have been washed, thus saving great wear and tear on the fabrics and increasing their length of life, is shown in the illustration. The stretcher can be made by anyone, a knowledge of woodcraft or art being unnecessary. If used, the device will prove to effect quite a saving in money, labor and worry in the course of a year.

Place a new and unused stocking, that properly fits the foot, flat on a heavy piece of cardboard or a wood board, if desired, and mark an outline of the stocking on the board with a pencil. Cut out the design with a penknife or heavy pair of scissors and smooth the edges. A design having

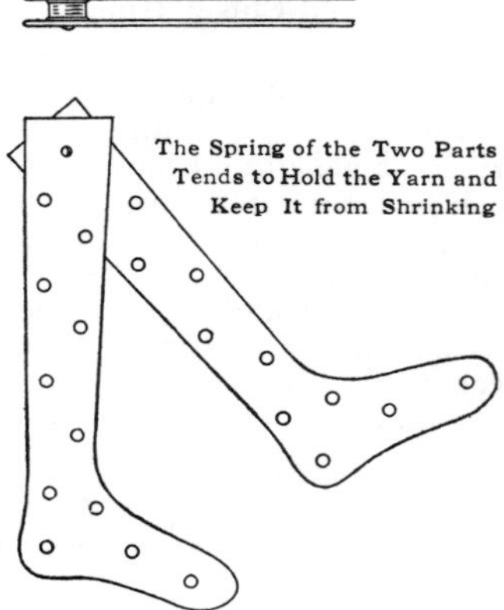

The Spring of the Two Parts Tends to Hold the Yarn and Keep It from Shrinking

the same shape and size as the stocking results. Duplicate boards can be easily made. Place a spool, such as used to hold the finest silk thread, near the upper end of the first form and on top of this place the second. Then drive a nail through the boards and spool and clinch it, or better still, use a small bolt. When the stockings are washed and the dampness wrung out as well as possible, stretch them over the boards and hang them up to dry. They will retain their shape and are easily ironed.—Contributed by Wm. P. Kennedy, Washington, D. C.

Stick Holder for a Chopping Block

Having a lot of branch wood, from ½ in. to 1 in. in diameter, to saw, and not wishing to bother with a sawbuck, I rigged up a chopping block, as shown in the sketch, by fastening a piece of board to one side of the block with

The Notched Board Fastened to the Chopping Block Turns It into a Sawbuck

small lag screws. The piece to be sawed was laid across the block in the notch. If the piece is held down on the block with one foot, the wood is very easily sawn.—Contributed by Wilfred B. Sylvester, Reading, Mass.

Cleaning Gold and Platinum

A good way to clean gold or platinum jewelry is to first brush with soapsuds, then dust magnesia powder over the article and allow it to dry. A few rubs with a cloth makes the article shine with great luster. As magnesia powder is highly inflammable, it must be kept away from fire.

A Twine Spool

The pieces of twine used in tying parcels delivered to a residence are either thrown away or tied together and wound into a ball for future use. The method I use for keeping the pieces of twine is to wind them over a discarded photographic-film spool. The spool was slipped on a finishing nail driven into the wall. The crank for turning the spool was made of a piece of wire, bent as shown and slipped into the slot end of the spool. One end of the first piece of string was tied

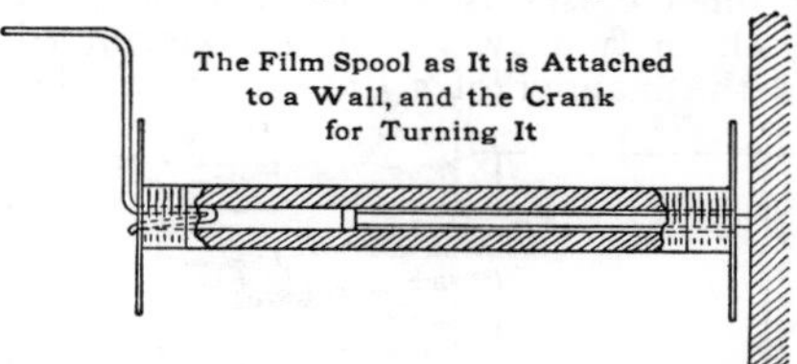

The Film Spool as It is Attached to a Wall, and the Crank for Turning It

to the core and then wound around it, the next piece tied to the first and wound up, and so on, as the strings were taken from the packages from time to time. When a string is needed for any purpose I always know where to find it, and it is easier to take it from the spool than from a ball.—Contributed by W. Resseguie, Susquehanna, Pa.

Reinforcing Chair Bottoms

Embossed-leather-board chair bottoms can be made as serviceable as leather in the following manner: Turn the chair upside down and fill the hollow beneath the seat with excelsior, soft rags or fine shavings, then nail a ¼-in. wood bottom over the filling with brads. Make the wood bottom ½ or ¾ in. larger than the opening. It will thus not be seen, and the seat will last as long as the chair.—Contributed by J. H. Sanford, Pasadena, California.

A Novelty Chain

An inexpensive chain for hanging painted glass panels, transparencies or photographs can be made by joining paper clips together to form the links. A box of 100 clips will make a chain about 10 ft. long. Such a chain can be made in a few minutes and a length of 10 ft. will hold about 4 lb.

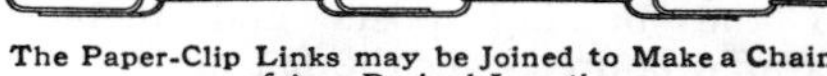

The Paper-Clip Links may be Joined to Make a Chain of Any Desired Length

If the chain is to be used for holding photographs, each inner loop end is bent out slightly.

Closet Holders for Linen

A combination drawer and shelf for a linen closet is much better than a shelf or a drawer. It is constructed in the manner of a drawer with sides

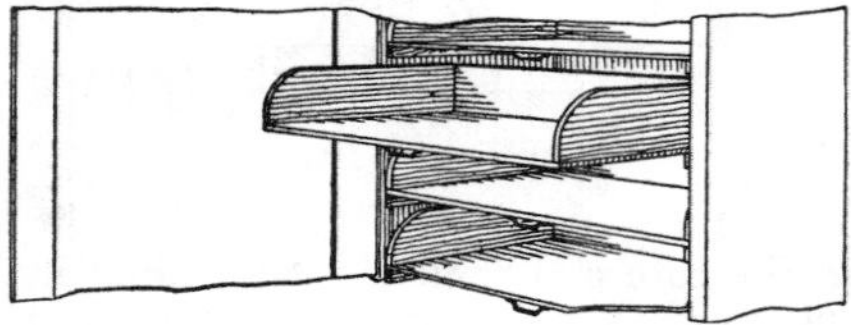

The Holder can be Pulled Out Like a Drawer and is as Accessible as a Shelf

and a back, the front being open and the ends of the sides cut rounding. A clip is attached to the under side of the bottom, near the front edge, to provide a means for pulling out the holder.

Sheets, towels, table cloths, napkins, etc., can be neatly piled on the holder and can be seen without digging down to the bottom. It has the advantage over the shelf that it can be pulled out without anything falling off, and the linen on the back part can be easily reached as well as that in front. The closet may contain as many holders as is necessary and should be provided with a door for keeping out dust.—Contributed by H. A. Sullwold, St. Paul, Minn.

Preserving Dry Batteries

The life of dry batteries, which are to be used in wet or damp places, may be considerably lengthened by being treated in the following manner:

The batteries are placed in glass jars a little wider and higher than themselves. A layer of dry sawdust is placed in the bottom, for the battery to rest on, and the sides are packed with sawdust to within ½ in. of the top. Waterproof wires are connected to the binding posts and melted paraffin poured over the battery to the top of the jar. The carbon and zinc terminals should be marked to avoid trouble when connecting several cells together. Batteries treated in this manner are waterproof and can be submerged in water if necessary.—Contributed by Olaf Tronnes, Evanston, Ill.

A Cleaner for Brass

In some recent laboratory experiments the following solution was found to cleanse brass very quickly without harm to the hands or the metal. An ounce of alum was put into a pint of boiling water and the solution rubbed on the brass with a cloth. Stains as well as tarnish were quickly removed. The solution is inexpensive and easily prepared. — Contributed by Loren Ward, Des Moines, Iowa.

Homemade Graduate

If a certain quantity of liquid is to be frequently measured out, it is best to have a graduate marked for this amount without any other markings upon it. To make a graduate for this purpose, procure a pickle or olive bottle of the type shown in the drawing and file a vertical line, A, on each side. These lines should be at least ⅛ in. wide. Place the bottle on a level surface and pour in the amount desired to be measured. Mark on each vertical line with a lead pencil and connect this mark or marks with lines, filed as shown at BB.—Contributed by James M. Kane, Doylestown, Pa.

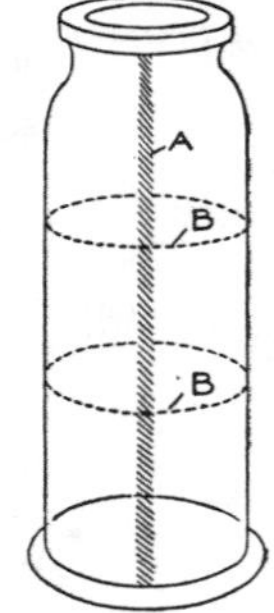

Mending a Break in Felt

A good way to mend partially broken felt or a felt hat is to hold a lighted match under the break and smooth out the crevice with the hand. The shellac in the felt is melted by the heat and runs together, mending the felt in such a way that the break is hardly noticeable. This method may also be used to mend felt articles in the laboratory.

Imitating Ebony on Oak

The wood is immersed for 48 hours in a warm solution of alum and sprinkled several times with the following mixture: One part of logwood of the best quality is boiled with 10 parts of water, then it is filtered through linen and the liquid evaporated at a low temperature until its volume is reduced by one-half. To every quart of this bath are added 10 to 15 drops of a saturate of soluble indigo entirely neutral in reaction.

Smaller pieces may be steeped for a time in this solution, then the wood is rubbed with a saturated and filtered solution of verdigris in warm, concentrated acetic acid, and this operation continued until a black color of the desired intensity is obtained. The oak wood dyed in this manner is very similar to real ebony.

Tongue Holder for a Boy's Wagon

To prevent any mishap when coasting in a boy's play wagon fasten the tongue with a coil spring so that it will be kept in a vertical position. The tongue is always out of the way when it is not used for drawing the wagon. The spring is only strong enough to hold the tongue, so that when this is used for pulling there is little or no tendency of the spring to draw the tongue upward. The coil spring is

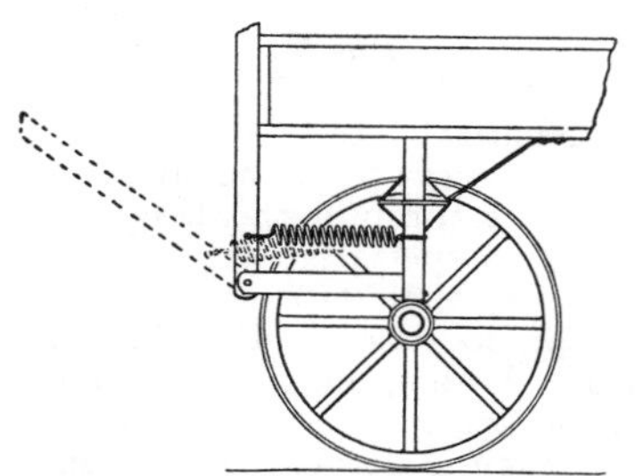

Holder for the Wagon Tongue to Keep It in a Vertical Position When Not in Use

fastened with one screweye in the tongue and one in the front axle.—Contributed by Wm. F. Benson, Brockton, Massachusetts.

Gluing Small Mitered Frames

The mechanic who attempts to fasten a mitered frame in the home workshop usually comes to grief. This is

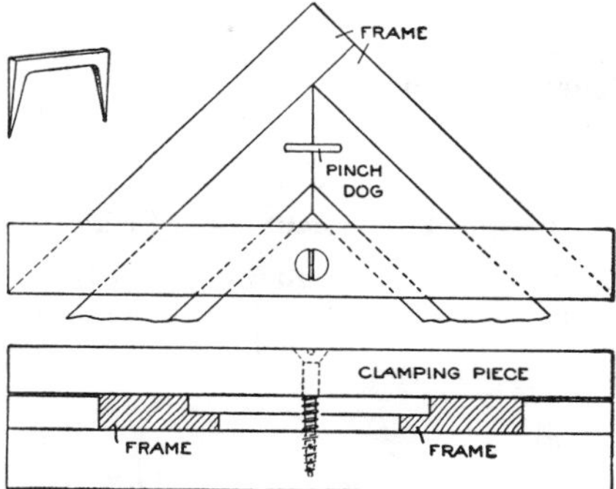

Clamp for Holding the Corner of a Frame While Gluing and Fastening the Mitered Joint

due to lack of proper facilities for holding the frame straight and out of wind, and for clamping or drawing the miter joint together after the glue has been applied. The little device shown in the sketch, if properly made and used, does away with the usual difficulties and annoyances. It consists of a triangular block of wood with raised strips on the two edges that make the right angle, and the clamping piece with the wood screw through the center on the long side. The raised strips are made somewhat thinner than the frame to be fastened, as the clamping piece should bear on the frame and not on the strips; the function of the strips being to hold the frame square. The triangular block should be large enough to take the corner of the frame and leave room enough for the wood screw that holds it in place on the block. Four of these blocks will be necessary and they should be used in conjunction with pinch dogs. These dogs come in different sizes and may be purchased at supply stores or made as shown. The outside of the legs should be straight and parallel and the inside tapered so as to draw the joint together.

When a joint is ready to be glued, a piece of paper is placed on the block under the joint to keep it from sticking. Apply the glue and push the two sides into the corner formed by the raised strips, the dog is then driven in lightly and the clamping piece screwed down tightly, and if the miter has been properly cut, a nice close-jointed and square corner will be the result.—Contributed by J. Shelly, Brooklyn, New York.

Handle Attachment for a Sickle

For cutting around flower beds or bushes and in close places I find that an extension handle for a sickle is

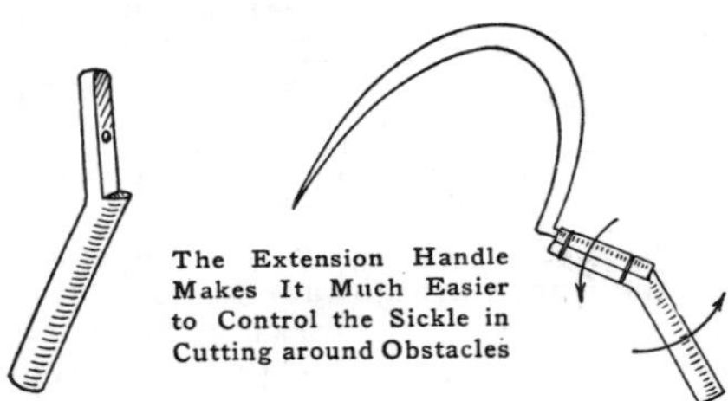
The Extension Handle Makes It Much Easier to Control the Sickle in Cutting around Obstacles

quite an assistance. The auxiliary handle is bound to the sickle handle with wire at the ends and is further fastened with a screw in the center. The arrows show the directions in which the hands should be moved in working the sickle.—Contributed by A. S. Thomas, Gordon, Can.

A Clothesline for Small Goods

Handkerchiefs and small pieces included in the week's laundry are usually quite troublesome to hang with the larger pieces, and for this

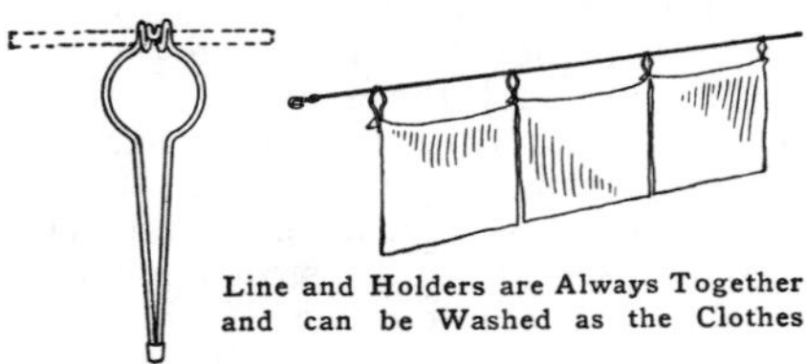
Line and Holders are Always Together and can be Washed as the Clothes

reason I constructed a special line for the small goods. A line was cut to fit between two porch posts and a hook made of galvanized wire tied to each end, staples being driven into the posts to receive them. Three or four wire grips were formed and attached to the line. It was only necessary to draw the corner of a handkerchief into the grip as it was wrung out, placing several in each grip. The line with its load was then carried out and attached between the porch posts. This made it unnecessary to look through the clothes for the small articles. It also prevented chilling the fingers and no pins were needed.—Contributed by R. D. Livingston, Hopkinton, Iowa.

Automatically Controlled Ice-Box Lights

Often the ice box is placed in a dark closet or some out-of-the-way place, and it is almost impossible to locate articles already in the box or put others away without considerable inconvenience on account of the lack of proper light. This difficulty can be easily overcome by mounting a small electric lamp in each of the different compartments of the box, which will

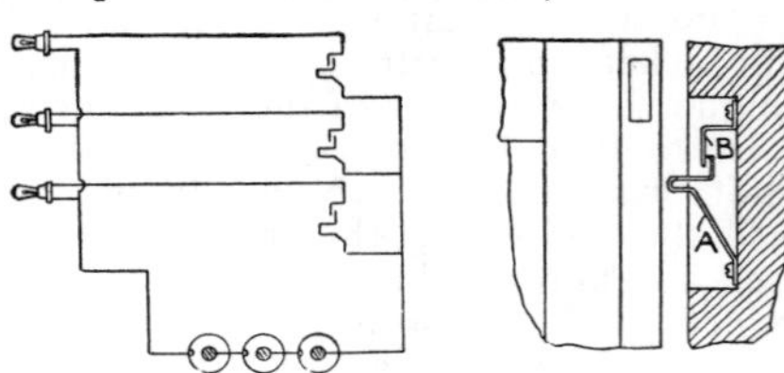

The Lamps will be Automatically Lighted When the Door of the Ice Box is Opened

be automatically lighted when the lid of the box is raised or the door opened. The circuit through the lamp is controlled by a special switch mounted in such a way that its contacts are open when the doors and lid of the box are closed. A diagram of the circuit is given in Fig. 1, which shows three lamps, each controlled by a separate switch, connected in parallel to a battery of several dry cells. The lamps should be of low voltage and need not be very high in candlepower. The number of cells needed in the battery will depend upon the voltage of the lamps. The voltage of the battery and the rated voltage of the lamps should be approximately the same.

A special switch that will serve the above purpose is shown in Fig. 2. It consists of two pieces of spring brass, A and B, about 3/8 in. wide, bent into the forms shown. These pieces are mounted in a recess cut in the jamb of the door or lid in such a way that the free end of the piece A is held away from the piece B when the door or lid is closed. When the lid of the box or the door is open the two springs come in contact and the lamp lights; upon closing the lid or door the contact is broken and the lamp goes out.

A good quality of rubber-insulated copper wire should be used in making the connections, and all parts should be as well protected from moisture and the possibilities of mechanical abuse as possible. It would be best to tape the lamps in the sockets with a piece of friction tape so as to prevent moisture getting into the socket and, perhaps, shortening the lamp. A short piece of brass tubing can be mounted around the lamp to protect it mechanically. Be sure to place the batteries where they will be kept dry.

A Bottle-Cap Lifter

To remove the crimped bottle cover so extensively used requires a special lifter, the corkscrew being of little use for this purpose. When a cap-cover remover is not at hand, prepare a pocketknife in the manner shown, and it makes an excellent substitute. It only requires a small notch filed in the heel of the blade, which does not interfere with the ordinary use of the knife in the least.—Contributed by John V. Loeffler, Evansville, Indiana.

¶Ants may be effectively destroyed by placing a coop with a chicken in it over the hill.

A Mechanical Bicycle Horn

The body of the horn A is made of metal, about 3 in. in diameter, with a screw cover. The shaft B, to which is attached a driving pulley, C, and a ratchet wheel, D, is fitted in holes drilled through the diameter of the body. The diaphragm E is clamped, between the edge of the body and the cover, on a seat made of rubber rings, F, and carries a contact device, G, that is riveted to its center. The diaphragm should be set so that the contact will touch the ends of the ratchets.

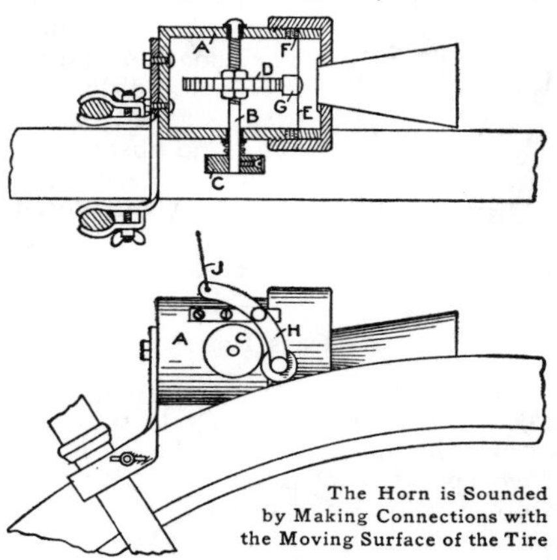

The Horn is Sounded by Making Connections with the Moving Surface of the Tire

A metal cone is fastened in an opening cut in the center of the cover, over the diaphragm. The back of the body is fitted with a bracket for attaching it to the front fork on a bicycle. The lever H carries an idler pulley which is forced against the bicycle tire and the pulley C by means of a cord, J.

Adjusting the diaphragm contact on the ratchet wheel will change the tone of the horn.—Contributed by P. Mertz, Jamaica, L. I.

Retarder for Plaster of Paris

When it is desired to lengthen the time of setting after preparing plaster of Paris, dissolve 1 oz. of citric acid in water used for mixing 100 lb. of plaster, and it will retard the setting for about three hours.

An Inkwell Stopper

A good way to keep an inkwell of the type shown in the sketch clean is to place a marble over the opening. The marble keeps out flies and dust, is easily rolled aside and is no obstacle to the pen entering the well. — Contributed by James M. Kane, Doylestown, Pennsylvania.

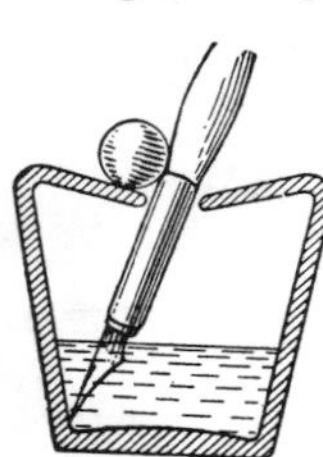

A Grass Rake

This adaptation of an ordinary iron rake for use on a lawn was the outcome of not having a lawn rake at hand. Two spools, each $1\frac{1}{2}$ in. in diameter, were procured and one forced on each end tooth of the rake. The spools were forced on the teeth just far enough to allow the rake to slide on the ground and prevent the other teeth from digging out the grass. The end of the spools may be rounded and smoothed so that they will slide easily on the ground.—Contributed by H. E. Gray, Montclair, N. J.

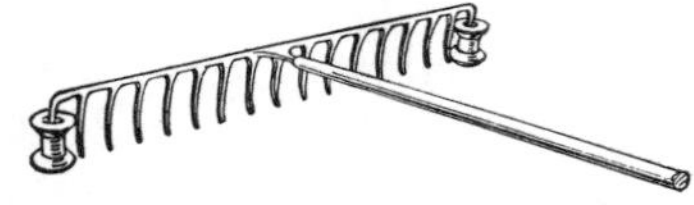

The Spools Prevent the Teeth from Injuring the Grass Roots as the Rake Passes over the Ground

A Staple Puller

A very simple way to pull a staple is to use the claws of an ordinary carpenter's hammer and a nail, as shown in the sketch. The staple can be removed quickly without being bent, and no damage to the material into which it was driven will result.

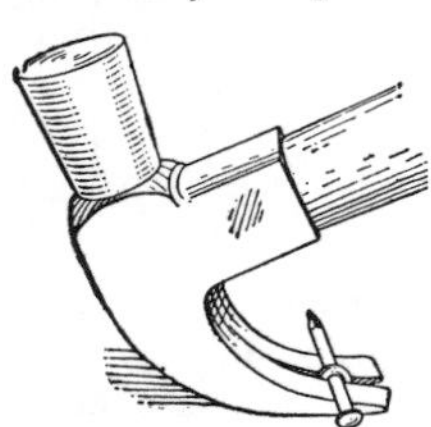

To Remove Acid Stains from Cloth

Apply pearlash directly to the stain, allowing it to set a minute or two, then boil the article in soap water for several minutes. The method is harmless and inexpensive, and can be used by anyone.

Repairing Rocker on a Chair

The tenons on the posts of a rocking chair being broken off so close to the rocker that it was impossible to make the ordinary repairs, four window-shade-roller brackets were used in the following manner: The metal was straightened so that it would lie flat and two brackets were used on the end of each post. This made a neat and strong repair.—Contributed by Chas. Schmidt, Baltimore, Md.

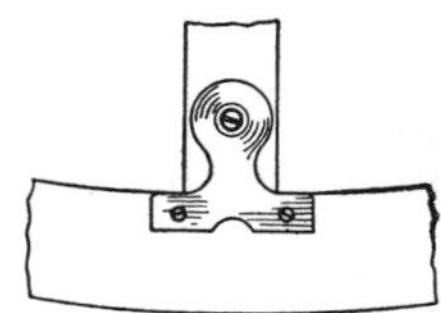

Electric-Lamp Reflector for a Target

An ordinary 1-lb. coffee can may be quickly fashioned into a most effective reflector for an electric bulb. The light is projected upon the target while the marksman's eyes are shielded. Of course, this device can be used for other purposes.

The can is shaped into a reflector by cutting it open along one side with a pair of snips, then following the circumference of the bottom halfway around on each side. Bend the flaps outward as far as desired and cut a hole in the bottom just large enough to insert the bulb, as shown.—Contributed by Burke Jenkins, Port Washington, L. I.

¶Linoleum may be renewed by applying floor wax in liquid form.

Making Small Taps

The owner of a private workshop has need for taps and occasionally wishes to make them, not because they are cheaper, but for the sake of experience or to get some special thread. In cutting the flutes, whether it be by hand or in a shaper, it is a good plan to give the flutes an angle, that is, to cut them, not parallel with the axis of the tap, but at an angle of 5 to 15 deg. with the center line. This makes the tap cut easier, giving it a wedge action instead of just simply pushing the metal off. The same method applies to counterbores and countersinks, which, when so made, take less power to drive.

Sink a Substitute for a Dishpan

On special occasions when company is entertained or in large families, it is almost impossible to wash all the dishes in an ordinary dishpan; in fact, the large platters will not go in at all, so I devised the following method as a substitute for a larger pan.

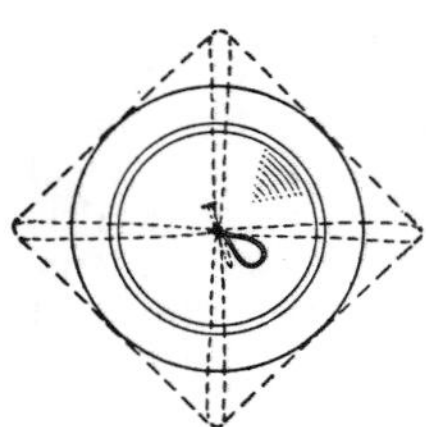

A tin disk was cut from the top of a tomato can with a can opener so as to be as round as possible, then a piece of cheesecloth was folded into an even square, the disk placed in the center and all four corners of the cloth drawn over to the center of the disk. A nail was driven through the center of the disk, to make a hole, through which a string was drawn with the nail and tied to it to form a loop on the head. This is used to stop the sink drain.

When this is put over the drain outlet the sink may be used as a dishpan. The same result could be obtained a little better with a piece of an old rubber boot or rubber coat, but usually this material is not at hand, and the cheesecloth will do almost as well. —Contributed by Hannah Jennings, Chicago.

How to Make Small Coil Springs

Procure a nut, having a small thread that will admit the size of the wire to be used in making the spring. Cut a small notch to the depth of the thread where the thread starts, and procure a smooth rod that will pass snugly through the threads of the nut. Shape one end of the rod to fit a carpenter's brace, if there is no drill chuck at hand, and drill a hole in the other end to admit one end of the spring wire.

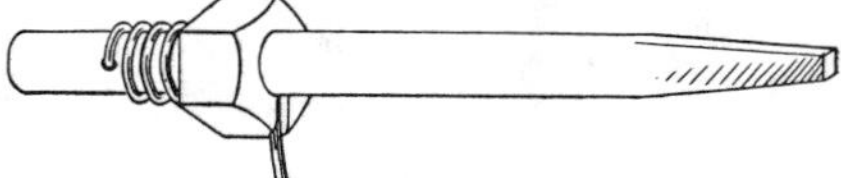

The Threads in the Nut Will Guide as Well as Coil the Spring Evenly

Bend the wire at right angles and insert the end in the hole. Place the end of the rod in the nut, which should be gripped in a vise, and turn the rod, at the same time seeing that the wire is guided into the notch cut at the start of the thread. The wire will follow the thread of the nut and make a perfect spring of an even opening throughout its length. Closed or open coils can be made by using a nut having the proper number of threads.—Contributed by A. Spencer, Kinston, N. C.

A Pruning-Saw Guard

The double-edged pruning saw with coarse teeth on one side and fine on the other would be far more widely used, if it were not for the fact that the unused edge so often injures the bark of the trunk when the saw is being used. A very satisfactory guard may be quickly made of a brass curtain rod by prying it apart slightly at the seam and cutting a suitable length to fit over the edge, as shown in the sketch. This will cling to the saw blade by its own tension.—Contributed by James H. Brundage, Katonah, N. Y.

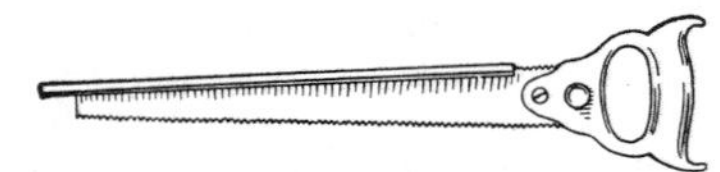

The Teeth on the Unused Edge are Covered with a Piece of Brass Curtain Rod

Home-Made Motion-Picture Camera and Projector

IN THREE PARTS—PART I

By CHARLES FRANK

Motion pictures are made and reproduced by means of a camera and projector, each having a similar mechanism that would seem entirely too complicated for the average person to construct at home, yet a correspondent of the Nickelodeon has devised a simple rotary cylinder shutter that can be substituted for the complicated parts. While this simple cylinder shutter is not claimed to be non-infringing on existing patents, yet, as it has no commercial value, there would be no objection on this score. The instruments described are nothing more than toys, and if the amateur photographer can secure a few dozen feet of animated photographs about the home that are dear to his heart, and reproduce them on a screen, it will have served its purpose. The camera and projector described uses standard film, $1\frac{3}{8}$ in. wide, with perforations every $\frac{3}{16}$ in.

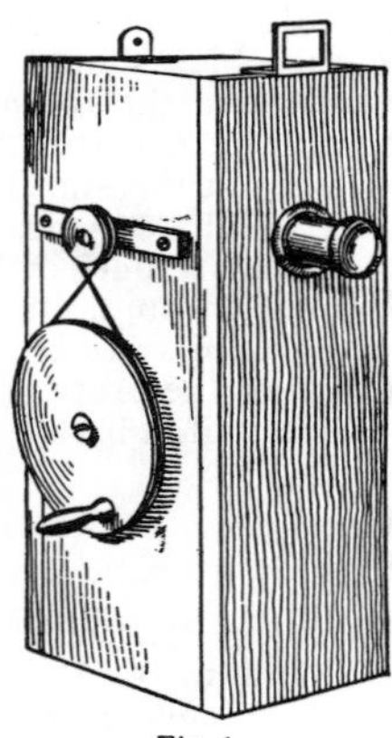

Fig. 1

The Camera

The ordinary hand camera for making still pictures consists of a light-tight box with a lens at one end and a sensitized plate or film at the other. The motion-picture camera (Fig. 1) is nothing more than a hand camera with a mechanical device for stepping a long roll of film through a space in the focal plane of the lens at a speed of about 16 pictures a second, and stopping the film long enough to make the requisite exposure on each division. The first thing to consider is the lens. A lens having ordinary speed for a hand camera, and one with about 3-in. focal length will give satisfactory results. If one does not care to purchase a lens, a small $1\frac{1}{2}$-in. or 2-in. reading glass can be used, if it is stopped down, or a lens may be taken from a hand camera. The width of the camera from front to back (W, Fig. 2) must be determined by the focal length of the lens. The dimensions given in the drawing are only approximate, and they can be changed if the camera is to be used in making an extra long film negative.

The roll of unexposed film (A, Fig. 2) is placed on a small shaft between U-shaped bearings, made of sheet metal and screwed to the top board of the camera. The lens B is set in the front board at a point 4 in. below the top. If a large roll of film is to be used, this distance must be greater to allow room for the film roll in the top of the camera. The cylinder C, which acts as a shutter and intermittent movement, revolves directly behind and in the path of the light passing through the lens. Partitions, DD, are set in grooves cut in the boards, forming the sides of the camera. These partitions are to keep the light, which may be diffused from the lens, from striking the film at either side of the shutter, and at the same time acting as guides for the film at the rear end of the camera. Their edges at the back are covered with black velvet. The back of the box is a hinged door, rabbeted on all edges, and opening at the side to allow the insertion and removal of the film, and also acting as a guide for the film when closed. A strip of black velvet, E, a little wider than the film, is pasted to the inside surface of the door, so that it bears lightly against the back edges of the partitions DD. The film passes between the edges of the partitions and the velvet on the door with some friction, which keeps it from moving except when pulled through with the roller shutter. A wire-staple guide, F, is fastened in the lower partition, through which the end of the film is passed before closing the door. The film as it is run through drops in folds in the bottom of the box.

The rotary cylinder shutter is the heart of the machine and should be made well and strictly according to the dimensions. The detail of this part is shown in Fig. 3. A rectangular opening is mortised through one of its diameters to admit light on the film when in certain positions. The cylinder is of wood with a ¼-in. steel rod inserted in the center of each end for axles. A small grooved pulley (G, Fig. 2), about 1 in. in diameter, is fastened to the outer end of one of these rods. The cylinder is revolved by a round belt from a drive wheel, H, 3 or 3½ in. in diameter and turned by the aid of a crankpin. Owing to the backward rotation of the cylinder, the belt must be crossed between the drive wheel H, and the pulley G. The projections or sprockets, Fig. 3, must be accurately set at a distance of ⅜ in. from the 90-deg. point, using the center of the mortised hole as a base. These projections can be pins or small staples, but they must not be over $\frac{1}{16}$ in. in size. The base of the sprockets must fit the hole in the film snugly, but the points should be slightly rounding, so that they will easily enter the perforations. When the upper sprocket, which is approaching the film, engages a perfora-

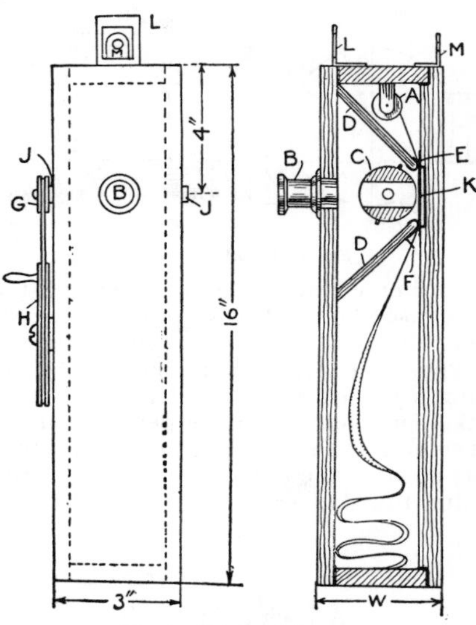

Fig. 2—Details of Camera

tion, just below the upper partition, it will carry the film downward until the sprocket disengages from the perforation at the lower partition. The distance of travel must be exactly ¾ in., as that is the height of each picture. The cylinder requires some adjustment to meet this condition; therefore the axles are made to revolve in holes bored in two strips of wood, JJ, which can be moved forward or backward to obtain the proper distance from the film. To allow for this movement, the axles pass through slots cut in the sides of the camera box instead of round holes. The strips JJ are fastened temporarily and when the correct position for the cylinder is found, they are permanently fastened to the box. Grooves, K, are cut through the black velvet and into the back of the door to allow a space for the sprockets to pass through freely. The inside of the box should be painted a dead black, and black paper pasted on all corners and joints. Black velvet is pasted in the rabbet of the door to insure a light-tight joint when the door is closed. The cylinder shutter is also painted a dead black inside and out.

The cylinder in revolving exposes the

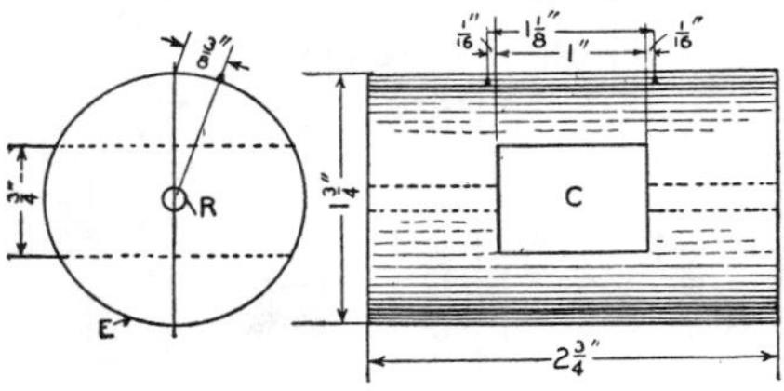

Fig. 3—Details of Shutter

film immediately behind it through the mortised hole. The sprockets or cylinder does not touch the film while the exposure is being made, but as the hole turns toward a perpendicular position, the sprockets catch the perforations of the film and it moves down ¾ in. Just as soon as the sprockets disengage the film, the shutter exposes the next section of film, and so on as rapidly as the cylinder is turned, but the average should be about 16 pictures per second.

A view finder must be supplied so the field covered by the lens can be determined. Such a finder is made of two pieces of metal, L and M, bent L-shaped and fastened to the top of the camera box. One of the pieces (L) has a rectangular opening 1 in. wide and ¾ in. high, and the other (M) is drilled with a ⅛-in. drill, the distance between the two pieces being the focal length of the lens. One eye applied to the ⅛-in. hole in the piece M will see through the rectangular hole in the piece L about the same field as covered by the lens. The pieces should be accurately placed and fastened on the box when the camera is set, so that the lens will throw the same portion of the picture on the space where the film passes as will be seen through the finder.

(To be continued)

A Swimming Raft

Swimming is learned only by experience and to get this experience one must not be afraid to trust himself in the water. This is sometimes accomplished by the use of a swimming raft or water wings. As the water wings need to be inflated frequently, I made a swimming raft instead, in the fol-

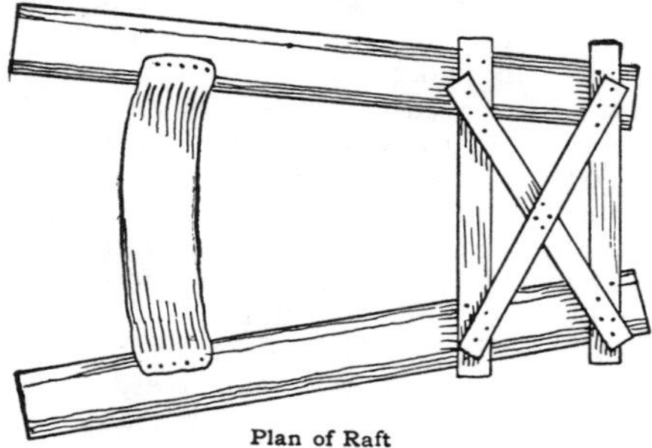

Plan of Raft

lowing manner: Two logs, about 6 or 7 ft. long and about 8 in. in diameter, were fastened together with large nails, as shown in the illustration, and a piece of burlap or other strong material was nailed across the center with slack enough for it to be partially submerged.

The middle of the band, its depth, etc., can be adjusted to suit the user. Be sure to remove all the roughness of the logs and boards with a rasp and sandpaper.—Contributed by W. P. Johnston, Sumner, Ill.

Removing Finger Marks on Books

Dampen a piece of wash leather and use it to rub pumice on the spot to be cleaned. Brush off the pumice and rub again with a piece of dry wash leather.

Tightening a Tennis Net

Anyone who has ever played tennis will readily see the advantage of the net-tightening device shown, in preference to the old method of pulling the net tight by hand. All that is necessary to make the device is 1 ft. of ordinary gas or water pipe, 8 or 10 in. of ½-in. iron bar, and two twenty-penny nails. The posts generally used are 6 by 6 in. About 4 in. from the top of the post bore a 1-in. hole, parallel with the direction the rope is to run. On the inside surface of the post bore four ¼-in. holes.

Drill a ½-in. hole 1 in. from one end of the pipe, and a ¼-in. hole 1 in. from the other end. Put the iron bar in the ½-in. hole, tie the rope around the pipe and bar at A and wind. With the leverage of the iron bar one can readily pull the net to any desired tightness. After the net is drawn in position, put one of the nails through the ¼-in. hole

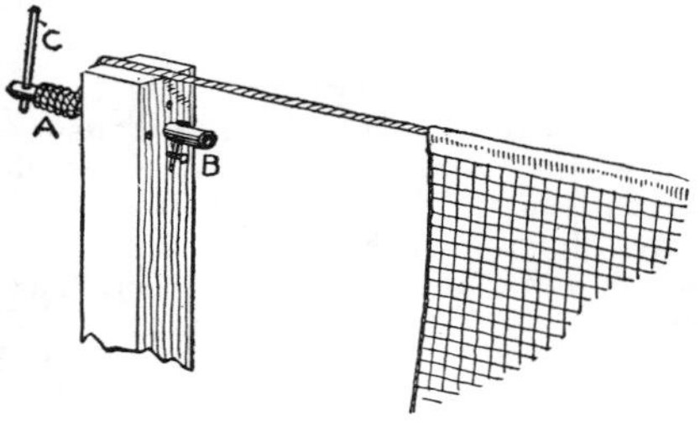

Tightener on Post

in the pipe and the other in one of the ¼-in. holes in the post.—Contributed by Wm. S. Looper, Gainesville, Ga.

Holding Fishing-Rod Joints Together

The addition of two or three screweyes properly placed in a jointed fishing rod of the ordinary type will prove decidedly worth while, as the joints will often pull out easily when they should not and stick tightly when they should pull apart.

Assemble the rod and bore small holes through the brass sockets into the joints as shown in Fig. 1 and place some screweyes into the holes. Mark the joints so that the holes in the joints and holes in the brass sockets will always be in the same position.

The screweyes prevent the joints from pulling out when an effort is made to free the line from some object in which it has become entangled. They also act as guides for the line. Should the joints fit too tightly, scrape the ends until they slip easily into the sock-

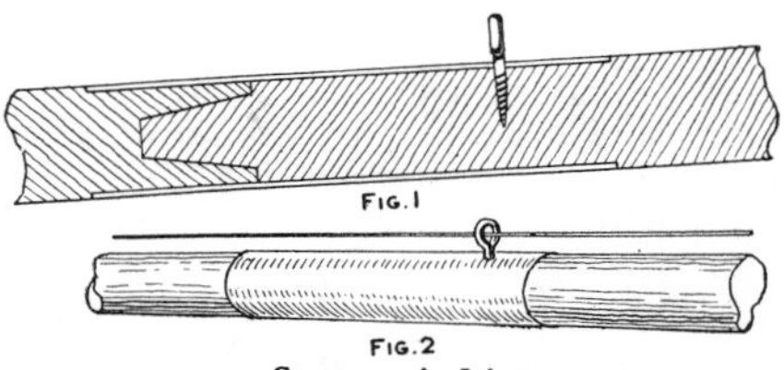

Screweye in Joint

ets, as the screweyes will hold them properly, even if they fit a little loose after the scraping.

Roller Skate on a Bicycle Wheel

When the front tire on a bicycle will not hold and needs to be taken to a repair shop, strap or tie a roller skate to the rim of the wheel, as shown, and no trouble will be experienced in wheeling or riding the bicycle to the shop.—Contributed by K. Chase Winslow, Elizabeth, N. J.

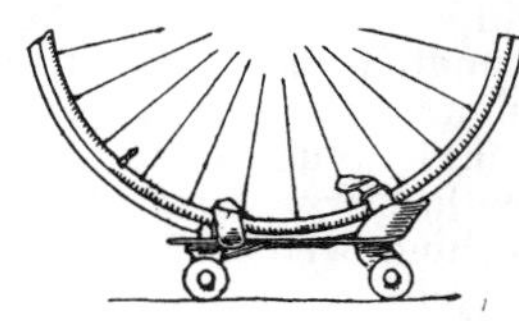

Rope Oarlocks

Having considerable trouble because of breaking of oarlocks, I devised a successful way by which the difficulty was

Piece of Rope in Place

overcome. The device is extremely simple and is nothing more than a piece of rope fastened to the gunwale as shown in the sketch.—Contributed by Arthur L. Chetlain, Rogers Park, Illinois.

Home-Made Motion-Picture Camera and Projector

IN THREE PARTS—PART II

Developing

After having exposed the film in the camera, the next steps are to develop and make a positive film from the negative. The developing and exposing of the film for the positive are the same as in ordinary photography for making negatives and lantern slides, the only difference being in the apparatus for handling the long films. One of the simplest ways of developing a long film is to use a large tray in connection with a cross arm having upright pins around which the film is wrapped in a continuous spiral. A film 100 ft. long would require a tray 18 by 22 in., with pins set in the cross arm about 3/8 in. apart. This method of developing is shown in Fig. 4.

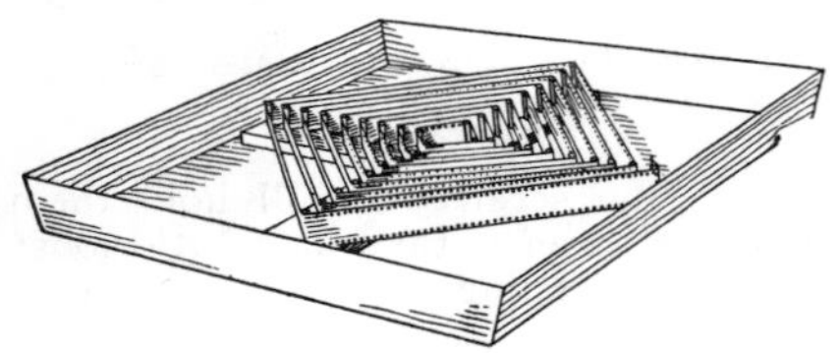

Fig. 4—Cross Arms with Pins

A long film can be developed in a small tray by using two flanged wheels or spools mounted on a frame (Fig. 5) that holds them directly above the liquid in the tray. The spools have a wood core or center with metal sides of sufficient diameter to take in the length of film to be developed. One end of the undeveloped film is attached to one spool and then wound upon it, then the other end is passed through the guides, gelatine side down, and fastened to the other spool. The film is first run slowly through a water bath until it is thoroughly saturated, then it is passed through the developing solution again and again until the proper density is secured. The trays can be easily removed and others substituted for fixing, washing, hardening and soaking, the film being passed through each solution in the same manner. Before developing either negative or positive film, small test strips should be run through the solution so that the proper timing and treating of the full-length strip will correspond to the test strip.

A reel should be prepared for drying the film. This can be made of small slats placed around two disks to form a drum (Fig. 6) about 1½ ft. in diameter and 2½ ft. long. After the film has been passed through the various solutions and is ready for drying, it is wound spirally around on the slats with the gelatine side out, and the whole hung up to dry.

Printing

The printing to make the transparency is accomplished by a very simple arrangement. The negative and positive films must be drawn through a space admitting light while their gelatine surfaces are in close contact. A box may be constructed in several ways, but the one shown in Fig. 7 illustrates the necessary parts and their relative positions.

The sprocket A is placed directly back of the opening B which may be regulated to admit the proper light. The sprocket can be purchased from a moving-picture stock house cheaply, but if the builder so desires, one can be made from wood turned up about 1 in.

Fig. 5—Developing Long Films

in diameter, or so that the circumference will receive sprockets at points $\frac{3}{16}$ in. apart. The sprockets are made of metal pins driven into the wood. Two rows of them are placed around the wood cylinder about $1\frac{1}{8}$ in. apart.

The cylinder is provided with a small metal shaft at each end which turns in round holes or bearings in the sides of the box. One of the shafts should project through the side of the box and have a grooved wheel, C, attached. The sprocket cylinder is driven by a smaller grooved wheel or pulley, D, to which a crank is attached for turning. The relative sizes of these wheels are determined by the speed of the exposure and the kind of light used. A 3-in. or 4-in. wheel on the cylinder sprocket shaft, driven by a pulley about 1 in. in

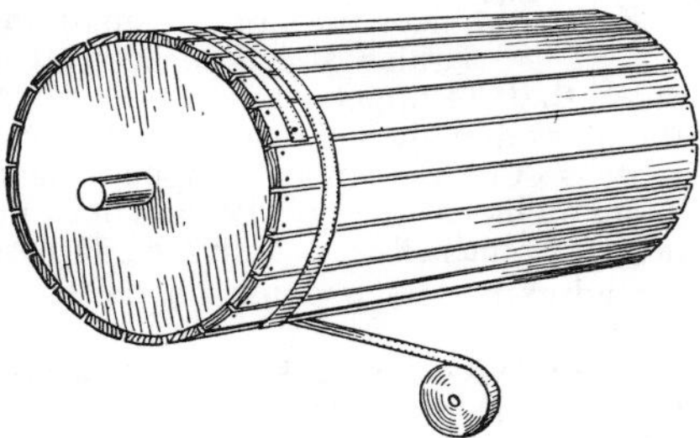

Fig. 6—Drying Reel

diameter, will be suitable under ordinary circumstances. The opening B may be adjusted by two metal slides which fit tightly in metal grooves fastened to the wood front. The metal grooves and slides can be made of tin and painted a dead black. The films after passing over the sprocket, fall into the bottom of the box, or, if very long films are to be made, the instrument can be used in the dark room and the light admitted only to the opening B, then the ends can be dropped into a basket or other receptacle at the bottom and the unprinted portions carried on reels above the box.

The speed of the exposure and the width of the opening B can be determined by making test strips. This can be done by setting the opening B to a certain width and turning the crank for

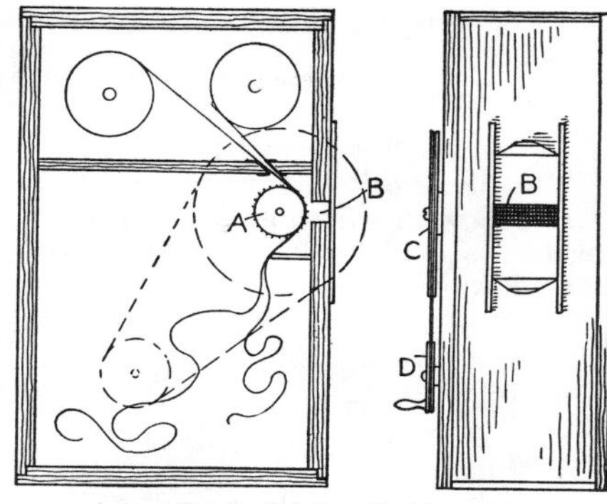

Fig. 7—Printing Machine

10 or 15 seconds and counting the number of revolutions. The proper exposure can be easily attained by this method.

(To be continued)

An Emergency Clamp

While making an extra large guitar I did not have clamps large enough to hold the top and bottom onto the sides while gluing, so I fastened three pieces of wood together, each piece being about 1 by 2 in., as shown in the sketch. Then I bored holes in both top and bottom pieces and inserted a piece of soft wire in the form of a loop, which, when twisted, drew the ends of the clamp together.—Contributed by Geo. E. Walsh, Buffalo, N. Y.

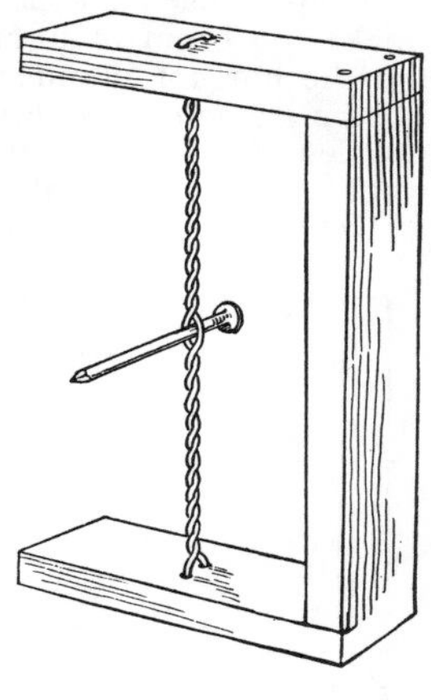

¶While camping, remember a hot stone wrapped up makes an excellent substitute for a hot-water bag.

Home-Made Motion-Picture Camera and Projector

IN THREE PARTS—PART III

The Projector

The film positives are projected on a screen with the same kind of a lantern as is used for lantern slides, with the addition of the device for stepping the film through, one picture at a time, and flashing light on each picture as it remains stationary for an instant. The projector (Fig. 8) is composed of a lamp house, a condensing lens to make the beam of light converge upon the film for illuminating it evenly, a film-stepping device, and a projecting lens for throwing the enlarged picture of the illuminated film upon a screen.

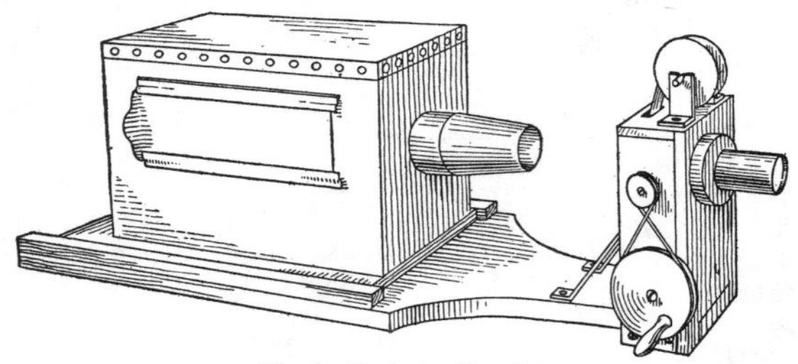
Fig. 8—Projector Complete

The lamp house is made of ordinary stovepipe metal and the dimensions given in the sketch are for a size suitable to use an acetylene or gas burner. The metal is laid out as shown by the pattern (Fig. 9) and bent on the dotted lines to form the sides and ends of the house. The joint may be riveted, or, if taken to a tinshop, lock-seamed. The cover is cut out as shown, the sides and ends having bent holes which are covered on the inside with perforated sheet metal, A. In order to deflect the light, a small angular strip, B, is riveted on so that its upper portion will cover the holes and allow a space for the heat to pass out. The cover may be hinged or set on like a cover on a can. The lamp house is attached to a sliding wood base for adjusting its position on the baseboard.

The condensing lenses are fixed into a metal barrel having a tapering end. This can be made of the same material

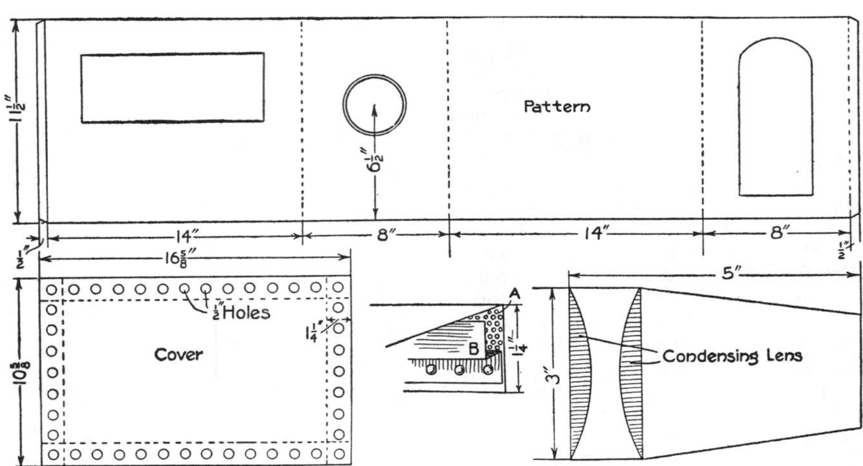

Fig. 9—Details of the Lamp House

as used in the lamp house. The parts can be rolled and a lock joint made at a local tinshop, or the pieces shaped over a wood form and riveted. Small L-shaped pieces are riveted to the in-

of the required size, or a lens of 12-in. focus enlarging a 1-in. film to about 6 ft. at a distance of 24 ft. A regular lens fitted in a metal tube can be purchased from a moving-picture stock

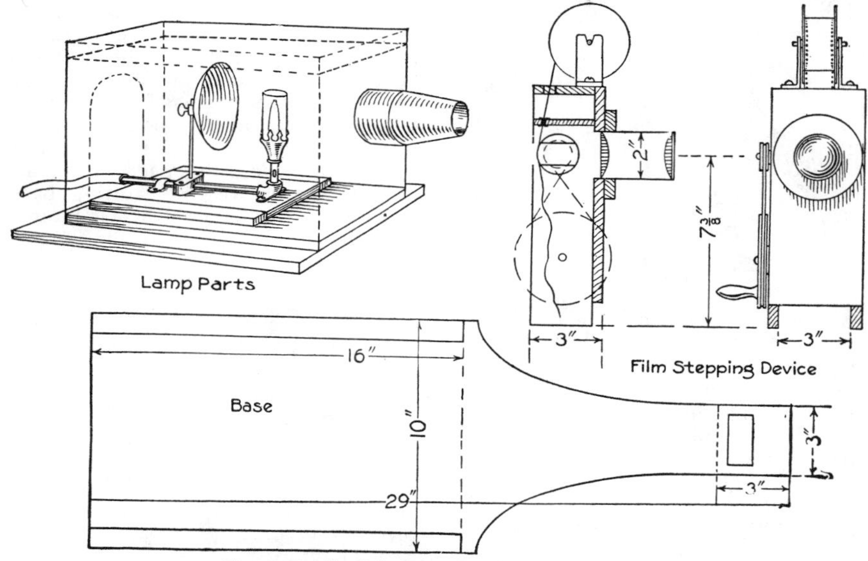

Fig. 10—Details of the Lamp, Stepping Device and Base

ner surfaces to hold each lens in place. A rim is turned up on the back end of the metal tube for attaching the lens barrel to the lamp house.

An ordinary mantle or acetylene burner is attached to a gas pipe that has for its base a drop elbow fastened to a sliding board similar to the slide of the lamp house on the baseboard. A good reflector should be attached to a standard just back of the burner. The standard is also fastened to the sliding board. The proper distance of the light from the condensing lens can be easily set by this adjusting device. This arrangement is shown in Fig. 10 in the diagram entitled "lamp parts."

The device for stepping the film is a duplicate of the one used in the camera as described in Part I, with the exception of the lens. The lens should be about 2 in. in diameter with such a focal length that will give a picture

house at a reasonable price. The box is made up similar to the camera box, but with a metal back instead of the wood. The intense heat from the light would quickly burn the wood and for this reason the light should be kept from the film while it is not in motion. The projecting lens barrel should be fitted snugly, yet loose enough for focusing.

The baseboard is cut as shown and the film-stepping device is firmly attached to the small end. The sides extend over the baseboard and are fastened with screws and braced with metal brackets. The slot in the small end of the baseboard is for the film to pass through. The film should have a tension the same as in the camera with velvet placed on the edges of the partitions. It is well to have a guide below the roller shutter to keep the film from encircling the roller as it turns.

Homemade Graining Tools

Desiring to do some fancy graining and having no tools at hand, I hastily made two of them from pieces of gar-

Tools Cut from Pieces of Garden Hose for Making Grains of Wood in Painted Surfaces

den hose, as shown in the sketch. Two pieces were cut from the hose, each 5 in. long, and the first one made as follows: A small hole, about 1/4 in. in diameter, was cut through the outside layer of rubber with a sharp knife at two points on opposite sides of the hose and exactly in the center for length. Around these holes rings of the rubber were cut out, or rather peeled off from the canvas part, the rings being $\frac{3}{16}$ in. wide, and the grooves, or parts removed, also $\frac{3}{16}$ in. wide. The hose will then appear as shown in the upper left-hand corner of the sketch.

To use this grainer, first paint the ground color, using a buff tint for imitation light oak, and allow it to dry, then put on a light coat of raw sienna, and while wet, take the prepared hose and draw it slowly over the length of wood, at the same time revolving the grainer slowly.

The other piece of hose, at the other corner, is made to take the place of a steel graining comb. The rubber is cut away lengthwise, leaving four segments, about 4 in. wide, on four sides of the hose. These segments are then notched out, like threads on a tap, each segment having a different number to the inch. These are used in the same manner as steel combs.—Contributed by A. H. Waychoff, Koenig, Colo.

Needle for Repairing Screens

In attaching patches to window or door screens, the work requires a continual shifting from one side to the other, or two persons, one on each side, must be present to pass the threaded needle back and forth. The operation can be easily simplified by using a bent needle, which has been heated and suitably shaped. The point of this needle can always be made to return to the side from which it entered, thereby avoiding the need of an assistant or the tiresome shifting back and forth.—Contributed by G. Jaques, Chicago, Ill.

An Emergency Tourniquet

A valuable addition to any shop medicine cabinet is the tourniquet. A device that will answer the purpose of the tourniquet can be made from an ordinary clothespin and a piece of binding tape, about 3/4 in. wide and 14 in. long. To stop the bleeding from a wound on a limb, pass the tape around the injured member between the wound and the blood supply. Pass the tape through the slot in the pin, wind the ends around the pin two or three times to prevent slipping, then turn the pin to draw up the tape tightly until the flow of blood is stopped.

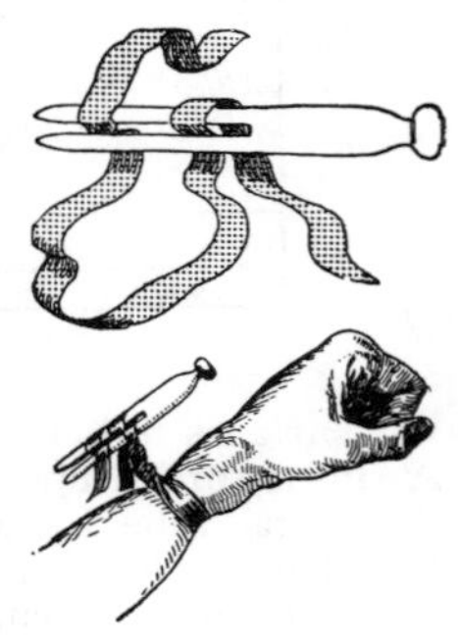

Mechanical Aid to Singers

Procure a large cigar box, of the square variety, and three ordinary drinking glasses with very thin walls and of different sizes, and place them in the box, as follows: Space them evenly, and drive three brads close to the circumference of each glass bottom, so that the glasses will have to be forced in between them. To prevent the glasses from touching the wood place a one-cent piece under each one.

A fourth glass is used, but from this the bottom must be removed. This can be done by saturating a string, or piece of yarn, in kerosene oil, wrapping it once around the glass near the bottom, then lighting it and allowing the string to burn out. The glass is then quickly dropped into cold water, which will remove the bottom.

A hole is cut in the cover of the box to receive the bottomless glass from the upper side, so that its lower edge will be flush with the under surface. Cut a slot, 3 in. long and 1/8 in. wide, in the cover near the back side.

To use, close the cover and at a distance of about 1/2 in. from the glass in the cover, or mouthpiece, sing into it. The glasses will impart to the voice a peculiar tone delightful to hear.—Contributed by J. B. Murphy, Plainfield, New Jersey.

Model Boat with Aerial Propeller

Procure or make a small model boat, 12 or 18 in. long, and place in the hold one or two cells of dry battery. Make a small platform in the stern and mount on it a small battery motor with the shaft parallel with the length of the boat and in the center. Directly above and parallel with the motor shaft run a shaft—a hatpin will do—in bearings fastened to the deck. Attach a drive pulley directly over the pulley on the motor and belt it up with a cord or rubber band. Purchase or make a propeller blade and attach it

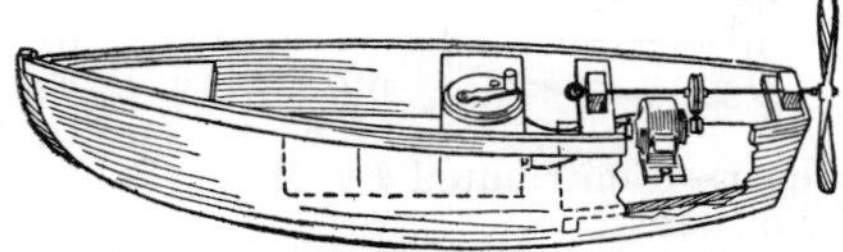

The Aerial Propeller is Driven by a Small Battery Motor Placed in the Boat

to the rear end of the shaft. A switch can be located on the deck for controlling the motor.—Contributed by Geo. B. Riker, Ft. Wayne, Ind.

Lantern-Slide Binding Machine

The machine shown in the illustration is very simple to make and when complete is one of the greatest time

A Machine That will Help to Bind Lantern Slides Quickly and Neatly

savers that a photographer can possess. The base is made of a piece of board, 9 in. long, 2 in. wide, and 7/8 in. thick. The uprights support a small bar upon which the roll of binding revolves. An old ink bottle filled with water and with some cotton stuffed in the neck serves as a moistener for the binding. The use of this machine insures a neat job in a very short space of time. The slide is always in the center of the binding. The end of the slide should run a little over the end of the base so that the binding may be fixed to the edge with the fingers, using a downward motion. The slide is then turned over on the other edge with a rolling motion and the operation repeated.—Contributed by Alvin G. Steier, Union Hill, N. Y.

Adjustable Film-Developing Machine

The simple homemade developing machine, shown in the illustration, can be easily made with three film spools,

Developing a Roll Film in a Tray with a Machine That Drives the Film around Rollers and through the Developing Liquid by Turning a Crank

some strong wire, and odd pieces of wood. It consists of an open frame, having two side pieces provided with slots down the center, sufficiently wide to allow an ordinary wood screw, of suitable size, to slide up or down freely. The two end-connecting pieces act as supports for the developing tray and should be made of sufficient length so the tray can pass freely between the sliding upright frame, made to fit in between the side pieces of the base. This frame can be adjusted to suit the length of film and is clamped in place at the desired position by wood screws, fitting in the long notches and screwed into the uprights. The two bottom rollers consist of film spools which are fastened in place by being slipped over a suitable wire, bent so the spool can enter the developing tray and the wire pass over the sides. Another bend at the outer end provides for the adjustment of the spools and for securing the wire in place by staples. The top spool is secured to a wire fitted with a crank at the outer end, so that in turning the wire, the spool will also turn, thereby driving the film. When placing the film on the machine, the sensitive side should face outward so it will not rub against the spools. The ends of the film may be connected with pins or ordinary paper fasteners.—Contributed by H. R. F. Richardson, Ottawa, Ont.

Preventing Loss of Fish from Covered Baskets

In the cover of fish baskets an opening is frequently made permitting the fish to be put in without lifting the cover. In traveling over rough places, or when the basket is full, some of the fish are likely to be shaken out, or may wiggle out of the basket. To guard against this, a leather flap can be provided covering the hole on the inside. At one end of the flap, four holes should be punched. It can then be placed in position and securely laced to the cover. The flap acts as a valve, allowing fish to be put into the basket, but preventing their escape.—Contributed by A. W. Cook, Kamela, Ore.

Repair for a Broken Lock Keeper

Having broken the recess half of a common cupboard lock, or latch, which was used to fasten a hinged storm window, I used a round-head wood screw as shown. The screw was easily placed, and it serves the purpose as well as the regular keeper.—Contributed by R. F. Pohle, Lynn, Mass.

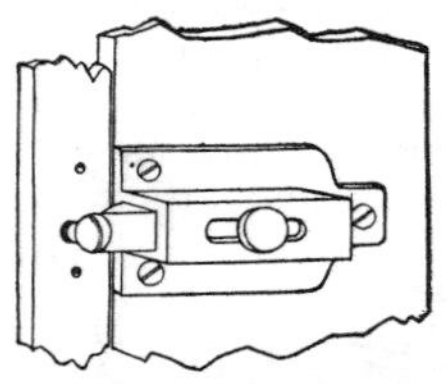

When using glue contained in screw-stoppered vessels it is advisable to smear a little vaseline on the thread to prevent the stopper from adhering to the container.

Throwing a Spot Light with the Lantern on Individuals of a Home Play, Which can be Given Brilliant Effects by the Use of the Tinted Celluloid in the Openings of the Revolving Wheel

Lantern for Spot and Colored Lights

The school play in pantomime is not complete unless the different parts of the play are illuminated in different colors, especially if the performers are clad in glittering garments. A spot light is also a feature not to be forgotten in singling out the star player or the one singing a song. The cost of a light for this purpose is entirely out of the reach of the average schoolboy, but if he has any ingenuity and a little time, a lantern for throwing those colored lights can be made at home, and the necessary parts will not cost much.

The metal necessary can be the ordinary stovepipe material, but if it is desired to have a fine-appearing lantern, procure what is called Russian iron. This metal has a gloss, and if used, it should be gone over from time to time with a rag soaked in oil, then wiped dry, to keep it from rusting. The pattern for the body of the lan-

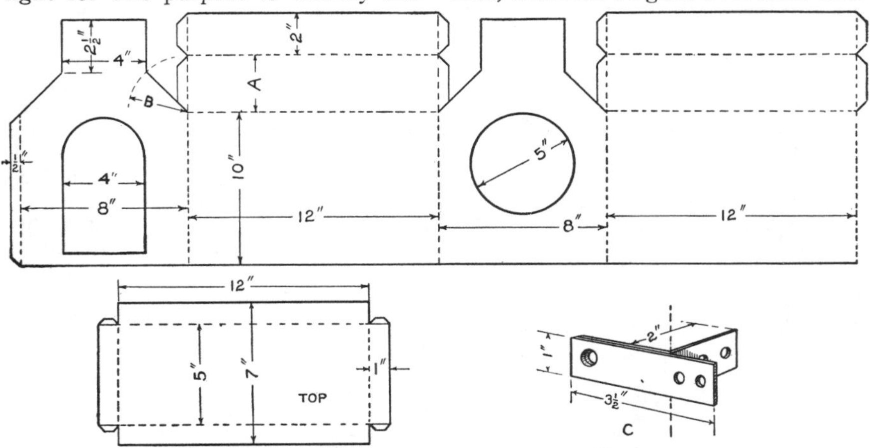

Pattern for Cutting the Metal to Form the Entire Lantern, or Lamp House, Also the Pattern for the Top and the Metal Bracket That Makes a Bearing for the Revolving Wheel, Having Openings Covered with Tinted Celluloid

tern, or lamp house, is shown with dimensions.

If metal, long enough for the whole length, cannot be procured, then make it in two pieces, being sure to allow ½-in.

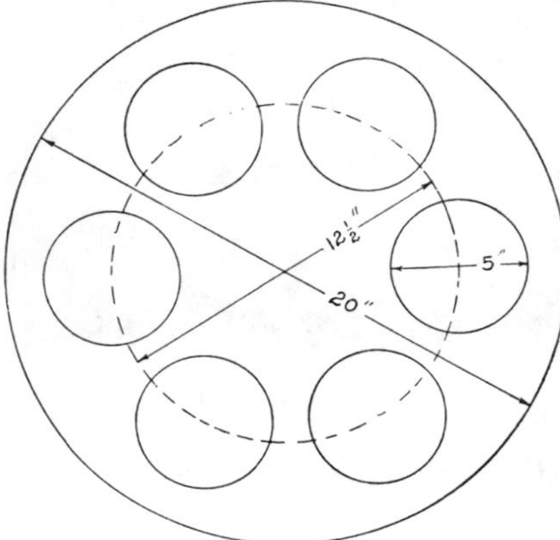

Pattern for the Revolving Wheel in Which Six Holes are Cut and Covered with Tinted Celluloid

end also on the second part, as shown on the first, for a riveted joint. The metal is bent on the dotted lines and cut out on the full ones. The distance between the lines A to be bent is equal to the radius B. The part A forms the sloping side of the top, and the 2-in. part at the top of the side extends vertically on the upper or vertical part, it being ½ in. narrower to provide an outlet for the heat.

An opening is cut in the rear end,

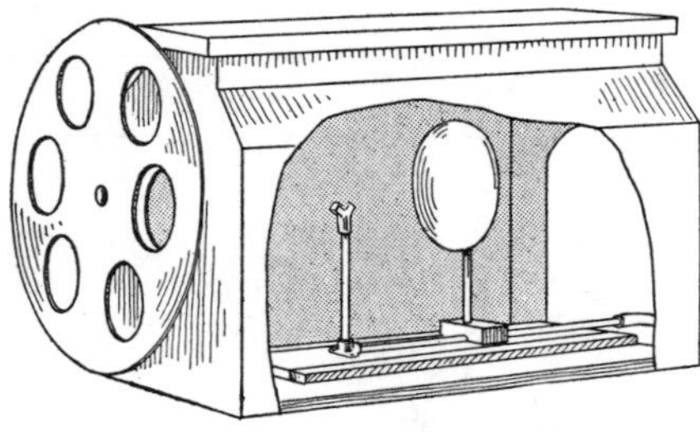

The Base of the Lantern is Provided with a Sliding Part Carrying the Light for Adjustment

as shown, also a hole, 5 in. in diameter, in the front end. The size of the round hole is optional, as it should be cut to suit the condensing lens provided. If a lens 5½ in. in diameter is used, then a 5-in. hole should be cut. This is enough difference in size to hold the lens from dropping through, while clips riveted on the inside of the lamp-house end will hold it in place. The lens is set in the hole with the curved side outward from the inside of the lamp house.

The top, or covering, is cut out of the same material as used in making the lamp house, the length being 12 in., and the sides are cut to extend ½ in. on each side of the ventilator. The edges, being turned down on the dotted lines, provide a covering to prevent any great amount of light from passing out through the ½-in. ventilating opening mentioned in connection with the side construction of the lantern. The 1-in. parts of the cover ends are turned down and riveted to the ends of the lamp house. The little extensions on the ends provide a means of riveting the side, to make a solid joint.

The arm C is made of a piece of ⅛ or $\frac{3}{16}$-in. metal, shaped as shown, to fit on the corner of the lamp house, where it is riveted. This provides a support and a place for an axis for the large revolving wheel holding the colored-celluloid disks.

The metal forming the lamp house is fastened on a baseboard, cut to snugly fit on the inside. The base has two cleats, nailed lengthwise to form a runway, 4 in. wide, into which another board is fitted to carry the burner. While the illustration shows an acetylene burner, any kind of light may be used so long as it is of a high candlepower. If manufactured gas is at hand, a gas burner with a mantle can be fitted, or a large tungsten electric light will give good results.

The wheel, carrying the colored disks, is made of the same kind of metal as used for the lamp house. The edges should be trimmed smooth, or, better still, turned over and hammered down to prevent injury to the hands while turning it. A washer should be used between this wheel and the arm C on a bolt used for the shaft, to make the wheel turn freely. The colored disks of celluloid are fastened to the outside of the wheel over the openings.

A yoke to support the lantern and provide a way for throwing the light in any direction, is made as shown. A line along which the lantern balances is determined by placing it on something round, as a broom stick, and the upper ends of the yoke are fastened on this line with loosely fitted bolts for pivots.

The lantern is set in front of the stage at the back of the room and the light is directed on the players, the colors being changed by turning the wheel. Sometimes good effects can be obtained by using the lantern in the wings, or for a fire dance, by placing it under the stage, throwing the light upward through grating or a heavy plate glass.

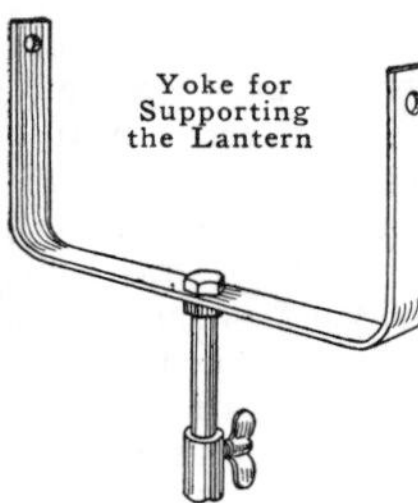

Yoke for Supporting the Lantern

Homemade Palette Knife

A corset steel makes a good substitute for a palette knife because of its flexibility. It gives better satisfaction if cut in the shape shown than if left straight. Should a handle be desired, one can be easily made by gluing two pieces of thin wood on the sides.—Contributed by James M. Kane, Doylestown, Pa.

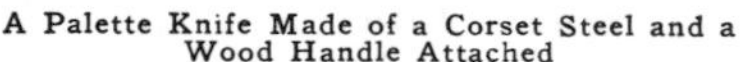

A Palette Knife Made of a Corset Steel and a Wood Handle Attached

ℭTo remove a white mark on wood having a wax surface, rub it lightly with a rag moistened in alcohol; then rub with a little raw linseed oil.

Self-Closing Gate

This gate is suspended from a horizontal bar by chains, and swings freely about a 1-in. gas pipe, placed vertically in the center of the gate. The chains are of the same length, being fastened equidistant from the pipe, the upper ends farther out than the lower. The distance depends on the weight of the gate and the desired force with which it should close. Any of the numerous styles of latches can be used, if desired.—Contributed by Kenneth Osborn, Loveland, Colo.

The Gate will Swing in Either Direction and Come to a Rest Where It Closes the Opening

A Poultry Shade

If a poultry yard is in an open space where the sun's rays will strike it squarely, a shade can be put up as follows: A piece of old carpet, rug, or canvas, fastened to the wire mesh with clothespins, will produce a shade at any place desired.—Contributed by Walter L. Kaufmann, Santa Ana, Cal.

Reflector for Viewing Scenery from a Car Window

Construct a box of pasteboard or thin wood, about 9 in. long, 3 in. wide and 2 in. thick, and fasten two pieces of mirror in the ends at an angle of 45 deg., both sloping in the same direction with their reflecting surfaces toward each other. An opening as large as the mirror is cut, facing it, in the box at the end A, and a small hole bored through at the end B so that it will center the mirror. Both of these apertures are covered with plain pieces of glass.

The Reflecting Device as It is Used in a Car Window for Viewing the Scenery Ahead

In use, the end A is placed outside of the car window and the user places an eye to the small hole B. It is impossible to be struck in the eye with a cinder or flying object.—Contributed by Mildred E. Thomas, Gordon, Can.

A Muskrat Trap

It is difficult to catch muskrats in an ordinary steel trap, as a broken bone allows them to sever the flesh and escape. During the summer these rats build a shelter for the winter constructed of moss and sticks placed on the river or lake bed, the top extending above the water level and the entrance being through a hole in the bottom near one side, while the passage itself is under water. It, therefore, only remains for the trapper to make one of these houses over into a huge wire trap so that the animal may be caught alive.

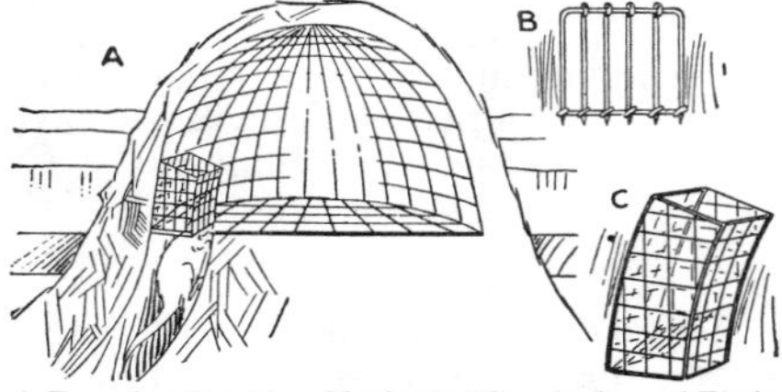

A Trap for Catching Muskrats Alive in One of Their Mounds Built of Moss and Sticks

The house A is prepared by removing the top and building the trap from heavy mesh wire which can be easily shaped, the joints being held together by binding the edges with wire. The passage is then fitted with a double trapdoor, the first, B, provided with sharp points on the swinging end, while the other is a falling cover. These two doors are placed in an entrance way, C, made of wire mesh and fastened over the passageway.

The muskrat comes up through the passage, pushing a bunch of moss or sticks and does not notice passing the trapdoors. The upper door is to keep the animals caught from getting at the first door.—Contributed by Vance Garrison, Bemidji, Minn.

A Casein Glue

Casein glues are splendid in woodworking, making cardboard articles, and when the composition is varied somewhat, make excellent cements for china and metals. Casein is made from the curd of soured milk after removal of the fat, and is put on the market in the form of a dry powder.

To make the glue, soak the casein powder two hours in an equal weight of hot water. To this gummy mass add about one-seventh the weight of the casein in borax which has been dissolved in very little hot water. Stir until all is dissolved after mixing borax and casein. This can be thinned with water to suit and is a good glue, but it can be made more adhesive by the addition of a little sodium arsenate. Any alkali, such as soda or ammonia, could be substituted for the borax.

To make a china cement, lime or water glass should be substituted for the borax. Addition of burnt magnesia increases the speed of hardening.

The Mile-O-View Camera

By T. B. LAMBERT

The Board Used Instead of a Tripod is Placed across the Backs of Two Car Seats

Many have tried, but heretofore no one has succeeded in taking panoramic views from the side of fast-moving trains or street cars. Motion pictures are easily obtained from the front or rear of moving trains, but none with the camera lens pointing at right angles, or nearly so, to the track. A complete apparatus for taking continuous and perfect panoramic pictures of any desired length as one travels through a country is too complicated to be described in detail within the limits of this article, but a simple arrangement, invented and constructed by the writer, will enable anyone to perform the experiment at practically no cost except for the film.

Some form of a roll-film camera is essential, and simply as a working basis, it will be assumed an ordinary camera is used, post-card camera in size, for which the following things will be required: A piece of thin black card, or hard rubber; a small board, and a piece of wire to be used as a crank.

Prepare the paper, or hard rubber, by cutting it to a size that will exactly cover the rear camera opening when the back of the camera is removed, which, in the case of a post-card size, is 6 in. long and 3¾ in. wide; then cut a narrow slot, about $\frac{3}{64}$ in. wide crosswise through the center of the material. This slot should extend to within about ½ in. of each edge, and the edges must be perfectly smooth and straight. If paper is used, glue it

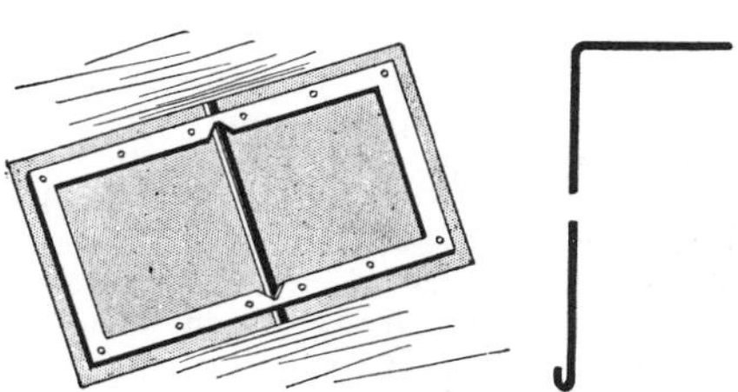

These Two Articles Constitute the Only Parts Necessary to Change a Camera into a Mile-O-View

to the opening in the camera. If hard rubber is used, it can be made up as shown and set in the camera opening.

This will bring the slot directly back of the lens center and at right angles to the direction in which the film moves when being rolled.

A board is prepared, about 4 ft. long, 10 in. wide and ¾ in. thick. This is to

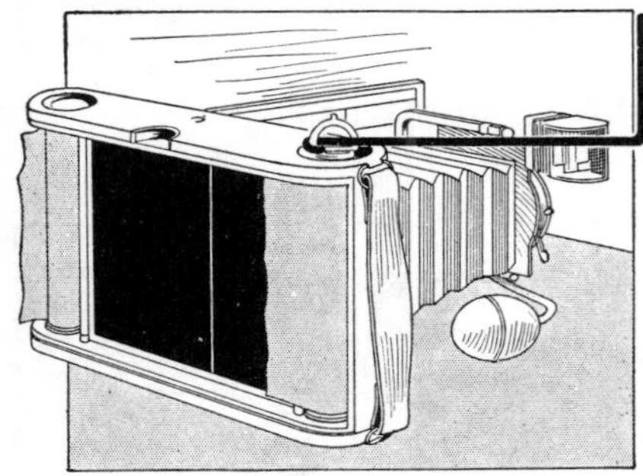

The Two Parts as They are Applied to an Ordinary Roll-Film Camera

take the place of a tripod, and it must have a small hole and suitable wing nut to attach the camera near the center. This length of board will reach from the back of one seat to another when it is placed to support the camera during the exposure.

A wire, about ⅛ in. in diameter, is bent, as shown, with a short hook on one end, and the other turned up at right angles, to serve as a handle. This wire, when hooked into the wing nut, will enable one to wind up the film at a fairly uniform speed. This completes all the necessary apparatus.

To take pictures with this panoramic outfit, load the camera in the usual way, but do not wind it up to exposure No. 1; stop at a point where the beginning of the film will be nearly opposite the narrow slot in the black paper, or rubber. This would be to stop the turning at about the time the hand pointer appears in the small back window. Attach the camera firmly to the board and brace up the lens end so that it will not easily shake with the movement of the car. Place the board across the backs of two adjacent seats, so that the camera will point out of the window at exactly right angles to the car.

When ready to expose, open the shutter wide, turn the crank that is hooked into the wing nut, and slowly wind up the film while the train is running. This will give a panoramic picture, continuous in character, and if the speed of turning is well judged, some very splendid views can be made.

The speed of turning the crank will be governed by the focal length of the lens and the speed of the train. For an average lens, the crank should be given one turn per second when the car is traveling about 15 miles an hour, or the average speed of a street car. A train traveling 30 miles an hour will require two turns of the crank per second. A good method of trying this out is to use one film as a test and turn the crank a few times and note its speed by the second, then stop and begin again at another speed for a few turns and so on, until the entire film is exposed, always noting the turns and time for each change, also the speed of the train. When the film is developed the one that shows best will give the proper number of turns per second.

The following points must be considered: The track should not be rough, and the camera must be perfectly steady and not twisted out of position by turning the crank, otherwise the resulting picture will be wavy. If the slot in the back board is not smooth and true, the picture will be streaked. Turning the film too fast will make the picture elongated, and too slowly, condensed. Should the camera be pointed otherwise than at right angles the picture will be distorted. This arrangement cannot be used to take moving objects except under special conditions. A picture of a passing train of cars can be made if the camera is stationary, but the wheels and drive rods will appear twisted out of shape. It is best for the experimenter to confine himself to scenery at the beginning, avoiding architectural objects, because a variation in speed of turning the crank to wind the film naturally distorts the architecture, which variation is not so noticeable in a scenic view.

A Photographic Worktable for Small Quarters

By K. V. REED

FLAT dwellers have no space at their disposal for a person to work at photography, and the bathroom must take the place of a dark room. As this was very inconvenient in my case, I constructed a table, that from all appearances was nothing more than a large-size kitchen worktable, and such a table can be used in case the builder does not care to construct it.

The table is turned upside down and the top removed by taking out the screws. The top is made of several pieces glued together and will remain in one piece. It is then hinged at one side to the top edge of the rail, so that it can be turned back like a trunk, or box, cover.

Boards are then nailed to the under edge of the rails. If a very neat job is required, these boards should be set inside on strips nailed to the inside surfaces of the rails, at the proper place to make the boards come flush with the under edges of the rails.

At the back side and in the center of the new bottom, a hole is cut, 6 or 7 in. square, and a box fastened beneath it, to form a bottom several inches below the main bottom. In this space bottles filled with solutions are kept. The main bottom should be painted with an acid-proof varnish.

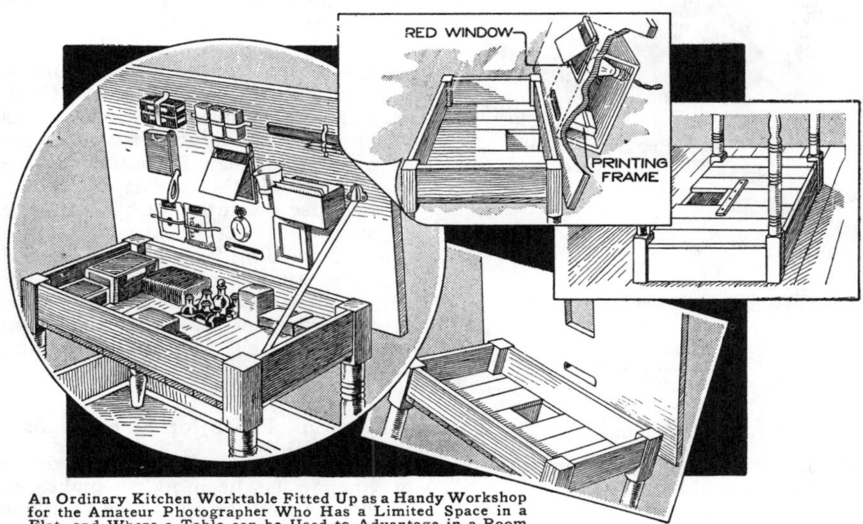

An Ordinary Kitchen Worktable Fitted Up as a Handy Workshop for the Amateur Photographer Who Has a Limited Space in a Flat, and Where a Table can be Used to Advantage in a Room

The space in the table is then divided, and partitions set up, which can be arranged to suit the builder.

Another attachment, which comes in exceedingly handy, is the ruby light.

This consists of a box, large enough to receive a printing frame at the bottom. Two holes are cut in the table top, at the right places to make a window for the light and a slit for the printing frame. When the table top is raised, the box with the light is fastened over the openings with hooks, the arrangement of which will depend on the size and shape of the box. In closing, the lamp box is removed, and pieces of board are set in the holes. This can be easily arranged, if the holes and blocks are cut on a slight slope, so that the latter when set in will not fall through the openings.

Back Thrust Prevented on Skis

To overcome the difficulty of skis slipping back when walking uphill either of the two devices shown is

Two Methods of Making an Attachment to Prevent the Backward Thrust of a Ski

good, if the attachments are fastened to the rear end of the skis.

The first represents a piece of horsehide, about 4 in. square, tacked on the ski and with the hair slanting backward. This will not interfere with going forward, but will retard any movement backward.

The other consists of a hinged portion that will enter the snow on a back thrust. As the ski end is thin, a block of wood must be attached to it on the upper side, and the projecting piece hinged to the block. The bevel at the end allows it to dig into the snow when the ski starts back. In going forward, it will swing out of the way freely.

Crystallization Shown on a Screen

The formation of chemical crystals can be shown in an interesting manner as follows: Spread a saturated solution of salt on a glass slide, or projection-lantern glass, and allow it to evaporate in the lantern's light or beneath a magnifying glass. The best substances to use are solutions of alum or sodium, alum being preferable. Ordinary table salt gives brilliant crystals which reflect the light to a marked degree. For regular formation, where the shape of the crystal is being studied, use a solution of hyposulphite of soda.

Many startling facts may be learned from the study of crystals in this manner, and watching them "grow" is great sport even to the chemist.—Contributed by L. T. Ward, Des Moines, Iowa.

Furniture Polish for Fine Woods

Boiled olive oil, to which a few drops of vinegar has been added, makes an excellent furniture polish for very fine woods. It will be found to work nicely on highly polished surfaces, and also for automobile bodies. It is applied in moderate quantities, and rubbed to a luster with a flannel cloth.

Enlarging Photographs

By A. E. SWOYER

When the photographer wishes to make an enlarged print from a small negative, he arranges a suitable light and condensers back of the negative and by means of a lens projects the resultant image upon a sheet of sensitive paper. Owing to the comparative weakness of the light, however, it is necessary either to use bromide paper or some of the faster brands of developing-out paper. If a more artistic medium is desired, a glass positive must first be made and enlarged to produce a negative from which the final prints will be made by contact. This process is somewhat clumsy and expensive, for if any retouching or doctoring is to be done, it must be upon a glass surface, either that of the two negatives or of the intermediate positive. As all of this work is done by transmitted light, there is the loss of fine detail common to all enlargements.

The difficulties incident to this process may be done away with by the use of a modification of the popular post-card projector; the alteration consisting simply in the substitution of a better lens for the cheap plate glass with which such instruments are usually fitted.

A contact print, preferably on glossy paper, ferrotyped, is made from the original negative by contact in the usual way; this is then placed in the modified projector and the image thrown upon a sensitive plate of the desired size. After a brief exposure, development will show an enlarged negative having every quality of the original.

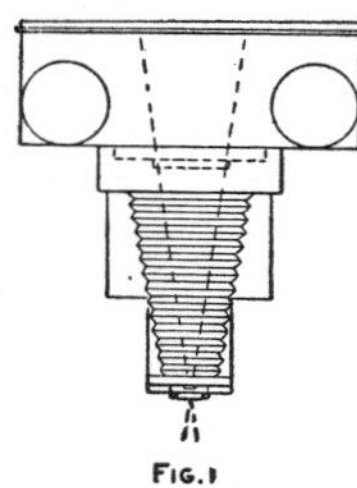

Fig. 1

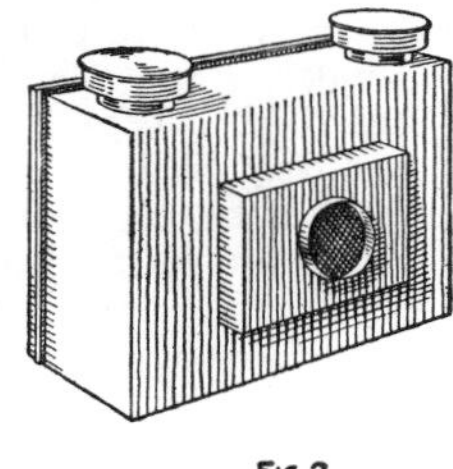

Fig. 2

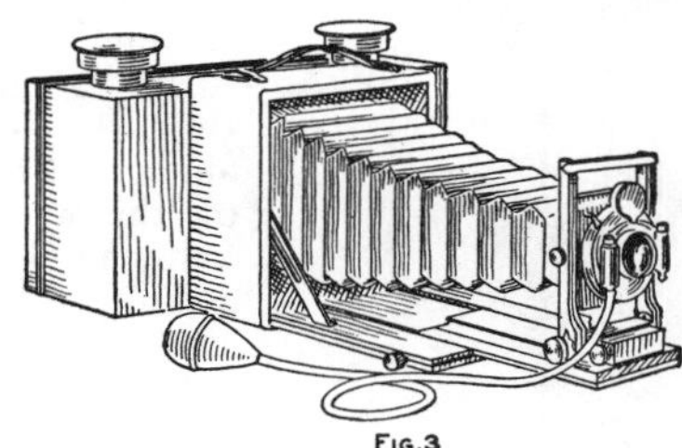

Fig. 3

An Ordinary Post-Card Projector Used Back of a Camera to Illuminate a Photograph Which is Enlarged on a Plate to Make a Negative Instead of a Print

The advantages of this process are obvious. In the first place, the comparative cheapness of the apparatus is a factor; in the second, the intermediate glass positive is eliminated, the print which is substituted for it providing a much better medium for retouching, faking or printing in. Transparent water colors in the less actinic shades may be used upon this print to control the final result, and if spoiled, it may be replaced at a negligible cost.

At first glance, it would appear as if

this method were simply a form of photographic copying; it is, in fact, the reverse. For in copying any object with a camera, the sensitive medium is behind the lens and the object to be copied is in front, and the size of the copy is therefore limited both by that of the camera and by its bellows draw. In the reflection process, the object to be copied is back of the lens and the sensitive medium is in front; as large a copy can be made with a small camera as with an eight by ten. It is really more convenient to work with a short-focus lens and a camera of limited bellows extension; the nearer the lens is to the back of the camera the larger will be the projected image.

The diagram (Fig. 1) shows that the size of the object to be enlarged does not depend upon the focal length of the lens used, as in ordinary enlarging, but simply upon the size of the opening in the front of the projector. The dotted lines are drawn from the edges of the card to be projected through the lens. Figure 2 is a sketch of a projector with the lens tube removed, so that it may be used with a camera as shown in Fig. 3.

Homemade Screen-Door Spring

A screen or storm-door spring can be easily made of spring-steel wire. The wire is bent to the shape shown in the sketch and two turns given to the coil as shown at A. The ends of the wire are fastened to the casing and door with staples. Two or three of these springs can be attached to one door where it is necessary to have more strength.—Contributed by Wm. Rosenberg, Watertown, Mass.

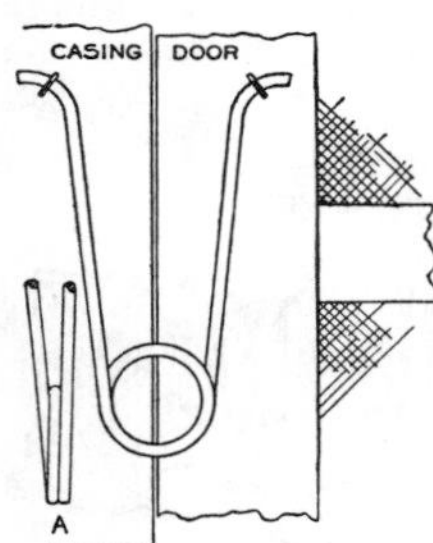

A Surprise Water Bottle

The performer produces a bottle and gives it with a glass to anyone in the audience, asking the person selected to take a drink of a very delicious concoction. When the person attempts to pour out the solution it is found to be frozen.

To perform this trick, the fluid must be previously made with a saturated solution of sulphate of soda and hot water. Fill a clean white bottle with the solution, taking care to cork the bottle while the liquid is hot. The liquid remains in a fluid state as long as the bottle is corked. When the bottle is shown, it appears to contain a liquid, and in handing it to a person the performer must be careful to take out the cork in time to allow it to solidify. In order to gain the proper time, pretend to be looking for a glass, make some remark about a sudden chill or feel the hand holding the bottle and say it is very cold. In the meantime, the air acting upon the solution has caused it to become fixed and immovable, and when the person attempts to pour it out, he finds it is impossible.

A Graduate Holder

A simple and easily constructed graduate holder in the form of a bracket placed in the corner of a dark room is shown in the sketch. The bracket not only holds the graduates securely, but allows them to drain perfectly and prevents dust settling on the inside, as they are suspended by the base. Holes of different size are cut in the board to accommodate large, medium and small graduates.

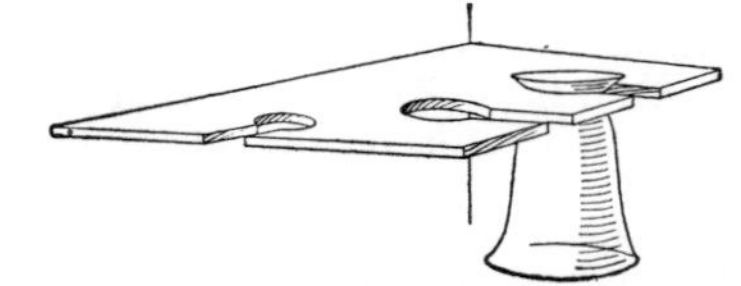

The Graduate Holder is Permanently Fastened in a Corner of the Dark Room

Homemade Enlarging Camera

The ordinary hand camera of the focusing type can be used to enlarge pictures from negatives of its own make. The requirement is a device to hold the negative rigid in a position in front of the camera lens, and at such a distance that the rays of light passing through the negative and lens will enter a box of sufficient size for the desired enlargement and focus plainly on a sheet of sensitive paper attached to the end of the box.

The first thing to do is to find the distance that is required from the camera lens to the paper enlargement to make the proper size, and the distance from the lens to the negative. A correspondent of Camera Craft gives the following rule for finding these dimensions: To find the distance between the lens and paper enlargement, add 1 to the number of times the picture is to be enlarged and multiply the result by the focus of the lens in inches. The example given is for a 6-in. focus lens. An example: A 4 by 5-in. negative enlarged to 8 by 10 in. is a two-time enlargement (four times in area); 2+1=3, and 3×6=18, the distance in inches of the lens from the sensitive paper. To find the distance of the lens to the negative, divide the above result, 18 in., by the number of times desired to enlarge, 18÷2=9, the distance in inches from the lens to the negative.

With these figures as a working basis, the box can be made in any size to use any focusing camera. The dimensions given in the drawing are for a 4 by 5-in. camera having a 6-in. focus lens, and to enlarge the pictures from a 4 by 5-in. negative to 8 by 10 in. In the first place make a box 8½ in. wide, 10½ in. deep and 14 in. long, inside measurement, using ¾-in. material, as shown in the sectional drawing A. One end is left open and in the center of the other a hole is cut 5 in. square.

The back end of the camera is placed over this hole as shown at B and ¼-in. strips nailed to the box end around the camera back to exclude all light. The camera must be centrally located.

The next to be made is the end board or easel, consisting of two pieces of ¾-in. material, one 8½ by 10½ in., which should fit easily into the end of the box, and a larger one, 10 by 12 in., the outside dimensions of the box, as shown at C. Nail the smaller piece

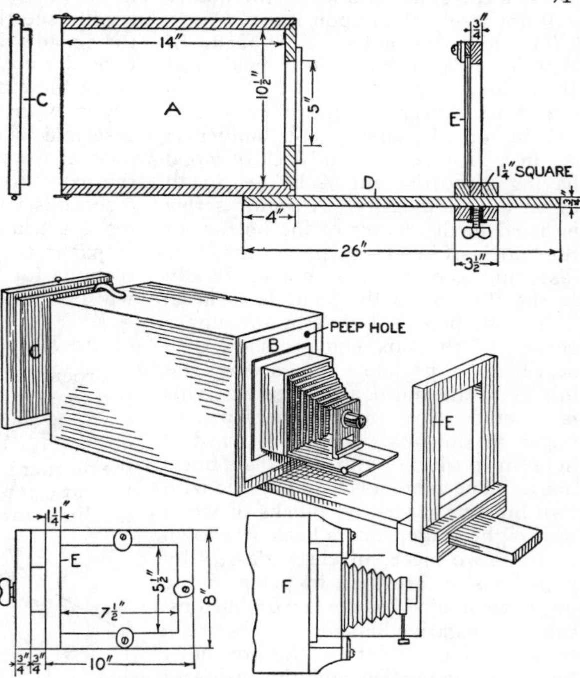

Details of Construction and Camera Complete

to the center of the large one, crossing the grain of wood in so doing. The end board is the easel upon which the sensitive paper is fastened with push pins, and should be covered with a sheet of white paper, pasting it on the $8\frac{1}{2}$ by $10\frac{1}{2}$-in. board with a thin coat of glue. The slide D is a piece of wood $\frac{3}{4}$ in. thick, $3\frac{1}{2}$ in. wide and 26 in. long. This is fastened to the under side of the box with four screws, placing it exactly in the center and parallel with the sides of the box. Be careful to have the slide parallel or the holder will not freely slide upon it.

The negative holder E is made of a piece of $\frac{3}{4}$-in. board, 8 in. wide and 10 in. long. A hole $5\frac{1}{2}$ by $7\frac{1}{2}$ in. is cut in its center, leaving a margin of $1\frac{1}{4}$ in. on all sides. This holder is set in a groove cut in a block of wood having a mortise cut $\frac{3}{4}$ by $3\frac{1}{2}$ in. to fit on the slide easily. A thumb screw is fitted in the center of the bottom of the block of wood. This is used for fastening the negative holder rigidly to the slide when the focus is secured.

A 1-in. hole is bored in the upper corner of the box end, as shown, to serve as a peephole for seeing the image on the end board or easel. This is covered before putting the sensitive paper in the box. The end board is held in position with two flat brass hooks. The camera is held in place with two buttons placed on blocks of wood the height of the camera back, as shown at F. Two pieces of clear glass, 6 by 8 in. in size, are held in place in the negative holder by means of buttons, the film negative being placed between them. All the joints in the box must be carefully puttied and the inside of the box blackened, which is done with a mixture of lampblack and alcohol, to which is added a small quantity of shellac to give it body.

A darkroom is not essential, a bathroom with the window covered over with orange paper will do, or even a large room with the shades drawn and pinned close to the window casing. It is best to leave a space in one of the windows to be covered with orange paper, doing the developing about 10 ft. from the source of light.

To operate the camera place it on the enlarging box, hook the easel in place, put a negative in the holder with the film side toward the lens. Take the outfit to a shady place outdoors, point the holder end at an unobstructed portion of the sky and look through the peephole. Rack the lens in and out to focus the picture. The easel should have heavy black lines drawn upon it inclosing parallelograms from 5 by 7 in. to 8 by 10 in., so that one can readily see the size of the enlargement to be made. When the focus is obtained take the outfit into the darkroom, remove the easel and fasten the sensitive paper with push pins. Replace the easel and take the outfit outdoors again, point it toward the clear sky and make the exposure, which should be at least 5 seconds with a 16 stop. It is best to make a trial exposure on a small strip of paper to find the proper time. Directions for the use of bromide papers will be found in each package.

An Easy Way to Make a Shelf

Procure an ordinary packing box and mark a line from corner to corner on both ends, as shown, from A to B in Fig. 1. Pull out all the nails from the corners that may cross the line. Nail the top to the box and saw it on the lines marked and two shelves will

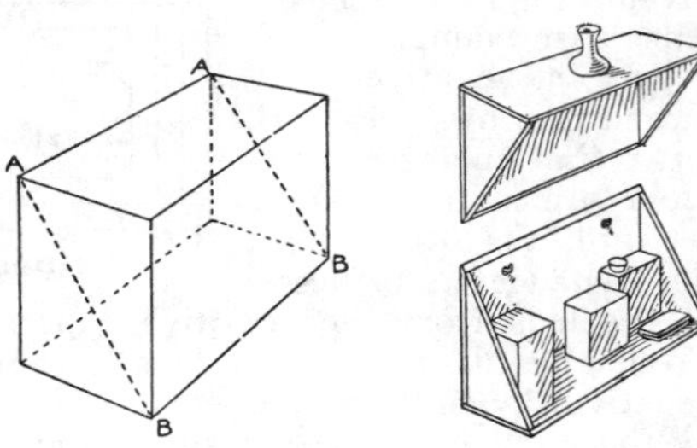

Two Shelves Made of One Box

be formed which may be used as shown in Fig. 2. Boxes dovetailed at the corners will make excellent shelves and look neat if painted.

Multiplying Attachment for a Camera

By J. C. MOORE

The hand camera suitable for this work is the kind commonly known as the reversible back, which is a detachable part that carries a ground glass for focusing and a place to insert the plate holders. When this part is removed, it will be seen that the back of the camera is mortised to prevent light from entering. Construct a frame to take the place of the back, but make it about ⅝ in. larger all around, and make one surface to fit the mortise of the camera box.

A back is now made and attached to the frame, to carry the ground-glass reversible back, so that it can be shifted over the center of focus for each small portion of the plate on which the picture is to be made. Measure the outside of the plate holder and, doubling the dimensions both ways, lay out a diagram on a piece of paper. Lay the plate holder on the paper and move it to the extreme left, then to the right, to see if the center of the plate will coincide with the center of the back. In the same manner locate the center in a vertical position. If the center lines do not coincide, increase the dimensions until this occurs. Mark, in the exact center, an opening the size of the plate and cut

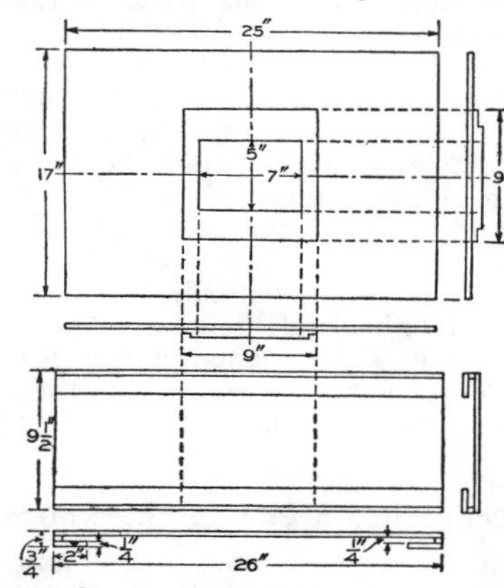

Manner of Laying Out the Pattern for the Back and Locating the Exact Center

out the wood. It is best to use a three-ply wood for making the back, but if this cannot be obtained, procure a dry piece of wood and mortise and glue strips to the ends to keep the wood from warping. Glue the frame to this

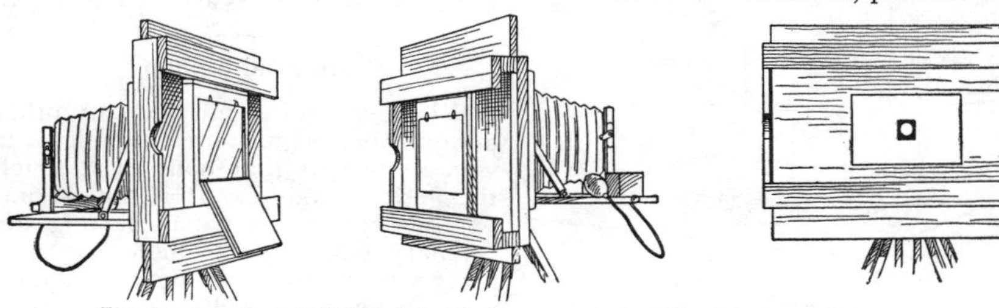

The Attachment as It is Fitted to the Camera and the Reversible Back in the Frame

back, over the opening, and make attachments to hold it to the camera in the same manner as the reversible back was attached.

If pictures of two or three different sizes are to be made, the opening in the new back should be fitted with as many new pieces as there are sizes of pictures, each to have an opening of corresponding size. For a 5 by 7-in. plate, 1⅛ by 1¼-in. pictures is a good size, as there will be room for 24 pictures on the plate with a small margin left for notes. The piece to fill the opening should be made of the same material as the back so that a smooth joint will result. As a board cannot be made smooth enough for a perfectly light-tight joint, the surface on the new back, over which the reversible back travels, must be covered with cloth—a piece of black velvet is suitable—to exclude all light as the plate holder is shifted over the back.

A frame is now made to carry the reversible back of the camera, the size of which will depend on the size of the other parts, as well as on the size of the camera to be used. This frame consists of two horizontal strips joined at the ends with grooved pieces, fitting the edge of the new back, so that it may be slid up and down in the grooves. The crosspieces are also rabbeted to receive the reversible back and allow it to be moved back and forth horizontally. The rabbet in the horizontal strips should not be so deep as to permit the extending edge to overlap the ground-glass frame, thus preventing it from moving back as the plate holder is inserted.

If the frame on the back and the reversible back fit tightly, they will remain in any position, but if they are loosely fitted, it will be necessary to provide some means to hold them. Small springs with pins may be fitted to the vertically moving frame to hold it in the position for the horizontal rows of pictures.

The ground glass should be marked for the size picture to be taken. The positions of the frame and plate carrier should also be marked so that the plate holder need not be taken out to find the location and focus for the next picture.

Connecting a Pipe to Sheet Metal

In the absence of a waste nut, an iron pipe can be easily fastened to sheet-metal work as shown in the

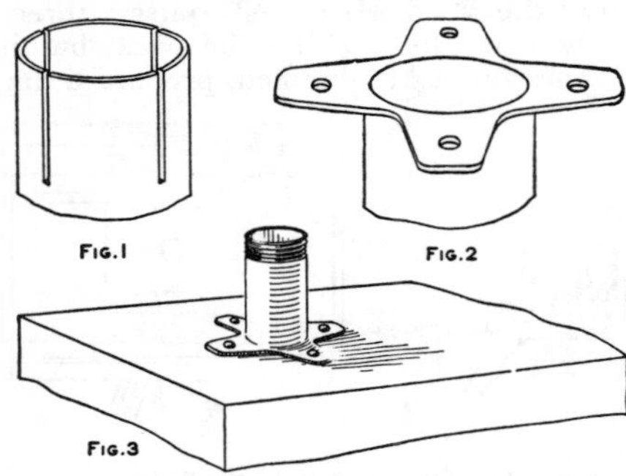

The End of the Pipe as It is Prepared to be Riveted on the Sheet Metal

sketch. The end of the pipe, Fig. 1, is slotted with a hacksaw to form four projections, which are turned outward and their ends rounded as shown in Fig. 2. The face of the projections are tinned and then riveted to the sheet-metal surface, as shown in Fig. 3. After soldering the joint, it will be as good or better than if a waste nut had been used.—Contributed by Lorin A. Brown, Washington, D. C.

An Acid Siphon

When siphoning off acids or other disagreeable or poisonous liquids, it is very important that none of it touch the flesh or mouth. It is almost impossible to do this when starting the ordinary siphon. A siphon that does away with this inconvenience and danger can be made as follows:

Procure a good Bunsen burner and two pieces of ¼-in. glass tube, one 2 ft. and the other 18 in. long. Heat the 2-ft. length at a point 8 in. from one end in the flame until it can be bent as shown at A. The other piece should be plugged at one end and then slowly and evenly heated at a point 10 in. from one end. When the glass is soft, blow slowly and steadily into the open end, at the same time turning the tube around in the flame. This will form a bulb, B. The ends of the glass tube are heated and bent as shown, at C and D, and then fused onto the piece A, as shown at E. This can be accomplished by heating the piece A at a point 4 in. from the unbent end. When the glass becomes soft, place one end of a short piece of tube in it and pull out into a thread. Break this off as close to the tube as possible, to make a hole in the tube. Heat the end of the tube D and also the glass around the hole, and when both become soft, they can be fused together.

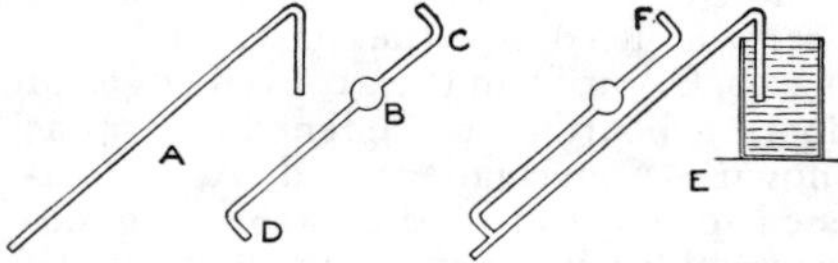

When Starting This Siphon It is Difficult for the Liquid to Touch the Mouth or Flesh

In use, close the end not in the liquid and, placing the mouth at F, exhaust the tube, thus filling it with the liquid. When the closed end is opened, the siphon will flow. The liquid collects in the bulb, and if a little care is used, none of it can reach the mouth.—Contributed by O. F. Tronnes, Evanston, Ill.

Bottle-Opening Trick

A local junk dealer, who was also known as the "strongest man in town," used to mystify the folks by opening a bottle, apparently with a stroke of his index finger. His audience saw his index finger strike the stopper, but did not see the knuckle of his second finger strike the eccentric at the point A, as shown in the sketch, causing it to fly up while his index finger B assisted the stopper out of the bottle mouth.

When trying the trick, it is best to select a bottle with a loose stopper, or else wear a glove, as the gentleman who demonstrated the trick had hands

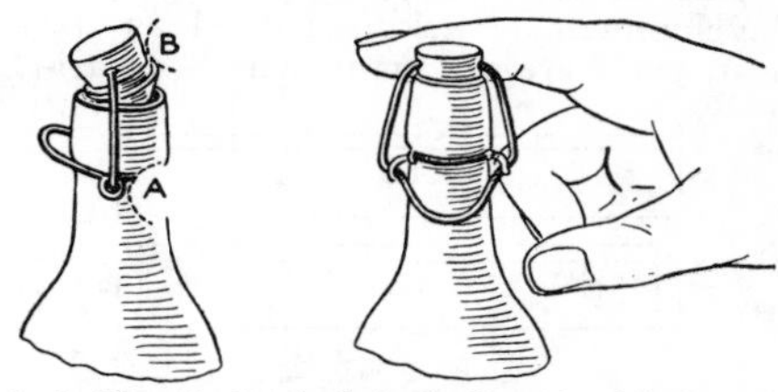

In Striking the Bottle Cork, the Knuckle of the Second Finger Loosens the Wire Lock

of the hard and horny type.—Contributed by James M. Kane, Doylestown, Pa.

Setting Colors in Fabrics

The colors of fabrics or other materials of any kind may be set by boiling the articles in the following solution: To 1 gal. of soft water add 1 oz. of ox gall. This solution should be boiling when the articles are dropped into it. A chemical reaction results and the colors are set or made nonfading. The process is harmless. Colors in wood may be treated in the same manner.

Towel-Roller Brackets

Very serviceable brackets for a towel roller can be made by using ordinary wire clothes hooks, as shown in the illustration. The roller is made of wood and two nails with their heads cut off, one in each end, form bearings to turn in the ends of the hooks. When it is desired to remove the roller, the hooks are sprung apart

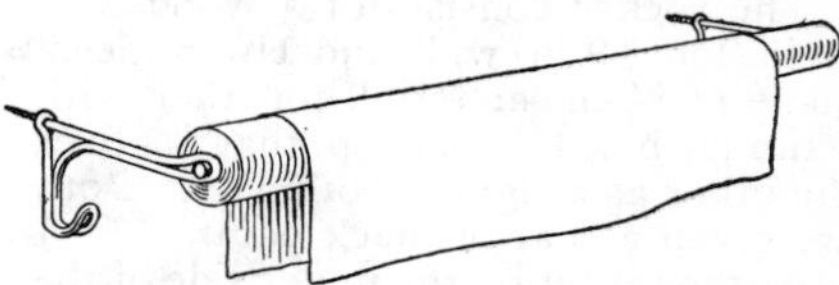
The Roller Brackets are Easily Adjusted in Any Location and Serve the Purpose Admirably

enough to allow it to drop out.—Contributed by Hugh Carmichael, West Lorne, Ont.

A Developing-Tray Rocker

The tank method of photographic development is acknowledged as the best, yet there are many who, for various reasons, still use the old-style tray method. For those who use the tray, a splendid and simple method that combines the good qualities of both the tank and tray is the tray-rocking device shown in the illustration.

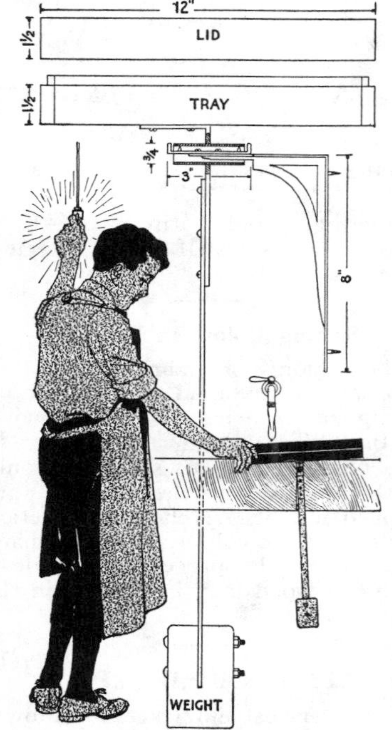

Developing-Tray Rocker to Keep the Liquid in Motion over the Plate Automatically

The rocker consists of a wood box, 13 in. long, 9 in. wide and 1½ in. deep, made of ⅜-in. material, together with a similar box 1½ in. deep, that fits over the other as a light-proof cover. Both are given a coat of black paint.

At the center on the under side of the tray part, a right angle made of strap iron is fastened with screws. On the part projecting down, a hole is drilled to receive a sleeve made of a brass tube which is soldered in place. An ordinary shelf bracket is procured, one end of which is filed and fitted with a strip of metal having both ends turned up slightly. Small-pointed pins are fastened in holes drilled near the turned-up part. The points of the pins serve as a knife-edge for the rocker. The extending end of the strap iron is fitted with a pendulum rod having a weight at the bottom.

The rocker is attached to the wall in a convenient place in the dark room. The tray with the developer and plate is placed in the box, which is light-tight, and the pendulum is started swinging.—Contributed by T. B. Lambert, Chicago.

An Adjustable Bookholder

A very satisfactory adjustable holder for books or letters can be constructed of ordinary materials. A board is used for the base, and two pieces, C, cut from the grooved edges of flooring boards, are fastened on top as shown. A permanent end, A, is fastened to one end of the base. A good-size holder is 19 in. long, 6 in. wide, made of material ¾ in. thick.

The movable slide B has two pieces attached to its under side, which are cut from the tongued edges of flooring boards. The piece D answers the double purpose of a handle and brace. A lock, E, is made of a bolt, having a long thread and a square head. A hole is bored from the under side through the brace, and a portion of the wood is cut out to admit the nut. A square place is cut out to admit the square bolt head in the bottom pieces. To lock the slide, simply screw the nut upward so that it will push the bolt head against the base.—Contributed by James M. Kane, Doylestown, Pa.

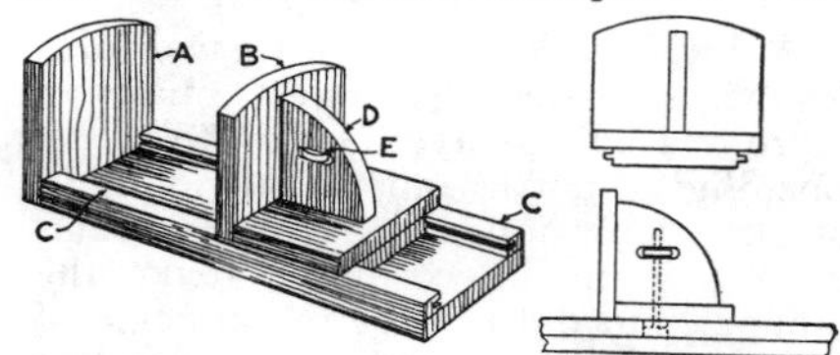

The Holder may be Used for Books or Letters and Papers as a File

An Old-Oak Stain

To make old oak of ash, elm, box alder, chestnut, maple, yew, and sycamore wood use a solution of copper acetate, or iron acetate. Either of these can be made by allowing a strong acid to come in contact with copper or iron. Acetic acid, or vinegar, will do for the acid. The chemical can be obtained from a local druggist if it is not desired to make the stain. By varying the strength of the solution, several shades may be obtained. A weak solution of iron acetate gives various brown hues. As the strength of the salt increases by concentration, the shades of brown darken.

Tablespoon End Used as Lemon Squeezer

In an emergency, the ordinary tablespoon can be used as a lemon squeezer by turning the lemon around the end

The Shape of the Spoon Bowl Produces the Same Effect as the Lemon Squeezer

of the spoon. This produces the same result as obtained with the regular squeezers, which act on the principle of extracting the juice by turning and crushing the lemon over a rough projection which approximately matches the shape of a half lemon.—Contributed by L. E. Turner, New York, N. Y.

A Back Stop for a Workbench

In planing small pieces on a bench, they usually have a tendency to tip up or slide around. This difficulty can be easily overcome by providing the bench with an extra back stop. For this purpose a discarded plane iron will do very well. Its edge should be notched so that it will easily enter the wood. The edges of its central slot should be

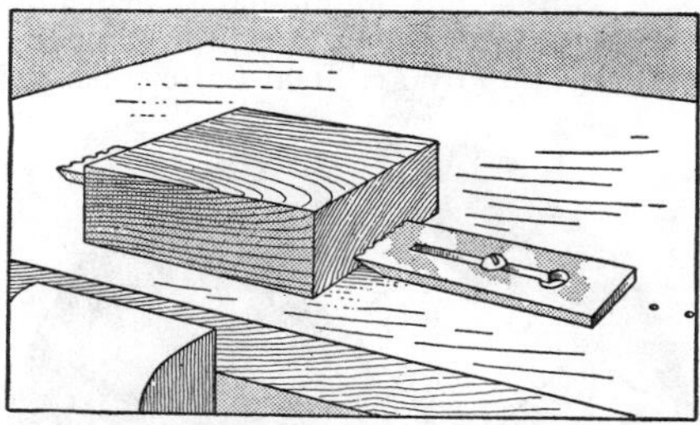

A Plane Bit Fastened to the Top of a Bench to Hold Blocks While Planing Them

beveled off, if an ordinary wood screw is used to fasten it to the bench. A series of holes, several inches apart and in line with the regular back stop, should be bored in the bench so the screw and iron can be readily changed, to fit varying lengths.—Contributed by C. S. Rice, Washington, D. C.

Croquet Mallets Protected by Metal Rings

Due to the severe service they are subjected to, croquet mallets very frequently split off at the ends, which spoils them for further use in accurate driving. To prevent this, metal bands may be placed

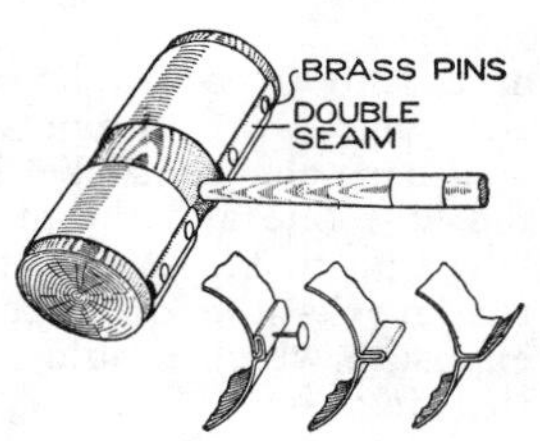

around the ends of the mallets. Thin sheet iron, or tin, can be used for this purpose. One end is bent up at right angles, the opposite end is provided with a loop to fit over the upright portion of the first end, and then the loop is closed up and hammered down to draw the metal tightly around the mallet. The ring is secured in place with several tacks, or short nails, driven through the seam.—Contributed by H. E. Stratmeyer, Rockville, Md.

Distance Marker for Printing Photographs

A convenient homemade printing device, or distance marker, for printing photographs by artificial light consists

The Same Distance with the Same Exposure will Always Produce Uniform Prints

of a smooth board on which twelve 1-in. marks are drawn, as shown. A wall-base electric socket is attached on the first line and the others are numbered up to 12. A trial test of a negative marks the distance and time of exposure which should be recorded on the negative. Such a device makes uniform prints possible and provides a means of recording time on negative-storage envelopes.—Contributed by Harold Davis, Altoona, Pa.

Mantel Picture Frames Made in Plaster

Procure a small oval or rectangular frame of a suitable size and use it as a pattern in making a mold. If it is not necessary to select an expensive frame, one that is straight without any floral designs is the best to use. Ordinary molding made into a frame will do as well, or a pattern, whittled out of wood in oval shape, will produce good results.

Make a flask out of any small box, and fill it with clay instead of molding sand. Make an impression of the frame in the clay, and the mold is ready for the plaster.

Procure four 8-oz. bottles, fill them with water, and tint the water in three of them red, green, and blue, with dyes. When purchasing the plaster of paris—2 lb. will do—also get some brass filings from a machine shop, and mix it with the plaster while in a dry state; then divide the lot into four parts of ½ lb. each, or equal parts.

Use the tinted water to mix the plaster and pour it into the mold. This will give the combinations red, green, blue, and white.

Picture frames made in this manner will stand enough polishing to keep the brass filings on the surface bright and shining, which gives a pretty effect.—Contributed by J. B. Murphy, Plainfield, N. J.

A Five-Pointed Star

There are many ways of making a five-pointed star, but the one illustrated is new and easy to apply. A long strip of paper, which should be transparent, is tied into a knot. When the ends A and B are drawn tightly, the paper strip takes the position shown in C. The end A is folded for-

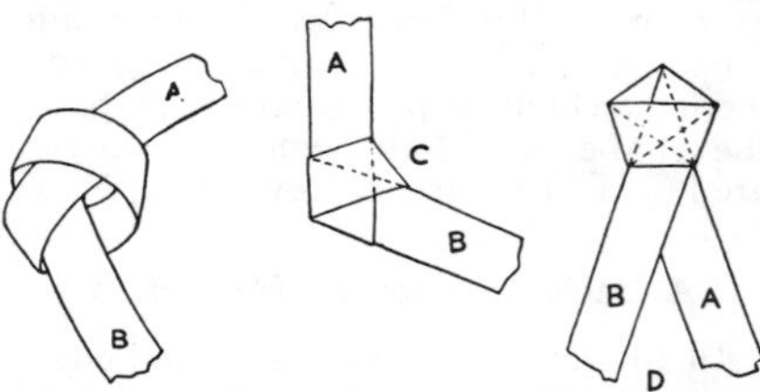

Holding the Knot to the Light a Star will be Seen, Shown by the Dotted Lines

ward, or in front of the knot; then the whole is turned over and it will take the position shown in D. Hold the paper to a good light and a perfect five-pointed star will be seen.—Contributed by J. J. Kolar, Maywood, Ill.

Fastening Portière Pole in a Doorway

A pole can be fastened between two supports, posts, or in a door casing neatly and without fixtures in the following manner: The pole is cut 1/8 in. shorter than the space between the casings, and a 5/16-in. hole is drilled in each end, one to a depth of 1 1/2 in. and the other 3/8 in. deep, a coil spring being placed in the deepest hole.

Screws are turned into the center of the location for the pole in the door jambs, allowing one screw head to project 1/8 in., and the other at least 1/4 inch.

To place the pole in position, put the end with the spring in the hole on the screw head projecting 1/4 in. and push the pole against the jamb, allowing the other end to pass over the

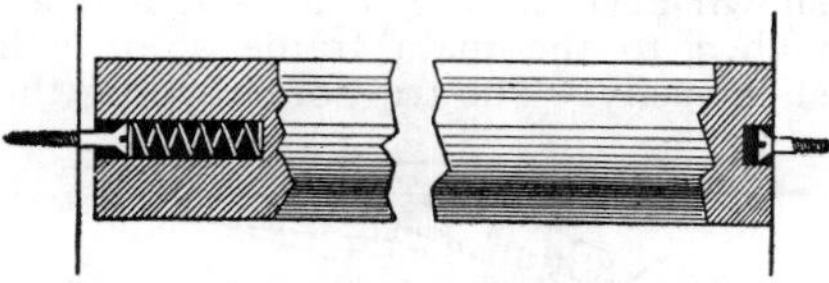

No Fixtures That will Show are Required with This Fastening of a Portière Pole

other projecting screw head until it slips into the hole by pressure from the spring. The spring will keep the pole in position.—Contributed by Ernest F. Dexter, Hartford, Conn.

Trick with Knives and Glasses

An interesting trick may be performed with three tumblers and three table knives. Place the tumblers in an equilateral triangle on a table so the knife ends, when the knives are laid between them, as shown in the plan sketch, are about 1 in. away from the tumblers. The trick is to arrange the knives so that they are supported by the tops of the three tumblers and nothing else. Most observers will say that it is impossible; some will try it and in most cases fail. It can be done, and the illustration shows how simply

Knives Placed in Such a Manner as to be Supported by the Three Glasses

it may be accomplished.—Contributed by R. Neland, Minneapolis, Minn.

A Scraper Handle

In using the ordinary steel-plate scraper, much inconvenience and cramping of the hands is experienced unless some suitable handle is attached. If a piece of scrap wood is taken and cut to a convenient shape, with a groove tightly fitting the scraper steel, greater pressure can be exerted and more effective work produced, without cramp-

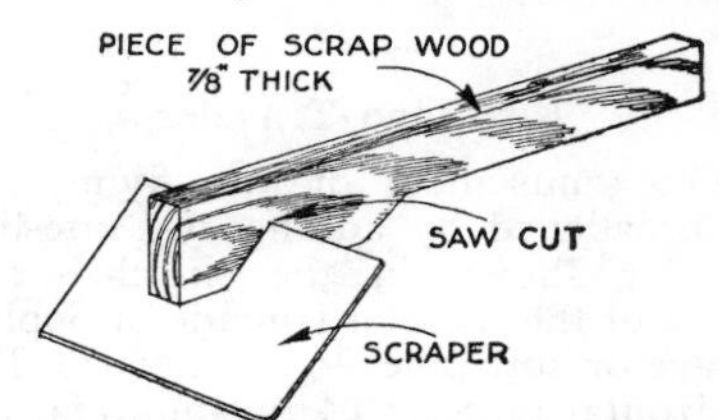

An Ordinary Piece of Board Shaped for a Handle and Notched for the Scraper Blade

ing the hands or tiring out the operator as readily.—Contributed by A. P. Nevin, Hancock, Mich.

Photographic Tray-Rocking Stand

Films develop better if the tray holding the solution is kept in motion or

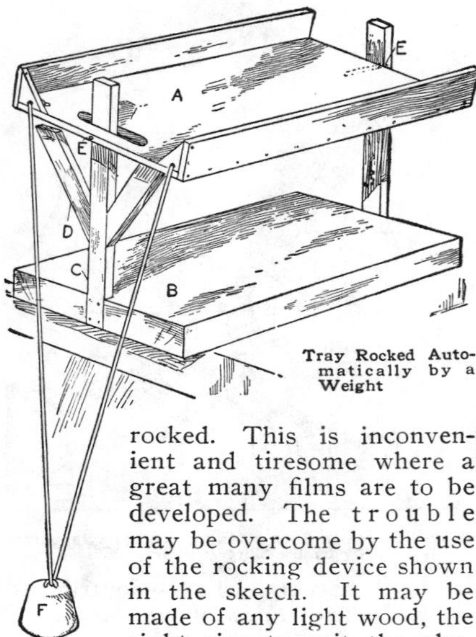

Tray Rocked Automatically by a Weight

rocked. This is inconvenient and tiresome where a great many films are to be developed. The trouble may be overcome by the use of the rocking device shown in the sketch. It may be made of any light wood, the right size to suit the photographer's needs.

The tray holder A is pivoted on the uprights C with pins EE. The uprights are fastened to a base, B. Two braces, D, one on each side of the upright C, limits the tip of the tray holder A. The weight F works as a pendulum, which automatically rocks the tray when set in motion.—Contributed by Abner B. Shaw, No. Dartmouth, Mass.

Kite-Line Traveler

The amusement of kite flying can be broadened by adding the kite-line traveler shown in the sketch. The frame of the traveler is made of poplar, spruce or soft pine, $\frac{1}{4}$ in. square. The horizontal piece is 24 in. long and the piece to which the wings are fastened is 8 in. long. This piece is cut so it will have a slight slant. The brace is a mitered piece, 13 in. long. The frame is fastened together with small brads, giving it the appearance shown in Fig. 1.

After the frame is finished, the traveler wheels are made and attached. They should be $\frac{1}{4}$ in. thick, about $1\frac{1}{4}$ in. in diameter, and have a groove cut $\frac{3}{16}$ in. into their faces. The pattern for cutting the bearings is shown in Fig. 4. These are bent at the places shown by the dotted lines and attached to the main frame stick as shown by BB in Fig. 3. The end view of the bearing is shown in Fig. 5. The metal is bent in as shown by AA, so that the wheel will rotate without much friction.

In Fig. 6 is shown the method of attaching the wings to the slanting frame part. The wings are made of light cardboard and each fastened with tacks to a wood arm, cut as shown. The large end of each arm is made to hinge in a piece of tin with brads AA.

Fasten a string to the ends of the arm pieces, as shown in Fig. 1, and attach a wire loop to the middle of the string, as shown in Fig. 3. The wire shown at L in Fig. 3 is bent and attached to the main frame so it will slide easily. The trip for dropping the

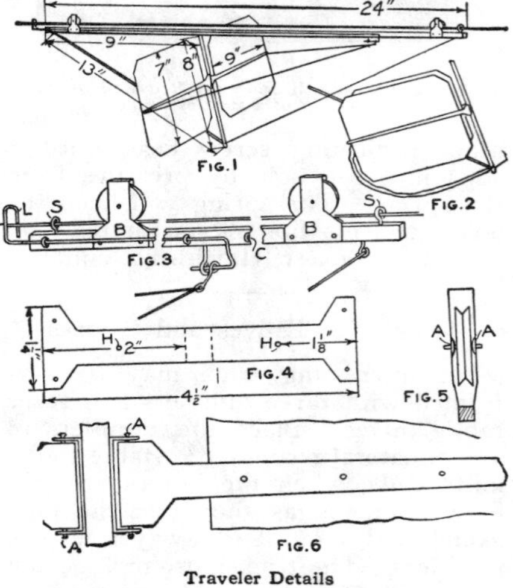

Traveler Details

wings, as shown in Fig. 2, is a small block of wood about 2 in. square and $\frac{1}{4}$ in. thick with a $\frac{1}{2}$-in. hole in the center. Slip the kite line through the hole before tying it to the kite. Place the trip about 100 ft. from the kite and wedge it to the string with a small piece of wood. The eyelets SS are necessary, as they make it impossible for the pulley to run off the string.

The traveler is first put on the kite string with the end having the loop L (Fig. 3) up, then, after letting out 100 ft. of string, the trip block is fastened in place and the kite tied to the end of the string. Hook the wire loop on the string attached to the ends of the wings in place in the wire catch of L, and it is ready for the flight. When the traveler reaches the trip, the loop L is pushed back, thus causing the end of the wire to slip out of wire loop and the wings to fall back as shown in Fig. 2, when the traveler descends ready to be set for another flight.—Contributed by Stanley C. Funk, Bellefontaine, Ohio.

A Mouse Trap

A simple mouse trap can be made of two lengths of steel wire. The spiral wire is $\frac{1}{16}$ in. in diameter and the center wire is of larger size The trap is set by pulling out the spring and catching the ends on the bends A and B. The bait is tied on at C. When the mouse puts his head through the coils and pulls the bait, the springs are released and his head is caught between the coils.

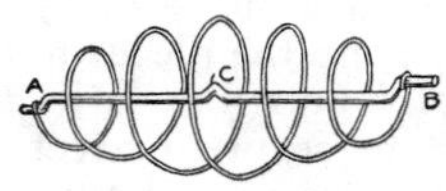

How to Make a Small Electric Furnace

The furnace consists of a large flower pot containing an ordinary clay crucible about 6 in. in height, the space between the two being packed with fireclay. Two ¾-in. holes are bored through the sides of the crucible about half way between the top and the bottom. Holes corresponding to these holes are molded in the fireclay, which should extend several inches above the top of the flower pot. A smaller crucible is placed inside of the large one for use in melting such metals as copper, brass and aluminum. With metals that will melt at a low degree of heat,

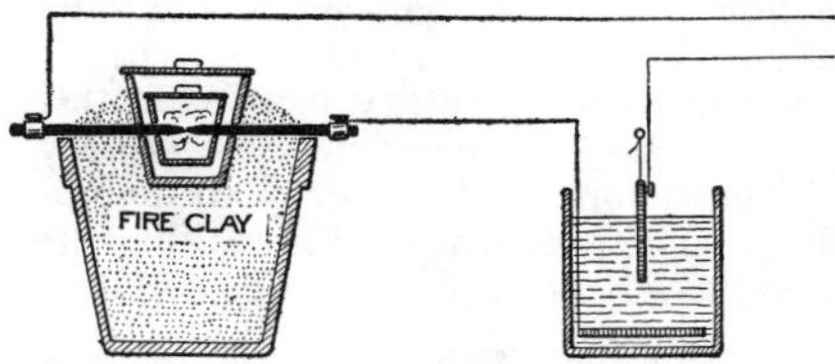

Electric Connections to Furnace

such as tin, lead or zinc, the large crucible can be used alone. Each crucible should be provided with a cover to confine the heat and keep out the air. The electrodes are ordinary arc-light carbons.

The furnace is run on an ordinary 110-volt lighting circuit and it is necessary to have a rheostat connected in series with it. A water rheostat as shown in the sketch will serve to regulate the current for this furnace. Small quantities of brass or aluminum can be melted in about 10 minutes in the furnace.—Contributed by Leonard Stebbins, Denver, Colo.

Repairing a Broken Knife Handle

A piece was broken from the pearl handle of my knife and I repaired it in the following manner: After cleaning both the edges of the pearl and the brass beneath, I run in enough solder to fill the place of the piece of pearl broken out. The solder was then filed, sandpapered and polished. The broken

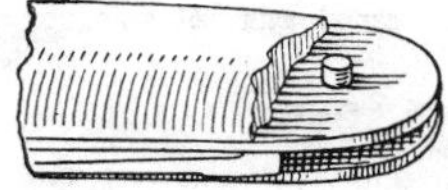

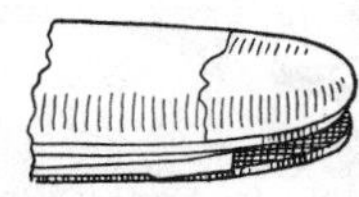

FIG.1 FIG.2

Repairing with Solder

part cannot be felt and it appears to be only an end decoration.—Contributed by W. A. Humphrey, Columbus, O.

Picture-Frame and Triangle Clamp

A picture frame or triangle is quite difficult to hold together when fitting the corners. It is still more difficult to hold them together while the glue dries. The clamp illustrated will be found quite satisfactory in solving this problem, and at the same time is very simple to construct and easy to manipulate. The material list for making the clamps and corner blocks is as follows:

Picture frame clamp:
- 4 pieces, 1¼ by 1¼ by 15 in.
- 2 pieces, 1¼ by 1¼ by 5 in.

Triangle clamp:
- 3 pieces, 1¼ by 1¼ by 10 in.
- 1 piece, 1¼ by 1¼ by 4 in.

Corner blocks:
- 4 pieces, ⅞ by 3½ by 3½ in.
- 8 pieces, ⅞ by 1 by 2 in.

The pieces mentioned are of oak, S-4-S.
- 1 piece ⅜-in. maple for dowels

Hardware:
- 10 bolts, ¼ by 2 in.
- 4 bolts, ¼ by 3 in.
- 2 bolts, ⅜ by 6 in.

The picture-frame clamp consists of the four arms A, B, C and D, Fig. 1. A ¼-in. hole is bored in one end of each piece, ½ in. from the end. A series of ⅜-in. holes, 1 in. apart, are bored along the center in each piece. The two short pieces, E and F, have two ¼-in. holes bored in their centers, ½ in. from each end. These pieces are bolted to the four arms with ¼-in. bolts as shown in the sketch. A ⅜-in. hole is bored in the middle of each piece E and F for one of the 6-in. bolts K.

The four corner blocks G, H, I and J, Fig. 1, have a ⅜-in. hole bored in the center of each and a dowel glued into it with the end projecting 1¼ in. on the under side and level with the surface on the upper side. Each of the corner blocks is fitted with two pieces like X, Fig. 2. Each of these pieces has one end round or a semicircle, and in its center a ¼-in. hole is bored. The other end has a ⅜-in. hole bored ½ in. from the end.

After making the small pieces, take the four corner blocks G, H, I and J and draw a line on the upper side in the center, with the grain of the wood, and mark the angles as follows, so that one-half the angle will be on each side of the centerline: On one end of the pieces G and H mark a 90-deg. angle, on the other end a 45-deg. angle, on the piece I mark a 90-deg. and 30-deg. angle and on J mark a 90-deg. and 60-deg. angle. Mark the number of degrees of each between the sides of the angle. Place two of the pieces marked X, Fig. 2, on each of the corner blocks, one piece on each side between the different angle lines, so their round ends will be toward the center and toward each other with a space of ¼ in. between them. Clamp the pieces to the corner blocks and bore the ¼-in. holes through them to secure perfect alinement. Put the bolts in and turn the pieces first to one angle and then the other, and while in the respective positions, bore the ⅜-in. holes ⅜ in. deep in the corner blocks. Glue a dowel in each ⅜-in. hole of the small

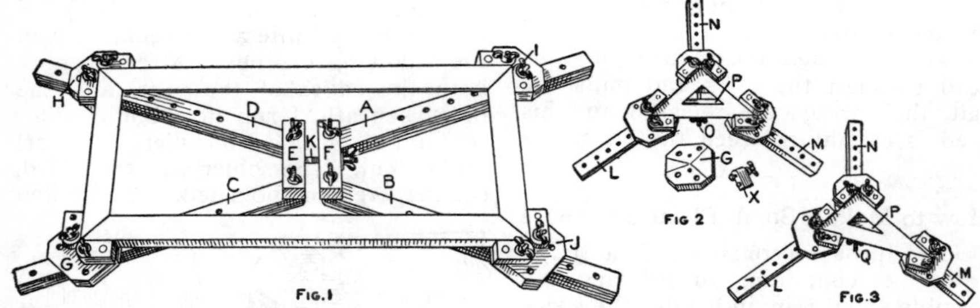

The Corner Blocks on Both Picture Frame and Triangle Clamps are so Constructed That They Hold the Molding together While Fitting the Corners and also Hold Them Securely While the Glue is Hardening

pieces, allowing it to project ¼ in. on the under side so it will fit in the ⅜-in. hole in the corner block. Be sure to countersink the holes for the heads of the bolts. All bolts should be fitted with wing nuts. All that is necessary to change from one angle to another is to loosen the nuts and swing the small pieces around so the dowel pins will drop into the other holes, then tighten the nuts.

The triangle clamp is made in the same manner as the picture-frame clamp, except that the arms L and M, Figs. 2 and 3, are half-lapped into the crosspiece P. The bolt O is ⅜ in. and the head is cut off. Drill a ⅛-in. hole in the bolt, ¼ in. from the end, and bore a ⅜-in. hole in the end of the arm N. Insert the headless bolt O in this hole and drive a nail through the side of the arm N, so it will pass through the hole drilled in the bolt. This keys the bolt in the end of the arm N.

To clamp a picture frame, set the corner blocks G, H, I and J to the 90-deg. angles and adjust them on the arms A, B, C and D to accommodate the size frame to be made, as shown in Fig. 1. Tighten the thumbnut on the bolt K, and this will draw all four corners together with the same pressure. The corners can then be examined to see if they fit properly. If they do not, saw in the joints with a backsaw until they do fit.

The triangles are clamped in the same way. The corner blocks are set to take the proper angles. The ends of the bolts should be slightly burred over so that the thumbnuts cannot be turned off.—Contributed by Chas. A. Pettit, Baltimore, Md.

Exterior Sliding Fly Screen

The method shown for fitting fly screens on the outside of the upper and lower sash permits the screen to be raised and held at different heights. Screweyes are turned into the outer strips, as shown in Fig. 1. The sides of the screen frame are grooved, Fig. 2, to allow it to slide up and down on the screweyes.

The screen can be raised and two of the screweyes turned from the normal vertical position, A, Fig. 3, to a horizontal position, B, to hold the frame at that point. By the use of a greater number of screweyes more places can be provided to support the screen at different heights.—Contributed by James M. Kane, Doylestown, Pa.

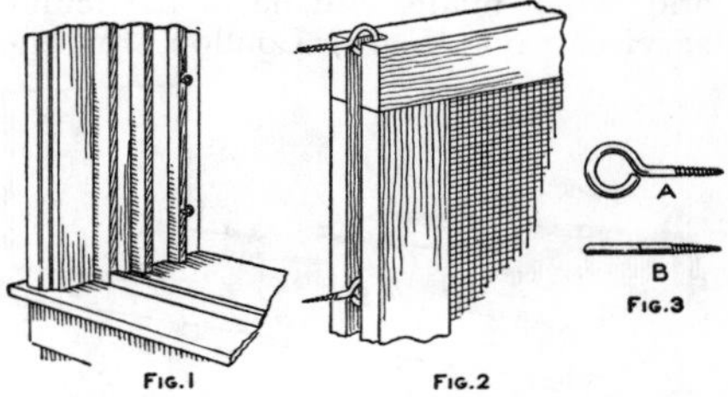

The Heads of the Screweyes in the Window-Frame Stop Slide in a Groove Cut in the Screen Frame

Bushing a Stovepipe in a Chimney Hole

When a stovepipe is too small for the hole in the chimney, a bushing can be made of the kind of metal tobacco boxes that are curved to fit in a pocket. Remove the tops and bottoms of the boxes and shove them in around the pipe. If such tobacco boxes are not at hand, tin cans of any kind can be used by melting off the tops and bottoms and bending the remaining cylindrical shells into proper shape.—Contributed by Elmer McConaughy, Dayton, O.

A Screweye Driver

An ordinary wire nail, 3 in. long, bent as shown and with its head filed square, makes a good tool for turning in screweyes. The square head is readily held in the chuck on most braces. The screweye can be turned in with greater speed than by the ordinary method.—Contributed by Robert T. Johnston, Buffalo, New York.

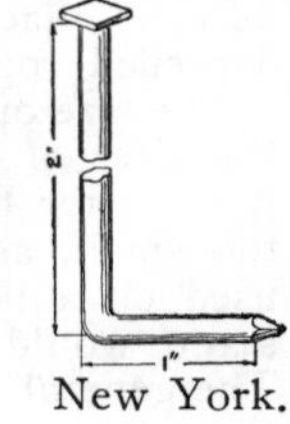

Copying Stand for Photographic Enlarging and Reducing

A camera stand or table, which can be put to many uses, is easily made and, when made, will be of particular service, says Work, London, for en-

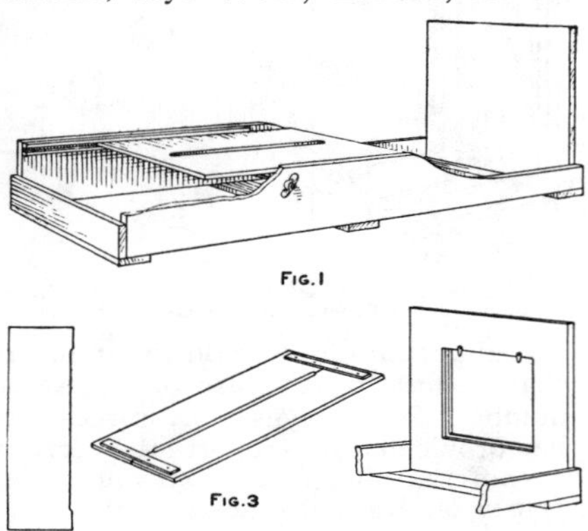

Camera Stand for Use in Copying and Enlarging, as Well as for Making Lantern Slides

larging, reducing, copying, and, with a slight modification, for making lantern slides by reduction.

Copying with a camera on a tripod is always a more or less complicated job, because of the ease with which a picture, being focused, may be thrown out of focus, and even out of the field of view, the camera not being attached to the same support as the picture. With the stand shown in the illustration, the picture is attached to the same support as the camera. This makes it possible to place the apparatus on a table, out in the open, or in any other suitable position, where the light may be best for the work. When used for enlarging with artificial light it will also be found convenient, as it may be placed in any position in a darkened room.

The size of the stand will depend on the sizes of pictures to be made, but it is better to have it too large than too small, as a small camera can be used on a large stand while a small stand would be of only limited use. The general appearance of the stand is shown in Fig. 1. The material list is as follows:

2 Sides, ½ in. by 9½ in. by 5 ft., S-2-S.
4 Crosspieces, ½ in. by 3 in. by 1 ft. 7 in., S-2-S.
4 Guides, ¾ in. by 1¼ in. by 2 ft. 6 in., S-2-S.
2 Bottom Pieces, 1 in. by 9 in. by 2 ft. 6 in., S-2-S.
1 Easel, ¾ in. by 1 ft. 6 in. by 2 ft., S-2-S.
2 Cleats, ½ in. by 1½ in. by 1 ft. 4 in., S-2-S.

Straight-grained soft pine or poplar is the best material to use. The side pieces should be narrowed at one end or to a point about halfway of their length. The extent of this narrowing will depend somewhat on circumstances. The guide pieces are then attached with screws, the two upper pieces so that they have their upper edges flush with the edges of the side boards.

The bottom piece, on which the camera is to be set, is made of the two pieces, cut as shown in Fig. 2, and joined with cleats, as in Fig. 3. The space left after part of one side of each board has been cut away, should be sufficient to make a slot which, when the boards are joined together, will admit the screw to hold the camera in place. A rod is run through holes bored in the sides, just below the two pairs of guides, and fitted with a wing nut for clamping the sliding bottom when a focus and the size of the picture is found.

In copying, the camera is attached to the bottom board and the picture is tacked to the easel. The camera is then focused roughly by means of the rack and pinion, the final, fine focusing being done by moving the sliding bottom board. For enlarging, the lantern is placed on the sliding bottom and the bromide paper tacked to the easel.

For lantern-slide work, which is reducing, it is necessary to cut an aperture in the easel, after the manner shown in Fig. 4. The edges of the opening have a rabbet to receive first a ground glass and then the negative, both being held in place with turn buttons. It is not necessary to have two easels, as this opening can be fitted with a piece to make a level surface when the apparatus is used for copying or enlarging.

To Make Whitewash Stick to Surfaces Coated

In using whitewash much difficulty is experienced in making it stick to the substance covered. A good way to prevent the coating from cracking and peeling off is to add 2 oz. of pure sodium chloride to every 1 gal. of whitewash mixture. This is not expensive, but should be secured at a drug store because some salts of sodium are not pure and will darken the whitewash. The sodium chloride should be added after the whitewash solution is made up. When this mixture is used in buildings it will destroy all vermin which it touches.

A Mechanical Camera

The young person who likes to draw will find the device illustrated of great assistance for outlining a portrait or a bit of scenery which can be filled in to make the picture. The camera consists of a box without a cover, about 12 in. long, 6 in. wide and 4 in. deep. An oblong hole is cut in one end, a small hole bored in the other, and a piece cut out of the lower edge so that one eye can be placed close to the hole. The oblong hole, shown by the dotted lines, is covered with a fine perforated cardboard, the kind used for working in mottoes with yarn. Supports are nailed in the corners of the box, their length being calculated to allow the operator to sit or stand, as desired.

The camera is used in the manner illustrated. If a portrait is to be drawn, then the one sitting for it must be quiet until the outlines are completed. The operator, looking through the hole, traces the lines on the cardboard between the perforations. When the outlines are drawn in this manner, the cardboard is removed and placed on the paper or cardboard used for the picture. The outline is then transferred by marking with a sharp-pointed

Outlining a Portrait on the Perforated Paper Placed over the Oblong Hole in the Camera

pencil through the perforations on the outlines as drawn. After separating the two pieces, the markings can be connected with a continuous line and an exact outline will be obtained which can be filled in as desired. The outline picture is a sample of work done with the camera.—Contributed by Florence Thomas, Gordon, Ont.

Gauge Attachment for a Pocket Rule

The base of the gauge A is cut from a block of hard wood, about 2½ in. long, 1 in. wide and ⅜ in. thick. A notch is cut in one side to admit the rule and the wedge B, which has a slot that slides on a pin in the base. A small metal clip keeps the wedge in place. The gauge can be readily set on the rule at any mark.

Plate Hangers

In hanging old china plates for decorative purposes use three large white dress hooks, placed at equal distances apart on the edge of the plate. The hanging wire or cord is run through them from the back side and drawn up tightly. These hooks are much better than the ordinary plate hanger, as they are small and will not show much on the plate.

An Electrically Operated Camera Shutter

It is often quite desirable to operate the shutter of a camera from a distance, especially in photographing birds and

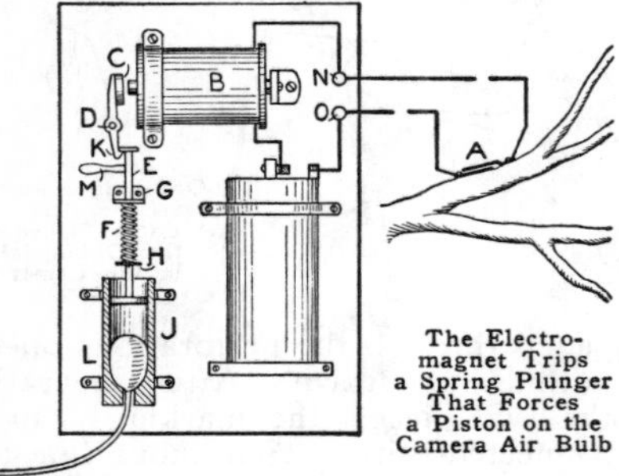

The Electromagnet Trips a Spring Plunger That Forces a Piston on the Camera Air Bulb

animals. The device shown in the accompanying sketch serves the above purpose very nicely, and its construction and operation are exceedingly simple. In brief, the operation is as follows: The switch A is mounted on the limb of a tree, in such a manner that it is not conspicuous, and connected in series with a magnet, B, and a battery by means of a piece of flexible conductor, such as lamp cord. The magnet B is energized when the switch is closed and attracts the iron armature C, which is mounted on an arm, pivoted at D. The lower end of this arm is in the form of a latch, which supports the rod E when it is raised to its upper position. The rod E when it is raised compresses the coiled spring F, which is held between the gauge G and the washer H mounted on the rod. A small coil spring holds the armature C away from the core of the magnet B. The lower end of the rod E is in the form of a piston operating in a wooden cylinder J. The rubber bulb at the end of the tube leading to the camera shutter is located in the lower end of the cylinder J. When the rod E is released by the latch K, it moves downward in the cylinder J, due to the action of the spring F, and compresses the bulb L, causing the shutter of the camera to be operated. A small handle, M, may be mounted on the rod to be used in raising it to the upper position. The component parts of this device may be mounted on a small wooden base by means of brass straps, and the terminals of the electric circuit connected to the binding posts N and O, as shown. The switch A may be dispensed with and a push button used in its place, as the operator may station himself several hundred feet away. It may be necessary to use a battery of more than one cell in such cases.

Electroplating without a Tank

Electroplating without a plating tank is made possible with the following easily homemade apparatus described in a German scientific magazine. It consists of a rubber ball, A, fitted at one end with a glass tube, B, which carries at the opposite end a small sponge. A rod, D, passes through the rubber ball, which is tightly corked at both ends, into the glass tube B and carries at that end the anode E. A small glass tube, F, also connects the rubber ball with the larger tube B. The connections from the battery to the cathode, G, the object to be plated, and to the projecting end of the anode-carrying rod, D, are made as shown. The rubber ball is filled with the electrolyte, and is squeezed so as to force the fluid

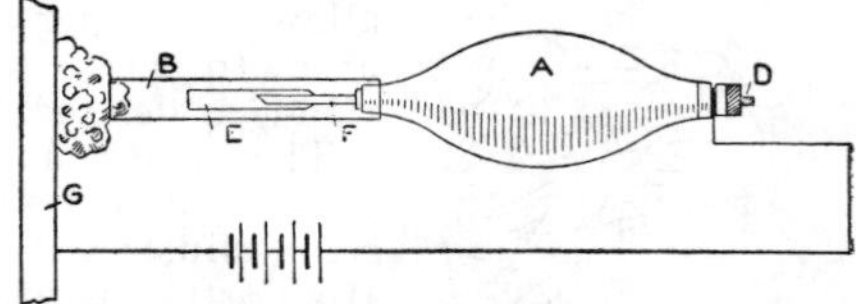

A Hand Tool for Applying a Plate Electrically to the Surface of Metal

through the small tube F, into the larger tube, B, filling it and soaking the sponge C. The current is then turned on, and by moving the wet sponge over the cathode G, the latter will be plated. Not only is this an interesting accessory for the amateur's laboratory, but it can be used in the industry where only parts of some object are to be plated, and where it is desired to remedy bad spots without putting the articles back into the bath.

A Milk-Bottle Tray

Bottled milk is difficult to deliver without knocking the bottles together when carrying them or while in a wagon. There are several kinds of wire baskets for carrying the bottles, but they all have the disadvantage of allowing the bottles to strike one another. A carrier not having this fault can be made very cheaply as follows: Procure a board 1 in. thick, 8 in. wide and 2 ft. long, plane and make it smooth, and use ordinary tin fruit or

Parts of Tin Cans Fastened to a Board for Holding Milk Bottles

vegetable cans for the bottle holders. Cut each can off 2½ in. from the bottom and smooth off the jagged edges with a file. Nail these in two rows on the board, starting 1 in. from each end. Attach a segment of a barrel hoop for a handle. The carrier can be painted as desired.—Contributed by G. H. Clemmons, Storm Lake, Iowa.

A Springboard

Select straight-grained hickory or ash for the springboards. These can be of any width to make up the board to 18 in. wide. The frame part may be of any material of the dimensions given in the sketch. The butt ends of the springboard should be well fastened to the crosspiece with screws, or, better still, small carriage bolts with the nuts on the under side.

The crosspiece at the rear is cut on the angle of the springboard. The front crosspiece is mortised into the frame, and the one near the center is laid on top of the two side rails.

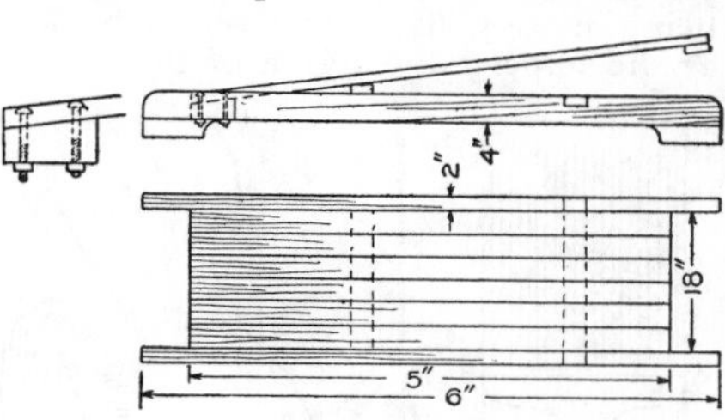

A Springboard for Use in Connection with a Vaulting Pole or for Turning Acts

The rear crosspiece is either fastened with large dowels or mortised into the sidepieces. This springboard will be of use in connection with a back-yard gymnasium for vaulting and doing turning acts.

Planing Rough-Grain Boards

The surface of a board having a grain that runs both ways is very hard to smooth with a plane. By sharpening the plane iron to a keen edge, then placing it in the plane with the cap reversed and set about $\frac{1}{32}$ in. from the cutting edge, I find that with a light cut the plane will smooth regardless of the direction of the grain.—Contributed by William Rollins, Wichita, Kansas.

Braces for Aeroplane Frames

In making model aeroplanes or gliders the brace shown will serve the purpose admirably. The size and strength of the metal used will depend on where it is to be used. The metal is bent

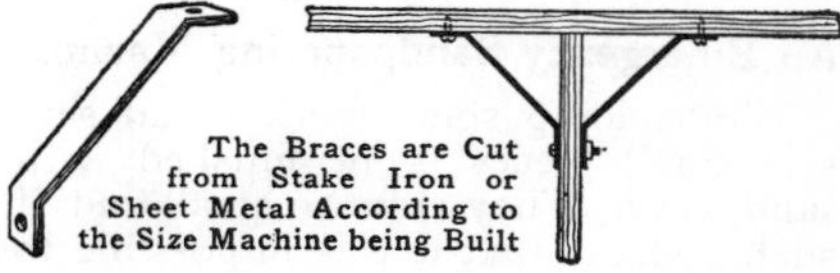

The Braces are Cut from Stake Iron or Sheet Metal According to the Size Machine being Built

into the shape shown with the use of a vise. The manner of attaching the braces is clearly shown.—Contributed by Francis Chetlain, Chicago.

A Puzzle Purse

The puzzle purse is made of four pieces of chamois, two of the pieces being merely flaps, one on each side at the upper edge. One of the pieces

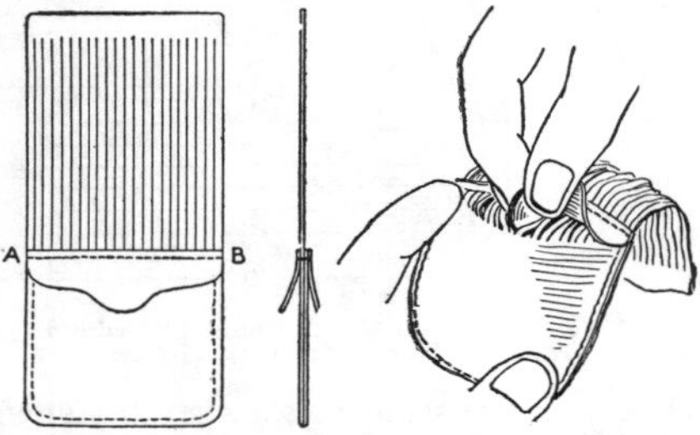

The Strips of Leather Sliding through the Stitches Make the Puzzle Part of the Purse

forming one side of the purse extends upward for about twice the height of the purse part. The part above the purse has a number of slits cut in it to make the width of each strip 1/8 in. These slits should be accurately cut in order that the purse may be opened easily. The other half is only the size of the purse proper. The upper edge of the latter piece and the flap on that side are stitched together to the flap on the opposite side, the threads of the stitches running between the strips of the long piece. These stitches are made on the line AB and around the edge.

To open the purse, take hold of each side on the purse part and draw the pieces apart. In doing so, the strips are drawn through the stitches so that they may be separated and a coin taken from the purse. A pull on each end will close the purse.—Contributed by Chas. Motton, Toronto, Ont.

An Emergency Sandpapering Machine

While doing some work I had several small pieces to be finished with sandpaper. They were so small and of such a shape that it was impossible to do the work by hand. Not having a sanding machine, I used a disk talking machine for the purpose. I placed a sheet of sandpaper over the disk and fastened it to the felt at the corners with pins. The machine was then set going at its highest rate of speed, and the articles were smoothed by holding them on the disk.—Contributed by Fred S. Barnard, Los Angeles, Cal.

A Developing Machine

The base of the developing machine consists of a wood tray with sloping ends and high sides, which is placed at the center and provides bearings for the wheel axle. The dimensions given in the sketch are for making a machine to develop a film about 29 in. long. The disk, or wheel, is cut from a board, 7/8 in. thick, and the attached crosspieces are cut from 1/4-in. dowels to make them 2 1/2 in. long. These are placed about 1 in. apart on the circumference of the disk.

An axle, fastened solidly in the wheel and adjusted in the bearings, is kept from slipping sideways by bushings made of a spool. A crank is attached to one end of the axle. Hot paraffin is applied to the inside of the tank part, to make it liquid-tight. Two pins or hooks are attached to one of the crosspieces to catch into the film end. If the wheel is the correct size, the same pins can be used for fastening the other end of the film.

The film is first attached to the

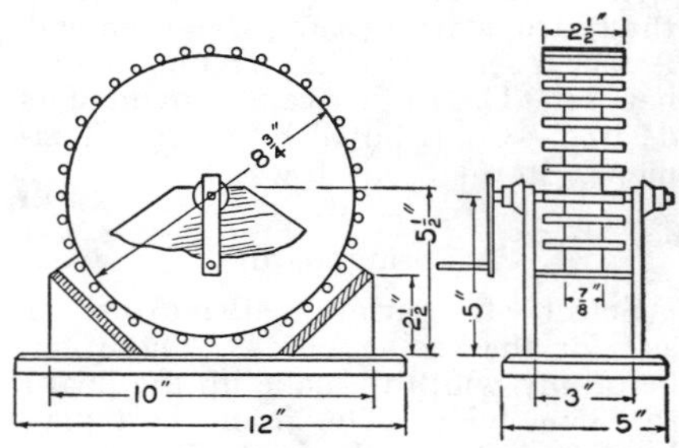

The Entire Length of Film is Placed on the Wheel Where It is Run through the Developer

wheel; then, while turning slowly, the developer is poured into the tray. Keep on turning the wheel until full development is obtained, then pour out the liquid and turn in fresh, clear water, and turn the wheel to wash out the developer. Remove the film and place it in the hypo bath.—Contributed by Raymond M. Bealer, Baltimore, Md.

A Stove-Wood Carrier

A handy wood carrier, for bringing wood and kindling from the basement or yard to the wood box in the house, may be made from a grain sack, as shown in the sketch. Use a complete sack and make rope handles at each end. When used, place only sufficient wood or kindling in it to permit the handles to come together over the top of the load. This will make a comfortable grip and it is no harder to carry than a medium-weight suitcase. When the wood is removed the carrier can be taken to the back yard and

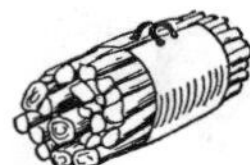

The Ropes at the Ends of the Sack Make a Handle to Carry It Like a Grip

shaken out, thus doing away with the dirt that usually results from other methods of filling wood boxes.—Contributed by Walter Nelson Kidston, Seattle, Wash.

A Pencil Sharpener

A pencil sharpened with the device shown will have a better point and one that will not break easily while being sharpened. The lower arm A is made from a strip of sheet steel, $\frac{1}{16}$ in. thick. An extension, 1/4 in. wide, is cut and bent in a circle to form the lower finger hold. The upper arm B forms the cutter, which is made from a piece of hacksaw blade. The teeth are ground off and the temper is drawn from the extension that forms the upper circle. A portion of the arm A is bent over, as shown at C, to form a support for the pencil point to rest upon. A hole, large enough for a pencil to turn in, is bored through a stick of hardwood, D, and tapered so that the center of the hole meets the inner edge of C. It is fastened to the lower arm with screws. A sharp cutting edge is ground

A Pencil Sharpener That will Make a Point without Breaking the Lead

on the blade which is then attached to the arm A with a rivet loosely enough to swing freely.—Contributed by J. V. Loeffler, Evansville, Ind.

Cleaning an Oilstone

Use kerosene oil and a sprinkling of emery flour and proceed to sharpen tools. It is not necessary to clean a stone thus treated before placing the tool on it, as the emery and kerosene will make a good surface on the stone as well as assisting in producing a sharp edge on the tool.—Contributed by James M. Kane, Doylestown, Pa.

Landing for Small Boats

Not having a landing for my small boat, I made a series of sectional platforms, rising 2 ft. above the bottom, which served the purpose well and were inexpensive. Each section is about 15 ft. long, 3 ft. wide, and 2 ft. high. The frame is made of material 2 in. thick and 4 in. wide, and on top is a floor made of boards, while the bottom consists of 2 by 4-in. crosspieces, nailed on 6 in. apart. Stones are laid on these crosspieces to moor it down in place. The whole landing is simple to make and it lasts a long

The Series of Platforms Make a Good Small-Boat Landing on a Slanting Beach

time, as the sections can be drawn out and stored during the winter.—Contributed by Henry Briggs, Lexington, Massachusetts.

Bearings for Model Work

For experimental work I use hangers or bearings made of sheet brass or copper, bent at right angles for strength

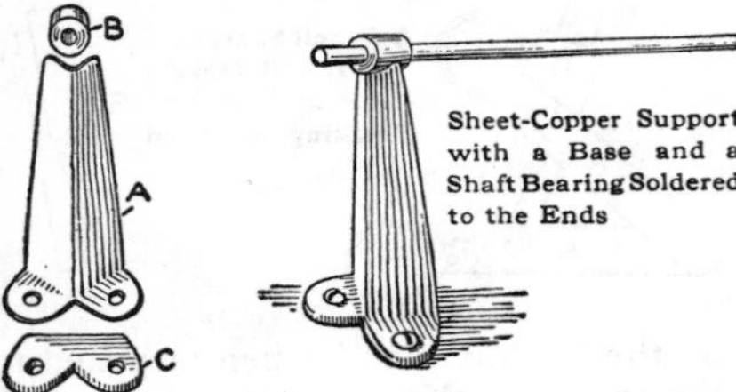

Sheet-Copper Support with a Base and a Shaft Bearing Soldered to the Ends

and capped with a box. The main part of the bearing A is shaped as shown, and the box B consists of a small piece cut from a brass rod and drilled for the size of the shaft. The box is soldered to the top end of A and the base C to the bottom end. When a large metal base is used for a certain model, the part A is attached directly to that base and the part C need not be used.

The bearings can be made in different heights, each of which will demand a corresponding size and thickness of the parts. Sheet brass or copper, $\frac{1}{32}$ in. thick, is about right for a bearing 3 in. high.—Contributed by W. E. Day, Pittsfield, Mass.

Holding the Tongue of a Shoe in Place

The tongue in a shoe will often slip down or over to one side or the other and expose the hose. To overcome

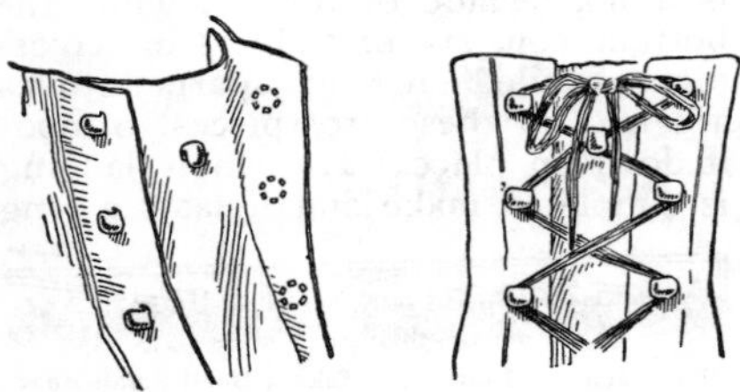

The Hook on the Tongue of the Shoe and Manner of Lacing to Hold the Tongue

this and have the tongue fit snugly in the right place, fasten a common lace clasp or hook near the top of the tongue, as shown in the illustration, so that in lacing the shoe the laces are passed under the hook to hold the tongue in place.

A Photo Vignetter

Procure a piece of heavy wire, one that is fairly stiff, says Camera Craft, and a pair of pliers and bend the wire with the pliers as shown in the illustration. After the loop is made to fit around the lens barrel the wire is bent at right angles at a point 6 in. below the circle. At a distance of 8 in. on the extending part of the wire it is bent as shown to form a clip for holding a sheet of cardboard.

The cardboard should be about 7 in. wide and of dark color, with one edge cut semicircular and notched. The

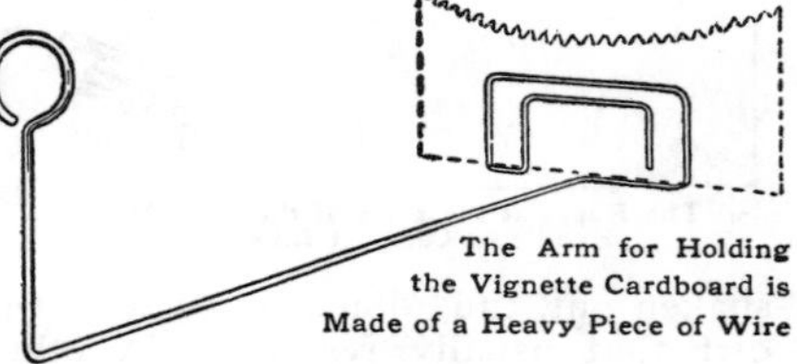

The Arm for Holding the Vignette Cardboard is Made of a Heavy Piece of Wire

size of the wire and the other measurements will depend upon the size and focal length of the lens. If a heavy vignetting card is required, it may be necessary to make the portion that encircles the lens double in length, bending it back upon itself to secure a firmer hold. This is a cheap and efficient vignetter that anyone can make in a few moments of spare time.

Pocket for the Inside of a Book Cover

Students or anyone wishing to retain notes on a subject will find it quite handy to have a large envelope pasted in the back of each textbook. Instead of having notes all through the book, they can be arranged in order and slipped into the envelope. If the book is accidentally dropped, the notes will not be lost.—Contributed by Harold Mynning, Chicago, Ill.

Cleaning Steel of Grease and Stains

Grease and stains can be easily removed from steel with a mixture of unslaked lime and chalk powder, by rubbing it on the steel with a dry cloth. The best proportion for the mixture, which is easily prepared, is 1 part of lime to 1 part of chalk powder. The powder should be used dry. It is kept in cans for future use and can be used over and over again.—Contributed by Loren Ward, Des Moines, Iowa.

An Electrically Ignited Flash Light for Making Photographs

The results obtained in a great many cases in trying to take pictures by flashlight are exceedingly unsatisfactory, as the expression on the faces of the people in the picture usually is strained or unnatural, due to the suspense in waiting for the flash. The following simple device avoids this difficulty because the flash is set off by means of electricity, so that the operator can control the flash from a distant point and thus be able to take the picture quite unawares to his subjects.

The construction of the device is as follows: Obtain a piece of rather heavy sheet iron, about 6 in. wide and 10 in. long. Bend this piece of iron into the form shown in the sketch, and fasten a wooden handle to it with a wood screw. Obtain a sheet of 1/8-in. sheet asbestos, the same size as the piece of sheet iron, and glue it to the inside surface of the curved piece of iron. It is best to fasten the four corners down by means of some small rivets with rather large washers under the heads next to the asbestos.

Now mount two pieces of sheet copper, 1/2 in. wide and 6 in. long, parallel with each other on the surface of the asbestos and 1 1/2 in. apart, so that their ends are even with the end of the piece of asbestos. These pieces of copper should be insulated from the piece of sheet iron, and there should be a small screw in one end of each and a small binding post mounted on the other end.

Procure a piece of lamp cord, 15 or 20 ft. in length. Fasten an ordinary plug to one end of this cord and the other end to the two binding posts.

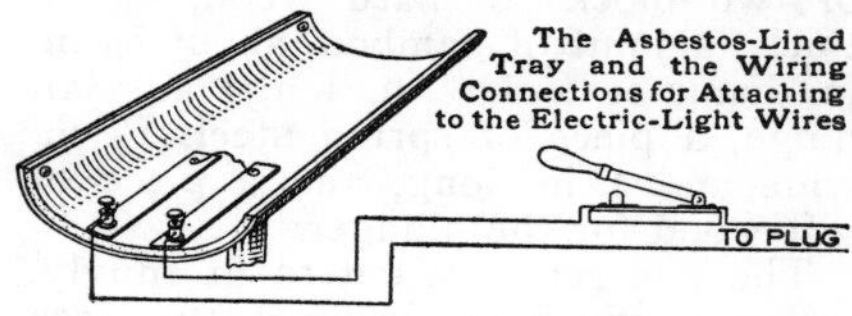

The Asbestos-Lined Tray and the Wiring Connections for Attaching to the Electric-Light Wires

Open one of the conductors in the cord at some point and introduce a single-pole switch, as shown in the sketch. Close the gap between the two pieces of copper by means of a piece of No. 32 gauge copper wire. Place the flash-light powder in position, but do not cover up the wire or have it in actual contact with the powder, and close the circuit. The operator may include himself in the picture by having a sufficiently long piece of lamp cord and the switch properly arranged.

A Simple Twine-Ball Holder

In looking for a place to put a twine ball I happened to see a tin funnel and it gave me the idea which I put into practice. I punched three holes at equal distances apart in its upper edge and attached three strings which were run to an apex and tied to a screw-eye in the ceiling. The end of the twine from the center of the ball was run through the funnel stem and allowed to hang as in an ordinary ball holder.—Contributed by W. C. Loy, Rochester, Ind.

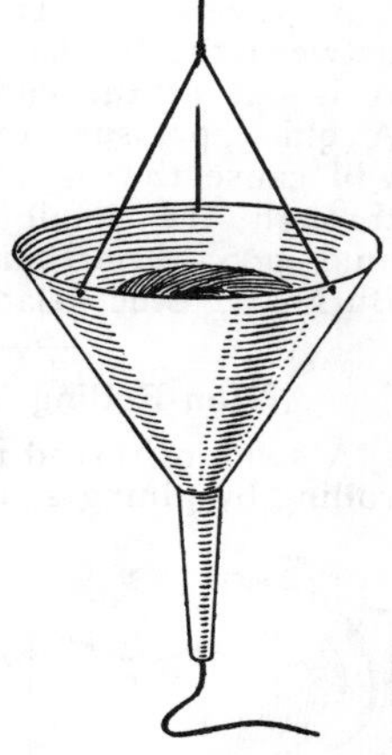

¶A filler for birch, red gum and beech can be made of 1 lb. of bleached shellac to each gallon of water.

A Toy Popgun

A toy popgun can be easily made of two blocks of hard wood, ½ in. thick; a joint of bamboo, about ⅞ in. in diameter and 6 in. long; a small hinge, a piece of spring steel, ½ in. wide and 1 in. long, and a piece of soft wood for the plunger.

The plunger A is cut to fit snugly, yet so it will move easily in the piece of bamboo B. One of the blocks of hard wood, C, is bored to fit one end of the bamboo, the other block has a ¼-in. hole bored, to center the hole in the first block. The two blocks are hinged and the spring latch attached as shown in the sketch. The spring has a hole drilled so it can be fastened with a screw to the outer block, and

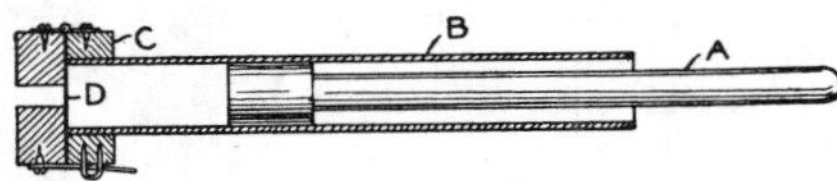

Detail of Popgun, Showing the Parts Assembled and Position of the Paper

a slot cut in the other end to slip over a staple driven into the block C.

A piece of paper, D, is placed in between the blocks while the plunger A is out at the end of the bamboo. A quick pressure on the plunger A will cause the paper D to break out through the small opening with a loud pop.—Contributed by Paul H. Burkhart, Blue Island, Ill.

A Non-Rolling Thread Spool

A spool of thread may be kept from rolling by gluing squares of cardboard to the ends. The squares should be a little larger than the spool. This will save many a step and much bending over to pick up the spool. The spool, when it falls, will stop where it landed.—Contributed by Katharine D. Morse, Syracuse, N. Y.

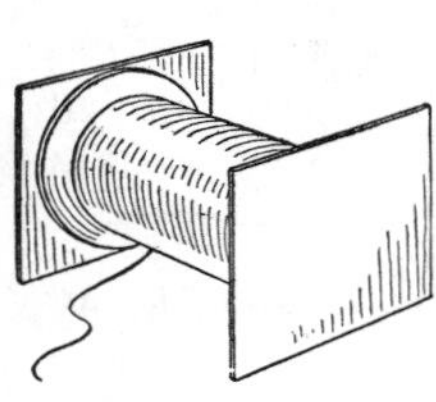

Shoe-Shining Stand

To anyone who finds it tiresome to shine his shoes while putting the foot on the rim of a bathtub, on a cook-

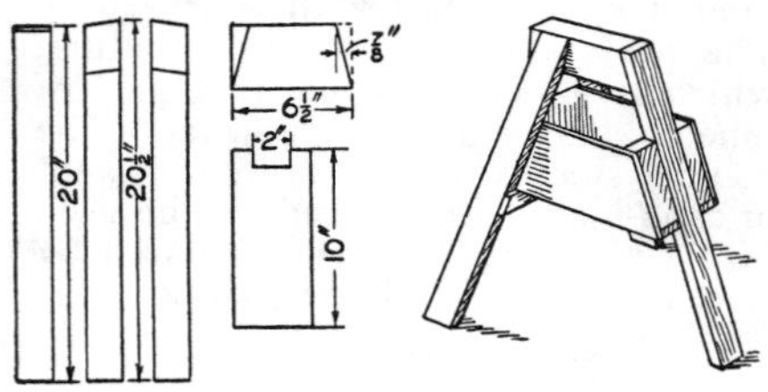

Dimensioned Parts and Completed Stand Which has a Box to Hold the Shining Outfit

stove or chair with a newspaper on it, the stand here described will afford relief and at the same time he will always have the shining outfit ready for use.

The whole is of pine, the foot rest being made of a piece 2 by 4 in.; the legs, of 1 by 2 in., and the bottom of the box, of ½ by 4¼ in. All other dimensions are given in the sketch. After the legs are attached and the bottom of the box in place, the sides are fitted and fastened with nails.—Contributed by Samuel Hughs, Berkeley, Cal.

Cutter Made of a Wafer Razor Blade

A useful instrument for seamstresses and makers of paper patterns and stencils can be made of a piece of steel

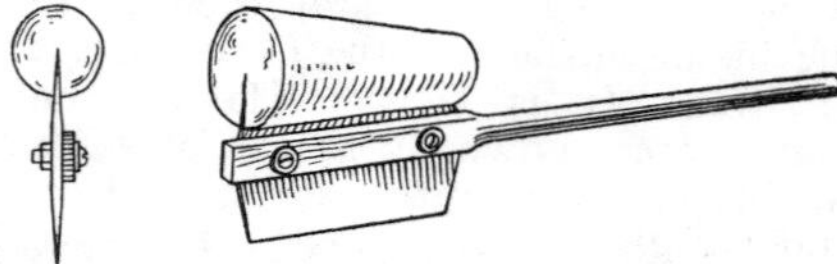

The Wafer Blade Attached to the Handle, the Top Edge being Protected with a Cork

or iron and a wafer razor blade. The end of the metal is flattened and two holes drilled to match the holes of the razor blade. Small screw bolts are used to attach the blade to the handle. Place a cork on one edge as a protection for the hand of the user.—Contributed by Maurice Baudier, New Orleans, La.

To Hold a Negative in a Printing Frame

When printing postal cards and working fast, it always bothered me to hold the negative in the printing frame while removing the card. To overcome this trouble I decided to contrive some arrangement to hold the negative in the frame when the back was removed. The device I made consists of a thin, flat spring, about 1/8 in. wide and as long as the width of the frame opening. Two lugs are formed and soldered to the ends, as shown in Fig. 1, for holding the plate, and a central lug is soldered on to provide a means of fastening the spring in position. A groove, about 1/16 in. deep, was cut in the opposite end of the frame to receive one end of the negative.

In use, slide the plate into the frame and into the lugs on the spring, and push the spring upward until the plate can be slipped into the slot at the opposite end of the frame. The pressure of the spring, as shown in Fig. 2, will hold the plate securely. The frame can be handled quite roughly and as fast as desired without any danger of the plate falling out.—Contributed by Thos. L. Parker, Wibaux, Montana.

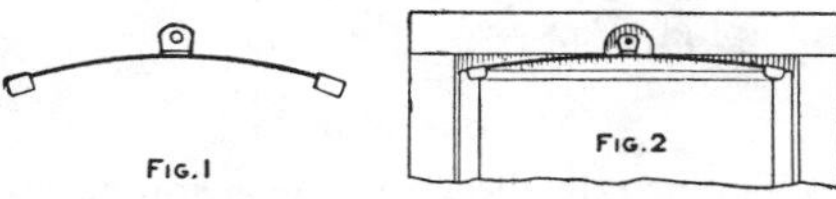

The Spring with Its Clips and Manner of Holding a Negative in a Printing Frame

---

A number of bright tin disks tied to the limbs of a fruit tree will prove an efficient means of driving away infesting birds.

How to Make an Electrolytic Interrupter

Obtain a glass jar or wide-mouth bottle about one-quart size. An ordinary round bottle will serve very nicely by having the top cut off, thus forming a glass jar. Make a top for the jar from a piece of 1/2-in. pine similar to the one shown in the illustration. The lower portion extends down inside the jar and serves to hold the top in place. Cut a slot in this top, 1/8 in. wide and 2 in. long. This slot should be cut at right angles to a diameter of the top and extend 1 in. on either side of the diameter. It should be about 1/2 in. from the center of the top. Directly opposite the center of the slot drill a 3/8-in hole, 1/2 in. from the center of the top. Drill a 1/4-in. hole in the center of the top to give ventilation to the jar. Boil the completed top in paraffin for a few minutes.

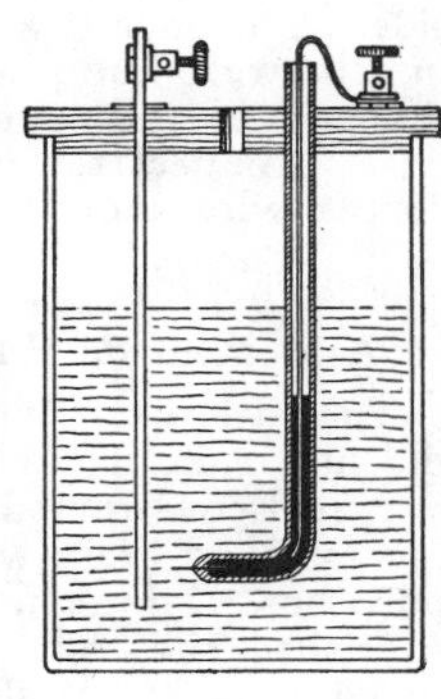

Obtain a piece of 1/8-in. sheet lead, 2 in. wide and about 1/2 in. longer than the depth of the jar. Mount a small binding post on one end of this piece of lead and then support it in the slot in the wooden top by means of two metal pins. The lower end of the piece of lead should be at least 1/2 in. from the bottom of the jar. Next get a piece of 3/8-in. glass tube and fuse a piece of platinum wire into one end.

Make sure the inside end of the platinum wire is not covered with the glass, and that the outside end protrudes a short distance beyond the end of the glass tube. Now bend about ¾ in. of the end of the glass tube which has the platinum in it over at right angles to the remainder of the tube. The tube should then be placed in the opening on the wooden top provided for it and a rubber band placed around it to prevent it dropping through the opening. The lower end of the tube should be a little higher than the lower end of the sheet of lead. A small quantity of mercury should be placed in the tube and a bare copper wire run down inside. The mercury affords a connection between the piece of platinum in the end of the tube and the copper wire. Connect the outside end of the copper wire under a binding post and the interrupter is complete with the exception of the solution.

The solution for the interrupter is dilute sulphuric acid made by mixing about four parts of water and one part of acid. In preparing this mixture, be sure to pour the acid into the water, not the water into the acid. The jar should be about two-thirds filled. At least 40 volts will be required for the satisfactory operation of the interrupter. The distance between the platinum point and the lead sheet may be adjusted by simply turning the glass tube.

No condenser will be required in operating an inductor coil with an interrupter of this kind. The make-and-break interrupter, if there is one in circuit, should of course be made inoperative by screwing up the contact point against the spring.

A Homemade Hand Drill Press

The little use I had for a drill press did not make it advisable to purchase one, so I constructed a device for drilling iron and brass which answered all purposes. A broken carpenter's brace furnished the chuck, which was fastened to a ½-in. shaft having a detachable crank. The shaft turns in a

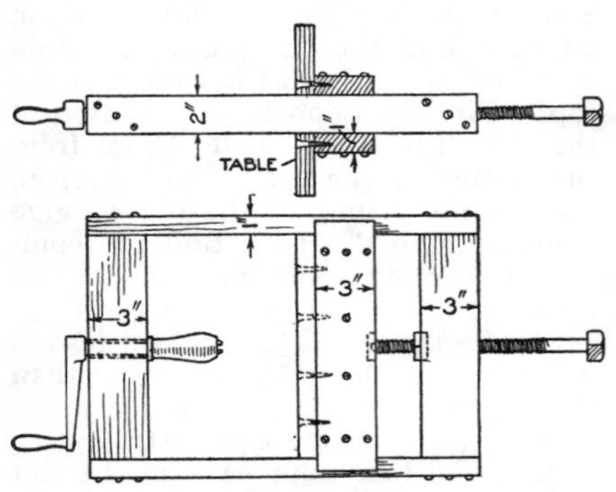

A Very Inexpensive Drill Press Frame Which Answers the Purpose Admirably

brass tube which is fitted tightly in a hole bored in the upright. The sliding part or table is forced up against the drill with a ½-in. machine bolt. The bolt turns in a square nut fastened in the opposite post. The end of the screw bears on a plate fastened on the under side of the table to prevent wear. A crank could be attached to this bolt so that it may be turned more easily.

The sliding or table part is made of a post similar to the end posts, but with guides attached so as to keep it in place. The holes for the chuck shaft and bolt should be bored on a line and exactly in the center of the posts.—Contributed by L. R. Kelley, Philadelphia, Pa.

A Hose Nozzle

The nozzle shown in the accompanying sketch was made from an empty tobacco can having an oval shape. I cut the can in two near the center and punched small holes in the bottom. I then cut a piece of ½-in. board to fit tightly in the end of the can and turned the edges of the tin down to hold it in place. A hole was bored in the center of the wood and a ½-in. hose coupling fitted in it. The water will swell the wood enough to make an absolutely watertight joint, but by using a little care in fitting it, the joint will be watertight without the swelling.

The holes being punched in straight lines, the nozzle throws a rectangular section of fine streams, which makes it possible to sprinkle close up to walks without wetting them. The friction is much less than in the ordinary hose nozzle, and consequently this nozzle delivers more water and also materially

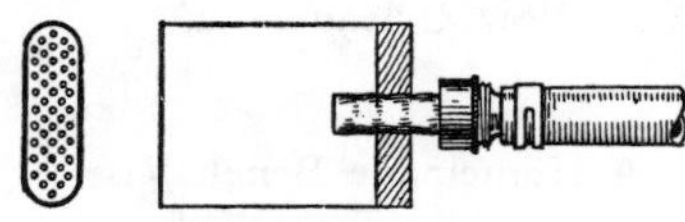

The Oval Form of the Box Makes It Possible to Sprinkle Close Up to Walks

reduces the strain on the hose.—Contributed by J. B. Downer, Seattle, Washington.

An Electric Water Heater

A simple electric water heater may be made as follows: Procure two sheets of copper, each 4 by 6 in., and place pieces of wood or other insulating material at the corners to keep them about $\frac{3}{4}$ in. apart. Bind them with cords, or, if the wood pieces are large enough, use screws so that there will be no contact between the plates. Attach wires to the plates with solder as shown, and make connections to a plug. Pour water in an earthenware

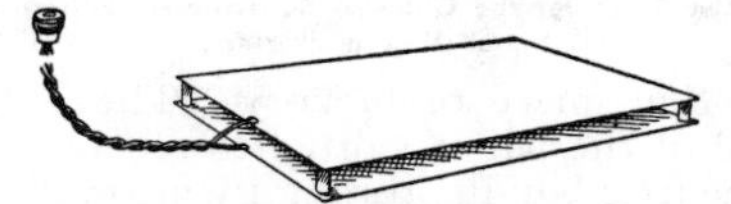

An Inexpensive Electric Water Heater Made of Two Copper Plates

jar, place the plates in it and turn the plug in a lamp socket. Do not use a metal vessel.—Contributed by G. Henry Jones, Sylacauga, Ala.

Frosting Glass

Procure a piece of flat iron similar to an iron hoop, bend it, as shown in the sketch, to make a piece 3 in. long and $1\frac{1}{4}$ in. wide and file one edge smooth. Sprinkle some fine lake sand over the glass, dampen the sand and rub the smooth edge of the iron band over the glass. It requires only a short time of

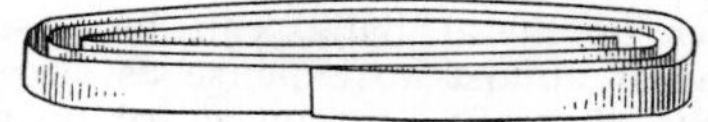

The Filed Edge on the Coiled Metal Retains the Sand Particles as It is Rubbed over the Glass Surface

rubbing to produce a beautiful frosted surface on the glass.—Contributed by M. E. Duggan, Kenosha, Wis.

Long Handle for a Dustpan

The dustpan is a rather unhandy utensil to use, especially for stout persons. One porter overcame this difficulty by attaching a long handle to the pan as shown in the illustration. The handle was taken from a discarded broom and a yoke of heavy wire was attached to it, the ends being bent to enter holes punched in the upturned edge of the pan. A stout cord, fastened to the handle and tied into the ring of the dustpan handle, keeps the pan from turning backward, and it is thus possible to push it or carry it with the long handle.

To Fasten Chair Legs

Chair legs often become loose when chairs are handled roughly, so that the glue is broken up. A small device made from a piece of pointed metal, A, which is securely fastened to the end of the chair leg by means of a screw, will hold the legs more firmly than wire or glue. When the

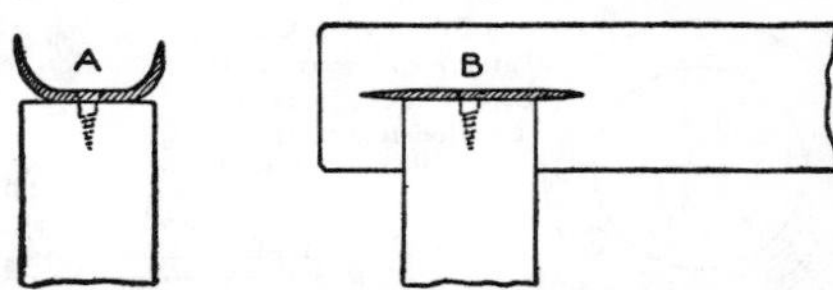

The Metal on the End of the Leg Fastens It Solidly in Place

leg is driven into the hole, the points are pushed into the wood B as the metal flattens.

Disk-Throwing Pistol

A pistol for throwing small disks of paper or metal balls, can be easily made at almost no expense as shown in the sketch. Two pieces of board,

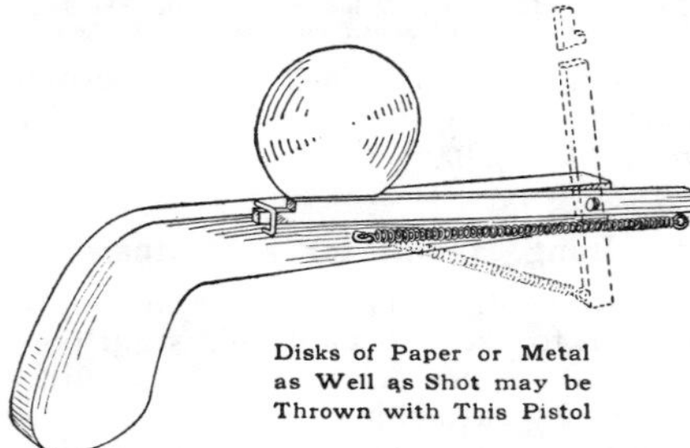

Disks of Paper or Metal as Well as Shot may be Thrown with This Pistol

one of which is shaped to the form of a pistol, are hinged together and a fairly strong spiral spring is fastened at the front end of the movable piece and the middle of the other. A slot is sawed in the movable piece to hold the disk, or a small round depression may be formed in it to receive a bean, pea, or shot. The movable arm is folded back and held in position by means of a stirrup of wire fastened on the other part. When the movable part is disengaged by pulling the stirrup away with the finger, the disk will be thrown with considerable force, depending on the strength of the spring.

Displaying Dye Colors

A certain druggist utilized old electric bulbs for displaying dye colors. Water was colored with a dye and the end of a bulb dipped into the liquid. Then the tip end was broken off, and

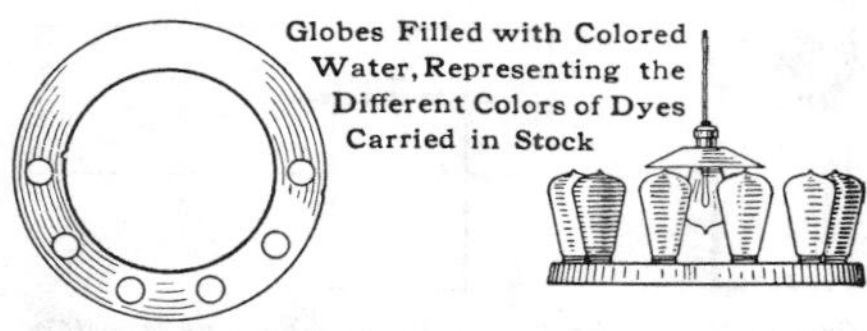

Globes Filled with Colored Water, Representing the Different Colors of Dyes Carried in Stock

the bulb being a vacuum, the colored water was drawn into it, and filled the globe. The point was then sealed with paraffin.

A ring-shaped piece, 15 in. in diameter and 2½ in. wide, was cut from a piece of board, and 1-in. holes bored, 2½ in. apart, in one-half of the ring. The globes holding the colored water were set in these holes and a light with a round shade placed in the center. It proved to be an attractive display and a good method of showing the colors.—Contributed by Maurice Baudier, New Orleans, La.

A Homemade Bench Vise

A serviceable and inexpensive bench vise can be made in the following manner: Procure a piece of hard wood, 1 in. thick, and shape it into an eccentric with an extending handle, as shown at A. The jaws B are made of material 2 in. thick, and the drawbar C is a 2

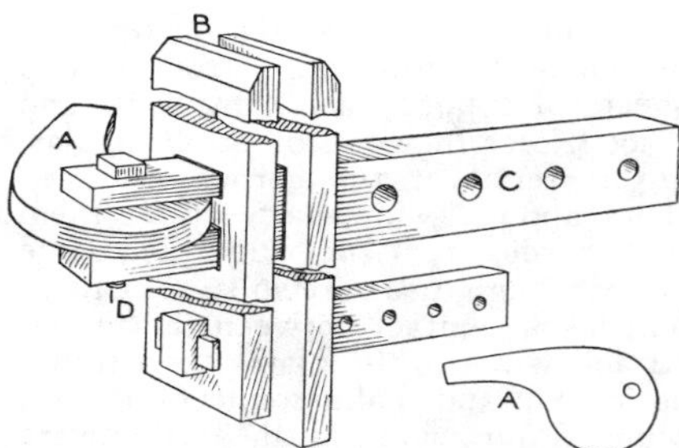

A Vise That can be Quickly Constructed Where No Bench Vise is at Hand

by 3-in. piece of hickory. The outer end of the bar is slotted to receive the eccentric handle, through which a bolt, D, passes to form a bearing. Holes are bored into the opposite end of the bar, 2 in. apart, into which a peg is inserted to come against the back side of the rear jaw. This provides an adjustment for a range of various thicknesses of material. Another bar is located at the bottom of the jaws to provide a means of keeping the jaws parallel. This bar is made in a similar manner to the bar C. The rear jaw can be fastened to the side of a bench, post, or any support that may be handy.—Contributed by Wm. S. Thompson, Columbia, Tenn.

Timing Photo Printing

Having hundreds of postals of a single subject to print, I made a perfect timing apparatus for exposing the prints from an old metronome and an old gong magnet. A disk, B, 20 in. in diameter, was made of heavy tin with two apertures, C C, each cut 7 in. in diameter, on a line with the center of the disk, and 2 in. from the edge. A large spool, F, was used to serve as a hub and also as a reel on which strong twine was wound, with a weight, E, attached to the free end.

The disk was bolted to the partition P of the darkroom, the partition having a hole, G, to coincide with the holes in the disk as it revolved. Four catch pins were fastened on the rim of the disk to engage a catch pin on the armature of the magnet. The gong and commutator were removed and the magnet placed in the position shown in the sketch. A strip of wood was fastened across the face of the metronome H, about 1 in. above the pendulum shaft or axle. On the inside of the center of the strip a small piece of wood was projected, with copper wire on one side only, to form a contact with a piece of flexible copper on the pendulum. Wiring was made as shown in the sketch and a switch used to stop the disk from revolving.

An ordinary postal-card printing frame, D, with a hinged back was used and placed on the shelf A, as shown. A hinge was made from heavy elastic bands to allow for two dozen cards in the frame at one time. As each card was printed it was taken out and dropped into the developer. The reel and metronome should be wound up after printing two dozen cards. The stops can be varied for any length of time by regulating the weight on the metronome. The disk and all woodwork must be painted a dull black. The circuit is completed on the return stroke of the pendulum, causing the magnet to attract the armature, which releases the catch, allowing a quarter turn of the disk.—Contributed by Frank W. Preston, Paterson, N. J.

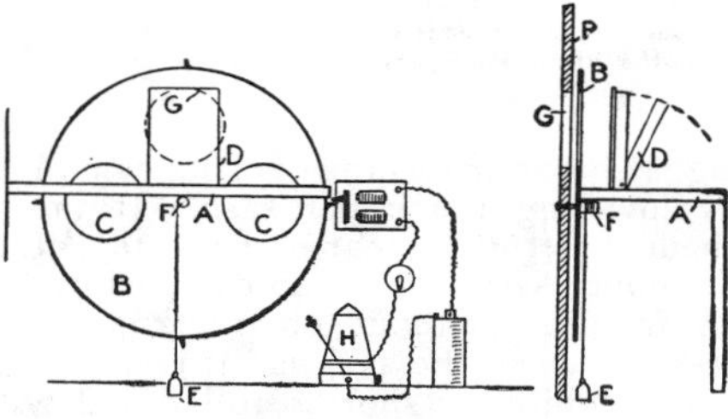

Details of Timing Apparatus

Pail Hook for a Pitcher Pump

When pumping water from the ordinary pitcher pump, the bucket must either be held to the spout or placed on the ground. The accompanying sketch shows how I arranged a hook, fastened over the collar of the pump, to take the bail of the bucket. The hook is made of ¼-in. round iron.—Contributed by Laurence B. Robbins, Harwich, Mass.

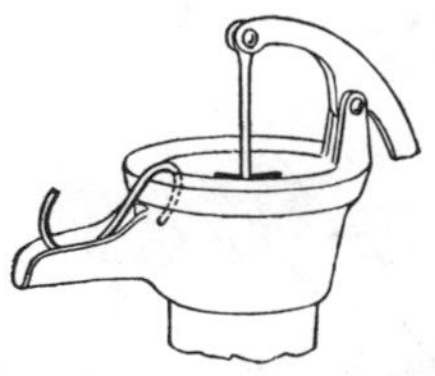

Shade Roller Attached to Upper Window Sash

Free circulation of air cannot be obtained through a window when the shade is attached to the window cas-

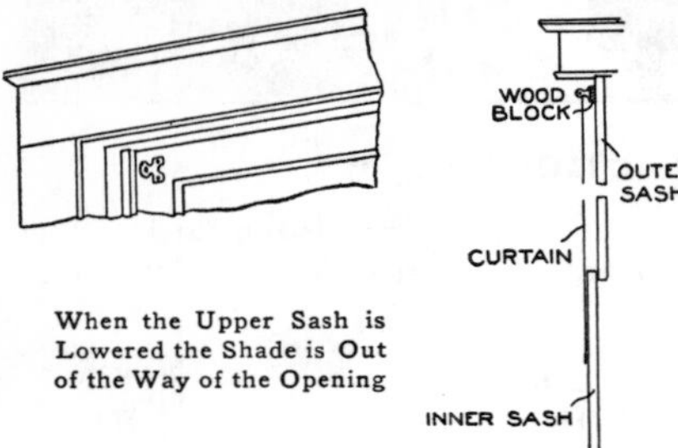

When the Upper Sash is Lowered the Shade is Out of the Way of the Opening

ing, as it partly fills the opening caused by lowering the upper sash. If the shade roller is attached to the top of the upper sash, the shade can perform its function without obstructing the opening when the sash is lowered. It only requires a shorter roller and a narrower shade. The roller brackets are attached in the usual manner, but, in order to have the shade hang vertically, a block, as wide as the lower sash frame, must be fastened under each bracket.

This arrangement also makes it much easier to put up a curtain, as the sash can be let down until the roller can be reached while standing on a chair.—Contributed by James M. Kane, Doylestown, Pa.

Flashing Hook

Having occasion to do a large amount of counter-flashing in a new wall where the mortar was soft and the joint too large to use an ordinary nail or the regular flashing hook, I made hooks from No. 24 gauge galvanized iron, having hooks of extra size and strength, as shown in the sketch. The size of the hook is 1¾ by 3⅛ in. On each side edge, 1⅛ in. from one end, I cut teeth, A A, and clipped the corners of the opposite end at an angle. The end at B was turned down at right angles and the points A A bent in the opposite direction. I placed the counter-flashing in the usual manner, with the projection B hanging down and the pointed end of the hook in the joint, and drove or pushed it in tightly. The points A A will catch on the under side of the brick and hold solidly.—Contributed by Ralph M. Chatham, Orleans, Indiana.

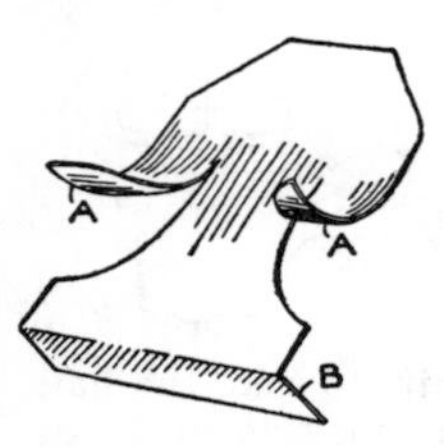

A Homemade Dibble

A dibble made of a round and sharp-pointed stick is the usual tool for making holes when setting tomato and other plants. I found by experience that a dibble made of a flat board would work much better and leave a

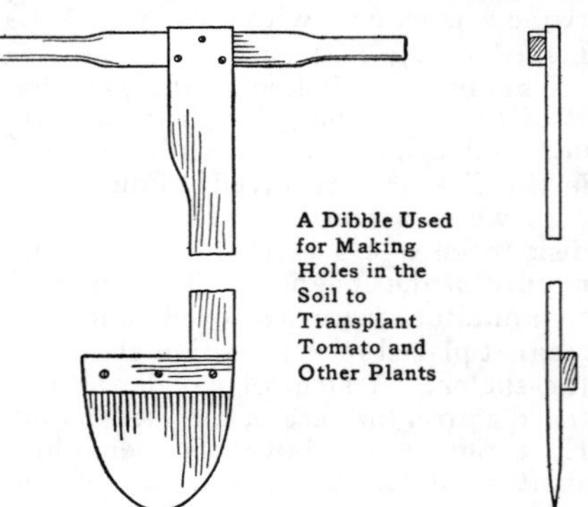

A Dibble Used for Making Holes in the Soil to Transplant Tomato and Other Plants

cleaner hole if worked into the earth with a horizontal swinging motion. The hole produced is just right for the plant. The illustration shows its construction.

Liquid Court-Plaster

A good liquid preparation for cuts and bruises that forms a covering like liquid court-plaster is made by mixing ¾ oz. of flexible collodion with ¼ oz. of ether. When this solution is applied to cuts it will not wash off. As the ether evaporates, add more to keep the mixture liquid.

A Substitute for Candles

One evening our electric light was cut off by a storm, and having no gas, candles, or oil lamps, a very good light was made in the following manner: A tablespoonful of lard was melted and poured in the top of a baking-powder can, and four strands of ordinary white wrapping twine were put into it, allowing one end to stand up for about ½ in. above the edge of the can. The end was lighted the same as a candle. —Contributed by B. E. Cole, Eureka, California.

A Poultry Coop

A barrel makes a good protection for a hen with a brood of chicks, if it is arranged as shown in the sketch. Procure a good barrel with a bottom and cut off each alternate stave at both ends close up to the first hoop. The lower openings thus formed make entrances for the chickens and the upper ones admit air and light. —Contributed by Wm. R. Konnan, Neillsville, Wis.

Preventing Mildew on Canvas

To prevent mildew on canvas, soak it in bluestone water, or if the mildew is already present, coat the parts well with ordinary soap and rub on powdered chalk, or whiting. A solution of corrosive sublimate, well weakened with water, will also prevent mildew, but owing to its poisonous nature it is best to use the former method.—Contributed by A. Ashmund Kelly, Malvern, Pa.

¶When the steel point of a compass is lost, a phonograph needle makes a good substitute.

Holder for Books in a Case

Very often it is found, after arranging the books in a case, that the rows are not complete and the books at the end are continually sliding down on the shelf. The sketch shows a very useful type of wire bracket to support the last book.

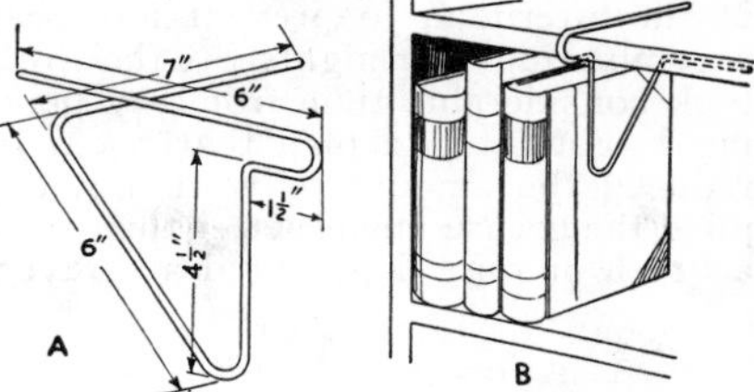

The Shape of the Wire Makes It Easily Applicable to Any Open Bookshelf

A brass wire, 26 in. long and about ⅛ in. in diameter, is bent, with the use of a vise or pliers, to the shape and dimensions shown at A. When the wire is placed on the bookshelf, as shown at B, it prevents the end book from falling. Its location can be changed as books are added to the shelf.—Contributed by John Y. Dunlop, Craighead, Scotland.

Laying Out a Dovetail Joint

With dividers and compass lay off the width of the board into twice as many parts as the dovetails wanted. Draw a light line, AB, across the board as far from the end as half the thickness of the board. On this line step off the divisions with the dividers, beginning with a half space or division. With the bevel square, set to a bevel of 1 in. in 3, draw lines through the division dots. This method will save much time and give accurate results.—Contributed by Joseph F. Parks, Wichita, Kan.

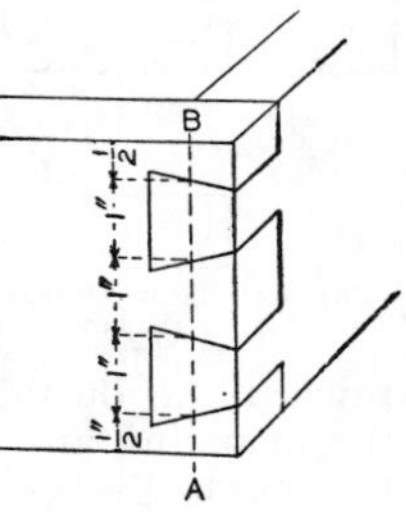

Oiling Bright Parts of Machinery

It is my duty to go over the bright parts on the machinery in my father's shop and give them a coat of oil late in the afternoon to prevent any rust accumulating over night. As the work took considerable time from my playing I thought of a plan that not only reduced the amount of work but applied the grease much better than with a brush or rag. I procured a sprayer,

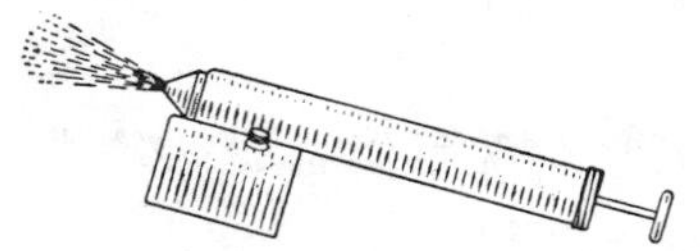

A Sprayer Filled with Oil Makes a Good Device for Coating the Bright Parts of Machinery

as shown in the sketch, and sprayed the oil on the bright parts.—Contributed by Waller Kaufman, Santa Ana, California.

Window Ventilator to Prevent Drafts

The ventilator consists of a piece of wood, about 8 in. wide, 3 in. thick and as long as the window is wide. Holes, 1¾ in. in diameter, are bored at regular intervals into one edge and these are connected with openings from one side as shown. The piece is set under the lower sash with the long openings

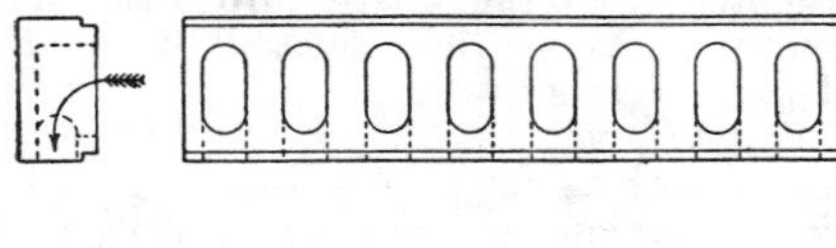

The Ventilator Prevents the Air from Entering a Room in a Straight Line

toward the outside. This will direct the incoming air currents upward into the room.

A Chisel Rack

Turn two large screweyes into the under side of a shelf, as far apart as is necessary, and slip a rod into the eyes. The rod may be kept from slipping out by threading each end and turning on a nut after it is in place. Hooks are made from heavy wire, in the shape of

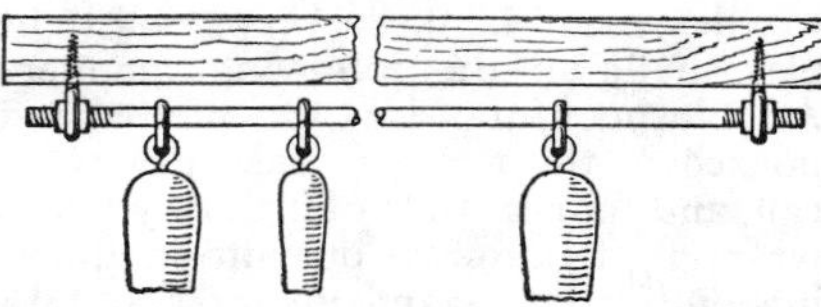

The Chisels are Kept Close at Hand and the Right Tool may be Quickly Found

the letter "S," and placed on the rod. A screweye is turned into the end of each chisel handle and used for hanging the tool on an S-hook. As many hooks are provided as there are tools in use. This method of hanging tools is especially adapted for the wood turner.—Contributed by Wallace E. Fisher, New York, N. Y.

Homemade Snap Hooks

Having had occasion to use several snap hooks of various sizes and being unable to find anything suitable for my purpose on the market, I procured several cotters of the desired sizes and by bending them over, as shown at A, and cutting them off, as at B, I had snap hooks which, besides answering my original purpose, have also found use as key rings and tool-chuck holders.—Contributed by Jos. J. Kolar, Maywood, Ill.

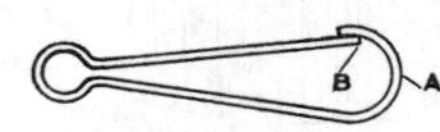

A Dropper and Cork for Medicine Bottles

A convenient way to accurately drop medicine and liquids without any other appliance than the cork is the following: Simply burn or puncture a smooth hole in the cork as shown. Pull the cork out slightly when the liquid is to be dropped, and when this is done, push the cork in and the bottle is sealed.

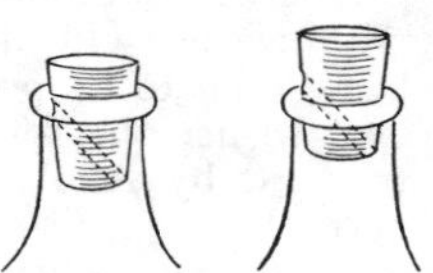

Repairing a Broken Oilstone

A broken oilstone can be repaired and made as good as new in the following manner: Warm the pieces by heating them on the top of a stove or gas heater, with a piece of heavy sheet metal placed on it so as to protect the stone from the direct heat of the flame. The heating should be done somewhat slowly or the stone will crack.

When the stone is warm wipe off the oil which the heat has driven out and apply a couple of coats of shellac to the broken ends. When the shellac is thoroughly dry, warm the stone again to melt the shellac, and clamp the pieces together. After cooling, the pieces will be found firmly stuck together.—Contributed by F. L. Sylvester, Reading, Mass.

Homemade Towel Roller

The towel roller is made of a piece of broom handle, 16 in. long, squared on both ends and a nail driven in the center of each end. Procure two small pieces of tin—disks about 1 in. in diameter will do—and drive a hole through the center of each with a wire nail. Cut from one edge of the disk down to the hole taking out a narrow V-shaped section.

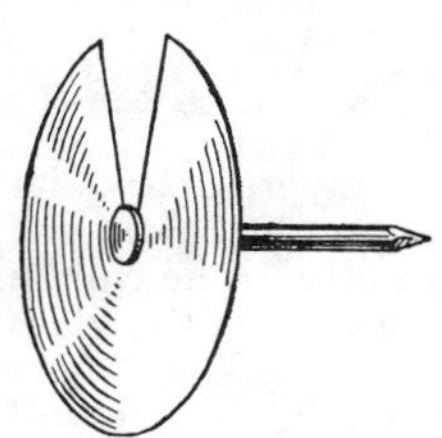

Fasten each disk to a block and nail these to any convenient wall at such a distance apart that the nail heads in the broomstick will slip down in the slots and rest in the holes in the centers of the disks, which form the bearings for the nail heads resting beyond the tin and next to the block.

With a little care the tin can be made to bulge outwardly in the center making room for the nail heads.—Contributed by L. Alberta Norrell, Augusta, Ga.

Clothesline Reel

The usual method of reeling up a clothesline and taking it in is quite a task and many times the lines are left out in the open from one wash day to another, due to neglect or forgetfulness. I made the arrangement shown in the sketch to take care of the line without any effort to the user.

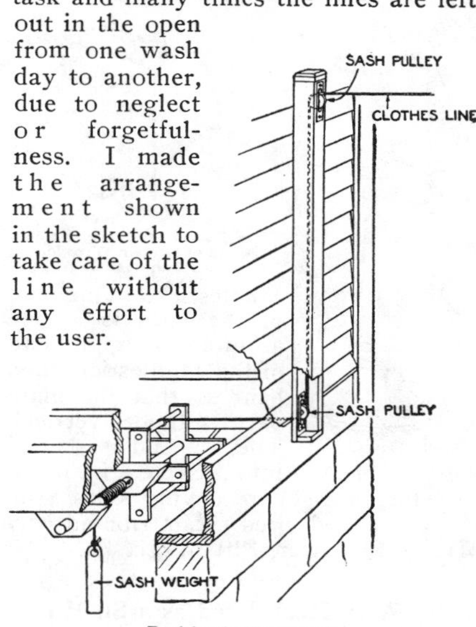

Reel in the Basement

All that is necessary with this arrangement is to take the end of the line and run it over the hooks or sheaves on the posts and make it secure around an awning fastener. When loosed, the weight in the basement will wind up the line.

A knot can be tied in the line near the reel to catch at a hole in the sill, which will prevent the strain on the reel. If the reel is made to wind up 4 ft. of line to each revolution and the sash-cord shaft is 3/4 in. in diameter, about 100 ft. of line can be taken up in a basement 7 ft. high.—Contributed by A. E. Little, Akron, O.

¶ Black-heart malleable iron derives its name from the fact that in annealing only the outer layers of carbon are oxidized, the carbon of the interior being simply changed to a black amorphous state.

A Candle-Shade Holder

A holder for either round or square shades can be easily constructed from a piece of heavy copper wire to fit on a

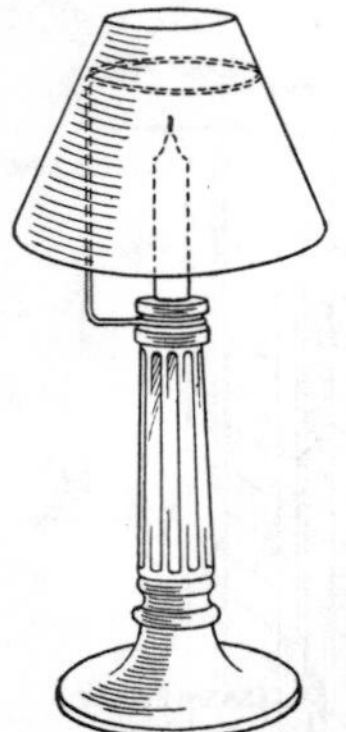

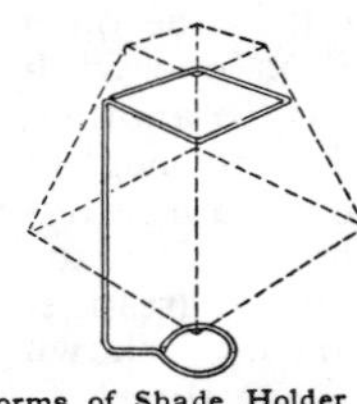

Two Forms of Shade Holder Made of Copper Wire for a Candlestick

candlestick. One end of the wire is looped around the upper end of the candlestick, then bent so that the main part will be vertical. The top end is shaped into a circle 2 in. in diameter or a square having sides 2 in. long, as desired.—Contributed by Harry Slosower, Pittsburgh, Pa.

Wire Mesh Used as a Shelf

In covering a window back of my lathe with wire mesh as a protection I also made a shelf for the tools between the window sill and the lathe bed of the same material. The mesh used was 1/4-in. The shelf is always clean, as the shavings and dirt fall through, and the tools may be readily picked up.—Contributed by J. H. Sanford, Pasadena, California.

Heel Plates

A good heel or toe plate can be made by driving ordinary thumb tacks into the leather of the shoe heel or sole. The shape can be varied by using tacks

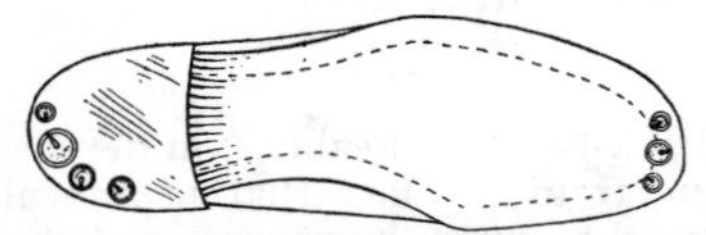

The Heads of the Tacks Form a Wearing Surface Equal to an Ordinary Heel Plate

having different-sized heads.—Contributed by James T. Gaffney, Chicago, Ill.

A Bright Dip for Metal

Articles of brass, copper and bronze may be given a bright luster by dipping them into a solution composed of 50 oz. of nitric acid, 25 oz. of sulphuric acid, liquid measure, and 1/2 oz. of soot and 1/2 oz. of salt, by weight. After the articles are dipped into the solution they are removed and thoroughly washed, then dried in sawdust to prevent streaks.

An Interesting Vacuum Experiment

A very interesting experiment may be performed with two drinking glasses, a small candle end and a piece of blotting paper, says the Pathfinder. The glasses must be the same size and of the thin-glass kind. The candle end is lighted and set in one glass; the blotting paper is well dampened and placed on top of the glass,

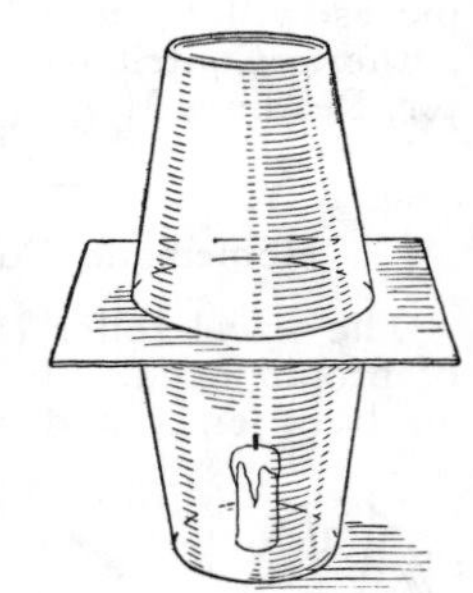

and the other glass inverted and its rim placed exactly over the lower one and pressed down tightly. The candle will burn up all the oxygen in the glass and go out.

The air in the glass being heated will expand and some of it will be forced out from under the moist paper, and then, as the portion remaining cools, it will contract and draw the upper glass on the paper and make an air-tight joint. The upper glass can then be taken up and the lower one will cling to it.

A Sliver Extractor

If a clipper for the finger nails becomes dull do not throw it away, but keep it in the tool box in a handy place. It is very useful for extracting slivers from the flesh.—Contributed by G. Wokenfuss, McCook, Neb.

Night Croquet Playing

Croquet playing became so interesting to us that we could not find time to do all our playing during the day. So at night we attach a candle to each of the wickets and also use one at each corner of the grounds. These light the grounds so that the game can be played nicely. The candles may be attached by wiring them to the wickets or by using small pasteboard boxes, similar to a pill box of sufficient size, and running a wire through the center or down the sides, which is hooked over the top to hold them upright on top of the ground. The latter way is the better as the candles may be pulled up in the day time and taken out of the way.—Contributed by Geo. Goodbrod, Union, Ore.

A Nursing-Bottle Holder

The ordinary nursing bottle with nipple necessitates holding the bottle in a certain position, and when the valve nipples are used, the bottle should be held far enough away to allow this valve free action. To accomplish this I constructed a very simple wire holder for the bottle as shown in the illustration. Ordinary telephone wire will hold any bottle. The wire is bent to hook on the side of the crib,

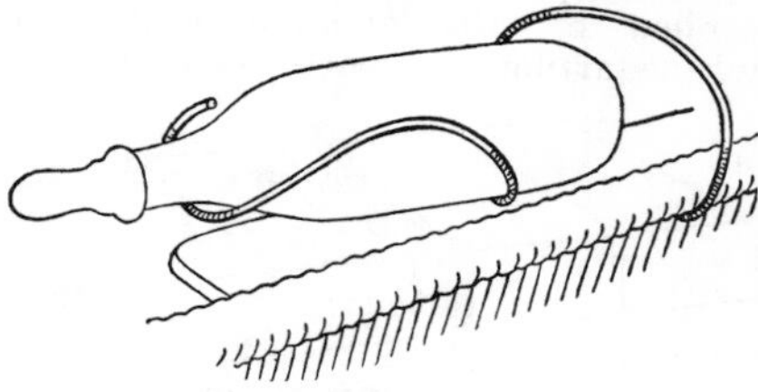

Nursing Bottle in Holder

cradle or cab.—Contributed by W. A. Humphrey, Columbus, O.

Milk-Ticket Holder

An ordinary spring mousetrap makes a good bread or milk-ticket holder. The wood part of the trap can be

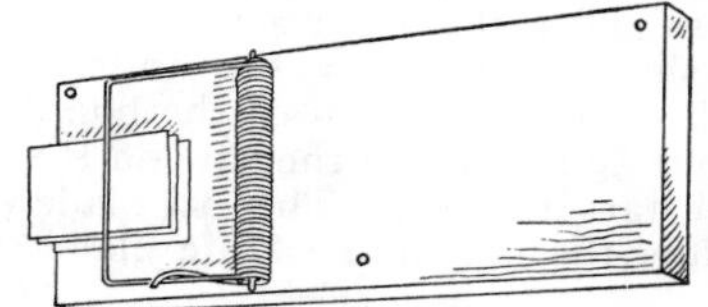

Trap Used as Ticket Holder

easily nailed or screwed to a door or window casing. The way the tickets are held is clearly shown in the sketch.

Joint for Cabinet Work

In making a cabinet containing 56 drawers of various sizes, I used the method shown in the sketch for making the frame. The horizontal strips A should be all fastened together when sawing the notches to fit over the uprights. The uprights B should be sawn in the same manner. It is best to round the front of the rear uprights slightly and also any other places where the drawers might strike when pushing them into place. The length of the runners C should be 1½ in. less than the length of the drawer.—Contributed by J. H. Dickson, Polk, Pa.

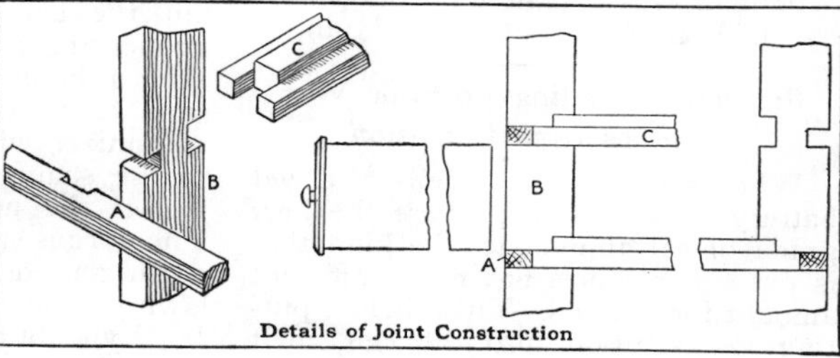

Details of Joint Construction

¶Do not expect accurate work unless you have accurate tools.

Starting a Saw Cut

A fine piece of woodwork is often spoiled by the amateur craftsman when starting a cut with a saw. As the

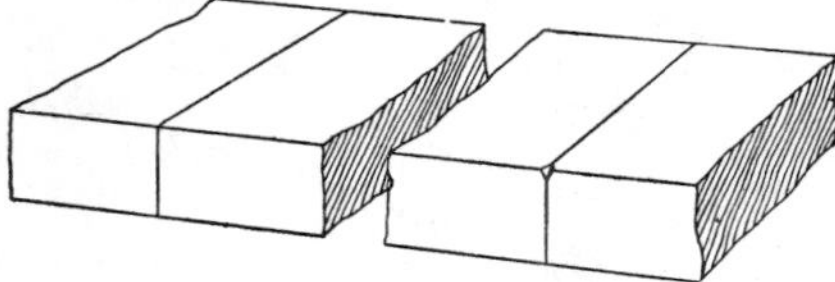

Starting a Saw on a Knife Cut will Prevent Roughing or Splintering the Edge

first stroke of the saw on the edge of the board is made, the teeth often break a splinter from the edge or the saw jumps to one side of the line, thereby making a rough and uneven cut. This can be avoided in a very simple way.

After marking the line, take a sharp knife and make a cut across the edge, as shown, and draw the knife down well over the corners of the board for about 1/8 in. Place the saw on the cut and start it slowly. The saw blade will follow the cut of the knife blade.

A Substitute Penholder

One evening when my wife was using the only penholder in the house I desired to do some writing and being in a hurry, I hastily made a substitute

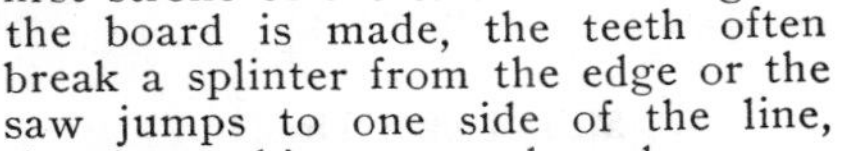

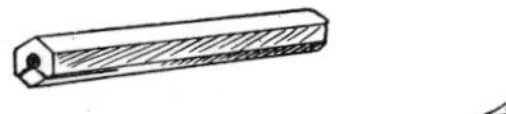

The End of the Pencil as It is Prepared to Receive the Pen

holder of a pencil. Two cuts were made in the butt end, as shown; the pen was then slipped in, the outside wound with a rubber band, and my penholder was complete.—Contributed by H. A. Sullwold, St. Paul, Minn.

Protecting Binding Posts on Wet Batteries from Corrosion

When recharging the cells of a wet battery it is best to procure the best grade of sal ammoniac, the kind that is put up in boxes having a sufficient amount for one cell. Then, before putting the solution into the cell, melt some paraffin used for preserving purposes and dip the upper end of the carbons, zinc, and the glass jar in it. This will apply a coat of insulating wax that will prevent any white deposit from working up on the parts and corroding the binding posts, or terminals.

The cells are then filled in the ordinary manner, after which the carbons and zincs are raised just far enough to admit a layer of common machine oil, about 3/8 in. thick. The oil not only prevents evaporation but aids greatly to keep the uncovered parts from corrosion.—Contributed by L. R. Kelley, Philadelphia, Pa.

A Cork Puller

A very simple and easy way to remove a stopper from a bottle, when a cork puller is not at hand, is to press two nails into the cork, as shown in the sketch, and, taking a firm hold on both nails, draw the cork out. Brads may be used on smaller corks. Large and tightly fitted corks may be drawn by gripping the nails with a pair of pliers.—Contributed by W. A. Jaquythe, Richmond, Cal.

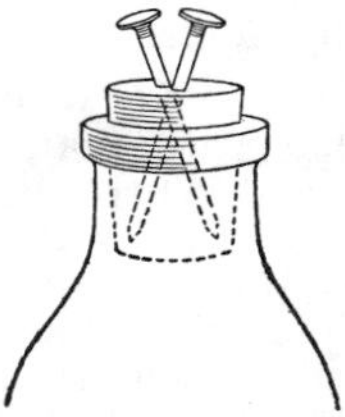

Holder for a Garden-Hose Nozzle

When sprinkling a lawn with an automatic spraying device on a hose nozzle it is necessary to have some kind of an arrangement to tilt the end at the proper angle. I find that a holder made of a heavy piece of galvanized wire bent in the shape shown can be used to set the nozzle at any angle. The wire is easily pushed into the earth and does no harm to the lawn.—Contributed by T. J. Ingram, Jr., Lynchburg, Va.

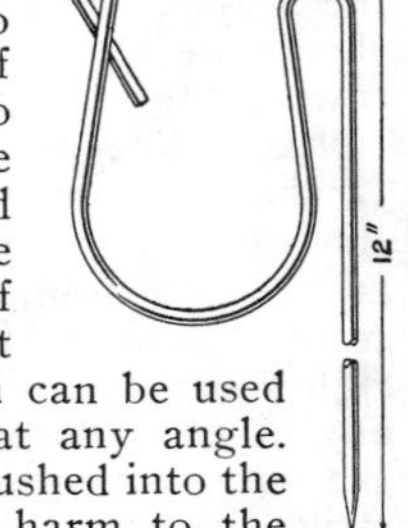

Alarm to Designate a Filled Storage Battery

When a storage battery is recharged, the completion of the recharging is marked by the development of gas in the cell. This fact is the basis of a simple electrical device which will ring a bell when the battery is fully charged. A glass tube bent as shown and having a small bulb near its upper end is inserted in the top of the cell, a small quantity of mercury being first introduced in the bend below the bulb. Wires extend down the upper tubing to within a short distance of the mercury. These wires are connected with binding posts so mounted that they can rest on top of the tube, whereupon the bell circuit is completed as shown. Small quantities of gas may develop

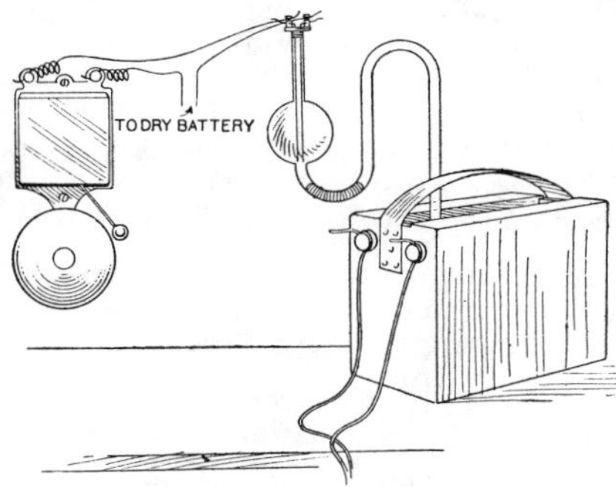

The Gas Generated by a Filled Storage Battery will Make Electric Connections and Sound an Alarm

during the charging of the cell, but if a small hole is pierced in the tube between the mercury and the cell, this gas will not exert pressure enough on the mercury to push it up and connect it with the wires, which will take place first when the development of gas becomes very active at the completion of the recharging.

Stretching Poultry Fencing

The woven-wire poultry fencing is an unusually difficult thing to handle and fasten on posts so that it will be taut and evenly stretched. The best method I have ever seen for drawing this fencing and holding it for nailing to a post is the use of the device shown in the sketch. It consists of a board, as long as the fencing is wide, with

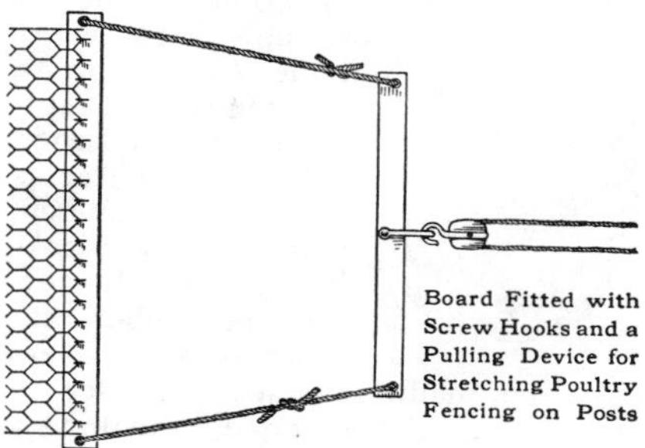

Board Fitted with Screw Hooks and a Pulling Device for Stretching Poultry Fencing on Posts

screw hooks set far enough apart to catch into the meshes of the wire, and a crosspiece attached to the board by pieces of rope at the ends and provided with a pulling loop in the center.—Contributed by Joseph C. Laackman, Meadow Brook, Pa.

A Centering Gauge

The centering gauge consists of a piece of celluloid on which several circles are drawn having different diameters, but all drawn from the same center. A small hole is made at the center to admit the point of a center punch. Two sets of circles may be drawn on one piece as shown, but the lines should be spaced far enough apart to allow the metal to be clearly seen through the celluloid. The sheet is placed on the end of a shaft and adjusted so that a ring will match the circumference of the shaft, then the center punch is set in the center hole

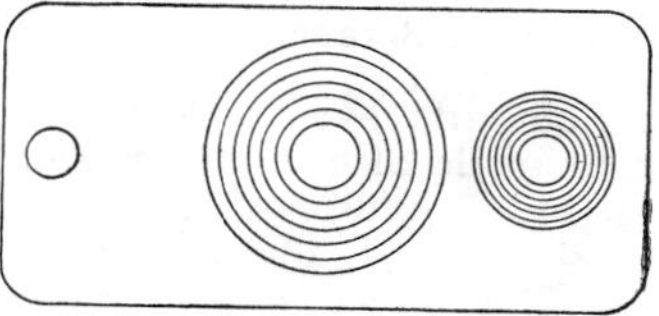

Circles Drawn on Celluloid to Adjust It on the End of a Shaft in Finding the Center

and struck with a hammer. The center punch for marking is shown in the sketch.—Contributed by Harry Holst, San Francisco, Cal.

Homemade Letters for Marking Bags

An initial marker for bags can be made of a beet or potato. Cut off enough of the vegetable to provide a flat surface of sufficient size and then cut out the letter as shown in the sketch, and use shoe blacking as ink. In cutting, remember that most of the letters must be made reversed in order to print right. For example, in making a B, draw it out on paper and cut it out, then lay the face of the pattern on the flat surface of the vegetable and cut around it.

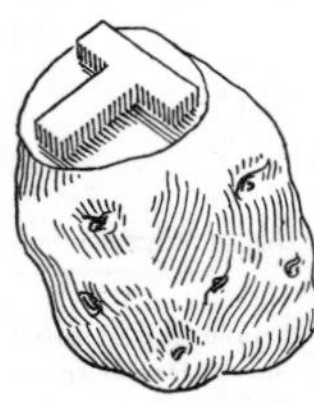

To Keep a Crease in a Soft Hat

The crease in a soft hat can be kept in proper shape with the aid of a paper clip. The clip is slipped over the fold inside of the hat which forms the bottom part of the crease.—Contributed by Jas. M. Kane, Doylestown, Pennsylvania.

Paper Clip on the Fold, Holding It in the Right Shape for the Outside Crease

A Shoe Scraper

A good boot and shoe scraper for a step can be made of a worn-out and discarded broom. Cut off the straws and strings as shown in the sketch, allowing one string to hold them together, and make the notch the width of the shoe. Tie the extending ends together, and mount the whole on a suitable block, or, if desired, a hole can be bored in the step to receive the handle, and the scraper thus securely attached.

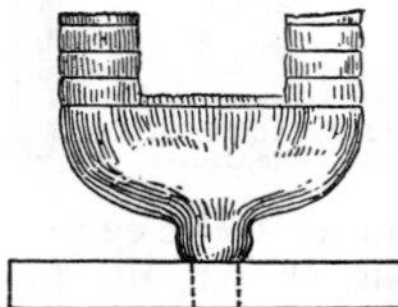

This makes an effective scraper for the bottom as well as the sides of shoes of almost any size.—Contributed by Jno. V. Loeffler, Evansville, Ind.

A Vegetable Slicer

A tin bucket or can makes a good slicer for vegetables when no other slicer is at hand. A number of slots are cut across one side of the can, and the lower edge of each slot slightly turned out to form a cutting edge. The vegetable is placed against the top of the can and pushed down over the slots. Each slot will cut off a slice which falls inside of the can.

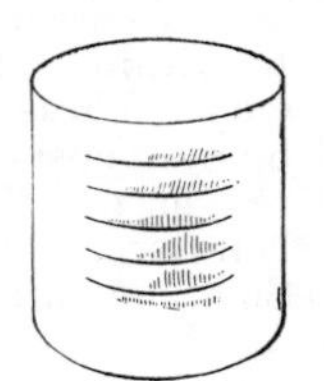

Bench Stop for Planing Thin Boards

A bench stop for planing thin boards with a hand plane may be made in the following manner: Procure a piece of strap iron about ¼ in. thick, 1½ or 2 in. wide, and about 6 in. long. File or grind one edge sharp on top and drill a ¼-in. hole through the center. Cut a slot in a board or in the workbench large enough to receive the stop A flat. Place enough strips of rubber or fit two coil springs, B, to raise the sharp edge out of the slot. Insert a screw in the hole of the stop and adjust it to the desired height by turning the screw up or down.

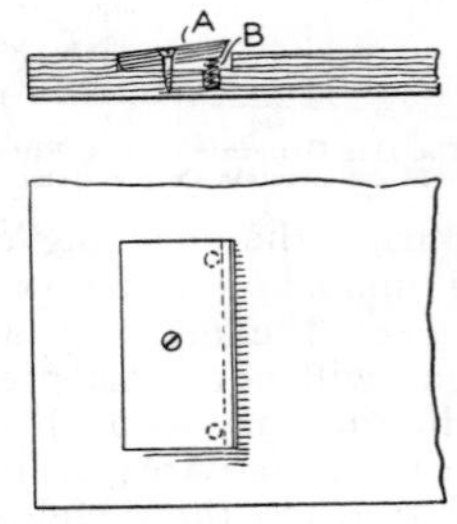

¶In a case of emergency, lemon juice may be used as soldering flux.

A Jardinière Pedestal

The pedestal may be made of any close-grained wood, such as basswood or maple, if the stain is to be walnut or mahogany, but it can also be constructed of quarter-sawed oak and finished in a waxed mission or varnished surface. The material required is as follows:

1 top, 12 by 12 by ⅞ in., S-2-S.
2 caps, 6 by 6 by ⅞ in., S-2-S.
1 upright, 18 by 4 by 4 in., S-4-S.
1 base, 8 by 8 by ⅞ in., S-2-S.

The top is centered and a circle, 11½ in. in diameter, is drawn upon it, and sawn out. The caps are also centered and circles drawn upon them, 5½ in. and 3½ in. in diameter. Saw them out on the larger circles and center them in a wood lathe and turn out the wood in the smaller circles to a depth of ½ in. The upright is then centered in the lathe and turned to 3½ in. in diameter for its full length.

The base and foot pieces are cut out as shown, fitted together and fastened with screws from the under side. One of the caps is mounted in the center on the base and the other cap in the center on the under side of the top. The upright is then placed in the turned-out parts of the caps and either glued or fastened with screws.

If light wood is used, the finish can be walnut or mahogany. A very

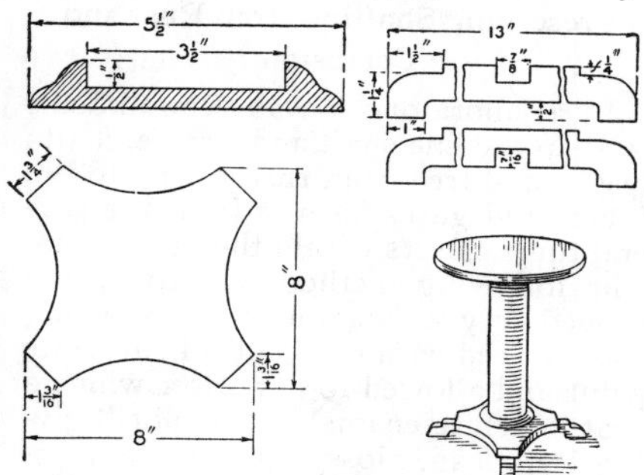

The Pedestal can be Made of a Wood Suitable for Finishing to Match Other Furniture

pretty finish can be worked out in pyrography, if one is familiar with that work.—Contributed by Russell T. Westbrook, Dover, N. J.

A Lawn-Tennis Marker

The liquid receptacle is a metal biscuit box, about 9 in. square and mounted on a wheel with a handle, the

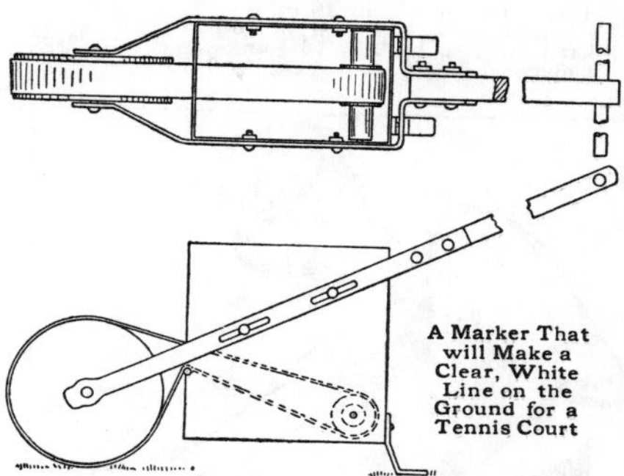

A Marker That will Make a Clear, White Line on the Ground for a Tennis Court

whole being similar to a wheelbarrow. The wheel is 7 in. in diameter and 2½ in. thick. The wheel and box are bolted between two pieces of strap iron in the manner shown, and the handle is attached back of the box. If the box is of very thin metal, boards should be placed within on the sides where it is fastened to the strap iron. A roller is pivoted in the box at the lower back corner and a canvas tape or band run over the roller and wheel in the manner of a belt. The tape should run through a slot cut in the front part of the box, about midway between the top and the bottom. The edges of the tin in the slot must be turned over and hammered down to make a smooth surface for the tape to run over.—Contributed by George N. Bertram, Toronto, Can.

Removing Tannin Stains from Teacups

A small portion of hyposulphite of soda mixed with vinegar will make a good cleaner for teacups having tannin stains. This process does not injure the finest china and is inexpensive. The same solution works quite well on clothes that are accidentally stained with tea. They should be washed out and dried quickly after its application in order to make this method most effective.—Contributed by Loren Ward, Des Moines, Iowa.

Woven-Top Stool

The material necessary for this stool is as follows:

4 legs, 1¾ by 1¾ by 16 in.
4 bottom rails, ⅞ by 1¾ by 16 in.
4 top rails, ⅞ by 2 by 16½ in.
4 diagonal braces, ⅞ by 1¾ by 6 in.

Weaving the Top of the Stool by Using a Wet Weaver of Reed

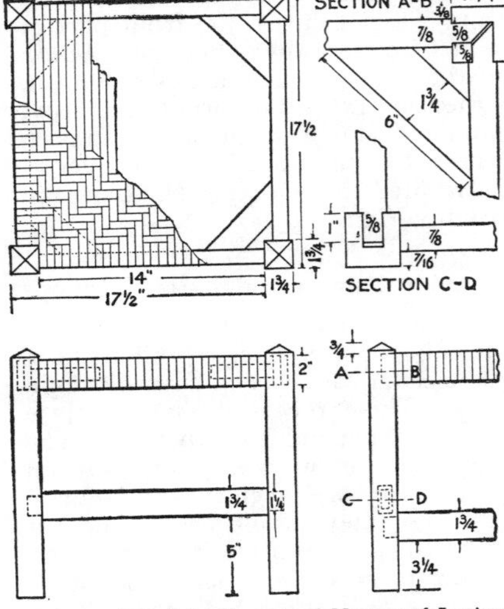

Construction of the Frame and Manner of Laying the Weavers for the Top

The legs are mortised so the top rails come level. The upper rails are tenoned on the sides only and beveled at the ends. For the bottom rails, the mortises are made one above the other, the rails being tenoned on all sides. The braces are cut at 45° on each end and glued into place.

In weaving the top, proceed as follows: Use a wet weaver and wrap one layer over the entire top, the strips being placed close together and tightly wound. Start the second layer at right angles to the first by going under one strip, then over three strips, under three, and so on, by threes, until that strip is finished. Start the second by going under two strips, then over three, under three, and so on, as before. The third strip should start by going under three, then over and under three, etc. Start the fourth by going over one, then under three, and over three, as in the preceding; the fifth, start over two, then under and over three, repeatedly. The sixth, and last of the series, begin over three and then continue, by threes, as before. Having finished one series, the remainder of the top should be completed in similar order. Good white shellac makes the best finish for the seat; the stool itself may be finished to suit.—Contributed by Russel Dodsworth, Erie, Pa.

Preserving Shafting from Rust and Corrosion

In a laboratory it was very difficult to keep the line shaft and countershafts bright and free from rust, owing to the fumes and gases issuing from the several fume closets within the same room. The following method was tried, and proved very satisfactory. The shafting was covered with two coats of flat white paint and allowed to dry, after which a coat of white enamel was applied, giving it a clean, glossy, and sanitary appearance. This eliminated all the trouble of cleaning it with emery cloth, and it also made it appear in harmony with the other furnishings of the laboratory. —Contributed by Geo. F. Stark, Norwich, N. Y.

Reed Furniture

By Chas. M. Miller

A Reed Basket

INASMUCH as there is a great demand for reed furniture and since good weavers are comparatively few in number, it would be well to learn the process of reed weaving. The weaving operations can be learned much better through the construction of some small article, such as a basket or jardinère cover. The center is the most difficult part of the basket making, and it is best to begin with wood bottoms, as the whole basket can be kept in a much better form due to the stiffness furnished by such a bottom. It is also an approach to the reed furniture which is woven on framework. The objectionable feature of the wood bottoms is the unfinished appearance of the wood edge showing through, but this can be overcome by the use of the roll shown in the illustration.

While the wood bottoms have been used for this class of work for a number of years, the roll is new and is very popular with those who have seen and used it. The roll can be placed in many ways on different-shaped baskets, and other reed pieces, so that it is best to master this piece of work thoroughly before attempting the other, or larger, pieces that will be described later, in other articles.

The description is for a basket 5 in. in diameter and 3 in. high, as shown in the illustration. A disk of wood, 1/4 in. thick and 5 in. in diameter, is required. Basswood makes the best bottom, but pine, or cedar, will do. Cut a board about 6 in. square, and draw diagonal lines on it intersecting at the center, then draw a circle, 5 in. in diameter, as shown in Fig. 1; also another circle, using the same center, 4 3/4 in. in diameter. Set compass points about 5/8 in. apart, and step off spaces on the inner

circle to make 24 points. This will have to be tried out more than once, to get the spaces to come out evenly and just have the right number of points. Holes are bored with a 1/8-in. bit, just inside of the inner circle, back of the places marked by the compass points, as shown in Fig. 2. Cut the board on the outside circle with a coping, or turn, saw, to make the circle, as in Fig. 3. Do not saw out the circle before boring the holes, as otherwise the disk might split out in places.

The reeds placed vertically are called spokes, and the horizontal ones are the weavers. For the spokes, what is called a No. 4 reed is used. Do not wet the spokes before putting them through the wood. Allow the ends to project about 5½ in. below the bottom, as shown in Fig. 4. Place the bottom, with the spokes, in water, and soak them thoroughly, especially the part below the bottom. About 15 minutes of soaking will be sufficient to make them pliable enough to bend over at right angles. It will not injure the wood bottom to soak it with the reeds. As shown at A, Figs. 4 and 5, each spoke below the wood bottom is bent down and back of the two nearest spokes, B and C, then out between the third and fourth spokes, C and D, and so on. The last two spokes, Y and Z, Fig. 6, are forced under the spokes A and B, respectively. In this illustration the spoke Y is shown as it is being inserted under the spoke A. When this operation is completed, the bottom will have the appearance of a fireworks pinwheel.

Continue the bending of the spokes, in the same direction, up and across the thickness of the wood in front of three other spokes and behind the fourth, as shown in Fig. 7. This would not cover the edge of the wood entirely, and, for this reason, other short spokes must be inserted in front of each of the first ones before it is brought up

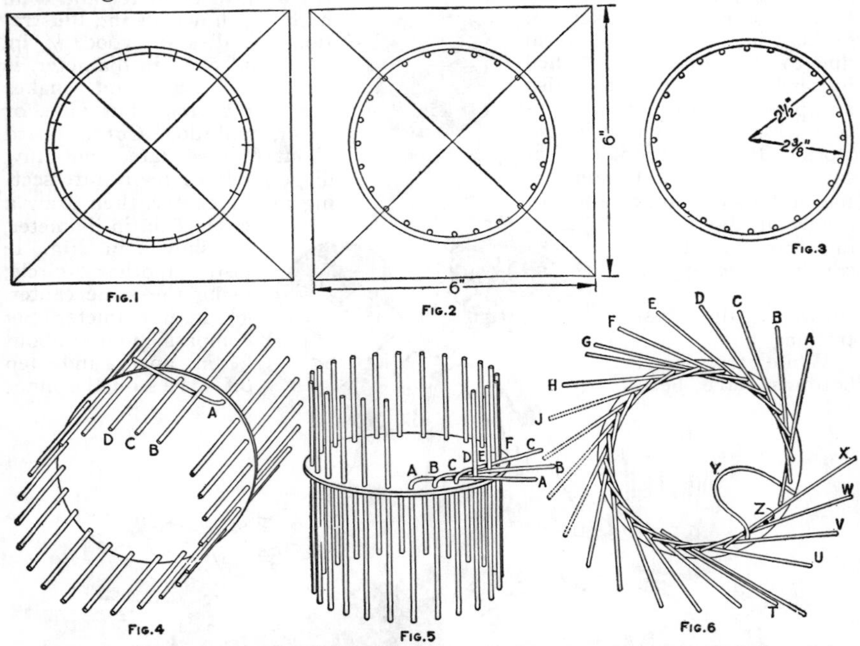

The Bottom is Cut from a Piece of Wood to Give Strength and to Avoid the Most Difficult Part of the Weaving; the Reeds are Attached to the Bottom and Their Lower Ends Bent as Shown

across the edge of the wood. These supplementary spokes should be about 4 in. long. The manner of inserting these spokes before making the bend is shown at G and T, Fig. 6. The double spokes must be pressed down flat, when brought up in place, without riding one on the other. If the ends are too long and interfere with the next pair, they can be cut off a little with a flat chisel, or knife, being careful not to make them too short, or the pieces will not stay in place. If there is still an open space, an extra, short spoke can be inserted to crowd the pieces together and fill up the space.

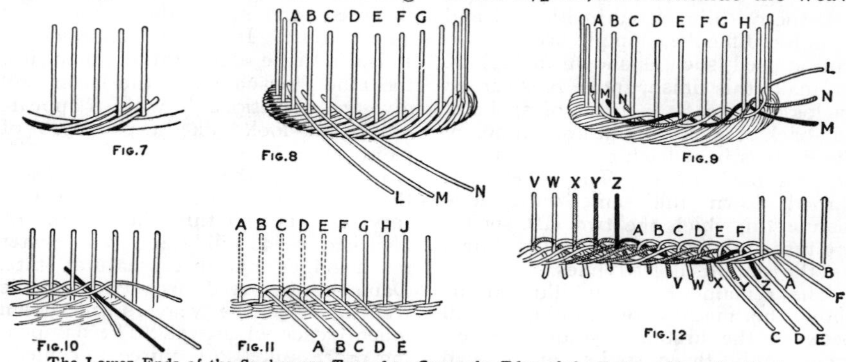

The Lower Ends of the Spokes are Turned to Cover the Edge of the Bottom, Then the Reeds are Woven into the Upright Spokes to the Right Height, Where They are Broken Down and Woven into a Top Border

When the roll is completed, insert three weavers, of No. 3 reed that has been soaked about 15 minutes, placing them between the spokes A and B, B and C, and C and D, as shown in Fig. 8. Pass weaver L in front of the spokes B and C, then back of D and out between D and E. Weaver M is passed in front of C and D, back of E and out in front of E and F. These operations are clearly shown in Fig. 9. The weaver N is placed in front of D and E, back of F and then in front of G and H. At this point the weaver L is used again. The weaver farthest behind each time is brought in front of the two spokes nearest to it, then behind the third and out in front of the next two spokes. Do not try to use weavers longer than 8 ft., which is about half the length of a reed. When a weaver is used up, press it back to the side a little, push in a new reed about 1½ in., and continue the weaving. This is clearly shown in Fig. 10. This weaving is known as the triple weave, which cinches down well and holds tightly. The first round should be carefully worked, so as to get the ends of the roll properly pressed down flat in place. Each throw of the weaver should be well pressed down.

The break-down-tight border is used for the finish at the top. The first operation in making this border is shown in Fig. 11. The spoke A is bent over back of spoke B and out between spokes B and C. The spoke B is bent over back of the spoke C and out between C and D, and so on, until the spoke E is turned down. Then take the end of the spoke A, Fig. 12, and lay it over B, C, D, and E, in front of F, back of G, and out between G and H. The end of spoke F is then brought down, also between G and H, but back of the end of A. The end of B takes a similar leap, passes behind H and out between H and J; then G is brought down behind the end of B, in the same manner as F was brought down back of A. The last four or five spokes are the most difficult to handle, as they must be forced through the first ones to correspond with those already in place. It is best not to pull the ends of A, B, C, and D down too tightly at first, keeping in mind that the last ones must be inserted under the first ones. The last standing spokes are represented by the full and shaded lines.

If the roll illustrated in Figs. 11 and 12 is too difficult, a simple break-down can be used, such as shown in Fig. 13. To make this finish, spoke A is turned back of spoke B, in front of spoke C and back of spoke D, but not out again. Spoke B is bent back of C, in front of D, and back of E. The others are turned down the same way. The manner in which the two last spokes are turned down and inserted is shown by the double dotted lines.

The remainder of the illustrations show the method of forming a roll between the first and second spokes, where only three spokes are turned down before the throwing-across process begins. The first three spokes turned down are shown in Fig. 14, and the throwing over, in Fig. 15. The second beginning is shown in Fig. 16. The finishing of this top is shown in Figs. 17 and 18. The full, heavy lines represent the final insertions, and the reed must be in quite a sharp loop to make the end enter the right place. It is then drawn down and forced in front of the other reed that passes out between the same spokes.

When the basket is dry, the long ends can be cut off close up with a knife, being careful not to cut a weaver. If there are hairy fibers sticking out they can be singed off over a gas, or other, flame that will not smut. If it requires bleaching, brush some chloride of lime, mixed in a little water, over the reeds and set in the sunlight for a short time. It is better to leave the finish a little dark rather than use too much bleaching, as the latter will give an objectionable whitish appearance that looks like a poor job of painting.

In working the reeds, do not leave them in the water longer than necessary, as this will turn them dark. A bleached reed will stand the water much longer than in the natural state. Dampen the reed frequently while weaving it, as the weavers pack down much closer when wet. The dampening process is also required to remedy the drying out caused by whisking the reeds through the air in weaving operations. A great variety of baskets can be made from this form, viz., low, tall, tapering vase forms, bowl shapes, etc., in plain or dark weaves.

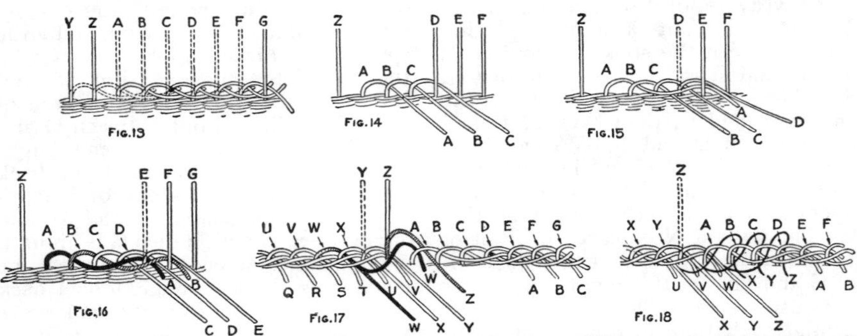

A Simple Break-Down Roll for the Top, Also a Method of Forming a Roll between the First and Second Spokes Where Only Three Spokes are Turned Down Before the Throwing-Across Process Begins

Wireless-Lighted Lamp Deception

Window displays of puzzling nature usually draw crowds. A lighted globe lying on its side in full view, yet apparently not connected to any source of electricity, could easily be arranged as a window display, deceiving the closest observer. A mirror, or window glass, backed with some opaque material, should be used for the foundation of the device. For the display lamp, it is best to use a 25 or 40-watt tungsten, as these will lie flatter on the glass than the larger sizes, and the deception will not be as easily discovered. The place where the brass cap of the lamp touches the glass should be marked and a small hole drilled through to the wire connecting the tungsten filament to the plug on the top of the lamp. At any suitable place, a hole should be drilled in the glass plate, no larger than is necessary, to permit two small cotton-covered magnet wires to pass through. One of the wires should be looped, passed through the hole in the cap and hooked onto the bare wire connecting with the plug on top of lamp. The other wire should be fastened to the brass cap, near the drilled hole, after which the lamp may be placed in position and the two wires connected to a source of electricity. If proper care has been taken and no crosses oc-

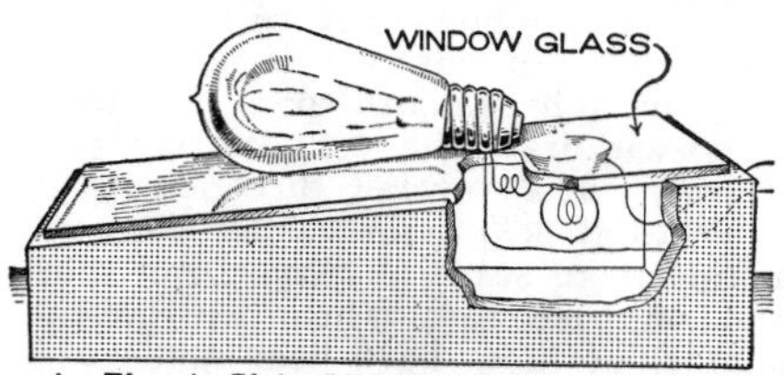

An Electric Globe Lighted on a Piece of Glass Makes a Good Window Attraction

cur, the lamp will light, and if the display is placed in the proper surroundings, it will prove very deceiving. To protect against a fuse blow-out from a short circuit, it is advisable to run another lamp in series with the display lamp, as shown.—Contributed by Clyde W. Epps, Mineola, Tex.

Live Bait Used in Fishing

With the simple device illustrated, no fisherman need worry over running short of bait or even regarding the usual repeated baiting of the hook. A small clear-glass bottle should be procured, and several hooks wired to it about the neck, or at each end, as desired or found best after several trials. After filling the bottle with water a live minnow is placed in it, and the bottle is sealed with a cork, which is notched around the edge to permit water to enter or leave the bottle without losing the bait. If live grasshoppers,

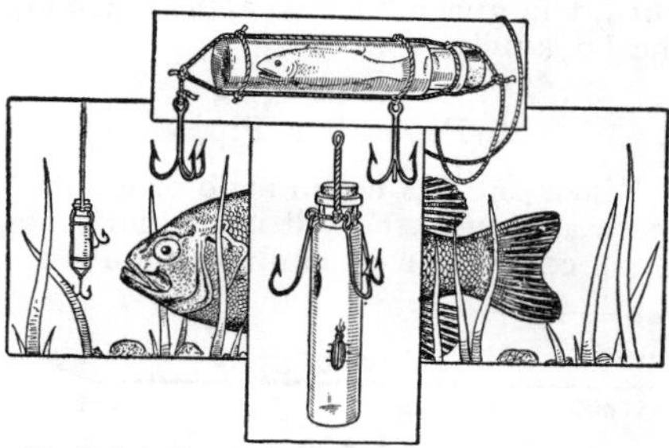

The Bait is Kept Alive and Unharmed in a Bottle Surrounded with Hooks

or similar bait, is desired the cork can be used unnotched to form a watertight stopper. As illuminated bait for night fishing, several fireflies can be put in the bottle.—Contributed by L. Wahrer, Tiffin, Ohio.

Bookrack

The material necessary for the illustrated bookrack is as follows:

2 end pieces, 5/8 by 5 1/4 by 6 in.
1 shelf, 5/8 by 5 1/4 by 13 in.

The shelf is cut rectangular, 5 1/4 in. wide by 14 1/2 in. long. Its two ends should then be provided with tenons 3/8 in. thick by 4 1/4 in. wide, and extending out 1/4 inch.

The end pieces, after being cut to the given dimensions, are marked off and

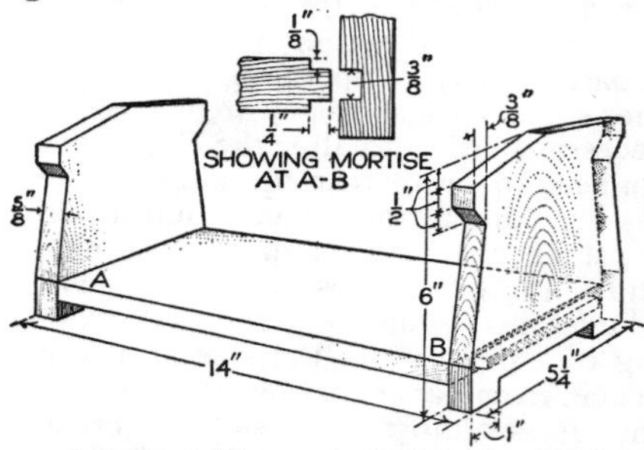

A Bookrack That can be Made in Any Wood to Match Other Furniture

cut out for mortises to fit the shelf tenons.

In assembling the parts, they are

glued in place, and clamped with hand screws until the glue has set. Any of the good mission stains, properly applied, will give a finished appearance to the bookrack.

A Paper Gas Pipe

When one fits up an attic or a back room as a workshop, it is seldom that a gas connection is available on about

The Tube is Run Out Horizontally from the Chandelier to the Wall Where the Drop is Connected

the same level as the workbench so that a Bunsen burner and soldering apparatus may be operated. To install the standard gas pipe, it would be necessary either to alter the chandelier connection or to tear up some of the plaster, the former plan resulting in a rather conspicuous display of pipe and the latter in considerable expense. The following method permits the rolling of a pipe, about the size of a lead pencil, from paper that becomes so stiff that it is almost impossible to crush it between the thumb and fingers. This small inconspicuous pipe may be run directly from the side of the valve on the chandelier to the wall, as shown in the sketch, thence down some corner formed by a door jamb or window frame, which protects it and renders it almost unnoticeable.

A good grade of tough Manila paper should be procured and cut into strips, about 18 in. long and wide enough to build up a tube at least $\frac{1}{32}$ in. in diameter. This will require from 4 to 6 in., according to the thickness of the paper. A piece of ¼-in. round iron or hard wood, 20 in. long, is procured and carefully oiled or greased. Apply a coat of strong fish glue to one of these pieces of paper, omitting a strip along one edge, about 1 in. wide. Using the outspread fingers of each hand, begin with the unglued edge and roll the paper around the wood. As it is impossible to get the paper uniformly tight with the fingers, select a smooth place on the table and then roll the newly formed tube forward by means of a piece of board, as shown in the illustration. On the return stroke lift the board. In this way it is possible to get a tight, smooth tube. Immediately withdraw the core, twisting it slightly in a reverse direction if it tends to stick. Before using the core again, make sure it is free from glue and regrease it. When a sufficient number of tubes have been made and hardened, neatly trim the ends off squarely, and then form an equal number of short tubes, about 2 in. long, by winding a strip of glued paper on a large wire nail until a diameter is reached that will fit snugly into the pipes already made. The joints may then be set up with strong glue and finally wrapped with two thicknesses of paper on the outside. The construction of these joints is shown in the cross section.

The connection with the chandelier can be made by means of a metal tube soldered in at a point where the regular valve will cut off all connection with the paper piping when it is not in use. This metal tube should be coated with thick shellac, and the paper tube slipped over it for 1 in. or more, after which the joint should be given several additional coats on the outside. A small regulating gas cock can be attached to the lower end of the piping, and if this is rigidly fastened to the wall, or casing, the connecting and disconnecting of the rubber tubing will not disturb the piping in any way.—Contributed by John D. Adams.

Rubbing Slats for a Washing Board

In an emergency, and to substitute something for a broken glass rubbing plate on an ordinary washing board, I fitted a series of 3/8-in. dowels horizontally across the board, closely together. This proved to be better than glass or zinc, as fabrics adhered to the wood dowels and caused them to revolve, making a more desirable rubbing surface and accomplishing the work of loosening the dirt in the fabric with far less effort than that necessary on the metal or glass board.—Contributed by H. M. Spamer, Vineland, N. J.

Catching Bugs Attracted by Light

Bugs, moths, and insects attracted by lights on summer evenings can be caught by means of sticky fly paper, suspended as shades around the lamps. Cuts in the shade allow the greater portion of the light to pass through and attract the bugs, which will surely be caught as they travel about the light onto the sticky paper. It is advisable to make two shades at the same time from a double sheet of the sticky paper, pasted, as when bought, with the sticky faces together so that the shades may be cut and handled easier.—Contributed by John J. Kolar, Maywood, Illinois.

Oilcans should be marked to indicate **the kind of oil in them.**

Needle Box for Talking Machines

An empty cigarette box can be easily changed to a useful container for talking-machine needles, as shown in the sketch. Take a fairly heavy card, trim it to the same length as the box, then bend and crease it, as shown at A, and glue the short, upright side to the inside of the box. Cut another card to the shape B, so that the depth C equals the inside depth of the box, and the side D is as long as its width. The side E should equal the inclined length of the card A, and is glued upon it when B is in position. The three compartments may be suitably labeled as indicated.—Contributed by V. A. Rettich, New York, N. Y.

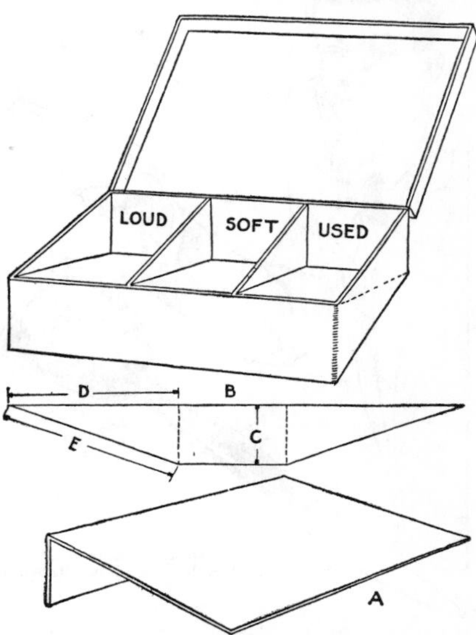

Three Compartments are Provided with Sloping Bottoms in a Neat Box for the Needles

Trick of Taking Dollar Bill from Apple

A rather pleasing, yet puzzling, deception is to pass a dollar bill into the interior of an examined lemon or apple. This can be accomplished in several ways, either mechanically or purely by sleight of hand. The mechanical method, of course, is the easier and really just as effective. In performing, a plate with three apples is first ex-

The Dollar Bill is Hidden in the Knife Handle That Cuts the Apple

hibited, and the audience is given choice of any one for use in the experiment. The selected one is tossed out for examination and then returned to the performer, who places it in full view of the spectators while he makes the dollar bill vanish. Taking the knife he cuts the apple into two pieces, requesting the audience to select one of them. Squeezing this piece he extracts the dollar bill therefrom. The entire secret is in the unsuspected article—the table knife.

The knife is prepared by boring out the wooden handle to make it hollow. Enough space must be made to hold a dollar bill. The knife lies on the plate with the fruit, the open end facing the performer. After the bill has been made to vanish and the examined apple returned to the entertainer, he takes it and cuts it in half. One of the halves is chosen, the performer impaling it on the end of the knife blade and holding it out to view. While still holding the knife he turns the blade downward and grasps the half apple and crushes it with a slight pass toward the knife-handle end where the bill is grasped along with the apple, which makes a perfect illusion of taking the bill out of the apple.

As to the disappearance of the dollar bill, there are many ways in which this may be accomplished. Perhaps the method requiring the least practice is to place the bill in the trousers pocket, and then show the audience that the latter is empty. This can be done by rolling the bill to small compass, and pushing it into the extreme upper corner of the pocket where it will remain undetected while the pocket is pulled out for inspection. Other combinations can be arranged with the use of the knife, which is simple to make and very inexpensive.

Guide for Making Buttonholes

It is almost impossible to make a perfect buttonhole in the ordinary manner by hand without a guide. The illustration shows a very simple guide that can be easily made by anyone. Procure two pieces of tin, or sheet brass, cut them as shown, and drill holes in them large enough for a needle, so that it will be easy to fasten them to the cloth with basting thread. Cut the buttonhole slot, then punch a hole at the end with an ordinary belt punch. Such a punch can be purchased from a local hardware dealer in any size. In making the buttonhole stitch, keep the

The Form of the Buttonhole is Cut in the Edges of the Two Pieces of Metal

needle close against the metal edge of the guide, as shown.—Contributed by A. L. Kerbaugh, Allentown, Pa.

¶An easy way to put varnish in the grooves of a tennis racket is to use a medicine dropper.

A Child's Playhouse

The child's playhouse is an expensive luxury, if it is purchased ready to set up, but by following the instructions given herewith a large and inexpensive one may be constructed.

Procure about 100 ft. of 1¾ by 1½-in. boards, and saw out pieces, as shown. With the use of iron brackets instead of nails, it will be found much easier to construct than if the corners are mortised and nailed or glued. The frame will also be much stronger.

When the frame is completed, burlap is tacked on to make the covering. The burlap can be purchased cheaply, and the best color to use is either green, red or brown. This material should be fastened on the different sections before they are hinged together. To prevent the burlap from unraveling, turn the edges under before tacking them down.

The Covered Framework can be Used In or Outdoors, as Desired, and When Set Up and the Wings Swung Back, It Presents the Appearance of a House

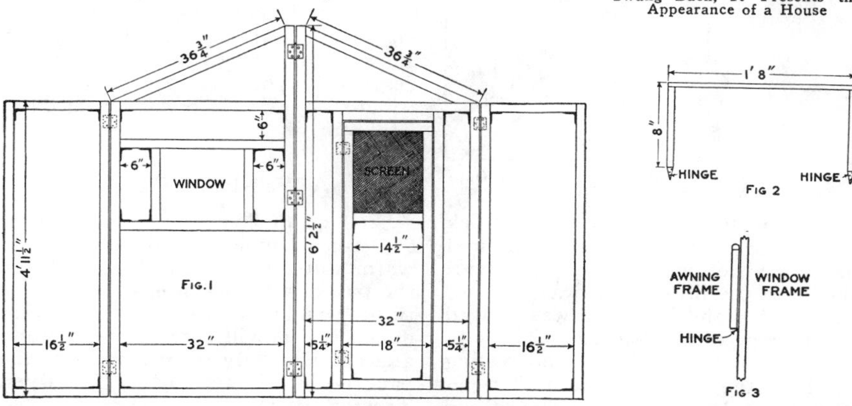

The Entire Framework is Held Together with Brackets, and is Hinged at the Joints, so That It can be Folded Up and Put into a Small Space, the Sections being Covered with Colored Burlap to Make Them Appear Solid. On the Right is Shown the Awning-Frame Construction

A piece of wire screen is used for the door. An old piece will do, if it is well coated with black or dark-green paint. It is then tacked on the inside of the door. Fasten the different parts together with the hinges. The hinges are fastened on the inside of the side wings, and on the outside of the two front pieces. With the hinges placed in this manner, the house can be folded into a small space.

For the one built by the writer, green burlap was used, and by trimming the door and window frames along the edges with white paint a very pretty effect was produced.

A small awning was made over the window, which improved the appearance very much. Roller shades on the door and window and an electric door bell completed a very neat and practical playhouse.

Removing Basketball from Closed-Bottom Receptacle

The closed-bottom basket used in the game of basketball is so high that it is difficult to remove the ball after a goal is made. Generally a long stick is used for this purpose, but I desired to have a better way, and the device shown in the illustration was the outcome. A light iron rod was hinged to the edge of the basket and bent to its inner shape, the lower end resting at about the center of the basket. A rope was attached to the lower end and run up and over a sheave pulley attached to the basket support, then down so it could be easily grasped. When a goal is made, it is only necessary to give a pull on the rope for throwing the ball out of the basket.—Contributed by Annie B. Currine, San Diego, Cal.

The Iron Rod in the Basket Throws the Ball Out When the Rope is Pulled

Testing Dry Batteries

For testing dry batteries or any low-voltage current, take an ordinary thermometer and wind around the mercury bulb enough wire to make about 10 ohms resistance. This will make a good tester. A dry cell of about 2 volts attached to the ends of the wire should generate enough heat to expand the mercury about four degrees in one-half minute.

This tester is not as fast as a voltmeter, nor has it as wide a range, but it is reasonably accurate, and by using a battery of known voltage, the winding can be increased or diminished to allow the mercury to expand as many degrees as desired per volt.—Contributed by E. H. Kimbrough, Bartlett, Kan.

A Wall-Paper Cleaner

To 1 qt. of flour add about 2 oz. of 90-per-cent ammonia and enough lukewarm water to make a dough. Wipe the paper with this preparation while turning and kneading it as in making dough. This will take up the dirt and a clean side is always presented to the paper.—Contributed by F. C. Myer, Tacoma, Wash.

A Trunk Mystery

Doubtless every person has seen the trunk mystery, the effect of which is as follows: A trunk, mounted upon four legs, is brought out on the stage and proven to be empty by turning it all the way around to show that there is nothing on the back, whereupon pieces of plate glass are placed along the back, sides, and front, the trunk is closed and given a swift turn and then opened, when to the amazement of all, a lady steps out appearing to come from nowhere. The secret of this trick is very simple, and the trunk can be made up very cheaply.

In the back of the trunk there is a movable panel with a shelf exactly the same size as the panel attached to its bottom, forming a right angle, the corner of which is hinged to the bottom of the trunk. The back panel can be turned in until it rests on the bottom of the trunk and, when this is done, the shelf part rises and takes its place, making the back of the trunk appear solid.

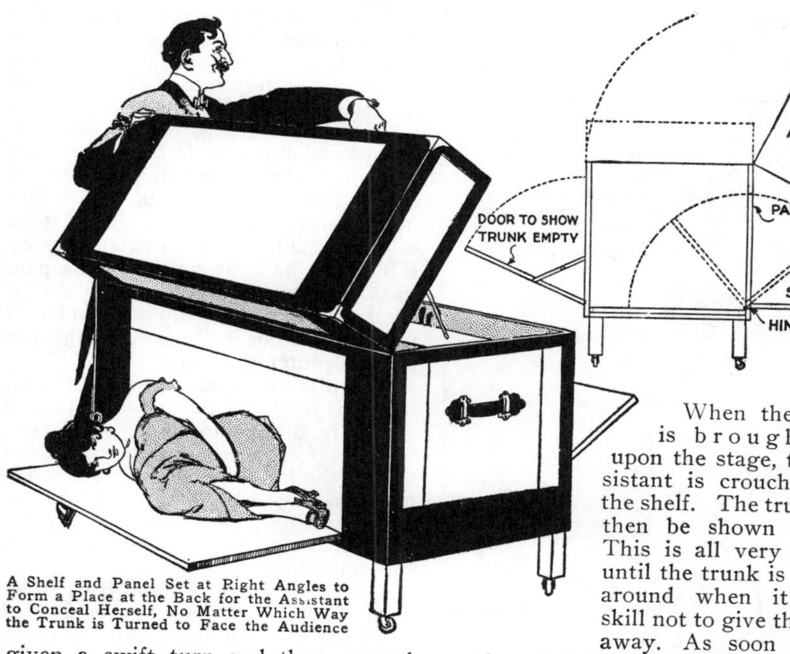

A Shelf and Panel Set at Right Angles to Form a Place at the Back for the Assistant to Conceal Herself, No Matter Which Way the Trunk is Turned to Face the Audience

When the trunk is brought out upon the stage, the assistant is crouching on the shelf. The trunk can then be shown empty. This is all very simple until the trunk is turned around when it takes skill not to give the trick away. As soon as the performer starts to turn the trunk around, the assistant shifts her weight on the panel, thus causing it to fall inward and bring the shelf up to make the back appear solid. The assistant is now in the trunk, and the back can be shown clear of any apparatus. When the trunk is turned to the front again, the lady repeats the previous operation in the opposite direction, thus bringing her body to the back of the trunk again.

To make the trick appear more difficult, glass plates are made to insert in the ends, front and back of the trunk. In making the trunk, have the back the same size as the bottom. Fit the piece of glass for the back into a light frame, similar to a window frame. This frame is hinged to the bottom of the trunk and is ½ in. smaller all around than the back of the trunk, so that the two pieces of glass can be put in the ends and also allow the back frame and glass to fall flush in the bottom of the trunk. A few rubber bumpers are fastened in the bottom of the trunk to catch the glass without noise as it falls. The best way to work this is for the performer to let the frame down with his right hand while he is closing up the front with his left.

As soon as the trunk is closed, the assistant again shifts her weight to cause the panel to fall in and then the trunk can be turned to show the back, or whirled around and turned to the front again, then opened up, whereupon the assistant steps out, bows to the audience, and leaves the stage.

How to Make a Candy-Floss Machine

Every person is familiar with candy floss, made at stands on fair grounds, or carnivals, in an expensive whirling

The Disk is Driven by a Small Battery Motor and Melted Sugar is Spun Out into Floss

machine. It is not necessary to wait for a fair or a carnival to have a bunch of candy floss, as it can be made at home much quicker than making taffy candy.

The device for making the candy floss consists of ordinary things that can be had in any home, and usually a boy has a battery motor of some kind that will furnish the power.

Procure a tin pan, the shape of an ordinary dish pan and of medium size; cut a hole about one-half the diameter of the pan in the bottom and solder in a conical-shaped piece similar to a cake pan, allowing it to extend up inside about half the height of the pan. Fasten supports to the pan so that a Bunsen burner can be set under it where the flame will pass through the conical center opening.

Mount a small battery motor with its shaft vertical, pulley end up, and centering the conical hole, on a base, which supports the pan. Procure a can cover, similar to that used on coffee cans, and fasten it with solder to the pulley on the motor shaft, being careful to locate it centrally so that it will run smoothly.

Close to the bottom and in the rim of the can cover, make a number of small holes with a prickpunch, or other sharp-pointed tool. Wire the motor to the battery, and the candy-floss machine is ready for use.

Light the burner, start the motor, and pour a little granulated sugar in the revolving can cover. As the sugar is melted, it will be spun out in floss form through the small holes into the pan receiver.—Contributed by Herbert Hahn, Chicago, Ill.

Enlarging Pictures

A very simple and sufficiently accurate way of enlarging pictures by means of a pencil holder and elastic is shown in the illustration. The picture to be enlarged is fastened to a table top or drawing board, and the paper on which it is to be drawn is placed directly below it. A small brad or tack is driven into the board at A, the location depending on the desired size of the enlarged picture, and the elastic is attached to it. The pencil holder B is fastened to the other end of the elastic over the drawing paper. A pointer, or a knot, is placed in the elastic at C. The pencil holder consists of a stick of wood turned into a handle with a hole bored centrally for a pencil.

In use, the pencil is moved over the drawing paper while the knot or pointer is watched, to keep it following the lines of the original drawing. The stretch of the elastic is sufficient to enlarge the parts equally, as well vertically as horizontally.—Contributed by Wm. Weitzsacker, Buffalo, N. Y.

The Size of the Enlarged Picture Depends on the Length of the Elastic and the Spacing of Pencil and Pointer

Distance Chart for Wireless Stations

The amateur wireless telegrapher may be troubled more or less regarding distances from other stations. The difficulty can be overcome by following a plan similar to that of a parcel-post map. A map should be selected covering the desired territory. With the home station as center, circles should be drawn to diameters corresponding in length to the scale used on the map. By measuring the distance other stations may be from any of these circles, their cross-country distance from the home station can be determined at a glance.—Contributed by E. L. Hartlett, Wausau, Wis.

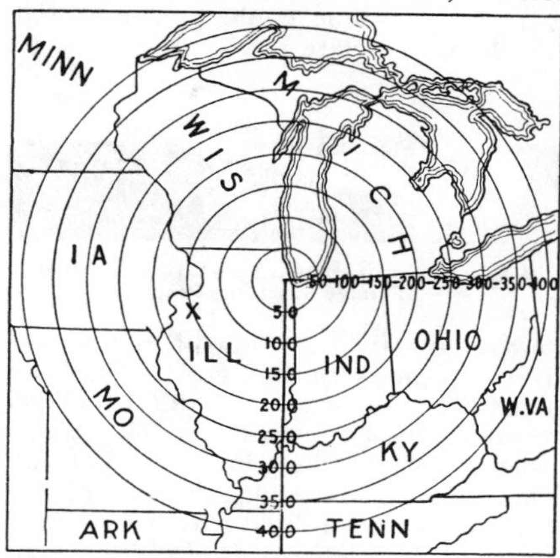

Circles on a Map the Same as for Parcel Post to Designate Wireless Distances

A Carrier for Fishhooks

Hooks that are attached to gut or short strings are difficult to carry and to keep in good shape for use on a line. I made a carrier that overcame this trouble, from a block of wood. The block is ½ in. in thickness with brads driven into one end, for engaging the loops on the gut or string, while the hook is caught on the opposite end, the block being just long enough for the short line. The hooks will be held securely, and the block can be carried in the pocket.—Contributed by Victor E. Carpenter, South Bend, Ind.

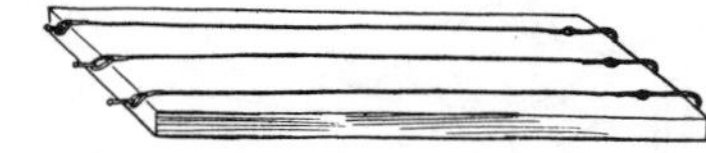

The String is Drawn Taut over the Block, and the Hooks are Caught in the Block End

A Substitute for a Pen

Recently I was hard pressed for a pen, and as none could be found and the hour was late it was necessary to find a substitute. I fashioned a pen from a piece of boxwood, and was agreeably surprised at the excellent results obtained with it. The wood was sharpened like a lead pencil at one end, and a groove was cut out of the tapered part to hold the ink.—Contributed by Richard F. Pohle, Lynn, Massachusetts.

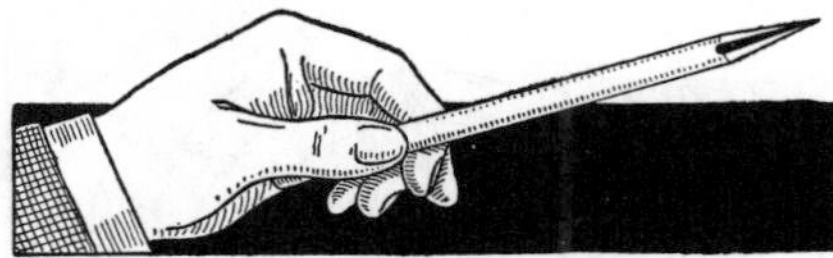

A Notch Cut in the Tapered Part of a Wood Stick Forms a Substitute Pen

---

¶A very convenient method of keeping shipping tags at hand is to slip them on a desk spindle.

A Bucket-Ball Game

This is a new indoor game which follows out in principle the regular baseball play. It is an exciting and interesting pastime, and while a certain amount of skill is required to score runs, a person who cannot play the regular game can score as many runs, and as often, as the best players in the national leagues.

Anyone that is just a little handy with tools can make the necessary parts for this game. The tools required are a hammer and a saw, and the materials consist of some finishing nails; three strips of wood, 6 ft. long, 2 in. wide, and 1 in. thick; two strips, 18 in. long, 4 in. wide, and 1 in. thick; four strips, 24 in. long, 2 in. wide, and 1 in. thick; two strips, 18 in. long, 2 in. wide, and 1 in. thick; two blocks, 4 in. square, and 1 in. thick, and four wood buckets.

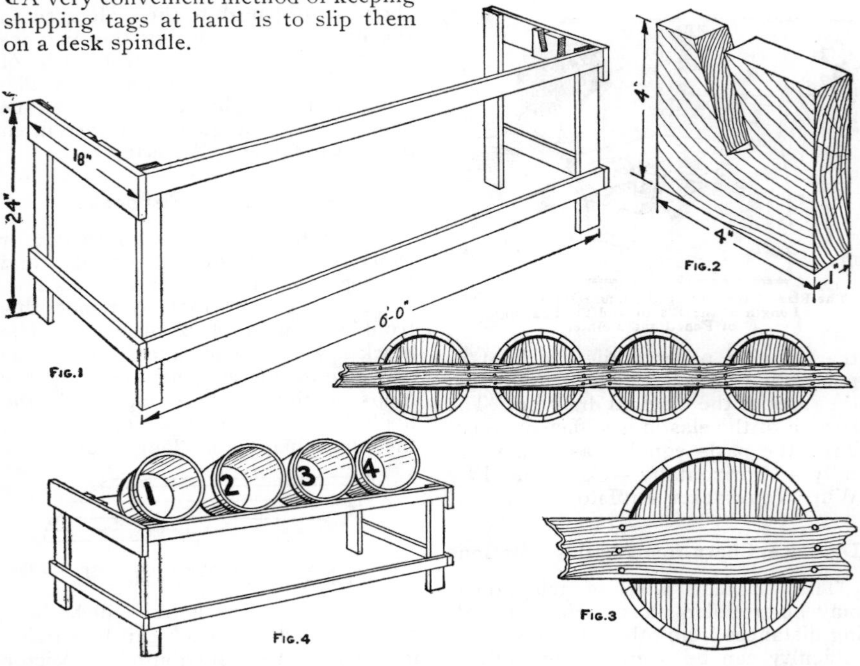

The Frame is Made Up without a Back, to Hold the Buckets at an Angle That Makes It Difficult to Toss the Ball So That It will Stay in Any One of Them

The Player must Throw the Ball So That It will Enter and Stay in One of the Buckets, Which Designates the Base Hits by the Number in Its Bottom

A frame is built up as shown, 6 ft. long, 18 in. wide, and 24 in. high, without a back. One of the long pieces is fastened to the bottoms of the buckets as shown, spacing the latter equally on the length of the piece. This piece is then set in notches cut in the blocks of wood at an angle of 45°. These blocks are fastened to the upper crosspieces at the ends of the frame. The upper part of the buckets rest on the upper front piece of the frame.

The rules for playing the game are as follows: Three baseballs are used. The players stand about 10 ft. distant and in front of the buckets. Each player, or side, is only permitted to throw three balls an inning, irrespective of the number of runs scored. Any kind of delivery is permitted, but an underhand throw will be found most successful. The buckets are numbered from 1 to 4, and represent, respectively, one, two, and three-base hits, and home runs. The one in which the ball stays designates the run.

Plays are figured as in a regular ball game. For instance, if a ball should stay in bucket No. 2 and the next in bucket No. 3, the first man would be forced home, counting one run, and leaving one man on third base. If the next ball stays in bucket No. 4, the man on third base is forced home, as well as the one who scored the home run, making three runs for that inning. The runs should be scored as made, to guard against confusion and argument.—Contributed by Walter Talley, Pottsville, Pa.

A Staple Puller

With nothing but ordinary tools the removing of staples is tedious and difficult work. If a suitable-sized wire nail is bent like a fishhook and the hook part driven under the staple, the latter can be easily pulled out by grasping and pulling the nail with a hammer in the usual way.—Contributed by R. Neland, Minneapolis, Minn.

A Dissolving Coin Trick

This is a very simple and effective trick. The articles required to perform the trick are, a glass of water, a silver dollar, a handkerchief and a watch crystal, or round piece of glass, the size of a silver dollar. Conceal the crystal in the palm of the hand and show the audience the dollar. Hold the handkerchief in one hand and place the hand holding the silver dollar and crystal under it so that the crystal can be grasped by the hand holding the handkerchief. Remove the dollar by holding it in the palm of the hand and slip it, unobserved, into a pocket.

Ask some one in the audience to hold the handkerchief with the inclosed crystal and ask him to let it drop into the glass of water as the handkerchief covers both. The falling glass can be heard, but upon removing the handkerchief nothing can be seen of the dollar or watch crystal. The circular glass disk cannot be seen in the water. —Contributed by Albert Biery, Spokane, Wash.

A Fruit-Jar Opener

The accompanying sketch shows a handy device for turning up and unscrewing the covers on glass fruit jars. The loop is slipped over the cover and the handle turned in the direction of the arrow. To unscrew the cover, the tool is turned over and the handle turned in the opposite direction.

The loop should be just large enough to slip over the cover easily.

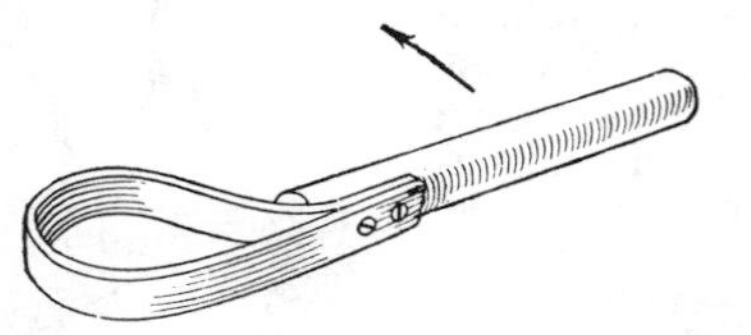

The Loop in the Leather Grips the Cap Tightly When the Handle is Turned as the Arrow Indicates

It is made of leather and fastened to the wood handle with screws.—Contributed by J. B. Downer, Seattle, Wash.

Anti-Tangle Safety Pin

A small disk of rubber or leather, placed on a safety pin as shown in Fig. 1, will prevent the fabric which is fastened by the pin from becoming tangled in the spring loop. The manner of using the pin is shown in Fig. 2.

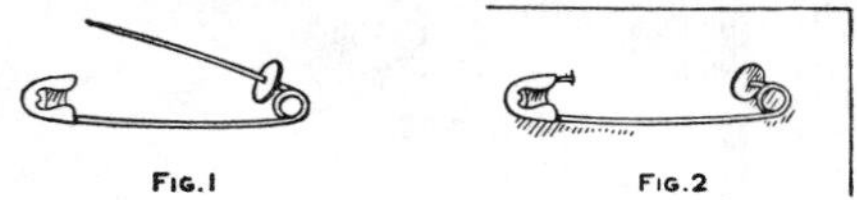

The Small Disk on the Pin Prevents the Goods from Becoming Tangled in the Coil

How to Nickel or Silverplate Iron by Friction

The following methods of plating iron with nickel and silver appeared in a recent issue of a German paper. In nickelplating iron, a thin coating of copper is first produced on it by rubbing on a solution of 20 parts sulphate of copper, 5 parts sulphuric acid and 100 parts of water. After the copper plate has been formed rub over it, with a rag, a solution of 3 parts tin, 6 parts nickel and 1 part iron in 100 parts of hydrochloric acid and 3 parts of sulphuric acid. If finally the object is rubbed with a rag that has been dipped in finely pulverized zinc, a nickel deposit will be formed on the copper. The thickness of the deposit of nickel can be increased by repeating the two last operations.

According to a recent patent, a silver coating can be produced by dissolving freshly precipitated chloride of silver in a solution of hyposulphite of soda, 1.1 parts to 10 parts of water, and adding to this solution 180 parts spirits of sal ammoniac and then stirring in 800 parts of finely washed chalk. This mixture is applied and rubbed until it dries on the object being silvered, and the result is a brilliant deposit of pure silver.

¶A good filling for cracks in old furniture is made of shellac, either melted by heat or dissolved in alcohol to make a thick paste.

A Homemade Cradle

The cradle shown in the sketch can be made quickly and easily at home and will be found far more serviceable than, and possessing several advantages over, the ones purchased. It is made of a clothes basket, an iron rod and two ordinary chairs. It can be taken down and the parts used for other purposes. The upper portion of the rod prevents the chairs from slipping. A light cloth can be placed over the rod, in tent fashion, to keep flies out, while at the same time permitting air for ventilation.—Contributed by Bert Verne, San Diego, Cal.

A Clothes Basket Supported with a Rod between Two Chairs Makes a Good Cradle

A Removable Post

It is often desirable to have football and baseball grounds in public parks roped in during the game, but after the game the ropes and stakes must be removed. To drive in iron stakes and then remove them is hard work and requires considerable time. The sketch shows a much better way. A piece of 2-in. pipe, about 18 in. long, is sunk level with the ground in the right location for a post. The post is made of 1½-in. pipe of the length desired. This will just fit inside of the 2-in. pipe. A wood plug is fitted in the upper end of the pipe in the ground to keep out dirt when the post is removed.—Contributed by Abner B. Shaw, N. Dartmouth, Mass.

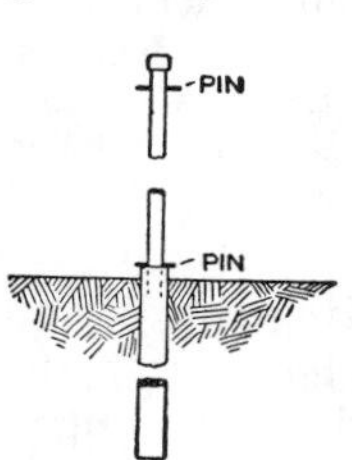

String-and-Ball Trick

The stopping of a ball on a string at any desired point is understood by almost every person, but to make one that can be worked only when the operator so desires is a mysterious trick. Procure a wooden ball, about 2 in. in diameter, and cut it into two equal parts. Insert a small peg in the flat surface of one half, a little to one side of the center, as shown, and allow the end to project about $\frac{3}{16}$ in. The flat surface of the other half is cut out concave, as shown, to make it ½ in. deep. The two halves are then glued together, and a hole is drilled centrally on the division line for a string to pass through.

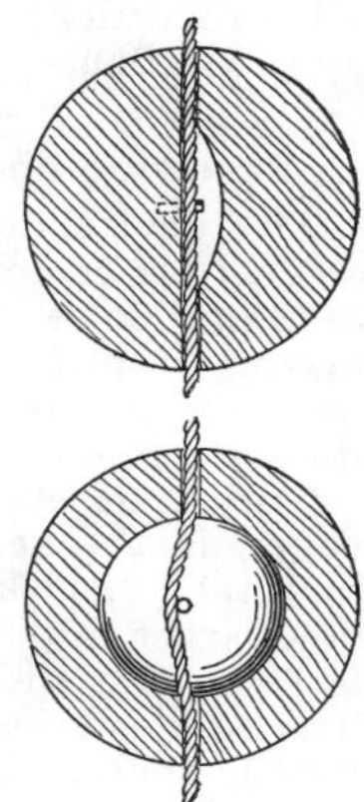

To do the trick, hold an end of the string in each hand tightly and draw it taut with the ball at the top, then slacken the string enough to allow the ball to slide down the string. To stop the ball at any point, pull the string taut.

Before handing the ball and string out for inspection, push the string from each side of the ball and turn it slightly to throw it off the peg. This will allow the string to pass freely through the ball, and it cannot be stopped at will. To replace the string reverse the operation.—Contributed by Wm. O. Swett, Chicago.

Wall-Paper Cleaner

The following mixture I have used with the best results for years. Thoroughly mix together 3 pt. of wheat flour and 1 pt. of powdered whiting, then add sufficient water to make a dough. To clean a dirty papered wall, take a piece of the dough that can be easily grasped in the hand, press it against the surface and make a long stroke downward. During the process of cleaning, keep kneading the dirt into the dough. The preparation can be mixed in any amount desired by using the proportions named.—Contributed by C. W. Bause, Jr., E. Troy, Wis.

Revolving Shaft without Power

The device illustrated seems paradoxical for it apparently works without any power being applied to it, making from two to three revolutions per hour, which, though slow, is nevertheless motion, requiring energy.

The shaft A is supported on the edges, in the bearings B and C, of a tank, D. A disk, E, having a central hole larger in diameter than the shaft, is located at the middle of the latter. The disk is supported by 12 or more cotton ropes, F. The tank is filled to the level G with water. The lower ropes, being immersed in the water, shrink and lift the disk slightly above the center in the position of an eccentric, as shown by the dotted lines in the sketch. The center of gravity of the disk in this position, being higher and slightly to one side of the shaft, the disk has a tendency to turn around. The motion drives the next rope into the water where it becomes soaked and shrinkage takes place again, lifting the disk to a higher position, while the rope coming out of the water dries

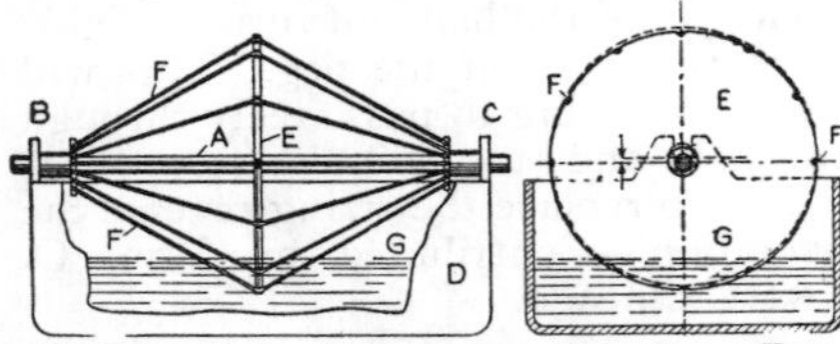

The Expansion and Contraction of the Ropes Keep the Disk Up and to One Side of the Center

out. The ropes emerging from the water but not yet thoroughly dry cause the upper part of the disk to be in an eccentric position laterally with reference to the center of the shaft, thus causing the center of gravity to be not only above but also slightly to one side.—Contributed by Charles Roberts, Brooklyn, N. Y.

A Paper-Bag Holder

A holder, to accommodate the different-sized bags used in a store, can be easily made of a board, 6 in. wide and 30 in. long. One edge of the board is cut with notches similar to the teeth of a ripsaw and their back-sloping edges are drilled to admit a nail point. A sufficient quantity of bags is placed in a pile and a nail is driven through the edge near their upper ends, and the projecting point of the nail is stuck into one of the holes. Proceed in the same manner with bags of other sizes. To remove a bag, take hold of the lower end of the outermost one and tear it from the nail. Be sure to drive the nails through the bags close to the top.—Contributed by Abner B. Shaw, N. Dartmouth, Mass.

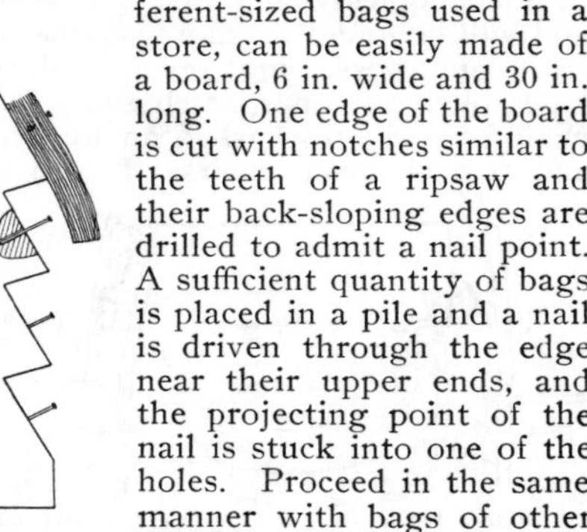

Covering for Chalk Trays

The chalk trays fitted at the lower edge of blackboards soon collect considerable chalk dust and the chalk sticks dropped into it are, therefore, disagreeable to handle. A simple way of keeping the sticks clean is to cover the trays with wire mesh which is shaped like a tray but not so deep as the chalk tray. Thus the chalk dust will fall through this screen and be out of the way of the sticks.

A Curtain Hanger

A close-coiled spring, about 1/4 in. in diameter, makes a much better hanger for a short curtain than a small rod. The spring should be about 1 in. shorter than the width of the window and fastened with screwhooks. The spring is preferable not only because it is less apt to tear the fabric, as it will give some if the curtain is pulled, but also for the reason that it is much easier to put it through the hem than the rod.—Contributed by Walter Ramm, New York City.

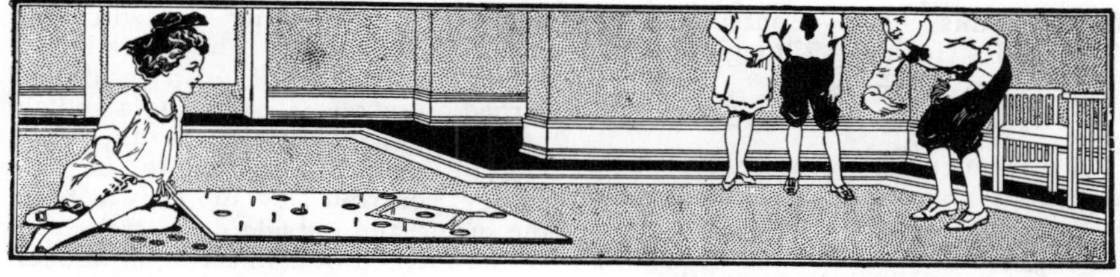

Joints for Model Aeroplane

In constructing model or toy aeroplanes the strips used are so slender that it is difficult to join them at the ends with brads without splitting them. If glue is used, there is danger of breaking two or more ribs, should it be necessary to remove a broken or defective rib.

An empty 22-gauge long cartridge can be formed into an elbow that will connect the framework accurately, give more strength than glue or brads, and allow a broken section to be removed without spoiling the other part of the framework. File off the end A, Fig. 1, so that the shell will form a straight tube, and file as shown in Fig. 2 with a three-cornered file. Then bend the two sections into the form shown in Fig. 3 and solder the adjacent edges. File off the rough spots and drill small holes, as shown, for the insertion of

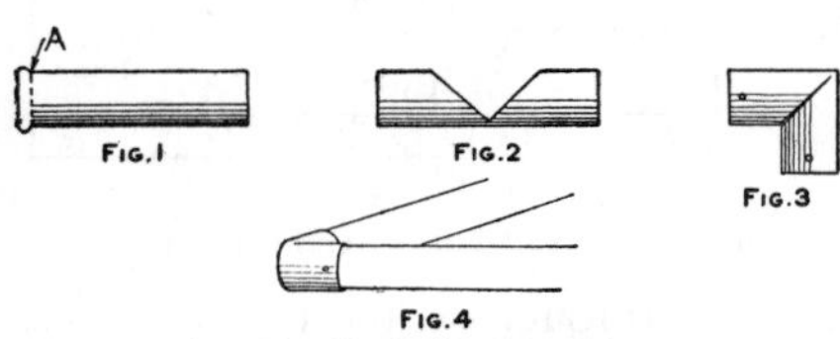

Cartridge Shells Used for Joints

pins to hold the wood strips. Much time in the building of model aeroplanes can be saved by keeping a supply of these elbows on hand.

ℭA deep rust on tools may be removed by soaking them in a strong, hot bath of potash and water for a half hour, then dipping them into a solution of 1 part muriatic acid in 2 parts cold water.

An Indoor Baseball Game

An indoor game of baseball may be played on a board 5 ft. long and 3 ft. wide. A diamond is laid off at one end of the board and pins represent-

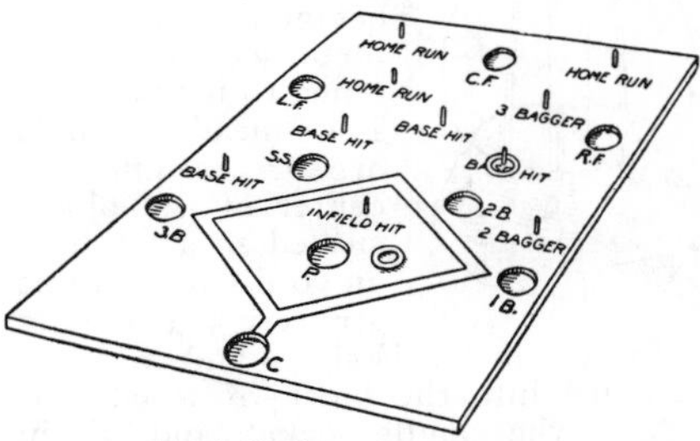

Baseball Diamond on a Board

ing the hits are attached to the board so they will project above the surface. The locations of the players are designated by holes bored part way in the wood with an expansive bit. These holes should be large enough to receive the rings easily. The rings may be gaskets or they may be made of rope, and should have an inside diameter of about 3 in.

Only two persons can play at this game. The distance from the board to the thrower may be from 10 to 100 ft., according to the size of the room. This distance should be marked and each thrower stand at the same place.

If the ring is thrown over one of the "base-hit" or "two-bagger" pegs, it shows the number of bases secured. Throwing a ring over one of the "home-run" pegs means a score, of course. The "infield hit" secures a base. If the ring slips into a hole, that counts one out. A player must throw until he has three outs. The score is kept for the runs made.—Contributed by Francis P. Hobart, Willoughby, O.

A Lantern for the Camp

A very desirable lantern for camp use is one that utilizes a candle instead of a lamp. Such a lantern can be made of an ordinary oil-lantern globe, a block of wood, some galvanized wire, a few nails, a metal collar, and a hood of zinc or tin. The block of wood is cut octagonally and the metal collar is fastened to it as shown. Four headless nails are driven into the center of the block, spaced so as to hold an ordinary candle securely. The wire is formed into a U-shape and the ends fastened into the block of wood outside of the candle socket, and within the globe circle. A conical piece of tin or zinc is formed to fit over the top of the globe as shown. As the candle does not require much draft there is no opening provided.—Contributed by Addison W. Baird, M. D., New York City.

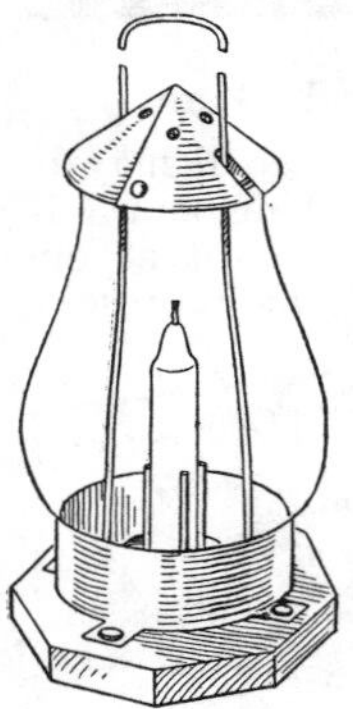

Electric Lights Controlled from Two or More Switches

Many times it is quite an advantage to have a lamp or group of lamps so connected that the current may be turned on or off by any one of a number of different switches. For example, the lights in a long hall or passage-way can be lighted or extinguished by operating a switch at either end of the hall; the lights in the upper and lower halls of a residence, turned on or off by operating a switch upstairs or downstairs as the case might demand; the lights in the garage, controlled by switches at both the inside and outside door, etc.

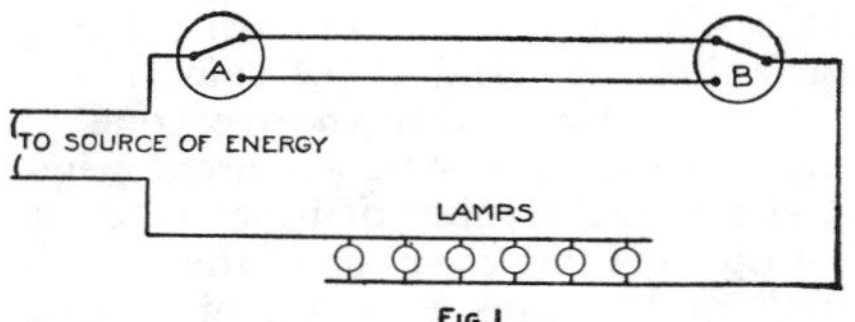

Fig. 1
Lamps Controlled from Two Switches

The method of connecting a number of lamps to a circuit so that they can be controlled from either of two switches is shown in Fig. 1. The switches, as illustrated in this drawing, are in such a position that the lamps will burn. If either of the switches be thrown to its other position (there are two positions for each switch), the circuit will be opened. The operation then of either switch will again close the circuit.

The method of connecting a number of lamps to a circuit so that they can be controlled by any number of switches is shown in Fig. 2. The switches are all in such a position that the lamps will burn. If any one of the switches be turned to its second position (all the switches have two positions), the circuit will be open. The dotted lines at switch C show the connections through switch C after it has been operated. Operating switch D then will again close the circuit, by using the dotted lines in switches C and D. The wiring for the control of lamps, as just indicated, must comply with the underwriters' requirements, and also city requirements, if the work be done in a place having city regulations for electric wiring.

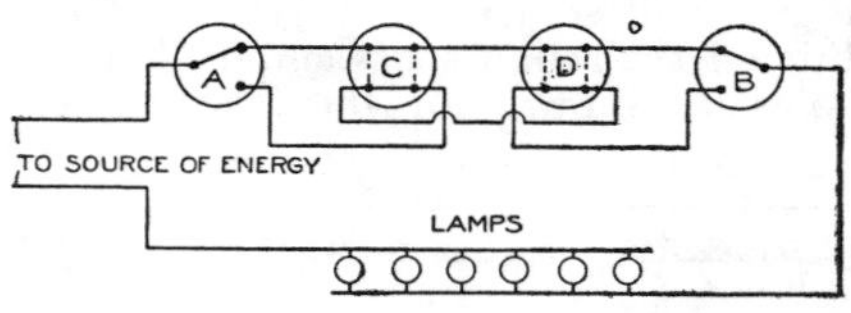

Fig. 2
Lamps Controlled by Any Number of Switches

¶Wire netting may be cut by laying it on the side edge of a spade and striking it with a hammer.

Electric Score Board for Indoor Games

A very satisfactory electric score board, for use in scoring basketball and other games played indoors, is shown in the illustration. It is constructed entirely of wood, but should be lined with asbestos board or sheathing. The dimensions are a matter of choice, but one 4 ft. long, 2 ft. wide and 18 in. deep is a good size. The back of the box is provided with two cleats, each 2½ ft. long, fastened at each end. This allows a projection of 3 in. at the top and bottom, for fastening the score board to the wall. The manner of construction is shown in Fig. 1, and a cross section of the box, in Fig. 2.

The front of the box should be fastened with screws so as to make its removal easy in case of repairs. This part of the box carries the frame for inserting the numbers and the words "Home Team" and "Visitors," as shown in Fig. 3. As the words are a permanent fixture, the cards carrying them are fastened to the front. At the end of these words a frame is constructed as shown in Fig. 4, in which the cards having the numbers are inserted in slides.

Numerals and letters can be cut out of heavy cardboard or tin. The design of a letter having sharp angles and straight edges, as shown in Fig. 5, is very easily cut out with a chisel. The method of cutting is shown in Fig. 6.

As portions of the letters and numerals, such as the center in an O, would fall out if cut entirely around, some way must be provided to hold the parts in place. The way to prepare stencils is to leave a portion uncut, which is known as a tie, and the letter will appear as shown in Fig. 7.

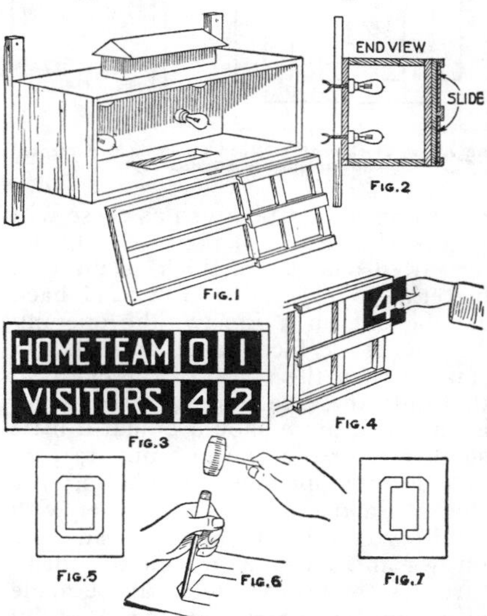

Electric Indoor Score Board, Showing Its Construction and Manner of Cutting Out the Letters and Numbers

The best method for making these letters and figures is to cut out the letter entirely, then to paste thin paper over the back and replace the parts removed by the cutting in their original position.—Contributed by James M. Kane, Doylestown, Pa.

A Mission Frame for an Alarm Clock

The old nickelplated alarm clock which usually adorns the kitchen mantel is, to say the least, not ornamental, and I improved the appearance of mine without lessening its usefulness by making a small case in mission style for it.

The sketch shows a design which is neat and easily made. Accurate dimensions cannot be given as these will vary with the size of the clock. Quarter-sawed oak, 1/4 in. thick, is the best material to use. The front and back can be cut on a jigsaw, the opening for the clock face being cut slightly smaller than the metal of the clock so that only the face shows. An opening in the back piece should be cut a little smaller than the one in front, to provide a free opening for winding the clock. Fasten the parts together with small round-head brass brads or screws and finish to match the furniture. A small desk clock can be made in a similar manner, using a cheap watch instead of the alarm clock.—Contributed by C. E. Hamann, Somerville, Mass.

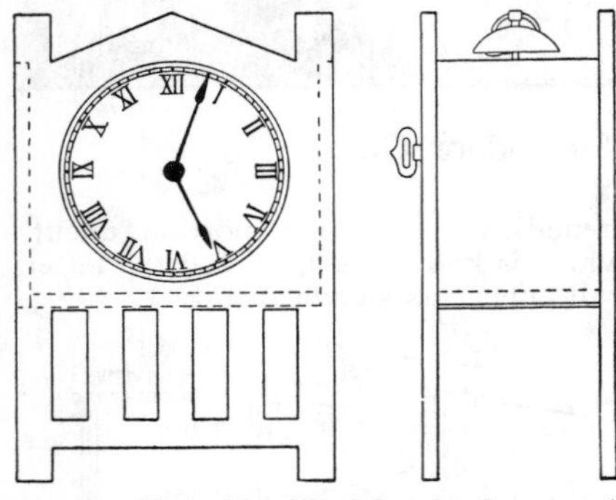
An Alarm Clock with a Wood Covering Ornamented and Finished in Mission Style

Mixing Sulphuric Acid

One of the first lessons given a student in chemistry is how to mix sulphuric acid with water. This would naturally be supposed to be very easy, yet, if it is not done right, it will surely result in injury to the person doing the mixing.

The specific gravity of sulphuric acid is 1.849 and, on account of its chemical attraction to water, great heat is set up or generated when the two are being mixed. If the acid is put into a jar and the water poured onto it, they will be temporarily separated, as the heavy acid will remain at the bottom, the chemical reaction taking place on the dividing line only. This soon generates heat which rapidly increases until steam is formed. Then the water boils over and finally becomes a bubbling volcano which readily ejects the contents of the jar. As the mixture at this moment is very hot, bad burns will be the result, which are aggravated by the biting of the acid; and clothing or anything that it comes in contact with will be ruined or badly damaged. Always remember this caution: add the acid to the water.

The following is the proper way to proceed in mixing sulphuric acid as well as other acids of lighter weight. Place the water in a jar and pour the acid in, a little at a time, stirring the mixture with a wooden stick. The mixing process will always heat the solution, which in many instances, must be allowed to cool before using.

A Chinese Pagoda

Fold the end of a long and narrow strip of paper over several times as shown in Fig. 1 and roll the entire length over a stick, then remove the roll and crease, or make it flat, as shown in Fig. 2. Make two cuts with a sharp knife centrally so that they reach to the several folds first made

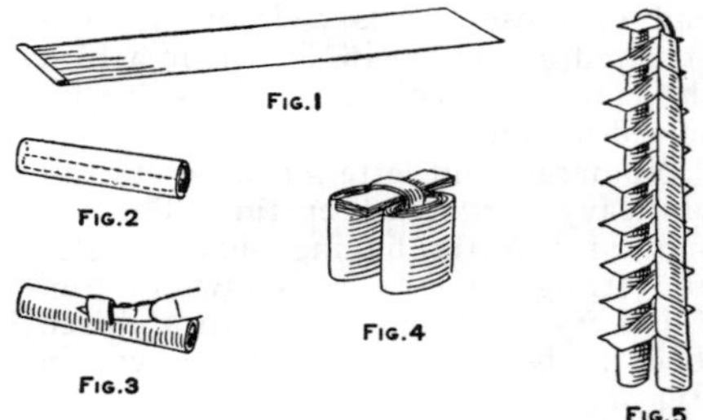

Stages in Making the Strip of Paper into the Finished Pagoda

on the inner end of the paper, then cut the fold in the paper between the cuts as shown in Fig. 3, and bend the ends over to form the shape in Fig. 4. Insert the knife blade under the first fold and draw it out until the paper takes the form in Fig. 5.

These pagodas can be made large or small, as desired, and also varied in several ways. Large ones can be formed and used as small tree ornaments. All that is necessary to make them high is to roll up one strip of paper on another in the rolling process.

In rolling up several strips, one on top of the other successively, various colored papers may be used and the appearance is greatly enhanced.—Contributed by Chas. C. Bradley, W. Toledo, O.

A Cuspidor Carrier

The task of handling cuspidors under all conditions is anything but pleasant, but the carrier shown in the sketch makes quite an improvement over ordinary methods. The carrier consists of an iron rod, 1/4 in. in diameter and 3 ft. long. One end is bent to fit around the neck of the cuspidor and the other is shaped into a handle.

Guide for Grinding a Plane Iron

When a plane iron has been sharpened a number of times, it often becomes so out of square that the edge cannot be made parallel with the bottom of the plane block, even by using the lateral adjustment. Where this happens, the plane iron must be reground. If an emery wheel mounted in a polishing head or lathe is at hand, this can be easily accomplished. Loosen the plane-iron cap and screw it down at right angles to the plane iron, also reverse the tool rest as shown in the sketch. In this way the work can be done better and more quickly than by the usual method.—Contributed by L. S. Uphoff, Schenectady, N. Y.

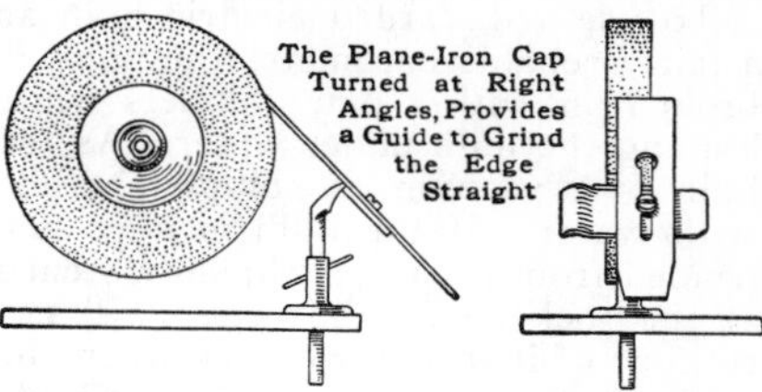

The Plane-Iron Cap Turned at Right Angles, Provides a Guide to Grind the Edge Straight

To Prevent Torch Lights from Smoking

In the shop or factory oil torches are sometimes used and much trouble is experienced by the excessive smoking of the flame. This occurs because too much carbon remains unburned, and can be remedied by first soaking the wick in a weak solution of acetic acid. A 5-per-cent solution can be purchased for a few cents at any drug store and will soak a great number of wicks. The acid is not poisonous unless taken internally.

A Lard and Fruit Presser

A very simple but handy device for pressing out lard, juices for jelly, or fruit for marmalade, is made from two boards, each 18 in. long, 3 in. wide and 1/2 in. thick, formed into the shape of paddles and hinged together. The hinge is made by running a wire through holes bored in one end of the paddles and twisting the ends together as shown. This presser will save the hands from stains and other effects of the juices.—Contributed by Julia A. White, Glenburg, Pa.

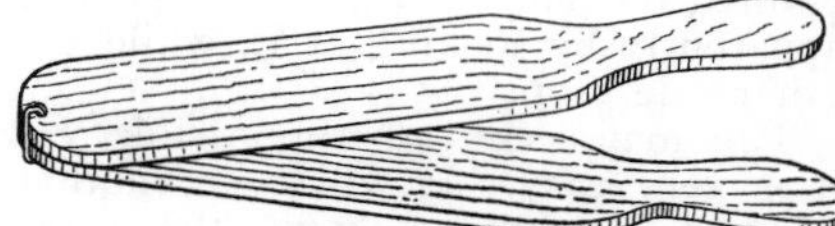

Two Paddles Hinged Together with a Piece of Wire Make a Presser for Lard and Fruits

An Electric-Light Bulb as Barometer

To use a discarded electric bulb as a fairly reliable barometer the point is broken off with a pair of pliers while holding the bulb under water. As the bulb is a vacuum, it completely fills with water. If the bulb is now suspended from a wire or thread fastened at the socket end, the water will not run out of it in fair weather when the atmospheric pressure is normal or high, but if the pressure falls, as happens when bad weather is approaching, the water will begin to bulge out of the small opening and sometimes a small drop may even fall off. When, with returning fair weather, the atmospheric pressure increases, the water can no longer bulge or drop out of the bulb.

A Swinging-Pendulum Trick

To swing a pendulum, picked out from a number of them at random, without touching it is a very puzzling trick. The articles necessary are a medium-sized table and a number of pendulums, some of which are suspended from a rod with their lower weighted ends inside of water and wine glasses placed on the table, and others attached to corks so that they will hang inside of bottles.

The spectators gather around the table which can be in full light. The performer sits at one side of the table with his hands flat on the top. A person may pick out any pendulum and ask him to swing it, which he will proceed to do without touching it, also making it strike the glass while it swings. Another pendulum may be pointed out and he will start that one apparently by looking at it, while the other one stops.

This may seem to be impossible, yet it is very easy. It will be seen that no two pendulums have the same length. A pendulum makes a certain number of swings in a given time, depending on its length. A long pendulum requires more time to complete its swing and will, therefore, make a less number of swings than a short one in the same time. It is only necessary to move the table slightly and watch the pendulum picked out until it be-

Any One Pendulum can be Made to Swing at Will by Moving the Table Slightly

gins to swing independently of the others, which soon happens. To make the longer pendulums swing, longer movements of the table top must be made. With a little practice anyone can become a skilled medium in pendulum swinging.—Contributed by James A. Hart, Philadelphia, Pa.

Applying a Strap Hinge

An ordinary strap hinge can be applied to a door or box cover in such a way that only one wing will show. Ordinarily the hinge opens as at A, and, on reversing it, the hinge will open to the limit as shown at B. If one wing is bent toward the other, as shown at C, the hinge may be applied as shown

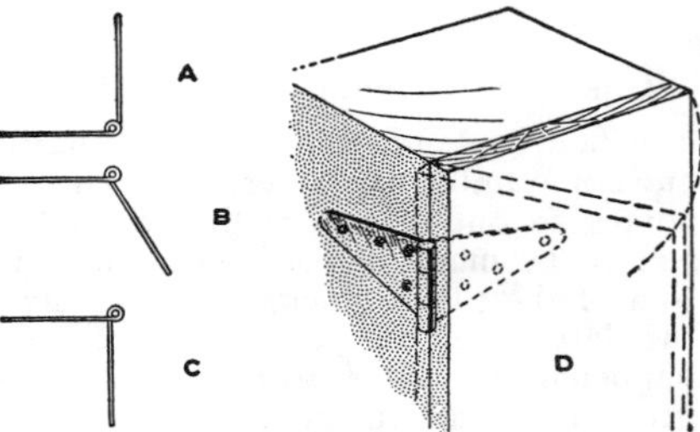

Reversing a Strap Hinge So That When It is Applied Only One Wing will Show

at D. As this process reverses the hinge, the screw holes must be countersunk on the opposite side.

Tricks Performed with Thumbs Tied Together

To have one's thumbs securely tied together by any person in an audience and examined by the spectators, then have some one throw a hoop or bicycle rim on one of the performer's arms as if the thumbs were not tied, seems impossible, yet this trick can be done, and its simplicity is its own protection, even though performed close to a committee selected from the audience. A stick can be held perpendicularly by anyone with one hand at each end and the performer can thrust his arms at the stick which passes between them with the thumbs apparently tied tightly together. The same effect is produced on the arm of any person, while the hands are tightly clasped, and before and after each movement the tied thumbs are examined by the committee.

The two cords used for the trick are made as follows: The first should be about 17 in. long, 1/4 in. in diameter at its center and tapering to points at the ends. The other cord is about 13 in. long, 1/8 in. in diameter in the center and also tapering at the ends. They are constructed of Chinese or Japanese paper, which is a soft, but very tough, fibrous texture. Cut the paper into strips, 1 in. wide, taking care that the grain, or rather the fiber, runs lengthwise. Beginning at one end, twist the paper on itself at an angle as in rolling the old-fashioned paper lamp lighter. Each turn should lap over the former about half of its width. When within 3 in. of the end of the first strip apply another by moistening the joining ends and continue the twisting. When the length given is reached, break off the strip and start back over the first in the opposite direction. Lay on enough layers to secure the diameter given. When finished, the cords should be strong enough to resist the pressure applied by the hands.

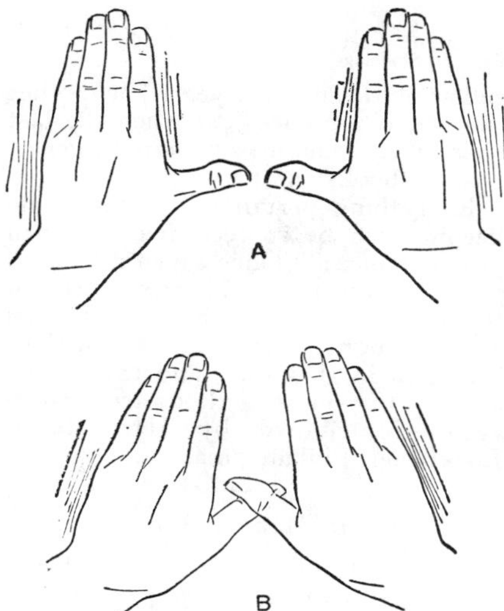

Manner of Crossing the Thumbs to Receive the Double Tie of the Cord

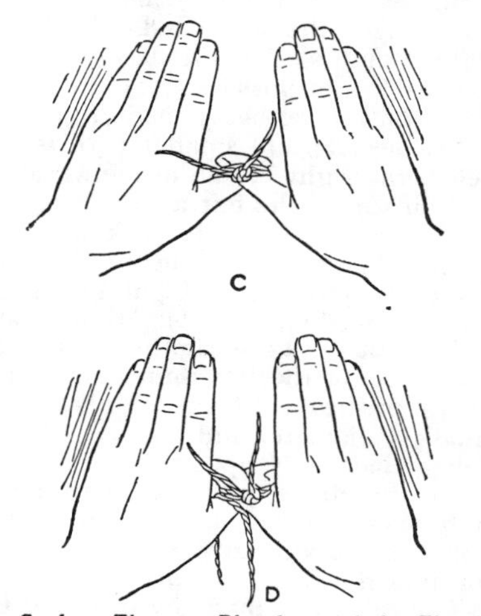

The Cords as They are Placed around the Thumbs and Tied in a Double Knot

With all fingers pressed together spread both thumbs away from the hands, as shown at A. Lay the right thumb across the left, as at B, the large knuckle bone of one lying directly over that of the other. The largest cord is laid over the crossing and both ends brought down, crossed under the thumbs, then up again, and tied in two knots on top of the right thumb, as at C. The trick in the tying is at this point. Just as the tie is being made pull the left thumb until the smallest-diameter joints reach the cord and pull down with the left hand. Push the right thumb so that the fleshy part enters as far as possible into the cords. Insist on the tie being made tightly.

The second and smaller cord is laid below the right thumb as shown at D, and on top of the left against the first cord, crossed, brought back and tied twice. When this is being done reverse the pushing and pulling as described, pushing the left thumb and pulling out on the right. Secure all the slack on the left thumb, the right being pushed into the cords at its smallest diameter and the second cord being tied high up and as near the right thumb as possible, with knots tightly drawn. If this second knot is not tight it will give trouble in performing the trick.

The release is made by bringing the tips of the fingers together and placing the thumbs into the palms. If the ties have been carefully made there will be no trouble to withdraw the left thumb as it is masked by the hands. The peculiar nature of the paper cord causes the loop from which the thumb was removed to remain open and rigid as a wire loop, and if the last tie was tightly drawn, the second cord will not slip down to close the loop. In approaching the hoop, stick, or arm, touch the thing to be passed with the finger tips and withdraw them, swaying backward a few times and, in the last swing before making the pass, remove the thumb from the loop. After passing, replace the thumb in the loop. In passing the object, open the finger tips, then close them and open the palms, and push the left thumb back into the loop, close the palms and apply a strain on both thumbs, then show the tie. Be careful to press both thumbs closely into the palms in passing so that they will not strike the object.

Always exhibit the tie from the back of the hands with the palms spread out. If there is any difficulty in drawing out or replacing the thumb in the loop, it is because the ties have not been properly made or tied when the thumbs were in the right place. It requires some practice to do the trick quickly.—Fayette.

A Way to Keep Home Accounts

An easy way to keep track of all the home expenses is by the popular card system. The index cards can be had at any stationery-supply house. Place the cards in a box on end and have a good supply of blanks back of them ready for use. Under, or back of, each letter place as many blanks as is necessary, and almost instantly any item of expense in the home may be found, such as the cost of coal for the year, drugs, meat, the cost of clothing for a child, and the account of the head of the family. The boy's account might read as follows under the letter J:

Johnnie		
Jan. 3	Shoes	$3.50
Jan. 15	Book	.45
Jan. 29	Hair cut	.25
Feb. 1	Stockings	.75

and so on through the year. The mother can see at a glance just when the last shoes were bought, and how much it cost for books and paper.

Everything pertaining to the home keeping can be so recorded and each year compared. Once given a trial no other bookkeeping will be required in the home where time counts. Children can be taught to keep account of their expenses in this way, and thus thrift and good business methods are encouraged.—Contributed by Harriette I. Lockwood, Philadelphia, Pa.

How to Make a Blowgun

Either a 12-in. length of a small curtain-rod tubing or a straight piece of small bamboo pole, cut off between the joints, can be used for the gun part of this simple device. If bamboo is used, see that it is cleaned out smoothly on the inside.

The dart used in the gun is shown

at A in the illustration. It is made by threading the eye of a darning needle full of yarn, clipping all the strands off to a uniform length of about 3/4 in., and then picking out the fibers into a brushlike mass above the needle's eye. Another needle or pin can be used for fuzzing the threads. The point to observe is that the brush is of somewhat larger diameter than the bore of the gun, so that when the needle is pushed into the mouth end the brush will be compressed and make an air-tight plug.

After thus inserting the dart, hold it as shown and give a quick, sharp blast of the breath into the gun. The dart will travel with great speed and accuracy for 20 ft. or more, and stick wherever it strikes. The point being

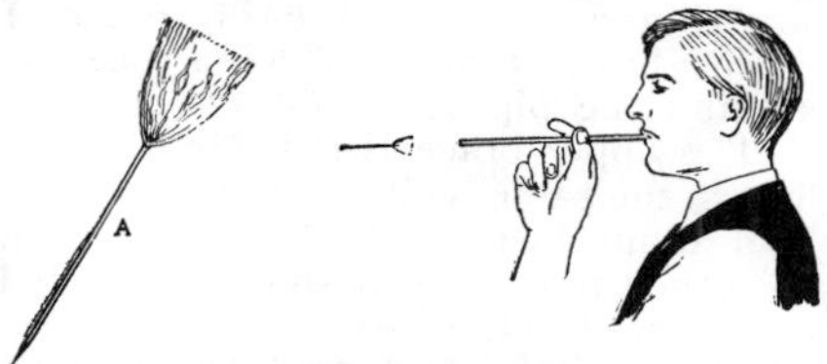

The Blowgun is Made of a Piece of Tubing, and the Dart of a Darning Needle

so small, it can be used in the house for shooting at a paper target pinned to the wall without injury to the plaster or woodwork.—Contributed by C. C. Fraser, Saginaw, Mich.

A Brush for Applying Soldering Acid

A good brush for applying acid to articles for soldering can be made of a piece of small copper pipe for the handle, and fine copper wire for the brush. To make the brush part, take a piece of cardboard, about 1 1/4 in. wide, and wind several turns of No. 28 gauge copper wire around it, then remove the coil, insert about 1/2 in. of it in the pipe, and flatten the latter to hold the wire. Clip the ends of the wire, and a brush will be had that ordinary acids will not affect. If only a short piece of pipe is available, it can be used as a ferrule and a handle made of wire or wood.—Contributed by A. R. Cunning, W. New Brighton, N. Y.

Inkwell and Penholder

An empty paste pot with a water well in the center makes an excellent inkwell and penholder. Fill the exterior well A with cement or plaster of paris, push the number of penholders to be held into the cement before it sets, moving them about occasionally to prevent the cement from sticking to them and to make the hole a little larger than the holder. The part B is for the ink.—Contributed by R. F. Pinkney, Lazareto del Mariel, Cuba.

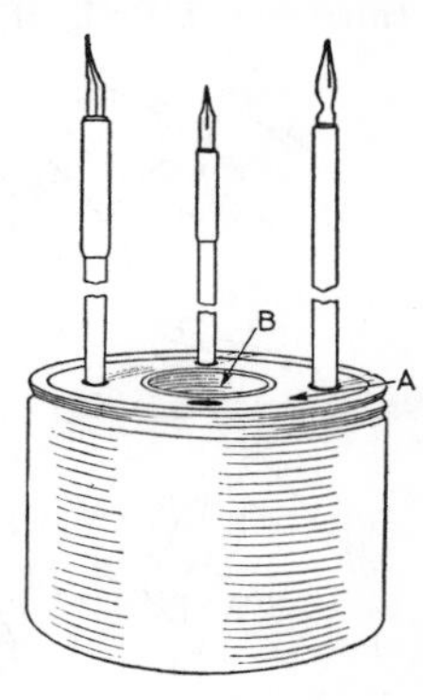

A Homemade Loose-Leaf Pocket Memorandum

The little memorandum illustrated herewith is very handy to carry in the coat or vest pocket for taking notes, etc. Loose leaves may be supplied with very little trouble. It consists of a fold of paper, cut as shown and pasted at the ends. The pocket thus formed will easily hold 2 doz.

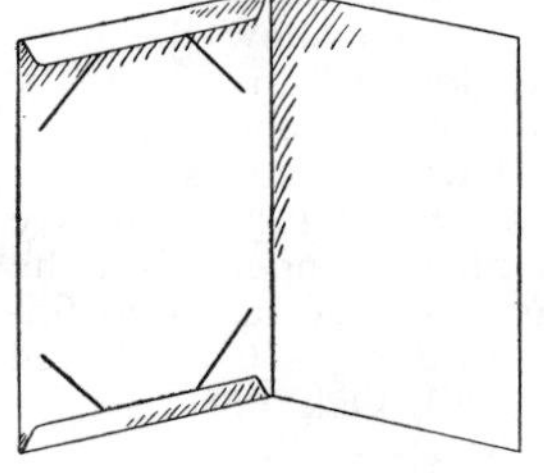

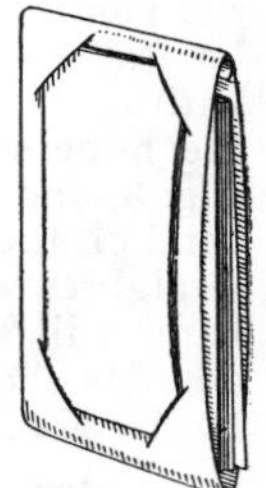

The Holder is Made of Heavy Manila Paper and will Stand Considerable Wear

sheets and the slits cut on the outside will admit 8 sheets.—Contributed by C. B. Hanson, Fitchburg, Mass.

¶An ideal cleaner for kid gloves is carbon tetrachloride.

Rubber-Band-Change Trick

The trick of changing a rubber band from the first and second fingers to the third and fourth, if done quickly, can

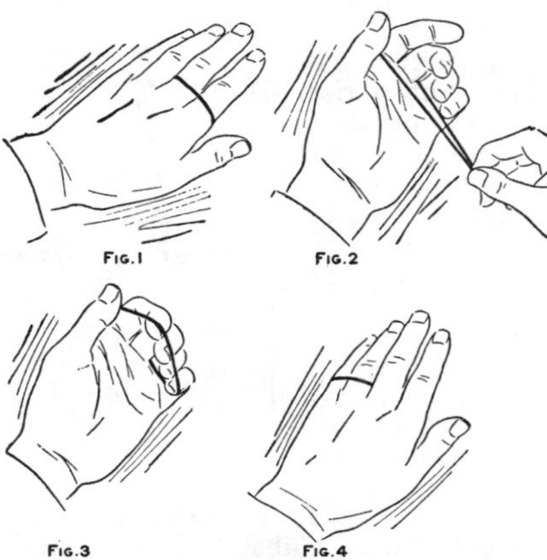

Transferring Rubber Band from the First Two Fingers to the Last Pair, Like Magic

be performed without detection by any one. The band on the first two fingers is shown to the spectator as in Fig. 1, with the back of the hand up. The hand is then turned over and the band drawn out quickly, as shown in Fig. 2, in a manner as to give the impression that the band is whole and on the two fingers. While doing this, quickly fold all the fingers so that their ends enter the band, and turn the hand over and let go the band, then show the back with the fingers doubled up. In reality the fingers will be in the band, as in Fig. 3, and the back will still show the band on the first two fingers. Quickly straighten out all the fingers, and the band will snap over the last two fingers, as shown in Fig. 4.—Contributed by E. K. Marshall, Oak Park, Ill.

A Swinging Electric-Light Bracket

The light bracket shown is both ornamental and useful and can be swung from one side of the room to the other in an instant, a feature that is of great value in a dimly lighted kitchen. It can be made of either brass or soft iron, but, for the sake of convenience, the description will be for one made of brass.

Procure four pieces of brass, 1 in. wide, 1/8 in. thick and 7 in. long, and bend them to the shape shown at A. These are to form the ceiling bracket. A 3/16-in. hole is drilled in the end of each piece to be against the ceiling. The other end is bent slightly concave and soldered to a brass collar, B, which is threaded on the inside. This collar must be of such a size that it will screw on the end of a brass pipe, C, 1 in. in outside diameter. The length of this pipe should be 18 or 20 inches.

The base D of the bracket is made of a brass bar, 1/8 in. thick, 1/2 in. wide and 45 in. long, a scroll being turned on 6 in. of its length at the globe end, and 3 in. of the other end turned up at right angles and soldered to a ring made of 1/16-in. brass that acts as a bearing around the pipe.

The upper brace E is made of 1/16-in. brass, the same width as the base piece and about 48 in. in length. Each end is turned into a scroll and then riveted or soldered to the base D and to the upper brass ring. The space between the base D, the brace E, and the pipe C is filled with any style of scroll or other brace that may suit the taste of the

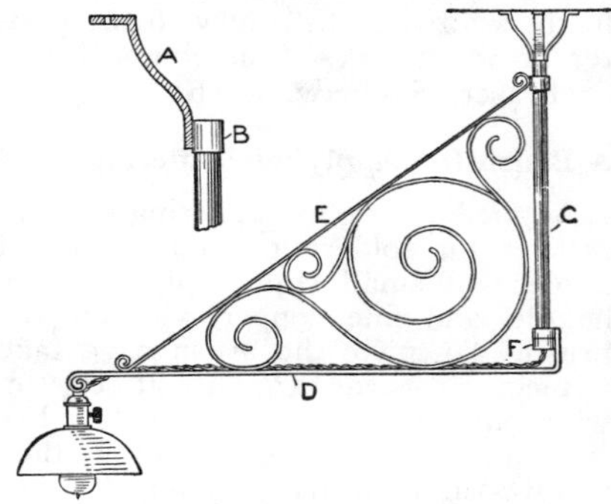

A Bracket Forming a Pendant and Swinging Arm to Change the Location of the Electric Light

maker, but the base D must be at right angles to the pipe C before the scroll is fastened in place.

A cap, F, is screwed to the lower end of the pipe, to keep the bracket in place. Ordinary flexible light cord is used to connect to the light which is swung to the scroll end of the base.—Contributed by F. L. Matter, Portland, Oregon.

Match Safe to Deliver One Match at a Time

A match safe that will deliver only one match at a time is constructed of two parts, the box or holder and the base, with slider. The box is diamond-shaped and of the size shown by the dimensions. The base, with slider, consists of two pieces, the baseboard and a standard which runs through the box diagonally on the longest dimension in a vertical position. A thumbtack is inserted in the standard near the top to prevent the box from being lifted entirely from the base.

The matches are filled into the box

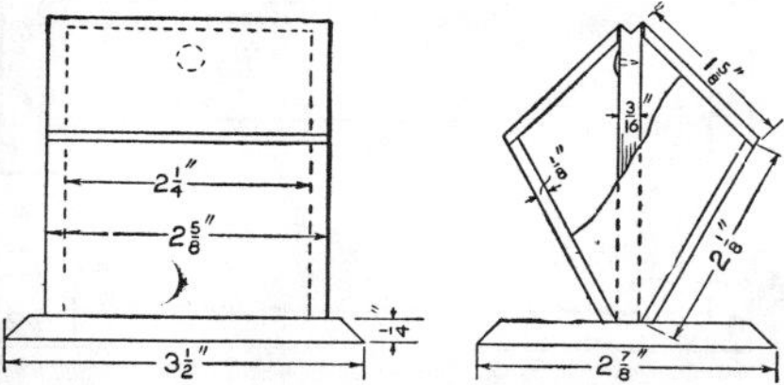

The Box Delivers Only One Match When It is Raised and Lowered on the Standard

on both sides of the standard. When a match is wanted, lift the box up and let it down again, and one match will be caught in the notch and raised out of the box. To prevent the box from tipping sideways when it is raised up, small pieces can be glued to the box ends on the inside and on both sides of the standard.—Contributed by A. S. Barrows, New Britain, Conn.

Cartridge Shells Used for Electrical Contacts

In making small switchboards, rheostats, and other electrical devices, I found a good use for old center-fire cartridge shells as shown in the sketch. A hole a little smaller than the diameter of the shell is made in the board and the shell is forced in. The proper wires are then soldered to the metal on the inside, or the wire may be placed inside of the shell and

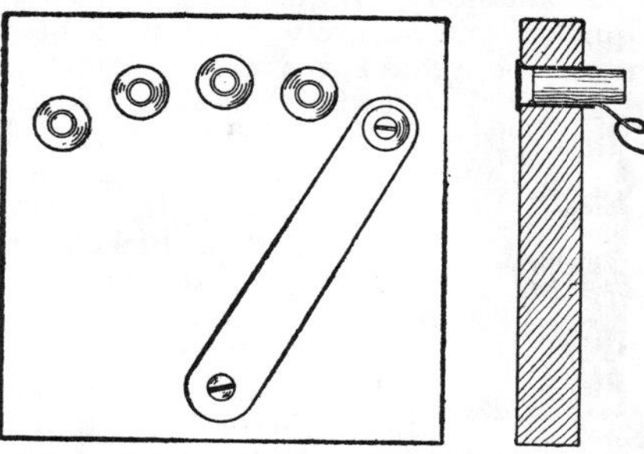

The Heads of the Cartridge Shells Make Good Contacts for a Switch Lever

held in contact by driving a wood plug in as indicated.—Contributed by W. O. Nettleton, Washington, D. C.

A Dowel-Turning Tool

The owner of a wood or metal lathe can easily construct a tool that will turn dowels of any size quickly. This tool, as described by a correspondent of Work, London, consists of a block of wood, shaped as shown at A, and a plane bit, B, attached with a wood screw. The hole in the collet C must be of such size that it will admit the rough stock freely but also prevent it from wabbling as the stick turns. The

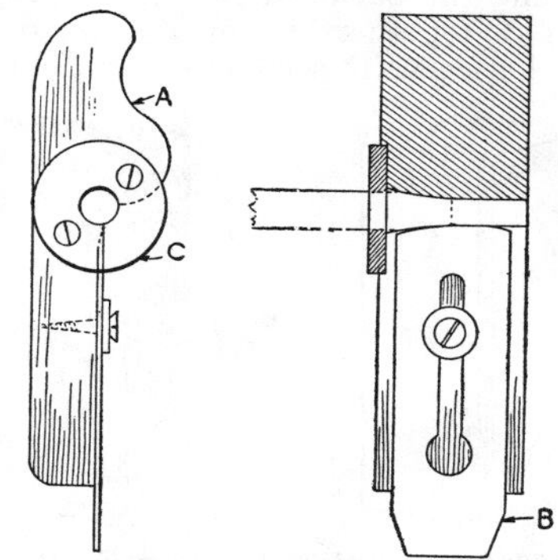

The Tool is Very Similar to a Plane and is Used] with a Lathe for Turning Dowels

stock is chucked in the ordinary manner and the tool is run on the outer end.

To Tie a Hammock

A method not generally known to quickly and securely hitch up a hammock between two trees, in camp or elsewhere, is shown in the sketch. Each end rope is given one or more turns around a tree trunk and then tucked under, as shown. The pull on the rope will draw it tightly against the rough bark on the tree. The harder the pull, the tighter the rope binds against the tree trunk. In this manner a hammock can be put up in a few moments and it is as readily taken down.—Contributed by Bert Morehouse, Des Moines, Iowa.

An Inexpensive File

Envelopes make a very inexpensive as well as a neat file for papers and letters if they are arranged and fastened together so that they can be kept in one packet. In making such a file procure as many envelopes as there will be headings in the file, also a number of strips of gummed tape, about 1½ in. long. There must be twice as many of these strips as there are envelopes.

Bind the backs of two envelopes, A and B, together leaving a space of ⅛ in. between the envelopes. Bind a

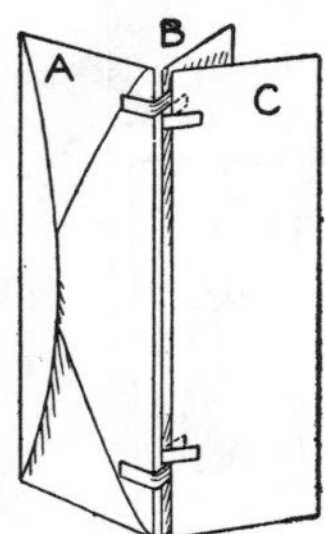

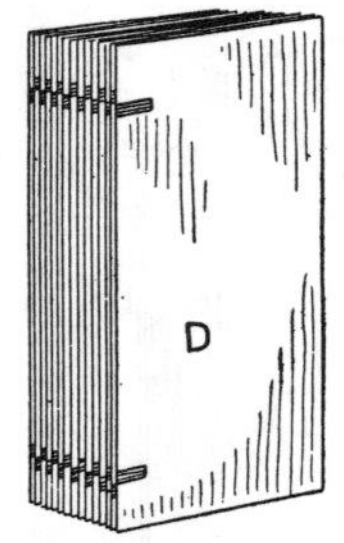

The File is Built Up of Envelopes Joined Together with Small Strips of Tape

third envelope, C, to B, and so on. The strips of tape from A to B and from B to C are on opposite sides of the envelope B. Continue binding until the required number of envelopes have been joined together. Assign a heading to each of the envelopes, and the file is ready for use. When completed it should appear as shown in D.—Contributed by Alfred Rice, Syracuse, N. Y.

Window-Shade Guides

The annoyance of a shade that will not run true on the roller and flops in the wind coming through an open window can be overcome by using guide wires as follows:

The stick in the hem on the lower edge of the shade is supplied with a screweye, A, at each end. A wire is run through the screweye and fastened in a vertical position on the casing

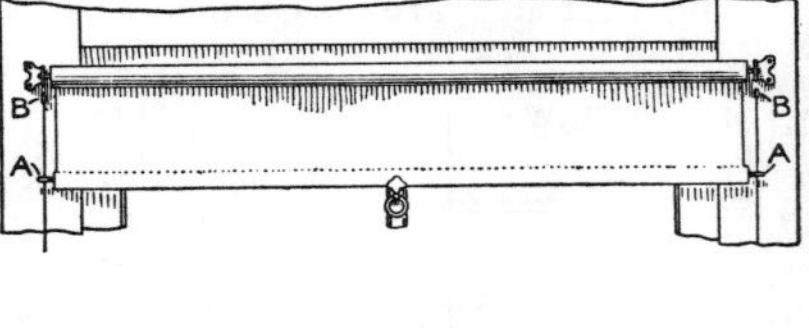

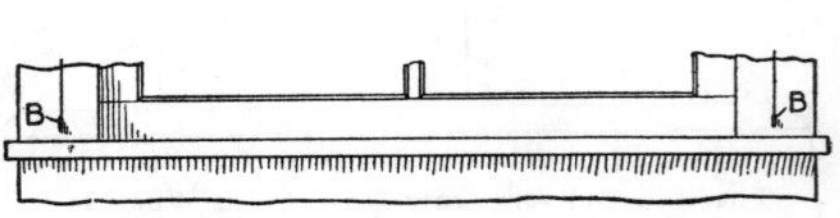

Two Parallel Guide Wires Hold the Stick of the Shade in Its Proper Place

with screweyes as shown by B, B. A second wire is similarly attached on the other side of the shade, taking care to have both wires parallel and true with the ends of the roller.—Contributed by George Lue, San Francisco, California.

Watering Plants at the Roots

An effective way to water rose bushes, shrubs or plants is to place an old cowhorn in the earth so that the small end will be near the roots of the plant and the large end level with the surface of the ground, and fill the horn with water. The small end of the horn should be cut off at such a point that the hole will be about the size of a lead pencil.—Contributed by Chas. L. Richards, Philadelphia, Pa.

How to Clean Jewelry

To cleanse articles of silver, gold, bronze and brass use a saturated solution of cyanide of potassium. To clean small articles, dip each one into the solution and rinse immediately in hot water; then dry and polish with a linen cloth. Larger articles are cleaned by rubbing the surface with a small tuft of cotton saturated in the solution. As cyanide of potassium is a deadly poison, care must be taken not to have it touch any sore spot on the flesh.—Contributed by G. A. Koerbis, U. S. S. "Vermont."

Runner for a Go-Cart

As the wheels of a go-cart do not push through the snow very easily and the cart, therefore, does not run in a straight direction, and as I did not care to purchase a sled, I instead fitted the

The Runners are Easily Applied to the Wheels of a Go-Cart and Hold Them Solidly

go-cart wheels with runners as shown in the sketch. I purchased a piece of machine steel of a diameter to fit the grooves in the wheels after the rubber tires were removed. This I cut and bent to the shape shown at A, making two runners, and applied one to each pair of wheels, front and rear, as shown at B. The runners kept the wheels immovable and caused the cart to glide over the snow as a sleigh. This runner will not interfere with the folding of a collapsible cart.—Contributed by Roy B. Hanaford, Detroit, Mich.

A Ring-Throwing Game

The board for this game is made of a cover from an old candy or lard pail, washed and painted black. When the paint is dry, place 50 pegs on the surface as shown and number them with white paint or by fastening numbers cut from paper below them. The numbering of the pegs is not consecutive, but low and high numbers distributed with the object in view of

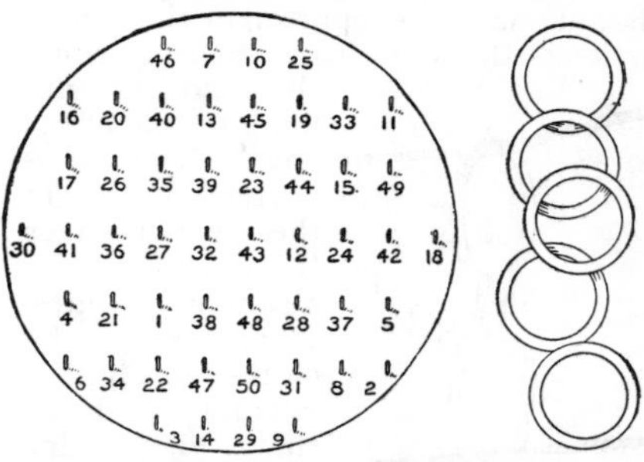

The Candy-Pail Cover with Pegs Numbered and a Set of Rings for Each Player

making it difficult to secure a high score.

Each player has a set of five rings, which are nothing else but rubber fruit-jar rings. These can be purchased at a grocery store. The board is hung on a wall or post, and the player stands about 5 or 6 ft. away and throws the rings, one at a time, trying to ring pegs having the highest numbers. The sum of the numbers corresponding to the pegs ringed counts toward the final score. Turns are taken by each player, and each time five rings are thrown. The score can be set at any amount, 500 being about right.—Contributed by Francis P. Hobart, Willoughby, O.

A Pen and Brush Holder

A sheet of corrugated paper is a handy thing to have on the writing desk, for the purpose of placing wet pens or brushes in its grooves. The paper absorbs the liquid, and the corrugations hold the pens or brushes in handy positions. A sheet of this paper

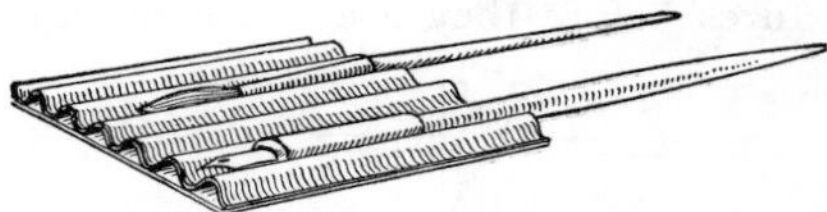

The Depressions in the Paper Hold the Pens or Brushes and Also Absorb the Excess Fluid

is almost as useful a desk accessory as a blotter.—Contributed by James M. Kane, Doylestown, Pa.

Supporter for a Double Clothesline

A double clothesline of any length should have a supporter in the center to keep the line from sagging when the clothes are hung on the lower one. The supporter shown in the sketch saves the wear from the strain on the lines. It also keeps the clothes in a higher current of air so that they dry quicker.

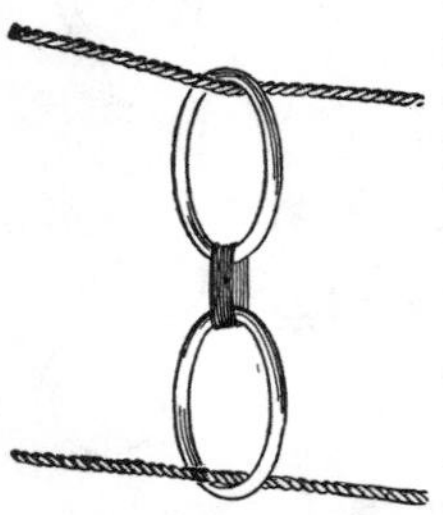

The supporter is made of two nickelplated rings measuring 2 in. in diameter. They are bound together as shown. The rings being nickelplated, the supporter will not rust the clothes. The clothes should be arranged on the lower line so that the supporter will rest in the center.—Contributed by Katharine D. Morse, Syracuse, New York.

Pincushion for the Arm

Those that have trouble in keeping the pincushion within reach while sewing, can remedy the trouble by making one to fit the wrist or arm. An ordinary pincushion is attached to a piece of cardboard and an elastic sewed to the cardboard edges so that it will fit on the arm. The pincushion is not in the way and is readily worn so that the pins are easier to reach than if pinned to the dress.—Contributed by Frank Sterrett, Portland, O.

Electric Test for Fixtures

A very useful device for testing out fixtures before they are connected up

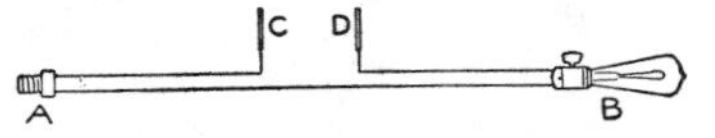

One Line of the Two Connecting Wires is Broken and the Ends Used as Terminals on the Fixture

can be easily made as follows: Two wires are run from a plug, A, one to a socket, B, and the other to terminate at C. The line from the other side of the socket B terminates at D.

In testing a fixture, the plug A is turned into a socket of some source of current, and a lamp is turned into the socket B. The terminal C is held to the metal covering of the fixture, while the end D is held to one of the wires. If there is a leak of current, the lamp at B and those of the fixture will light up.—Contributed by Fred Schumacher, Brooklyn, N. Y.

Opening for Steam in a Utensil Cover

When cooking certain foods the ordinary cover on a vessel confines too much steam, while if no cover at all is used, too much will escape, hence a cover which is provided with a vent is very desirable. The cover attachment shown in the illustration is evidently well adapted for service on such occasions and can be easily made as follows:

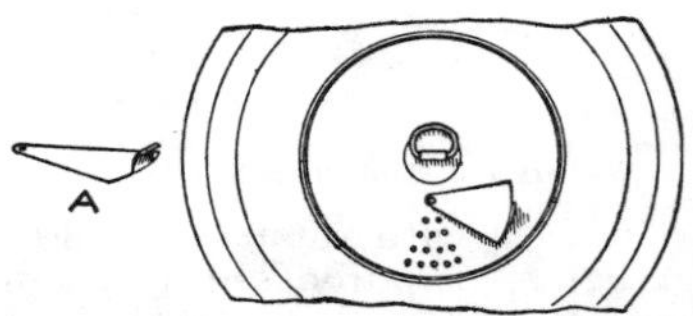

The Small Triangular Surface Provided with Holes for Releasing Surplus Steam is Covered with a Cap

Lay out a small triangle on some level part of the cover and punch several holes inside of the lines. Cut a cap, A, from a piece of tin to cover the holes. A small projection on the edge of the cap serves to swing it one way or the other, as needed, and it is fastened loosely to the cover with a soft-copper rivet, so that it may be easily opened.

Drying Seeds

A good way to dry tomato, cantaloupe, and other seeds is to put them on blotters. They will quickly dry in this manner and will not become moldy, as the blotter soaks up the moisture.—Contributed by Theodore Becker, Kansas City, Mo.

Cleaning Clothes by Boiling Them

When cleaning clothes by boiling them in a boiler over a fire, fit in a false bottom to keep the clothes from touching the bottom. The false bottom should be perforated with holes, 3/8-in. in diameter and 1 in. apart, over the entire piece. Fasten four legs, each about 2 in. long, to the under side to make a space between the bottoms. In washing, all that is necessary is to place the clothes in the boiler and boil them. The dirt will come loose and settle through the holes and on the boiler bottom.

An Emergency Tack Puller

One day I had to pull some tacks but had no tack puller at hand. An idea came to me to use the kitchen

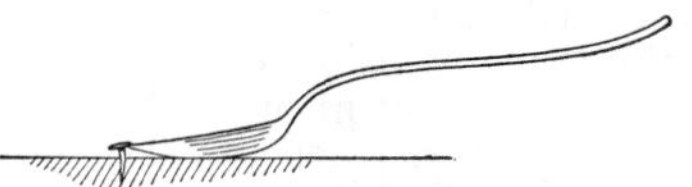

The Point of a Spoon will Easily Pull a Tack from Soft Wood

spoon, and I found that it worked even better than a regular tack puller. The ordinary kitchen spoon usually has an edge sharp enough to get under any tack.—Contributed by H. D. Harkins, St. Louis, Mo.

A Puzzle with Figures

This puzzle is to arrange all the figures or digits, from 1 to 9 inclusively, in two rows, each containing all the digits, so that the sum in addition as well as the remainder in subtraction will have nine figures, in which all the digits are represented. There are several solutions to the puzzle, and the following is one of them:

371294568
216397845

The sum of the foregoing numbers and the remainder, when the lower row is subtracted from the upper, will both have nine figures and include all the digits from 1 to 9.—Contributed by Walter Bennett, Detroit, Mich.

To Fasten Loose Table Legs

When legs of an ordinary table become loose and unsteady they may be easily repaired as shown in the sketch.

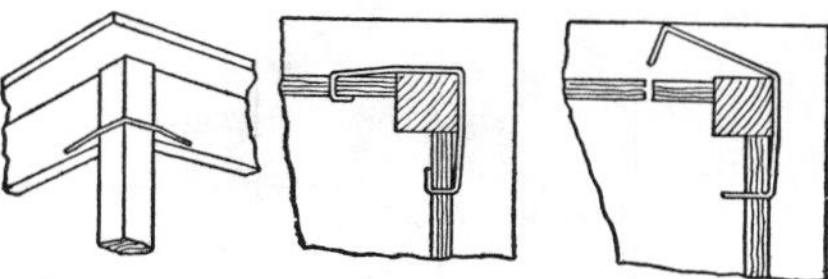

A Piece of Wire Bent around the Leg of a Table will Make It Rigid

Nails do not hold well in such places and glue will not stand much washing.

The method of making the repair is to drill 1/8-in. holes through the rails on each side of the leg and insert pieces of galvanized wire of a size to fit the holes. After the wire is inserted, the ends are bent over. The illustration clearly shows the repair.—Contributed by Edwin C. Wright, Newport, Ky.

Washbasin Holder

A piece of wire formed into the shape shown in the sketch makes a handy hook to hold a washbasin when it is not in use. This keeps it out of the way and out of the dirty water which might be thrown into the kitchen sink. — Contributed by F. C. Althen, Anamosa, Iowa.

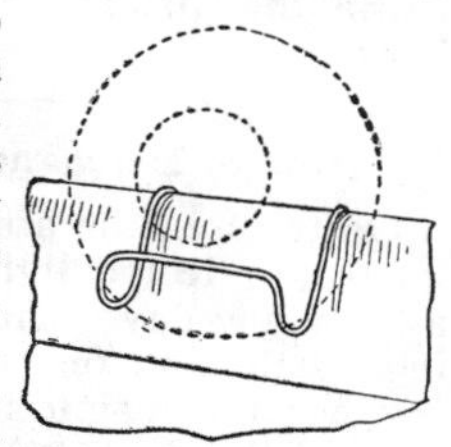

A Cleaner for Canvas Shoes

One of the most economical cleansers for canvas shoes is oxide of zinc. Mix a small quantity of the powder with water, to the consistency of thin paste, and apply it to the canvas with an old toothbrush, rubbing it in thoroughly. Then set the shoes aside to dry before wearing them.—Contributed by Katharine D. Morse, Syracuse, N. Y.

¶A good substitute currycomb can be made of corncobs tied together tightly.

Ruling Blank Books

A special ruling for a blank book can be drawn by using a thin piece of sheet metal or cardboard, cut as shown

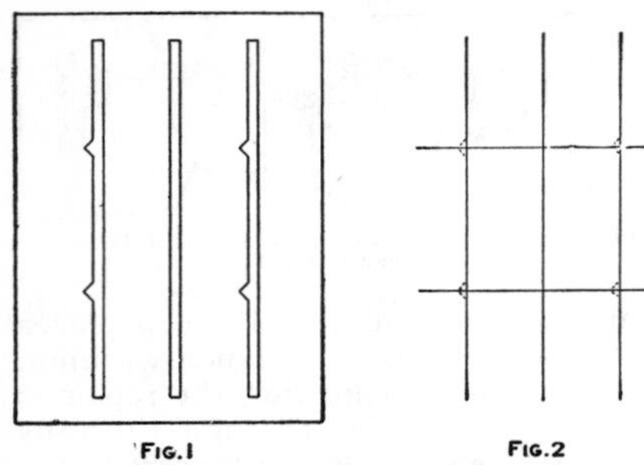

A Template Having Slots Cut for Drawing Special Vertical and Horizontal Lines on Pages

in Fig. 1, for a template. The pencil is drawn along one edge of the cut-out so that it will make lines as shown in Fig. 2.

If horizontal lines are required, cut notches on the edge for the location of each line as shown. When the vertical lines are drawn, these notches will mark the places for the horizontal lines.

How to Demagnetize a Watch

Quite often the attendants or a visitor to an electric-light plant discovers after a few days that his watch is losing a half hour or more a day by having become magnetized by the dynamos. In stations where the old types of machines are still in use there is a great deal more danger from what is called "stray" magnetic fields than in those where modern machines are installed.

The jeweler demagnetizes a watch in the following way: He has a piece of soft iron with an opening cut in its center of such shape and size as to receive the watch, and with a fine wire wound about it. After the watch has been placed in position, an alternating current, that is, one whose direction is changing at regular intervals, is sent through the winding, and thus a magnetic field is produced that also changes in direction as the current reverses. The current is gradually reduced in value and the magnetism originally possessed by the watch is removed. When an alternating current is not available, a direct current may be used, its direction being rapidly reversed by what is known as a "polarity changer."

Anyone can demagnetize his own watch, however, with very little trouble and no expense by a much simpler method. Procure a piece of heavy linen thread about 3 ft. long, attach one end of it to the ring of the watch, hold the other end and turn the watch around until the thread is twisted at least one hundred times. Now allow the thread to unwind, and as the watch revolves, pass it back and forth near a powerful electromagnet. The field magnet of a good-sized generator or motor will answer. The machine should be in operation, or at least there should be a current in the windings about the fields, when you attempt to demagnetize the watch. While the thread is unwinding, and the watch moved in the magnetic field, gradually withdraw from the magnet so that when the watch ceases to revolve, it is just outside of the field.

Always be sure to keep the watch revolving while it is in the magnetic field, otherwise the results will be very unsatisfactory, and more harm than good may result.

A Pencil Holder

Procure a piece of paper, 7 in. long and 4 in. wide, and roll it one time around a lead pencil, then coat the remaining surface of the paper with glue. Roll this around the pencil and a tube is formed, which will hold a

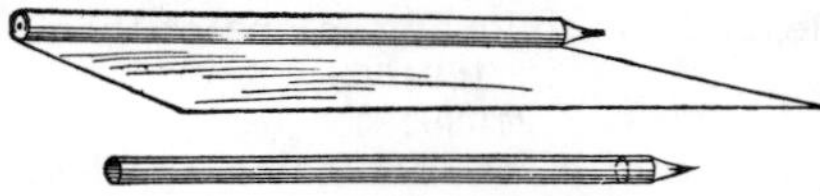

A Stub of a Pencil can be Easily Held in the Tube for Writing

pencil or even pieces of pencil down to ½ in. in length.—Contributed by W. D. Brooks, Paterson, N. J.

A Poultry-Food Chopper

The illustration shows a handy device for cutting roots for food, and for chopping and mixing stale bread, potatoes, peelings, refuse fruit, etc., for poultry. Any blacksmith can make the chopper at little cost. For the cutting blades use two pieces of steel a little heavier than oil-barrel hoops, each 1½ in. wide and 8 in. long. Procure a ½-in. iron rod, about 3 ft. long, bend one end in the shape of a spade

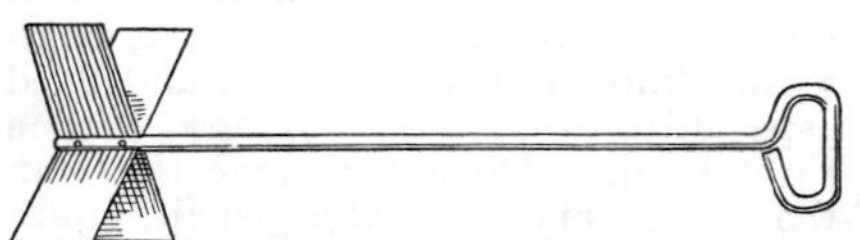

The Chopper Consists of a Rod Handle to Which Blades are Attached by Riveting or Welding

handle and split the other end for a distance of about 2½ in.

Sharpen one edge of each blade and curve the metal slightly. Lay the two blades together with the convex sides touching in the center and insert them in the slit in the handle end. They are riveted or welded in place. Heat and bend the blades at right angles.

Many of the materials mentioned for poultry foods may be chopped in an ordinary pail having a strong bottom, but it is best to make a box, about 1½ ft. square and with a plank bottom, for use with the chopper.

A Small Spring Hinge

Box covers or small doors that are seldom used can be supplied with a small spring hinge as shown in the illustration. The hinge is made of a piece of spring wire which is formed similar to a staple with a coil or complete turn given to the wire in the

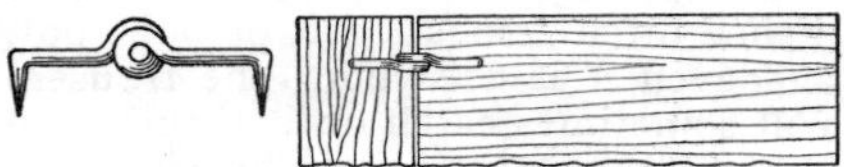

The Shape of the Hinge, and the Manner of Attaching It to a Cover or Door

center. It is attached by driving the points, one into the door and the other into the casing.

Shoestring End

When the tips slip from shoelaces, new ones may be readily made of fine wire. The wire is run through the end of the lace, Fig. 1, and the two ends

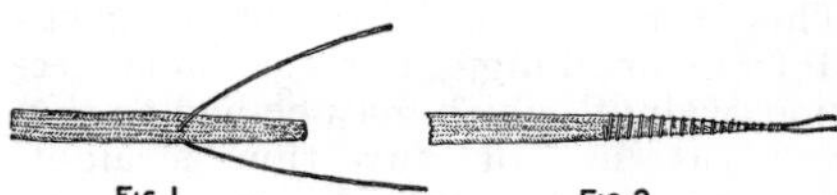

The Wire Prevents the Lace from Raveling and Makes a Tip for Easily Entering the Eyelets

are twisted tightly together as shown in Fig. 2. This covers the end of the lace and makes a tip that is easily passed through the eyelets.

Threads on Wood Shafts

In model making it is quite necessary at times to have threads on a wood shaft. These can be made quite

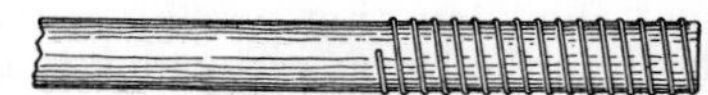

The Wire Forms a Thread That in Many Instances is Quite Serviceable for Model Making

satisfactorily by coiling a wire around the shaft where the threads are wanted, and driving the ends into the wood.

A Glass Breaker

After cutting glass, and especially where a small strip is to be removed, the part must be broken away in small

The Nut is Set to the Thickness of the Glass and Used to Break Pieces Away

pieces. The accompanying sketch shows a very useful tool for this purpose. The tool is made of a piece of metal having a bolt fastened to it at one end whose nut can be adjusted to the thickness of the glass.

¶Old discarded blueprints can be made white and used for sketching by dipping them in a solution of soda and water, in the proportions of 4 oz. of soda to each gallon of water.

Wood Postal Cards

The card consists of three pieces, or three-ply, veneer. The grain of the outside veneer runs lengthwise, while that of the inside piece runs crosswise. This makes the card straight and keeps it from breaking. For the inner section, walnut, which may be had as thin as 1/64 in., or any thin straight-grained veneer may be used. Two pieces of veneer, about 3¾ in. wide and 6 in. long; one piece, 6 in. wide and 3¾ in. long,—the length being with the grain of the wood—and two blocks of wood, known as cauls, of the same size or a little larger, and about ⅞ in. thick, are required.

The veneer is laid flat on a board and cut with a sharp knife or fine saw along the edge of a ruler. The three pieces are glued together in the following manner. Use ordinary hot glue, not too thin, but thin enough to run freely from the brush. The glue is applied evenly on both sides of the inner piece only, and this is then stood on edge until the glue chills. Then the cauls are heated. This is best done on a stove, or on stove lids over a gas fire. While the blocks are being heated, put one veneer on either side of the middle piece, and a piece of thin paper on each side to keep the glue from the cauls. A hand screw or vise should be opened to almost the distance required. One of the cauls is now laid flat, the veneers upon it and the other caul on top. This should be done quickly. Then clamp the whole firmly together. While the full pressure is only needed for about two hours, the pieces should be allowed to dry between the cauls for, say, a day or two, so that they will keep straight. The size of the finished card is 3⅜ in. by 5½ in. It is cut and planed to size while lying flat on a board, the plane being pushed along on its side on the bench top. To dress or clean, clamp one side to the bench. While a scraper blade may be used to advantage, it is not essential, as a block of wood and sandpaper will do. The thinner it is dressed the better. The sharp edges should be removed with sandpaper. The writing on a wood card is not done in the ordinary manner, as the ink would run. The surface must be prepared, which also gives a finish to the wood. Melt some wax or paraffin in a suitable vessel and cover the surface of the wood, using a brush or rag. The lines for the address on one side are then drawn, and the writing is done with a hard lead pencil. When through writing on one side, cover it with some strong aniline stain. (Aniline, dissolved in hot water, commonly known as water stain and used especially to stain mahogany, is the right kind.) Do not remove the wax that was raised by the pencil point. Brush the stain over until the whole side is covered. When dry, repeat on the other side. In about an hour the wax may be scraped off with a dull scraper or some other dull instrument. After every particle of wax has been removed, the card is given a good rubbing with a clean, soft rag. It is well to protect the hands as well as the table during the process.—Contributed by Chas. Schapmeier, Baltimore, Md.

Fastening Screws in Tile and Brick Walls

A simple way to fasten screws in tile or brick walls is to drill holes, not too large, for the screws, then tear up some paper, wet it and make a pulp. Pack this pulp tightly in the hole and turn in the screws. The screws will stand a great deal of strain.—Contributed by John Thomas, Brantford, Ont.

Shoe Pull Made of an Eyelet

The pulling-on strap at the back of a shoe often comes loose, or pulls out, and even if it does not, the trousers will sometimes catch on it if the strap is not tucked inside of the shoe. A very simple way to overcome these troubles is to remove the straps and substitute eyelets. A buttonhook will then serve admirably in pulling the shoe onto the foot.

Holder for a Set of Sadirons

A very attractive holder for a set of sadirons and their handle can be made as shown in the illustration, although the design may be changed if desired. The holder consists of a shield-shaped back, which is fastened to the wall in a convenient place and has a shelf with openings for the irons attached to it. The shelf is made in two pieces, the bottom part being covered with a heavy piece of tin while the upper is cut out to receive the irons.

The irons are placed on the upper piece in such positions that they will be attractively displayed and evenly located, and then a lead-pencil mark is drawn around their base. Openings are cut in the wood on these marks and the board fastened on top of the tin-covered shelf. An ordinary brass

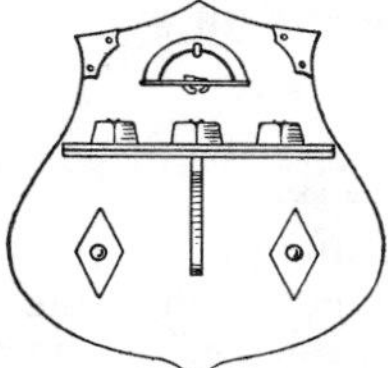

An Ornamented Bracket Shelf for Holding a Complete Set of Sadirons and Their Handle

bracket is used in the center beneath the shelf, to keep it from sagging.

The shield is fastened to the wall with two screws, over which two brushed-brass, diamond-shaped pieces are fastened with large brass tacks, to cover the screw heads. The corners of the shield may be ornamented with brushed-brass designs, and the wood finished as desired. The irons can be set in the holder while hot without fear of burning any part, and they will present a very neat appearance.—Contributed by G. E. Martin, Hastings, Nebraska.

A Garden Roller

A garden roller for digging the earth and crushing clods is easily made of the following material: One round piece of wood, 10 in. in diameter and 18 in. long; two pieces of wood, each 56 in. long, 2½ in. wide and 1¼ in. thick; one piece, 21 in. long, 2 in. wide and 1 in. thick; two ½-in. lag screws, 6

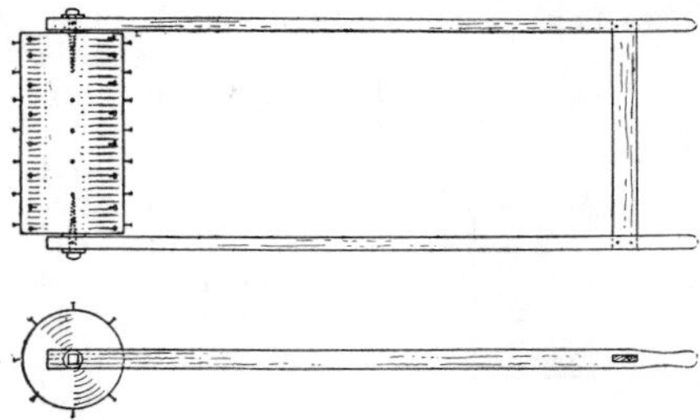

A Roller for Crushing Clods and Digging the Earth in Garden Making

in. long, and a quantity of 8-penny nails.

The short piece of wood is fitted between the two long pieces with tenon-and-mortise joints to serve as a handle at one end and the roller is fastened between the side pieces at the opposite end to revolve on the lag screws. The nails are driven into the roller so that they project about 1 in.

A Substitute for Glaziers' Points

Ordinary small staples make good substitutes for glaziers' tacks. The points of the staples should be drawn apart slightly, as shown at A, to give them a greater holding area and at the same time make them easier to drive. These points seem to hold the glass better than the regular glaziers' points,

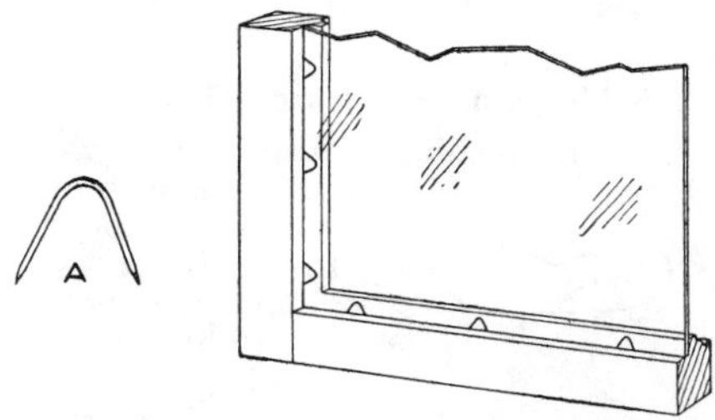

Double-Pointed Tacks, or Staples, with the Points Spread, Used as Substitutes for Glaziers' Points

consequently the putty will not crack and loosen, and renewing is avoided. —Contributed by Edward Sieja, Chicago.

Water-Heating Coil in a Furnace Pipe

The accompanying sketch shows a plan I adopted for conserving the waste heat from my furnace. I found that I was able to put a coil into the smoke pipe, which was about 8 in. in diameter, and thus heat water for domestic purposes. It will be seen that the coil is spiral in shape rather than cylindrical, as the latter would leave a free passage up the center and therefore would not bring enough gases into contact with the coil.

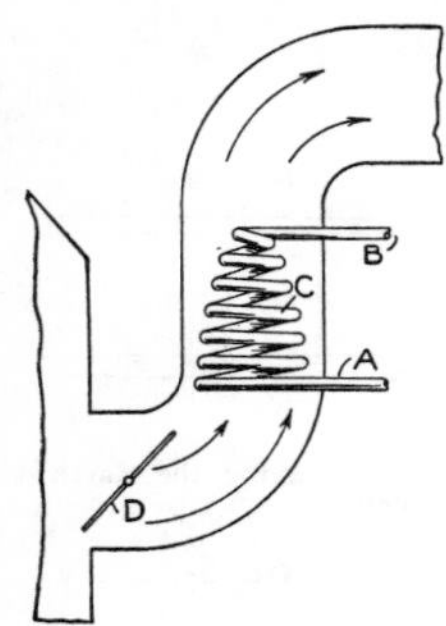

In addition to this coil I have a gas heater near the tank which is used only in case the demand for hot water exceeds the capacity of the coil, which is naturally not as efficient per unit of length as one directly within the firepot would be. It has the advantage of not absorbing heat which should go to make steam, but only that which would otherwise be wasted. The heating surface of the coil is much greater than would be possible within the firepot, which in a measure compensates for its lower efficiency.—Contributed by W. E. Morey, Chicago.

A Homemade Marking Gauge

A 3/8-in. bushing is turned into the side outlet of a 3/8-in. tee. The bushing is then tapped to receive a 7/16-in. wing bolt. A tight-fitting wood plug is driven into the throughway of the tee and the ends ground off flush on the emery wheel. A slot, 5/16-in. square, is then cut through the wood plug just under the bushing. Two pieces of flat steel, each 1/4 in. wide by 1/8 in. thick and 1/8 in. longer than the tee, are fitted in the slot cut in the plug as shown in the sketch. The outer end of each piece is bent at right angles and sharpened. After the points have been drawn out to the right distance, the wing bolt is turned to hold them in that position.—Contributed by C. Molloy, Philadelphia, Pa.

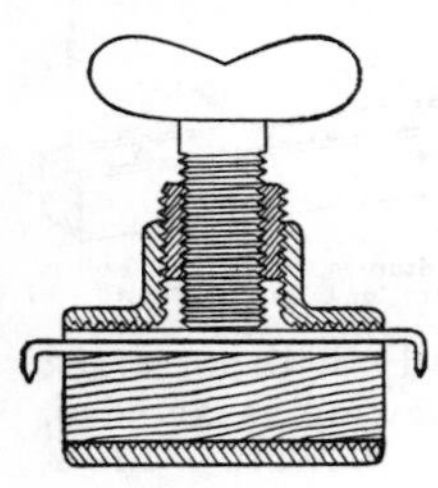

Protecting Brush Handles from Paint

A very efficient method to prevent paint from running down on a paint-brush handle and on the hand is to cut a hollow rubber ball in half, Fig. 1, make a hole in the center to fit the brush handle and attach it as shown in Fig. 2. One ball will fit up two brushes. The cup shape catches the paint and prevents it from getting on the handle.—Contributed by O. H. Meyer, Churdon, Iowa.

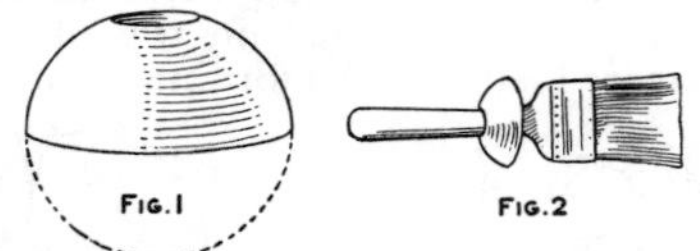

The Shape of the Ball Forms a Cup to Catch the Paint from the Brush

A Tie-Pin Holder

Having lost several tie pins by theft or by their falling out I made a little device to securely hold the pin in the tie. This device makes it almost impossible to pull the pin out and it cannot be lost accidentally. The device is made of a small safety pin, bent as shown, with one arm, A, longer than the other, B. The arm A is put on the pin first or upward, and attached as shown at C. When pulling on the tie pin the arms of the holder tend to draw together and clamp it on the pin.—Contributed by Robert C. Knox, Colorado Springs, Colo.

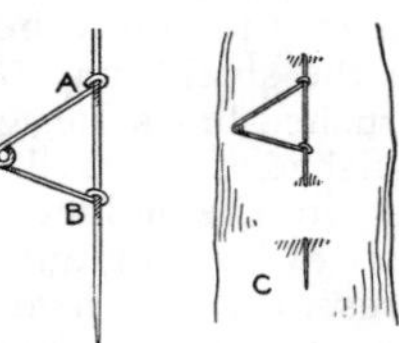

Hulling Walnuts

When gathering my winter supply of walnuts, I found that they could not be hulled readily by hand. Not knowing of any machine designed for the purpose, I tried running them through a corn sheller and found it to do the work nicely. The sheller not only hulled them, but separated the nuts from the hulls, the nuts being carried out through the cob opening and the hulls dropping through the grain spout.—Contributed by Irl R. Hicks, Hallsville, Mo.

How to Make a Small Vise Screw

Procure an ordinary lag screw, as shown in Fig. 1, cut off the pointed end and file the threads into the shape

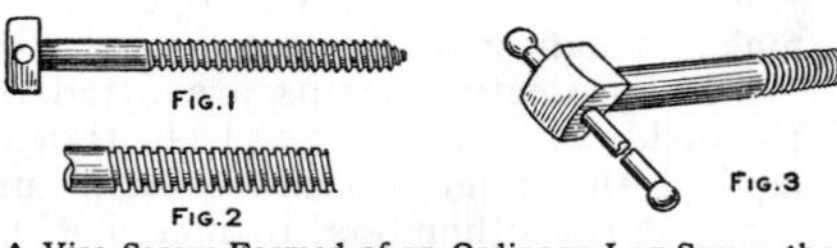

A Vise Screw Formed of an Ordinary Lag Screw, the Threads being Made Square and a Handle Attached

shown in Fig. 2. A hole is drilled through the head and a handle put in, as shown in Fig. 3. This makes a good substitute screw when the original screw for a small vise is broken.—Contributed by James M. Kane, Doylestown, Pa.

A Medicine-Spoon Holder

When a dropper is not at hand it is difficult to drop medicine in a spoon while holding it, and the shape of the spoon will not permit its being set down. A shoe horn used as shown in

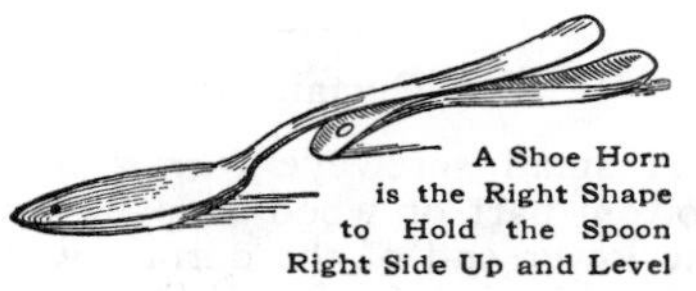
A Shoe Horn is the Right Shape to Hold the Spoon Right Side Up and Level

the sketch will hold the spoon right side up and in a position to hold the liquid.—Contributed by Maurice Baudier, New Orleans, La.

Knife Holder on a Frying Pan

Instead of laying a knife on the stove or carrying it to a table or elsewhere while frying anything in a pan,

The Shape of the Clip and Manner of Attaching It to a Frying Pan

make a clip to fit the edge of the pan for holding the knife when it is not in use. The clip is easily made of brass wire and when attached to a frying pan it will save many steps.—Contributed by John C. Harlacker, Jr., Cumberland, B. C.

A Broom for Sweeping Out Corners in Steps

Sweeping the corners of steps is one of the greatest difficulties of the housewife, or others who have a number of stairs to sweep. I have made this task easy in a very simple manner. I secured a used broom, the longer and newer the better, and cut the straws off diagonally across the sweeping edge. The pointed part will easily clean out the corners in steps or in a room.—Contributed by W. A. Stamaman, Berlin, Ontario.

Removing a Cork from a Bottle

A cork that has been pushed into a bottle accidentally or otherwise can be easily removed in the following manner: Tie several knots in one end of a string to form a large cluster and drop it into the bottle, holding on to the other end of the string. Turn the bottle over so that the cork will fall to the opening in the neck, then pull on the string. The cluster formed by the knots at the end of the string will easily draw out the cork.—Contributed by Frank Hart, Chicago, Ill.

Filing Flat Surfaces

Anyone who has used a file knows what skill is required to produce flat surfaces. A fixture which is nothing

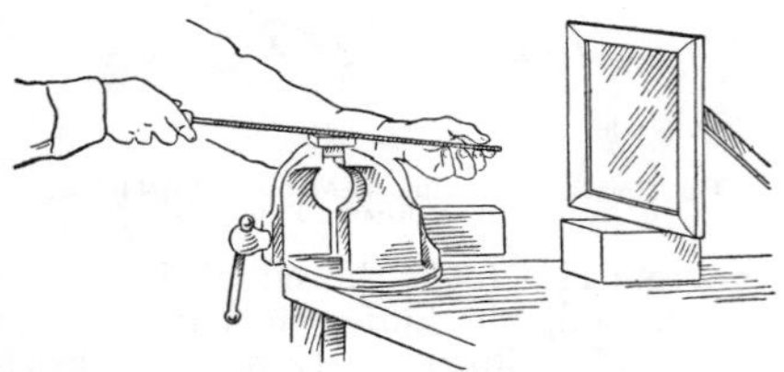

The File can be Seen in the Mirror and Its Direction Controlled for Filing Flat Surfaces

more than a mirror properly placed enables the operator to sight along the file and see at all times just how the file is running.—Contributed by A. F. Stearns, Madison, Wis.

Tacking a Screen on a Frame

Screen wire is very difficult material to fasten on a frame so that it becomes taut. To make it taut and even drive the tacks as follows: First tack the screen on one side of the frame, taking care to leave no slack between the tacks, which should be about 1 ft. apart. Fasten the opposite side by stretching the screen with one hand and with the other place the tack through the meshes and push the point as far as possible toward the outer edge of the screen frame as shown in the sketch. Drive the tack so that it will enter the wood straight, which will draw the screen taut. After having thus fastened the screen to two opposite sides of the frame with tacks 1 ft. apart, other tacks are driven in midway between the first ones, stretching the screen and driving the tacks as before described, until a sufficient number of tacks are driven into either side. Then both ends are attached in the same manner.—Contributed by Bertram S. Barnes, Santa Barbara, Cal.

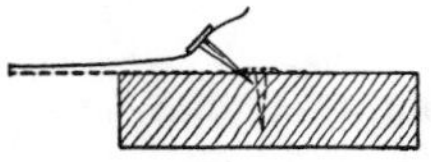

Safety Tips on Chair Rockers

Some rocking chairs are so constructed that when the person occupying it gives a hard tilt backward, the chair tips over or dangerously near it. A rubber-tipped screw turned into the under side of each rocker, near the rear end, will prevent the chair from tipping too far back.

Portable and Folding Bookcase or Closet

Two packing boxes hinged as shown and fitted with casters make a very convenient portable closet. It can be folded flat against a wall or fitted into a corner. If furnished with shelves, it can be used as a bookcase or tool closet, and when fully opened, it makes a handy workbench.

Two projecting strips are fitted on the inside of one box so as to fit tightly against the inner top and bottom surfaces of the other box, to increase the rigidity of the box when closed. The addition of casters makes the opening,

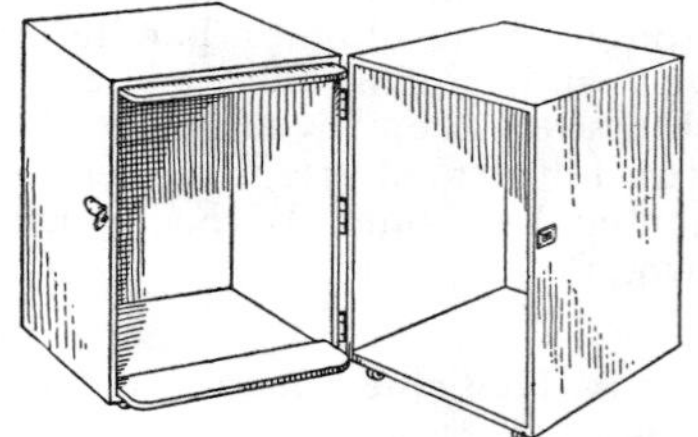

The Two Boxes are Joined on One Edge with Hinges and with a Hasp, if Desired, on the Other

closing and pushing about very easy. An ornamental hasp or lock can be fitted if desired.

A Curtain Stop

A small screweye turned into the bottom part or wood strip inclosed in the lower end of the curtain will prevent this end from winding over the top roller when the curtain is quickly released and rolls to the top.—Contributed by D. O. C. Kersten, Detroit, Michigan.

An Alarm for a Sleepwalker

A little girl in our family would walk in her sleep and it caused us no little worry lest she might leave the house without our knowing it. I therefore rigged up an alarm device to ring a bell should she leave the room. The device consisted of a bell and battery in a circuit, and a switch which was attached to one door casing. A string was stretched across the doorway and attached to the switch lever in such a manner as to pull it closed when the string was pushed through the doorway opening. —Contributed by J. Woodburn, Toronto, Canada.

A Kraut and Root Grinder

The grinder is intended mainly for chopping cabbage when making sauerkraut, but it is also of much service in grinding vegetables and roots to be cooked for poultry.

The base A is made of a plank, at least 1 ft. wide and 4 ft. long, with a 9¼ by 9½-in. hole cut in the center. The grinding part, or cylinder, is made of wood, 3 in. in diameter and 9 in. long, with 8-penny nails, spaced $\frac{3}{16}$ in. apart, driven partly into it and then cut off so as to leave ¼ in. projecting. The cylinder is turned by means of a crank attached to the end of the shaft.

A hopper, B, is constructed, 4 by 9½ in. inside measurement at the bottom, and as large as necessary at the top. A space is provided at the bottom as shown to receive the concave C, which consists of a 1-in. board, 3 to 4 in. wide and 9 in. long, with nails driven in and cut off as described for the cylinder.

The hopper is securely fastened on top of the baseboard and over the cylinder. The concave is slipped into place and held with wedges or by driving two nails in just far enough to fasten it temporarily. The concave can be adjusted for grinding the different vegetable products, or replaced at any time with a new one.

The ends of the base are supported on boxes, or legs may be provided if desired. When grinding cabbage, cut the heads into quarters and remove the hearts. Press the cabbage on the cylinder and turn the crank. Fine bits of cabbage, suitable for sauerkraut, will be the result.—Contributed by J. G. Allshouse, Avonmore, Pa.

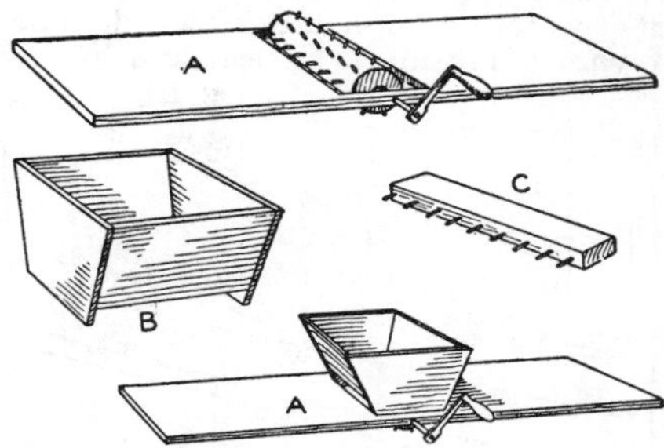

The Grinder will Easily Reduce Cabbage Heads to Bits Suitable for Sauerkraut

Opening for Air at the Top of a Shade

Procure an extra long shade and cut two openings in the end to be used at the top. The openings may be cut square or ornamental as desired, leaving a strip at each side and one in the center. These strips are reinforced by gluing on some of the same material as the shade or pieces of tape.

A shade made in this manner permits the air to enter the room unhindered when the top sash is lowered and at the same time obstructs the view of passers-by.—Contributed by Warren E. Crane, Cleveland, O.

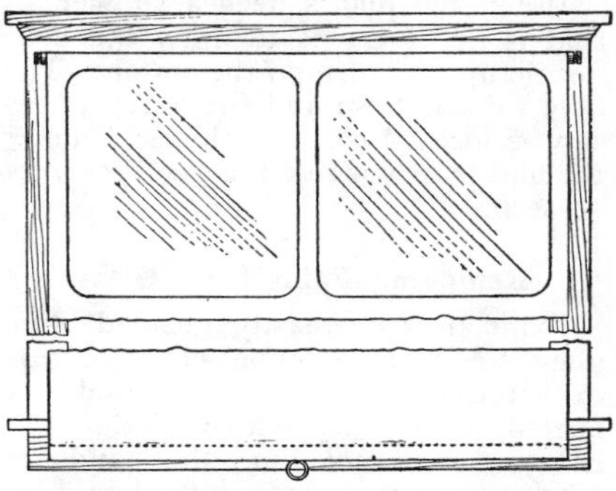
When the Shade is Pulled Down the Openings Coincide with the Opening over the Upper Sash

Hose Attachment for Watering Window Plants

The window garden of the house has its watering difficulties which one owner overcame in a neat and handy

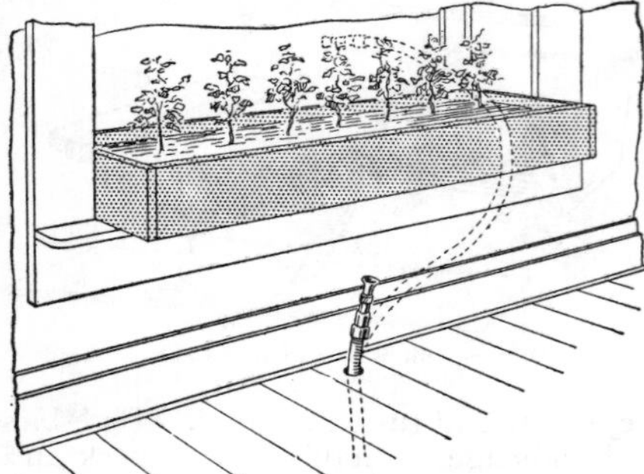
The Hose is Automatically Run on a Reel by a Weight beneath the Floor

manner. A hose on a weighted reel was attached to the joists in the basement under the floor near the window flower pots. The weight on the reel kept the hose wound on it and the nozzle end which projects through the floor is large enough to hold it from passing through the hole bored for the hose. A long stem valve was provided with the wheel attached above the floor for turning the water on and off.

When the plants need a shower all that is necessary is to draw the hose nozzle up and turn on the water. The hole for the hose and the valve wheel can be located close to the wall under the flower tray where they will scarcely be seen.

Removing Paint from Glass

Paint may be easily cleaned from glass by using a 50-per-cent solution of acetic acid. The acid should be heated and applied with a cloth. The hot acid will not hurt the hands or fabrics, nor the glass, but should be kept from children who might drink of it. The solution is made of commercial acetic acid and heated by adding hot water. The acid is inexpensive and can be purchased at any local drug store.

To Prevent Baking Ovens from Scorching

A good method to prevent baking ovens from scorching or burning pastry is to sprinkle a mixture of sand and salt on the bottom where the pans are placed. This affords a way of radiating the heat evenly. The mixture also absorbs fruit juices, which may be spilled in the course of cooking. The covering is easily changed, which keeps the oven clean. The best proportion is half salt and half sand.

Horn Candle Sconce

The person who cares for things unusual will find the candle sconce made of a cowhorn a suitable fixture for the den. A well shaped and not too large cowhorn is selected, and prepared by first partly filling it with paper, packed in tightly, then filling it to the top with plaster of Paris, in which a candle socket is formed.

The bracket is made of strips of metal, formed as shown and riveted together where they touch each other, the back piece being fastened with screws to a wall board. The metal may be brass or copper and finished in

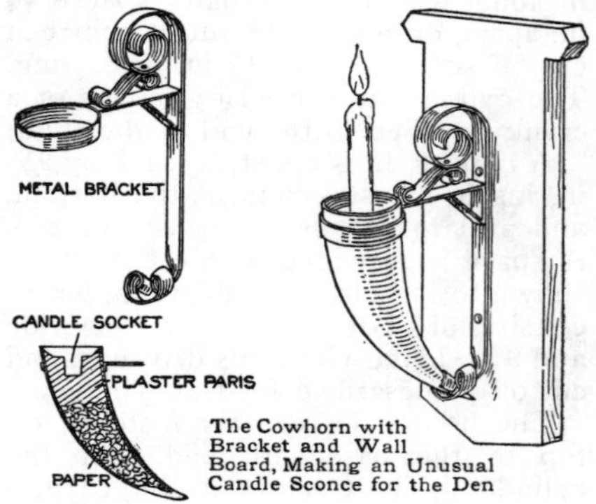

The Cowhorn with Bracket and Wall Board, Making an Unusual Candle Sconce for the Den

nickel, antique, bronze, or given a brush finish. The wooden wall piece can be finished in any style desired.

ℭWhite spots on furniture can be removed by rubbing the wood with ammonia.

How to Make a Copper Stencil for Marking Laundry

A stencil suitable for marking laundry may be easily made as follows: First procure a small sheet of "stencil sheet copper," about 1 in. wide and 4 in. long. Dip this sheet of copper in a vessel containing some melted beeswax, so that both sides will be evenly covered with a thin coat of the wax when it cools. The design—name, monogram or figure—that is wanted in the stencil should now be drawn upon a piece of thin white paper, the reverse side of the paper blackened with graphite, and then laid on the stencil plate with the design in the center of the plate, whereupon the design is lightly traced with a blunt point on the thin wax coating. After the paper is removed, trace the design on the wax surface with a pointed instrument, but not completely, the lines being broken at more or less regular intervals, to form "holders" so that, after etching, the design cannot fall out.

Next lay the stencil in a small shallow dish and pour a small quantity of fresh nitric acid over it. Keep the air bubbles removed from the surface by means of a piece of soft feather. The design will be eaten away in a very short time, where the wax has been removed, and this may be readily observed by holding the stencil plate up to the light. The acid should then be rinsed off with water, and the wax removed by heating and wiping it off with a cloth. The stencil may be given a final cleaning in a dish of benzine or gasoline, which will remove any remaining wax.

A Brass Pin Tray

A novelty pin tray can be easily made of a piece of No. 24 gauge sheet brass or copper, 5 in. in diameter. The metal is annealed and polished with fine emery cloth, which is given a circular motion to produce a frosted effect. The necessary tools are a 1-in. hardwood board with a 2½-in. hole bored in it, and a round piece of hard wood, 1⅞ or 2 in. in diameter, with the ends sawn off square.

Place the sheet metal centrally over the hole in the board and set one end of the round stick in the center of the metal. Drive the stick with a hammer until a recess about 1 in. deep is made in the center. The edge of the metal will wrinkle up as shown in the sketch. It is scarcely possible to make two trays alike, as the edge almost invariably will buckle in a different manner.—Contributed by F. Van Eps, Plainfield, N. J.

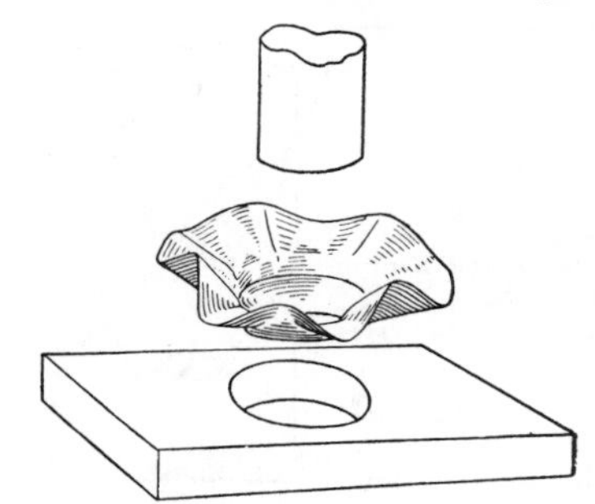

The Former and Method of Using It to Produce a Wrinkled Edge on the Tray

A Homemade Exerciser

A weight machine for exercising the muscles of the arms is easily constructed by using two screw hooks, 5 in. long, and two small pulleys, 2½ in. in diameter. An awning pulley can be used for this purpose. The hole at the top of the hanger will allow the pulley to freely turn at almost any angle. A paving brick or a piece of metal can be used as a weight for each rope.—Contributed by Sterling R. Speirs, St. Louis, Mo.

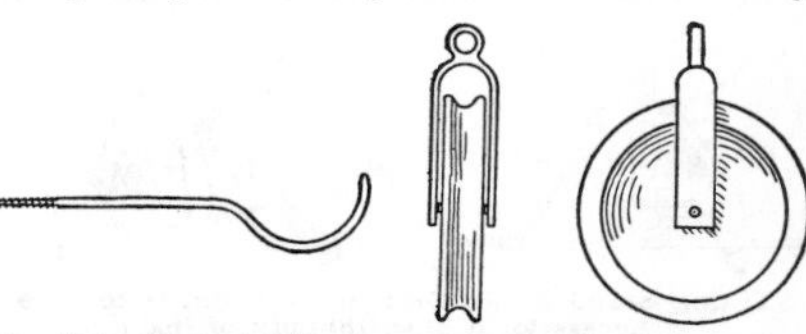

The Yoke of the Pulley is so Arranged as to Make It Move in All Positions on the Hook

A Book Covering

New books can be quickly and neatly covered to keep them clean by cutting a paper large enough to cover the back and sides when the book is closed, allowing 1 in. extra at each end to be turned over the front and back edges, then pasting on corners cut from used envelopes. The paper jacket can be slipped on or off easily when the book is opened, and it will keep a new cover clean while the book is being handled.—Contributed by Dr. John A. Cohalan, Philadelphia.

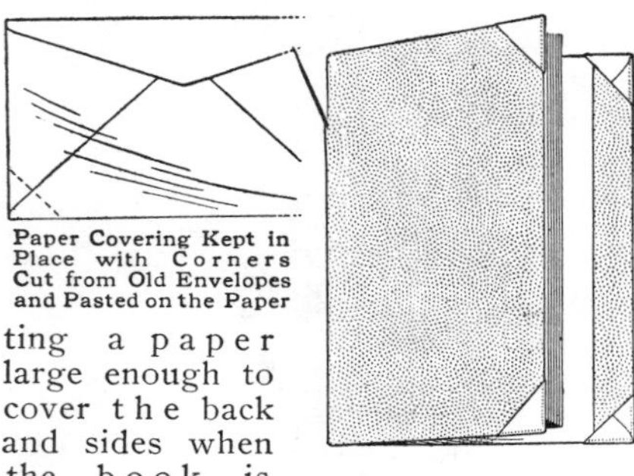

Paper Covering Kept in Place with Corners Cut from Old Envelopes and Pasted on the Paper

A Tilting Inkstand

An ink-bottle stand, that can be tilted or adjusted so that the pen will always be filled with a sufficient quantity of ink even when little of it remains in the bottle, as shown in the sketch, can be easily made by the amateur. The base may consist of a square piece of sheet brass, which has soldered or riveted to its center two pieces of spring brass, placed crosswise and bent upward so as to form clips to hold the bottle firmly. The legs are made of two lengths of wire, of sufficient stiffness, and are shaped to form holders for lead pencils and penholders. One pair of the legs may be soldered to the brass plate and the opposite side of the latter rolled over the other pair so as to allow them either to stand upright or be depressed in order to tilt the stand, when the ink supply in the bottle gets low.

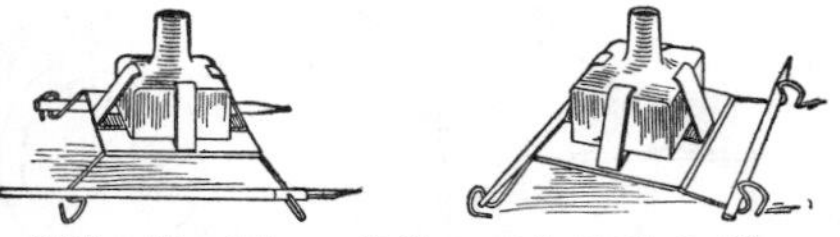

Tilting Stand for an Ordinary Ink Bottle to Give Access for a Small Supply of Ink

A Ring Trick

The trick to be described is one of the simplest and at the same time one of the most effective, and but little "make-ready" is required to perform it. The magician, while sitting in a chair, allows his hands to be tied together behind the back of the chair. A ring is placed between his lips which he claims to be able to slip on his finger without untying his hands. This, to the audience, seems practically impossible, but it is easily accomplished.

A screen is placed in front of the performer before the trick is started, so that the audience will not see how it is done. As soon as he is hidden from view, he tilts his head forward and drops the ring in his lap. He then allows the ring to drop to the seat of the chair between his legs. The chair is tilted backward slightly, and he raises himself to allow the ring to slip to the back part of the chair seat, where he catches it in his hands and slips it on the finger. Any one finger may be mentioned, as he can slip the ring as readily on one as on another. Use a leather-bottom chair, if possible, as the least noise will then be made when the ring is dropped.—Contributed by Abner B. Shaw, N. Dartmouth, Massachusetts.

Removing Old Putty

A very effective way to remove old putty from window panes or other articles is to apply a red-hot iron, as follows: The iron should be made of a broken file or cold chisel and the point heated quite hot. This is run over the surface of the putty, which will crack and fall off. Be careful not to let the hot iron touch the glass, as the heat may cause the latter to break.

How to Make a Water Wheel

The materials used in the construction of this water wheel are such as the average amateur mechanic may pick up or secure from a junk pile. The drawings in Fig. 1 clearly show the way the wheel is built. The nozzle, Fig. 2, is made of pipe and fittings and is adjustable to concentrate the stream so as to get the full efficiency of the weight and velocity of the water. The cap on the end of the nipple is drilled to receive the pin point filed on the end of the 1/4-in. rod. The parts of this nozzle are a 1/2-in. tee, connected to the source of water supply; a plug, drilled to snugly fit the 1/4-in. rod, and fitted into one end of the straight part of the tee; and a 1/2-in. nipple of sufficient length to make the dimension shown in the sketch. The nipple has a long thread to receive two 1/2-in. locknuts, which clamp the nozzle to the sheet-metal covering, as shown in Fig. 1.

The buckets, Fig. 3, are formed of some easily melted, but not too soft metal alloy which can be cast in plaster molds. They are attached with rivets to the circumference of a 1/16-in. thick sheet-metal disk of the diameter given in Fig. 1. This disk is fastened to a 1/4-in. shaft, 6 in. long, with two collars, one on each side of the disk, both being riveted to the disk and pinned to the shaft. The bearings AA are made of 3/4-in. pipe, each 2 1/4 in. long. Long threads are cut on these to turn through the two 3/4-in. waste nuts BB, which provides a way to adjust the buckets centrally with the stream of water, and to take up any side motion. The pipe is babbitted and drilled for oil holes. The runner or wheel must be well balanced, as the speed will be from 2,000 to 2,500 revolutions per minute with ordinary city pressure. In balancing the wheel, instead of adding an extra weight, a part of the disk is filed out on one edge. The inclosing sides are made of wood—cypress preferred—having the dimensions given, and two 7/8 by 1 1/2-in. pieces are attached to the bottom outside surfaces for mounting the wheel. The curved part is covered with galvanized sheet metal.

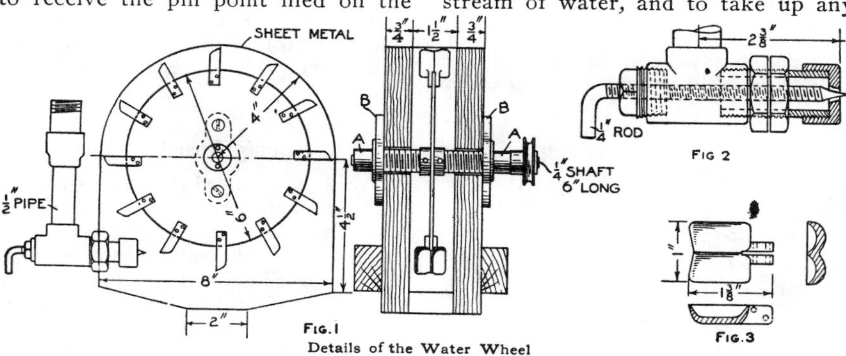

Details of the Water Wheel

The drawing shows a wheel of

small diameter, but having considerable power. Greater power may be obtained by increasing the size of the jet and the diameter of the wheel, but the use of too many buckets results

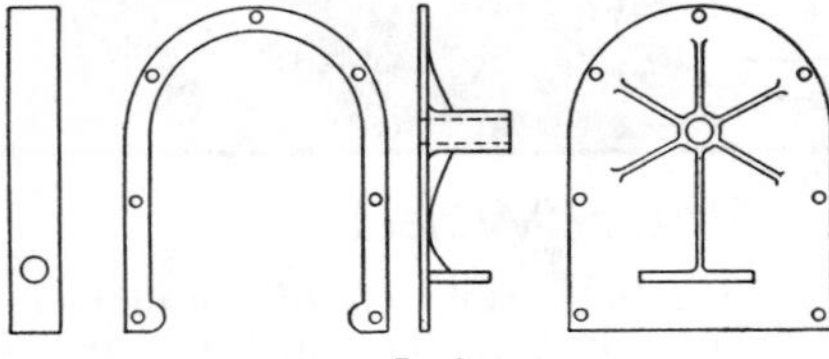

Metal Casing Instead of Wood

in decrease of power. One bucket should be just entering the stream of water, when the working bucket is at a point at right angles to the stream. The water should divide equally exactly on the center of the bucket and get out of the way as soon as possible. Any stagnant water in the case, or dead water in the bucket, is detrimental to the power. A free exit for the water is made at the bottom of the case, as shown.

The construction of the case may be varied and, instead of wood, metal sides and frame may be used. Where the builder cares to make a more substantial wheel and has access to a foundry, the metal parts can be made as shown in Fig. 4. The parts are in this instance fastened together with machine screws. Patterns are made and taken to a foundry for the castings, which are then machined to have close fitting joints.—Contributed by R. H. Franklin, Unnatosa, Wis.

An Interesting Experiment

Take an ordinary board, 2 or 3 ft. long, such as a bread board, and place it on the table so that about one-third

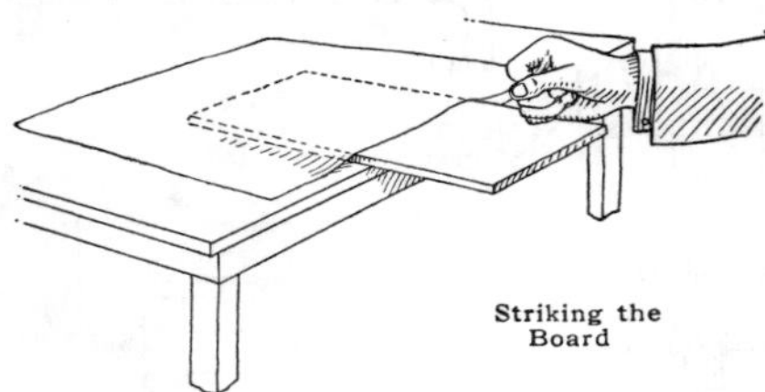
Striking the Board

of its length will project over the edge. Unfold a newspaper and lay it on the table over the board as shown in the sketch. Anyone not familiar with the experiment would suppose the board could be knocked off by hitting it on the outer end. It would appear to be easy to do, but try it. Unless you are prepared to break the board you will probably not be able to knock the board off.

The reason is that when the board is struck it forces the other end up and the newspaper along with it. This causes a momentary vacuum to be formed under the paper, and the pressure of the air above, which is about 15 lb. to the square inch, prevents the board from coming up. This is an entertaining trick to play at an evening party, and also makes a simple and interesting school experiment.

Ironing-Board Holder

An ironing board that had been used on two chairs was cut off square on one end and a piece of heavy sheet metal cut and bent into the shape shown in Fig. 1. The square end of the board was fitted into the socket formed by the sheet metal. After attaching the socket to the wall with screws the board was easily put in

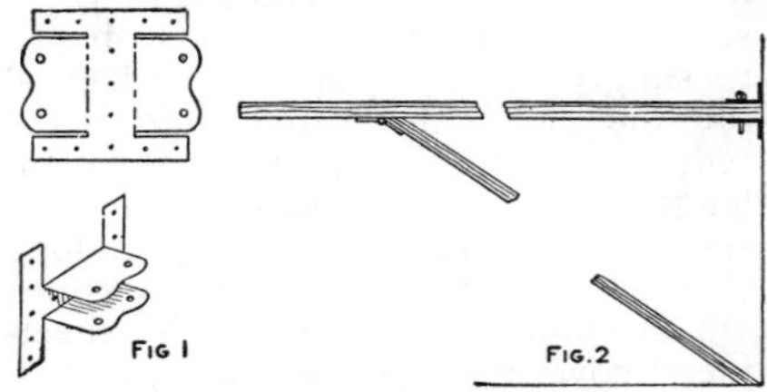

Socket and Manner of Holding Board

place as shown in Fig. 2. The brace is hinged to the under side of the board. —Contributed by L. G. Swett, Rochester, N. Y.

How to Make a Water Motor

By EDWARD SILJA

After making several different styles of water motors I found the one illustrated to be the most powerful as well as the simplest and most inexpensive to make. It can be constructed in the following manner: A disk, as shown in Fig. 1, cut from sheet iron or brass, $\frac{1}{16}$ in. thick and 9¾ in. in diameter, constitutes the main part of the wheel. The circumference is divided into 24 equal parts, and a depth line marked which is 8¼ in. in diameter. Notches are cut to the depth line, similar to the teeth of a rip saw, one edge being on a line with the center of the wheel and the other running from the top of one tooth to the base of the preceding tooth.

A ¼-in. hole is drilled in the center of the disk and the metal strengthened with a flange, placed on each side of the disk and fastened with screws or rivets. A ¼-in. steel rod is used for the shaft.

The cups, or buckets, are shaped in a die which can be cast or built up of two pieces, as desired. Both of these dies are shown in Fig. 2. The one at A is made of two pieces riveted together.

If a foundry is near, a pattern can be made for a casting, as shown at B.

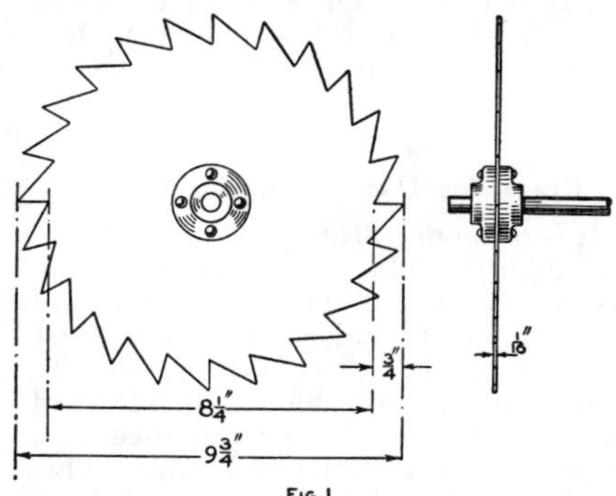

Fig. 1

Metal Disk with a Saw-Tooth Circumference That Constitutes the Main Body of the Wheel

The die is used in the manner shown in Fig. 3. A strip of galvanized metal is placed over the depressions in the die and a ball-peen hammer used to

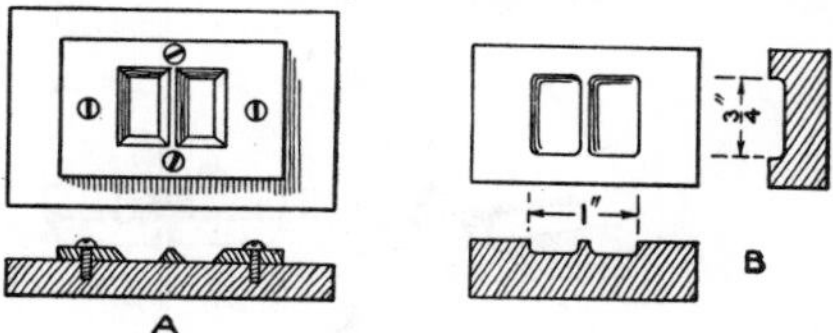

Fig. 2

Two Ways of Making the Dies to Shape the Sheet-Metal Water Cups

drive the metal into the die. Cups, or buckets, are thus formed which are soldered to the edge of the teeth on a line with the center of the disk, as

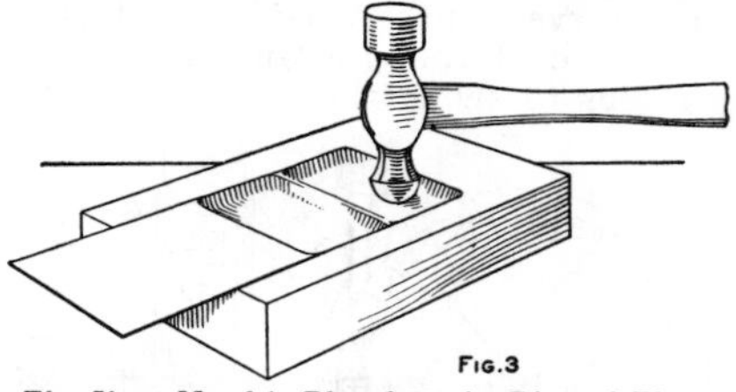

Fig. 3

The Sheet Metal is Placed on the Die and Then Hammered into Shape

shown in Fig. 4. As there are 24 notches in the disk, 24 cups will be necessary to fill them.

The cups are made in pairs or in two sections, which is a better construction than the single cup. The water from the nozzle first strikes the center between the cups, then divides and produces a double force.

When this part of the work is finished it is well to balance the wheel, which can be done by filing off some of the metal on the heavy side or adding a little solder to the light side. This will be necessary to provide an easy-running wheel that will not cause any unnecessary wear on the bearings.

The housing for the wheel consists of two wood pieces, about ¾-in. thick and cut to the shape shown in Fig. 5. Grooves are cut in one surface of each piece, to receive the edges of a strip of galvanized metal, as shown at A. The grooves are cut with a specially constructed saw, shown in Fig. 6. It consists of a piece of wood, 6 in. long,

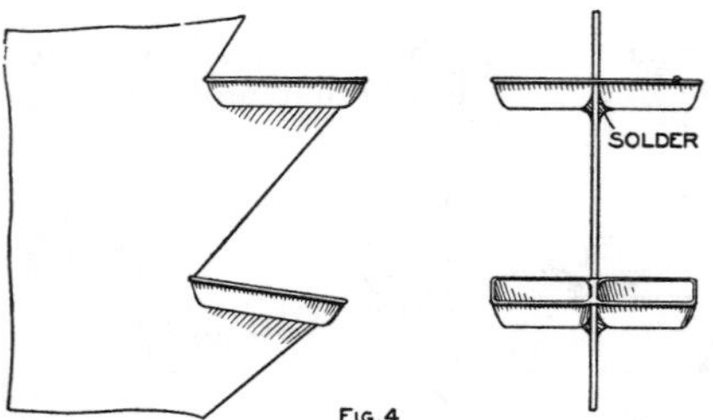

The Water Cups are Fastened to the Teeth on the Metal Disk with Solder

1½ in. wide and ½ in. thick, the end being cut on an arc of a circle whose diameter is 10 in. A piece of a broken hacksaw blade is fastened with screws to the curved end. A nail is used as a center pivot, forming a 5-in. and a 5¾-in. radius to swing the saw on in cut-

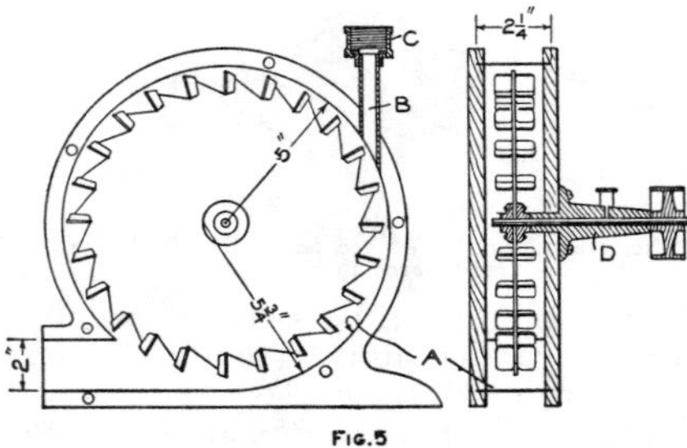

The Housing for the Wheel with a Connection to Attach the Motor on an Ordinary Faucet

ting the groove. After inserting the strip of galvanized metal, A, Fig. 5, the sides are clamped together with bolts about 3¼ in. long.

A piece of pipe, B, Fig. 5, having an opening ⅜-in. in diameter, is soldered onto the metal strip A. An ordinary

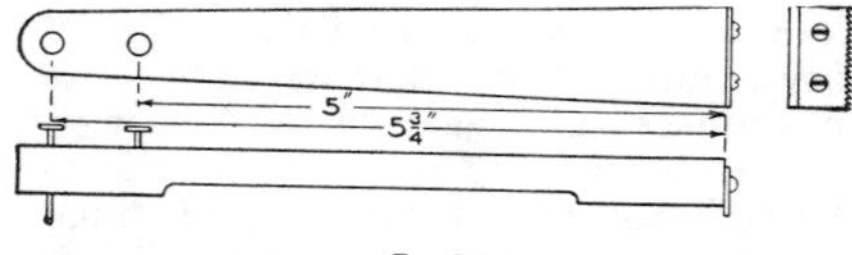

Construction of the Saw for Making the Groove to Receive the Metal Strip in the Sides

garden-hose coupling, C, is soldered to the end of the pipe.

A bearing, D, shaped as shown, is fastened to one of the wood sides with screws, the wheel shaft is run into it, and the parts assembled. A wheel, either grooved or flat, 2½ or 3 in. in diameter, is placed on the shaft. The hose coupling makes it easy to connect the motor directly to the water faucet.

An Application for Small Wounds

Pure wintergreen oil makes a good local application for all small wounds, bites, scratches, abrasions, etc. There is no germ or microbe, animal or vegetable, dead or living, that can withstand this oil, and at the same time it is not injurious to living tissues. A few drops gently rubbed in where there is apt to be any infection is sufficient.

An infection always follows the wound of a bullet or the scratch of a brass pin, with irritation extending up the limb or part threatening tetanus or lockjaw. These symptoms are manifested by spasmodic pains which shoot upward, but are quickly subdued, if the oil is applied along the track of the pain or infection. This oil is equally effective when locally applied to tendons or ligaments which have been unduly strained.

An ounce of the pure oil does not cost much, and it should be kept in every shop and household. If 5 or 10 per cent of olive oil is added to it, the oil will have more body and will last longer.—Contributed by Dr. E. R. Ellis, Detroit, Mich.

Cores for Use in Babbitt Metal

It is often necessary in making things of babbitt metal to core out some of the parts. A very good core is made of common salt and glue. Mix just enough of the glue into the salt to make a stiff paste, which is then formed into the desired shape or molded in a core box and allowed to harden. This kind of a core can be removed from the casting by soaking it in warm water, which will dissolve the salt and leave the desired hole.—Contributed by H. F. Hopkins, N. Girard, Pa.

How to Build a Wind Vane with an Electric Indicator

Quite often it is practically impossible to ascertain the direction of the wind by observing an ordinary wind vane on account of the necessity of locating the vane at such a height that it may give a true indication. By means of the device shown in Fig. 2, the position of the vane may be determined without actually looking at the vane itself and the indicating device may be located almost anywhere and independently of the position of the wind vane.

The principle upon which the device operates is that of the Wheatstone bridge. The position of the moving contact A, Fig. 1, is controlled by the wind vane. This contact is made to move over a specially constructed resistance R, Fig. 2. A second movable contact, B, is controlled by the observer and moves over a second resistance, identical with that over which the contact A moves. These two resistances are connected so as to form the two main branches of a Wheatstone bridge; the points A and B are connected to the current-detecting device, which may be a galvanometer or telephone receiver, and current is supplied by a number of dry cells.

In order to obtain a balance—that is, no current through the receiver—the points A and B must occupy corresponding positions on their respective resistances. If the two resistances over which the points A and B move are mounted in the same position with respect to the cardinal points of the compass, then the points themselves will always be in the same position with respect to the cardinal points when a balance is obtained. The arrow head on the wind vane and the point A are made to occupy corresponding positions, and hence the position of the point B, when no current passes through the receiver, is an indication of the direction in which the wind vane is pointing.

The principal parts in the construction of the device are shown in the illustration, and the following description of their construction may be of interest to those who contemplate building the indicator.

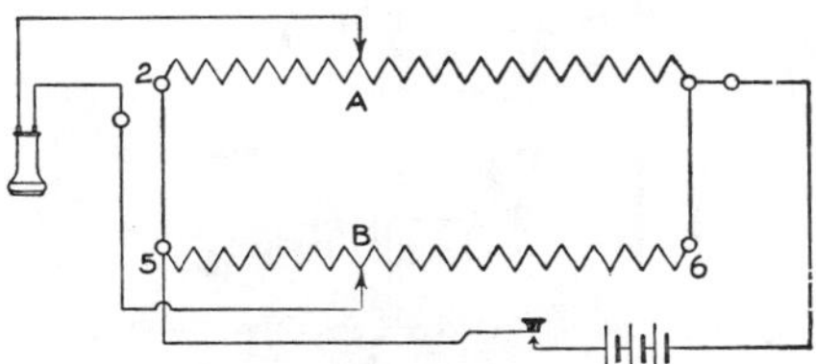

Fig. 1—The Diagram of a Wheatstone Bridge Which Shows the Points of Contact So Placed That a Balance is Obtained

Procure two pieces of $\frac{1}{16}$-in. hard rubber, 1½ in. wide by 24 in. long. Clamp these, side by side, between two boards and smooth down their edges and ends, and then file small slots in the edges with the edge of a three-cornered file. These slots should all be equally spaced about $\frac{3}{32}$ in. apart. Have the pieces clamped together while filing the slots and mark one edge top and one end right so that the pieces may be mounted alike. Now procure a small quantity of No. 20 gauge bare manganin wire. Fasten one end of this wire to one end of the pieces of rubber by winding it in and out through three or four small holes and then wind it around the piece, placing the various turns in the small slots that were filed in the edges. After completing the winding, fasten the end just as the starting end was attached. Wind the second piece of rubber in a similar manner and make sure to have the length of the free ends in each case the same. Obtain a cylinder of some kind, about 8 in. in diameter, warm the pieces of rubber by dipping them in hot water, bend them around the cylinder and allow them to cool.

A containing case, similar to that shown in cross section in the upper portion of Fig. 2 should now be constructed from a good quality of tin or copper. The inside diameter of this case should be about 1 in. more than the outside diameter of the resistance ring R, and it should be about 3 in. deep. The top C may be made

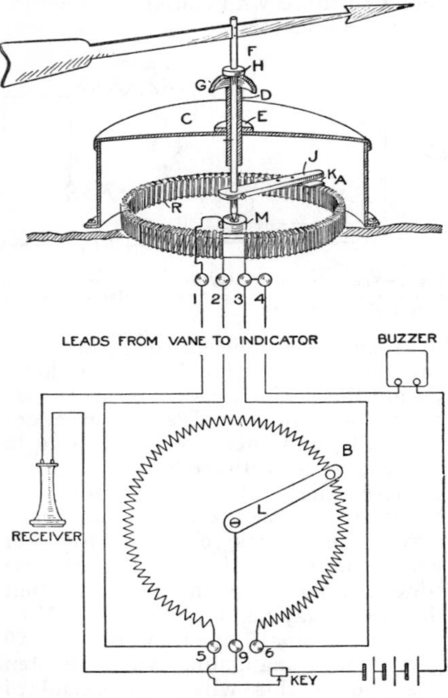

Fig. 2—The Weather Vane with Resistance Coil, and Diagram of Indicator Which is Identical with That of the Vane

curved as shown in the illustration, and should be fastened to the case proper by a number of small machine screws. The base of this case may be made so that the whole device can be mounted on the top of a pole.

Mount a piece of ¼-in. steel rod, about ½ in. long, with a conical hole in one end, in the center of the bottom of the case as shown by M. A number of supports, similar to the one shown, should be made from some ¼-in. hard rubber and fastened to the sides of the case, to support the resistance ring. The dimensions of these supports should be such that the ends of the piece of rubber, forming the ring, are against each other when it is in place. The upper edge of the ring should be about 2 in. above the bottom of the case.

Next, mount a piece of brass tube, D, in the exact center of the top and perpendicular to it. A washer, E, may also be soldered to the top so as to aid in holding the tube. Procure a piece of steel rod, F, that will fit in the tube D and turn freely. Sharpen one end of this rod and mount a brass wind vane on the other end. A small metal cup, G, may be soldered to a washer, H, and the whole mounted on the steel rod F in an inverted position as shown, which will prevent water from getting down inside the case along the rod. The cup G may be soldered directly to the rod. Make a small arm, J, of brass, and fasten a piece of light spring, K, to one side of it, near the outer end, then mount the arm on the steel rod so that it is parallel to the vane and its outer end points in the same direction as the arrow on the vane. The free end of the light spring on the arm J should be broad enough to bridge the gap between adjacent turns of wire on the resistance ring. Four bindings should then be mounted on the inside of the case and all insulated from it with the exception of number 1. Numbers 2 and 3 are connected to the ends of the winding and number 4 is connected to number 3.

A second outfit should now be constructed, identical with the one just described except that it should have a flat top with a circular scale mounted on it, and the arm L should be controlled by a small handle in the center of the scale. The position of the contact B may be indicated on the scale by a slender pointer, attached to the handle controlling the arm L.

Four leads of equal resistance should be used in connecting the two devices and the connections made as shown. An ordinary buzzer placed in the battery circuit will produce an interrupted current through the bridge circuit and a balance will be obtained by adjusting the contact point B until a minimum hum is heard in the telephone receiver.

Planting Seeds in Egg Shells

When growing flower plants from seeds, start them in halves of shells from hard-boiled eggs. When the time comes to transplant them, they can be easily removed by allowing the dirt in the shell to become hard and then breaking off the shell, whereupon the plant is placed in the ground.

A pasteboard box provided with holes large enough to support the egg shells can be used to hold them, unless egg crates are at hand. Two large seeds such as nasturtiums and sweet peas can be planted in one shell, and four seeds of the smaller varieties.—Contributed by Katharine D. Morse, Syracuse, N. Y.

Locating Drip Pan under a Refrigerator

In replacing the drip pan of an ice box or refrigerator it is often necessary to bend over in locating it under the drip pipe. This trouble may be done away with by fastening two strips of wood in a V-shape to the floor beneath the refrigerator. When the pan is shoved under, it will strike one

Strips on Floor under Refrigerator

strip and slide along until it strikes the other. Then the pan is sure to be under the drip pipe.—Contributed by Lloyd A. Phelan, Beachmont, Mass.

Windmill for Light Power

The windmill shown in the sketch is one that will always face the wind, and it never requires adjustment. It

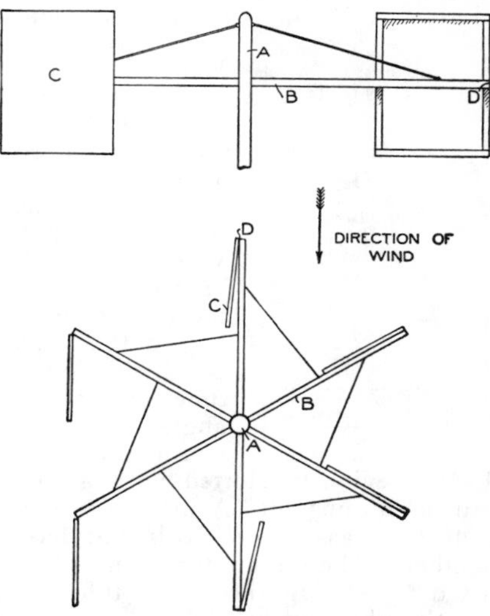

Frames Hinged to the Arms

consists of a vertical shaft, A, provided with a number of arms, B, on which are hinged square sails, C. These sails are preferably made of wood frames covered with canvas. They are provided with hinges, D, attached to the ends of the arms in such a way that they offer resistance to the wind on one side of the wheel, while they move edgewise against the wind on the other side, as shown. The shaft of the mill can either be run in bearings set on an upright post, the lower end of the shaft turning on a conical bearing, or collars may be used on the bearings to keep it in position. The power can be transmitted with gears or by a flat belt over a pulley.

A wheel of this kind is not adapted for high speed, but direct-connected to a pump or other slow-working machinery will prove very efficient.—Contributed by Edward Hanson, Kane, Pennsylvania.

A Small Bunsen Burner

An excellent bunsen burner for small work can be made as follows: Draw a glass tube to the shape shown, to produce a fine hollow point. Mark carefully with a file and break at A and then at B. Bore or burn a hole in a cork to fit the tube. Cut a V-shaped notch in the side of the cork extending to the hole. Bend the lower tube at right angles and insert it in a wood block, previously slotted with a saw to make a snug fit. A little glue will hold the glass tubes, cork and base together. The air mixture can be adjusted by sliding the upper tube before the glue sets.

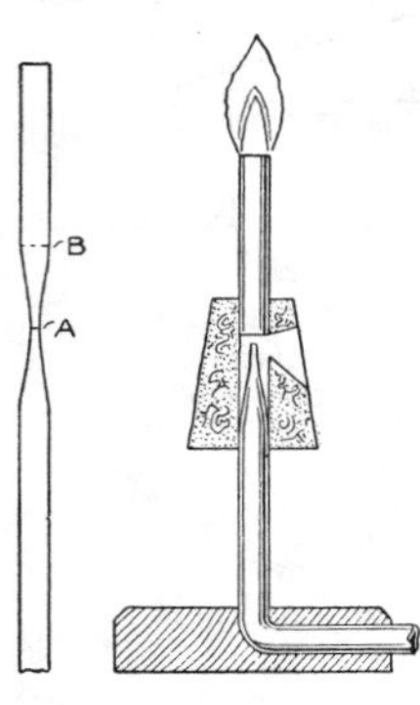

The burner is especially adapted to continuous work, such as sealing packages, etc. The flame will not discolor the wax.—Contributed by E. P. Ferté, Spokane, Wash.

The Hindoo Sand Trick

This is one of the many tricks for which the Hindoos are famous, and was long kept a secret by them. It consists of placing ordinary sand in a basin full of water, stirring the water and taking out the sand in handfuls perfectly dry. It need scarcely be said that without previous preparation, it is impossible to do so.

Take 2 lb. of fine silver sand, place it in a frying pan and heat well over a clear fire. When the sand is thoroughly heated, place a small piece of grease or wax—the composition of a paraffin candle preferred—in the sand, stirring it well to get it thoroughly mixed, then allow the sand to cool. When this sand is placed in a basin of water, it will be apparently dry when taken out. It is very important that only a small portion of the adherent be used so that it cannot be detected when the sand is examined by the audience. The explanation is that the grease or wax coating on each sand particle repels the water.—Contributed by Mighty Oaks, Oshkosh, Wis.

A Kite-Line Cutaway for Toy Parachutes

The cutaway is made of a small piece of board, a cigar-box lid, an old yardstick or a piece of lath, which should be about 6 in. long. Common carpet wire staples are used to hold it on the string. The under side has a wire bent into such a shape as to form a loop at the forward end over the kite string, then running back through the two staples at the one side and through two staples at the other side.

The parachute should have a small wire ring fastened at the weight end so as to fasten in the carrier, and

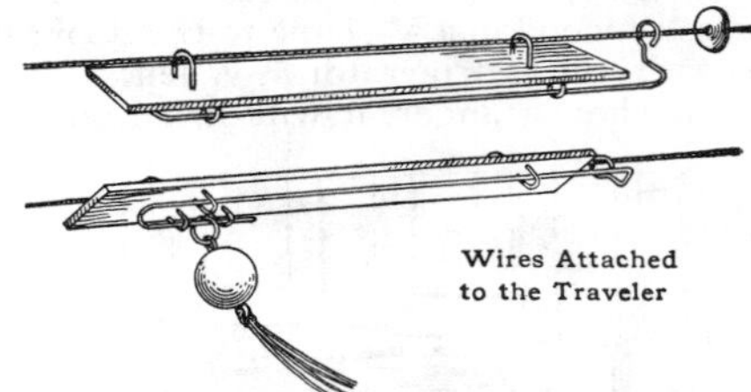

Wires Attached to the Traveler

should be put between the two staples that are closest together on the under side of the carrier. A small nail or button—anything larger than the loop in the wire—should be attached to the kite string a few feet from the kite. When the parachute is carried up the kite string, the knob on the string will strike the loop of the wire on the carrier, which releases the parachute and allows it to drop. The carrier will return of its own weight to the lower end of the string.—Contributed by I. O. Lansing, Lincoln, Neb.

A Cherry Pitter

Procure an ordinary quill feather and cut the tip off to form a small hole. Do not remove so much of the end that the cherry stone can stick in it. The hole must be slightly smaller than the cherry stone. Push the quill through the center of the cherry and the stone will come out easily.—Contributed by Harold Wynning, Chicago, Ill.

To Hold a Fish while Removing the Scales

Insert a screwdriver or ice pick in a fish as shown, and the scales can be removed much better and quicker than in any other way. The handle of the

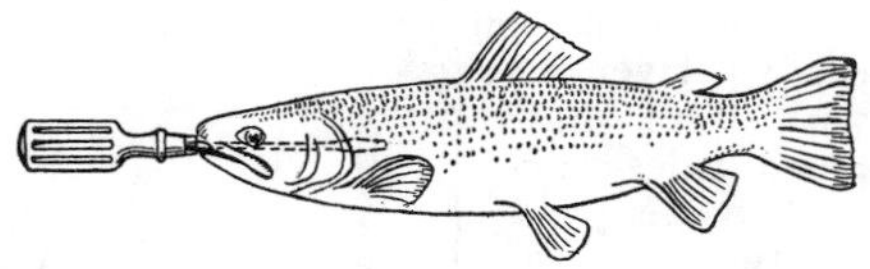

Holding Fish for Scaling

screwdriver affords an efficient grip so that the fish can be held firmly on the board and every scale can be removed.

Carrying Stone Jars

The handholds on stone jars are usually not large enough to carry the jars safely when they are full. If the handles of an old galvanized tub are riveted to a leather strap long enough to reach under the bottom and almost to the top on each side, the jar can be handled without danger of being dropped. The fingers are placed in the handles to carry the weight, while the thumbs are used to keep the jar from tipping. By placing a buckle near one end, the strap may be used for carrying a jar of any size.—Contributed by C. H. Floyd, Elwood, Ind.

Vibrator for a Spark Coil

If you do not have the time to make a vibrator or electrolytic interrupter for a spark coil, a common electric door-

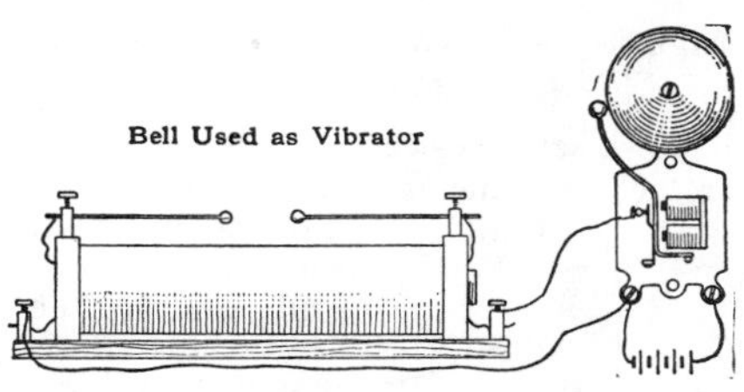

Bell Used as Vibrator

bell makes a good substitute. Connect one of the primary wires to the binding-post of the bell that is not insulated from the frame, and the other primary wire to the adjusting screw on the make-and-break contact of the bell, as shown in the sketch. The connections are made from the batteries to the bell in the usual manner.—Contributed by Ralph Tarshis, Brooklyn, N. Y.

Head Rest for a Chair

While seated in a chair a person very often desires to lay the head back in resting. A support for the head is lacking in the low-back rockers and ordinary chairs. A detachable, padded support can be easily made at home for placing on any low-back chair and used as a head rest.

The support standards can be made of wood or metal as desired. If metal

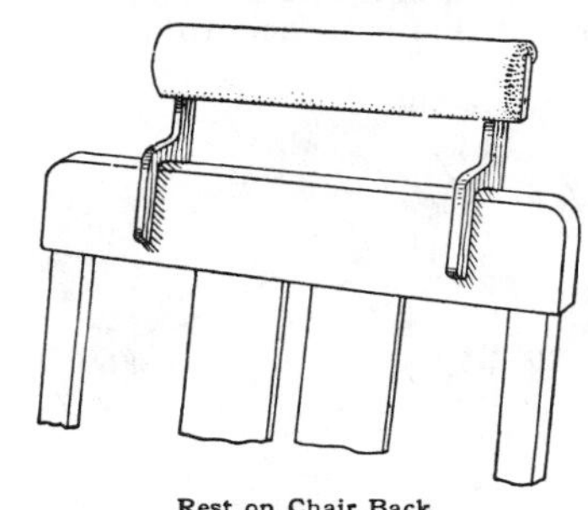

Rest on Chair Back

is used, the rest will have some springiness, which combined with the pad will insure much greater comfort than the hard rigid back. A cloth or paper is placed over the back of the chair to prevent marring of the varnish or wood.

Lighting a Lawn Mower for Use at Night

Those who desire to do so, or must, for lack of time during the day, may use their lawn mower at night and light the front of their machine with an ordinary bicycle lamp. The arm to hold the lamp can be attached with screws to the handle as shown in the sketch. It is easily made from a piece of hoop or bar iron.—Contributed by Samuel F. Reid, Minneapolis, Minn.

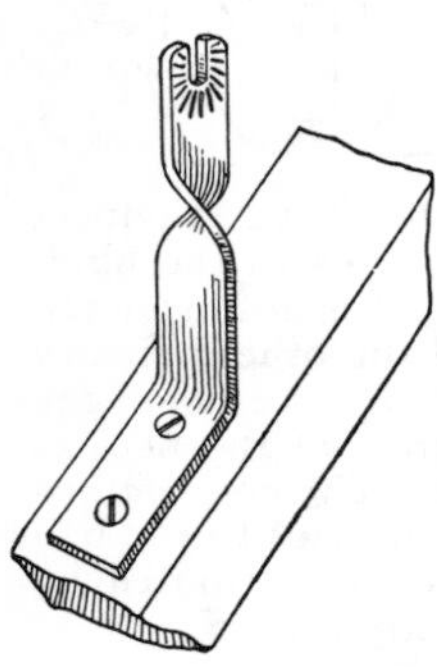

Tying a Rosette in a Couch-Cover Corner

In the accompanying illustration is shown a very simple method of tying a rosette in the corner of a couch cover. The use of the average couch cover as a throw-over leaves a large corner which drags upon the floor. To dispose of this extra length and at the same time make an artistic corner, the Upholsterer suggests the following method:

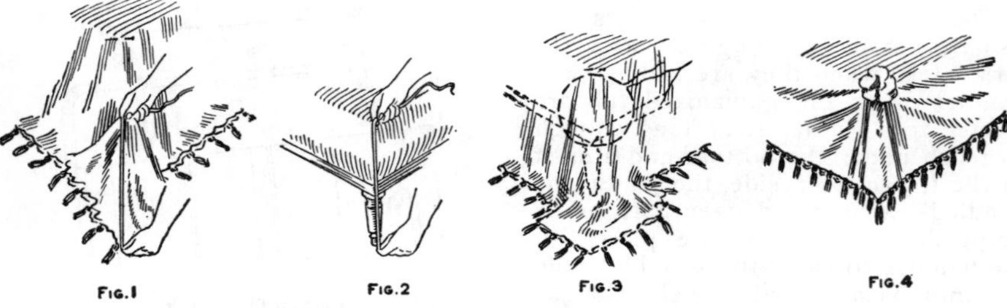

Different Stages in Tying the Rosette

Spread the couch cover on the couch so that the surplus is evenly divided between the sides and ends, and pass a pin through the cover to show each corner as in Fig. 1. Measure the distance from each corner of the couch to the floor, Fig. 2, and measuring from the point of the corner, mark the same distance by the insertion of another pin, repeating in all four corners. The distance between the two pins at each corner now defines the amount of surplus that is to be taken up. Chalk a circle to include the portion between these two pins, as shown in Fig. 3, and with a circular needle and stout stitching twine run a shirring thread around the circle, and when this is drawn tightly and tied, the surplus is formed into a rosette, while the corner may be draped into an artistic cascade, as shown in Fig. 4.

Driving Screws

A wood screw having the threads hammered flat on two sides can be easily driven in with the flattened sides parallel to the grain of the wood. When the screw is turned a quarter turn the remaining threads cross the grain and hold as well as if they had been turned in all the way. This is an especial advantage where something is wanted which is easily inserted and will hold better than a nail.—Contributed by P. D. Merrill, Chicago.

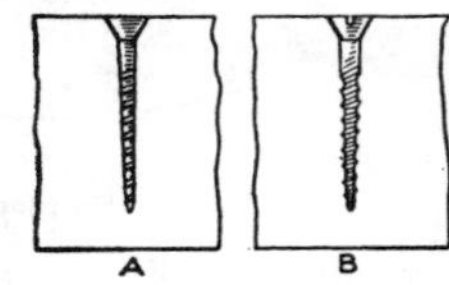

A Power Windmill

The windmill shown is somewhat different from the ordinary kind. It is not a toy, nor does it approach in size the ordinary farm windmill, but is a compromise between the two, and in a good strong wind, will supply power enough to run a washing machine, a small dynamo, an emery wheel, or any other device used in the home workshop. The wheel is about 5 ft. in diameter, with eight blades. The over-all length is about 6 feet.

The windmill is easily made and the cost is within the means of the average boy. There is not a part used in its construction that cannot be found about an ordinary manual-training shop. The most difficult parts of the construction will be described in

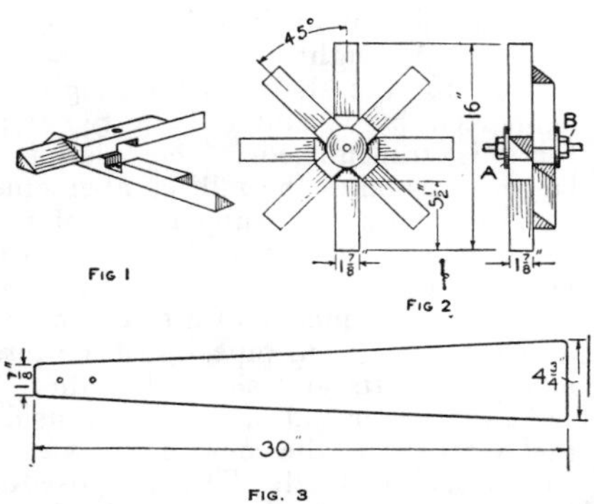

The Hub Consists of Two Parts, Each Having Four Arms for Holding the Blades

detail. Symmetry and smoothness of design should be preserved and the parts made as light as possible consistent with strength and durability.

The Wheel

As shown in the drawings, the wheel has eight blades. Ordinarily the use of eight blades makes it difficult to

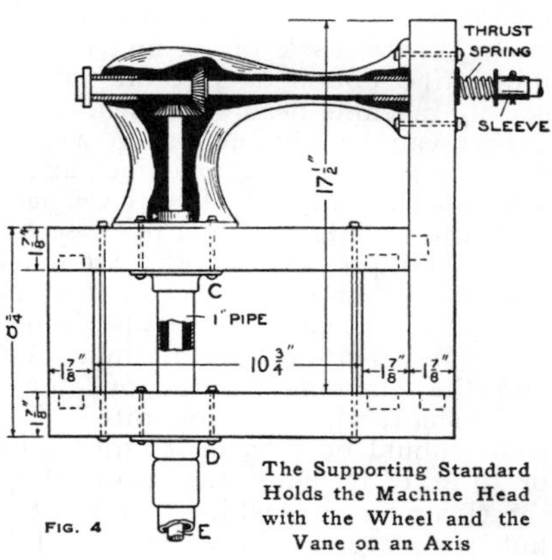

The Supporting Standard Holds the Machine Head with the Wheel and the Vane on an Axis

construct a hub of sufficient strength to carry them. Where so many blades radiate from a common center it is almost impossible to provide an anchorage for each blade. To provide a maximum of strength coupled with simplicity of design, the plan of using two hubs of four arms each was adopted in the construction of this mill. The ordinary hub of four arms is simple to make and quite strong. Four pieces of straight-grained oak, each 16 in. long and 1⅞ in. square, are used in constructing the hubs. The manner of notching each pair of pieces together is shown in Fig. 1. The slope for the blades is made to run in opposite directions on the ends of each crosspiece. The slope is formed by cutting out a triangular piece, as shown.

The two hubs, thus formed, are mounted on the shaft, one behind the other, in such positions that the arms will be evenly divided for space in the wheel circle. These details are shown in Fig. 2. The blades, Fig. 3, are made of thin basswood or hard maple, and each is fastened in its place by means of two 3/8-in. bolts, in addition to which a few brads are driven in to prevent the thin blades from warping.

The Gears

This windmill was designed to transmit power by means of shafts and gear wheels, rather than with cranks and reciprocating pump rods, such as are used on ordinary farm mills. To obtain this result, an old sewing machine head was used. Such a part can be obtained from a junk dealer or a sewing-machine agent. The head is stripped of its base plate with the shuttle gearing; likewise the needle rod, presser foot, etc., are taken from the front end of the head along with the faceplate. The horizontal shaft and gear wheel are taken out and the bearings reamed out for a 1/2-in. shaft, which is substituted. The shaft should be 2 ft. in length, and 8 or 10 in. of its outer end threaded for the clamping nuts which hold the two hubs in place, as shown at A and B, Fig. 2. The gear wheel is also bored out and remounted on the new shaft.

The supporting standard is constructed of oak, with mortise-and-tenon joints, as shown in Fig. 4. The width of the pieces will depend on the kind of sewing-machine head used. It may be necessary also to slightly change the dimensions. The machine head is fastened on the support with bolts. A sleeve and thrust spring are mounted on the shaft, as shown. The sleeve is made of brass tubing, of a size to fit snugly on the shaft. A cotter will keep it in place. The sleeve serves as a collar for the thrust spring, which is placed between the sleeve and the standard. This arrangement acts as a buffer to take up the end thrust on the shaft caused by the varying pressure of the wind on the wheel.

The Vane

To keep the wheel facing the wind at all times, a vane must be provided. It is made of basswood or hard maple, as shown in Fig. 5. It is not built up solid, air spaces being left between the slats to reduce the wind resistance. Unless built in this manner, the vane is liable to twist off in a gale. The horizontal slats are 1/4 in. thick, and the upright and cross braces 3/8 in. thick, while the long arm connecting the vane to the supporting standard is 1/2 in. thick.

The supporting standard, carrying the wheel and the vane, must revolve about a vertical axis with the changes in the wind, and this vertical axis is supplied in the form of a piece of gas pipe which runs through the supporting standard at the points marked C and D, Fig. 4. Ordinary pipe fittings, called flanges, are bolted to the frame at these points. The coupling in the gas pipe beneath the supporting standard serves as a stationary collar to support the weight of the whole mill. The vane should be placed correctly to balance the weight of the wheel.

The shaft passes through the framework of the mill on the inside of the pipe, as shown at E. A 3/8-in. soft-steel or wrought-iron rod is satisfactory for the shaft, as no weight is supported by it and only a twisting force is transmitted. The use of a larger rod makes the mill cumbersome and unwieldy. The upper end of the shaft is fastened to the shaft that projects from the under side of the machine head by means of a sleeve made of a piece of 3/8-in. pipe. Two cotters hold the shafts and sleeve together.

At the lower end of the shaft, inside the workshop, the device shown in Fig. 6 is installed. The purpose of this appliance is to provide a horizontal shaft upon which pulleys or driving gears may be mounted. The device is constructed of another sewing-machine head similar to the one already described. The head is cut in two and the separate parts mounted on suitable supports. The gap between the sawed portions permits a pulley to be fastened on the shaft to serve as the main drive. The wheel propelled by the treadle of the sewing machine will make a good drive wheel. The small handwheel, originally mounted on the machine-head shaft, is left intact. This arrangement gives two sizes of drive wheels. Heavy sewing-machine belts will serve to transmit the power.

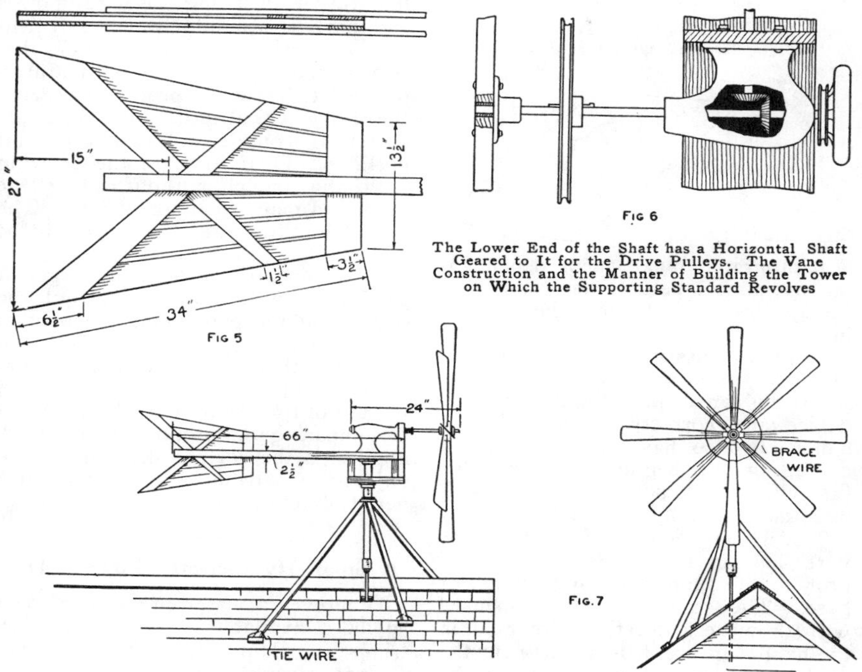

The Lower End of the Shaft has a Horizontal Shaft Geared to It for the Drive Pulleys. The Vane Construction and the Manner of Building the Tower on Which the Supporting Standard Revolves

The Tower

The tower can be built up in any manner to suit the conditions. Ordinarily sticks, 2 in. square, are suitable. These are well braced with wire and fastened securely to the roof of the shop. The arrangement of the tower with the mill is shown in Fig. 7.

Telegraph Code on Typewriter Keys

A very simple and practical method of transcribing wireless time and other messages on the typewriter without having such perfect knowledge of the Morse system as to be able to immediately translate it into the common alphabet is the following: The characters of the Morse system are inscribed on small slips of paper—thus, three dots (. . .), for the letter S; two dashes (- -), for the letter M, etc.—and these slips are pasted on the corresponding keys of the typewriter. The operator puts on his receiver, and the proper key is struck as he hears the corresponding Morse letter. As there are no capitals, spacing between words, or even punctuation, the manipulation of the typewriter is much simplified, and it is easily learned to record the signals as fast as they are heard.

An Aid in Sketching Profiles

The means usually employed by most beginners to obtain the correct outline of an object, such as tracing or a pantograph, make them dependent on mechanical help rather than train the eye to form and proportion a drawing correctly. The device shown not only greatly assists the beginner, but actually trains him toward a point where he can dispense with any such device and correctly sketch by free hand. It also has the effect of encouraging the beginner, because his first efforts will not be complete failures, as is usually the case.

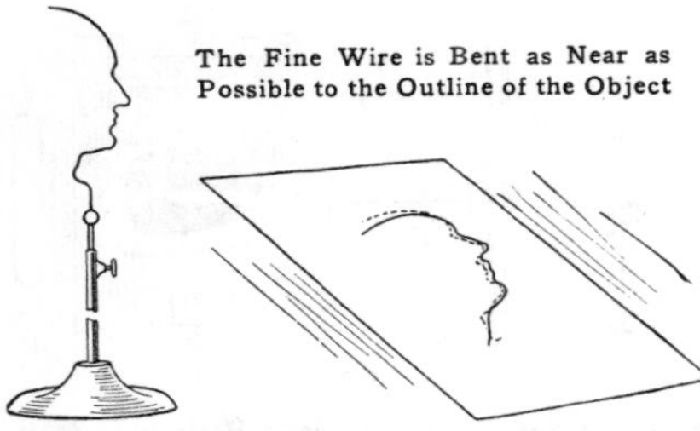
The Fine Wire is Bent as Near as Possible to the Outline of the Object

The device consists of a rather fine wire bent in the shape of a human profile and supported on a stand or base. The stand may be dispensed with, however, and the wire held in the hand. In use, it is placed near the model or person whose profile is to be drawn; then, after closing one eye, it is set at a position where it will correspond to the features of the model. This enables one to note the variations between the wire and the model's features. For instance, the forehead may recede from the wire at the top, or the nose may have a different slant or shape.

The paper on which the drawing is to be made should have a faint outline drawn by laying the wire upon it and marking around it with a soft pencil. Having noted the variations between the wire and the features, proceed to draw the profile, observing the same variations, and when the sketch is completed, erase the faint outlines. Then compare the drawing with the model without using the wire, and make final corrections. The dotted line indicates the outline to be erased.

The drawing may be made larger or smaller than the bent wire, but the outline on the paper must be kept in exactly the same proportion. It is not necessary that the wire be bent so that it represents perfect features. With the use of this device one forms a habit of comparing and proportioning, which applies to the correct sketching of all objects.—Contributed by Will L. Burner, Columbus, Ohio.

A Small Hydroelectric-Power Plant

Wherever a water pressure of over 30 lb. is available a small hydroelectric-power plant will produce sufficient electric current for any light work, such as charging storage batteries, operating sewing and washing machines, toys, etc. The design is for a 6-in. hydraulic motor of the Pelton type, which will operate well on almost all city-water pressures, and at

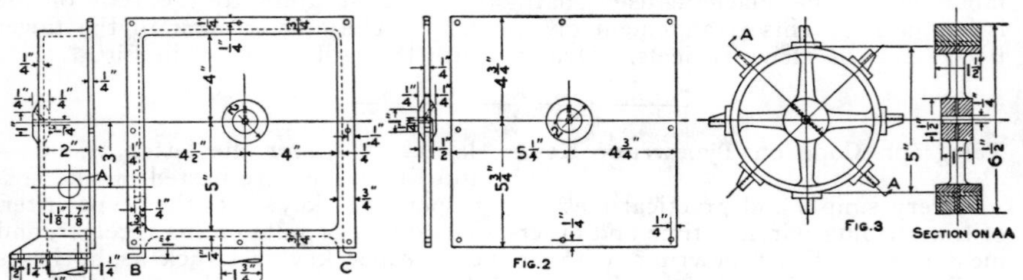

Layout for the Casing, Cover and Wheel for the Construction of a Hydraulic Motor That will Drive a Small Dynamo, to Produce Current for Experimental Purposes, to Charge Storage Cells or to Run Electric Toys

80 lb. will drive a 100-watt generator to its full output.

The castings may be procured from any foundry cheaply, so that these parts need not trouble the builder. The patterns can be constructed easily and are not so complicated that they will tear the molds when being removed. They are made from well seasoned white pine, 1/4 in. thick. Fill in all sharp corners with small fillets. All the patterns should taper slightly from the parting line.

The motor casing is shown in Fig. 1. It is made with a wide flange so that the cover plate can be bolted to it. The lug A is to give additional strength and thickness to the side so that it may be drilled and tapped for the nozzle. The legs B and C are for bolting the case to a base or support. The outlet pipe is of lead, 1 3/4 in. outside diameter, and the hole for it in the case can be either drilled or cored. Solder the pipe flush with the inside of the casing. Drill and tap the holes around the flange for 8, 32 bolts. The shaft hole must be drilled very carefully. Drill 1/4-in. holes in the feet. The oil holes are 1/8 in. in diameter. File the surface of the flange smooth and also the inside shoulder of the bearing lug. Drill and tap the nozzle hole for a 3/4-in. pipe thread.

The cover plate is shown in Fig. 2. This is bolted to the casing with 8, 32 brass bolts, 1/2 in. long. The holes for them are drilled 3/16 in. in diameter. A shallow hole, for the end of the shaft to fit in, is drilled in the lug, as shown.

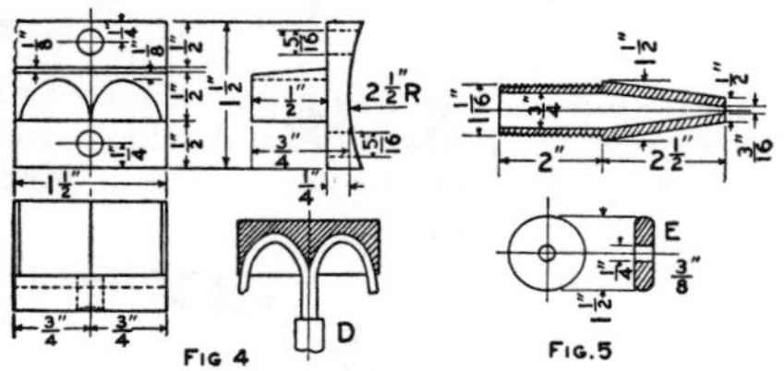

The Best Shape of the Buckets to Take Up the Force of the Water

It does not pass all the way through the plate. File the inside face of the lug smooth and also the edge of the plate where it joins the casing.

The wheel, with brackets attached, is shown in Fig. 3. This style of wheel need not be followed out closely. Bore the hub centrally for a 1/4-in.

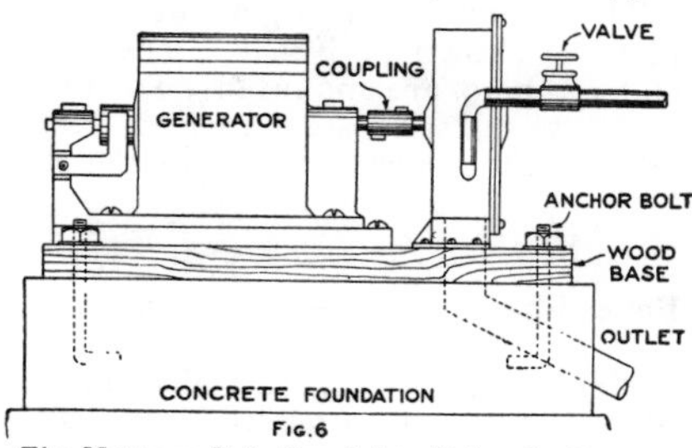

The Motor as It is Coupled to Drive the Dynamo, and the Water Connections

shaft and fit in two setscrews. Drill and tap the rim for the buckets with a 1/4-in. standard tap. The buckets must be evenly spaced and bolted on to make the wheel balance.

The buckets are shown in Fig. 4. They may be cast from iron or babbitt. The sharp ridge in the center provides for a deviation of the water jet as it flows on the bucket. The ridge divides the bucket into two equal lobes which turn each division of the jet through almost 180 deg., using all the kinetic energy in the jet. This is shown at D. The dividing ridge must lie in the plane of the revolution, so that each bucket will enter the center of the jet. The buckets being evenly spaced on the periphery of the wheel, only one at a time receives the force of the jet, the one in front and the one behind clearing the jet.

The nozzle is shown in Fig. 5. It can be made of iron or brass. The inside gradually tapers from 3/4 to 3/16 in. It has a 3/4-in. pipe thread and is screwed into the hole in the case from the inside and is secured with a lock nut. Enough additional threaded portion is left protruding to allow the supply pipe to be connected.

When assembling the motor, fasten the wheel to the shaft with the two setscrews, and place a metal washer, E, on each side of the wheel. Place the wheel in the casing and screw the cover plate in place. A thin rubber gasket should be placed between the cover and the casing to provide a water-tight joint.

The general arrangement of the plant is shown in Fig. 6. The motor and dynamo are mounted on a heavy wood base, which in turn is firmly bolted to a concrete foundation. Level up the two machines by the use of thin washers on the bolts between the base and machine. A heavy sleeve and setscrews are used to connect the two shafts. The connection to the water supply is made with ¾-in. pipe, with a globe valve in it to regulate the flow of water. Any dynamo of about 100-watt output can be used.

Paper Shades for Electric-Light Globes

The appearance of an electric-light globe can be very prettily improved by making a shade of crêpe paper of any

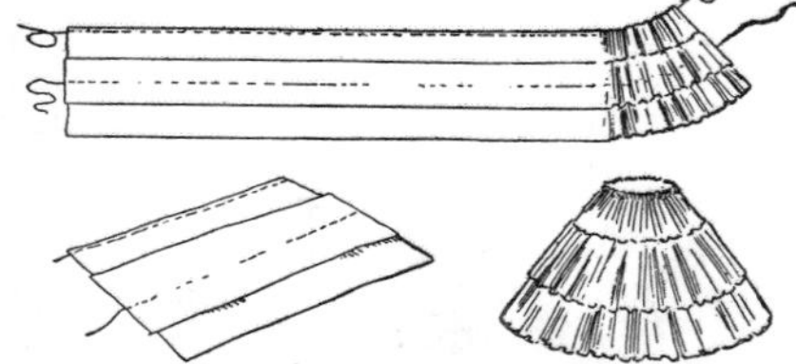

Two Pieces of Crêpe Paper Stitched Together and Ruffled, to Make a Fancy Electric-Light Shade

desired color for each one. Canary-colored crêpe produces a soft, mellow effect. Pale blue, yellow, red and, in fact, all the colors can be used, making a very pleasing variety.

The body of the shade is made of a piece of paper about 5½ in. wide and 3½ ft. long. The width will vary with the length of the globe to be covered, and it is best to have it full, as the edge can be trimmed even with the lower end of the globe afterward. Another piece of the same color is cut 2½ in. wide and of the same length. This piece makes the ruffle.

The smaller piece is placed on the larger centrally, and both are stitched together with a running stitch, using a needle and cotton thread. A plain running stitch is also made ¼ in. from one edge of the larger strip. The material is gathered along both threads. This operation makes the material shrink in length. Wrap it around the globe, pulling the threads taut so that the ends of the paper will just meet. Tie the threads and clip off the extending ends. If the paper extends beyond the end of the globe, trim it off with the shears. Ruffle the two edges of the narrow strip and the lower edge of the larger one. This operation is simply stretching the edge of the crêpe to cause it to stand out.—Contributed by Jas. A. Hart, Philadelphia, Pa.

Renewing the Markings on Graduates

Graduates that have been in use a long time, especially for measuring alkalies, become unreadable. The graduations are easily restored in the following manner: Moisten a small piece of absorbent cotton with a solution of white shellac, cut in alcohol. Rub this well into all the etched parts and allow to dry for about two minutes, then rub in a fine whiting or litharge with an old toothbrush. If red is desired, use rouge; if black is preferred, use lampblack or powdered graphite. When dry, wipe off the excess pigment with a cloth moistened in alcohol.—Contributed by A. C. Norris, Rockford, Ill.

Repairing a Broken Ball-Clasp Purse

Having occasion to repair a purse of the ordinary ball-clasp kind where one of the stems was broken off and lost, I first had some trouble in finding a way to repair it. I started to take off the remaining stem in an

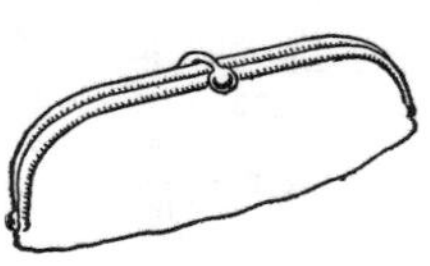

attempt to replace the locking device with another kind, and in bending it down toward the opposite side, I happened to close the purse and found that it locked just as well as if there had been two balls on it. I have since repaired two other purses in the same manner and found that they worked well.

The idea is to bend the remaining clasp over until it is low enough to come in contact with and to spring over the other side, thus giving the same snap and holding qualities as before.—Contributed by W. C. Loy, Rochester, Ind.

Automatic Valve for a Funnel

Where liquid is run through a funnel into an opaque bottle or earthen jug, the filling cannot be watched, and if not watched constantly, the vessel will overflow. This can be obviated by applying the automatic valve to the funnel stem, as shown. A washer support is soldered or otherwise fastened in the upper end of the stem, or at the base of the sloping part, and a crossbar is fastened to its upper surface across the hole. The crossbar is centrally drilled to receive a small rod or wire, to which is attached a valve that will cover the hole in the washer. A cork is stuck on the lower end of the rod. The location of the cork on the rod should be at a point a little below the level to which the bottle or vessel is to be filled.—Contributed by H. W. Hilton, Hopington, B. C.

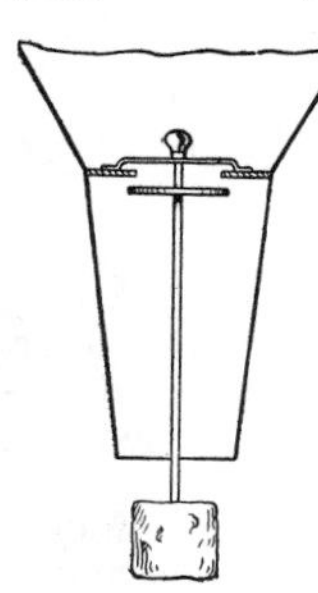

Chisel Holder for Whetting

To obtain the proper slope and apply a fine cutting edge, the plane iron or chisel must be held at the proper slope while grinding, and especially so when whetting. The illustration shows a holder to keep the iron or chisel at the proper slope. It consists of a block of wood with a sloping cut at the right angle to make two pieces. One of these pieces is permanently fastened to the strip at the back,

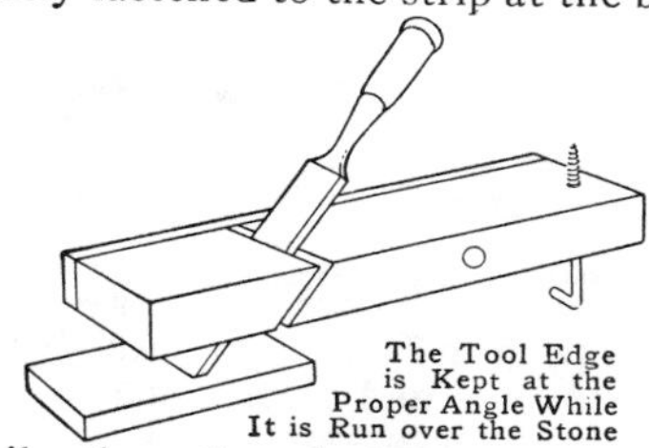

The Tool Edge is Kept at the Proper Angle While It is Run over the Stone

while the other is held with a bolt passing through a notch in the strip for adjusting or clamping. The rear end of the back piece is fitted with a large screw hook or L-hook to provide a slide to keep the rear end of the holder at the right height. The iron or chisel is inserted between the sloping edges of the blocks and clamped in place, then the L-screw is adjusted for height to secure the proper angle on the stone. It is then only necessary to move the block and tool back and forth over the stone.

A Large Hole in a Small Piece of Paper

It would seem impossible to cut a hole in a piece of paper, 2 in. wide and 3 in. long, large enough to allow a person's body to pass through it, but if carefully cut as shown by the lines in the sketch, one will find with surprise that the paper can be extended so that the feat is easily accomplished. Make the cuts about 1/8 in. apart and

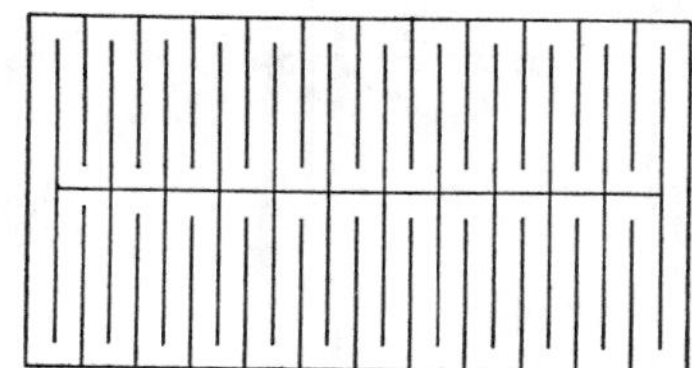

The Slits Cut in the Paper Allow It to Expand Several Times the Size of the Original

these will allow the paper to expand several times its size.—Contributed by H. Martine Warner, E. Orange, N. J.

Homemade Bunsen Burner

The amateur craftsman, at some time or other, needs a hot flame for certain kinds of work, and a Bunsen or

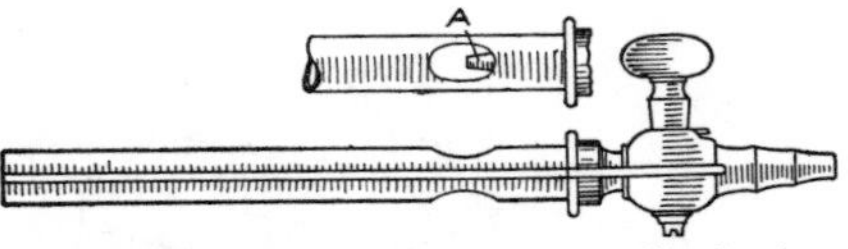

Bunsen-Burner Attachment for Use with Illuminating Gas Taken from the House Mains

alcohol flame is brought into service. The gasoline and alcohol flames have their drawbacks, one of which is the starting of the burner and the waiting for the heat. They are also unhandy in directing the flame on parts of the work. As I desired a burner for quick work and one whose flame I could direct at any angle, for repoussé and chasing on copper and silversmith's work, I made the one shown in the sketch to attach to a hose and connected it with the gas pipe of the illuminating system in the house. It consists of a hose connection into which a piece of pipe, 5 in. long, is fitted. The hose connection is also fitted with a small nozzle, A, for the gas, and the pipe has an opening through it at the end of the nozzle.—Contributed by John Koestner, Brooklyn, N. Y.

Cane-Seat Cleaner

A rapid and practical method of removing stains and discolorations from the cane seats of chairs, wickerwork, etc., is to use oxalic acid and powdered pumice.

Dissolve oxalic-acid crystals in hot water and saturate a small stiff brush in it, then dip the brush in the powdered pumice and rub the discolored cane briskly with the brush.—Contributed by W. F. Jaquythe, Richmond, California.

Shade-Roller and Curtain-Pole Bracket

The main advantage of this shade bracket is that a person can lower it for adjusting the shade or in changing curtains while standing on the floor, thus eliminating the use of a step ladder and the danger possibly attending such use.

The front elevation of a window with bracket attachment in position is shown in Fig. 1, and a cross section in Fig. 2. The position of the curtain pole when the brackets are lowered is shown by the dotted lines. A detail sketch of the support end is given in Fig. 3 and one bracket is shown in Fig. 4.

The curtain pole A is fastened to the brackets B with ¼-in. dowel pins, C.

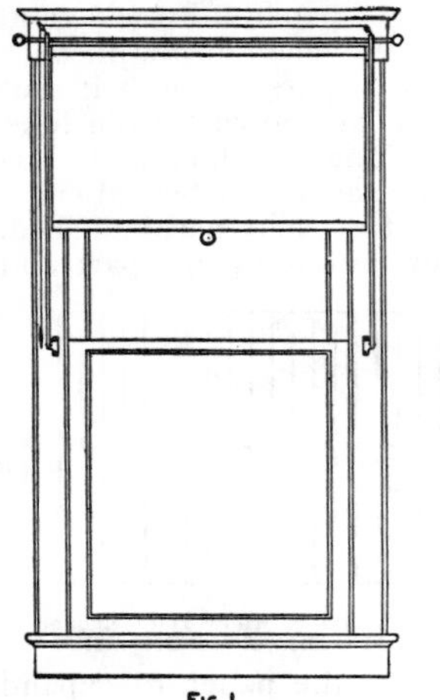

The Brackets as They are Attached to a Window Casing for Lowering the Curtain Pole

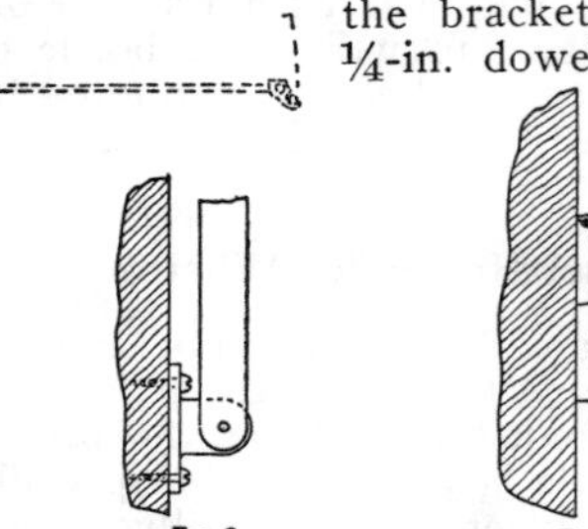

The Attachments, Supports and Brackets for Holding both Curtain Pole and Shade Roller

These pins and the pole keep the brackets from spreading at the top, so that a shade roller, D, may have its attachments fastened to the inner sides of the brackets. A small pulley, E, is attached to the window casing above the right bracket and a double pulley is located above the left, cords being passed through them, down along the casing to a point within easy reach, and fastened in any manner desired.

All that is necessary to change the curtains or fix a shade is to loosen the cord and allow the brackets to drop down until they may be easily reached. —Contributed by James F. Napier, Montreal, Can.

Planing Arrow Sticks

While making some bows one day I discovered I had no suitable dowel sticks for the arrows, so I started to make them out of ¼-in. square stock. I found it rather difficult to plane these pieces until I hit upon the scheme

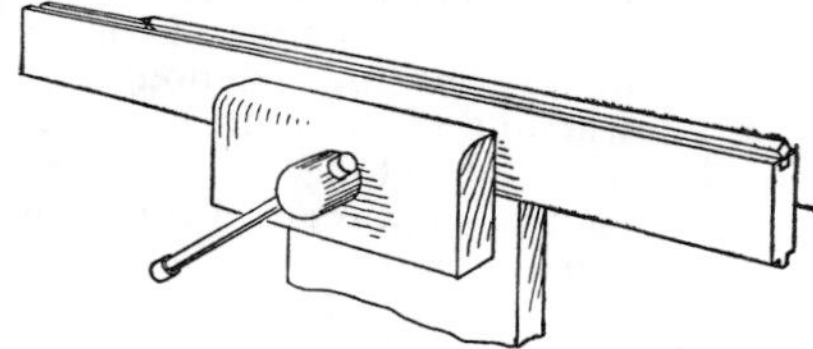

Planing the Corners from Square Stock by Placing Them in the Groove of a Flooring Board

shown in the sketch. I procured a piece of ordinary tongue-and-groove flooring and clamped it in the bench vise, then drove a nail in the groove to act as a stop, and in no time I had the sticks planed into arrows.—Contributed by J. F. Culverwell, Washington, District of Columbia.

To Clean Shellac from a Brush

Put the brush in a strong, warm solution of borax and water, and then wash in clean, warm water. If the bristles have become hard, allow the brush to remain in the solution until soft, keeping the solution warm in the meantime; then wash it out in warm water.—Contributed by N. J. Shattuck, Woburn, Mass.

Lathe Dogs

In the absence of a full equipment of lathe dogs the amateur can make them cheaply from pieces of iron pipe.

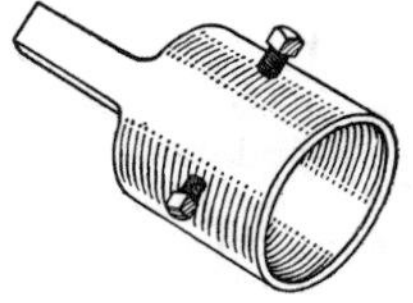

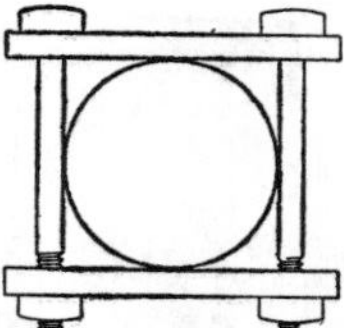

Two Forms of Lathe Dogs That are Quickly and Cheaply Constructed

One of these is shown in the sketch. A section of pipe, 1½ in. to 3 in. long, is partly cut away, as shown, leaving a projection of metal 1 in. wide. One or more setscrews are fitted in the round part, and the dog is complete.

A dog, or driver, may also be made of two U-clamps and two bolts as shown. This is especially useful for large work, where the cost of a dog would be prohibitive. After these two clamps are bolted on the work to be turned a bolt is attached in the faceplate that bears against the clamp, thus turning the work.

To Remove a Splinter from the Flesh

Quite frequently small particles of steel, splinters, or thorns are run into the flesh and cannot be removed with the fingers. These can be readily removed in the following manner: Press the eye of an ordinary needle over the protruding end, then turn the needle

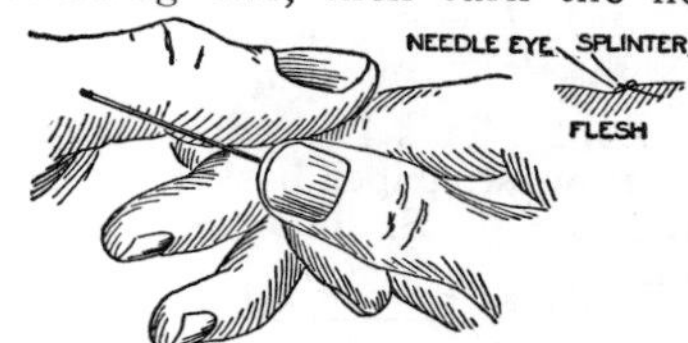

The Eye of a Needle Slipped over a Thorn for Removing It from the Flesh

until the edges bind or clinch. While in this position, raise the needle and out comes the splinter.

¶A fine luster can be given to zinc by rubbing it with kerosene or a weak solution of sulphuric acid.

Holders for Displaying Magazines

Papers and magazines often are sold in drug stores where the display space usually is limited, especially in the window. The method used by one druggist gave space for the magazines in the window without interfering with the other goods.

The back of the window was arranged with rows of hooks, three hooks for each magazine, two at the top edges and one in the center at the bottom. The magazine is easily slipped into these holders, and the whole presents a tidy appearance. The hooks are the ordinary screwhooks that can be obtained from a hardware or furniture store.—Contributed by T. F. Monaghan, Philadelphia, Pa.

Waste-Paper Basket

The covering of a broken demijohn was used in the manner shown as a waste-paper basket. The glass was broken out and the covering soaked in water, after which the splints were turned down and tied with a cord. This I found to make a first-class waste-paper basket. — Contributed by A. S. Thomas, Gordon, Canada.

Lettering Photographs

Amateur photographers often write, or print, the names of the subjects on the mounts, or in the albums, with white ink or scratch it on the negative so that it will print in the picture.

A very good method is to take ordinary black ink and do the lettering on the sensitive paper before it is printed under the negative, being careful not to scratch the paper. After printing the paper to the proper shade the toning and fixing baths will wash away the ink and leave the lettering in white.

The lettering is easily accomplished and a post card can be sent with any message desired on any negative, the inscription being printed on the paper so that the negative is unharmed for other printing.—Contributed by Henry J. Marion, Pontiac, Mich.

A Stamp Moistener

A handy stamp moistener and envelope sealer can be made by procuring a small medicine bottle or glass vial and inserting a piece of felt or other wicking material in the place of the stopper, and filling it with water.

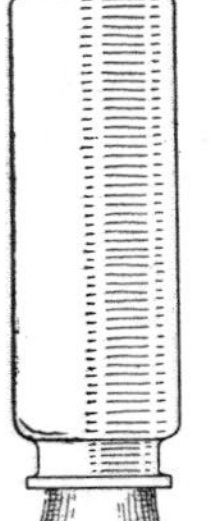

This moistener will be found handy for a small office where the mail is quite heavy, but not big enough to warrant the purchasing of a sealing machine. This moistener is sanitary and replaces the wet sponge.—Contributed by Theo. J. Becker, Kansas City, Mo.

A Window Lock

A very neat window lock can be made of sheet steel, ½ in. wide. One piece, shaped like a saw tooth, is fastened to the sash, and the other, which is bent to form a catch over the tooth projection and ends in a curved top for a finger hold, is attached to the window casing. The illustration clearly shows how the lock is attached.—Contributed by Lee B. Green, Cleveland, O.

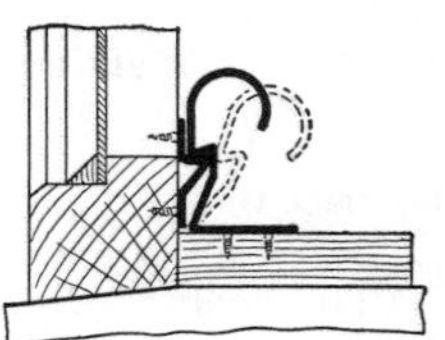

¶Georgia pine should be filled with white shellac.

Varnished Candles Burn Longer

The heated tallow or wax of a candle runs down the sides and this results in a considerable waste. This waste can be stopped by coating the new candles with white varnish and laying them aside for a few days to harden. The varnish will keep the melted tallow or wax from running away and it is used in the wick.

Guides for a Mill File

Having a large number of wires to file true on the end I devised a way to do this with the use of some old worn-out and discarded files that had good cutting edges. A piece of sheet copper, about the same length as the files, was bent to fit over one edge and both sides of the file, allowing both edges to project about 1/4 in. This made a guide that prevented the edge of the file from slipping off the end of

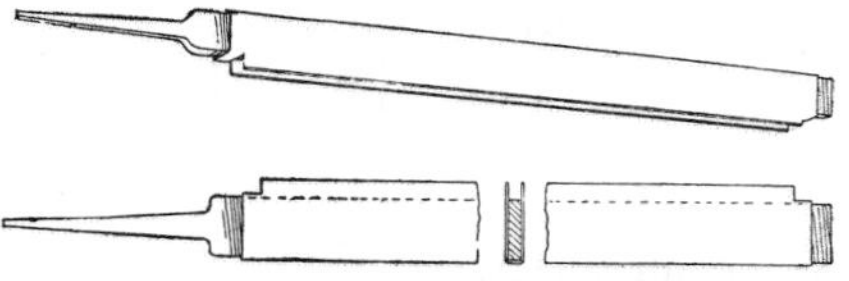

Guide for Using the Edge of Worn-Out Files on Small Round or Square Stock

the wire. The guide was held in place on the file by cutting a slit in the projecting edges, about 1/4 in. from the end, and turning these separated parts back on the file.

If such a guide is fitted tightly on a file, the edges of worn-out files can be used for such work, and the file cannot slip off and mar the sides of the work. —Contributed by A. R. Drury, Hampton, Ill.

A Simple Motion-Picture Machine

The drum A is a piece of wood, 1 3/4 in. long and 1 3/16 in. in diameter, supported on the end of a round stick, B, which can be made in one piece with the drum, if a wood lathe is at hand, but a piece cut from a curtain pole and a lead pencil inserted in a hole bored in the end will answer the purpose. Be sure to have the diameter of the drum 1 3/16 inches.

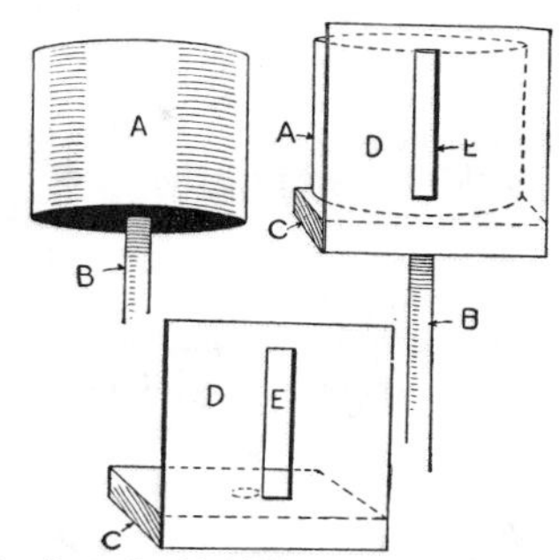

The Parts for Making the Revolving Drum for Holding the Strip of Pictures

Provide a base piece, C, 1/2 in. thick and 2 in. square, and fasten a piece of cardboard having a slit E, as shown. The cardboard should be 2 in. wide and 2 1/2 in. high, the slit being cut 1/2 in. in width, 1/4 in. from the top and 3/4 in. from the bottom. A hole is bored in the center of the block to admit the standard B easily.

The next step is to provide the picture and attach it to the drum. A picture of a boy pounding cobblestones is shown in the sketch, at F, which should be made on a strip of paper 4 3/8 in. long. This is glued or attached with rubber bands to the drum. The drawing can be enlarged in pen and ink, or can be reproduced as it is, if a hand camera is at hand, and a print used on the drum.

The Different Positions of the Picture will Appear in Action When Turning with the Drum

It is only necessary to put the parts together, grasp the base in one hand and turn the support B with the other, when, looking through the slot E, the boy is seen pounding the stones. Various pictures can be made and the strips changed.—Contributed by C. C. Fraser, Saginaw, Mich

Substitute for Cleats on Boards

The necessity for using more than one cleat for fastening two boards together may be done away with by using the device shown in the sketch. The center cleat prevents the boards from buckling while the sides are tightly held by these simple flat fasteners. The fasteners are made of tin cut as indicated, slipped between the edges of the boards and the parts bent over and tacked. Where the strain is not too great the holders may be used without a cleat, making an effective flat fastening.—Contributed by W. O. Nettleton, Washington, D. C.

The Metal Clips Hold the Edges of the Boards Together Closely and Quite Rigidly

Attaching Door Knobs to Locks

When putting a lock on a door it is often difficult to press the two knobs together tightly enough to prevent them from rattling and still be able to insert the screw into the shank. By using a piece of board, 1 in. thick, 6 in. wide and 1 ft. or more in length, with a V-shaped piece cut out of one side, the knobs can be easily forced and held together while the screw is inserted.—Contributed by H. Musgrave, Sidney, British Columbia.

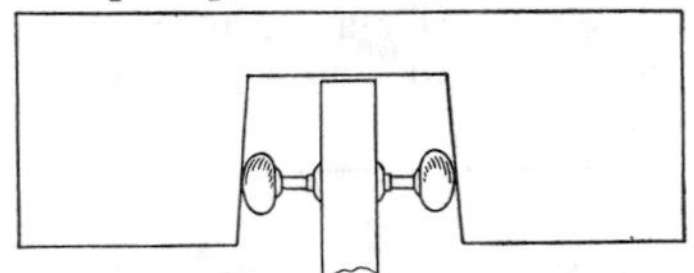

The Sloping Edges in the Notch Forces the Knobs Together and Holds Them While Inserting the Screws

A Finger-Nail Buffer

The flywheel on a sewing machine is usually turned with a semicircular face and this makes a good base on which to apply a piece of chamois skin for use in buffing nails. A strip of the chamois is cut the length of the wheel's circumference and small holes pierced in its edges, through which strings are run to hold it to the rim of the wheel. The chamois can then be removed or left on the wheel as desired. Run the machine and hold the nail on the buffer. When there is a free wheel on the machine this makes an excellent buffing device.

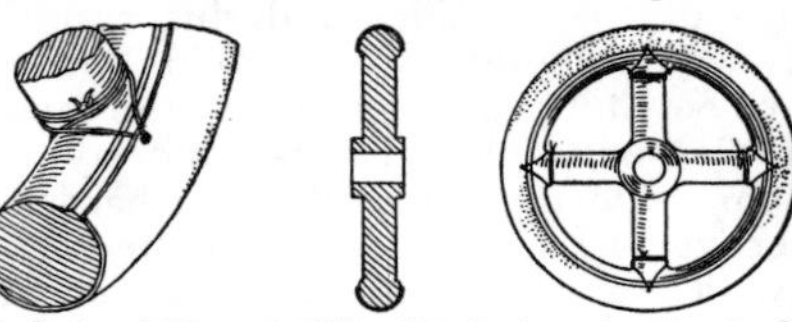

A Strip of Chamois Skin Attached to the Flywheel of a Sewing Machine for a Buffer

Grinding Chisel Edges

A cold chisel ground with a rounding edge, as shown, will last twice as long and do better work than one that is ground straight, because it will not wedge, and the cutting edge, having a better support, will not chip off.—Contributed by F. G. Marbach, Cleveland, O.

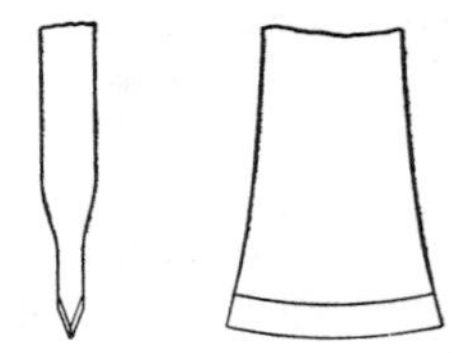

Reducing Amperage of a Fuse Wire

It is sometimes necessary to use an electrical fuse of smaller amperage than those at hand, and for experimental work this is often the case. A smaller amperage may be readily made from a larger-size wire by making a nick in it with the cutting edge of pliers, or with a knife. The illustration shows how to reduce the size of a 10-ampere fuse to make it five amperes.—Contributed by Louis Litsky, Brooklyn, N. Y.

10 AMPERES 5 AMPERES

The Amperes of a Fuse Reduced by Making a Nick in the Lead Wire

Dip-Plating Process

The various ways of doing dip plating are practically the same method, the coating fluid consisting of essentially the same materials.

The tank or crucible, as it may be called, consists of a piece of 3-in. gas pipe, 9 in. long, threaded at both ends, one end being fitted with a screw cap and the other with a pipe flange. This part is shown in Fig. 1. A piece of sheet metal is cut in the shape shown in Fig. 2 and bent to form a cone, so that the smaller end will fit snugly around the pipe and the base be 9 in. in diameter. The joined edges are riveted together. The assembled parts will appear as shown in Fig. 3.

The metal used for plating consists of bismuth, 4 oz.; antimony, 4 oz., and pure block tin, 10 lb. Place the antimony in the crucible and melt it, then add the tin and bismuth. A flame from an ordinary gasoline burner will be sufficient to heat the crucible.

Clean the article to be coated by rinsing it in strong caustic potash, which will remove all grime and grease, then dip it in a strong solution of sal ammoniac and water. Dry it and then dip it in the melted metal, allowing it to remain there about 1 minute, then remove and plunge it in a bath made of 1 lb. of sal ammoniac

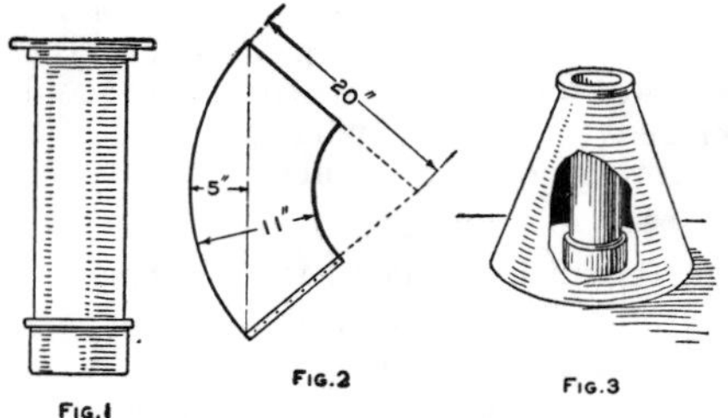

The Parts to Make the Crucible Consist of Pipe and Fittings and a Piece of Sheet Metal

and 1 gal. of water. The article is then dried in sawdust.

The coating put on in this manner is a nice, shiny plate that will stand a lot of wear. No polishing or grinding is necessary.—Contributed by A. H. Waychoff, Lyons, Colo.

A Model Steam-Turbine Boat

A piece of thin board, or shingle, is cut to the shape of a boat and two standards are fastened to it. The standards have notches cut in them to hold

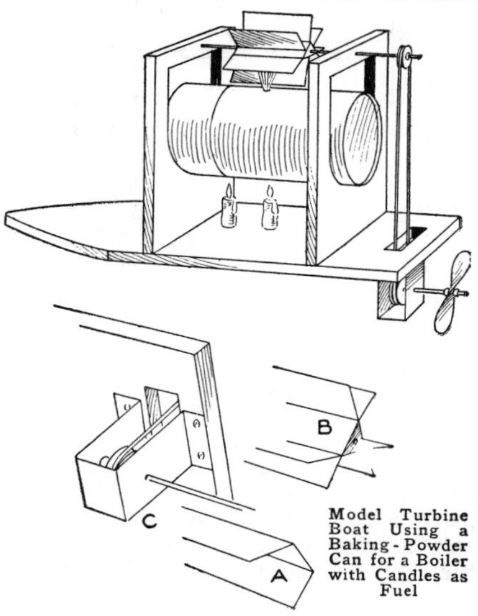

Model Turbine Boat Using a Baking-Powder Can for a Boiler with Candles as Fuel

an ordinary baking-powder can which is used for the boiler. The lid of the can is soldered on, and a small hole punched in one side with an awl. Two candles are used to heat the water.

The turbine is constructed on an axle made of a hatpin which runs through the top of the standards for bearings. The paddles are made of cardboard, or better still, pieces of thin sheet tin, cut and bent as shown at A, and three of these are attached to a three-cornered block of wood fastened to the shaft, as shown at B. The manner of attaching the shaft for the propeller is shown at C. The propeller consists of a piece of tin, slightly twisted and attached to the shaft with solder. The pulleys are located as shown and connected with a string band. The hole made in the can should be pointed to one side of the turbine shaft so that the escaping steam will strike one side of the paddles on the turbine.—Contributed by McKinley Wood, Ava, N. Y.

Plant Shelf for a Window

An ingenious and simple method of putting up window shelves for winter plants so that the window casing and

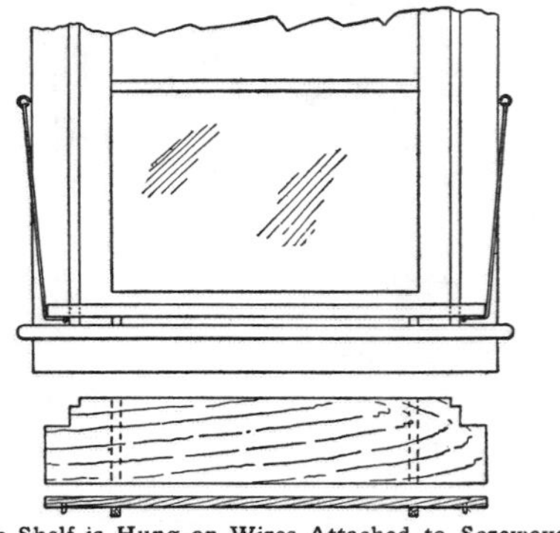

The Shelf is Hung on Wires Attached to Screweyes Placed in the Facing Edge

facing are not marred is shown in the sketch. The materials required are one shelf, about 8 in. wide, 1½ yd. of picture wire, two screweyes, two fence staples, and two strips of wood, to raise the shelf slightly from the window sill. The board for the shelf is cut to fit the window frame and casing. The picture wire, screweyes and staples are attached as shown. When cleaning the window the shelf can be drawn out of the way.—Contributed by H. C. Dixon, Johnstown, Pa.

A Camera Support

A device which, in many instances, will take the place of a tripod, can be made of a brass wood screw and can be carried in the pocket as easily as a pencil. The screw should be 3 or 4 in.

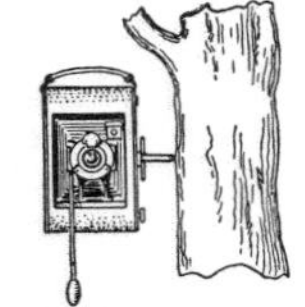

Substitute for a Camera Tripod That can be Carried in the Pocket Like a Pencil

long and ¼ in. in diameter. Cut off the head and thread the end about ½ in. to fit the socket in the camera. Drill a ⅛-in. hole through the metal just below the threaded part and insert a short piece of ⅛-in. wire. Slip a washer over the end, down to the wire, and fasten it with solder.

The device can be turned into a tree, post or a stick thrust into the ground, and the camera screwed onto it and adjusted to any angle.—Contributed by O. D. Turner, Seattle, Wash.

Combination Tool for Amateur Draftsmen

A common 6-in. mill file can be converted into a very useful tool for an amateur draftsman. Grind the end of the file as shown in the sketch and use it for prying out thumbtacks that are driven in too tightly. Grind the base of the tang into a knife blade for sharpening pencils, shaving chalk, opening envelopes, etc. Shape, by careful grinding, the part A for cutting and trimming sheets. Grind one edge of the file round and polish it for smoothing and burnishing purposes. Grind a sharp point on the tang for per-

A Tool Made of a File Combining Several Tools Which are Used by a Draftsman

forating sheets. A piece of rubber stuck on the tang end answers the double purpose of a protector and eraser. The file part is used for finishing points on pencils.

Varnishing Bases for Electric Apparatus

It is quite difficult to keep from making finger marks on freshly varnished boards used as bases on electric devices. It is easily avoided, however, by procuring a large spool and fastening it to the bottom of the base with a wood screw. The spool will serve as a handle while the varnish is applied, and also makes a stand for the board while the varnish dries.—Contributed by Jacob Laudan, Louisville, Ky.

Waterproof Shoe Dressing

Melt some tallow and, while it is hot, put in some scraps of rubber from old rubber shoes or boots. Be careful to select rubber that is free from cloth. Put in as much of the rubber as the tallow will absorb. Stir freely while it is melting, and keep it away from any flames. Allow it to cool and set away for future use. Take enough for immediate use and warm it sufficiently so that it may be applied with a brush.—Contributed by F. S. Cummings, Detroit, Mich.

An Adjustable Bench Stop

A simple adjustable bench stop for light work may be made from a piece of 1-in. broom handle and a piece of piano wire. Plane a flat surface on the broom stick and drill two $\frac{1}{16}$-in. holes, about 1/4 in. deep, 1/4 in. from each end. Bend the ends of the wire to enter the holes and have the wire of such length as to give it a slight curve between

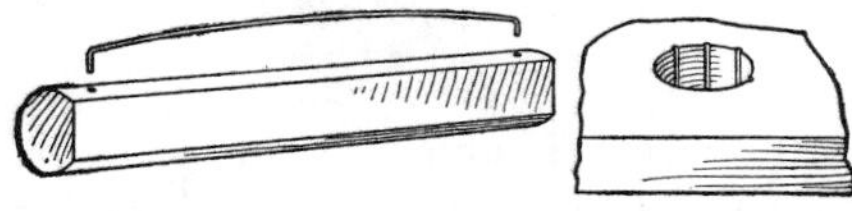

The Spring Wire will Hold the Stop at Any Desired Position for Height

the ends when it is in place on the stick.

Bore a 1-in. hole through the bench top where it is desired to use the stop and cut several grooves, as shown, in the walls of the hole with a compass saw. The spring wire will slide into a groove and hold the stick wherever it is set. The position of the face can be changed by inserting the stick so that the wire will enter the right groove.—Contributed by Alan H. Andrews, Fall River, Mass.

A Crochet Hook

In making some kinds of lace work different-sized hooks must be used as the work proceeds. Considerable time will be lost in changing from one hook to another, if they are separate. The best way is to mount all the hooks necessary on one handle, as shown in the sketch. The handle part is made of a large wire or small rod, bent to the

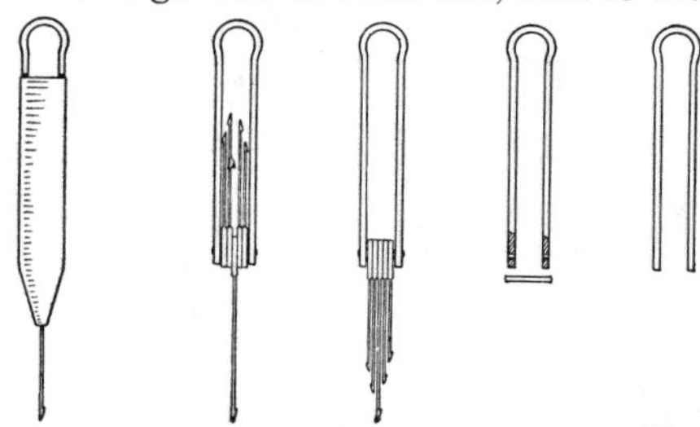

A Crochet-Hook Handle for Holding Several Hooks That are Required for Some Lace Work

shape shown and with holes drilled through the ends for a small rivet. The ends of the hooks are drilled or bent to fit on the rivet. A small tin ferrule is made to slip over the handle and the hooks not in use. All hooks but the one in use are turned back into the handle and the ferrule slipped into place.—Contributed by Miss Nita S. Ingle, W. Toledo, O.

Writing Board for Children

A writing desk for a child can be easily made as shown in the sketch. The materials necessary are a board of suitable size, two screwhooks, four screweyes and a pair of rods for braces. The hooks are screwed into the back of a chair and the screweyes into the board, as shown. This desk is instantly attached or taken down when desired. If the chair is light and apt

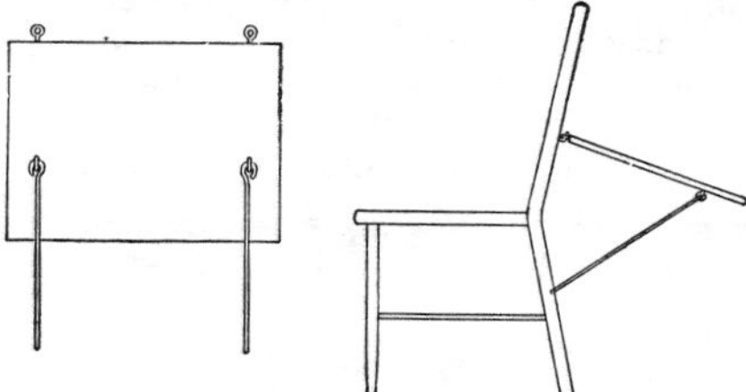

The Writing Board is Easily Attached to, or Detached from, an Ordinary Chair Back

to tip over, make the rods long enough to reach to the floor.—Contributed by John V. Loeffler, Evansville, Ind.

Geometric Principle in Line Division

When sketching a plan, if any one of the first few lines drawn is found to be the proper length, then this line can be

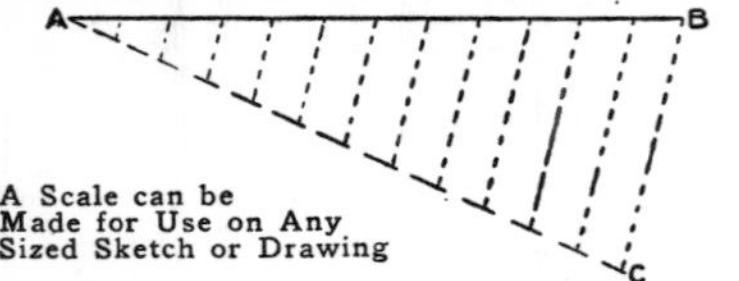

A Scale can be Made for Use on Any Sized Sketch or Drawing

made into a scale by the geometric rule for dividing a given line into equal parts.

Suppose, for example, the line AB, which is to represent 12 ft., is found to be 1 ft. long. Draw a line, AC, at any angle from the point A and step off on it 12 equal parts, beginning at A. The last point, or the one at C, is connected to the end B, then eleven other lines are drawn parallel with CB. Thus AB will make a scale of 1 in. to each 1 ft.—Contributed by James M. Kane, Doylestown, Pa.

Repairing a Broken Whip

Procure a piece of thin tin—the metal taken from a discarded fruit can will do—and cut it about 2½ in. long and wide enough to encircle the break. Notch the ends like saw teeth and remove any sharp edges with a file. Place the tin on the break and tie temporarily. Wind the whole from end to end with a waxed linen thread, such as used by harness makers. The threads lying alternately on the whip and on metal at the notched ends eliminate any possibility of the parts working loose. A break near the small and flexible end of a whip is repaired in the same manner, using a quill instead

The Repair on a Whip Made with a Notched Ferrule and a Waxed Thread

of the tin. In either case, do not let the edges of the splicing material meet, and it will clamp tightly on the whip. —Contributed by W. S. Kingsley, W. Gouldsboro, Me.

Repairing a Worn Thimble

Silver thimbles are easily worn through at the end, and they can be quickly repaired by soldering from the inside. A very neat repair can be made with an alcohol lamp and a blowpipe by using a little silver solder. Borax or resin is used as a flux.

A Small Torch

A small torch, that will give a very fine and hot smokeless flame, can be made from a piece of glass tube, about 4 in. long, and 4 ft. of rubber tubing. The glass tube is heated in the center

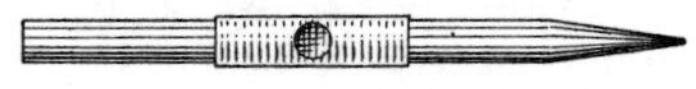

A Torch Made of Glass and Rubber Tubing, to be Used on an Ordinary Gas Jet

until it is red, then the ends drawn apart so that the tube will have a small diameter. After the glass has cooled, make a small scratch with a file on the thin part and break it. One of the pointed ends is connected to a straight piece of glass tube with a short piece of the rubber tube, as shown in the sketch. A small hole is cut in the side of the piece of rubber to admit air to the gas. The torch is connected to an ordinary gas jet.—Contributed by E. K. Marshall, Oak Park, Ill.

Fountain Attachment for an Ordinary Pen

A quite efficient fountain pen may be quickly made by bending an ordinary

The Space between the Pens Forms the Fountain, Which is Sufficient for Considerable Writing

pen, as shown at A, and inserting it in the holder opposite to the regular pen, as shown at B. For best results, the point of the auxiliary pen should just touch the regular pen.—Contributed by Thos. L. Parker, Wibaux, Mont.

¶A little water added to oil paint will make a flat or lusterless finish and will do no harm to the paint, as the water evaporates in time.

Homemade Cut Press

The person who has a little ability in making wood cuts with a knife will find it very interesting to make the press shown in the sketch. A fair job of printing can be done with the press, using printer's ink spread on a piece of glass with a hand ink roller, such as can be purchased cheaply of any dealer in printing supplies.

The press may have a base, A, of any size to suit, but one 1½ in. thick, 6 in. wide, and 12 in. long will be found to serve best for most purposes. It must be smooth and level. Hard wood, such as maple, beech, or birch, is best for all parts. The post B is 1¼ in. thick, 2 in. wide, and 5 in. long. Before setting it, slot the upper end for the end of the lever. This is done by making a saw cut, 1¾ in. deep, ⅝ in. from either side and cutting out the core to make a slot ¾ in. wide. A ¼-in. hole is then bored through the prongs to receive a stove bolt that connects them with the lever. The post is fastened with screws and glue in a notch cut in the center of the base end.

The lever C is made of a piece of wood ¼ in. square and 10 in. long. At the forward end the sides are pared away to form a tongue, or tenon, that will pass between the prongs of the upright, and a hole is bored through it to match those in the prongs. The entire upper surface of the lever is rounded and the under surface is rounded, beginning 6 in. from the tenon end. Glue to the under side of the lever a block, D, at the end of the under, flat surface. The block should be about 1¼ in. square by 1½ in. long. If the under side of the base is crowning, either level it with a plane or nail cleats across the ends for feet. A washer is used with the stove bolt in connecting the lever and post.

The cuts are made of small blocks

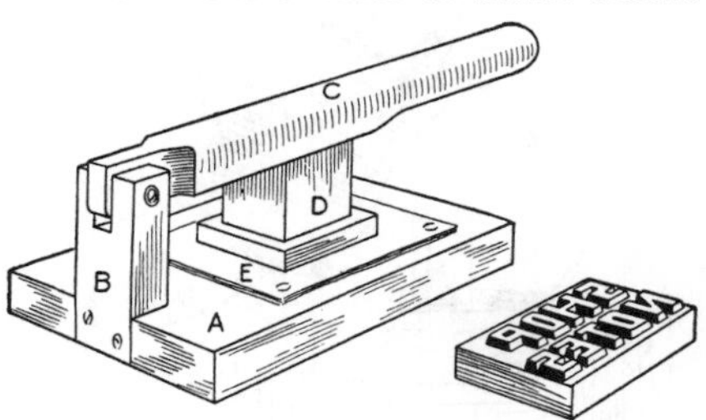

A Hand Press for Printing from Cuts Made of Wood, Using Ordinary Printer's Ink

of wood, about ¾ in. thick and of a size to take the characters desired. These blocks must be level and the printing side made smooth with very fine sandpaper, or a scraper, before the characters are laid out. Boxwood is best for cuts, but pearwood, applewood, birch, or maple will do very well. Mark out the characters backward, using the pencil very lightly. Then, with the small blade of a knife, made as sharp as possible, cut around the outlines, holding the knife slanting, and remove the adjacent wood by cutting in at a reverse angle to meet the boundary cut. Gradually deepen the cuts around the characters until they stand in relief about ⅛ in., then score V-shaped grooves, checkerboard fashion, across the remaining high surface that is not a part of the design, and chip out the resulting small blocks to bring the entire secondary surface of the block to a uniform level with the portions adjoining the characters.

A touch of glue to the back of the cut will set it securely enough to the bottom of the block D for printing, and allow its removal without injury when desired. To get a uniform impression in printing, place paper on the base, as at E, to the thickness required. For controlling the printing position on the stock paper, pins or tacks can be stuck into the base and each sheet to be printed laid against these guides.—Contributed by Chelsea Curtis Frazier, Saginaw, Mich.

An Electrical Testing Instrument for Experimenters

The amateur having an ordinary flash light can make an instrument that will serve for a variety of purposes. It is only necessary to solder a piece

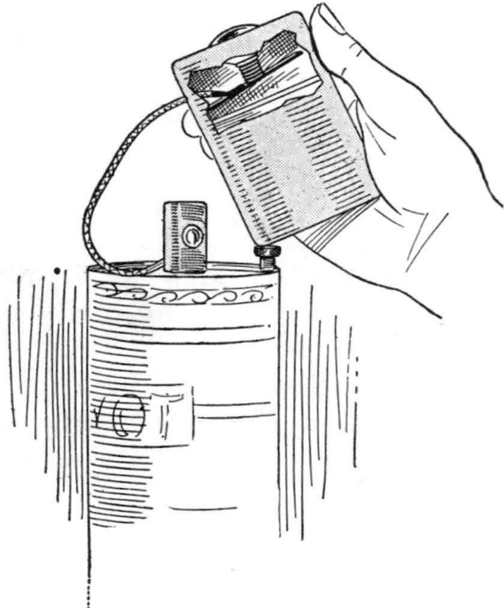

An Instrument Made of an Electrical Pocket Flash Light for Testing Circuits and Instruments

of lamp cord to the spring of the battery which comes in contact with the lamp, and pass the end through a hole drilled in the top of the case. The end can be fitted with a cord tip.

To test batteries, take the flash light in the right hand and press the button, lighting the lamp, then place the bottom of the flash light on one binding post and the cord on the other. If the light burns brilliantly, the battery is dead, but if it burns dimly or goes out the battery is good.

It may happen that the experimenter's telegraph line is out of order and the trouble cannot be found. The sounder may be tested out by disconnecting the wires from the instrument and placing the bottom of the flash light on one binding post and the cord on the other. If the light goes out, the trouble does not lie in the sounder, but in some other part of the line. The line may be tested in a similar manner if one end is short-circuited and the flash light connected to the other.

A tester of this kind cannot be used on long lines, or on instruments of much resistance, as their resistance will overcome that of the light. Keep in mind the fact that the lamp will always burn on an open circuit and go out on a closed circuit.

Softening the Tone of a Talking Machine

An effective mute, for use on any disk talking machine, can be made by clamping an ordinary wood clothespin on the head of the setscrew that holds the needle. Thus the tone will be softened a great deal more than by the use of a wood needle.

The record of a stringed instrument, such as a violin, will be almost exactly reproduced. It will also eliminate almost all the scratching sound caused by a steel needle.—Contributed by C. M. Reeves, Los Angeles, Cal.

¶An antenna should be made of wire larger than No. 14 gauge.

A Musical Doorbell

By H. MARCELLE

IN the construction of this doorbell it is best to purchase a small instrument known as the "tubaphone." It consists of a rack with several pieces of brass tubing cut to different lengths to give the proper tones as they are struck. Such an instrument with eight tubes will play almost any tune, and can be purchased from 50 cents up, depending on the size. Brass tubes can be purchased, cut, and toned, but the time taken in doing this is worth more than the price of the instrument, and no changes are necessary in it to make the doorbell.

Several strips of pine, 2 in. wide and 7/8 in. thick, are procured for the framework. The tubes are placed on a table top, 1 in. apart and with their lower ends on a line at right angles to their length. Allow a space of 1 in. outside the first and last tube, and cut a piece of the wood to this length, allowing sufficient additional material to fasten on the ends of two uprights, which are cut long enough to admit the longest tube and allow sufficient room for a large roller and space at the top to swing the tubes.

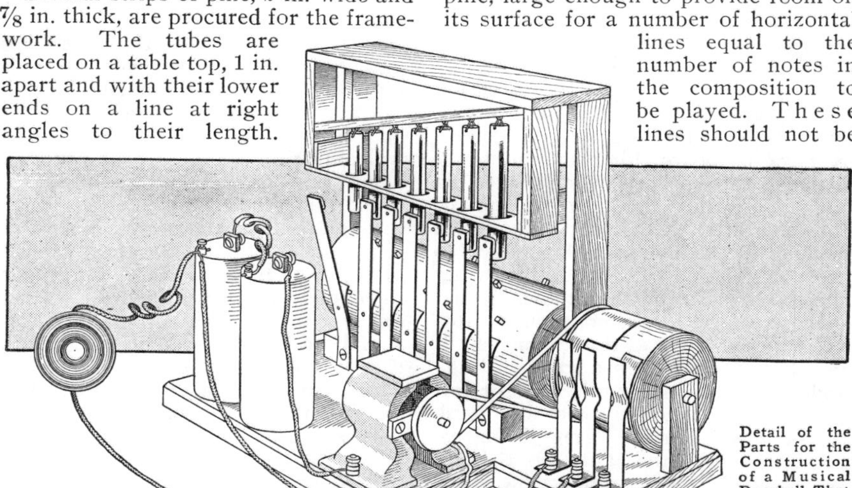

Detail of the Parts for the Construction of a Musical Doorbell That will Play the Music on Brass Tubes with One Touch of a Push Button

A base is cut from a board, 7/8 in. thick and of sufficient size to admit the roller and tube rack, together with a small battery motor. The tube rack is fastened to the back of this base by making a tenon on the lower end of each upright, and a mortise in the baseboard to receive it.

A roller is turned from a piece of soft pine, large enough to provide room on its surface for a number of horizontal lines equal to the number of notes in the composition to be played. These lines should not be too close together. Supposing the music it is desired to play has 15 notes in its composition, then 15 horizontal lines must be spaced evenly on the surface of the roller. The length of the roller should be a free-working fit between the uprights. A 1/4-in. steel rod is run through its center for a shaft,

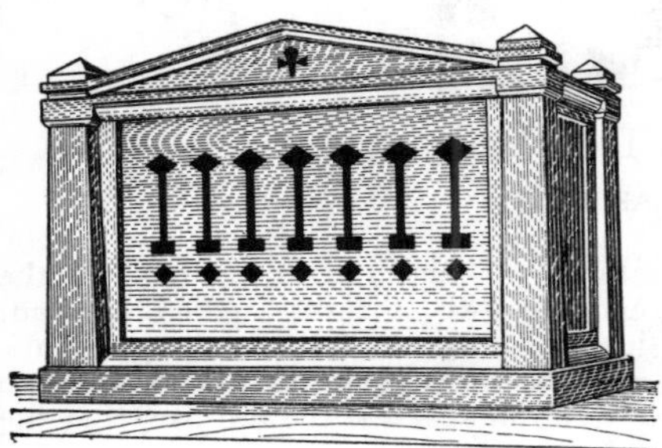

The Appearance of the Doorbell Is That of a Mission Clock on a Mantel

allowing sufficient ends for the bearings, and, in addition, at one end sufficient length for a pulley.

The motor is lined up on the base, so that its pulley wheel will run a belt on the large wheel of the roller. The current is turned on after making belt and wiring connections, a lead pencil is held directly centering the place where each tube hangs, and a line is drawn on the circumference of the roller.

A 1/8-in. hole is drilled through each tube, near one end, and a piece of catgut string run into it to make a hanger. A piece of board, long enough to fit between the uprights when placed on the slope formed by the upper ends of the tubes after their lower ends are set straight on a line at right angles to their length, and wide enough to swing the tubes clear of the frame, is fastened in place, as shown. Small screw eyes are turned into the under side of this board, at even spacings of 1 in., and used to swing the tubes by the catgut strings. Another piece of board, the same width as the former, is placed, perfectly horizontal, between the uprights a short distance above the lower ends of the hanging tubes. Evenly spaced holes are bored in this crosspiece to admit the ends of the tubes. The holes should be of such size that when they are lined with a piece of felt, the tubes will have a little play without touching the sides at any point.

The hammers are each made of a strip of sheet brass, having a length that will extend from the base to a short distance above the lower ends of the tubes. A hole is drilled in each end of the strip, the lower one being of a size to fasten it to the base crosspiece with a round-head wood screw. The hole in the upper end is used to fasten a small block of wood with a screw, for the hammer head. A small strip of felt is glued to the striking side of the block. Another piece of brass, used for a trip, is fastened to the center part of each long piece with rivets, so that its upper end will be near the center of the roller for height, and strike the end of a small peg driven into the roller. The length of these pieces, in fact, of all pieces, will depend on the length of the tubes in the tubaphone and the size roller required for the music.

The setting of the pegs in the roller requires some patience in order to get the tune correct, but one mistake will be of more value than an hour's description. The pegs can be procured from a shoemaker. If the roller is of pine, they can be driven into the wood of the roller with a hammer.

With ordinary connections to the push button and motor, the mechanism will only run while the push button is being pressed. A device that will cause the piece of music to be played through to the finish after the push button is pushed for a short time, consists of a turned piece of wood fastened to the outside surface of the driving wheel on the roller. This piece of wood should be carefully set, so that its outside surface will be true as it revolves. Three brushes, made of copper strips, are fastened to the base. The length of these brushes will depend on the size of the roller and height of the block of wood. They should be evenly spaced and fastened, so that they will be insulated from each other. One strip of brass, or copper, is fastened around the turned piece of wood. This strip must be as wide as two brushes, except for a short distance to make a break in the electrical circuit. The notch in the strip, to make this break, should be on the outside edge where it will disconnect the center brush, and its location on the turned piece of wood should be on a line with the end and the beginning of the pegs for the music. Another short strip is fastened to the turned piece of wood, where it will make a contact with the first brush when the second or middle brush is in the notch, or disconnected, and is connected to the other notched strip with a piece of wire run beneath the wood.

The wiring shown will make it possible to start the motor with the push button which will turn the roll far enough to connect the center brush; then the roller will turn until the music is played, at which point it will stop and remain in rest until the push button again makes the contact.

The entire mechanism can be made to set on the mantel or shelf, incased like a mission clock, and the wires running to it may be concealed.

Replacing Buckle Tongues

Having several buckles without tongues I tried to repair them with pieces of wire, but could not get them to bend short enough to fasten around the buckle frame. Some cotters were at hand and seeing them gave me the idea of using one leg, with the eye part, as a tongue. By using the proper-sized cotter, a substantial and quickly made repair will be the result. —Contributed by Everett Hoar, Bowmanville, Ont.

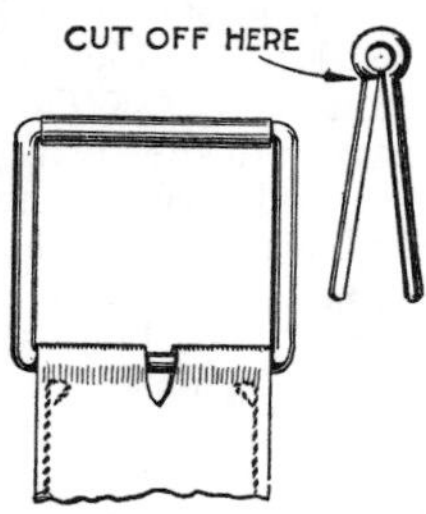

ℭBread crumbs thoroughly rubbed over a pencil drawing will remove most of the dirt and without disturbing the pencil lines.

Drying Towels in Photographer's Dark Room

In doing a large amount of photographic work the towel becomes wet, and to dry the hands on it is impossible. To obviate this annoyance, I made a galvanized-iron pipe, about 2 ft. long and 8 in. in diameter, with a disk, or circular piece, of metal about 10 in. in diameter soldered on each end to form flanges. One flange was fastened to the wall of the dark room in a convenient place to support the device. On the inside of the spool, or towel support, an ordinary incandescent electric globe was placed. The heat of the lamp would easily dry 12 in. of the towel, and when the dry part was pulled down for use another wet portion was brought into position for drying.

An Electric Globe Makes Heat in the Spool for Drying a Portion of the Towel

Those who have tried to handle gelatin dry plates with moist hands will readily appreciate the value of this simple contrivance. The lamp in the spool is connected on the switch with the ruby light, so that it is not forgotten, when leaving the room, to turn it out.—Contributed by T. B. Lambert, Chicago.

An Electric Chime Clock

By JOHN E. MAHLMEISTER

In the construction of this clock one perfectly good and accurate alarm clock and the works of an old or discarded one are used. The clock for the accurate time is set into a frame, or casing, made of thin boards which have a circular opening cut in them to fit

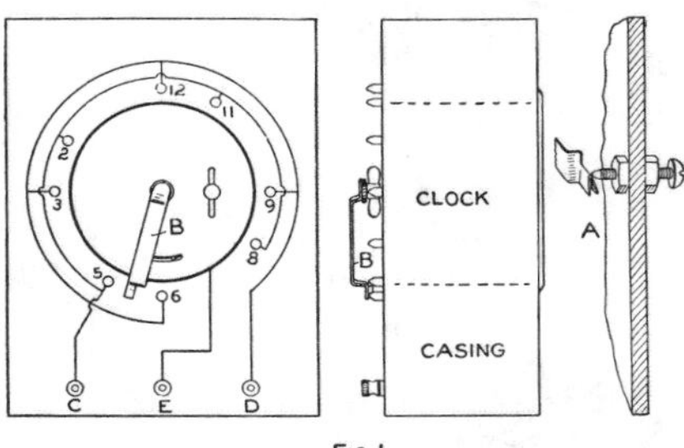

Fig. 1

The Alarm Clock in Its Case and the Location of the Contact Pins and Contact Lever

snugly on the outside casing of the clock. The back of the clock and casing are shown in Fig. 1. A circular line is drawn on the casing, about 1 in. larger in diameter than the clock, and brass machine screws with two nuts clamping on the wood back, as shown at A, are set at intervals so as to be opposite, or just back of, the hour marks 2, 3, 5, 6, 8, 9, 11, and 12. A contact spring, B, is shaped as shown and soldered to the knurled knob on the back

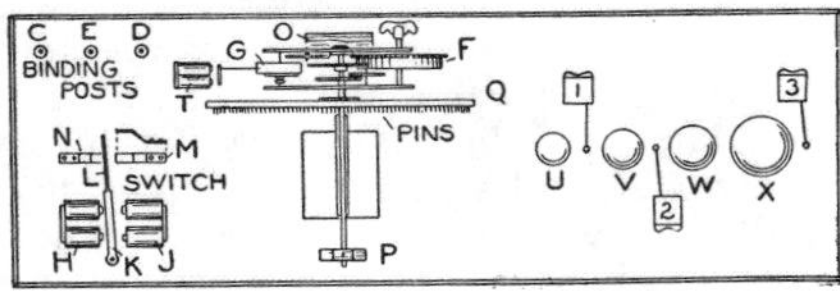

Fig. 2

Location of the Clock Works, Magnets, Binding Posts, Gongs and Strikers on the Baseboard

of the clock used for setting the hands in a position where it will travel or be parallel with the minute hand. The end of the contact spring should be shaped so that it will slide over the points of the screws easily, but in good contact. The ends of the screws should be filed to a slightly rounding point. The wiring diagram for this part of the apparatus is clearly shown, and the terminals are connected to binding posts C and D. The binding post E is connected to the metal part of the clock.

The chime part is made entirely separate and can be located at any reasonable distance from the clock. It is propelled by the works from an old clock, as shown at F, Fig. 2. The old clock is prepared for use by removing the hands, balance wheel and escapement so that the wheels will turn freely. To prevent the works from running too fast, a piece of sheet brass, G, is soldered to the shaft running at the highest speed. The brass should be as large as the space will admit. It forms a fan to catch the air and retard the speed, and also provides a means of stopping the works by the electric mechanism.

The parts for the gongs and electrical apparatus are supported on a baseboard, 3/4 in. thick, 6 in. wide, and 18 in. long. The automatic switch is located at one end of the base, and consists of two sets of magnets, H and J, with an armature, K, to which is attached a stiff contact wire, L. This wire is to make contact with the spring M when the armature is drawn by the magnets J, and with N when drawn by the magnets H. The springs M and N are made of thin sheet brass, bent as shown, and mounted on the base.

A piece of wood, O, on which to mount the works of the old clock is mortised into the base. Another standard, P, of the same height as O, is also mortised into the base to provide a bearing for the end of the shaft which carries the wood disk Q, the opposite end of the shaft being connected by means of a ferrule and soldered to the end of the minute-hand shaft. The shaft should be well lined up, so that it will turn freely. The wood disk is 1/4 in. thick and about 6 in. in diameter.

Mark four circles on the face of the disk, near the outside edge and 1/4 in. apart. Step off the outside circle into 150 parts and draw a radial line from each mark across the four circular lines with the straight edge on the center of the disk. An arc of the disk is shown in Fig. 3, where trip pins are driven in for making the electric contacts. This part of the arc shows the method of locating the pins for the hour from 3 to 4 o'clock, with the intermediate pins for the quarter, half, and three-quarter-hour contacts. The intermediate pins are arranged in the same manner for all hours, but the hour pins, on the second circle, run from 1 pin to 12 pins consecutively. Ordinary pins, with the heads cut off, are used and should be driven in accurately on the division lines to secure proper results.

The arrangement of the springs is shown in Fig. 4. These springs, when pressed together, will close the circuit for ringing the gongs. They are made of thin sheet brass, bent as shown at R, and fastened to a piece, or block, of hard wood with screws, as shown at S. The springs numbered 3, 5, 7, and 9 are the ones made as shown at R for sliding over the pins in the disk Q, and their ends should clear the face of the disk about 1/8 in. The springs 1, 2, 4, 6, and 8 are about 1/2 in. shorter and have their ends bent up at right angles so that they will almost touch the long ones. The spring 1 should be a little shorter than 2. When fastening the

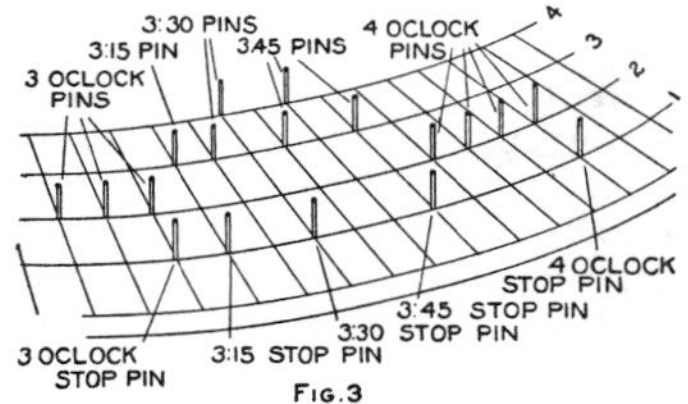

The Pins are Accurately Set in Four Circular Lines and on Radial Lines

springs to the block of wood, be sure that no two springs touch and that each one is separated from the other to form no contact until the pins in the wheel force them together. The block is then fastened to the base under and parallel with the shaft carrying the disk Q, as shown.

The starting and stopping of the clockwork F is accomplished by means of a set of bell magnets, arranged, as

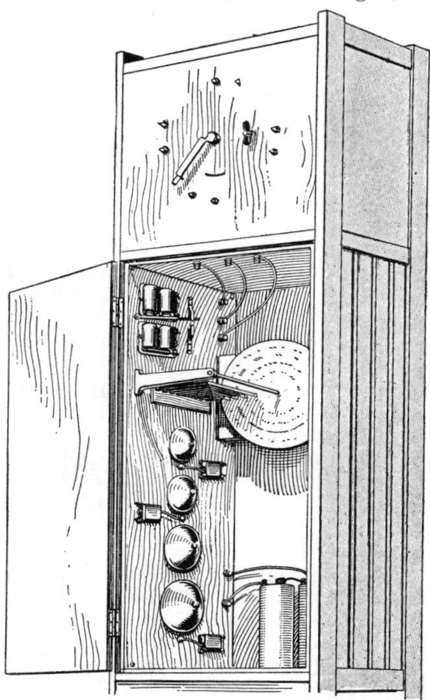
The Parts Constructing the Chime are Placed in the Clock Frame below the Works

shown at T, Fig. 2, with the wire attached to the armature bent to touch the brass wing of the fan G. The armature must not vibrate, but stay against the magnet cores while the current is flowing through them, thus allowing the clock wheels to turn, and as soon as the current is cut off, the armature will spring back and stop the wheels.

Arrange four gongs, U, V, W, and X, as shown in Fig. 2, and also three bell magnets with clappers 1, 2 and 3. These gongs should be selected for tone as in a chime clock. The connections to the bell magnets 1, 2, and 3 should be direct to the binding posts so that the armature will not vibrate, but give one stroke. For instance, bell magnet 1 should produce one stroke on the gong U when the current is on, and one stroke on the gong V when

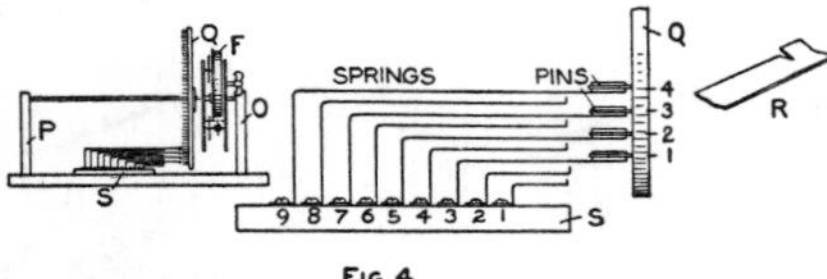

Fig. 4

The Contact Springs are Operated by the Pins on the Disk Wheel

the current breaks. The magnets 2 should cause the clapper to strike once on the gong V when the current is on, and to make one stroke on the gong W when the current is broken. The magnets 3 produce only one stroke on the gong X at a time, which is used to sound the hours.

The parts are connected up electrically as shown in Fig. 5. The lines between the clock, Fig. 1, and the bell-ringing part, Fig. 2, are connected from C to C, D to D, and E, Fig. 1, to the zinc of a battery and from the carbon to E, Fig. 2. Two dry cells will be sufficient for the current.

The working of the mechanism is as follows: Suppose the time is 6 minutes of 3 o'clock and the contact spring on the back is near the 11 pin. As soon as it touches the pin, the armature K of the switch will be drawn in contact with the spring N, then when the contact spring touches the 12 pin, the current will flow into the

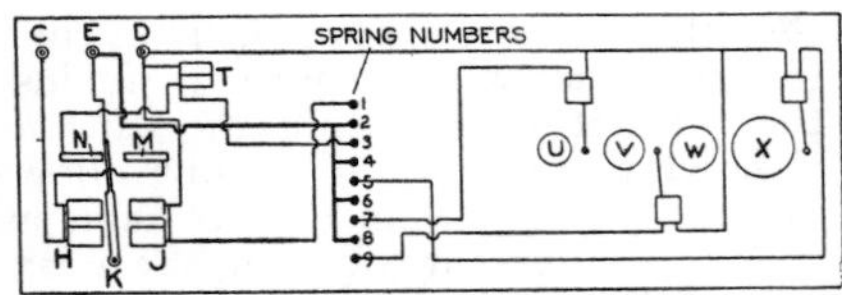

Fig. 5

The Wiring Diagram for the Location of the Wires on the Under Side of the Base

magnets T and release the wheels of the clockwork F, which turns the disk Q, and the three pins in the second row will pass over the spring 5 and press it in contact with the spring 4 three times, causing the gong X to toll out 3 o'clock. As the contact spring B will be on the contact pin 12 for about 1 minute, the wheels of the clockwork F would continue to turn and the bells ring, if it were not for the stop pin located on the outside, or first, circle of the disk Q, which pin is set in line with the last pin in the set of pins for the hour, or, in this instance, in line with the third pin. When the stop pin has passed the spring, the connection through the magnets T is broken and the clockwork F stops instantly. When the spring B strikes the 2 o'clock pin, or 10 minutes after 3 o'clock, the armature K is drawn over to N, and at the 3 pin, or 15 minutes after 3 o'clock, the bells U, V, and W will ring and then the stop pin will break the current, and so on, at every 15 minutes of the 12 hours.

Hinges Used to Substitute Night Bolt

One of the safest devices for bolting, or locking, a door against intruders is to use two sets of hinges. The extra set is fastened to the door and frame in the same way but directly opposite the regular hinges. It may be necessary to file the extra hinges and pins in order to separate and bring the parts together easily. The usual door lock need not be used with this arrangement, as the hinges are exposed only on the inside of the room and cannot be tampered with from without.

Propellers for a Hand Sled

Desiring to propel my hand sled with power transmitted by cranks and wheels, I set about to procure the necessary materials. Two medium-sized buggy wheels were found in the back yard of a blacksmith shop, which were procured for a nominal price. The fellies of these wheels were removed, the tenons cut from the spokes and nails substituted, which were driven in their ends so that about ½ in. of the body with the head projected. The heads were then removed and the nail ends sharpened.

The hubs were plugged with pieces

of wood, whittled to tightly fit the holes. A hole was then bored exactly central through each plug for a ½-in. rod. This size rod was procured and bent to form a crank, the bearing end being threaded for a distance equal to the length of the hub.

Two pieces or blocks of wood, 2 in. square and 4 in. long, were used as bearings. These were bored centrally through the long way, to receive the ½-in. rod just loose enough to make a good bearing. These bearings were supported by a pair of braces made of strap iron, about ¼ in. thick and ¾ in. wide. The length of the iron will depend on the size of the wheels and the height of the sled runner. The braces were shaped as shown. The center of the bearing hole must be as high from the surface of the ground as the distance the spoke ends are from the center of the hub hole.

The crank is then run through the bearing hole and a nut run on the threads and a washer placed against the nut. The wheel is then slipped on the axle, and another washer and nut run on tightly. Both wheels, bearings, cranks, and brackets are

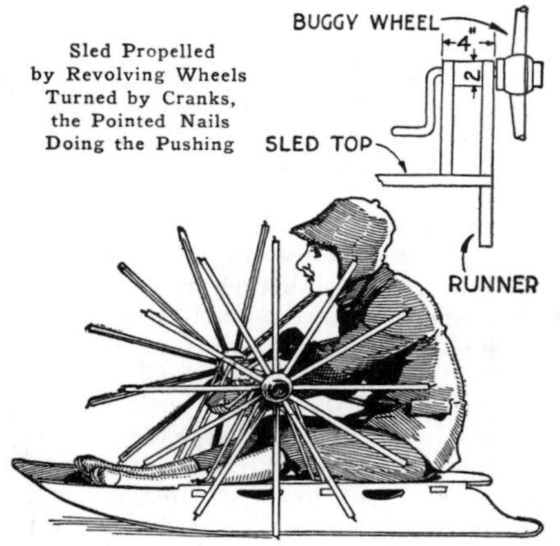

Sled Propelled by Revolving Wheels Turned by Cranks, the Pointed Nails Doing the Pushing

made alike. The brackets are fastened with small bolts to the sled top. —Contributed by Justin Stewart, Wallingford, Conn.

A Self-Feeding Match Box

With the addition of the simple device here illustrated, any match box can be converted into one of the self-

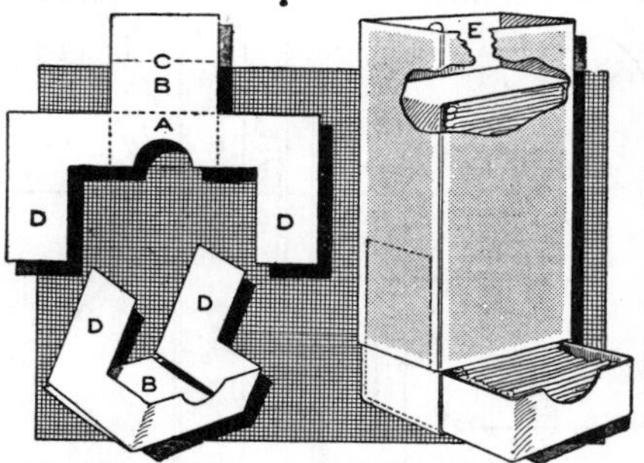

The Attachment Consists of a Receptacle Fitting into the End of a Match Box

feeding type. A piece of tin, or cardboard, is cut, as shown at A, the exact size depending on the match box used. The piece cut out is folded on the dotted lines, the cover on the match box is removed, and the part B pushed into the end of the box beneath the matches. The part B is twice as long as the depth of the box, therefore it enters the box as far as the line C. The flaps D rest against the outside of the box, and are held in place by the box cover. The matches feed into the box formed of the tin or cardboard as fast as used, while the burnt ones can be placed in the upper part E.

Corks-in-a-Box Trick

Procure a pill box and a clean cork. Cut two disks from the cork to fit in the box, and fasten one of the pieces centrally to the inside bottom of the pill box with glue.

To perform the trick, put the loose disk in with the one that is fast, and then open the box to show both corks. Close the box and in doing so turn it over, then open and only one cork will be seen. Be careful not to show the inside of the other part of the box with the cork that is fastened.—Contributed by Fred B. Spoolstra, Yonkers, N. Y.

A Disk-Armature Motor

One of the simplest motors to make is the disk motor, its construction requiring a wood base, a brass disk, a 3-in. horseshoe magnet, and some mercury.

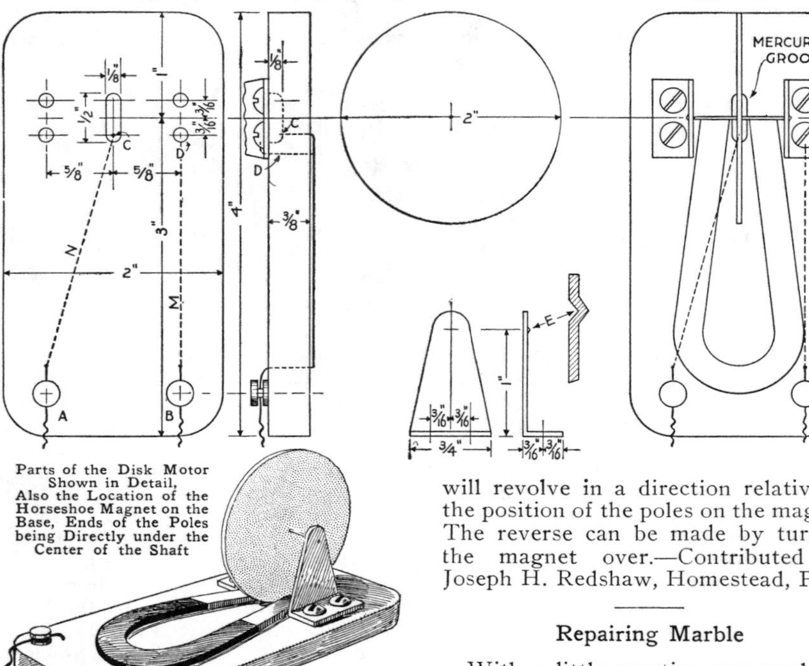

Parts of the Disk Motor Shown in Detail, Also the Location of the Horseshoe Magnet on the Base, Ends of the Poles being Directly under the Center of the Shaft

The base is made of hard wood, in the proportions shown in the sketch. The leading-in wires are connected to the binding posts A and B, and from these connections are made, on the bottom of the base, from A to the groove C cut in the upper surface of the base for the mercury, and from B to one screw, D, of one bearing. The end of the former wire must be clean and project into the end of the groove, where it will be surrounded with mercury.

The bearings consist of thin sheet brass, cut to the dimensions shown, the bearing part being made with a well-pointed center punch, as at E. The disk wheel is made of sheet brass, 2 in. in diameter, and a needle, with the eye broken off and pointed, is used for the shaft. The needle shaft can be placed in position by springing the bearings apart at the top.

When the current is applied, the disk will revolve in a direction relative to the position of the poles on the magnet. The reverse can be made by turning the magnet over.—Contributed by Joseph H. Redshaw, Homestead, Pa.

Repairing Marble

With a little practice any mechanic can repair holes, cracks or chipped places on marble slabs, so that the patched place cannot be detected from the natural marble. Use the following mixture as a base for the filler: Water glass, 10 parts; calcined magnesite, 2 parts, and powdered marble, 4 parts. These should be mixed thoroughly to a semifluid paste. Fill the crack or hole and smooth off level, then with a camel's-hair brush and colors, made of aniline in alcohol, work out the veins, body colors, etc., as near to the natural marble as possible. It will depend on the application of the colors whether the repair can be seen or not. Artificial-marble slabs can be formed from this mixture.—Contributed by A. E. Soderlund, New York City.

The Construction of a Simple Wireless Telephone Set

By A. E. ANDREWS

In Two Parts — Part I

Among the various methods for the transmission of speech electrically, without wire, from one point to another, the so-called "inductivity" system, which utilizes the principles of electromagnetic induction, is perhaps the simplest, because it requires no special apparatus. Since this system is so simple in construction, and its operation can be easily understood by one whose knowledge of electricity is limited, a description will be given of how to construct and connect the necessary apparatus required at a station for both transmitting and receiving a message.

Before taking up the actual construction and proper connection of the various pieces of apparatus, it will be well to explain the electrical operation of the system. If a conductor be moved in a magnetic field in any direction other than parallel to the field, there will be an electrical pressure induced in the conductor, and this induced electrical pressure will produce a current in an electrical circuit of which the conductor is a part, provided the circuit be complete, or closed, just as the electrical pressure produced in the battery due to the chemical action in the battery will produce a current in a circuit connected to the terminals of the battery. A simple experiment to illustrate the fact that there is an induced electrical pressure set up in a conductor when it is moved in a magnetic field may be performed as follows: Take a wire, AB, as shown in Fig. 1, and connect its terminals to a galvanometer, G, as shown. If no galvanometer can be obtained, a simple one can be made by supporting a small compass needle inside a coil composed of about 100 turns of small wire. The terminals of the winding on the coil of the galvanometer should be connected to the terminals of the conductor AB, as shown in Fig. 1. If now the conductor AB be moved up and down past the end of the magnet N, there will be an electrical pressure induced in the conductor, and this electrical pressure will produce a current in the winding of the galvanometer

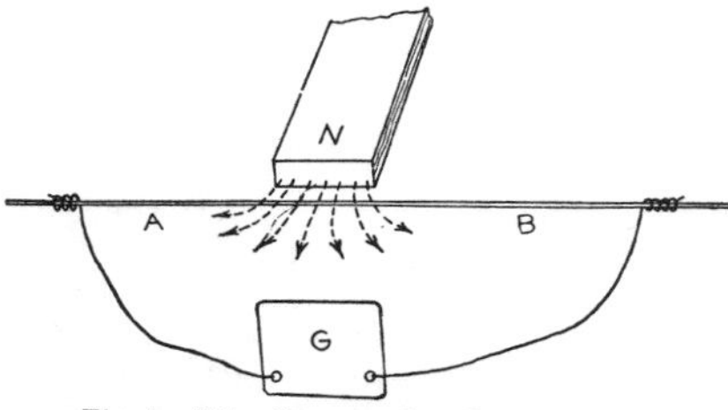

Fig. 1 — Wire Connected to Galvanometer

G, which will cause the magnetic needle suspended in the center of the coil to be acted upon by a magnetic force tending to move it from its initial position, or position of rest. It will be found that this induced electrical pressure will exist only as long as the conductor AB is moving with respect to the magnetic field of the magnet N, as there will be no deflection of the galvanometer needle when the motion of the conductor ceases, indicating there is no current in the galvanometer winding, and hence no induced electrical pressure. It will also be found that the direction in which the magnetic needle of the galvanometer is deflected changes as the direction of motion of the conductor changes with respect to the magnet, indicating that there is a change in the direction of the current in the winding of the galvanometer, and since the direction of this current is dependent upon the direction in which the induced electrical pressure acts, there must have been a change in the direction of this pressure due to a change in the direction of motion of the conductor. The same results can be obtained by moving the magnet, allowing the conductor AB to remain stationary, the only requirement being a relative movement of the conductor and the magnetic field created by the magnet.

It is not necessary that the magnetic field be created by a permanent magnet. It can be produced by a current

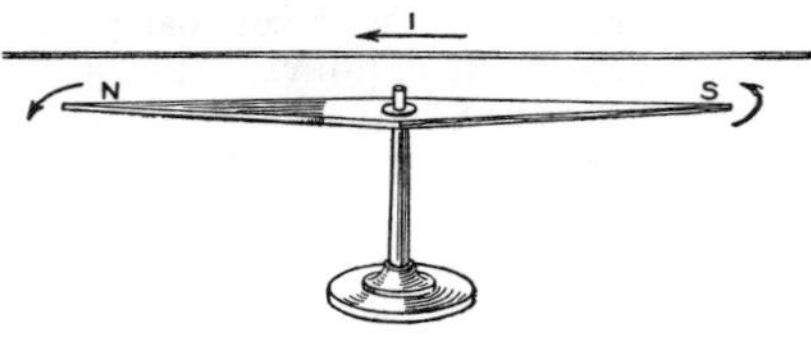

Fig. 2—Compass Needle Test

in a conductor. The fact that there is a magnetic field surrounding a conductor in which there is a current can be shown by a simple experiment, as illustrated in Fig. 2. If a wire be placed above a compass needle and parallel to the direction of the compass needle and a current be sent through the wire in the direction indicated by the arrow I, there will be a force acting on the compass needle tending to turn the needle at right angles to the wire. The amount the needle is turned will depend upon the value of the current in the wire. There is a definite relation between the direction of the current in the wire and the direction of the magnetic field surrounding the wire, because a reversal of current in the conductor will result in a reversal in the direction in which the compass needle is deflected. Remembering that the direction of a magnetic field can be determined by placing a magnetic needle in the field and noting the direction in which the N-pole of the needle points, this being taken as the positive direction, if one looks along a conductor in which there is a current and the current be from the observer, the direction of the magnetic field about the conductor will be clockwise. Imagine a conductor carrying a current and that you are looking at a cross-section of this conductor (see Fig. 3), and the direction of the current in the conductor is from you (this being indicated in the figure by the cross inside the circle), then the lines of force of the magnetic field will be concentric circles about the conductor, they being nearer together near the conductor, indicating the strength of the field is greatest near the conductor. A compass needle placed above the conductor would place itself in such a position that the N-pole would point toward the right and the S-pole toward the left. If the needle be placed below the conductor, the N-pole would point to the left and the S-pole to the right, indicating that the direction of the magnetic field above the conductor is just the reverse of what it is below the conductor.

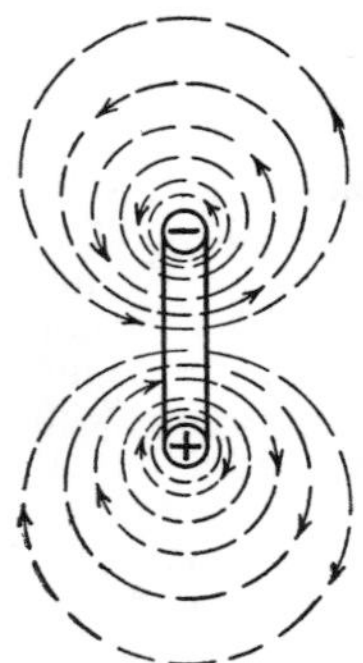

Fig. 4—Reversed Lines of Force

The strength of the magnetic field produced by a current in a conductor can be greatly increased by forming the conductor into a coil. Figure 4 shows the cross-section of a coil composed of a single turn of wire. The current in the upper cross-section is just the reverse of what it is in the lower cross-section, as indicated by the cross and dash inside the two circles. As a result of the direction of current

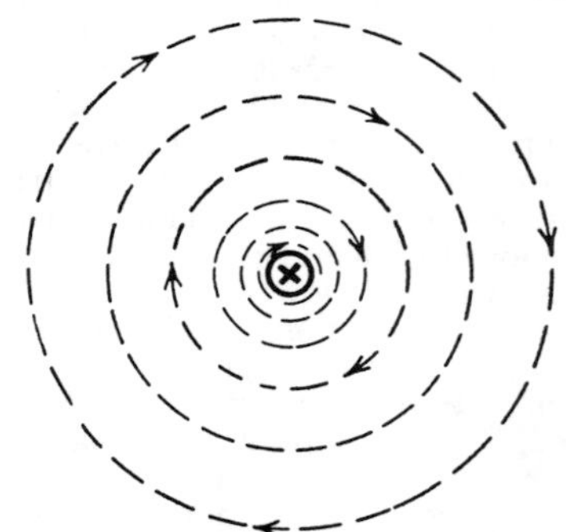

Fig. 3—Lines of Force

in the two cross-sections being different, the direction of the magnetic field about these two cross-sections will be different, one being clockwise, and the other counter-clockwise. It will be observed, however, that all the lines of force pass through the center of the coil in the same direction, or the magnetic field inside the coil is due to the combined action of the various parts of the conductor forming the complete turn. This magnetic field can be increased in value, without increasing the current in the conductor, by adding more turns to the coil.

A cross-section through a coil composed of eight turns placed side by side is shown in Fig. 5. The greater part of the magnetic lines created by each turn pass through the remaining turns as shown in the figure, instead of passing around the conductor in which the current exists that creates them. This results in the total num-

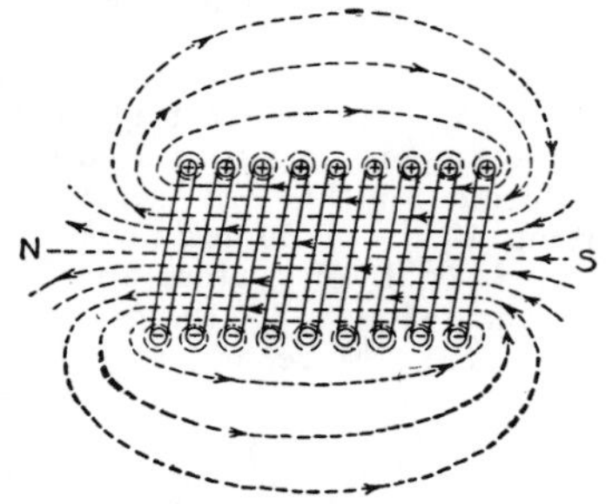

Fig. 5—Magnetic Lines Passing through Center

ber of lines passing through the coil per unit of cross-sectional area being greater than it was for a single turn, although the value of the current in the conductor has remained constant, the only change being an increase in the number of turns forming the coil.

If a conductor be moved by the end of a coil similar to that shown in Fig. 5, when there is a current in the winding of the coil, there will be an electrical pressure induced in the conductor, just the same as though it were moved by the end of a permanent magnet. The polarity of the coil is marked in Fig. 5. The magnetic lines pass from the S-pole to the N-pole through the coil and from the N-pole to the S-pole outside the coil, just as they do in a permanent magnet.

How to Lock a Tenoned Joint

A tenon placed in a blind mortise can be permanently fastened, when putting the joints together, by two

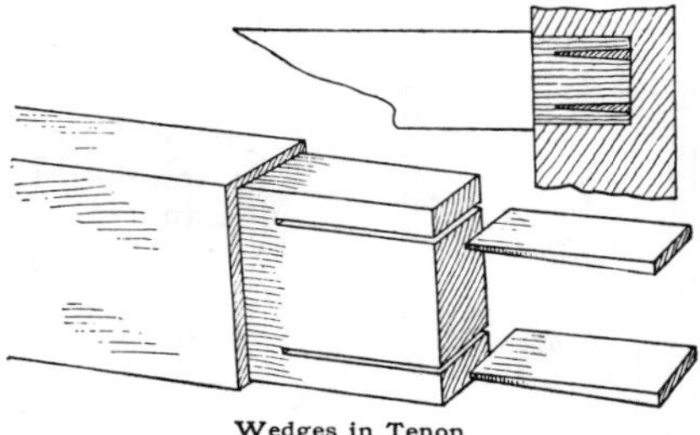

Wedges in Tenon

wedges driven in the end grain of the wood. In some cases, where the wood to be used is very dry and brittle, it is advisable to dip the tenon in warm water before applying the glue. The glue must be applied immediately after the tenon is removed from the water, and then inserted in the mortise. The sketch shows the application of the wedges. The bottom of the mortise drives the wedges as the tenon is forced in place.

Fitting a Large Cork in a Small Bottle

When necessary, a large cork may be made to fit a small bottle, if treated as shown in the sketch. Two wedge-shaped sections are cut from the cork, at right angles to each other, as shown in Fig. 1. The points are then squeezed together (Fig. 2) and the end inserted

Reducing Size of Cork

in the bottle (Fig. 3). Wet the cork slightly and the operation will be easier.—Contributed by James M. Kane, Doylestown, Pa.

A Homemade Wet Battery

Procure a large water bottle and have a glass cutter cut the top off so that the lower portion will form a jar about 8½ in. high. Next obtain two pieces of carbon, about 8 in. long, 4 in. wide and ¼ in. thick. Melt up some old scrap zinc and mold a piece having the same dimensions as the pieces of carbon. The mold for casting the zinc may be made by nailing some ¼-in. strips of wood on a piece of dry board, forming a shallow box, 4 in. wide and 8 in. long. Remove all the impurities from the surface of the zinc when it is melted, with a metal spoon or piece of tin. Before filling the mold with the metal, place a piece of No. 14 gauge bare copper wire through a small hole in one of the end pieces forming the mold, and allow it to project several inches inside, and make sure the mold is perfectly level. The zinc will run around the end of the wire, which is to afford a means of connecting the zinc plate to one of the binding posts forming the terminals of the cell.

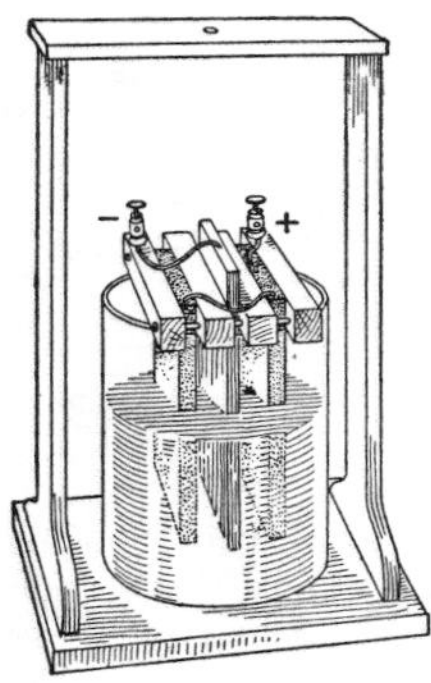

Cut from some hard wood four pieces a little longer than the outside diameter of the glass jar, two of them ½ by ½ in., and two, ½ by ⅝ in. Drill a ⅛-in. hole in each end of all four pieces, the holes being perpendicular to the ½-in. dimension in each case, and about ⅜ in. from the end. Boil all the pieces for several minutes in paraffin and stand them up on end to drain. Procure two ⅛-in. brass bolts, 3½ in. long, which are to be used in clamping the elements of the cell together. The two smaller pieces of wood should be placed on each side of one end of the zinc, then the carbon pieces and the larger pieces of wood outside the carbon pieces. The carbon plates should be connected together and then connected to a binding post which forms the positive terminal of the cell. If unable to obtain pieces of carbon of the required dimensions, a number of ordinary electric-light carbons may be used. Get about ten ½-in. carbons, without the copper coating, if possible; if not, file all the copper off. Cut these carbons off, forming 8-in. lengths. File the top ends of the carbons flat and so that they all become equal in thickness, and clamp them in place by means of the brass bolts. If rods are used, they should all be connected together by means of a piece of copper wire and then to a binding post.

The plates may now be hung in the jar, the wooden pieces resting on the top of the jar and acting as a support. The solution for this cell is made by dissolving ½ lb. of potassium bichromate in ½ gal. of water, and then adding very slowly ½ lb. of strong sulphuric acid. More or less solution may be made by using the proper proportion of each ingredient.

This cell will have a voltage of two volts, a rather low internal resistance, and will be capable of delivering a large current. If it should begin to show signs of exhaustion, a little more acid may be added.

A chemical action goes on in this cell regardless of whether it supplies current to an external circuit or not, and for this reason the elements should be removed from the solution and hung directly over the jar when the cell is not in use. A simple device for this purpose may be constructed as shown. A cord may be passed through the opening in the crossbar at the top and its lower end attached to the elements. When the elements are drawn out of the solution, the upper end of the cord may be fastened in some manner. This frame can, of course, be made longer, so it will accommodate a number of cells.

The Construction of a Simple Wireless Telephone Set

By A. E. ANDREWS

In Two Parts—Part II

If two coils of wire be placed parallel to each other as shown in Fig. 6, and a current be passed through the winding of one of them, say A, a part of the magnetic lines of force created by this current will pass through the other coil B. These lines of magnetic force must cut across the turns of wire of the coil in which there is no current as the magnetic field is being created, and as a result there will be an electrical pressure produced in the winding of the coil carrying no current. When the current in coil A is discontinued, the magnetic field created by this current is destroyed or it contracts to zero, and the magnetic lines again cut the various turns composing the winding of coil B. The direction in which the magnetic lines of force and the winding of coil B move with respect to each other is just the reverse, when the current in the winding of coil A is increasing, to what it is when the current in the winding of the coil A is decreasing. Any change in the value of the current in the winding of coil A will result in a change in the number of magnetic lines of force linked with the winding of the coil B, and as a result of this change in the number of lines linked with the winding of coil B there will be an induced electrical pressure set up in coil B. The direction of this induced electrical pressure will depend upon whether the current in the winding of coil A is increasing or decreasing in value. When the current in the winding of coil A is increasing in value, the electrical pressure induced in the winding of coil B will be in such a direction that the current produced by this induced electrical pressure will pass around the winding of coil B in the opposite direction to that in which the current passes around the winding of coil A. Or the current produced by the induced electrical pressure tends to produce a magnetic field opposite in direction to the one created by the current in the winding of coil A. When the current in the winding of A is decreasing in value, the induced pressure in the winding of the coil B is just the reverse of what it was in the previous case and the current produced by this induced pressure passes around the winding of the coil B in the same direction as the current passes around the winding of coil A. The current produced by the induced electrical pressure aids the current in the winding of coil A in producing a magnetic field. In general the current resulting from the induced pressure always passes around the circuit in such a direction as to produce a magnetic effect which will oppose a change in the value of the magnetic field causing the induced electrical pressure.

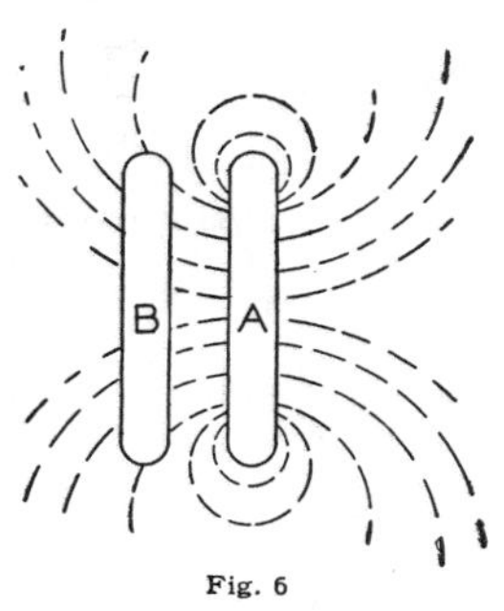

Fig. 6

There will be an induced pressure in the winding of coil B, due to a change in the value of the current in the winding of coil A, as long as the coil B remains in the magnetic field of the coil A and its plane is not parallel to magnetic lines; or, in other words, coil B must always be in such a position that some of the magnetic lines created by the current in coil A will pass through the winding of coil B.

If a telephone transmitter and a battery be connected in series with the winding of coil A, a fluctuating or varying current can be made to pass through the winding by causing the diaphragm of the transmitter to vibrate by speaking into the mouthpiece of the transmitter. This varying current will set up a varying magnetic field and there will be an induced electrical pressure set up in coil B, if it be properly placed with respect to coil A. A receiver connected in series with the winding of coil B will be subjected to the action of a varying current due to the induced electrical pressure in the winding of coil B and as a result, the diaphragm of the receiver will vibrate in unison with that of the transmitter, and speech can thus be transmitted. The connection just described should be somewhat modified and a little more equipment used in order to give the best results.

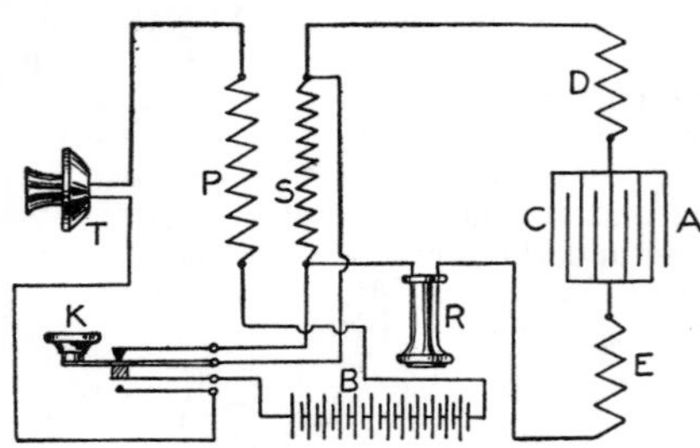

Fig. 7—Sending and Receiving Equipment

Figure 7 shows the complete sending and receiving equipment, a complete outfit of this kind being required for each station. The transmitter T and the receiver R may be an ordinary local battery transmitter and receiver, although a high-resistance receiver will give better results. The induction coil with the windings, marked P and S, may be any commercial type of induction coil as used in a magneto telephone instrument, but a coil with a high-wound secondary will give better results. The push button K is to be used in closing the transmitter circuit when the set is being used for transmitting, the key being depressed, and for shorting out the high resistance secondary winding when the set is used in receiving, the key being in the normal position. Ten dry cells should be connected in series and used to supply current to the transmitter circuit, as shown by B in the figure. The receiver R, secondary winding of the induction coil S, and the winding of coil A used in transmitting and receiving the magnetic effects, are all connected in series. The winding of the coil A consists of two parts, D and E, as shown in the figure, with two of their ends connected together by means of a condenser, C, having a capacity of about 2 micro-farads. Each of these parts should consist of about 200 turns of No. 22 gauge silk-covered copper wire, wound on an ordinary bicycle rim. The inside end of one winding should be connected to the outside of the other by means of the condenser, the two coils being wound in the same direction. The condenser C can be procured at a small cost from almost any telephone company.

To talk, two of the instruments are placed 25 or 30 ft. apart, and they may be placed in different rooms as walls and other ordinary obstructions that do not interfere with the production of the magnetic field about the transmitting coil, have no effect upon the operation. Pressing the button K at the transmitting station, closes the transmitter circuit and removes the shunt from about the secondary winding of the induction. Any vibration of the transmitter will cause a varying current to pass through the primary winding P, which in turn induces an electrical pressure in the secondary winding S, and this pressure causes a varying current to pass through the coil A. The varying current in the winding of the coil A produces a varying magnetic field which acts upon the receiving coil, inducing an electrical pressure in it and producing a current through the receiver at the receiving station.

A filing coherer, adapted to close a local relay circuit and ring an ordinary bell, may be used with the sets just described for signaling between stations.

An Electric Incubator

Where electric current is available, it can be used to heat an incubator much better and cleanlier than the kerosene lamp. The materials are inexpensive and the cost should be no more than for the ordinary kind of heater.

First of all the box part must be made of very dry wood, ½ in. thick. The material should be matched, as the cost of the operation depends upon the construction of the box. The proper size for an 80-egg incubator is 2 ft. square and 1 ft. high. If a larger one is desired, the dimensions may be varied to suit, but it is not necessary to make it any higher for a larger one. If it is desired to have a window in the door, care must be taken to make it a good fit. The top, as shown in the sketch, is made without hinges so that it can be readily set on and removed. This makes it handy in case of repairing the heater and cleaning the box. The inside of the box, with the exception of the bottom, should be covered with asbestos paper.

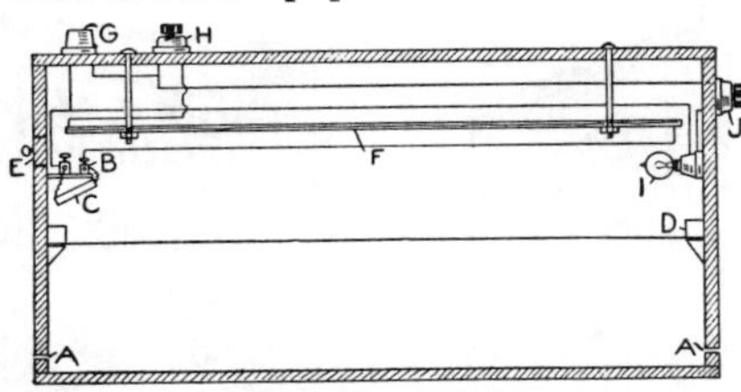

Fig. 1—Box Details

After the box is finished, fit it with a tray, 1½ ft. by 1 ft. 10¾ in. A tray having these dimensions will slide easily in the box. This is an essential feature of the hatching. The frame of the tray D, Fig. 1, consists of wood, ¾ by ¾ in., with a bottom made of wire mesh. The mesh should be firmly

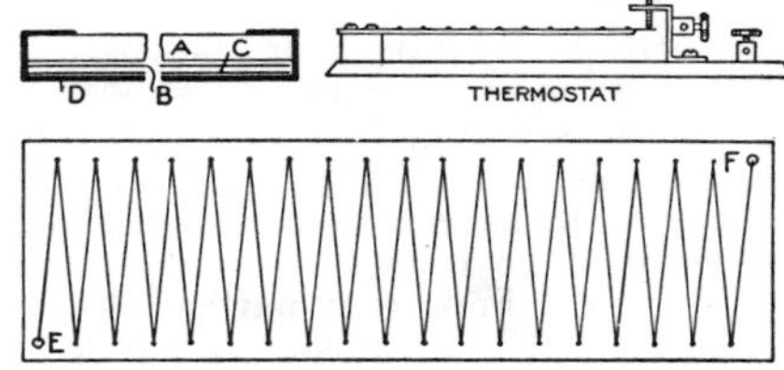

Fig. 2—Heater Details

attached, so that it will not give away when full of eggs. Runners for the tray are placed 4½ in. from the bottom of the box. When the tray is put in place, it will not touch the back. This small space is left for the chicks to fall into the nursery below. About 4 in. below the tray four holes are bored, A A, ⅛ in. in diameter, one on each side of the box. These holes admit fresh air to the eggs.

The electric heater is just large enough to allow a space about ½ in. on all edges. This makes it 23 in. square. A piece of ¼-in. asbestos of the above size should be secured, on which to place the heating wire. The amount of wire depends on the size and kind. As it is not necessary to heat the wire very hot, iron or steel wire may be used. The length of wire may be determined by the following method:

Wind the wire on a long stick, making sure that no one coil touches its neighbor. Connect one wire of the current supply at one end of the coil and run the other end of the current supply along the coils, starting at the extreme opposite end and drawing toward the center until the iron wire gets too hot to hold with the bare hand. This will be the right length of wire to use. The length being known, a number of tacks are placed in the asbestos board to hold the wire, as shown in Fig. 2. Cover the wire with a sheet of asbestos and attach binding-posts, E and F, at each end.

The asbestos inclosing the heating wires is covered with a thin piece of sheet iron, which is made to fit tightly over the bottom and sides. This will spread the heat evenly. Be careful to have the binding-posts insulated from the sheet metal. In the cross section of the heater, Fig. 2, A represents the 1/4-in. asbestos board; B, the heater wire; C, the asbestos paper, and D the sheet-metal covering.

The most important part of the incubator is the thermostat which regulates the current to maintain a steady heat. It is not advisable to make this instrument, as a good one can be purchased for less than $1. Place the thermostat in the end of the box at B, Fig. 1. A small door, E, is made in the box for easy adjustment of the thumbscrews.

Suspend the heater from the cover of the box with bolts 2 3/4 in. long, as shown in Fig. 1. A base receptacle, G, and a snap switch, H, are fastened on top of the cover and connected up to the thermostat B, the condenser C, the heater F, and lamp I, as shown. Another snap switch, J, is used on the light only. The condenser C is to prevent sparking, thus saving the platinum points on the screws. Do not use more than a 2-cp. lamp for lighting purposes, as a brighter light blinds the young chicks.

The incubator should be run for a day or two so that the current may be well regulated before placing the eggs in the tray. The incubator is operated the same as with lamp heat.—Contributed by M. Miller, Lansing, Mich.

A Cover for Magazines

As soon as Popular Mechanics, or any other magazine of similar size, arrives and before any member of the family looks through it, strip off the front cover and carefully remove the narrow strip on the back as shown in Fig. 1. Strengthen the back with a piece of bookbinding tissue, A, Fig. 2, and then paste a piece of heavy manila paper, B, over the covers and back. Over this paste a piece of dark blue cambric, Fig. 3, carefully turning the edges even with the book. The picture from the cover and the date added to

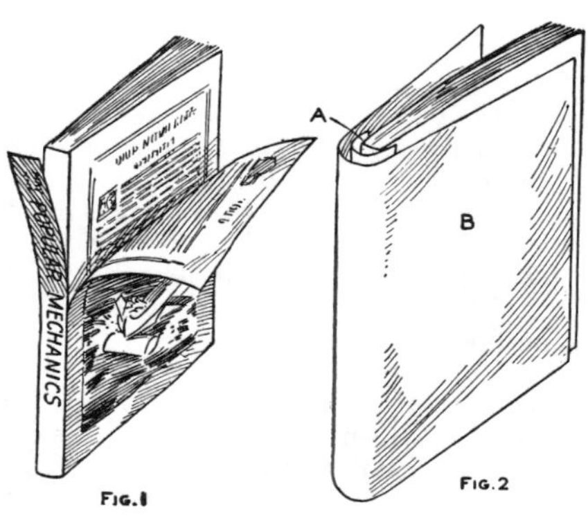

Removing the Cover, and Binding with Heavy Paper

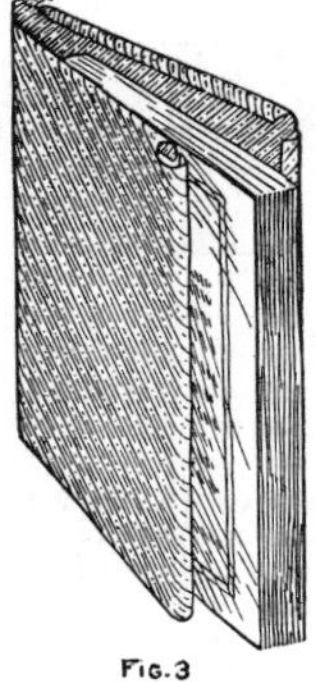

Cloth Cover and Paper Cover Attached

the left corner of the picture are neatly pasted on, Fig. 4, and the narrow strip is glued to the back.

The book is put under a heavy weight for several hours. Thus a neat, strong cover, which looks well in a bookcase, is secured at very little expense. The eager handling by every member of the family cannot soil or deface the cover.—Contributed by Katharine D. Morse, Syracuse, N. Y.

An Optical Illusion

A very deceiving illusion can be contrived with a bit of wire, a rubber band and a toothpick. An ordinary straight hairpin will serve instead of the wire. The hairpin or wire is bent as shown in the illustration, and the rubber band then placed on the inverted U-shaped part. A toothpick is inserted through

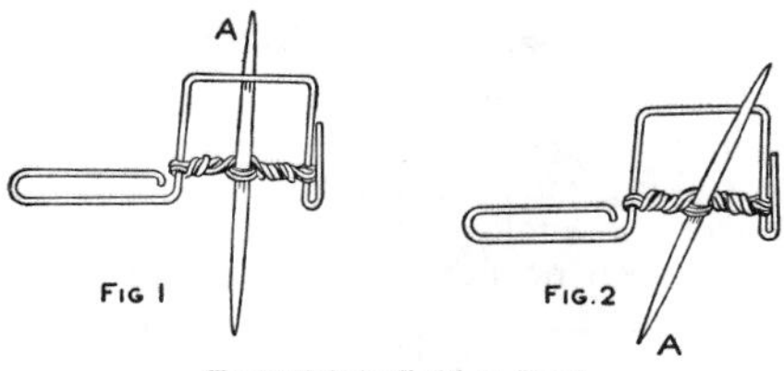

Toothpick in Rubber Band

the rubber band and a few turns taken by slipping the toothpick back and forth so it will pass the wire.

Hold the wire straight in front of the eyes, and, using the forefinger of the right hand, turn the end of the toothpick A, Fig. 1, down until it almost reaches the opposite point A, Fig. 2, and let the finger slip off. It will appear as if the toothpick passed through the wire.—Contributed by H. H. Windsor, Jr.

Temperature Alarm

The falling temperature of a room during the night may result in a very bad cold for the occupant. This may be prevented by the use of an alarm to awaken the sleeper and warn him to close the window. An alarm can be made as follows: Take a glass tube about 4 in. long and 1/4 in. in diameter and close one end, used for the bottom, with sealing wax, in which

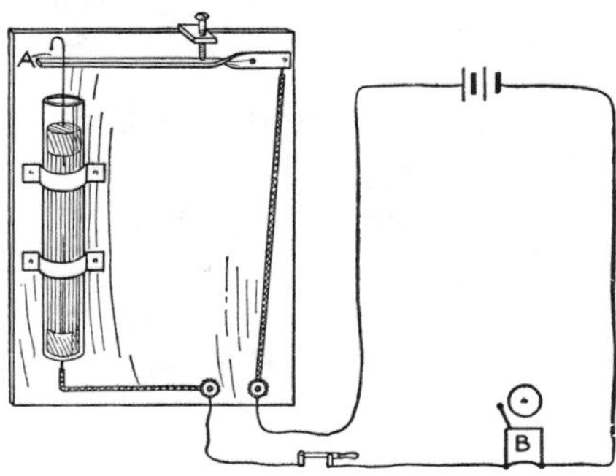

The Alarm and Wiring Diagram

the bare end of a No. 20 gauge magnet wire is inserted. The tube is almost filled with mercury. On the mercury a float of wax is placed in which a bare piece of the same magnet wire is inserted and bent as shown in the sketch. The tube of mercury is fastened to a base with two clips of metal. At the upper end of this base the adjustable lever A is attached. The electric connections are made as shown in the sketch.

Should the temperature fall during the night, the mercury will contract, the float descend and the circuit close, so that the bell will ring. The adjustable lever allows setting the alarm for various differences of temperature. —Contributed by Klyce Fuzzelle, Rogers, Ark.

Paper Smoother and Penwiper

A convenient paper smoother and penwiper can be easily made as follows: Procure a common celluloid harness ring, A, about 1 1/2 in. in diameter and fasten a penwiper, B, to it. The wiper is made of arts-crafts leather, doubled and filled with pieces of chamois. They are held in place

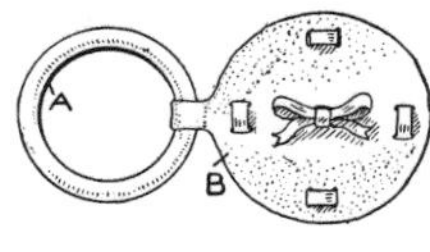

with a ribbon or cord tied as shown. The roughened paper caused by erasing can be easily smoothed with the ring.—Contributed by G. H. Holter, Jasper, Minn.

Stereoscopic Pictures with an Ordinary Camera

Make a small table as wide as the camera is long and 3 in. longer than the camera is wide. Sink a screw nut in the center of the under side to engage the regular tripod screw. Fasten a double or two-way spirit level on the front left-hand corner. Nail strips on both ends and on the rear side, to form a shallow box with three sides. The illustration shows the construction quite plainly. This device was used by a correspondent of Camera Craft as follows: The table was fastened to the tripod and carefully leveled. The camera is placed at one side, bringing the back snugly into the corner on that side. Make the exposure, change the film, slide the camera over to the other side and make another exposure. The table being 3 in. longer than the camera is wide, the lens will be moved exactly 3 in. when the camera is moved over to the other side. Three inches is the separation of the lenses in stereoscopic cameras and the negatives made as above will be the same.

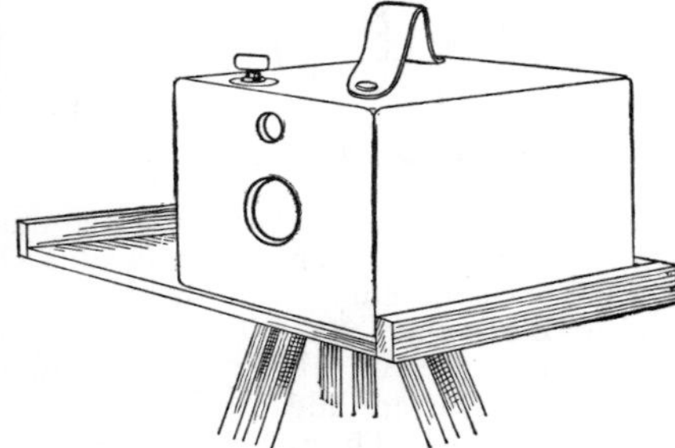
Table on Tripod for Camera

As the negatives must be sized, it is necessary to use films. A camera using films 3½ by 3½ in. will make negatives that can be trimmed ¼ in. on each side to make prints 3 by 3¼ in. Each two negatives making a pair are fastened together, properly transposed, by folding a narrow strip of black paper like a long, V-shaped trough, pasting it, and putting one on the bottom of the two negatives, as they lie side by side, and one at the top, saddle fashion. This can be done still easier by using strips of passe-partout binding, or strips used for binding lantern slides. If so desired, the use of black paper can be carried farther by cutting the top strip of binding paper in such a way that it gives the round corners to the top of the prints. A narrow strip through the center and a binding of black paper along the two end edges make a mask unnecessary in printing.

How to Make a Paper Drinking Cup

Every person should understand the simple method of making a paper drinking cup. It may be necessary at times to make quick use of medicine and with no cup or spoon convenient, the pyramid-shaped cup shown in the sketch is a useful emergency utensil.

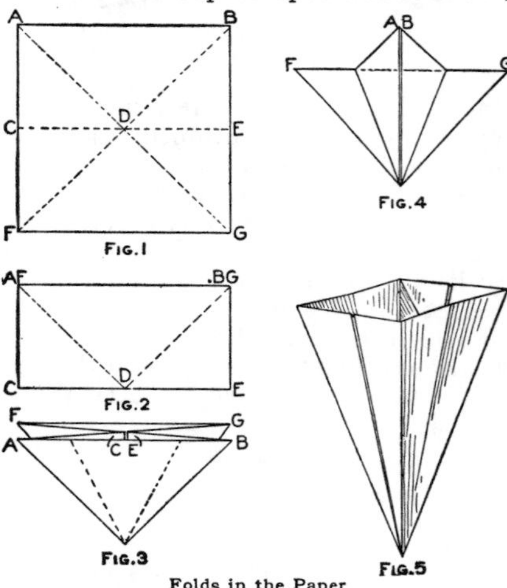

Folds in the Paper

The paper cup is made as follows: Cut the paper into a square and crease it on the dotted lines, A G, F B, and C D E, as shown in Fig. 1. Fold the paper in half through the line C D E to form a rectangle, Fig. 2. Fold points C and E inward until they meet inside the triangle to form the shape shown in Fig. 3. This makes four distinct corners, F, G, A and B. Fold the paper over on the dotted line and bring the points A and B together as in Fig. 4. The extreme edges meet in the central line indicated. Reverse the paper and fold the points G and F in like manner. Turn the points A B and F G inward and fold on the dotted line, and you will have a perfect pyramid-shaped cup as shown in Fig. 5.—Contributed by Miss Margaret S. Humphreville, Mt. Pleasant, O.

A Hand Corn Sheller

A very handy device for shelling corn, and especially popcorn, can be made of a 1-in. board on which is fas-

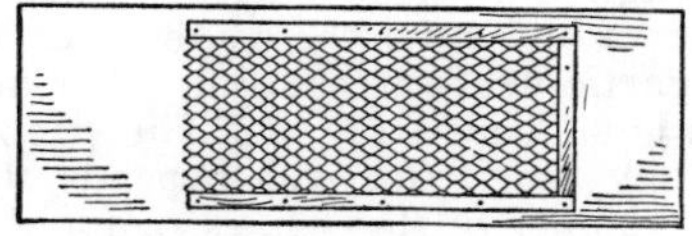

Metal Lath on a Board

tened a piece of metal lath. The edges of the metal lath are bound with a strip of wood nailed to the board.—Contributed by Ulysses Flacy, Long Beach, California.

A Shaft Coupling

In connecting a small ⅛-hp. motor to a small air pump where both shafts were ⅜ in. in diameter, I quickly made a coupling that would save the wear on the machines, as follows. The coupling was made of a piece of ¾-in. brass rod with a ⅜-in. hole drilled through its center. One end of the hole was enlarged to 7-16 in. for about ⅞ in. The end of the coupling having the small hole was slipped on the pump shaft and fastened with two setscrews. The other end was drilled to take a pin loosely, the pin fitting tightly in a hole drilled in the motor shaft. The pin was bent at one end so as to keep it from falling out and the other end fitted with two nuts. The motor shaft

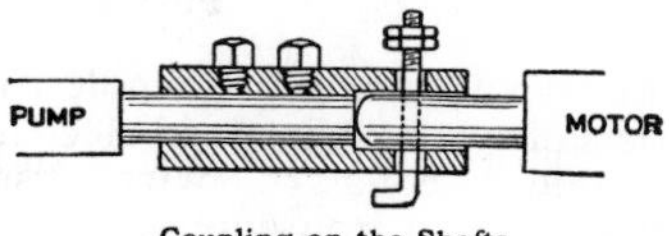

Coupling on the Shafts

being a little loose in the coupling, gave it a chance to work free without binding.—Contributed by Leo J. Werner, New York City.

Reading the Date of a Worn Coin

The date and denomination of a coin worn smooth can be determined in the following manner: Take an ordinary coal shovel, or a piece of sheet metal, and place it in a hot fire. Allow it to become red hot, then remove, and place the coin on the hot surface of the metal. Any figures or letters can be readily seen when heated in this manner. This test seldom fails even when the inscriptions have been worn so smooth that they are invisible to the naked eye.

Making a Knife an Easy Opener

The large blade of my knife being so hard to open placed me in constant risk of breaking my thumbnail. To overcome this difficulty, I ground a notch in the handle as shown in the sketch. After smoothing it up with a round file and fine sandpaper, I had just as good a job as if the knife had been made that way, and it is very easy to open it, as it can be done with the thumb and forefinger. Anyone can improve

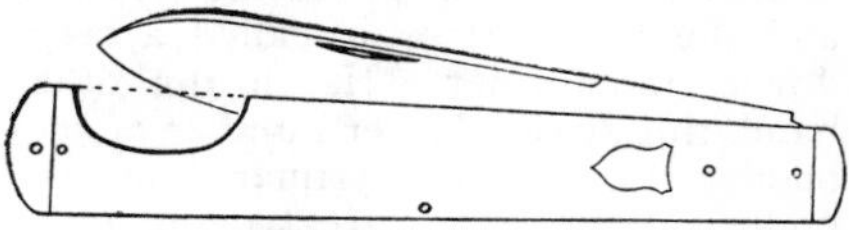

Notch in the Handle

his knife in this way, but be careful not to cut the notch back of the point of the small blade.—Contributed by C. M. Mahood, Warren, Pa.

Construction of a Small Bell-Ringing Transformer

By A. E. ANDREWS

Part I—Fundamental Principles

The transformer in its simplest form consists of two separate and electrically independent coils of wire, usually wound upon an iron core.

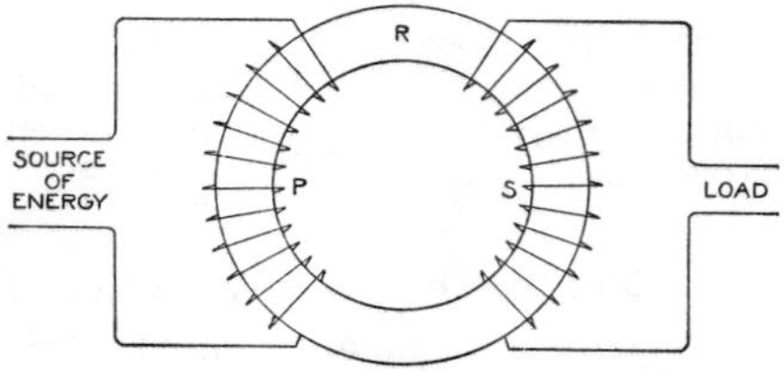

Fig. 1—Two Coils on an Iron Ring

Figure 1 shows two coils, P and S, placed upon an iron ring, R. One of these coils is connected to some source of energy, such as an alternating-current generator, or an alternating-current lighting circuit, receiving its energy therefrom. The other coil is connected to a load to which it delivers alternating current. The coil of the transformer that is connected to the source of energy is called the primary coil, and the one that is connected to the load, the secondary coil.

The electrical pressure (voltage) at which current is supplied by the secondary bears a definite relation to the electrical pressure at which current is supplied to the primary. This relation, as will be explained later, is practically the same as the relation between the number of turns in the secondary and primary coils. If there are a smaller number of turns in the secondary coil than there are in the primary, the secondary voltage is less than the primary, and the transformer is called a step-down transformer. If, on the other hand, there are a larger number of secondary turns than of primary, the secondary voltage is greater than the primary voltage, and the transformer is called a step-up transformer.

The transfer of electrical energy from the primary coil to the secondary coil of a transformer is based upon the fundamental principles of electromagnetism and electromagnetic induction, and it will be necessary to investigate these principles before we can understand the operation of the transformer.

A magnet is a body, which, when freely suspended, assumes approximately a north and south position. The end of the magnet that points north is called the north pole, while the end that points south is called the south pole. The region surrounding a magnet is called a magnetic field. In this field the magnetism is supposed to flow along a large number of imaginary lines, called lines of force, and these lines are all supposed to emanate from the north pole of the magnet, pass through the medium surrounding the magnet and enter the south pole. The magnetic field surrounding a bar magnet is shown in Fig. 2. The strength of any magnetic field depends upon the number of these lines of force per unit area (square centimeter), the area being taken perpendicular to the direction of the lines.

In 1812, Oersted discovered that a compass needle, which is nothing but a permanent magnet freely suspended or supported, when placed near a conductor in which there was a direct

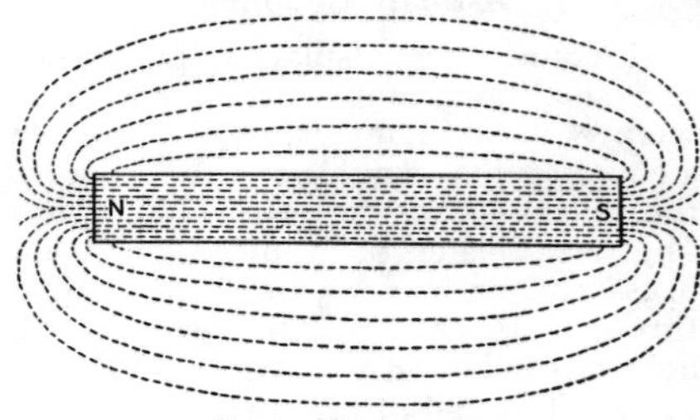

Fig. 2—Magnetic Field

current, was acted upon by a force that tended to bring the needle into a position at right angles to the conductor. This simple experiment proved to

Oersted that there was a magnetic field produced by the current in the conductor. He also found that there was a definite relation between the direction of the current in the conductor, and the direction in which the north pole of the compass needle pointed. If the compass needle is allowed to come to rest in the earth's magnetic field, and a conductor is placed above it, the conductor being parallel to the needle, and a current then sent through the conductor, the needle will be deflected from its position of rest. Reversing the current in the conductor, reverses the direction in which the needle is deflected. If the needle be allowed to come to rest while there is a current in the conductor, and this current is then increased, it will be found that the deflection of the needle will be increased, but not in direct proportion to the increase in the current. Hence the strength of this magnetic field surrounding the conductor depends upon the value of the current in the conductor, and the direction of the field depends upon the direction of the current.

If a conductor be passed through a piece of cardboard, as shown in Fig. 3, and a current sent through it in the direction indicated by the arrow A, a compass needle, moved about the conductor in the path indicated by the dotted line, will always assume such a position that the north pole points around the conductor in a clockwise direction as you look down on the cardboard. If the current be reversed, the direction assumed by the compass needle will be reversed. Looking along a conductor in the direction of the current, the magnetic field will consist of magnetic lines encircling the conductor. These lines will be con-

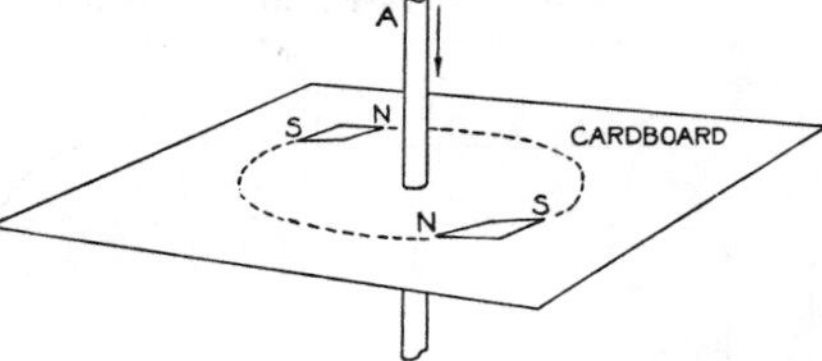

Fig. 3—Magnetic Field around Conductor

centric circles, as a general rule, except when they are distorted by the presence of other magnets or magnetic materials, and their direction will be clockwise.

The strength of the magnetic field at any point near this conductor will depend upon the value of the current in the conductor, and the distance the point is from the conductor. The magnetic field surrounding a conductor is shown in Fig. 4. The plus sign indicates that the direction of the current is from you. The strength of a magnetic field due to a current in a conductor can be greatly increased by forming a coil of the conductor. Each turn of the coil then produces a certain number of lines, and the greater part of these lines pass through the center of the coil, as shown in Fig. 5. The field strength inside such a coil is dependent upon the number of turns in the coil, and the value of the current in these turns. Increasing the number of turns in the coil increases the number of magnetic lines passing through

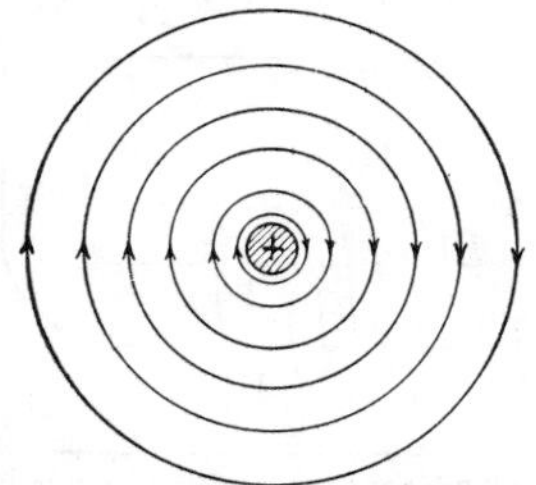
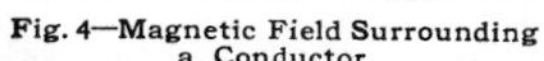
Fig. 4—Magnetic Field Surrounding a Conductor

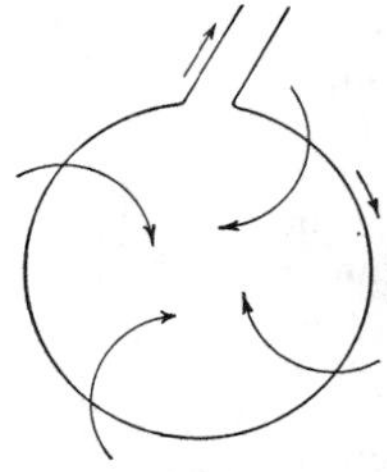
Fig. 5—Magnetic Field about a Coil

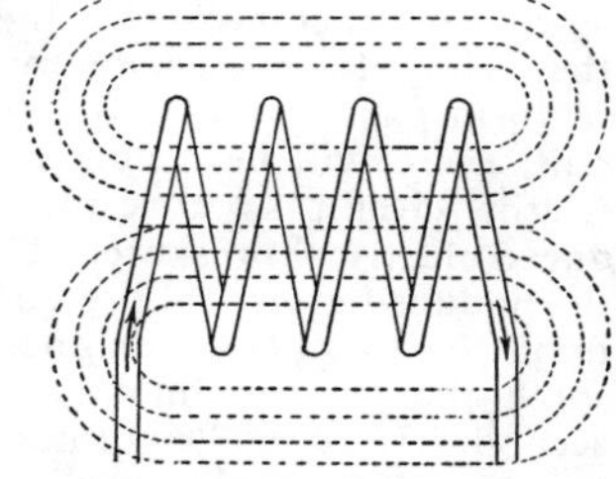
Fig. 6—A Coil about a Magnetic Circuit through Iron and Air

the center of the coil, as shown in Fig. 6. If the current be decreased in value, the field strength is decreased, and if the current be reversed in direction, the magnetic field is reversed in direction. The number of magnetic lines passing through the solenoid depends also upon the kind of material composing the core of the solenoid, in addition to the number of turns and the value of the current in these turns. The number of lines per unit area inside a solenoid with an air core can be multiplied several times by introducing a soft-iron core. If this core be extended as shown in Fig. 7, the magnetic circuit (the path through which the magnetic lines pass) may be completed through it. The larger part of the total number of lines will pass through the iron, as it is a much better conductor of magnetism than air.

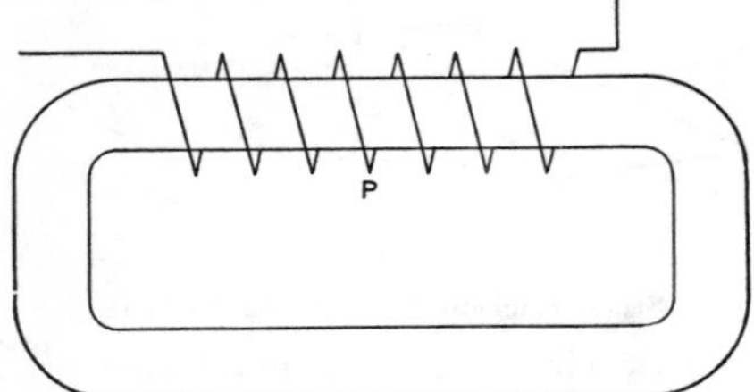

Fig. 7— A Coil about a Magnetic Circuit through Iron

In 1831, Michael Faraday discovered that there was an electrical pressure induced in an electrical conductor when it was moved in a magnetic field so that it cut some of the lines forming the field. If this conductor be made to form part of a closed electrical circuit, there will be a current produced in the circuit as a result of the induced electrical pressure. The value of this induced electrical pressure depends upon the number of magnetic lines of force that the conductor cuts in one second. If 100,000,000 lines are cut in one second, an electrical pressure of one volt is produced. The direction of the induced pressure depends upon the direction of the movement of the conductor and the direction of the lines of force in the magnetic field; reversing either the direction of the magnetic field or the motion of the conductor, reverses the direction of the induced pressure. If both the direction of the magnetic field, and the direction of the motion of the conductor be reversed, there is no change in the direction of the induced pressure, for there is then no change in the relative directions of the two. The same results can be obtained by moving the magnetic field with respect to the conductor in such a way that the lines of force of the field cut the conductor.

If a permanent magnet be thrust into a coil of wire, there will be an electrical pressure set up in the coil so long as the turns of wire forming the coil are cutting the lines of force that are produced by the magnet. When the magnet is withdrawn, the induced electrical pressure will be reversed in direction, since the direction of cutting is reversed. A magnetic field may be produced through a coil of wire by winding it on the magnetic circuit shown in Fig. 8. Now any change of current in the coil P will cause a change in the number of magnetic lines passing through S and hence there will be an induced electrical pressure set up in S so long as the number of lines passing through it is changing. The pressure induced in each of the turns comprising the coil S depends upon the change in the number of magnetic lines through it.

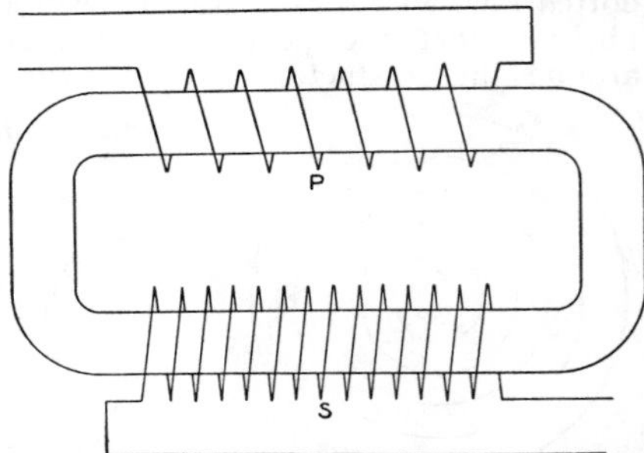

Fig. 8—Two Coils about a Magnetic Circuit through Iron

Let us now consider a condition of operation when there is no current in the secondary coil and the primary coil is connected to some source of electrical energy. When this is the case the current in the primary coil is not determined by Ohm's law, which states that the current is equal to the electrical pressure divided by the resistance, but is considerably less in value, for the following reason. The magnetic lines of force produced by the current in the primary induces an electrical pressure in the primary winding itself, the direction of which is always opposite to the impressed pressure, or the one producing the current. As a result of this induced pressure being set up in the primary, the effective pressure acting in the circuit is decreased. At the same time there is an electrical pressure induced in the secondary winding in the same direction as that induced in the primary.

If the secondary circuit be connected to a load, there will be a current in the secondary winding, which will pass around the magnetic circuit in the opposite direction to the primary current, and as a result will decrease the number of lines passing through the primary coil. This will in turn decrease the electrical pressure induced in the primary coil, and a larger current will exist in the primary winding than there was before any current was taken from the secondary coil. The decrease in induced pressure is small, but it is always ample to allow the required increase in primary current. There is, at the same time, a small decrease in the secondary pressure.

When the transformer is operating on no load, with no current in the secondary coil, the induced pressure in the primary coil is practically equal to the impressed pressure and hence a very small current will be taken from the source of energy. It is apparent now that if the primary and secondary coils have the same number of turns, the induced electrical pressure in each of these coils will be the same, assuming, of course, that all the magnetic lines that pass through the primary also pass through the secondary coil, and vice versa, or the secondary pressure is practically the same as the pressure impressed on the primary. If the number of turns in the secondary coil is greater or less than the number of turns in the primary, the magnetic lines will be cut a greater or less number of times by the secondary coil, and hence the induced pressure will be greater or less, depending upon the relation of the number of turns in the two coils.

Spirit Photographs

Print some photographs in the usual way on printing-out paper, then fix them in a solution of 1 oz. hyposulphite of soda and 8 oz. of water, and wash them thoroughly. While the prints are still wet, immerse them in a saturated solution of bichloride of mercury. Be very careful to wash the hands and trays after using the mercury solution, as it is poisonous. When the print is placed in the mercury solution, the picture vanishes completely. Leave the prints in this bath just long enough for the image to disappear, and then wash and dry them thoroughly. Soak some clean blotting paper in the hyposulphite-of-soda solution and allow it to dry. You are now ready to perform the magic-photograph trick.

To cause the spirit photograph to appear, cut a piece of blotting paper the same size as the prepared print and moisten it, then hold the apparently blank piece of paper in contact with it. The picture will come out clear and plain, and if thoroughly washed out it will remain permanently.

¶Saturate a small piece of cotton batting in glue and wrap it around a nail, then place it in a hole previously made in a plaster wall. When the glue dries, the nail will remain permanently.

Construction of a Small Bell-Ringing Transformer

By A. E. ANDREWS

PART II — Construction

Transformers may be divided into two main groups, the classification being made according to the relation between the magnetic circuit of the transformer and the primary and secondary windings. When the two windings surround the magnetic circuit of a transformer, as indicated in Fig. 9, the transformer is said to be of core type. If the magnetic circuit surrounds the windings, as indicated in Fig. 10, the transformer is said to be of the shell type. The following instructions are for a shell-type transformer.

WINDINGS

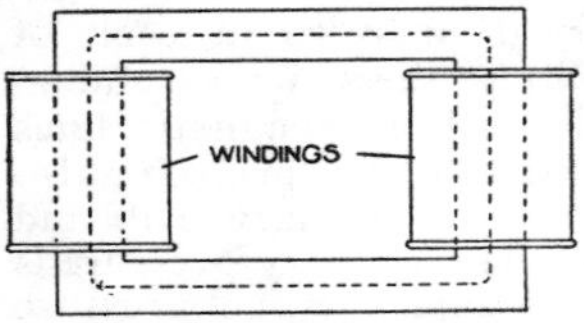

Fig. 9 — Core-Type Transformer

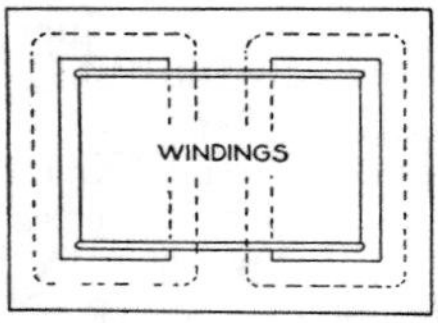

WINDINGS

Fig. 10 — Shell-Type Transformer

Any mass of magnetic material, such as a piece of soft iron, when placed in a magnetic field that is produced by an alternating current, will be rapidly magnetized and demagnetized, the rapidity of the change depending upon the frequency of the current producing the field. When a piece of iron is magnetized and demagnetized, as just stated, there will be a certain amount of heat generated in it and this heat represents energy that must come from the electrical circuit producing the magnetic field in which the iron is placed.

The heat that is generated in the iron is due to two causes: First, the hysteresis loss which is due to a property of the iron that causes the magnetism in the iron to lag behind the magnetizing influence, or the changes that are constantly taking place in the field strength due to the alternating current. This loss cannot be entirely eliminated, but it may be reduced to a very low value by using a soft grade of iron, or one having what is called a low hysteretic constant. Second, the eddy-current loss which is due to the circulation of currents through the mass of metal. These currents are due to unequal electromotive forces set up in the different parts of the piece of metal when there is a change in the strength of the field in which the metal is placed. This loss cannot be entirely eliminated, but it can be greatly reduced by breaking the mass of metal up into parts and insulating these parts from each other, which results in the paths in which the eddy currents originally circulated being destroyed to a certain extent.

The breaking up of the metal is usually made in such a way that the joints between the various parts are parallel to the direction of the magnetic field. When the joints are made in this way, they offer less opposition to the magnetizing force. This is one of the principal reasons why induction-coil cores are made up of a bundle of wires instead of a solid piece. These wires are annealed or softened to reduce the hysteresis loss that would occur. The combined hysteresis and eddy-current losses, which are spoken of as the iron losses, will of course be very small in the transformer you are going to construct, but the above discussion is given to show why the magnetic circuits of transformers are built up from sheets of soft iron, called laminations. The core is said to be laminated.

The dimensions of the complete magnetic circuit, of the transformer you are going to construct, are given in

Fig. 11. The primary and secondary windings are both to be placed about the center portion C, and it is apparent that the winding of these coils would be very tedious if the wire had to be passed back and forth through the openings A and B. This procedure in winding can be prevented by first forming the part of the magnetic circuit upon which the windings are placed; then wind on the coils and, after they are completed, finish building up the magnetic circuit with pieces cut to the proper size and shape.

Procure a small quantity of soft, thin sheet iron and cut out a sufficient number of rectangular pieces, 3 in. by 4¼ in., to make a pile ¾ in. in height when firmly pressed together. Now cut a rectangular notch in each of these pieces, 2 in. wide and 3⅝ in. long. The sides of this notch can be cut with a pair of tinner's shears, and the end can be cut with a sharp cold-chisel. Be careful not to bend either piece any more than you can help. The outside piece, or the one in which the notch is cut, should have dimensions corresponding to those given in Fig. 12. When all of these pieces have been cut, as indicated above, the rectangular pieces, 2 in. by 3⅝ in., that were cut out to form the notch in the larger pieces, should have two of their corners cut away, so as to form pieces whose dimensions correspond to those given in Fig. 13. These last pieces are to form the core and part of the end of the transformer. Now make sure that all the edges of the pieces are perfectly smooth and that they are all of the same size; then give each one a coat of very thin shellac.

Now cut from a piece of insulating fiber, that is about $\frac{1}{16}$ in. thick, two pieces whose dimensions correspond to those given in Fig. 14. When these pieces are completed, the core of the transformer can be assembled as follows: Place the T-shaped pieces, whose dimensions correspond to those given in Fig. 13, through the openings in the pieces of insulation, alternate pieces being put through the openings from opposite sides. The distance from outside to outside of the pieces of insulation should be exactly the same as the length of the vertical portion of the T-shaped pieces forming the core, or 3 in.

Cut from some soft wood four pieces having cross sections whose dimensions correspond to those given in Fig. 15, and of such a length that they will just slip down between the two pieces of insulation. These pieces should now be placed on the four sides of the iron core and covered with several layers of heavy insulating cloth. Each layer of the cloth should be shellacked as it is put on, which will increase the insulation and at the same time help in holding the wooden pieces in place. You are now ready to start winding the transformer.

The secondary, which is the low-voltage side in this case, as you are using the transformer to reduce or step down the voltage, will have the smaller number of turns, and larger wire should be used in winding it than in the primary, as it will carry a larger current. On account of the secondary being of larger wire, it will be placed on the core first. For this winding you will need a small quantity of No. 26 B. & S. gauge, single cotton-covered wire.

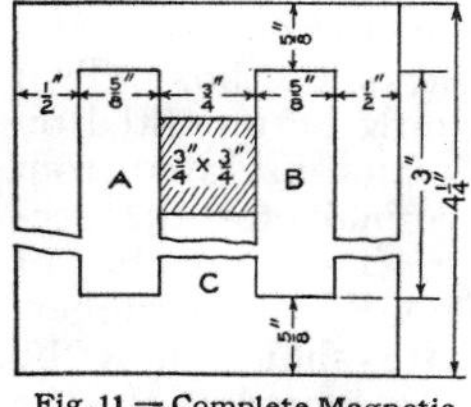

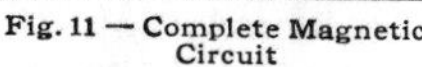
Fig. 11 — Complete Magnetic Circuit

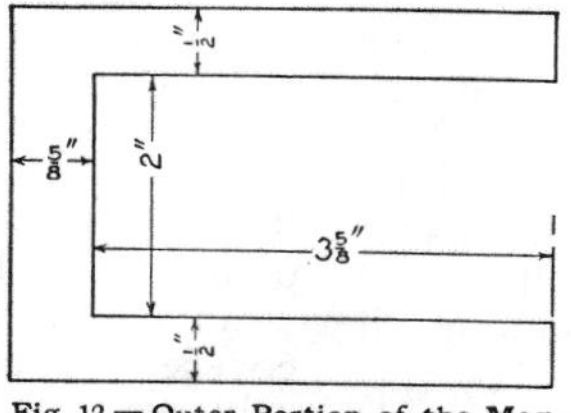

Fig. 12 — Outer Portion of the Magnetic Circuit

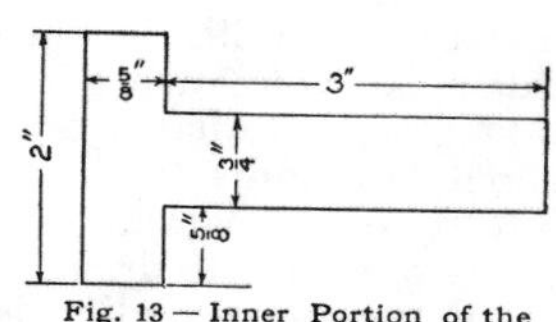

Fig. 13 — Inner Portion of the Magnetic Circuit

Drill a small hole through one of the insulating washers, down close to the cloth covering the core, being careful at the same time to keep the hole as far

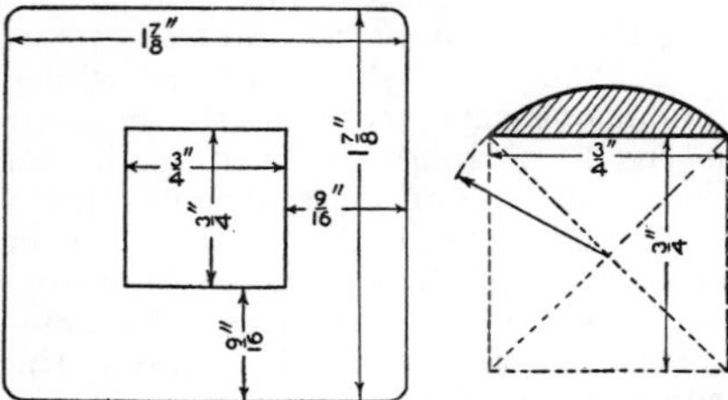

Fig. 14—Insulating Washer Fig. 15—Wood Filler

from the metal part of the core as possible. Pass the end of a short piece of No. 18 or 20 B. & S. gauge, double cotton-covered wire through this opening and solder it to the end of the No. 26 wire. Insulate the joint with a piece of paraffin paper or cloth, and bind the piece of heavy wire to the core of the transformer with a piece of linen thread.

Now wind the No. 26 wire on the core as evenly as possible, to within about 1/8 in. of the end of the spool. Place over the first layer two layers of paraffin paper and wind on a second layer of wire. Three layers should give you the required number of turns in the secondary winding and a resistance of approximately 3½ ohms. The end of the secondary winding should be terminated in the same way as the winding was started. Outside of the completed secondary winding place at least six layers of paraffin paper, or several layers of insulating cloth. The paraffin paper used should be approximately five mills in thickness. You can make your own paraffin paper by taking a good quality of writing paper about two mills thick and dipping it into some hot paraffin, then hanging it up by one edge to drain.

The primary winding is to be made from No. 34 B. & S. gauge, single silk-covered copper wire. The inside end of this winding should be started in the same way as the secondary, but at the end opposite to the one where the secondary terminated. Wind about 240 turns on each layer and place one layer of paraffin paper between each layer of wire. The primary winding should have at least 12 layers, and the outside end should be terminated as the inside end. Outside of the completed windings, place several layers of insulating cloth to serve as an insulation, and at the same time provide a mechanical protection for the windings.

The outside part of the magnetic circuit can now be put in place. When the U-shaped pieces are all in place, the magnetic circuit will have the form and dimensions shown in Fig. 11. A clamp should now be made for each end of the transformer, to hold the pieces forming the magnetic circuit together, and at the same time give an easy means of mounting the transformer. Cut from a piece of sheet iron, about 1/16 in. in thickness, two pieces whose dimensions correspond to those given in Fig. 16, and two pieces whose dimensions correspond to those given in Fig. 17. Drill the holes in these pieces as indicated, and bend the larger ones into the form shown in Fig. 18. These pieces can now be clamped across the ends of the transformer with small bolts, as shown in Fig. 19.

A box should now be made from sheet iron to hold the transformer. The box should be of such dimensions that it will be at least 1/8 in. from the transformer at all points. This box should be provided with a cover that can be easily removed.

Now mount the transformer in the box by means of small bolts, that pass through the holes in the supports and holes in the bottom of the box. Two binding-posts can now be mounted on one end of the box, and insulated from it, to serve as terminals for the secondary winding. Two pieces of stranded No. 14 B. & S. gauge, rubber-covered copper wire should now be soldered to the terminals of the primary circuit and passed out through insulating bushings mounted in holes cut in the end of the box opposite to the one upon which the binding-posts were mounted. These heavy wires should be firmly fastened to the iron part of the transformer inside the box, so that any outside strain placed upon them will not, in time, break them loose from the smaller wires. Be sure to insulate all joints and wires well inside the box.

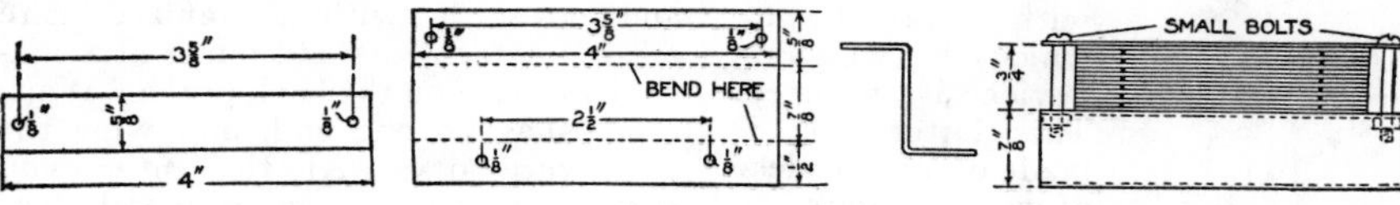

Fig. 16—Upper Clamping Pieces

Fig. 17—Lower Clamping Pieces and Mounting Supports

Fig. 18—Shape of Support

Fig. 19—Method of Clamping Transformer Together

A circuit can now be run from a 110-volt lighting or power circuit, observing the same rules as though you were wiring for lights, and connected to the heavy wires, or primary circuit. The binding-posts, or secondary winding should be connected to the bell circuit and the transformer is complete and ready to operate. You may have to change the adjustment of the bells, but after a little adjustment they will operate quite satisfactorily.

Mirror Hinged to Window Casing

A shaving mirror is usually placed on a window sash to avoid shadows as much as possible. This is very inconvenient and many times the mirror is broken by a fall. A good way to avoid shadows and have the mirror handy is to hinge it to the window casing. This can be done with screw-eyes, A, and screwhooks, B. The screweyes are turned into the frame of the mirror and the screwhooks into the window casing. Two screwhooks can also be turned into the casing on the opposite side of the window, if desired, so that the mirror can be used on either side.—Contributed by James D. McKenna, New Britain, Conn.

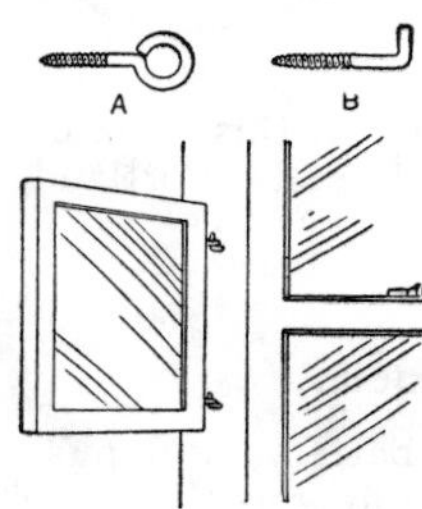

A Cleaning Bath for Silverware

A good way to clean silverware of all coloring by eggs or other substances is to place the silver articles in a kettle of boiling water containing a few pieces of zinc. An electrolytic action is produced by the zinc, water and silver which decomposes the sulphides on the silver and leaves it well cleaned. No silver is taken away by this method.—Contributed by Loren Ward, Des Moines, Iowa.

To Prevent Poultry Water from Freezing

The method shown in the sketch is used by me in cold weather to keep the drinking water for the poultry from freezing. The device consists of a part of a barrel inverted and set over the fountain, and a tubular lantern. A small opening is cut in one side of the barrel through which the fowl can reach the water.—Contributed by P. C. Fish, Kansas City, Mo.

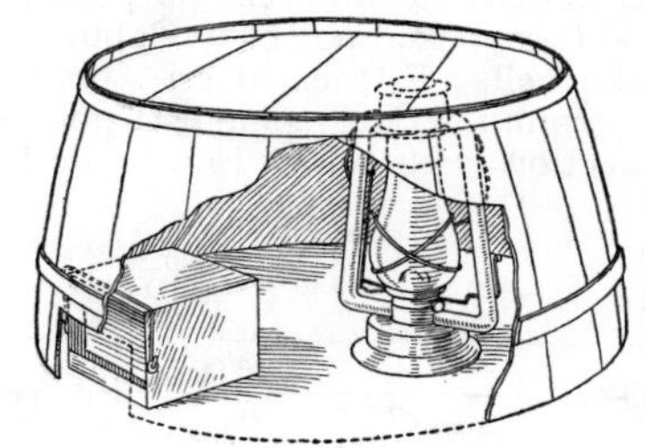

Lantern and Fountain in Half Barrel

How to Make a Letter Scale

A reliable letter scale that can be easily made is shown in the sketch. It consists of a wide-neck bottle filled with water into which the weighing device is inserted. This latter part is made of a light piece of wood weighted on the lower end, to keep it in a stable, upright position, and a piece of cardboard is tacked to the other. The wood is placed in the water, and known weights are used on the cardboard while calibrating.

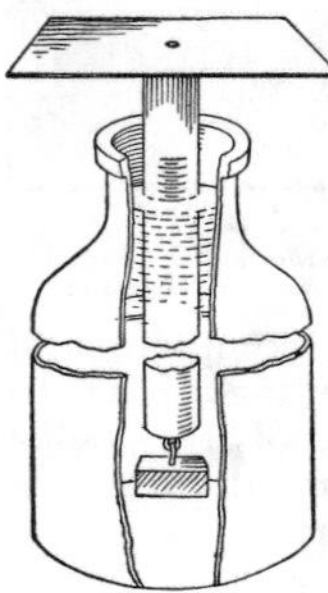

The first line is marked at the water level when there is no weight on the cardboard, and then a known weight placed on the top and another mark made at the water level, and so on, until a sufficient number of ½-oz. and ounce-divisions have been marked. The wood should be well coated with shellac varnish before it is placed in the water.—Contributed by Francis Chetlain, Chicago.

Summer Dish Washing

A labor-saving method in dish washing for a summer day is as follows: Construct a substantial wood frame and cover it with galvanized wire mesh. Attach legs and put it in a convenient place on the back porch. Wash the dishes on one end, and wipe the silverware dry. At the outer end spread a towel over the wire and place the dishes turned down upon it to dry, and cover them with another towel.—Contributed by L. Alberta Norrell, Tifton, Ga.

Nozzle Angle for Lawn Sprinkling

Where there is no prop or water sprinkler at hand for tilting the nozzle of a hose, start to tie a knot in the hose, as shown in the sketch, but do not draw it up tightly. The hose nozzle can be tilted to any angle in this manner.—Contributed by S. J. Eddy, Portland, Oregon.

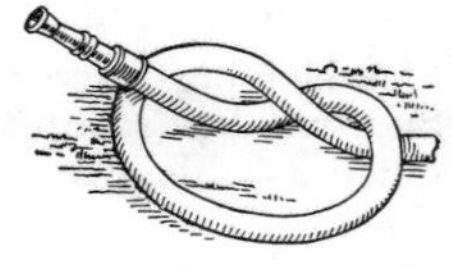

Simple Methods of Connecting Call Bells

The following diagrams will indicate a few of the various methods that may be employed in connecting up electric bells for different purposes, A, B and C representing the push buttons; D, the bells; E, the batteries, and G, the ground. The simplest possible connection is shown in Fig. 1, the bell D, battery E, and push button A, are all connected in series. The operation of the bell is independent of the order in which the bell, battery, and push button are placed, so long as there is a complete circuit when the push button is pressed. One of the wires in this circuit may be done away with by completing the circuit through the ground, as shown in Fig. 2. Connecting a bell as shown in this diagram often results in quite a saving of wire. The proper connections for operating one bell from either of two push

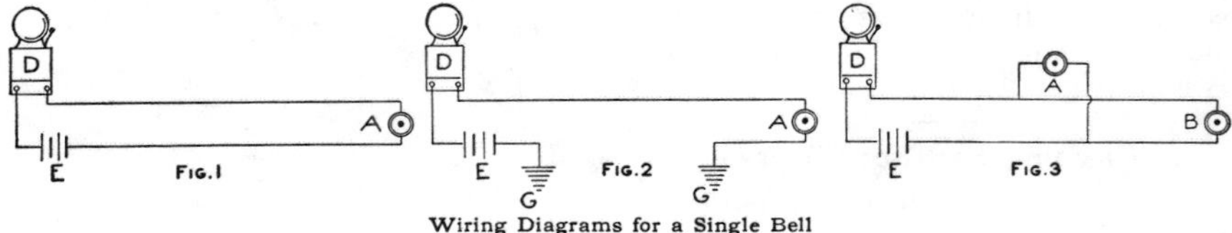

Wiring Diagrams for a Single Bell

buttons, A or B, is shown in Fig. 3. Two bells, D, operated from a single push button, C, are connected as shown

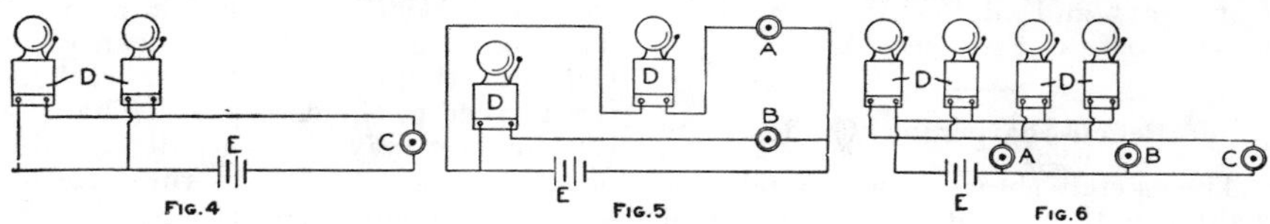

Wiring Diagram for Two or More Bells

in Fig. 4. The two bells, D, are shown connected in parallel, which requires more wire than if they were connected in series. If they be connected in series, one or the other should have its make-and-break contact closed. The bell whose circuit remains unchanged will intercept the current for the other bell in series with it. The operating of the bells is more satisfactory, however, when they are in parallel, and each taking current from the battery independent of the other.

The diagram, Fig. 5, shows the proper connections for operating two bells from two independent push buttons, each push button operating a particular bell. Any number of bells operated from any number of push buttons, all of the bells being rung from any one of the push buttons, are connected as shown in Fig. 6. Such a circuit can be used as a fire alarm or time call in a factory, the operation of the circuit being controlled from any one of a number of different points.

The proper connections for what is called a return-call circuit is shown in Fig. 7. The circuit is so arranged that the bell at one end is controlled by the push button at the other end. Such

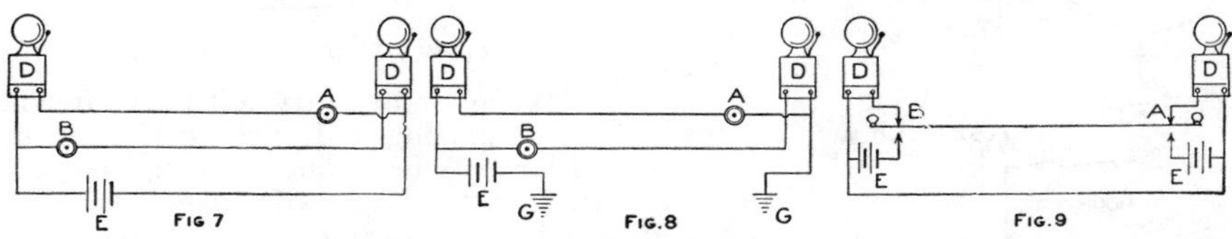

Wiring Diagrams for Return-Call Bells

a circuit can be used in transmitting signals in either direction. A ground return-call circuit is shown in Fig. 8. In the circuits shown in Figs. 7 and 8, only one battery is needed.

The connections of a two-wire metallic return-call circuit are shown in Fig. 9. A special push button must be used in this circuit, and in this case two batteries are used instead of one, as in Figs. 7 and 8. This circuit may be changed to a ground return-call circuit by using the earth as a conductor instead of either wire. There are, of course, numerous other methods that may be used in connecting call bells, but the connections shown in the diagrams are perhaps the most common.

Refrigerator for Dry and Warm Climates

Set a bowl containing butter, cream or fruit in a saucer and cover the bowl with a moistened napkin, allowing the edges to hang in a larger saucer filled with water, and place the whole in the air out of the sun's rays. The article to be kept cool may also be placed in a pan with an earthenware crock turned over it and covered with a small towel or cloth, the edges of which extend into another outer pan partly filled with water.

The method can be applied on a larger scale by using a shallow galvanized pan which will contain many articles and more water. This manner of cooling is especially adapted to camping parties and will prevent sloppy butter, sour milk and spoiling fruit. The articles are also kept free from ants and flies.—Contributed by C. B. Hosford, Swansea, Ariz.

Pencil-Sharpening Guide

The sketch shows how a guide for making a true point on a lead pencil may be made of a block of wood. The hole, which should be large enough to allow the pencil to be turned easily, is bored at the proper angle to form the desired point on the pencil. The long side of the block serves as a guide for the knife blade, while the projection at the bottom acts as a stop. The guide insures an even point and is easily manipulated. It is held in the palm of the left hand and the pencil is turned with the thumb and forefinger, while the knife is held against the face of the block, cutting edge downward, and worked up and down with the right hand.

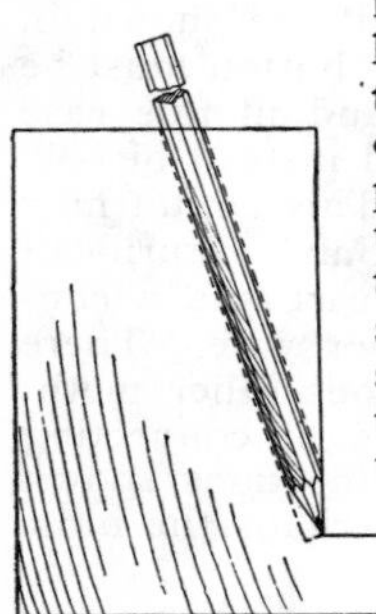

Homemade Hinges

When making a chicken house recently I had forgotten to procure hinges. When searching the "junk" box I found some little metal brackets such as used for holding spring roller shades. Attaching these as shown, I made a good substitute hinge. A pair of the brackets having no slots were selected. A 2½-in. wire nail with a washer was placed in the hole and driven into the top of the door, 1 in. from its back edge. The other bracket was placed on the bottom of the door in a similar manner. The door was placed in an open position and the prongs of the brackets were nailed to the door post. The bottom bracket may also be nailed to the floor and the top one to the lintel.—Contributed by Robert Smith, E. Burnaby, B. C.

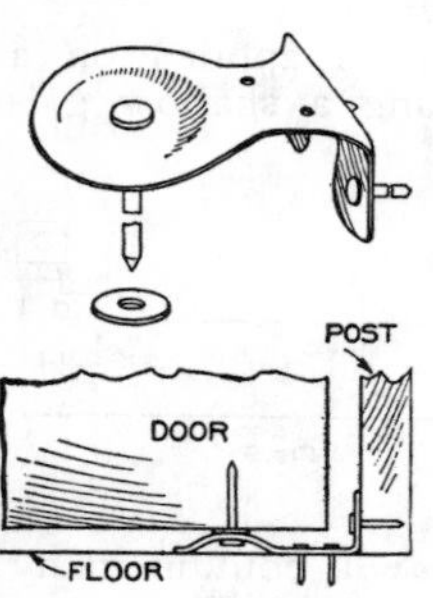

Skimmer for Bottled Milk

The cream that rises on the milk in an ordinary milk bottle cannot be removed easily. Where a small family desires to use the cream for coffee, the skimmer shown in the sketch is very handy.

The cone is made of metal—tin, brass or copper—which can be nickelplated, the seam being soldered. The cone is 2 in. deep with a diameter at the top of 1⅜ in. A handle can be made of a discarded sugar or teaspoon, which is soldered to the cone. Insert the cone in the bottle far enough for the cream to flow into it and then withdraw. Cream will gather about 3 in. deep on rich milk. The milk can be used for cooking. A piece of wire can be used for a handle instead of the spoon.—Contributed by Victor Labadie, Dallas, Texas.

How to Preserve Putty

Having some putty left over after a job of glazing and wishing to keep it without its becoming dried up, I tried wrapping it in paraffin paper such as used to wrap butter. I found this method to be a decided success, the oil being prevented from drying out. —Contributed by Levi R. Markwood, Fairview, Pa.

How to Build a Simple Electric Motor

By A. G. McCLURE

An exceedingly simple and inexpensive motor that may be used in operating small toys can be constructed as follows: First procure a good permanent magnet, about 5 in. long and about 1½ in. between the inside edges at the open end. This magnet should be at least ½ in. thick, and if it cannot be had in one piece, two or more may be placed side by side, like poles being placed together. The writer was unable to procure ready-made magnets, so one was formed and magnetized. Obtain a piece of tungsten or some other good-grade steel, ½ in. by ½ in., and about 11 in. long. Bend this piece into the form of a U, with the inner edges 1¾ in. apart. Square off both ends and drill two small holes in the outside surface of each end, at AA, about ⅜ in. from the end. Tap these holes for small machine screws. Drill the hole B with a small drill, about $\frac{1}{16}$ in., in the center of the lower portion of the U and ream it out. The piece should now be clamped with a good pair of blacksmith's tongs,—a block of iron being placed between the ends to keep the pressure of the tongs from drawing them together—heated to a cherry red and then plunged into a bath of oil. It can then be magnetized by placing it in contact with a permanent magnet.

Next obtain a piece of ⅛-in. brass, about ½ in. wide and 5½ in. long. Drill two holes in each end of the piece to match those drilled in the ends of the magnet, also one in the center, and tap it for a ⅛-in. machine screw. Now bend this piece into the form shown. Provide a machine screw, S, for the hole C and drill a small tapered hole in the end of the screw.

Obtain a small quantity of soft sheet iron and cut a sufficient number of pieces similar to that shown at D to make a pile ½ in. high. Cut two

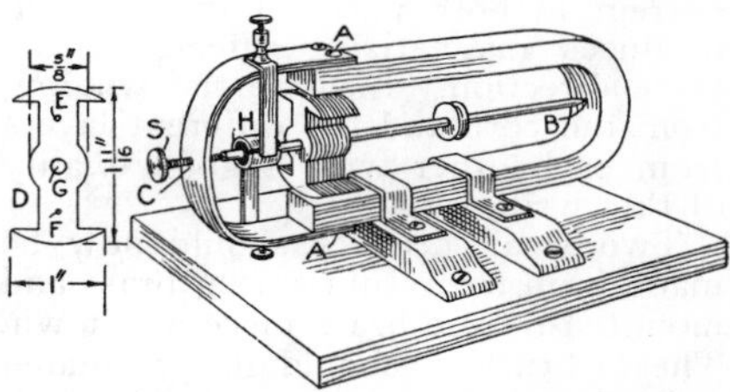

Detail of Armature Laminations, and Completed Parts Assembled, but without Armature Windings

pieces of the same size from some thin sheet brass. Now place all of these pieces in a pile, the brass pieces being on the outside, and clamp them securely, then drill the two small holes, E and F. Place two small copper rivets in these holes and rivet the heads down before removing the clamp. Drill a ⅛-in. hole, G, through this piece, the armature, for the shaft to pass through. Procure a piece of ⅛-in. steel rod, about 6 in. long. Sharpen one end so that it will enter the hole B, then cut the other end off and sharpen it so that it will enter the opening made in the end of the screw S. The armature may now be soldered to this shaft, its left-hand surface being flush with the ends of the magnet.

A small commutator, H, should now be made as follows: Obtain a piece of thin brass tubing about ⅝ in. in diameter. Turn down a piece of hard rubber so that the tube will fit tightly on it. Drill a hole in this piece of rubber of such a size that it will have to be forced on the steel shaft. Saw two longitudinal slots in the brass tube diametrically opposite each other and then bind these two pieces in place on the piece of rubber with some heavy linen thread wrapped around each end. The armature is now ready to wind. Get a small quantity of No. 22 gauge cotton-covered wire, solder one end to one of the segments of the commutator, then wind one end of the armature full and cross over and wind the other end full, soldering the end of the wire to the second commutator segment. Make sure to wind both ends of the armature in the same direction so the current in both parts of the winding produces magnetizing effects in the same direction. Insulate the winding from the core and the different layers from each other with a good quality of thin writing paper.

Two small brushes should now be made from some thin spring brass and mounted on the brass piece as shown. These brushes should be insulated from the piece of brass and two small binding posts should be provided for making connections to them. The position of the commutator and brushes should be such that the brushes move from one segment to the other when the ends of the armature are directly in line with the ends of the permanent magnet.

A small pulley should be mounted upon the shaft to be used in transmitting the power. The whole device may be mounted in a horizontal position on a wooden base as shown, and the motor is complete.

How to Make a Humidity Indicator

A simple weather indicator that may be used in determining the condition of the atmosphere may be made as follows: Dress a small figure, in the form of a doll, with a piece of cloth, previously dipped in the following solution: Chloride of cobalt, 30 parts by weight; sodium chloride, 15 parts; gum arabic, 7½ parts; calcium chloride, 4½ parts, and water, 400 parts. This cloth will change color as the amount of moisture in the atmosphere changes, the change being due to the cobalt salt, which, in dry air, is lavender blue. As the moisture in the atmosphere increases, the color changes first to bluish red, then light red and finally pink, according to the amount of moisture. With a decrease in moisture, the colors change in the reverse order to that given above, and the blue color returns when the air becomes dry.

The "Q" Trick

Lay out the form of the capital letter Q with coins on a table and ask someone in the audience to select a number and then ask that person to count up from one until the number is reached, beginning at A and stopping on the circle, for instance at B, then counting back again beginning with one, but, instead of counting on the tail, pass it and go around the circle, say, to C. The performer gives these instructions to the person doing the counting. The one selecting the number must not tell the performer what the number is, and the latter is to leave the room while the counting proceeds. The performer, before leaving the room, is to tell which coin will be the last one counted.

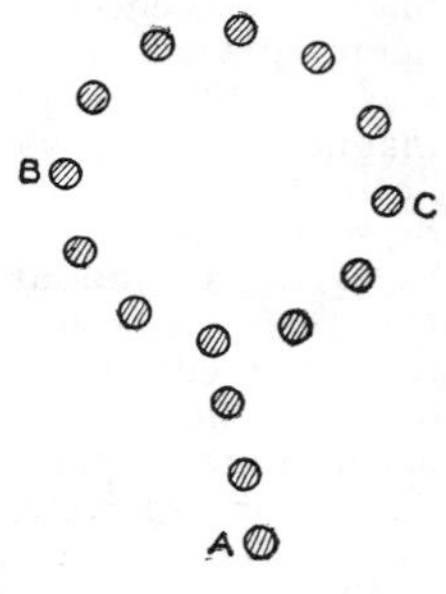

Take, for example, the number 7. Counting from A to B there are just 7 coins and counting back the last number or 7 will be at C. Try 9 for the number and the last one counted will also be C. The number of coins in the tail represents the number of coins in the circle from the intersection of the tail and circle to the last number counted. For instance, the sketch shows 4 coins in the tail, therefore the last coin counted in the circle will be at C or the fourth coin from the intersection of the tail and circle.

By slipping another coin in the tail the location of the last coin counted is changed, thereby eliminating any chance of exposing the trick by locating the same coin in the circle every time. This can be done secretly without being noticed.

To Keep Ants Away From Food

Suspend a shelf, breadbox or rack with wire around which is tied a piece of cotton cloth, saturated with a mineral oil. The ants will not cross the oil-soaked cloth.

Some strong wire hooks attached to the rack or shelf answer well to hang small articles on, such as bacon, bags of sugar, syrup cans, etc.—Contributed by C. B. Hosford, Swansea, Ariz.

Vaulting-Pole Holder

An adjusting device for a vaulting pole that can be easily fixed at any point on a round pole by using a wedge and ring, is shown in the sketch. The wedge carries a pin on which to place the cross pole. The

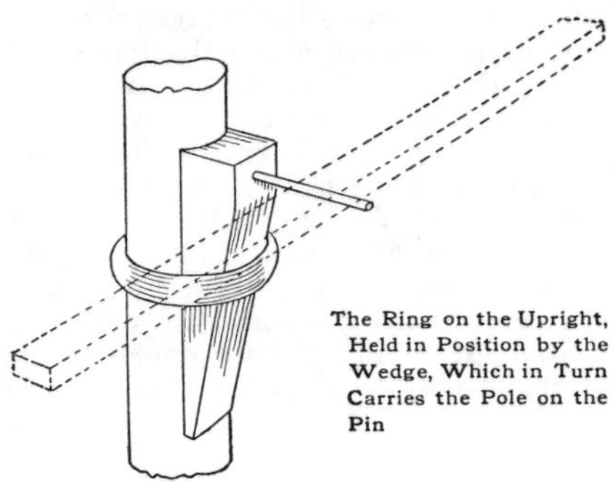

The Ring on the Upright, Held in Position by the Wedge, Which in Turn Carries the Pole on the Pin

manner of using this device as well as its construction is clearly indicated. —Contributed by Sterling R. Speirs, St. Louis, Mo.

Flying Model Aeroplane for a Display

A novelty for a window display is made of a model aeroplane flying by its own power. To control the direction and make the model fly in a circle

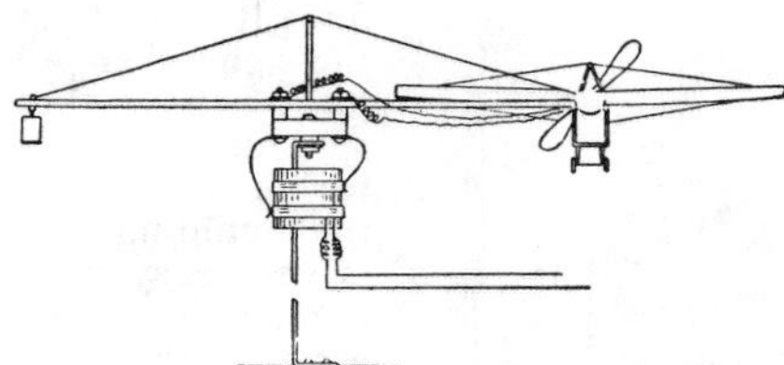

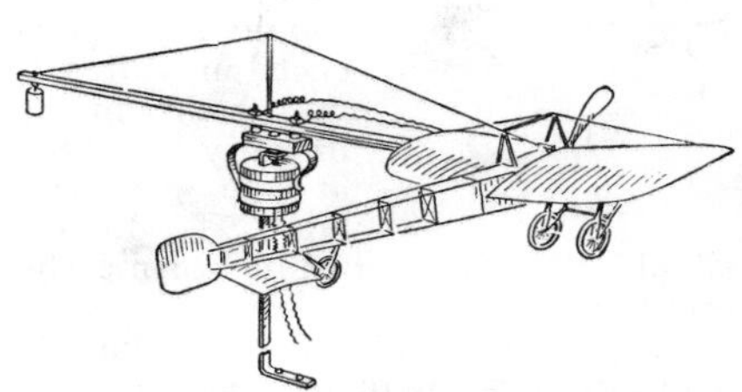

Detail of Parts Showing Wire Connections and Model in Flight around the Central Axis

it is fastened to a long stick or beam which is pivoted in the center. The one shown was pivoted to a roller-skate wheel which in turn was fastened to a metal standard. The beam was attached to the skate wheel with two small bolts which were insulated and carried two brushes as commutator contacts.

The commutator rings were made of heavy brass strips, fastened to a round piece of wood which was attached to the metal standard. The wires from the current supply were connected to the commutator rings. From the brushes connecting wires were carried along the beam to the aeroplane motor which was a small battery motor with propeller.

The opposite end of the beam was weighted to balance it. The first sketch shows the parts and the manner of making the connections. The aeroplane is driven in a circular path by its own power in a realistic manner.

An Electric Time Light

Although the modern alarm clock is a wonderfully effective piece of mechanism, it is, to say the least, very abrupt in its manner. It seldom confines its efforts to the chamber of its owner, but spreads its disturbance all over the building. It is very easy for a person to arise early in the summer and no greater difficulty should be experienced in winter, if the bedroom is brightly lighted at the proper hour. To do this simply and automatically became the problem.

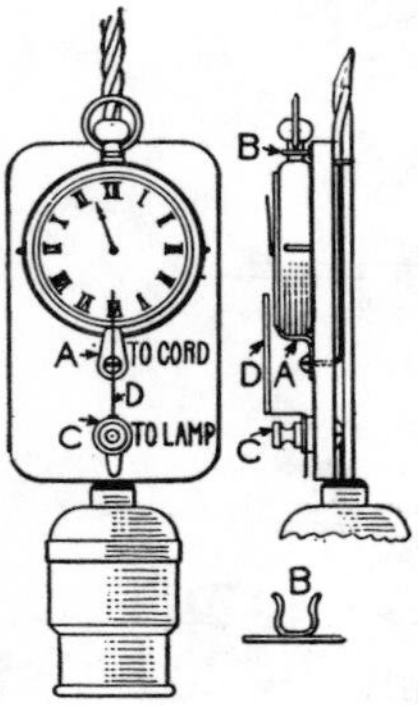

The first thought was to obtain one of those clock-actuated electric-light switches, such as the stores use, but this would not do, because it meant some unsightly wiring around the room. It was then remembered how, in the course of some experiments, an ordinary incandescent light was operated through a piece of No. 36 gauge wire without any sign of heating. If, then, a wire only 1/200 in. in diameter were of ample carrying capacity, surely a dollar watch would be sufficient to make the connection. Such being the case, the whole mechanism could readily be attached to the drop cord of a lamp directly above the socket, thus obviating any additional wiring. This all proved to be true, and the whole was made and attached in the course of a couple of hours.

While one might feel enthusiastic about this small and easily contrived affair, it is scarcely to be presumed that it would operate so effectively on one who had spent the larger part of the night tripping the "light fantastic," or in undue conviviality. An ordinary 16-cp. globe has thus far operated perfectly, and a 40-watt tungsten lamp would, if not too far away, surely awaken the hardest sleeper of sober habits.

The base of the mechanism is a small piece of 1/4-in. hard wood, upon which is fastened a small brass bracket, A, bent so as to hold the watch from slipping down. A small clip, B, was then arranged so as to grip the neck of the watch after its lower edge had been placed against A, and a small brad at either side prevented lateral movement. In this way the watch was held firmly, yet in a manner that would permit its being taken out instantly when necessary. The glass and minute hand were removed. The brass bolt from an exhausted dry cell was placed at C, so as to clamp a small copper washer to which was soldered a narrow strip of copper, D, about 1/16 in. wide and cut from a leaf of an old dynamo brush. This strip is arranged so as to wipe the hour hand as it travels past, but being so thin, it has no appreciable effect on the time keeping. As illustrated, the device is set for six o'clock, but by loosening the nut C an hour's adjustment either way may be had. It is a very simple matter, however, to arrange the device so it will operate at any hour. In connecting up, one end of the drop cord is removed from the socket and attached to A, which throws the current through the watch, thence along the hand and down D to C, from where it is carried by a short piece of wire to the socket again. As there are so many circuits through the watch, the small current required for one light does not affect it in any way. Thus far, no trouble has been experienced in making this delicate connection with 110 volts, but if any should develop, the contacts may be tipped with the small pieces of platinum taken from a burned-out globe.

¶The meat of a white English walnut may be easily removed by heating the nut in an oven or on top of a stove, then using a knife to pry the shell open.

A Small Shocking Machine

AN amusing as well as instructive shocking machine, usually called a medical coil, can be easily constructed from a discarded buzzer or electric bell, four binding posts, some pieces of insulated wire, two carbon rods, and a rheostat.

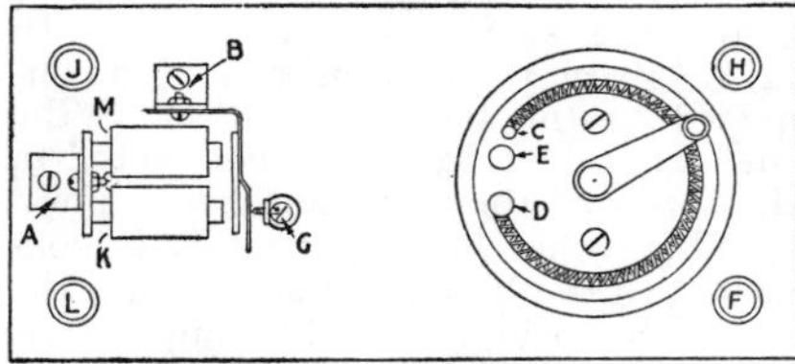

Fig. 1

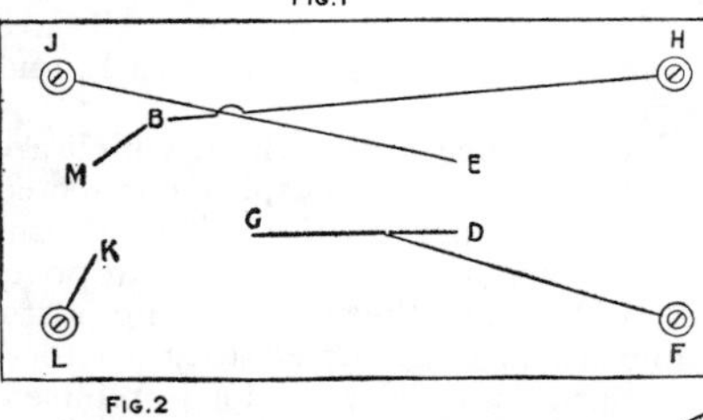

Fig. 2

The Base upon Which the Buzzer and Rheostat are Fastened, and the Electrical Connections

A base for attaching the parts is made of a piece of poplar, 10 in. long, 5 in. wide, and ½ in. thick, which can be finished as desired, but a good method is to shape the edge like molding and give it a mahogany stain, and when dry apply a coat of white shellac, which should be allowed to dry a day, whereupon the surface is rubbed with prepared wax. When the base is ready, mount the buzzer at one end. This can be easily done by making an L-shaped piece of metal, A, which is fastened to the base with a screw, and to the yoke of the magnet coil with a small bolt. If the armature and its connections are also used from the buzzer, the height of the coils must be taken in consideration. These parts are fastened in position as shown, using an L-shaped piece of metal, B, for the spring end. The screw holding the armature spring to the base, as well as the vibrator screw, should be of such a length that it will

Fig. 3

The Shocking Coil as It is Used for Amusement, or in the Manner a Current is Given a Patient

Left: The Rheostat That is Used to Regulate the Flow of Current in the Carbon Hand Pieces

enter the base far enough to permit a connection for a wire in a countersunk hole bored in the base from the under side. Binding posts are placed in the corners of the base in holes countersunk from the under side for the screw heads.

The rheostat is of the miniature-battery type, which has a round base and a coil of resistance wire with a lever passing over the coil. Such a rheostat can be purchased from an electrical store, but if the person constructing the shocking machine desires to make one, it is not difficult if a lathe is at hand.

To make the rheostat, turn up a disk, about 3 in. in diameter, from a piece of hard wood, such as oak, maple, or walnut, and form a circular groove in the upper surface, about 3/8 in. inside of the circumference. The groove is to admit a circular coil of resistance wire, and in making it, be sure to have it the proper size to take the coil snugly. The coil can be of any size, and to make it, resistance wire is wound around a piece of wire used as a mandrel. If the coil is 1/4 in., or a trifle smaller, in diameter, it will make a good size. Be sure that the depth of the groove is such that it will allow a part of the coils of the resistance wire to project above the surface of the wood disk. The coil of wire should be just long enough to fit in the groove and allow a 1-in. space between the ends, one of which is anchored to the base, at C, the other being attached to the binding post D. Drill a hole through the center of the disk and fasten a lever, taken from a switch, or one made of a piece of sheet brass, that will extend from the center to the outside of the disk, or over the resistance-wire coil. A small handle is attached to the outer end. A connection is made from the center support of the lever to the binding post E.

The connections for the buzzer and rheostat are made on the under side of the base, where grooves are cut to run the wires in, so that they will be below the surface of the wood. In the diagram, the binding post F is connected to the binding post D of the rheostat, which in turn is connected to the screw of the make-and-break point G. The other binding post H is connected to the bracket B supporting the armature spring. The binding post E of the rheostat is connected to the base binding post J. The magnet coils are connected, as shown, from K to L, and from M to B.

The two pieces of carbon, which are used for the hand pieces, are connected with silk-insulated wire. These connections are made to the binding posts F and H. The other two binding posts, J and L, are connected to a battery. The carbons used may be purchased, or taken from an old battery. Two or more dry cells are used for the current. The rheostat controls the amount of current passing through the hand pieces.—Contributed by Gilbert Crossley, Erie, Pa.

Secret Compartment in Ordinary Table Drawer

It is frequently desired to have some handy place for storing valuables where there is but little chance of discovering them. Secret drawers in tables usually require special and expensive changes, but with only a few simple changes on a regular drawer of any ordinary table, a secret compartment can be made which is as secure as can ordinarily be figured on, outside of a steel safe. Having chosen the desired table, a partition should be placed across the entire back part of the drawer, allowing for necessary space in the secret compartment. This partition should resemble the real back of the drawer as closely as it is

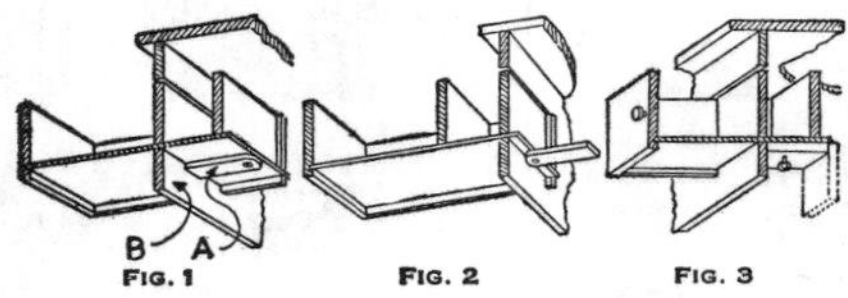

Two Positions of the Strip for Holding, or Giving Access to, the Secret Part, and a Hinged Strip

possible to make it. The compartment must not be too wide, for the resulting small width of the front part of the drawer might then arouse suspicion. On the lower side of the secret compartment a strip of wood, A, should be attached with a screw, as shown in Fig. 1, allowing sufficient looseness so the strip may be turned end for end when necessary. With the strip set as shown, it will strike the front side B of the table when the drawer is pulled out, leaving the secret compartment still hidden. In order to expose this, it will be necessary to turn the strip, as shown in Fig. 2, when the drawer can be pulled out to its full length.

It being necessary that the strip A be as long as the secret compartment is wide, to fully expose this, there may be cases where the drawer is not wide enough to allow the strip A to turn around. In that case the strip can be hinged to the back of the drawer as shown in Fig. 3. When it is hanging down, as shown by the dotted outline, the drawer may be pulled out to its full extent. When it is desired to lock the secret compartment, the hinged strip must be swung up in position, and fastened. An ordinary thumbscrew or eye can be used which, by a turn or two, will either release it or fasten it in place.—Contributed by Paul Durst, Detroit, Mich.

Inflating Handballs

When handballs become "dead," or no longer bounce freely, they may frequently be restored by inflating them with air. This can be done by means of a bulb attached to a hypodermic needle. The needle must be inserted through the soft plug which every inflated ball has, and which can be discovered by pressure. After the ball is inflated and the needle extracted, the soft rubber closes around the fine hole, preventing the escape of the air. If a leak is found, which allows the air to escape too rapidly, a repair can be made with a single-tube tire outfit.—Contributed by A. B. Wegener, Camden, N. J.

A Garden-Bed Scarecrow

A very neat and successful scarecrow for garden beds can be made as follows: A number of corks are pro-

The Fluttering Feathers Attached to the String with Corks Scare the Birds Away

cured, and a feather is stuck in each end of them, as shown. These are tied to a string, spacing them from 1 to 2 ft. apart, and the string is hung over the beds. The slightest breeze will keep them fluttering, and no bird will come to rest on the beds.—Contributed by M. T. Canary, Chicago.

Measuring the Length of Wire Wound on a Spool

When winding magnet spools on a lathe, the exact amount of wire used can be easily determined by means of the device shown in the illustration. The large reel from which the wire is obtained is conveniently placed on a loose mandrel, or rod, near the lathe, and in line with the spool which is to be wound. A grooved idler wheel, the ex-

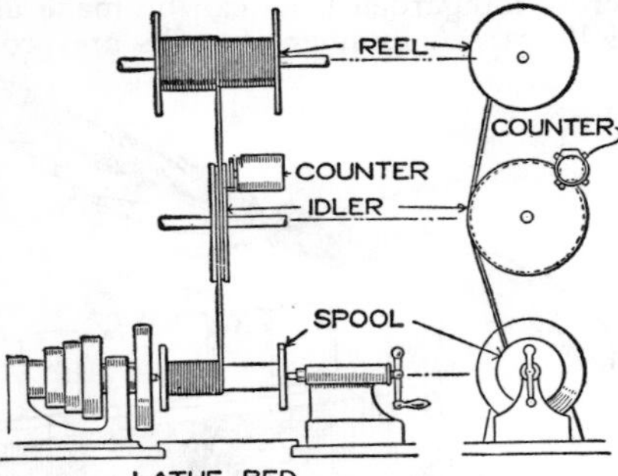

Measuring the Length of Wire on a Spool with the Use of an Idler and Counter

act diameter of which is known, is supported between the spool and wire reel so it may freely revolve; the number of its revolutions should be obtained, automatically, by a revolution counter. When using the device, the wire from the reel is placed once around the idler to insure the necessary grip to prevent it from sliding; then it is led to the spool. The exact diameter of the idler being known and the number of revolutions indicated, the true length of the wire wound on the spools can be easily determined by the following formula: Length of wire on spool in feet equals circumference of idler in feet times number of revolutions of idler.—Contributed by C. Swayne, St. Louis, Mo.

Homemade Lawn Sprinkler

With a short length of old hose, a serviceable lawn sprinkler can be quickly and easily made. One end is provided with a regular coupling for connecting it to the line of good hose. The other end is turned up for several inches, and securely wired to the main

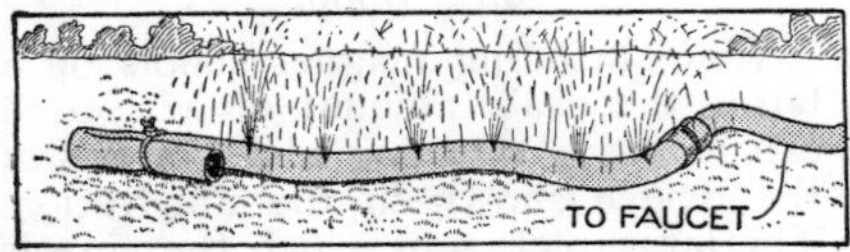

The Slots Cut in the Hose will Produce a Very Fine Spray of Water

part, thereby shutting off any flow through it. Several cuts are made into it, about halfway across and 6 in. apart. If the water is forced in, the only means of escape will be through the slots, which will produce fine sprays, giving as good service as a manufactured sprinkler.—Contributed by A. B. Shaw, N. Dartmouth, Mass.

Homemade Toy Bank

The little bank illustrated is not exactly burglar-proof, but once put together it cannot be opened except by the destruction of one of the units of which it is composed. It requires but little skill to make, and would be a good problem for manual training, as it offers an excellent opportunity for teaching certain rudiments of woodworking by the application method.

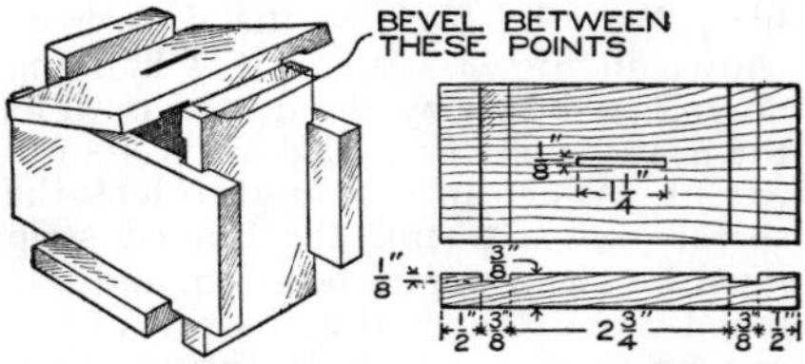

Six Pieces of Wood as They are Put Together to Form a Toy Bank

In its construction, six pieces of hard wood, of the dimensions shown in the sketch, are required. White wood will do if there is no hard wood at hand. The coin slot is 1/8 in. wide by 1 1/4 in. long, and is cut in only one piece.

No difficulty will be experienced in putting the first five pieces together, but the sixth, or top, piece, shown in the sketch, will not go in, because the bottom edge of the raised side will strike the inside of the piece to the right. By beveling this edge with a chisel from top to bottom between the dadoes, or grooves, it can be forced down quite a distance and sprung in place by placing a block of wood on the high side and striking it a sharp blow with a heavy hammer.—Contributed by J. A. Shelly, Brooklyn, New York.

An Electric Anemometer

By Wm. H. DETTMAN

The construction of this instrument is so simple that any amateur can make one, and if accurate calibrations are desired, these can be marked by comparison with a standard anemometer, while both are placed in the wind.

The Indicator

The case of the indicator is built of thin wood—the material of an old cigar box will do—9 in. long, 6 in. wide and 1½ in. deep. If cigar-box material is used, it must first be soaked in warm water to remove the paper. If a cover is to be used on the box, a slot, on an arc of a circle, must be cut through it to show the scale beneath. The arc is determined by the length of the needle from a center over the axis on which the needle swings. When the box is completed, smooth up the outside surface with fine sandpaper and give it a coat of stain.

The core of the magnet is made by winding several layers of bond paper around a pencil of sufficient size to make an inside diameter of slightly over ¼ in., and a tube 2 in. long. Each layer of the paper is glued to the preceding layer.

Two flanges or disks are attached to the tube to form a spool for the wire. The disks are cut from thin wood, 1¼ in. square, and a hole bored through their centers so that each will fit on the tube tightly. One of them is glued to one end of the tube and the other fastened at a point ½ in. from the opposite end. The space between the disks is filled with seven layers of No. 22 gauge insulated magnet wire, allowing sufficient ends of the wire to project for connections. The finished coil is located in the box, as shown at A, Fig. 1.

The core for the coil is cut from a piece of ¼-in. iron rod, 1¼ in. long, and a slot is cut in each end, ¼ in. deep, into which brass strips are inserted and soldered, or otherwise fastened. The strips of brass are $\frac{3}{16}$ in. wide, one 1½ in. long and the other ¾ in. Two $\frac{1}{16}$-in. holes are drilled in the end of the long piece, and one $\frac{1}{16}$-in. hole in the end of the short piece. The complete core with the brass ends is shown in Fig. 2.

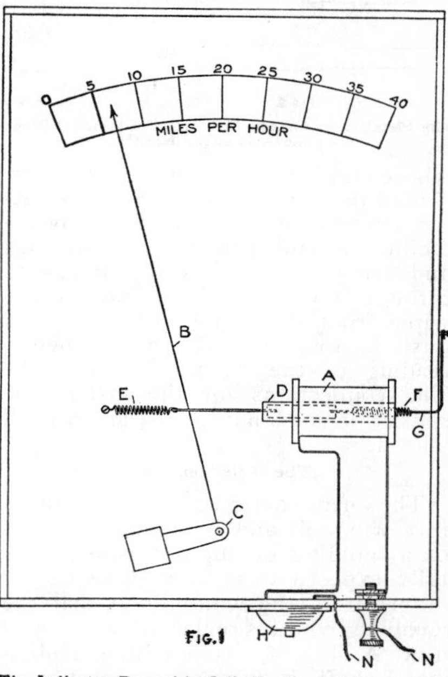

The Indicator Box with Coil, Needle and Scale, as It is Used in Connection with the Anemometer

The needle B, Fig. 1, is made of a copper or brass wire, about 6 in. long, and is mounted on an axis at C. The detail of the bearing for the axis is shown in Fig. 3. The axis D is a piece of wood fitted in the U-shaped piece of brass and made to turn on brads as bearings, the center being pierced to receive the end of the needle. After locating the bearing for the axis C, Fig. 1, it is fastened in place so that the upper end or pointer of the needle will travel over the scale. The needle is then attached to the bearing after having been passed through the inner hole of the longer brass strip of the core, and the coil is fitted with the core in the manner shown at D. A light brass coil spring is attached to each end of the core, as shown at E and F, the latter being held with a string, G,

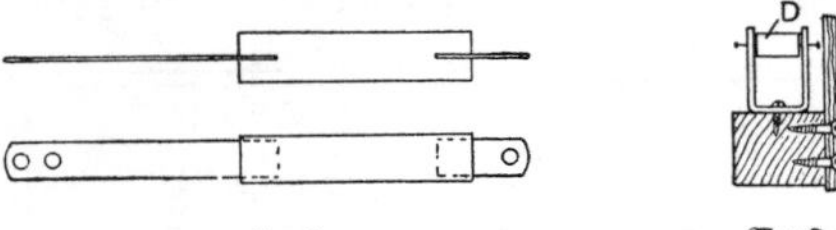

The Metal Core for the Coil and the Bearing Block for the Axis of the Needle

whose end is tied to a brad on the outside of the box, for adjustment. A better device could be substituted by attaching the end of the spring F to a nut and using a knurled-head bolt passed through the box side. One of the wires from the coil is attached to a push button, H, to be used when a reading of the instrument is made. The connections for the instrument consist of one binding post and a push button.

The Anemometer

The anemometer resembles a miniature windmill and is mounted on top of a building or support where it is fully exposed to the air currents. It differs from the windmill in that the revolving wheel is replaced by a cupped disk, A, Fig. 4, fitted with a sliding metal shaft, B, which is supported on crosspieces, CC, between the main frame pieces DD. The latter pieces carry a vane at the opposite end. The frame pieces are ½ in. thick, 2¼ in.

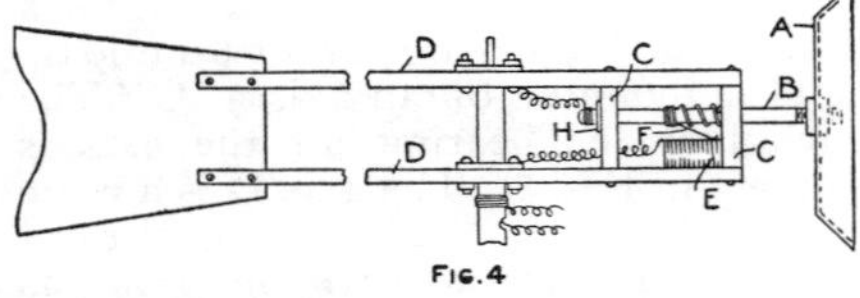

The Anemometer as It is Mounted on a Standard Similar to a Small Windmill Weather Vane

wide and 36 in. long, and the crosspieces have the same width and thickness and are 4 in. long.

A variable-resistance coil, E, is made as follows and fastened in the main frame. The core of this coil is a piece of wood, 2 in. square and 4 in. long, and wound with No. 18 gauge single-wound cotton-covered german-silver wire. The winding should begin ¼ in. from one end of the core and finish ¼ in. from the other, making the length of the coil 3½ in. The ends of the wire are secured by winding them around the heads of brads driven into the core. A small portion of the insulation is removed from the wire on one side of the coil. This may be done with a piece of emery cloth or sandpaper. A sliding spring contact, F, is attached to the sliding shaft B, the end of which is pressed firmly on the bared portion of the wire coil. One end of a coil spring, which is slipped on the shaft between the pieces CC, is attached to the end crosspiece, and the other end is fastened to the sliding shaft so as to keep the shaft and disk out, and the flange H against the second crosspiece, when there is no air current applied to the disk A.

The insulation of the standard upon which the anemometer turns is shown in Fig. 5. The standard J is made of a piece of ½-in. pipe, suitably and rigidly attached to the building or support, and the upper end, around which the anemometer revolves to keep in the direction of the air currents, is fitted with a plug of wood to insulate the ¼-in. brass rod K. A bearing and electric-wire connection plate, L, is made of brass, ⅛ in. thick, 2 in. wide and 4 in. long. The bearing and connection plate M are made in a similar manner. The surface of the holes in these plates, bearing against the pipe J and the brass rod K, make the two connections for the wires from the variable-resistance coil E, Fig. 4, located on the main frame, to the wire connections between the two instruments. These wires should be weather-proof, insulated, attached as shown, and running to and connecting the indicator with the anemometer at NN, Fig. 1.

Two or more dry cells must be connected in the line, and when a reading is desired. the button H, Fig. 1, is pushed, which causes the current to flow through the lines and draw the magnet core D in the coil, in proportion to the magnetic force induced by the amount of current passing through the resistance in the coils on E, Fig. 4, from the contact into which the spring F is brought by the wind pressure on the disk A.

How to Make Stick Shellac

It is often desired to use shellac in solid or stick form, and to get it into this shape by melting and molding requires considerable time. A much quicker method is to place the shellac in a shallow box, spread it out in a thin layer and play the flame from a Bunsen burner upon it until the mass is melted and run together. Allow it to stand a few seconds, then, with moistened fingers, fold it over and over and shape it with the fingers. It is possible to make a stick 8 or 10 in. long and 5/8 in. in diameter in about 5 minutes.—Contributed by J. H. Beeber, Rochester, N. Y.

Substitute for a Hose Reel

Not having the room to spare for the ordinary hose reel, I used as a substitute a piece of wire bent into the shape of a letter S and with its aid coiled the hose in a manner to expel the water and leave it in shape for storing.

The hook A is sprung around the hose about 5 ft. from the connection joint and remains there permanently. The end of the hose with the connection C is then brought around in a circle and forced into the hook B. This forms the start for the coil and

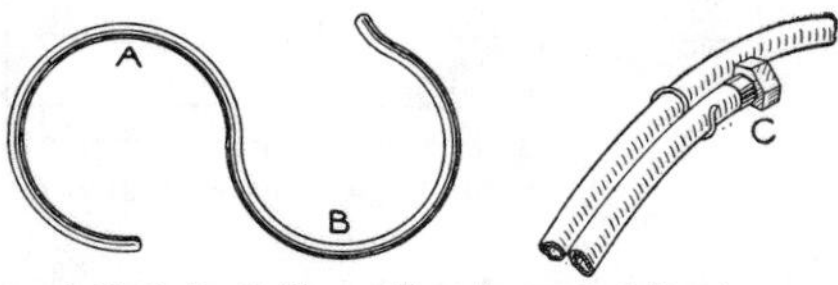

A Hook for Coiling a Hose Instead of Turning It on a Reel

the hose is easily rolled up to the nozzle, the water being expelled during the operation.—Contributed by F. H. Aldrich, Toledo, Ohio.

Addressing a Roll of Papers

When addressing rolled-up papers it is difficult to write on the curved surface. The papers also have a tendency

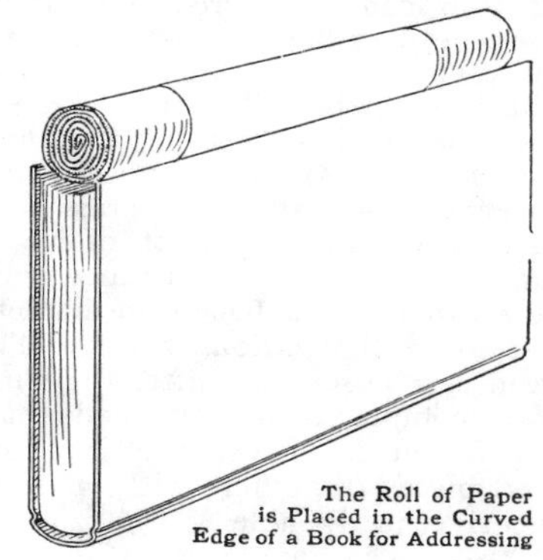
The Roll of Paper is Placed in the Curved Edge of a Book for Addressing

to roll away. By placing the roll in the hollow on the front edge of a large book, as shown in the sketch, it will be found easy to write on the wrapper.—Contributed by W. P. Shaw, Toronto, Canada.

Repairing the Bruised Sides of a Motorboat

When the sides of a boat become scored or bruised scrape the parts clean and fill the depressions with wood cement. The wood cement or stick cement, as it is called, can be procured from a paint store. Heat the cement with a blowtorch and apply it to the bruised parts. Use a heated putty knife to smooth the cement and make the surface level. After sandpapering the fills and applying a coat of paint the boat sides will look as good as new. The cement will not chip or fall out.—Contributed by Henry Beck, Bronx, New York.

How to Make an Electric Lamp Flasher

Procure two pieces of metal, one of brass and the other of sheet iron, 5 in. long, $\frac{1}{2}$ in. wide, and $\frac{1}{32}$ in., or just a little more, in thickness. Bend the brass strip into the form shown in Fig. 1, then place the brass piece on top of the iron and drill the holes A and B indicated in Fig. 2. After the brass piece has been bent, as shown in Fig. 1, it will of course be shorter than the iron strip and the iron strip must be cut off, or a brass strip a little longer than 5 in. can be secured and cut the same length as the iron strip after it is bent. The holes A and B should be $\frac{3}{32}$ in. in diameter. The next thing to do will be to wind a heating coil about the brass strip. Wrap a very thin layer of sheet asbestos about the brass strip, and wind on the strip 18 ft. of No. 34 gauge bare superior resistance wire. Use a thread about .006 in. in diameter to separate the various turns. This thread can be removed after the winding is completed and the ends have been fastened. Rivet the iron and brass pieces together with a small brass rivet in the hole A, Fig. 2. After the two pieces are riveted together bend them into the form shown in Fig. 4 and then drill the two $\frac{1}{8}$-in. holes C and D, as shown in Fig. 2. Tap the hole B, Fig. 2, to take a small machine screw.

The base is constructed as follows: Procure a piece of slate, $5\frac{3}{8}$ in. long, $1\frac{1}{2}$ in. wide, and $\frac{1}{2}$ in. in thickness. Drill the holes indicated in Fig. 3. The four corner holes are for mounting the flasher in its containing case, and should be about $\frac{1}{8}$ in. in diameter. The holes E, F, G, and H should be $\frac{1}{8}$ in. in diameter and countersunk with a $\frac{3}{8}$-in. square-ended drill, on the under side, to a depth of $\frac{3}{16}$ or $\frac{1}{4}$ in. Cut from some $\frac{1}{16}$-in. sheet brass a piece $1\frac{3}{8}$ in. long, and $\frac{1}{2}$ in. wide. Drill two $\frac{1}{8}$-in. holes in this piece, $\frac{7}{8}$ in. apart and equally spaced from the ends. Procure four $\frac{1}{8}$-in. brass bolts, two $\frac{1}{2}$ in. in length, and two 1 in. in length. Secure four small washers and two additional nuts. Mount the combined iron and brass strip on the slate base, using a long and short bolt as shown in Fig. 4. One terminal of the winding should be placed under the head of the bolt J. Place a washer, K, between the head of the bolt and the wire. The brass strip L can now be mounted in a similar manner, as shown in Fig. 4. Place the other end of the winding under the head of the bolt M.

Obtain a small screw, N, Fig. 4, of such a length that its point will reach the brass strip L when the screw is placed in the hole B, Fig. 2. A lock nut, O, should be provided for this screw so that it will remain in adjustment. The point of the screw and the point on the brass plate where the screw touches should be of platinum, as the brass will not withstand the high temperature of the arc formed when the circuit is broken.

A metal box should now be provided to serve as a containing case and the flasher is complete. This box should be of such design and construction that it will comply with the requirements of the electrical inspection department having jurisdiction over the locality where the flasher is to be used.

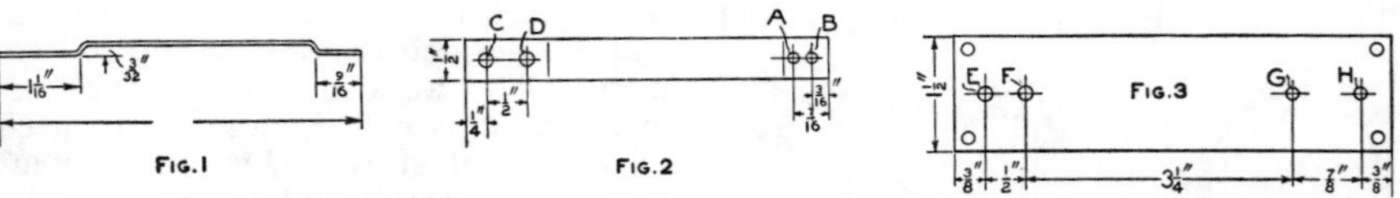

Dimensions of the Brass Strip and Mounting Base, Showing the Location of the Holes and the Shape of the Brass Strip to Receive the Coil of Wire

The flasher should be connected in series with the lamp, the wires being fastened under the nuts on the bolts P and R, Fig. 4, and the screw N adjusted so that it lacks a small fraction of an inch of making contact with the brass plate when there is no current in the winding. When the switch is turned on there will be a current through the lamp and winding in series. The brass strip will be heated more than the iron and it will expand more, thus forcing the point of the screw N down upon the brass plate, which will result in the winding about the brass strip being shorted and the full voltage will be impressed upon the lamp, and it will burn at normal candlepower. When the coil is shorted there will of course be no current in its winding and the brass strip will cool down, the screw N will finally be drawn away from contact with the brass plate, and the winding again connected in series with the lamp. The lamp will apparently go out when the

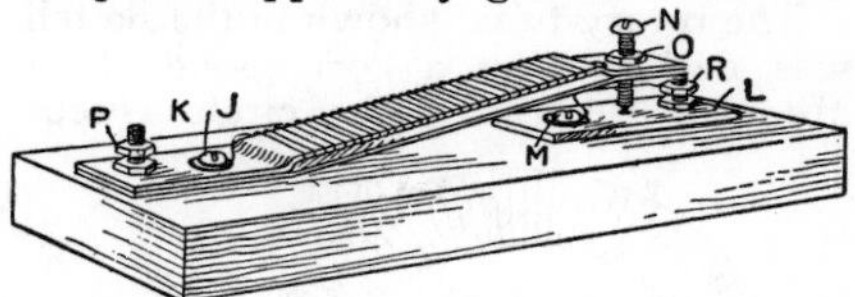

Fig. 4
The Assembled Parts Showing the Complete Flasher and Electric Connections with Adjusting Screw

winding is in series with it, as the total resistance of the lamp and winding combined will not permit sufficient current to pass through the lamp to make its filament glow. The time the lamp is on and off may be varied to a certain extent by adjusting the screw N.

Timing Photograph Prints

An amateur photographer insists that a timing clock in the darkroom is a needless luxury. In order to time printing exposures, which he does with a pendant tungsten light under a reflecting shade, he simply fastens the electric-light cord so that the lamp and shade will act like a pendulum bob which beats the seconds. Of course he makes no effort to be exact, but if the distance between the lamp and the point of suspension of the cord be about 39 or 40 in., the beats will be very nearly seconds. When the light is turned on, it is started swinging, and the operator can thus easily count seconds with sufficient accuracy, and, besides, it readily furnishes a guide for duplicating printing results.

The same principle can be applied to camera exposures, if so desired, by the following plan. Select some suitable place on the under side of the tripod plate, as, for instance, the screw head, and fasten a small string, having a weight attached to it about 39 in. from the point of support. Like the swinging lamp, this device too, will beat seconds. For convenience, one of the tripod legs may be marked to indicate the length of string needed, so that the operator at any time can quickly fasten a string, measure off the right length on the tripod leg, attach a bunch of keys, a knife, or any other convenient weight, even a small stone, and have a second-beating pendulum for time exposures.—Contributed by F. B. Lambert, Chicago.

Supports for Camp-Fire Utensils

The sketch shows how to make a standard or support to hold cooking utensils over a camp fire. The main part or stake is made of a piece of gas pipe, on one end of which is turned an ordinary coupling, Fig. 1. This is used to furnish a strong head when the stake is driven into the ground. The rings and supports for the utensils are

A Piece of Gas Pipe Constitutes the Standard with Wires Attached for Holding the Utensils

made of heavy wire bent into the shape required to hold the respective vessels. The sketch, Fig. 2, shows the manner of shaping the wires.

A Rotary Tuning Coil

The rotary tuner shown in the sketch was designed by a correspondent of Modern Electrics. The circle is cut from ¾-in. stock, 1 in. wide and well covered with insulating material. It is then wound with No. 24 single cotton-covered copper wire so that the coils will lie flat. All the arms are of ¼-in. square brass. The supports are smaller in section. Sliders are mounted on the ends of the long arms and are kept in place by setscrews.

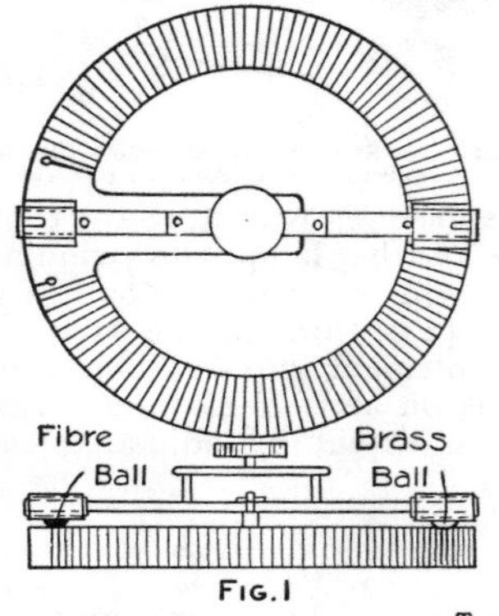

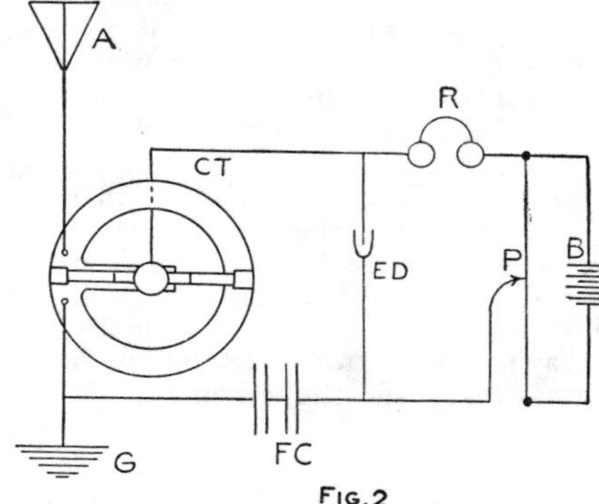

Tuning Coil and Wiring Diagram

The insulation on the wire is removed with a small piece of sandpaper pasted on a block of wood. This should be temporarily fastened to the revolving lever at the point where the contact is wanted, then the lever is turned until the insulation is removed. The wiring diagram shows the location of the tuning coil in the line.

Preparing Sheet Music for Turning

Each page on sheet music having three or more pages should be cut ¼ in. shorter than the preceding page, as shown by the dotted lines in the sketch. This will enable the player to quickly turn the pages one at a time. —Contributed by Chas. Homewood, Waterloo, Ia.

Leaves Cut for Turning

Toy Parachute Cut-Away for Kite Lines

An interesting pastime while flying kites is to attach large toy parachutes to the lines and have some device to drop them when they are at a great height. In Fig. 1 is shown how the parachute is dropped by the burning of a piece of punk.

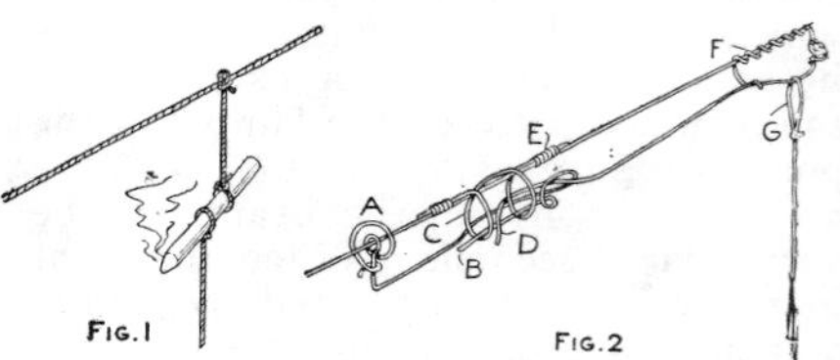

Two Parachute Drops

Another method is shown in Fig. 2. It is only necessary to send a piece of paper or cardboard along the line and when it strikes the wire coil A (Fig. 2) the part B slides out of the loops C, the end D will then fall and disengage the loop G on the end of the parachute string. The wires E and F are twisted around the kite string.—Contributed by Thos. De Loof, Grand Rapids, Michigan.

How to Make an Electric Furnace

A small electric furnace that will be very serviceable in a laboratory may be made as follows:

First procure a small clay flowerpot, about 4 in. in diameter at the bottom, and also a small clay crucible, about 2 in. in diameter at the bottom and at least 1 in. less in height than the flowerpot, and having as nearly as possible the same slope to its sides as the pot. Now obtain a small quantity of asbestos compound and pack it around the small crucible inside the flowerpot. Make sure the crucible is in the exact center of the flowerpot and that their tops are even with each other. Assuming that ordinary electric-light carbons are to be used, which are about 1/2 in. in diameter, drill two 5/8-in. holes, exactly opposite each other, through the walls of the flowerpot and asbestos compound so that they enter the crucible about 3/4 in. above its bottom on the inside. A suitable lid for the furnace may be made from 1/4-in. sheet asbestos and should be large enough to cover the top of the flowerpot.

The feeds and supports for the carbon electrodes are constructed as follows: Procure two pieces of 1/8-in. brass, 1 in. wide and 9 in. long. Cut a 1/8-in. groove lengthwise in the center of these pieces to within 1 1/2 in. of each end, as shown in Fig. 1. Drill four 1/8-in. holes, AA, in each piece, a 3/8-in. hole, B, in one end and a 3/16-in. hole, C, in the other end. Now bend the ends up at right angles to the remainder of the piece along the dotted lines shown at D and E. Next obtain two 3/8-in. rods, 10 3/16 in. long. Turn one end of each down to a 3/16-in. diameter for a distance of 3/8 in. From that point thread the same end of the rods for a distance of 6 in. Drill a 1/16-in. hole in each end of the rods a little less than 1/4 in. from the ends. The dimensions of the rods are given in Fig. 2. Two small rubber or wooden handles, similar to the one shown in Fig. 3, should now be made and fastened to the large ends of the rods by means of 1/16-in. steel pins. Obtain two pieces of brass of approximately the following dimensions: 1 in. by 1 in. by 3 in. Drill four holes in each of these pieces as shown in Fig. 4. The hole H should be just large enough to allow the carbon to enter, or about 1/2 in. in diameter. The hole G should be tapped to take a 1/4-in. machine screw, the hole F should be threaded so that the threaded rods will enter, and a small binding post should be mounted on a lug fastened in the hole J. Cut away one end of this piece as shown in Fig. 4 until it is a little less than 1/8 in. in thickness, or so it will enter the grooves cut in the brass strips.

The parts of the furnace are now ready to assemble, which may be done as follows: Procure a piece of well seasoned board, hard wood if possible, about 1 in. thick, 8 in. wide and perhaps 20 in. long. Cover one side of this board and the edges with some 1/8-in. sheet asbestos. Now place the flowerpot in the exact center and then mount the grooved brass strips one on either side of it with the longest dimension parallel to the longest dimen-

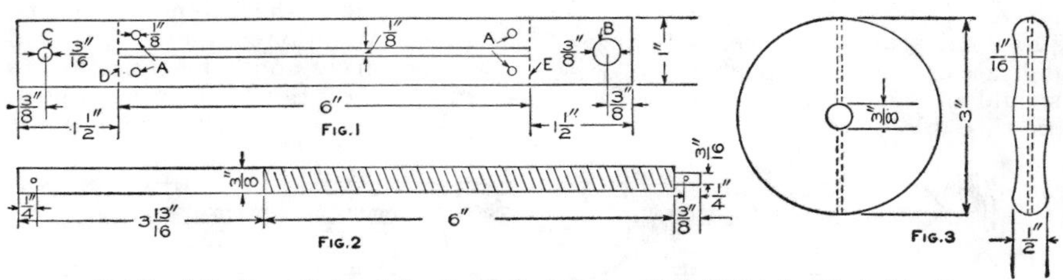

Details of the Base, Rod and Handle for Each Carbon Feed, Which is Attached to the Large Base on One Side of the Furnace

sion of the board and the inside end about 1 in. from the side of the pot. The end with the $\frac{3}{16}$-in. holes should be next to the pot. Assemble the parts of the carbon feeds and then cut out some circular disks of asbestos to place under the flowerpot so as to raise it to such a position that the holes in its sides will be on a line with the carbon rods. Three long screws should now be placed in the board, forming the base, in such a position as to hold the flowerpot always in place. This completes the furnace proper, which is shown in Fig. 5. The furnace can now be put into operation provided there is a suitable current rheostat to connect in series with the carbon arc to prevent an excessive current being taken from the line. If such a rheostat is not available, a serviceable one may be made as follows:

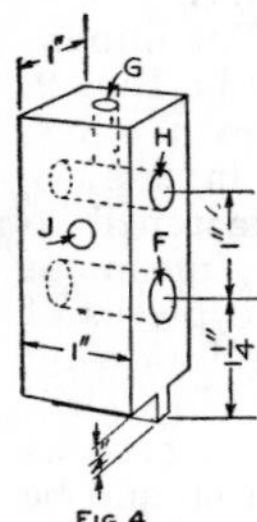

Fig. 4

Obtain two pieces of $\frac{1}{16}$-in. sheet iron, 6 by 6 in., that are to form the end plates. Cut off the corners of one piece so as to form an octagon and drill a number of $\frac{1}{8}$-in. and $\frac{1}{4}$-in. holes in it, as shown in Fig. 6. Bend the corners of the other piece down along the dotted lines marked L, Fig. 7, and then make a second bend in each corner along the dotted lines K, so that the outermost portion of the corner is parallel to the main portion of the piece. Drill a number of $\frac{1}{8}$-in. holes in this piece as indicated. A 3-in. opening should be cut in the center of this piece to give access to the interior of the completed rheostat. Now obtain eight $\frac{3}{8}$-in. iron rods, 10 in. long. Drill and tap each end of these rods to accommodate a $\frac{1}{8}$-in. machine screw. Wrap several layers of thin sheet asbestos around each rod and tie it in place with some thread. These rods should now be fastened between the end plates by means of a number of iron machine screws. Mount four back-connected binding posts on the plate shown in Fig. 6, making sure they are insulated from the plate by means of suitable bushings and washers.

Procure a small quantity of No. 14 gauge iron wire. Fasten one end of the wire under the head of the screw holding one of the binding posts in place and then wind it around the rods about 20 times, making the distance between the turns equal to the diameter of the wire. After winding on the 20 turns, attach a short piece of wire to the main wire and fasten the free end of the short piece to one of the other binding posts. Wind on 20 more turns, and make another connection to the third binding post, then complete the

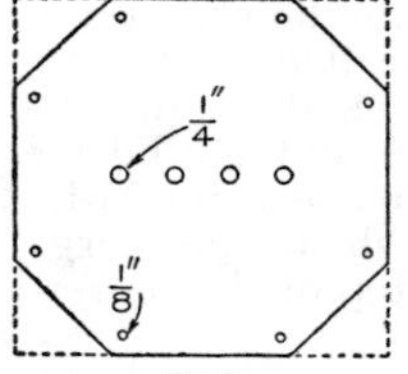

Fig. 6

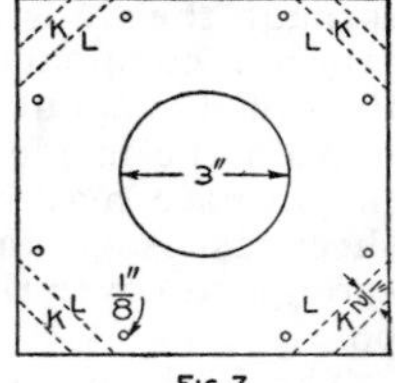

Fig. 7

Detail of the Upper and Lower End Plates That are Used in Making a Rheostat

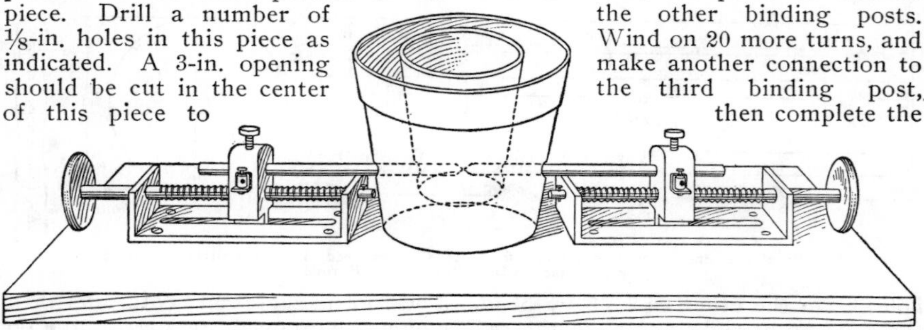

Fig. 5

The Furnace Consists of a Flowerpot in Which a Crucible is Set, and on Either Side the Carbon Holders are Fastened to the Base

winding and attach the end to the remaining binding post. Different amounts of this resistance can now be connected in series with the arc by changing the connections from one binding post to another. The rheostat may be located on a bracket fastened to the wall, but care must be taken not to place it in such a position that it will come into contact with inflammable material. As an extra precaution, the circuit should be properly fused.

Cleaning Brass Articles

Embossed or undercut brass work may be easily cleaned by boiling the pieces in a strong solution of caustic soda or lye, and then immersing them in a mixture of hydrochloric acid, 6 parts; water, 2 parts, and nitric acid, 1 part, until they become covered with a dark deposit. Take them from the solution and remove the black substance with a fine scratch brush. After cleaned in this manner, rinse in hot water and dry in hot sawdust.

A fine orange-yellow tinge may be given to the brass by substituting an equivalent weight of powdered alum for the nitric acid in the solution.—Contributed by Mrs. Richard F. Pohle, E. Lynn, Mass.

A Whetting Block

A handy tool gauge for sharpening the various tools about the household is made of a block of wood with the sides of one end cut sloping in different degrees so that each will serve to secure the proper slant of the cutting edge on a certain tool.

The block of wood with the corners cut is shown in Fig. 1, and the manner of whetting a chisel is shown in Fig. 2.—Contributed by Will Parker, Wibaux, Mont.

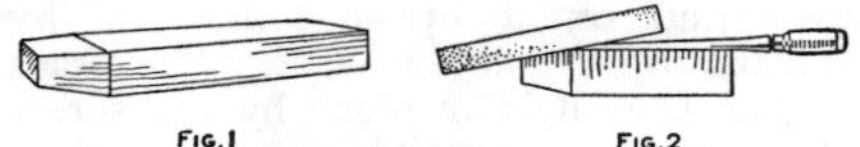

The Sloping Edges on the Block of Wood and the Manner of Whetting a Chisel

¶A cardboard cut the same size as a page and fastened with paper clips in the center of a magazine will prevent the pages from folding over when the magazine is placed in a bookcase.

Submarine Photographs

A photographer at a seashore resort, wishing to increase his sales of souvenir postal cards, rigged up a device for producing negatives to make "submarine" pictures. The device consisted of an aquarium, about 40 in. long, 18 in. high and 6 in. wide. The aquarium was designed to stand on edge or the narrow way, and was equipped with rocks, living sea moss, kelp, and some fish, and the bottom was covered with sand and shells.

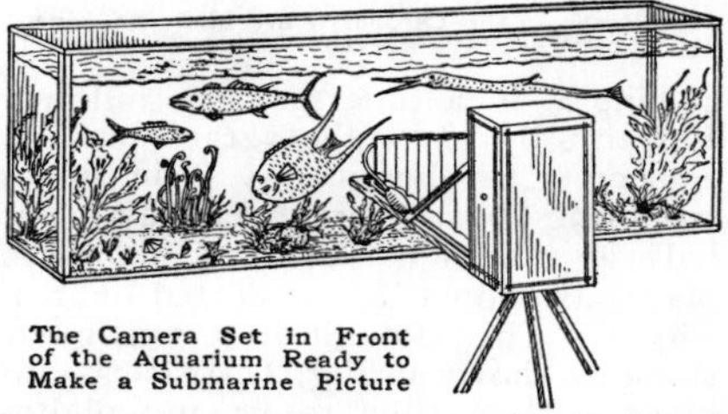

The Camera Set in Front of the Aquarium Ready to Make a Submarine Picture

A canvas was hung back of the aquarium and the camera set in front at such a distance as to make a negative of only the water and the prepared sea bottom. Very fine views that will give the appearance of being made at the bottom of the sea can be produced.

Mending Paper-Pulp Utensils

Pails, washtubs, and other receptacles made of paper pulp, when cut and worn, may be easily mended with adhesive tape. After this is applied to the place to be mended, give the mended part a coating of paint, and when the paint has dried, the surface is given another coat to match the color of the article mended. Leaks may be entirely stopped in this way at a very reasonable cost.—Contributed by Katharine D. Morse, Syracuse, N. Y.

A Homemade Mailing Tube

A photograph or manuscript may be sent through the mail unmounted without the danger of being broken by

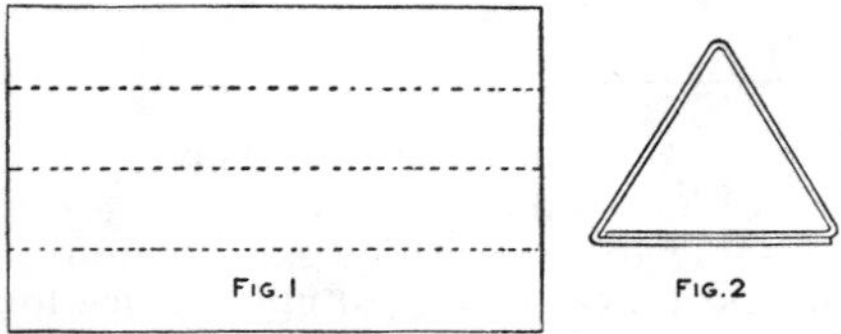

The Bends in the Cardboard are Made on Lines Equal Distances Apart to Form a Triangle

placing it in a tube made as follows: For an 8 by 10-in. photograph procure a piece of cardboard 6 by 10 in., plain mounting board preferred, and cut halfway through the card in three places as shown by the dotted lines in Fig. 1. Then fold it in a triangular shape as shown in Fig. 2. It is easy to make such a tube to fit any photograph or manuscript to be mailed.—Contributed by A. H. Schaefer, Buffalo, N. Y.

Cutter for Lace Leather

Lace leather may be easily cut with an ordinary pocket knife having a U-shaped block fitted on the edge of the blade. The width of the opening should be exactly the same as the thickness of the leather and the width of the lace is determined by the distance between the blade and the depth of the notch. Several places can be provided for the blade to cut different widths of lacing.—Contributed by A. K. Runkle, Kinsman, O.

Refinishing Chairs

When refinishing chairs, a good way to get at the bottom part is to turn the chair upside down and place its seat on the seat of another chair. The legs and rungs can thus be easily cleaned and varnished.—Contributed by A. Mandeville, Ware, Mass.

An Electric Gas Lighter

A very simple and inexpensive electric gas-lighting device is shown in the accompanying illustration. The gas is ignited by means of an electric spark which is produced between the two parts A and B of an electric circuit. This circuit is composed of a source of electrical energy, such as a number of dry cells, a kick coil, the connecting leads, and a special operating switch for opening and closing the circuit to produce the spark. The circuit is normally open, but as the lever controlling the gas valve is moved from one position to the other, by pulling the chains, the lever C is caused to move through a certain arc. Now, as this lever C moves, its upper end passes the projecting point B, which is attached to the upper portion of the burner, and the electric circuit will be completed and broken. Just as the point A leaves contact with the point B an arc will be produced. This arc is greatly intensified by the kick coil, which acts as a sort of reservoir in which energy is stored while the circuit is closed, and upon opening the circuit this stored energy is given out by the kick coil and increases the size of the arc.

The points A and B should both be made of platinum, as other metals will not withstand the extremely high temperature of the arc. Pieces of platinum that will serve very nicely for the purpose may be obtained from an old incandescent lamp. The piece B is mounted on a brass collar, D, by means of a small screw, E. The brass collar D is held in place by the screw F, which draws the two ends together. This collar must be insulated from the stem or fixture by some thin sheets of mica. The upper end of the piece of platinum B should be just high enough to come within the lower edge of the gas flame.

Now mount an arm, C, on the valve stem so that it stands in a vertical position when the lever to which the chains are attached is in a horizontal position. Bend this arm into the form shown in the figure and cut its upper end off so that it is about ½ in. below the outwardly projecting end of the piece of platinum B. Drill a small hole in the upper end of C, and insert a piece of platinum and run some solder around it.

Then the complete burner and valve are mounted on the gas fixture, and from the collar D an insulated wire is run to the point where the battery and kick coil are to be located. The gas fixture itself is to form one side of the electric circuit, and one terminal of the battery should be connected to the gas pipe as shown in the figure.

A kick coil may be made as follows: Procure a small quantity of rather small soft-iron wire and cut a sufficient number of 8-in. lengths to make a bundle about ⅞ in. in diameter. From some good writing paper make a tube, 8 in. long and ⅞ in. in outside diameter. Use at least six layers of paper and glue the various layers together in forming this paper tube. After the tube has dried thoroughly, fill it with the pieces of iron wire until it is perfectly hard. Cut from some ½-in. hard wood, two pieces, 3 in. square, and drill a ⅞-in. hole in the center of each of these to a depth of ⅜ in. Now glue these pieces to the completed core and the winding can begin as soon as the glue is dry. Wind on this spool six layers of double cotton-covered No. 18 gauge wire, insulating the various layers from each other with several thicknesses of good writing paper. This coil is then mounted on a wooden base and suitable terminals provided.

At least four dry cells will be required to give satisfactory results. Bear in mind that the gas must be escaping from the burner when the arc is formed. The adjustment of the arm A, as given above, may result in the gas valve being closed when the arc is formed, and the device will then fail to operate. If this is the case, the arm C should be loosened and moved back so that the circuit is broken at a later time while the valve is being moved from the "off" to "on" position. The circuit should be closed for some little time before it is opened so that some energy may be stored in the kick coil. If the wire A is made long enough to

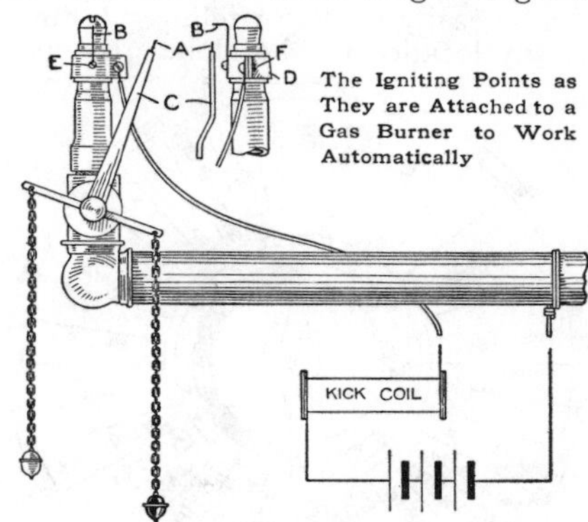

The Igniting Points as They are Attached to a Gas Burner to Work Automatically

project a short distance above B, it will result in the circuit being closed for a longer time than it would if they just touched.

Stretching Tight-Fitting Shoes

A tight-fitting shoe can be stretched by filling it tightly with oats dampened in water and packing some old paper in the top. The grain will quickly swell and, as the leather will get softened by the dampness, the shoe will be rapidly stretched. Allow time for the oats to dry out before removing them. —Contributed by Fred L. King, Islip, New York.

Pad for a Percolator

To prevent heating the bowl of a percolator and burning the handle, as often happens when it is placed on a stove, use an ordinary asbestos pad with a hole cut in the center as shown, just large enough to admit the foot of the percolator.—Contributed by Mrs. G. W. Coplin, Bay City, Mich.

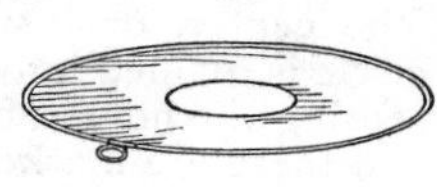

¶If a motorcycle engine is raced while on the stand, the cylinder will heat, often with the result that it is ruined.

Compass Time Chart

A very instructive little instrument can be easily made for telling the time of any location on the globe. Its con-

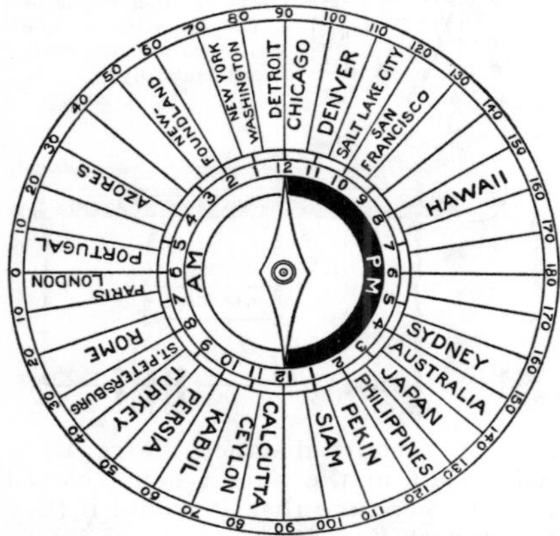

A Time Chart for Telling the Hour of the Day at Any Place on the Globe

struction is extremely simple. Draw a circle, about 1½ in. in diameter, on a piece of paper and then draw a larger circle, about 4 in. in diameter, around the first one. Divide the circles into 36 equal parts and draw lines from one circle to the other like the spokes in a wheel. These divisions will be 10 deg., or 40 minutes of time, apart. They should be numbered around the outside, commencing at a point marked 0 and marking the numbers by tens each way until they meet at 180 deg.

Using a map of the eastern and western hemispheres, write the names of the different cities on the globe in their respective degrees of longitude. The center, or inside, of the smaller circle is divided into 24 divisions representing the hours of the day and night, and these are marked from 1 to 12, the left side being forenoon, and the right, afternoon. The noon mark must be set on the line nearest to the location in which the instrument is to be used. For instance, if the instrument is to be used in Chicago, it is set as shown in the sketch.

The disk is mounted on a thin piece of board and a pin is driven through the center from the back side so as to make a projecting point on the upper side on which to place the magnetized needle of a compass. The needle may be taken from any cheap compass.

All that is necessary to do, to tell what time it is in any other city or country, is to turn the instrument so that the name of that place points toward the sun, when the north end of the compass needle will point on the disk to the time it is in that city or locality.—Contributed by Henry J. Marion, Pontiac, Mich.

Reversing Switch for Small Motors

A reversing switch made as follows will be found very serviceable in reversing the direction of the rotation of small motors, changing the polarity of electromagnets, etc.

A diagram of the connections to the switch and on the switch base is given in the sketch, and in this particular case the switch is shown connected to a small toy motor. The field of the motor is represented by A, the armature by B; and C, D, E, and F are four binding posts mounted on the base of the switch; G, H, and I are three contacts; J and K are terminals of the switch blades, and L a single-pole switch. The two blades of the reversing switch have their lower ends fastened to the terminals J and K, and their upper ends, which are indicated by arrow heads, may be moved over the contacts G, H, and I. For the position of the reversing switch shown by the full lines, J is connected to G and K to H. When the switch is thrown to the right-hand position, as shown by the dotted lines, J is connected to H and K to I. It is obvious that the direction of the current through the armature B will be reversed when the reversing switch is thrown from one position to the other. The direction in which the armature rotates will change, due to the reversal in direction of the current through it. The same results could be obtained by reversing the current in the field winding A. But it must always be borne in mind that in order to reverse the direction of rotation, the current must be reversed in the armature only or in the field only, not in both.

The above switch may be constructed as follows: First, procure a piece of well-seasoned hard wood, say maple, ½ in. thick, 2½ in. wide and 4 in. long. Round off the corners and the edges of this piece on one side and drill the holes indicated in the sketch. The four corner holes should be of such a size as to accommodate the screws used in mounting four small back-connected binding posts. The remaining holes should be ⅛ in. All these holes should be countersunk with a ⅜-in. bit to a depth of ¼ in. on the under side.

Cut from some $\frac{1}{16}$-in. sheet brass two pieces, 2¾ in. long, ½ in. wide at one end and ¼ in. at the other, and round their ends. Drill a ⅛-in. hole through the larger end of each of these pieces, ¼ in. from the end, and also a hole through each, 1¼ in. from the narrow end. The last two holes should be threaded for ⅛-in. machine screws. Obtain five ⅛-in. brass bolts, ½ in. long. File the heads of three of these bolts down to a thickness of approximately $\frac{1}{16}$ in. and mount them in the holes G, H and I. Before mounting anything on the base the grooves indicated by the heavy dotted lines should be cut in the under side so that the various points may be properly connected by conductors placed in the grooves. Now mount the two pieces of sheet brass upon the base by means of the remaining two bolts, which should pass through the holes J and K. A $\frac{1}{16}$-in. washer should be placed between the pieces of brass and the wooden base.

Procure a piece of ⅛-in. fiber, 1¼ in. long and ⅜ in. broad. Drill two ⅛-in. holes in this piece, one in each end, so that they are 1 in. apart. Drill a third ⅛-in. hole in the center and fasten a small handle to the piece of fiber. Now mount this piece upon the two pieces of brass that form the blades of the switch by means of two small ⅛-in. brass machine screws.

Two small brads should be driven into the wooden base so as to prevent the possibility of the switch blades

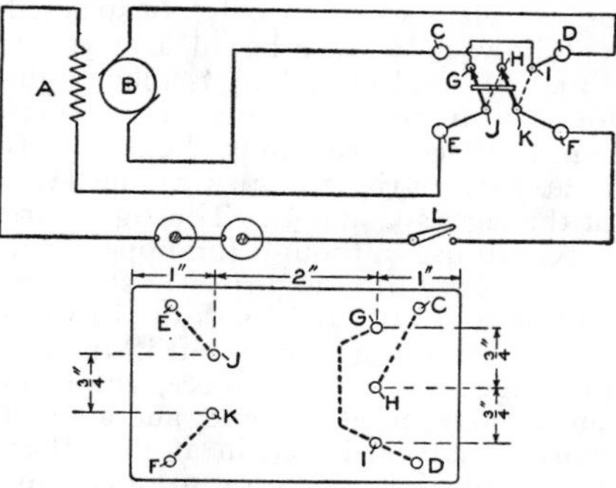

Diagram of the Wiring to a Small Motor and the Details of the Switch

moving beyond their proper position. Two pieces of $\frac{1}{16}$-in. fiber should be placed between the heads of the screws G and H, and H and I, to prevent the ends of the switch blades from dropping down on the wooden base.

Adjustable Rod for Potted Plants

Procure a brass sash-curtain rod of the telescoping kind and stick the solid part into the soil close to the plant and tie it to the rod. As the plant grows move the tubular part of the rod upward to correspond with the height of the plant. This makes a good support and is not so unsightly as a stick.—Contributed by Gertrude M. Bender, Utica, N. Y.

Wrench for Different-Size Nuts

A very handy wrench can be made from a piece of square bar, shaped as shown and fitted with a handle. The joint at A may be halved and riveted or a weld made as desired. The size

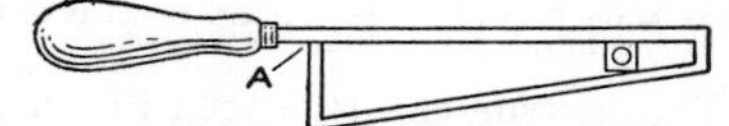

The Sloping Notch in the Wrench Permits Its Use on Nuts of Various Size

of the bar and the space between the parts will depend on the size of nuts to be turned.

A Simple Sextant

A sextant for measuring the latitude of any place can be easily constructed as follows: While a board, 1 in. thick, 6 in. wide, and 12 in. long is about right for the instrument, any dimensions can be used, providing the line AB is at perfect right angles to the level of the sights C and D. The sights are better to use, although the upper edge of the board, if it is perfectly straight, will do as well. If it is desired to use sights, a slight groove is cut in the upper edge; a V-shaped piece, cut from tin, is fastened at one end, and a small pointed nail is driven in at the other. In doing this, be sure to level the bottom of the V-notch and nail point so that in drawing the line AB it will be at perfect right angles to a line between the sights. A tack is driven into the side of the board at the upper edge, a line fastened to it and a weight tied to the lower end which should swing below the lower edge of the board.

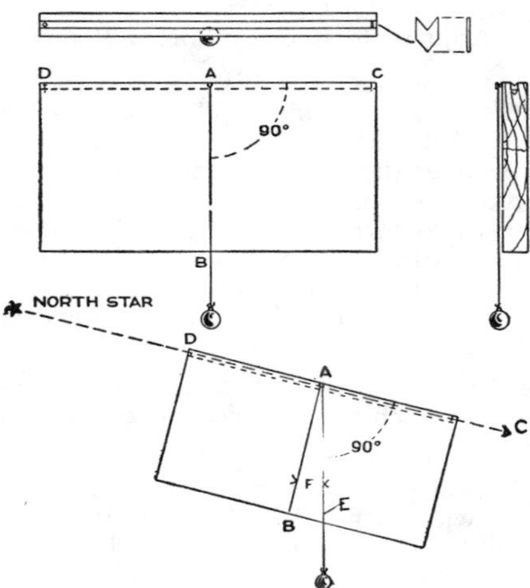

The Main Part of the Instrument Consists of a Board with a Plumb Attached

The instrument is placed in such a manner that the North Star is sighted, as shown, and the point on the lower edge of the board is marked where the line E comes to rest. A line is then drawn from A to the point marked and the angle F is measured with a protractor. The number of degrees in this angle will be approximately equal to

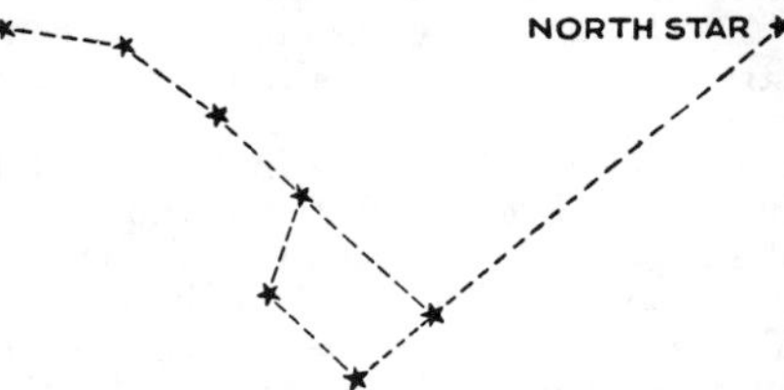

The Two Stars at the End of the Great Dipper are Pointers to the North Star

the number of degrees in the latitude of that place.

The North Star is easily located by reason of its position relative to the Great Dipper, as shown by the diagram.—Contributed by Carlos Harrison, Anderson, Ind.

How to Make a Taper Ferrule

Having occasion to make a taper ferrule of irregular form, a pattern from which to cut the material was made as follows: A mandrel of the desired shape was made, a piece of writing paper, soaked in water, wrapped around the mandrel, and a piece of twine wound over it, coil after coil like the thread on a spool. This was allowed to dry thoroughly, using a little heat. The string was then removed and a longitudinal cut made in the paper while on the mandrel. When opened this paper formed the pattern.

A piece of metal was cut from the pattern and the edges were brought together and brazed with spelter. The point of the mandrel was driven through a piece of block tin, about ½ in. thick. The mandrel was then removed, the ferrule was placed on it, and both then started in the hole made in the tin and driven through it. As the mandrel with the ferrule passed through the tin, the metal was shaped exactly to the mandrel. It is best to oil the hole in the tin slightly. Tin is preferable as it is harder.—Contributed by James H. Beebee, Rochester, N. Y.

How to Make a Continuously Ringing Bell

The bell shown in the accompanying diagram is known as the continuously ringing type, and has quite a field of usefulness in connection with burglar alarms, door-bell signals, telephone signals, etc. The operation of the bell proper is identical with that of the ordinary vibrating bell and, in addition, there is a circuit controlled by the armature of the bell, which is normally open, but becomes closed as soon as the armature is drawn over. The closing of this circuit by the operation of the armature amounts to keeping the push button in the bell circuit depressed, and the bell will continue to ring until the latch A is restored by pulling the cord B.

Any ordinary vibrating bell may be converted into a continuously ringing bell as follows: In the armature, C, mount a short metal pin, D, and round off its under side slightly. A latch, A, should now be constructed similar to the one shown in the sketch and mounted in such a position that its left end will rest on the outer end of the pin D when the armature, C, of the bell is in its extreme outer position. The length of the latch should be such that its left end will drop off the end of the pin D, due to the action of the spring E, when the armature C is drawn over

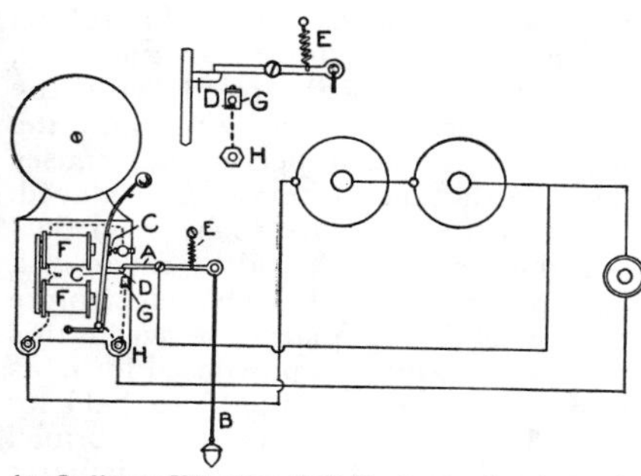

An Ordinary Vibrating Bell Used as a Continuously Ringing Bell, and the Wiring Diagram

by the electromagnets F, thus allowing it to come into contact with a spring G, which is electrically connected to the terminal of the bell marked H. The latch A is connected to one side of the line, as shown in the sketch, so as to include the bell winding and battery in a local circuit that is formed by the latch coming in contact with the spring G. The end of the latch should not interfere with the free operation of the armature when it is resting on the spring G. A cord, B, attached to the outer end of the latch, is used in restoring it, and at the same time stopping the bell from ringing. The tension in the spring E should be so adjusted that the operation of the latch is sure and firm, yet not too stiff.

A Mission-Style Inkstand

Having a couple of good-sized ink bottles of the ordinary type lying

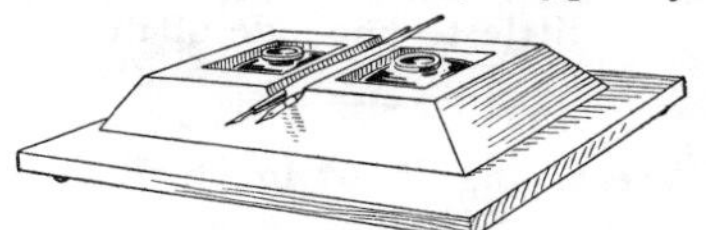

Two Pieces of Pine Shaped to Receive the Inkwells and Finished in Mission Style

around, I fashioned a mission-style stand for them out of a piece of yellow pine, 2 in. wide and 3 in. long, set on another piece of pine large enough to project all around on all four sides of the block, for a base. The wells were cut out with a wood chisel, and the parts fastened together with screws. The supports were four brass-head or upholsterer's tacks. The finish was flat black.—Contributed by James M. Kane, Doylestown, Pa.

Raising Dents in Wood

The imprint of a hammer on finely finished wood caused by a glancing blow, or otherwise, may be removed in the following manner: Pour enough wood alcohol on the dented spot to cover it, then light the alcohol and allow it to burn out. The heat will expand the wood and raise it enough so that the spot can be planed and smoothed in the usual manner.—Contributed by W. F. Elwell, Waltham, Massachusetts.

Carrying Two Pails in One Hand

When it is necessary to carry two small filled pails in one hand and a package in the other it will be found a very difficult job, if the contents are liquid. Procure a stick of sufficient size to carry the weight of the pails and cut a small notch in each end to admit the bail. Place a pail on each end of the stick and take hold in the center, or, if the pails are not equally filled, a little to one side of the center.

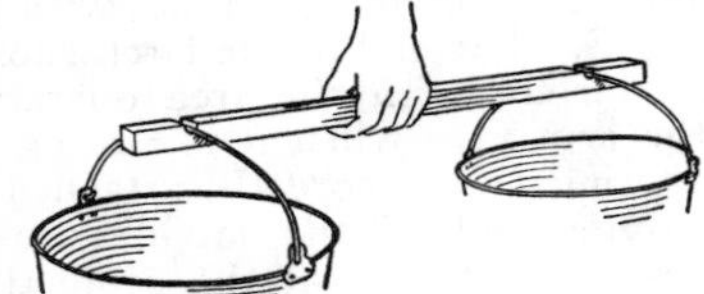

Two Filled Pails can be Readily Carried by Placing the Bails on the Ends of a Stick

Preserving Paint in Open Cans

To keep paint from drying out in an open can it is necessary to exclude the air from the oil. This can be done by procuring an air-tight paper sack, which is tested by blowing into it. Set the can into the sack and tie it tightly with a cord. Mixed paint will be kept in a working state in this manner.

Jelly-Straining Stand

Procure a board, 7/8 in. thick and 18 in. square, and cut a hole, about 1 ft. in diameter, in the center. Fasten posts, 4 ft. long, to each corner. Screw hooks are located around the edge of the hole to catch into the cloth used for holding the fruit. The stand is high enough to be convenient and admit a vessel beneath to catch the juice.

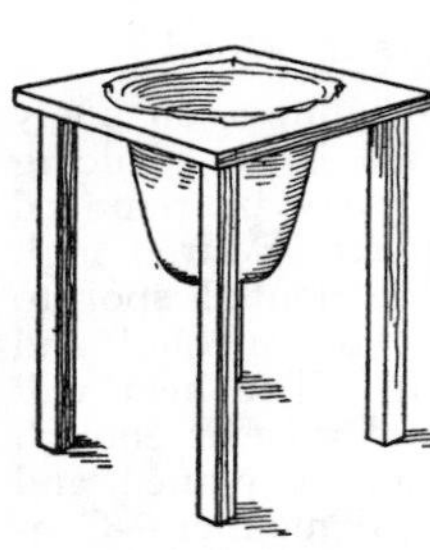

Renewing Dry Batteries

It is a well-known fact that dry cells commence to deteriorate from the time they are manufactured, and it is a matter of considerable uncertainty in purchasing cells to know whether they will continue to be efficient for their supposed natural life under the existing conditions of service, or for only a small part of this period. When the voltage of a dry cell falls below a certain value it is usually discarded and replaced by a new one, which often means quite an expense. The following simple suggestion will enable one to renew the prematurely exhausted cell with very little trouble and slight expense, so that its period of usefulness will be extended for a length of time, at least equal to that for which it could be used if put into service immediately after its manufacture.

The procedure in renewing the cell is as follows: A casing is placed outside of the zinc-containing case, having inside dimensions a little greater than the zinc cup. The space between the zinc cup and case is filled with a dry electrolyte, which, upon the addition of moisture, sets up a chemical action with the exterior surface of the zinc, and the latter having been perforated, causes electrical action to be again produced.

The casing, or cup, to be used outside the zinc cup should be made of a waterproof material. The electrolyte instead of being placed between this cup and the zinc in a powdered form, as might be expected, should be held by several layers of blotting paper, formed into a cylinder of the proper diameter to fit snugly on the outside of the zinc cup. This porous cup should be impregnated with a solution containing the following materials in the approximate amounts given: Muriate of ammonia, 10 parts; bichromate of potash, 4 parts, and chloride of sodium, 4 parts. After the porous cup has thoroughly soaked in the above solution it should be dried by passing a roller over its external surface when it is mounted on a wooden cylinder of proper diameter. The moisture-proof cup may be formed outside the porous cup by covering the latter with several coats of waterproofing paste and winding on several thicknesses of common manila paper, each layer of paper being treated with the paste. A disk of cardboard, properly treated, should be placed in the end of the cylinder to form the bottom, and the edge of the manila paper folded in over it and pasted in place.

The pasteboard covering surrounding the zinc cup of the cell should be removed and the surface of the zinc thoroughly cleaned. The coal tar in the top of the zinc cup should be removed by tapping around the edge with a hammer, and a large number of small holes should be made in the walls of the cup with a sharp instrument. Then put the cell within the porous cup and fill the top with clear water, preferably rain water. A chemical reaction will immediately take place between the outer surface of the zinc and the chemicals contained in the material forming the porous cup, and the terminal voltage of the cell will be practically the same as it was when the cell was new. The water, of course, must be replenished from time to time on account of evaporation, and the useful life of the cell can be prolonged for a considerable time. A part cross section of a cell treated as described above is shown in the accompanying sketch.

Workbench Equipment for a Table Top

The average home mechanic with a few tools seldom has a place to work and is usually without a workbench. As this was my case, I constructed a bench equipment that I could easily clamp to the kitchen or other table and thus have the necessary tools at hand for work. A plank, 2 in. thick, 10 in. wide and 18 in. long, was planed and

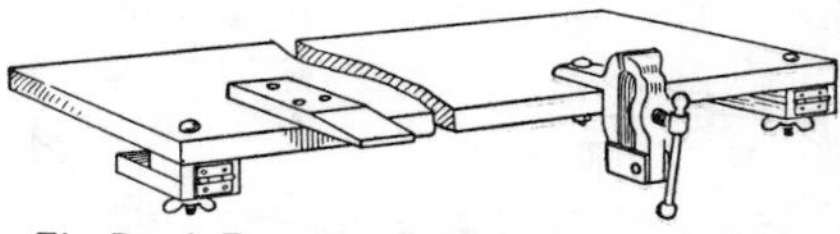

The Bench Top can be Quickly Attached to Any Table Top without Harming It

smoothed up on all sides, and a vise and a bench pin were fastened on one edge.

To the under side of the same edge two blocks were securely fastened, as shown, and to these blocks two other pieces were fastened with hinges. With a bolt, running through from the top, and a thumb nut used underneath, these pieces are used as clamps for holding the bench to the table top. The top can be removed and set away in a closet when not in use.—Contributed by Wm. H. Hathaway, Nutley, N. J.

A Nonsticking Drawer Guide

The guide shown is nonbinding and has been found thoroughly practical after several years' use on furniture. The guide A consists of a piece of wood, about 1⅛ in. square, with a concave cut in its upper edge, the width being about ¾ in. and the depth such as not to cut through the extending end projecting over the crossbar B.

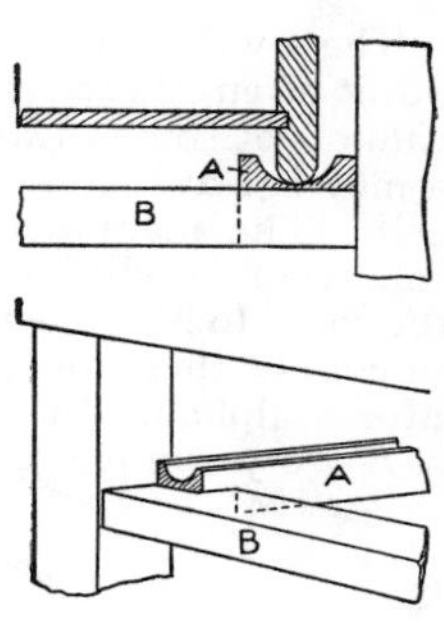

The drawer sides have a half-round edge on the bottom edge to run in the groove in the guide. The difference in width between the groove in the guide and the rounding edge on the drawer side causes the drawer always to ride snugly without binding as the wood expands or contracts with changes in the weather.—Contributed by Herman Hermann, Portland, Ind.

A Milk Stool

The stool is made of three pieces of board and a piece of round, or stake, iron. The appearance and manner of

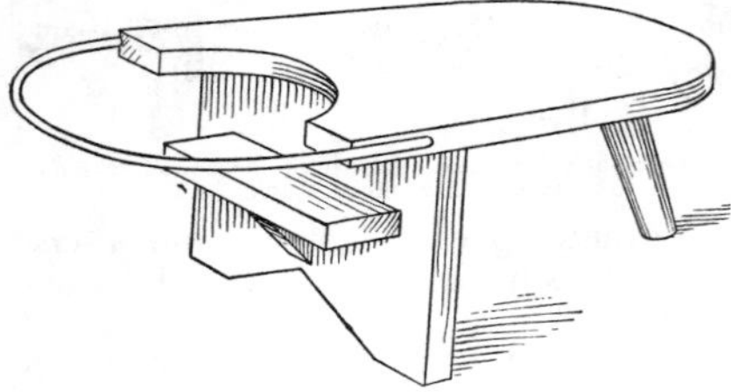

A Milk Stool Having a Place to Keep the Bucket Clean and at the Right Height

construction are clearly shown in the illustration. The seat board is sawed out to fit the circumference of the bucket to be used, and the iron is also bent to this curve and fastened to the board as shown. The little shelf on the front support holds the bucket at the right height, and keeps it clean and out of the way of the cow's foot while milking.

Sounder for Wireless-Telegraph Messages

The owner of an amateur wireless outfit often has reason to regret that he cannot let some of his friends listen to a message at the same time as he himself. The magnifier described in the following permits all those present in the room to hear the message, provided, of course, they are able to interpret the Morse alphabet by sound.

A very simple means, making the

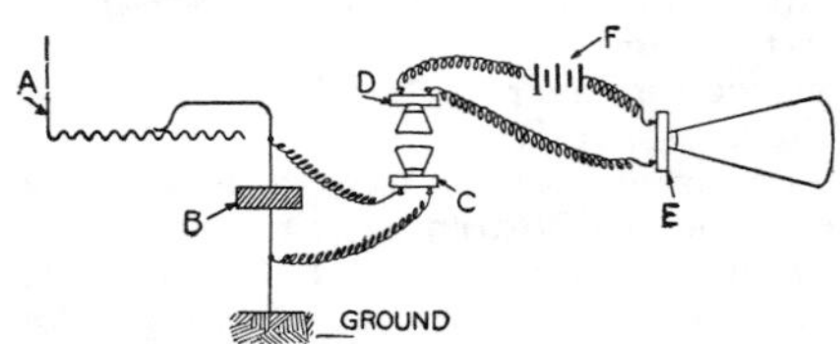

The Phonograph Horn as It is Connected to a Detector for Transmitting the Messages

message audible at a distance of about 10 ft., is to attach a phonograph horn, or a horn of cardboard or metal, to the telephone receiver, but a much better arrangement can be made as shown in the diagram, in which A represents the antenna or aerial; B, the detector, and C, the receiver. Procure a small microphone, D, placing its mouthpiece closely against the receiver—for the sake of clearness the two are separated in the diagram—and connect the former with a battery, F, of two or three dry cells, in series with the microphone of an ordinary telephone transmitter provided with a large horn. The effect obtained by this simple means will be surprising.

Joint for Mission Furniture

The mortise for this joint is made in the usual manner, the only requirements being that the mortise is run through the piece, and the tenon is cut 1/8 in. shorter than the depth of the

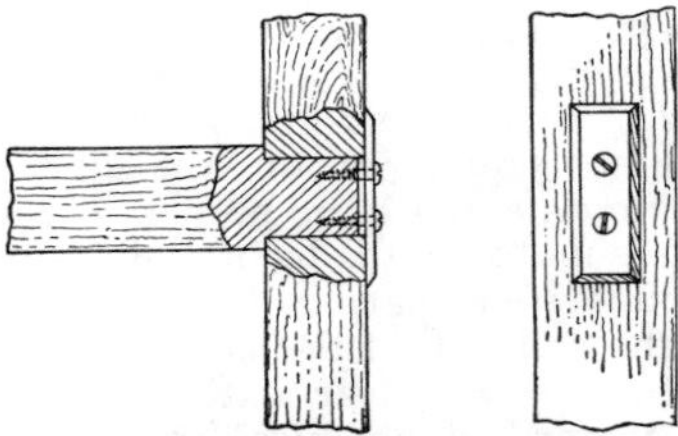

Metal Covering and Holder for a Tenon and Mortise Joint on Mission Furniture

mortise or the width of the piece it is entering. The end of the tenon and the mortise is then covered with a piece of metal, fastened with screws as shown. The metal can be of any desired material and beveled on the edges. This makes a very good knockdown joint for mission furniture.—Contributed by H. R. Allen, Cheyenne, Wyoming.

A Towel Roller

A substantial, convenient and nonrusting towel roller can be made from 8 or 9 of the familiar wood handles on bundle carriers and a length of brass curtain rod. The bracket ends can be shaped from any piece of wood of suitable dimensions. The rollers and ends can be finished as desired.—Contributed by F. E. S., E. Lynn, Mass.

An Electric Shaving Mug

The general use of electricity in the home has opened up a new field in the way of heating and cooking utensils. While these utensils are sold by electric-supply houses, some of them can be easily made at home and answer the purpose just as nicely. One of these is the electric shaving mug.

A mug that will stand heat is the first thing required, and an aluminum cup of standard shape and design, which can be bought in almost every town, will do perfectly well. These cups are spun from a flat sheet and have no seams to open and leak, and it is necessary that no holes be drilled in the cup as it is impossible to make such a hole watertight. The heating element must be fastened to the mug with a clamp. The clamp will also allow the heating coil to be removed for repairs without injury to the mug. The bottoms of these mugs have a flange which makes a recessed part and in this the heating element is placed.

The legs of the mug are made of sheet brass as shown in Fig. 1, one of the three having an enlargement near its center with a hole for an insulating button (Fig. 2), of "transite" or some other material, to hold the supply cord in place.

The clamp for holding the heating coil in place is shown in Fig. 3. This clamp has a screw in the center to tighten it in place. The legs and clamp may be nickelplated if desired.

The heating coil is shown in Fig. 4 which is a coil of flat "Nichrome" wire, or ribbon as it is called, 12 ft. long, $\frac{1}{16}$ in. wide and 3/1000 in. thick. This is equal in cross section to a No. 26 gauge wire. To wind this coil, procure a block of wood, ⅞ in. thick and about 4 in. square, with a ½-in. hole in the center for an axis or pivot. Clamp a ½-in. rod in a vise so that the block can be rotated about it. Begin at the center and fasten one end of the ribbon to the block, leaving about 2 in. projecting for a connection, then proceed to wind the ribbon in a spiral coil, separating each turn from the preceding one with a strand of asbestos cord. A small section of the coil is shown in Fig. 5, in which A, or the light part, represents the asbestos insulation, and B, or the black lines, the heating element. The insulation may be obtained by untwisting some ⅛-in. round asbestos packing and using one of the strands. This cord insulates each turn of the ribbon from the other and the current must travel through the whole coil without jumping across from one turn to the other. The whole coil must be closely wound to get it into the limited space at the bottom of the mug.

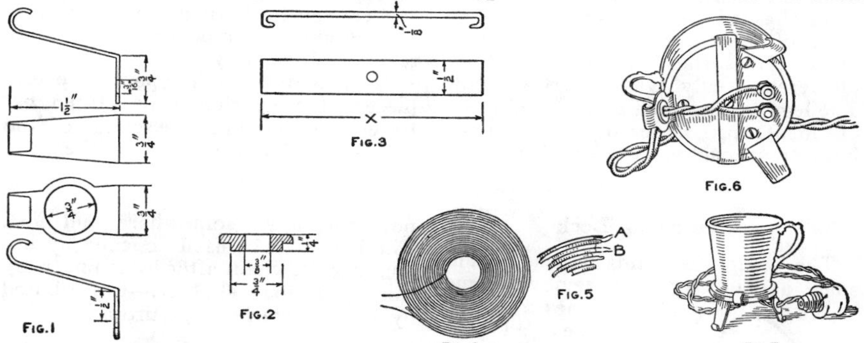

Detail of the Parts for the Construction of an Electric Shaving Mug. The Heating of Sufficient Water for a Shave can be Accomplished at a Nominal Cost

Before taking the coil from the block, rub into its surface a little asbestos retort cement, or a cement composed of a mixture of silicate of soda and silica, or glass sand. This mixture, when dry, will tend to hold the coil together and the current may be passed through the coil to test it as well as to bake it in its coiled shape.

The support for the heating coil is made of a piece of $\frac{5}{16}$-in. asbestos wood or transite. Cut it to fit into the recessed bottom of the mug, then with a chisel remove the material in the top to form a depression $\frac{1}{16}$ in. deep to receive the coil with its top flush. The leads of the coil are run through the disk. The surface of the coil is then plastered evenly with retort cement. The legs are fastened to a second piece of insulating material with roundhead brass machine screws, ½ in. long, with nuts. The heads of these screws are shown in Fig. 6, the nuts being above the brass and between the two insulating pieces.

The ends of the heating ribbon are brought through the lower insulating disk and attached to binding posts as shown. The leads may be covered with tape to prevent any short circuit.

The mug uses 3½ amperes at 110 volts, either direct or alternating current, and it will cost about 3 cents an hour to operate it. Care should be taken to use a separable attachment for connecting, as an ordinary lamp socket may be burned out by turning off the current, it being adapted only to a small capacity.

In assembling the parts, several pieces of mica should be placed between the coil and the metal of the mug to insulate the coil from the mug.

A Handbag Lock

The pickpocket finds it easy to unsnap a handbag and remove some of the contents, especially in crowded places. To make it less easy for the pickpocket, I fixed my mother's handbag as shown in the sketch. I used a chain which had served its way holding a small coin purse—any small chain will do—by passing it through the links that hold the handle and winding it once or twice around the snap fasteners to hold them securely closed.

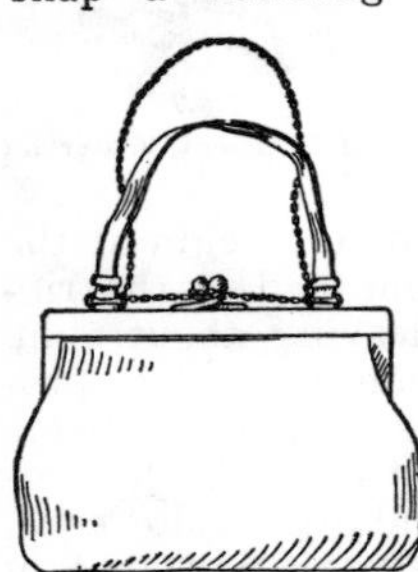

The chain may be either shortened enough to make it convenient to hold with the handle of the handbag, or may be left long and used over the shoulder under the coat, thus making it possible to have both hands free for shopping while the handbag hangs by the side. This leaves a person free from the worry of taking care that the bag is not laid down somewhere and lost. The bag may be easily opened by unwinding the chain after loosening it by raising the bag slightly.—Contributed by Wm. Waterhouse, Aurora, Ill.

An Emery-Cloth Holder

Emery cloth in sheets is very easily spoiled around a workbench. Oil or other fluids used on work are apt to drop on it and when wet for a short time the abrasive is useless. The illustration shows a tin holder, A, that can be placed on the under side of the bench where space is not required for drawer room.

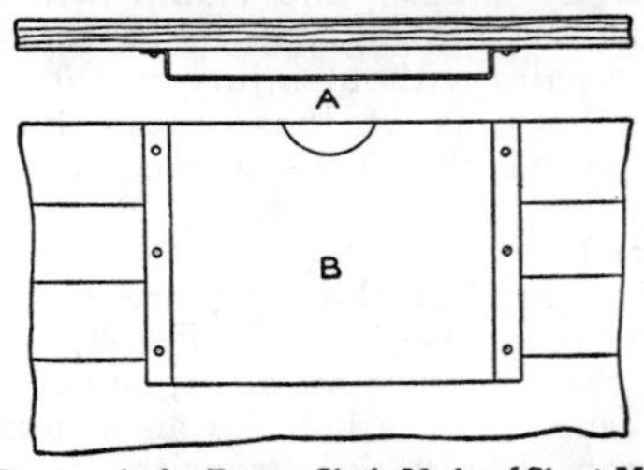

A Receptacle for Emery Cloth Made of Sheet Metal or Tin and Fastened to a Bench

The portion cut out of the bottom

of the holder B is to enable the workman to easily grasp the sheets of emery cloth. As the holder is on the under side of the bench, there is little danger of any liquid or other substance spoiling the sheets. The sheets are also within easy reach.—Contributed by F. W. Bently, Huron, S. D.

The Operation of the Compass

After trying to tell a few small boys what a compass is, they wanted a practical illustration—something they could see. Not having a compass or knowing where to locate one handily, I used a piece of cork with needles and a needle for a pivot and found it very satisfactory. The method used is shown in the sketch.

It is best not to magnetize both needles unless care is exercised in maintaining pole relationship, or they will oppose each other and not point to the north. The extreme ends or the heads of the needles must be opposites, the head of one negative and the head of the other positive.

If a good compass is brought carelessly in contact with a magnet, the poles may become reversed and the north end will no longer point to the north but to the south until the current has been reversed again by bringing the opposite pole of the magnet in contact with the compass.—Contributed by W. H. Albright, Bellevue, O.

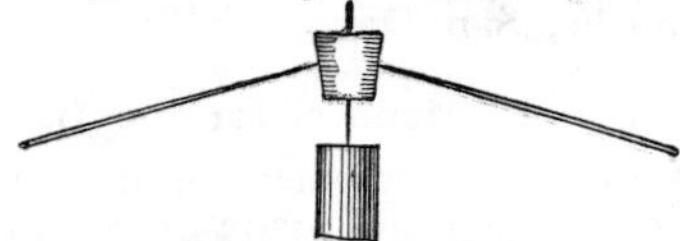

Two Large Needles in a Cork Balanced on a Central Needle to Make Them Revolve Easily

Thawing Out Frozen Pipes

When the water pipes connecting a range boiler become frozen, get a plumber and avoid an explosion of the water back. If, however, the frozen pipe is a cold-water pipe in no way connected with the hot-water boiler, it can be thawed out as follows:

Procure some grain alcohol—not denatured or wood alcohol—and after turning the spigot upward or upside down, as shown, open it and pour in the alcohol. When the water begins to flow turn it to its proper position.—Contributed by James M. Kane, Doylestown, Pa.

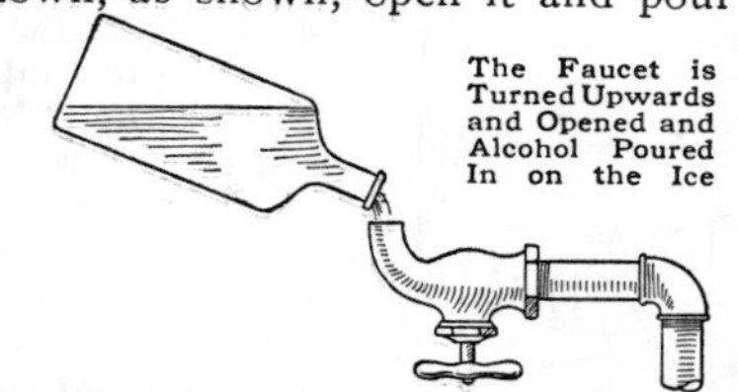

The Faucet is Turned Upwards and Opened and Alcohol Poured In on the Ice

A Wire Clothespin

The pin is made of galvanized wire, A, 8 or 10 in. long, wound spirally, B, on a round surface, such as a broom handle, to make the holding part. The ends are fastened together as shown. The space between the spiral turns makes the cloth-holding part.—Contributed by Wesley H. Freeman, Palestine, Tex.

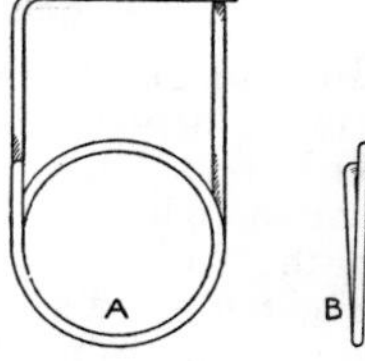

Vent for Pouring Heavy Liquids

A tube placed in a jug or bottle as shown in the sketch will assist greatly in removing molasses or heavy liquids. The tube can be placed in the receptacle without getting the liquid inside by holding a finger over the outer end. The air can easily enter without disturbing the flow of the liquid.—Contributed by Homer Payear, Owensboro, Ky.

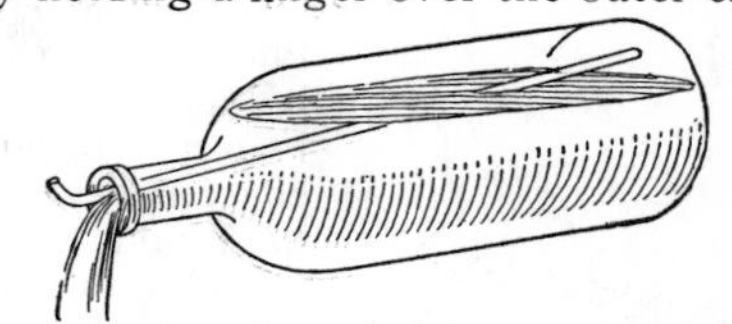

The Vacuum Caused by the Flow of Heavy Liquids is Easily Overcome by the Air Tube

A Hat Hanger

Procure a piece of 1/8-in. wire, about 3 ft. long, bend it into the shape shown in the sketch, and sharpen the projecting end. Drive this into the wall above a coat hanger. This provides a better hat hanger than the ordinary hook.—Contributed by John D. Watt, Roxbury, Mass.

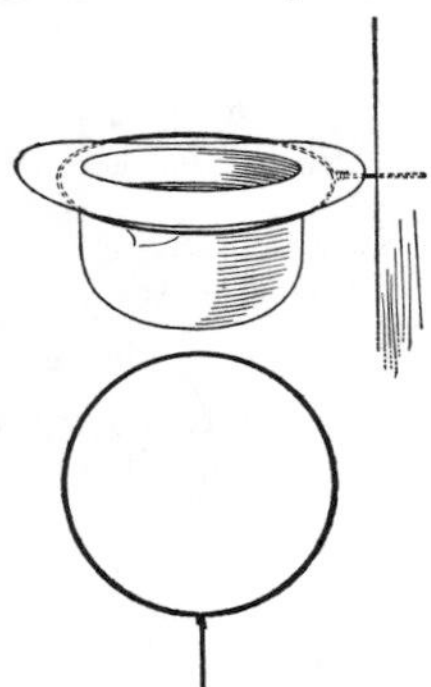

Repairing a Broken Tenon on a Chair Post

Instead of cutting off the four posts to make new tenons where one tenon was broken I used a metal piece made from a short length of bicycle tubing, as shown. The tube was slotted two ways to make four parts which were turned out and flattened. The remaining end of the tube was slipped over the broken post and the four parts were fastened with screws to the under side of the chair seat.—Contributed by Chas. H. Roberts, Calumet, Mich.

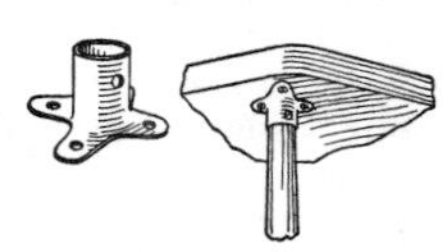

Substitute for an Iron-Holder Knob

The wood knob on the holder for my irons became charred from the heat and finally broke away from the pin. The pin would get so hot in continued use that it could not be moved without burning my fingers. I remedied the difficulty by attaching a short string to the handle and the pin. A pull on the string with the forefinger readily released the iron. I have found this better than the knob, as it is handier to use.—Contributed by Mrs. H. C. Dixon, Johnstown, Pa.

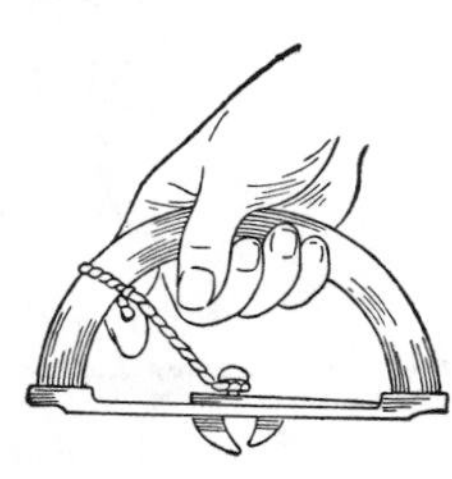

An Egg-Frying Pan

The frying of eggs in an ordinary frying pan is accompanied with some difficulty in removing them when they are cooked without breaking the yolk. Then, sometimes, the pan is too hot and the egg sticks to the pan and the top remains uncooked. A much better way is to shape a piece of sheet metal or tin as shown in the sketch to place the egg in and use it in the ordinary pan. It will not burn the egg, and the egg can be lifted out of the pan and easily slipped on a plate or toast when it is cooked.—Contributed by W. A. Jaquythe, San Diego, Cal.

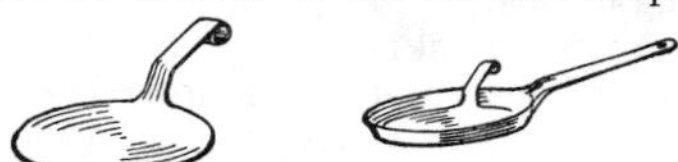

A Metal Plate for Use in an Ordinary Frying Pan to Cook Eggs without Scorching Them

A Sander Mandrel for the Lathe

A cylindrical sander for use in the lathe can be easily made of two pieces of wood, turned to a diameter that will take the stock size of sandpaper, and clamped together with pinch dogs at the ends. One edge of the sandpaper is clamped between the pieces and then it is wrapped around the wood, the opposite edge being glued to the starting edge, as shown at A. The dimensions given are for a 9 by 12-in. sheet of sandpaper. The sander is easily placed in the lathe centers when needed, and the sandpaper may be replaced at any time.—Contributed by James T. Gaffney, Chicago.

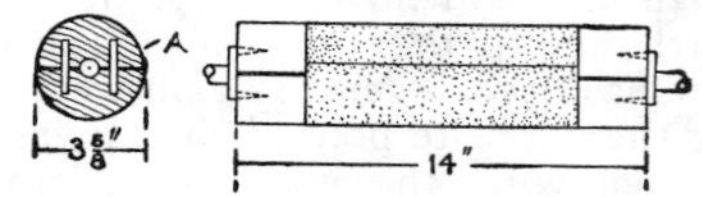

A Wood Mandrel for Attaching Regular Sheets of Sandpaper to Make a Lathe Sander

How to Construct a Simple Galvanometer

A galvanometer is an instrument used to detect the presence of an electrical current in a circuit or to measure the value of the current in amperes. The operation of practically all galvanometers is based upon the same principle, and they differ chiefly in mechanical construction and the relative arrangement of their different parts.

A very simple galvanometer, that will give quite satisfactory results, under favorable conditions, may be constructed as follows: Turn from a piece of hard wood a ring having dimensions corresponding to those given in the cross section, Fig. 1. Fill the groove in this ring to within 1/8 in. of the top with No. 18 gauge double-cotton-covered copper wire, insulating the different layers from each other by means of a layer of good bond paper. The winding may be started by drilling a small hole through the side of the groove, as close to the bottom as possible, and allowing about 6 in. of the wire to protrude through it. The outside end may be terminated in a similar manner, and the two ends should be on the same side of the ring, or as near each other as possible. A protecting covering of bookbinder's paper is placed over the winding and the completed ring given a coat of shellac. The electric current to be detected or measured is to pass around the winding of this coil and produce an effect upon a compass needle mounted in its center. In order that the current may produce a maximum effect upon the needle, the coil should be mounted in a vertical position.

The base upon which the ring is to be mounted may be cut from some 1/2-in. hard wood. It should be circular in form and about 5 in. in diameter, and have its upper edge rounded off and shellacked to improve its appearance. The ring is mounted in a vertical position on this base, which may be done as follows: Cut a flat surface on each of the flanges of the ring so that it will stand in a vertical position and the terminals of the winding will be as near as possible to the

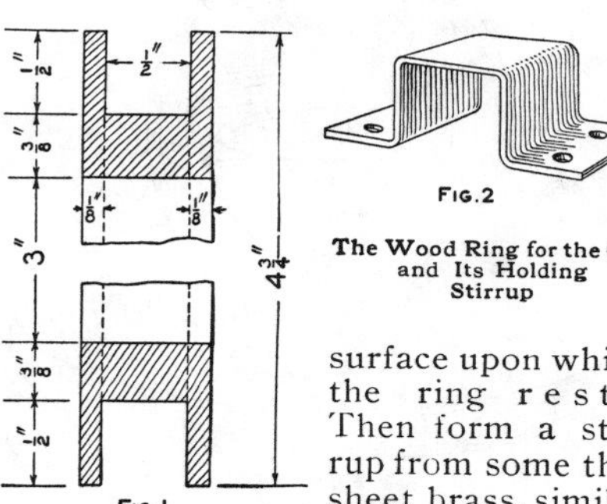

The Wood Ring for the Coil and Its Holding Stirrup

surface upon which the ring rests. Then form a stirrup from some thin sheet brass, similar to that shown in Fig. 2, so that it will fit tightly over the ring and its outwardly projecting ends will rest upon the base of the instrument. Small wood screws are used in fastening the stirrup to the base. The fastening may be made more secure by cutting a groove across the inside of the ring for the stirrup to fit in, Fig. 3, thus preventing the possibility of the ring moving through the stirrup. Two holes should be drilled in the base for the terminals of the winding to pass through, and it would be best to cut two grooves in the side of the ring for these wires so as to prevent their coming into contact with the metal stirrup. Two back-connected binding posts, A and B, Fig. 3, are mounted on the base and the ends of the winding attached to them. The wires should be placed in grooves cut in the under side of the base, and the screws used in fastening the binding posts should be countersunk.

A short compass needle is then mounted on a suitable supporting pivot in the center of the coil. This compass needle will always come to rest in an approximate north and south position when it is acted upon by the earth's magnetic field alone. If now the plane of the coil be placed in such a position that it is parallel to the direction of the compass needle (no current in the coil), the magnetic field that will be produced when a current is sent through the winding will be perpendic-

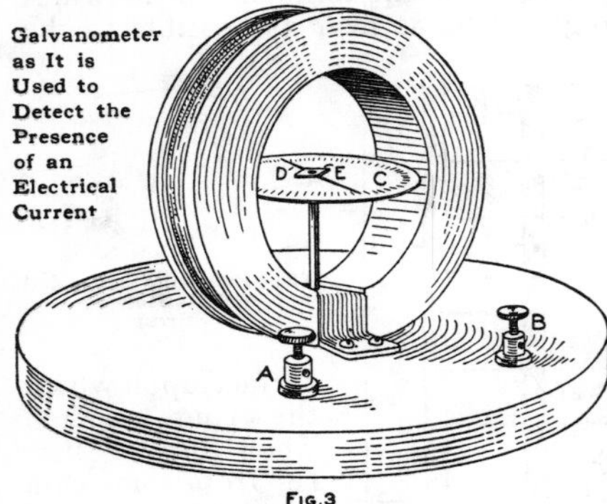

Galvanometer as It is Used to Detect the Presence of an Electrical Current

Fig. 3

ular to the magnetic field of the earth and there will be a force, due to this particular current, tending to turn the compass needle around perpendicularly to its original position. There will be a deflection of the needle for all values of current in the coil, and this deflection will vary in value as the current in the coil varies. The mere fact that the compass needle is deflected due to a current in the coil gives a means of detecting a current in any circuit of which the coil is a part, and the degree of this deflection affords a means of measuring the current, the value of the different deflections in terms of the current in the coil having been experimentally determined by sending a known current through the coil and noting the positions of the compass needle for each value of current used.

In order to determine the deflection of the needle, a scale, C, Fig. 3, must be mounted directly under the compass needle and a pointer, D, attached to the compass needle so that any movement of the needle results in an equal angular displacement of the pointer. The compass needle, E, should be short and quite heavy, say, 5/8 in. in length, 1/16 in. in thickness and 1/4 in. in width at its center, and tapering to a point at its ends. It should be made of a good grade of steel, tempered and then magnetized by means of a powerful electromagnet. The reason for making the compass needle short is that it will then operate in practically a uniform magnetic field, which exists only at the center of the coil. On account of the needle being so short and in view of the fact that it comes to rest parallel to the coil for its zero position, it is best to use a pointer attached to the needle to determine its deflection, as this pointer can be made much longer than the needle, and any movement of the needle may be more easily detected, as the end of the pointer moves through a much larger distance than the end of the needle, and since it may be attached to the needle, at right angles to the needle's axis, the end of the pointer will be off to one side of the coil and its movement may be easily observed. The pointer should be made of some nonmagnetic material, such as aluminum or brass, and it should be as long as it may be conveniently made. A suitable box with a glass cover may be provided in which the needle, pointer and scale may be housed. The construction of this box will be left entirely to the ingenuity of the one making the instrument.

In order to use this instrument as an ammeter, it will be necessary to calibrate it, which consists in determining the position of the pointer for various values of current through the coil. It will be necessary to obtain the use of a direct-current ammeter for this purpose. The winding of the galvanometer, ammeter, battery and a variable resistance of some kind should

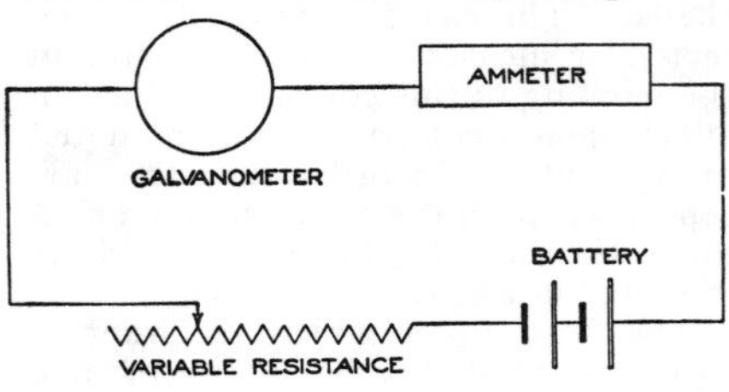

Fig. 4

The Electric Circuit, Showing Connections for Finding the Value of a Current in Calibrating

all be connected in series as shown in the diagram, Fig. 4. Allow the compass needle to come to rest under the influence of the earth's magnetic field and then turn the coil into such a position that it is as nearly parallel with the needle as possible. This corresponds to the zero position, and the instrument must always be in this position when it is used. The position of the ends of the pointer is now marked on the scale for different values of current, first with the current in one direction and then in the opposite direction. The deflection of the needle will, of course, reverse when the current is reversed.

The effect produced by any current upon the compass needle can be changed by changing the number of turns in the coil. In measuring a large current, a few turns of large wire would be required, and in measuring a small current, a large number of turns of small wire could be used. In other words, the size of the wire will depend upon the current it is to carry and the number of turns in the coil will depend upon the magnetic effect the current is to produce, which is proportional to the product of the number of turns and the current, called the ampere-turns.

Experiments with Camphor

Place a few scrapings from gum camphor in a tumbler of water and watch the phenomenon. The scrapings will go through all kinds of rapid motions as if they were alive. A drop of turpentine, or any oil, will stop their maneuvers. This experiment will show how quickly oil spreads over the surface of water.

Boiling Cracked Eggs

Eggs with the shells cracked can be boiled in the ordinary manner without danger of the white boiling out, if they are first wrapped in tissue paper. As soon as the paper becomes wet it will cling so tightly to the shell that the cracks are effectively closed.

A Trousers Hanger

A very serviceable hanger can be easily made of two clothespins of the clip type and about 2 ft. of large wire.

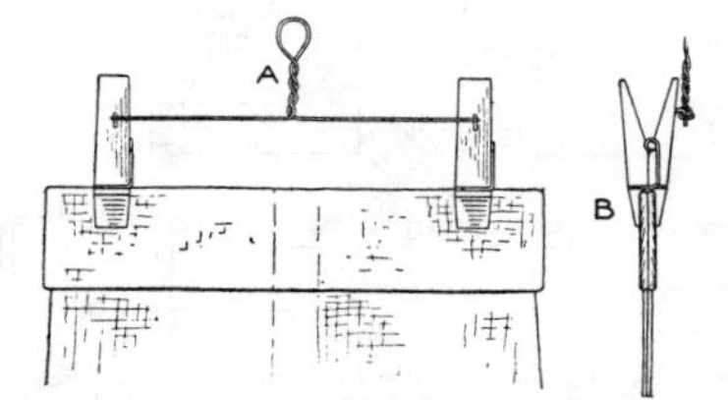

Clothesline Clips Joined Together with a Wire and Used as a Trousers Hanger

The wire should be bent into the shape shown at A with a loop about 1 in. in diameter as a hanger. The ends of the wire are slipped under the hooks on the sides of the clothespins, which are fastened to the trousers as shown in B.—Contributed by Olaf Tronnes, Evanston, Ill.

Removing Tight-Fitting Can Covers

Tight-fitting covers on lard and similar pails can be readily removed by tying a stout cord loosely below the cover, then placing an ordinary nail under the cord and twisting it. This will tighten the cord around the can evenly, which will loosen the cover.

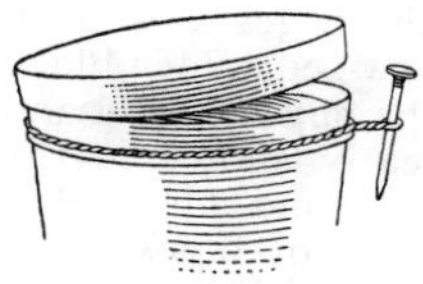

A Skimming Spoon

A handy skimming spoon can be made very quickly of an ordinary spoon of any size desired. Slits are sawn across the bowl in the manner shown, using a hacksaw. The illustration is self-explanatory.—Contributed by G. H. Holter, Jasper, Minn.

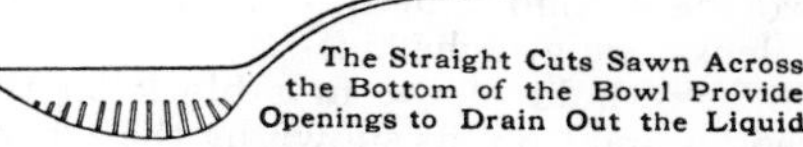

The Straight Cuts Sawn Across the Bottom of the Bowl Provide Openings to Drain Out the Liquid

How to Make Falling Blocks

Procure a thin board large enough to cut six blocks, 2 in. wide and 3 in. long; also 2 yd. of cotton tape, 1/4 in.

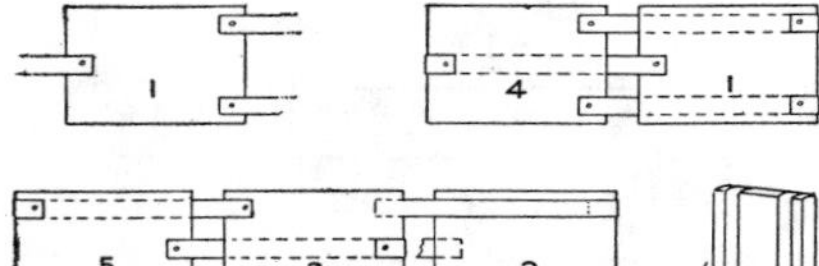

Set of Blocks Joined with Tape So That They Appear to Fall from the Top

wide, and some very small tacks. Cut the board into pieces of the size mentioned, and number two of them on both surfaces, 1, 2, 3, and 4. Cut off three pieces of tape, 4 3/4 in. long, and on the side of block 1 tack one piece of tape in the center at one end, and the other two pieces at each edge on the opposite end, all being on one side of the block as shown. Take the other block and lay the side numbered 4 up, then draw the two strips of tape on the edges of block 1 under it and back to the end of the surface on block 4, and tack them on this surface at the edges as shown. The center tape is passed under block 4 and turned over the opposite end and tacked. This is clearly shown in the sketch. Thus the second block will hang from either end of block 1 by simply folding them together and separating the ends.

Mark the sides of the third block 5 and 6, and place it with the two others so that the sides numbered 2, 3, and 5 will be up. Cut off three more pieces of tape, 4 3/4 in. long, and tack them on as shown, being careful not to tack through any of the first three pieces. Put on the fourth block in the same manner as the third block was attached to the second, and so on, until all the blocks are attached.

Take hold of the first block on the edges and tip it as shown by the arrow. The second block will then fall as shown by the second arrow, and the third block falls away in the same manner, and so on, down to the end.—Contributed by Wayne Nutting, Minneapolis, Minn.

Writing Name Reversed on Paper Placed on Forehead

The following is an entertaining experiment in a party of young people. One of those present is asked if he can write his name, and will, of course, answer "yes." He is then subjected to the following test: He is asked to sit down in a chair, a paper, folded several times, is placed on his forehead, a lead pencil is handed him and he is asked to write his name on the paper. As little time as possible to reflect should be left him; if he hesitates, he should be told to just go ahead, and in most cases it will be found that he starts writing his name at the left temple and, to the amusement of the others present, writes it in the way of many left-handed persons, that is, so that it is legible only when held in front of a mirror, unless one is practiced in reading reversed writing.

Use for an Old Table

An old table of the extension type, that may have a post broken, can be used against the wall in a kitchen as a work table. If there is a damaged part, that side is removed by sawing the crosspieces of the table in two and attaching it to the wall against the leaf

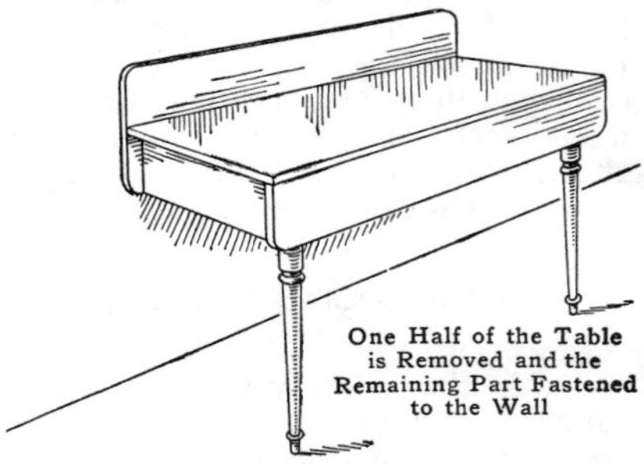

One Half of the Table is Removed and the Remaining Part Fastened to the Wall

which is turned in a reverse position.—Contributed by A. S. Thomas, Gordon, Can.

How to Make a Small Rheostat

In operating small motors there is as a rule no means provided for regulating their speed, and this often is quite a disadvantage, especially in the case of toy motors such as used on miniature electric locomotives. The speed, of course, can be regulated by changing the number of cells of battery by means of a special switch, but then all the cells are not used the same amount and some of them may be completely exhausted before the others show any appreciable depreciation. If a small transformer is used with a number of taps taken off the secondary winding, the voltage impressed upon the motor, and consequently the speed, can be changed by varying the amount of the secondary winding across which the motor is connected.

But in both these cases there is no means of varying the speed gradually. This can, however, be accomplished by means of a small rheostat placed in series with the motor. The rheostat acts in an electrical circuit in just the same way a valve does in a hydraulic circuit. It consists of a resistance, which can be easily varied in value, placed in the circuit connecting the motor with the source of electrical energy. A diagram of the rheostat is shown in Fig. 1, in which A represents the armature of the motor; B, the field; C, the rheostat, and D, the source of electrical energy. When the handle E is in such a position that the max-

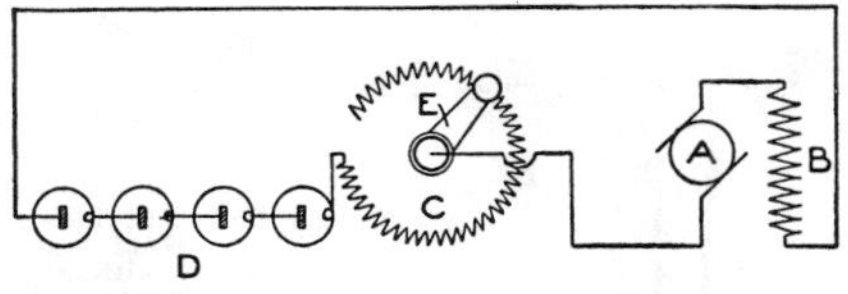

Fig. I
Diagram Showing the Connections for a Small Motor Where a Rheostat Is in the Line

imum amount of resistance is in circuit there will be a minimum circuit through the field and armature of the motor, and its speed will be a minimum. As the resistance of the rheostat is decreased, the current increases and the motor speeds up, reaching a maximum value when the resistance of the rheostat has been reduced to zero value. Such a rheostat may be used in combination with a special switch

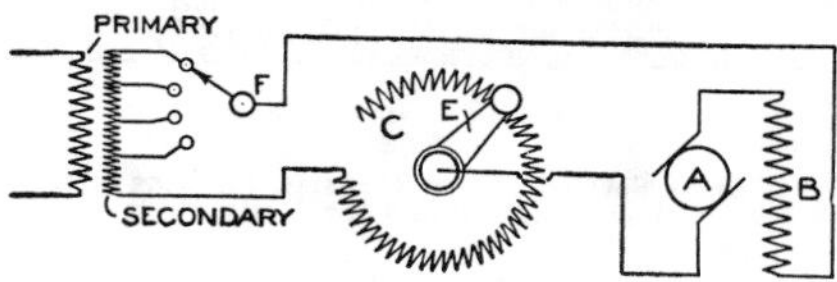

Fig. 2
Diagram of a Small Motor Where a Rheostat and Switch Are in the Line

F., as shown in Fig. 2. The switch gives a means of varying the voltage and the rheostat takes care of the desired changes in speed occurring between those produced by the variations in voltage.

A very simple and inexpensive rheostat may be constructed as follows: Procure a piece of thin fiber, about 1/16 in. thick, 1/2 in. wide and approximately 10 in. long. Wind on this piece of fiber, after the edges have all been smoothed down, a piece of No. 22 gauge cotton-covered resistance wire, starting about 1/4 in. from one end and winding the various turns fairly close together to within 1/4 in. of the other end. The ends of the wire may be secured by passing them through several small holes drilled in the piece of fiber, and should protrude 3 or 4 in. for connecting to binding posts that will be mounted upon the base of the rheostat.

Now form this piece of fiber into a complete ring by bending it around some round object, the flat side being toward the object. Determine as accurately as possible the diameter of the ring thus formed and also its thickness. Obtain a piece of well seasoned hard wood, 1/2 in. thick and 4 1/2 in. square. Round off the corners and upper edges of this block and mark out on it two circles whose diameters correspond to the inside and outside diameters of the fiber ring. The centers of these circles should be in the center of the block. Carefully saw out the two circles so that the space between the inside and outside portions will just accommodate the fiber ring. Obtain a second piece of hard wood,

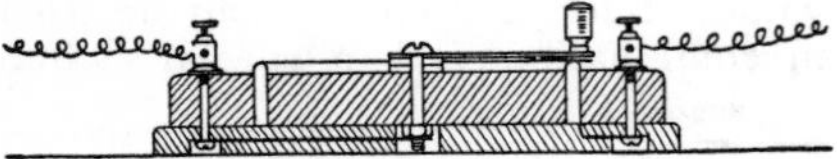

Fig. 3
A Cross Section of the Rheostat, Showing the Connections through the Resistance

¼ in. thick and 4¾ in. square, round off its corners and upper edges and mount the other pieces upon it by means of several small wood screws, which should pass up from the under side and be well countersunk. Place the fiber ring in the groove, but, before doing so, drill a hole in the base proper for one end of the wire to pass through. Two small back-connected binding posts should be mounted in the corners. One of these should be connected to the end of the winding and the other to a small bolt in the center of the base that serves to hold the handle or movable arm of the rheostat in place. These connecting leads should all be placed in grooves cut in the under side of the base.

The movable arm of the rheostat may be made from a piece of $\frac{1}{16}$-in. sheet brass, and should have the following approximate dimensions: length, 2 in.; breadth ½ in. at one end, and ¼ in. at the other. Obtain a ⅛-in. brass bolt, about 1 in. long, also several washers. Drill a hole in the larger end of the piece of brass to accommodate the bolt and also in the center of the wooden base. Countersink the hole in the base on the under side with a ½-in. bit to a depth of ¼ in. On the under side of the piece of brass, and near its narrow end, solder a piece of thin spring brass so that its free end will rest upon the upper edge of the fiber ring. A small handle may be mounted upon the upper side of the movable arm. Now mount the arm on the base by means of the bolt, placing several washers between it and the upper surface of the base, so that its outer end will be raised above the edge of the fiber ring. Solder a short piece of thin brass to the nut that is to be placed on the lower end of the bolt, and cut a recess in the countersunk portion of the hole in the base to accommodate it. When the bolt has been screwed down sufficiently tight a locknut may be put on, or the first nut soldered to the end of the bolt. If possible, it would be best to use a spring washer, or two, between the arm and base.

The insulation should now be removed from the wire on the upper edge of the fiber ring with a piece of fine sandpaper, so that the spring on the under side of the movable arm may make contact with the winding. The rheostat is now complete with the exception of a coat of shellac. A cross-sectional view of the completed rheostat is shown in Fig. 3.

Folding Arms for Clothesline Posts

The inconvenience of using a number of clothesline posts and the limited space available resulted in the making of a clothesline post as shown in the sketch. The entire line is supported on two posts, which should be about 6 in. square and are set in concrete. The upper ends of the posts are equipped with two arms, hinged to the sides of the posts in such a manner that the inside ends of the arms will meet on

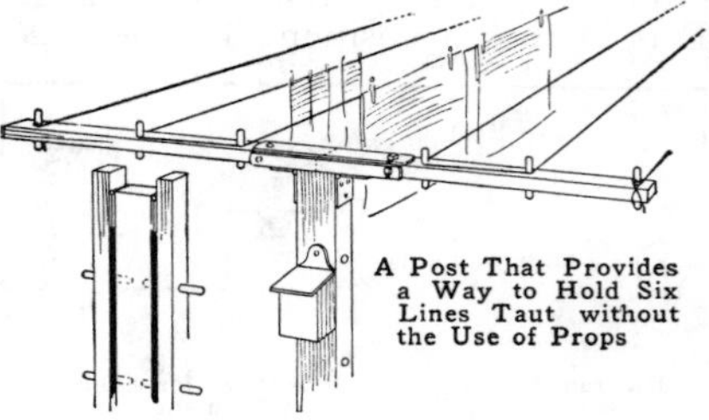

A Post That Provides a Way to Hold Six Lines Taut without the Use of Props

top of the post when they are in a horizontal position. Each arm is provided with three wood pins, equally spaced for the line. The arms are supported in a horizontal position by two bars of metal at the center, as shown.

Holes are bored into the sides of the posts to receive the pins when the arms are at rest.

A small box is fastened to one post, to provide a place for the clothesline and the clothespins. The line, when put up, gives space for an entire washing without the use of a prop, as the line can be drawn taut enough to hold the garments.—Contributed by Olaf Tronnes, Evanston, Ill.

A Folding Bookrack

Having need of a bookrack which I could pack away in my trunk and still have room for my clothes, I made one as follows: I procured a piece of pine, $5/8$ in. thick, 6 in. wide and 18 in. long, and laid out the plan on one side. Holes were drilled in the edges, $3/4$ in. from the ends, to receive $1\frac{1}{2}$-in. round-head brass screws. The design for the ends was sawn out with a scroll saw and the edges smoothed up with fine sand-

The Ends of the Rack Turn Down, Making a Straight Board

paper, whereupon the surfaces were stained and given a coat of wax. The screws were put in place to make the ends turn on them as on a bearing. In use the ends were turned up.—Contributed by Spencer Hall, Baltimore, Maryland.

A Simple Balance

Having use for a balance in a laboratory and being unable to procure any scales at the time, I hastily rigged up a device that served the purpose as well, as the work did not require very great precision. An elastic band and a short piece of string was procured and the band cut open. The string was then fastened around the beaker as shown, and the whole suspended from a shelf.

Into the beaker was then poured 100 cubic centimeters of water and the stretch of the elastic band noted by the

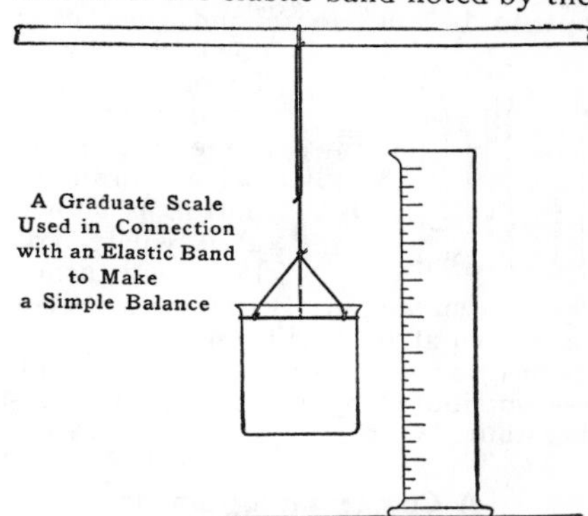

A Graduate Scale Used in Connection with an Elastic Band to Make a Simple Balance

displacement of a knot in the string in respect to the scale on a graduate, placed beside the beaker. The length of the elastic was then changed until the knot was exactly opposite the 100-division mark on the graduate scale. Then, since the elongation of the elastic band follows Hook's law, the extension of the band to the amount of one scale division means an added weight of one gram in the beaker.—Contributed by L. Horle, Newark, New Jersey.

An Ink Eraser

A good knife eraser for ink can be made from a discarded or broken ruling pen. One of the parts, or nibs, is cut off close to the handle and the remaining one sharpened on both edges at the point. This instrument is better than a knife or the regular scratcher, because the cutting edge will shave the surface of the paper or tracing cloth and not roughen or cut it. Erasing done with this knife will readily take

One of the Nibs on the Ruling Pen Sharpened and Used as an Eraser

ink without further preparation of the surface.—Contributed by Warren E. Crane, Cleveland, O.

Gate Fasteners

Buttons on gates or small doors are apt to become loose and then drop down, thereby allowing the gate or door to become unfastened. The ordinary button is shown at A where it is loose and turned by its own weight. If the button is cut as shown at B, it will remain fastened, even if it is loose on the screw or nail.—Contributed by A. S. Thomas, Amherstburg, Ont.

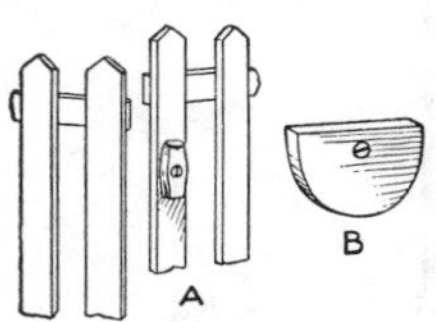

A Compensating Siphon

The homemade siphon shown in the sketch consists of two rubber corks and a glass tube with a rubber hose connected to it. The cork A is used as a bearing and support on the edge of the tank. The position of the cork B on the tube determines the distance that the mouth of the tube will be under the surface of the liquid, also to some extent the sensitiveness of the apparatus. However, the principle of the device is the buoyant effect of the water and the lever action of the rubber tube which is attached.

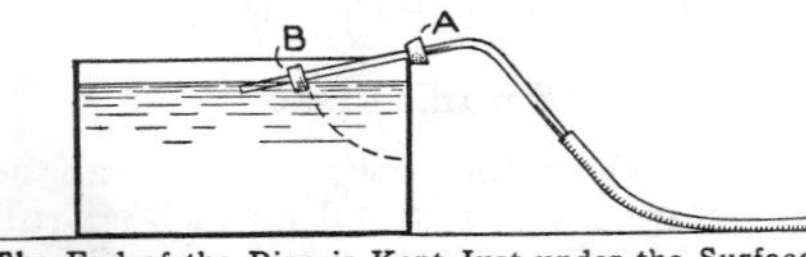

The End of the Pipe is Kept Just under the Surface of the Liquid at all Times

The one that I made had a tube 14 in. long, and the cork B was 1¾ in. in diameter, 1 in. thick, and weighed about $\frac{1}{10}$ of a pound. The practical application of this siphon will be found in sieve tests where it is necessary to collect the residue on the bottom of the tank while drawing off the liquid at the surface, also in oil-storage tanks where it is not wished to disturb the dirt or other residue which collects on the bottom of the tank.—Contributed by James Hemphill, Jr., Duquesne, Pennsylvania.

A Polarity Indicator

Lines in a cable or the ends of connections at a distance from the battery must be tested to determine the polarity. Where a large amount of this work is to be done, as in automobile and motorboat repairing, it is necessary to have an indicator to save time. A cheap indicator for this purpose can be made of a 6-in. test tube having its ends sealed and inclosing a saturated solution of ammonium chloride (sal ammoniac) and water. The sealed ends are made by inserting a piece of wire through a cork and, after forcing this tightly into the end of the test tube, covering it with sealing wax.

To use, connect the terminals to the battery lines, and the end of the wire in the solution giving off bubbles is the negative wire.—Contributed by H. S. Parker, Brooklyn, N. Y.

A Simple Pocket Indicator for Finding the Negative Wire in Battery Cable Lines

Small Steam-Engine Cylinders Made from Seamless Brass Tubing

In making a small steam engine it was desired to use seamless brass tubing for the cylinders. To have them exactly alike a piece of tubing of the right size and of sufficient length for both cylinders was fitted on a wood mandrel, A, and the ends trued up in a lathe. As these cylinders were to fit into holes bored in a steel bedplate, it was necessary to have a flange at one end. A groove was turned in the tubing B in the center, and as a final operation a parting tool was used on the line CD. This resulted in a pair of cylinders flanged to fit the bedplate.—Contributed by Harry F. Lowe, Washington, D. C.

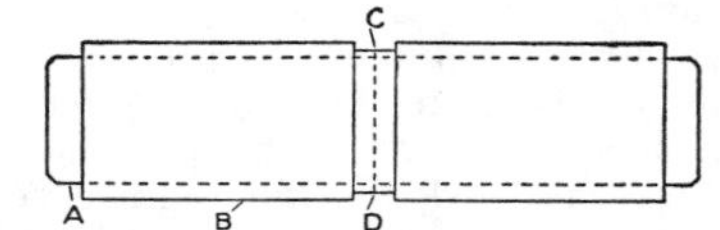

A Wood Mandrel Used to Face the Ends and Turn Flanges on Tubing for Cylinders

A Pocket Direct-Current Voltmeter

The assembled drawings of a very simple voltmeter are shown in Fig. 1, and its operation is as follows: The moving portion consists of a pointer, or needle, A; a small permanent magnet, or armature, B, and a counterweight, C, mounted upon a small steel shaft, D. The ends of this steel shaft are pointed and rest in bearings provided in the U-shaped piece of brass E, which is rigidly fastened to the fiber base F, by means of two screws. The permanent magnet B, carried on the shaft D, is at all times under the magnetic influence of the permanent horseshoe magnet, G, which is fastened, by means of thin brass straps, H H, and small screws, to the base F, so that the ends of the armature B are directly above the poles of the horseshoe magnet. The armature B will assume the position shown in the sketch when it is acted upon by the permanent magnet G alone and the moving system is perfectly balanced. A solenoid, J, is mounted in the position shown. When there is a current in its winding its soft-iron core will become magnetized and the magnetic pole produced at the lower end will produce a magnetic force upon the armature B, with the result that the armature will be rotated either in a clockwise or counter-clockwise direction, depending upon its polarity and the polarity of the end of the core adjacent to it. Thus, if the left end of the armature has north polarity, the right end south polarity, and the lower end of the core is magnetized to a south polarity the armature will be rotated clockwise, for the left end, or north pole, will be attracted by the lower end of the iron core, which is a south pole, and the right end will be repelled. This is in accordance with one of the fundamental laws of magnetism which states that magnetic poles of unlike polarity attract each other and those of like polarity repel each other. The amount the armature B is rotated will depend upon the relative effects of the pole of the solenoid and the permanent magnet G. The strength of the pole of the solenoid will depend upon the current in its winding and the number of times the current passes around the core, or the number of turns in the winding. In other words, the strength of the pole of the solenoid

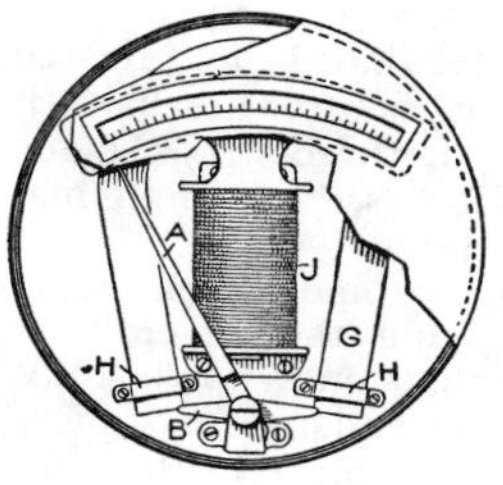

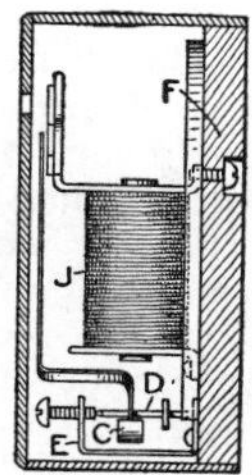

FIG. 1

The Parts as They are Assembled to Make a Pocket Voltmeter for Direct Currents

varies as the product of the current and the number of turns, which is called the ampere-turns. The same magnetic effect can be produced by a large current passing through a few turns or a small current passing through a relatively large number of turns. This simple relation of current and turns gives a means of adjusting the current capacity of the instrument so that a full-scale deflection of the needle will correspond to any desired maximum current. The instrument may be used as either a voltmeter or as an ammeter, and its operation will be identical in each case. The resistance of the voltmeter, however, will be many times the resistance of the ammeter, as it will be connected directly across the line, while the ammeter will always be in series in the circuit in which it is desired to measure the current. The following description and suggestion as to how to proceed in the construction of this instrument may be useful to those who undertake to build one. All the minor details and some of the dimensions will be omitted in the description, but these can be easily supplied.

Procure a piece of hard rubber or fiber, about 1/4 in. in thickness and of sufficient size to cut from it a disk, 2 1/2 in. in diameter. Make a small horseshoe magnet from a piece of the very best steel obtainable, and magnetize it to as high a strength as possible. This magnet is made of a piece of steel, 1/8 in. thick, about 3/8 in. in breadth, and of such length that the overall lengthwise dimension of the completed magnet will be about 1 7/8 in. and the distance between the inside edges of the ends a little greater than 1/2 in. Fasten the completed magnet to the base F by means of two or three straps, made from some thin brass, and small machine or wood screws.

Then cut from some 1/16-in. sheet brass a piece having the general appearance and dimensions shown at A, Fig. 2. Bend the ends of this piece over at right angles to the center portion along the dotted lines. Drill the hole at the upper end and thread it for a 1/16-in. machine screw. By means of a pointed drill, make a small recess at the lower end directly opposite the first hole. This small recess is to form the lower bearing for the shaft supporting the moving system, while a small recess cut centrally in the end of a screw, mounted in the upper hole, will form the upper bearing. The screw placed in the upper hole need be only about 3/16 in. long. The holes in the two wings are for mounting this piece upon the fiber base, as shown in Fig. 1.

The shaft for supporting the moving system is made of a piece of a hatpin. It is about 1 3/16 in. long and its ends are pointed so that they will turn freely in the bearings provided for them.

The armature is cut from a piece of 1/16-in. sheet steel. It is made about 3/4 in. long, 5/16 in. wide at the center, tapering to 1/8 in. at the ends. A hole is drilled in its center so that it may be forced onto the shaft. It is mounted so that its lower surface comes about 1/4 in. from the lower end of the shaft.

Then cut from some very thin brass a piece, that is to form the needle, 1/4 in. wide at one end and tapered to a point at the other, the total length being about 3 in. Drill a hole in the large end of this piece, the same size as the shaft and 1/2 in. from the end. This piece is not fastened to the shaft until some of the other parts are completed.

The spool upon which the winding is to be placed is made as follows: Procure a piece of very soft wrought iron, 1 1/4 in. long and 1/4 in. in diameter, to form the core. The ends of the spool are made of thin brass and are dimensioned as shown in Fig. 2, at B and C. The piece shown at B is to form the lower end of the spool, and is bent at right angles along the dotted line. The two holes at the lower edge are for attaching the end of the spool to the fiber base. The piece shown at C forms the upper end of the spool and at the same time a back upon which the scale of the instrument is mounted. The holes in the lower edge are threaded for small machine screws, as it will be necessary to fasten this piece to the base by means of screws that pass through the base from the under side, as shown in Fig. 1. Bend the upper and lower portion of the piece over at right angles to the center portion along the dotted lines. Make sure that the large hole in the center of each end piece is of such size that it will fit very tight on the end of the wrought-iron core. Force the end pieces onto the ends of the core a short distance, say, 1/16 in., and hammer down the edges of the core so that the end pieces cannot be easily removed. In fastening the ends to the core be sure that the parts that are to rest upon the base are parallel with each other and extend in opposite directions; also that the ends are at right angles to the core. Then insulate the inner portions of the completed spool with several thicknesses of onion-skin paper, or any good-quality, thin writing paper, and shellac. The winding will be described later.

Mount the spool and support for the bearings upon the base so that they occupy the positions, relative to each other, indicated in Fig. 1. A paper scale is then mounted upon the brass base provided for it by means of some thin shellac. The upper and lower lines for the scale can now be drawn upon the paper, using the center of the screw at the lower end of the needle as a center. These lines are best placed about ⅛ in. apart and not nearer the edge of the base than ¼ inches.

The needle is bent over at right angles $\frac{5}{16}$ in. from the center of the shaft. Another right-angle bend in the needle is then made so that the pointed end will be about $\frac{1}{16}$ in. above the surface of the scale when the large end of the needle is fastened to the shaft ⅜ in. from the upper end of the latter. Turn the needle on the shaft so that the pointer is at the left end of the scale when the moving system is at rest. The shaft must be exactly vertical when this adjustment is made. Cut the end of the needle down until its end is midway between the two scale lines. Solder the needle to the shaft, and then place a sufficient quantity of solder on the broad end to balance the system perfectly and allow it to come to rest in any position when the armature B is not influenced by any magnetic field.

A containing case for the instrument may be made as follows: Make a cylinder from some thin sheet brass, having exactly the same inside diameter as the base, and a height a little greater than the vertical distance from the lower surface of the base to the upper surface of the needle. Also a disk from some thin sheet brass, having a diameter ⅛ in. greater than the outside diameter of the cylinder. Round off the edges of this disk and cut a curved slot in it directly over the scale, about ⅜ in. wide and of the same length and form as the scale. Solder the disk to one end of the cylinder, placing the solder all on the inside. To prevent moisture from entering the case, fasten a piece of thin glass on the under side of the slot in the disk by means of some shellac and several pieces of brass soldered to the disk and bent down onto the glass. The case can now be fastened to the base by means of several screws, passing through its lower end into the edge of the base. Two small binding posts are mounted on the outside of the case, about 90 deg. apart and well insulated from each other and from the case, to serve as terminals for the instrument.

The instrument is now complete with the exception of the winding. Since this is to be a voltmeter and it is always desirable that a voltmeter take as small a current as possible, the winding must consist of a relatively large number of turns of small wire, each turn carrying a small current. The difference in the construction of different instruments necessitates that their winding contain a different number of turns in order that a given voltage may produce a full-scale deflection. A little experimenting with different windings is the easiest means of determining the proper size of wire and number of turns to meet individual requirements. After adjusting the winding so that the maximum voltage it is desired to measure produces a full-scale deflection, the scale is calibrated by marking the positions of the needle in accordance with those of the needle of a standard instrument connected in parallel with it. In marking the scale of an ammeter, connect the instruments in series. Remember that if the instrument is to be used as an ammeter, it must have as low a resistance as possible and that to prevent undue heating, the wire must have ample cross section.

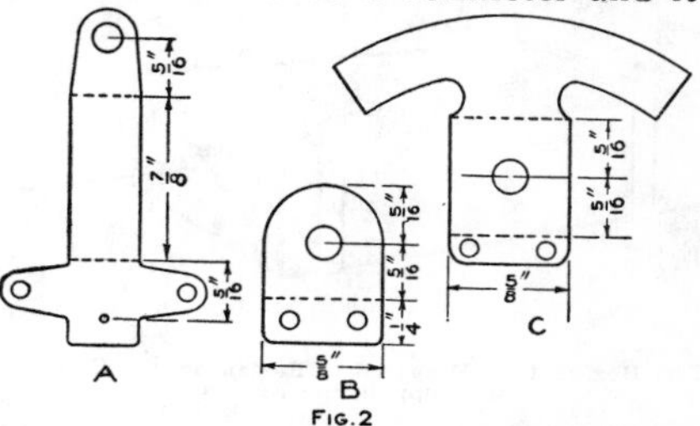

Fig. 2
Details of the Supports for the Coil and for the Needle, or Pointer, Shaft

If difficulty is experienced due to the continuous vibration of the needle, although the current be practically constant, this trouble can be greatly reduced by mounting a paper wind vane on the moving system, which will tend to dampen its movement.

Falling Leaves in a Nature Scene

Use an ordinary pasteboard box, a shoe box or larger, and cut out one end. Fasten the box to the ceiling by

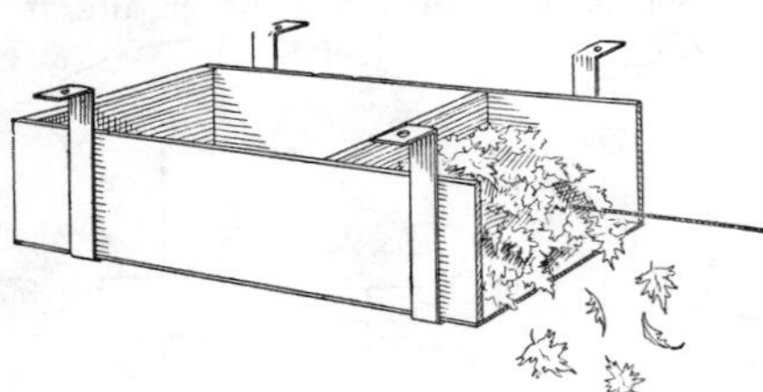

The Box as It is Prepared to Fasten on the Ceiling for Dropping the Leaves

means of pasteboard strips. One end of these strips is pasted on the bottom of the box and the other ends tacked to the ceiling. Fit a piece of board, ½ in. thick, into the open end of the box so that it will slide easily back and forth on the inside. Place this slide in the back of the box, attach a string to it and run this through double tacks placed in the ceiling and to the side wings.

Have the box almost full of autumn leaves, and when the slide is pulled slowly by the operator, they will be pushed, one or two at a time, out of the open end, and will drift down to the stage as naturally as if falling from trees, making quite a realistic scene.—Contributed by Miss S. E. Jocelyn, New Haven, Conn.

Home or Traveling Utility Bed Pocket

The pocket is made of cretonne with wire hooks attached on the upper edge.

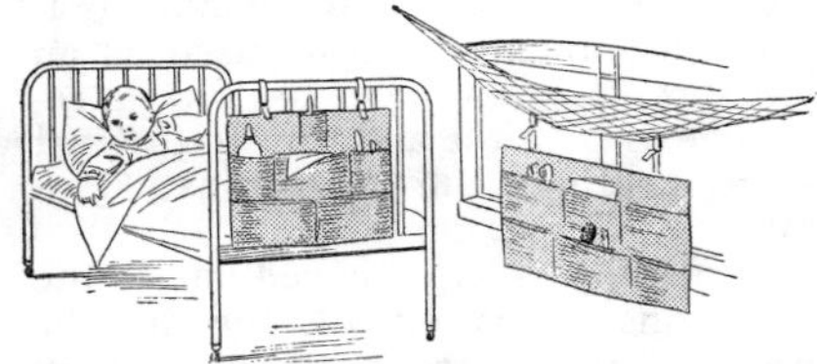

Various Pockets for the Change Garments for Use at Home or in Traveling

The compartments are arranged as needs may require. It can be hooked on the head, foot or side rail of the bed or used, as shown, in a sleeping car. It provides a place to keep the slippers, gown and other necessities, and can be rolled up and put in a bag.—Contributed by Harriette I. Lockwood, Philadelphia, Pa.

A Paper Perforator

In an emergency an ordinary hacksaw blade may be made to serve very acceptably as a paper perforator. The toothed edge is applied to the paper and the reverse edge tapped with a mallet or hammer. A considerable number of sheets may be perforated at one time, depending of course on the thickness and softness of the paper.

Turning Brass Rings

Occasionally an amateur has need of brass rings of round cross section, and if their construction is not understood, the task is a difficult one. If a piece of brass tubing, an old bushing or a cored piece is at hand, a part of the work is already done. If not, a piece of stock with large enough outside diameter should be chucked in the lathe and drilled out with the right size of drill. A tin or pasteboard template should be prepared the size of the ring section—a half circle is best, and it is easiest made by drilling a hole in the tin and cutting it in two. An inside boring tool and a turning tool are necessary. It is preferable to shape the inside first, cutting it out roughly and checking up with the template. The amount of inside cutting is shown in the drawing. A hard scraper and emery cloth may be used for smoothing and polishing.

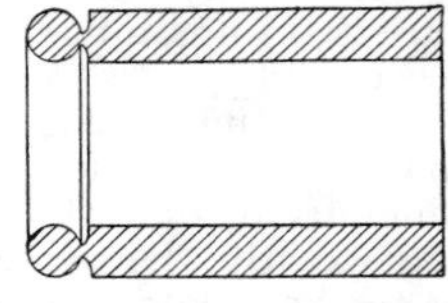

Turn and polish the outside and finally turn as far down on the inner quarter as can be done without cutting off the finish, then polish and cut it off. It only requires a little filing to smooth up the rim of rough metal left.

The Electric Globes, as They Light beneath the Spray, Illuminate the Top, and the Light Follows the Streams of Water So That They Appear Like Streams of Light

An Electric Fountain

By WALTER P. BUTLER

To make the grounds as attractive as possible for a lawn party given one night, I constructed an electric fountain which at first appeared to be an expensive proposition, but when completed the desired effect was produced without any expense whatever, as I had the things used in its construction on hand.

A light frame, 9 in. square, was made, of 3/4-in. material, as shown in Fig. 1, and a grooved pulley was attached exactly in the center on the under side of the crosspiece. A turned stick, A, 2 in. in diameter and 2 1/2 in. long, was fastened to the face of the pulley so that it turned true as the pulley and frame revolved. A hole was then bored centrally through the three parts, the frame crosspiece, the pulley, and the turned stick, of a size to fit a spindle about 3/8 in. in diameter.

A box was procured. large enough for the frame to turn in freely, and a block of wood was fastened centrally in its bottom, which had a 3/8-in. pin set in a hole bored in the center. The pin may be of hard wood, but it is better to use metal. A bolt, or piece of rod, will answer the purpose of a pin very well.

A small battery motor—I had one on hand and did not need to purchase one—was fastened to one side of the box so that its pulley was in line with the pulley on the lower surface of the frame. The batteries to run the motor were placed in the corner of the box, where the revolving frame would not touch them. The motor may be of larger current capacity, however, and run direct on the current used for the lamps.

About 1/2 in. from the lower end of the turned piece A, a brass strip was fastened around it. This work should be neatly done, and the joint soldered and smoothed, so that the outer surface will not catch on the brush used to make the contact. This ring can be better made by cutting the width from a piece of brass tubing of a size to fit on the turned stick A. About 1 1/2 in. from the lower end four segments of a circle were fastened so as to make a space of about 1/4 in. between their ends. This construction is clearly shown in Fig. 2. A cross section, showing the wire connections from the brass ring and segments to the lamps and where they lead out on top, is shown at B. The contact brushes consist of brass strips fastened with bolts to an upright, C, made of wood and attached to one edge of the block in the bottom of the box. Two nuts are used on each bolt, between which are fastened the lead wires from a source of current.

The wiring diagram is shown in Fig. 3. The wire D from the ring is run to the brass base of each lamp, of which there are four. The wires E, from each segment, are connected with solder to each screw ferrule of the lamps, and the ends are left bare and open, as shown, between the lamps.

A lamp is fastened to each corner of the frame on top, as shown in Fig. 4, with a piece of wire wrapped once around the screw ferrule and the extending ends held with staples. The wire used should be heavily insulated or, if it is of iron, a rubber tube slipped over it. A piece of tin, or bright metal, is placed beneath each globe for a reflector.

A glass plate was used to cover the box, and a lawn spray of the fountain type was placed on the glass. The globes, as they light beneath the spray, illuminate the top and the light

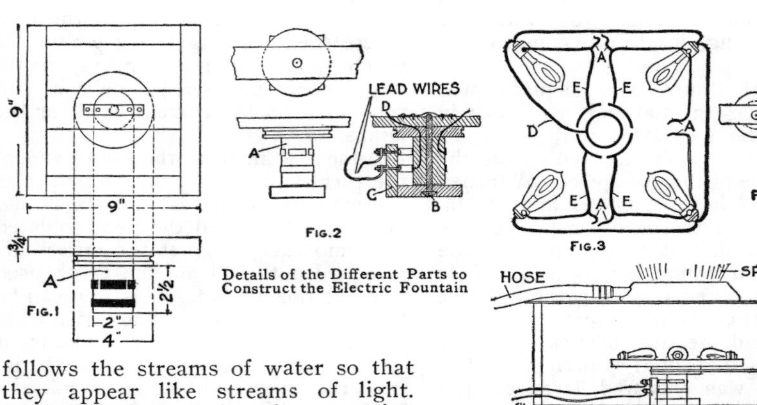

Details of the Different Parts to Construct the Electric Fountain

follows the streams of water so that they appear like streams of light. Each light is turned on in succession as the frame revolves within the box, and by using globes of different colors, an exceedingly beautiful effect is obtained. If the bared ends of the wires are twisted together between the globes, these will all glow at once.

A Mystery Coin Box

The effect of this trick is as follows: A small metal box, just large enough to hold a half dollar and about ½ in. high, with a cover that fits snugly over the top, is passed out to be examined, and when handed back to the performer he places it on the finger ends of his left hand, and a half dollar is dropped into it and the cover put on. The box is then shaken to prove that the coin is still there. The performer then taps the box with his fingers and picks it up with the other hand and the coin will appear to have fallen through the bottom. Both the coin and box are then handed out for examination.

This seemingly impossible effect is made when the performer places the cover on the box. The box is resting on the fingers of the left hand and the cover is held between the thumb and forefinger of the right hand, but just before placing the cover on, the box is turned over with the right thumb, and the cover is placed on the bottom instead of the top.

The trick can be done within a foot of the spectators without their seeing the deception. It is a good plan to hide the box with the right hand when placing the cover, although this is not necessary.

How to Make a Small Series Motor

The motor here described has been constructed and found to give very good results. It is simple to build and the materials required can be easily obtained. The armature core and field, or frame, are made of laminated iron, instead of being cast as is often done by the manufacturers, which is a decided advantage, as certain losses are thereby reduced, and its operation will be improved by this type of construction especially if used on an alternating-current circuit.

The machine will be divided into three main parts, the construction of each of which will be taken up in turn and the method of procedure discussed in detail. These parts are the completed armature, the field and bearings, and the brushes together with suitable terminals and connections.

The armature core is constructed from a number of pieces, having dimensions that correspond to those given in A, Fig. 1. These pieces are cut from thin annealed sheet iron, in sufficient number to make a pile, ¾ in. high, when placed on top of each other and firmly clamped. It would, no doubt, be best to first lay out one of these pieces very carefully and then cut it out and mark out the other pieces with the first one as a pattern, being careful to file off all the rough edges on each piece.

Now obtain a piece of ¼-in. iron or brass rod, 3¼ in. long, that is to serve as a shaft upon which to mount the armature and commutator. This rod is threaded for a distance of ⅞ in. on one end and 1⅞ in. on the other. Procure five brass nuts, ⅛ in. in thickness, to fit the threads on the rod. If possible have the ends of the rod centered before the threads are cut, for reasons to be given later. Place one of the nuts on that end of the shaft that is threaded for ⅞ in., and in such a position that its inner surface is ¾ in. from the end of the rod. Solder this nut to the rod when it is in the proper place and remove all extra solder. Drill a ¼-in. hole in each of the armature stampings and place them on the shaft, clamping them together with three small clamps, one on each ex-

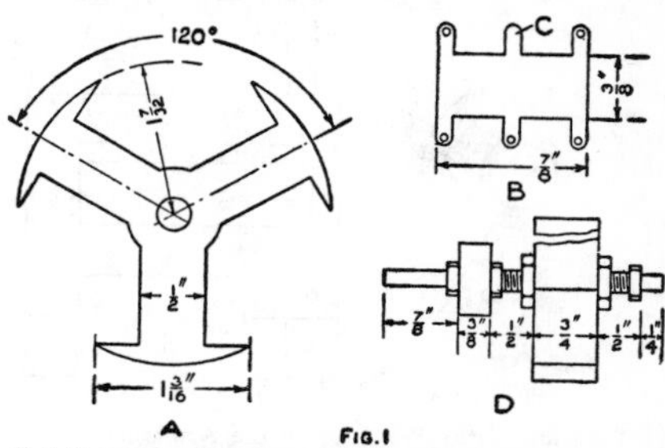

Details of the Armature Laminations and the Commutator Segments, and the Method of Mounting Armature Core and Commutator

tension or pole. Then place a second nut on the shaft and draw it up tight against the last stamping placed in position, and solder it to the shaft. Next wind two or three layers of good strong tape around each of the rectangular portions of the armature and then remove the clamps. Make sure that all the edges of the different laminations are perfectly even before applying the tape.

The shaft is then placed between two centers to determine whether the core is approximately balanced and runs true. If the armature core is unbalanced or not true, the trouble should be corrected before proceeding with the remainder of the armature construction. The armature winding is not to be put on the core until the commutator has been constructed and mounted on the shaft.

The commutator consists of three pieces of thin sheet brass similar to that shown at B, Fig 1, mounted on the surface of a cylinder of insulating material, ⅜ in. long and ⅞ in. in diameter. A ¼-in. hole is drilled lengthwise through the cylinder of insulating material. Bend the pieces of brass around the outside of the cylinder, and turn all the lugs, except the center one, marked C, over at right angles and put a small nail or screw through the holes in the ends of the lugs into the cylinder. These pieces of brass are equally spaced around the cylinder so that all the lugs, not turned down, project in the same direction.

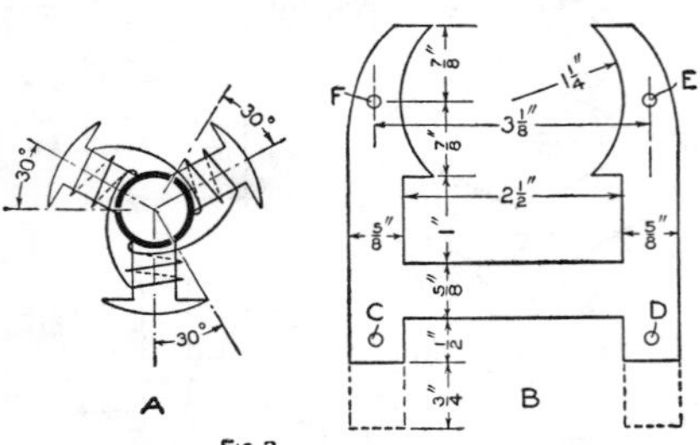

Diagram of the Winding on the Armature and Detail of the Field Laminations

tion. Now place a nut on the end of the shaft that extends the greatest distance through the armature, so that its outside surface is ½ in. from the surface of the end of the armature core next to it, and solder the nut to the shaft. Place the commutator on the shaft so that the projections on the pieces of brass are toward the armature core and the spaces between the ends of the pieces occupy the position relative to the cores, shown at A, Fig. 2. Another nut is then placed on the shaft and drawn up tight against the cylinder. The proper spacing of the various parts on the shaft of the machine is shown at D, Fig. 1. Another small nut is placed on the end of the shaft, away from the commutator, so that its outside surface is ½ in. from the surface of the end of the armature core.

The threads on that part of the shaft extending beyond the last nut on each end are now filed off, which can be easily done by placing the shaft between the centers of a lathe and revolving it quite rapidly, the file being applied to the parts that are to be cut down.

Obtain a small quantity of No. 22 gauge single-cotton-covered copper wire and wind four layers on each of the three legs, or poles, of the armature core, insulating the layers from each other and the entire winding from the core by means of paper and shellac. The three coils are wound in the same direction about their respective cores and each winding is started at the center of the armature with 2 or 3 in. of wire extending out toward the commutator. The outside end of each winding will terminate at the end of the coil toward the center of the armature, if an even number of layers is wound on, and is securely fastened by means of two or three turns of heavy thread. The inside end of one coil is then connected to the outside end of the next one, and so on. These connections can be easily made, and at the same time the proper connections made to the commutator, by cutting the inside end of one coil and the outside end of the next so that they will reach the lug on the nearest segment of the commutator, with about ¼ in. to spare, then removing the insulation from each for about ⅛ in. and soldering them both to the same lug. The arrangement of the winding is shown at A, Fig. 2. Connect all of the coils and segments in this manner, and the armature of the motor is complete.

The field or frame of the machine is made from a number of laminations whose dimensions correspond to those given in B, Fig. 2. As many laminations are used in the construction of the frame as the number of pieces in the armature, if iron of the same thickness is used. Four of the laminations have extensions at their lower corners to correspond to the parts shown by the dotted lines in B, Fig. 2. Place all of these laminations in a pile and clamp them rigidly together, then drill the four holes, indicated by the letters C, D, E and F, with a 3/16-in. drill. Two of the pieces with the extensions on them are placed in the bottom of the pile and the other two on top.

Place a 3/16-in. bolt through each of the lower holes and draw up the nuts on them tight. Procure two pieces of 3/16-in. rod, 1½ in. long, and thread each end for a distance of ½ in. Get 8 nuts for these rods, about ⅛ in. thick and ⅝ in. across the face, if possible. Both sides of these nuts are filed down flat. Put the threaded rods through the two upper holes in the field frame and place a nut on each end and draw them tight, leaving an equal length of rod protruding from each side.

Obtain two pieces of 1/8-in. brass, 5/8 in. wide, one 4 3/4 in. long and the other 5 3/4 in. long. Bend these pieces into the forms shown at A, Fig. 3. Drill a 3/16-in. hole in each end of both pieces so that they may be mounted upon the ends of the rods protruding from the field frame. The exact center of the space the armature is to occupy is then marked on each of these pieces, and a hole is drilled in each, having the same diameter as the ends of the armature shaft.

The extensions on the outside laminations are bent over at right angles to the main portion of the frame, thus forming a base upon which the motor may rest. Holes may be drilled in the extensions after they are bent over to be used in mounting the frame upon a wooden base.

Procure about 1/2 lb. of No. 18 gauge single-cotton-covered copper wire and wind it on the lower center portion of the frame until the depth of the winding is about 1/2 in. Be careful to insulate the winding well and, to insure mechanical protection, place a layer of adhesive tape outside. About 4 or 5 in. of wire is allowed at each end for making connections. It is best to have these ends terminate on the commutator side of the frame.

The brushes for the machine are made from some thin sheet copper or brass, and are shaped and dimensioned approximately as shown at B, Fig. 3. Two pieces of hard rubber, or fiber, 1/2 in. square and 7/8 in. long, serve as mountings for the brushes. These pieces of insulation are mounted in the corners of the armature support, at the commutator end, by means of two small screws in each. Mount the brushes on these pieces so that their free ends bear on the commutator exactly opposite each other. One brush is mounted on the upper end of its support and the other brush on the lower end of its support. This is shown at C, Fig. 3. Two small binding posts are mounted at the same time as the brushes, and are electrically connected to the brushes, thus affording an easy means of making a connection to the

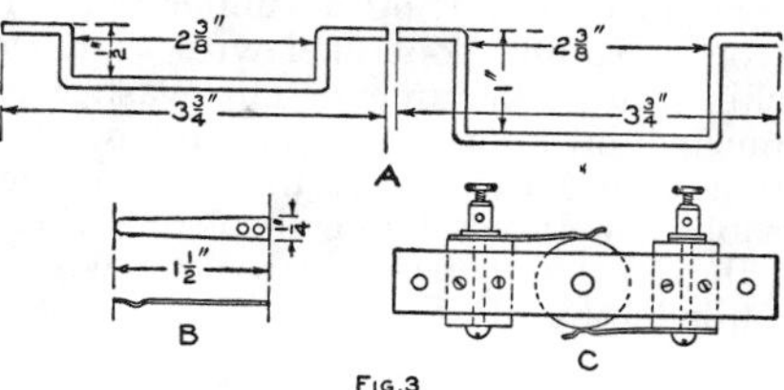

Detail of the Armature Supports and the Brushes, and the Manner of Mounting the Brushes

armature. The brushes are so mounted as to bear firmly upon the commutator.

To operate the motor, connect the armature and field windings in series, and the combination to a source of electromotive force of several volts. If it is desired to reverse the direction of rotation, reverse the connections of either the armature or field windings, but not both. The motor may be mounted on a neat wooden base and the connections all brought down to a reversing switch, which may also be mounted on the same base as the motor. The speed can be varied by changing the impressed voltage, or by connecting a variable resistance in the armature circuit, such as a wire rheostat.

A small pulley may be made and attached to the armature shaft so that the motor may be used in driving various kinds of toys.

Cooler for Milk and Butter

An earthen jar or crock, with a cover, set in a box containing moist sand will keep butter and milk in hot weather better than a refrigerator. The sand must be kept moist at all times. — Edwin J. Bachman, Jr., Fullerton, Pa.

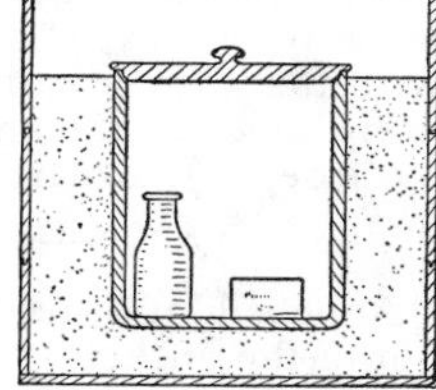

Rubber Bumper on a Water Faucet

Sometimes a dish is broken by striking it on the faucet. This is easily remedied by cutting a rubber washer from a rubber-boot heel with a sharp chisel and a hammer. The washer is pushed into place on the end of the faucet, and the dishes may strike the rubber without being broken.—Contributed by Harriette I. Lockwood, Philadelphia, Pa.

Boring a Clean-Edged Hole

When boring a hole in wood, withdraw the bit as soon as the worm shows, then start the worm in the hole on the opposite side and finish boring the hole. It will then have clean edges on both sides of the wood. Often the bit pushes splinters of wood ahead of it, when passing through, but by using the method described this is avoided.

Drilling Thin Metal

In drilling very thin stock the drill, if not properly ground, will tear the metal and leave a ragged edge. To cut a hole through neatly the drill should be ground as illustrated. The center A should extend about $\frac{1}{64}$ in. beyond the points B. The point A locates the center and the sharp points B cut out the disk of metal. Holes have been neatly and quickly made with this drill grinding in metal measuring .002 in. thickness.—Contributed by Joseph J. Kolar, Maywood, Ill.

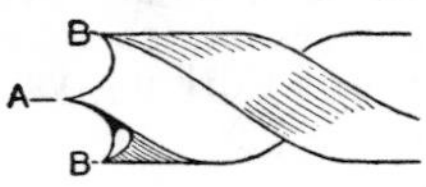

¶A pencil may be kept from falling out of the pocket by wrapping a couple of turns of tape around it or by wrapping it with a small rubber band.

Flexible-Cord Adjuster for an Electrical Flatiron

When using an electrical flatiron the flexible cord frequently gets under the iron, causing much trouble for the user, and mussing up the clothing. The cord can be kept out of the way by fastening a pulley to the ironing board and attaching a coil spring to the electric cord between the pulley and the electric-fixture socket. A coil spring that will draw out about 3 ft. should be used.—Contributed by Herbert Blandford, Elmira, N. Y.

A Wood Clothes Peg

If clothes that are slightly damp are hung on a nail or metal peg, a rust stain that is almost impossible to remove will be the result. To prevent this, drive a nail with the head removed into the wall or cleat, and place a wood peg over it. The peg may be turned up or whittled out with a pocket knife and the hole bored with a hand drill.—Contributed by Wm. A. Robinson, Waynesboro, Pa.

To Make Scratch Pads of Old Labels

Labels and blank paper of uniform size, that would otherwise be cast aside, can be turned into handy scratch pads by placing them between blocks of wood, secured by a wood clamp, and applying paste on two edges, then pressing a strip of paper on the pasted portions. The edges to be pasted should project a trifle beyond the edges of the blocks.

How to Make an Electric Heater

The electric heater described in this article is very simple to construct, its operation exceedingly satisfactory, and the necessary material easily procured at a small cost at most electrical-supply stores. The few tools needed are usually found about every home, and the heater may be constructed by any ingenious person.

Procure 6 porcelain tubes, 20 in. long and approximately $\frac{13}{16}$ in. in diameter. On each of these tubes wind 25 ft. of bare No. 26 gauge "Climax" resistance wire. The various turns should be uniformly distributed along the tubes and not allowed to come into contact with each other, which can be prevented by placing a thin, narrow coat of plaster of Paris along the side of each of the tubes immediately after the winding has been put on. Several inches of free wire should be allowed at each end, for making connections, and the first and last turns on each tube should be securely fastened to the tube by several turns of binding wire. It would be best not to extend the winding nearer the ends of the tubes than 3/4 in.

Cut from some heavy tin, or other thin sheet metal, two disks, 6 in. in diameter, and punch six $\frac{5}{16}$-in. holes in each of the disks at equal distances and within 3/4 in. of the outer edge. Punch two 1/8-in. holes in one of these disks, to be used in mounting a porcelain socket, and also one 1/2-in. hole through which the wires may be led to the socket, as shown in Fig. 1. In the other disk punch four 1/8-in. holes, for mounting two porcelain single-pole snap switches, and two 1/2-in. holes, for leading the wires through to the switches, as shown in Fig. 2.

Cut off six lengths of $\frac{5}{16}$-in. iron rod, 22 in. long, and thread both ends of each piece for a length of 1 1/4 in. Fasten the porcelain tubes between the metal disks, by placing one of the rods through each of the tubes and allowing the ends to extend through the $\frac{5}{16}$-in. holes in the outer edge of the disks. A nut should be placed on each end of all the rods and drawn up so that the length of rod protruding at each end is the same. Obtain two single-pole snap switches and a porcelain socket, and mount them on the ends by means of some small stove bolts.

The windings on the porcelain tubes should be connected as follows: Let

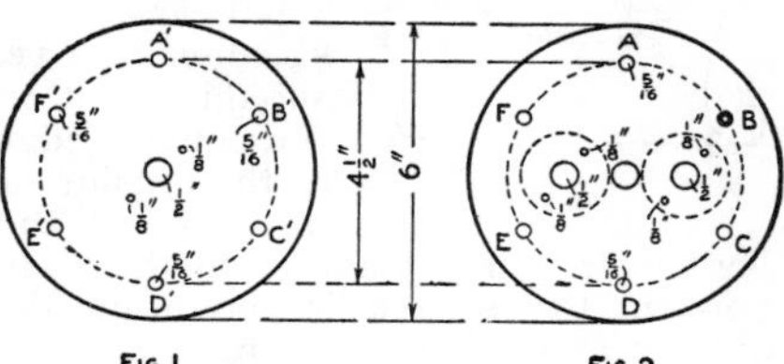

Detail of the Two Ends on the Heater Giving Dimensions and the Location of Parts

the windings be designated by the letters A, B, C, D, E, and F, and their position be that indicated in Figs. 1 and 2. The primes indicate the ends of the windings at the socket end, and the letters without the primes indicate the ends of the windings at the switch end of the heater. The ends A and D should be connected directly together. The ends B and C to the clips of the right-hand snap switch, and E and F, to the clips of the left-hand snap switch. The ends F′, A′, and B′ should be connected to one terminal of the socket, and C′, D′, and E′ to the other terminal of the socket. Electrical connection is made to the winding by means of a plug and piece of lamp cord. It is obvious that the windings A and D will be connected as soon as the plug is screwed into the socket, if the circuit is closed at all other points, and the windings B and C, and E and F are controlled by the right and left-hand snap switches, respectively. Make sure all the connections are properly insulated, and that there is little chance of a short circuit occurring.

After the socket and snap switches have been connected to the windings, two more thin disks, the same diameter as the first, may be fitted over the ends and held in place by two units on the end of each rod, a nut being placed on each side of the disks. A better way of mounting these disks would be by small machine screws that enter threaded holes in the ends of the rods. These last disks are not absolutely necessary, but they will add some to the appearance of the completed heater. Four small ears, about 5/8 in. square, should be cut on the outer edge of the outside or inside disks and bent over at right angles to the main portion, to be used in mounting the outside case of the heater.

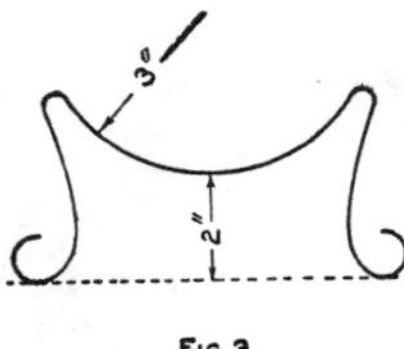

Fig. 3

Cut from a sheet of 1/8-in. asbestos a piece just long enough to fit between the inside disks and wide enough to cover the three lower windings C, D, and E. The object of this piece of asbestos is to protect the surface upon which the heater will stand from excessive heat, since it is to rest in a horizontal position.

Obtain a piece of perforated, thin sheet metal, 19½ in. wide and long enough to reach from one outside disk to the other. Bend this into a cylinder and fasten it to the lugs on the disks by means of small screws or bolts.

The legs may be made of 1/8-in. strap iron, 5/8 in. wide, bent into the form shown in Fig. 3. These pieces may be attached to the perforated cylinder, before it is mounted on the heater proper, by means of several small bolts. The piece of asbestos should be wired to the cylinder after the heater is all assembled, so that it will always remain in the lower part of the cylinder and serve the purpose for which it is intended.

The heater, as described above, is constructed for a 110-volt circuit, which is the voltage commonly used in electric lighting. The total consumption of the heater will be approximately 600 watts, each part consuming about 1/3 of the total, or 200 watts. If it is desired to wind the heater for a 220-volt circuit, 25 ft. of No. 29 gauge "Climax" resistance wire should be used on each tube.

A Molding-Sawing Block Used on a Bench

Having occasion to saw some short pieces of molding, I experienced considerable trouble in holding them without a vise until I made a block, as shown in the sketch. This answered the purpose as well as a vise. The block is not fastened in any manner, but is simply pushed against the edge of the bench or table and held with the hand. It should be about 9 in. wide and 1 ft. long, with strips 2 in. thick at each edge.—Contributed by W. F. Brodnax, Jr., Bethlehem, Pa.

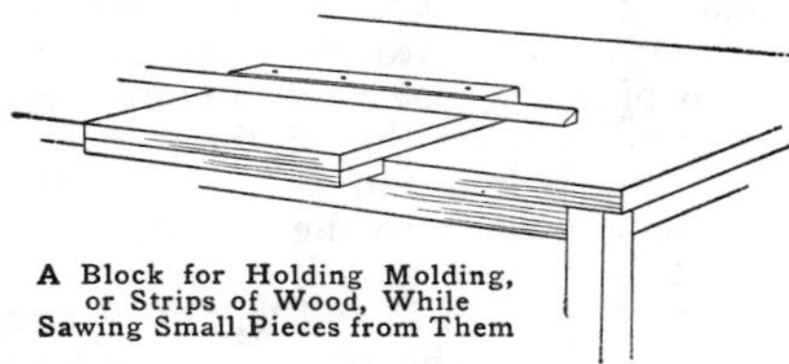
A Block for Holding Molding, or Strips of Wood, While Sawing Small Pieces from Them

Pipe Caps Used as Castings for Engine Pistons

Desiring to make a small piston for a model engine and not caring to make a pattern and send it away to have a casting made, I thought of using ordinary pipe caps, these being both inexpensive and of a quality adapted to machining.

The cylinder bore was 1½ in. in diameter, so I secured a standard pipe cap for 1¼-in. pipe which gave an outside diameter of about 1⅝ in. The cap, not having sufficient depth for holding in a chuck, was screwed on a short piece of pipe and then trued in the lathe chuck. The outside surface was turned to a diameter of 1½ in., then removed from the pipe, reversed and chucked again, and the threads bored out to reduce the walls to 1/8 in. This made an excellent piston for a single-acting engine.—Contributed by Harry F. Lowe, Washington, D. C.

An Electric Horn

A simple electric horn for use on a bicycle, automobile, or for other purposes, can be constructed as shown in Fig. 1. The size will of course depend somewhat on the use for which it is intended, but one with the diaphragm 1¾ in. in diameter and the horn 5 in. long and 4 in. in diameter, at the large end, will be sufficient for most purposes. This will make the instrument 7½ or 8 in. in over-all length.

The horn proper, A, Fig. 1, is constructed first. This can be formed from sheet brass. To lay out the metal to the desired size draw a cross section, as ABCD, Fig. 2, then project the lines AC and BD until they meet at E. Strike two arcs of circles on the brass sheet, using EC as radius for the inner one and EA for the outer. Measure off FG and HJ equal to 3¼ times DC and AB, respectively, and cut out FGJH. Roll and lap ¼ in. at the edges and solder the joint neatly.

After smoothing the edges on the ends, solder a very thin disk of ferrotype metal, B, Fig. 1, to the small end of the horn. This is used for the diaphragm. Cut out a ring, C, from ¼-in. hard fiber and bevel it on the inside edge to fit the horn. Also make a disk of fiber, D, having the same outside diameter as the ring C. These parts form the ends for a brass cylinder E, which is made in two parts or halves joined on the lines shown in Fig. 3. Fasten one of the halves, F, Fig. 3, to the fiber ring C and disk D, Fig. 1, with small screws, the other half to be put in place after the instrument is completed and adjusted.

A small support, G, is cut from fiber and fastened in as shown. A pair of magnets of about 50 ohms are mounted on this support. The parts from an old bell or buzzer may be used, which consist of a soft-iron armature, H, Fig. 1, having a strap of spring brass, J, attached by soldering and pivoted at K, with an adjusting screw, L, to set the tension. Another U-shaped spring-brass strip, M, constitutes the current breaker, which has an adjusting screw, N. The points of contact on the current breaker should be tipped

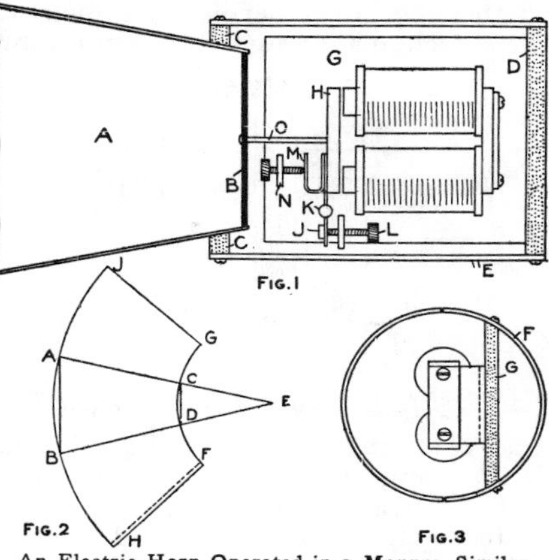

An Electric Horn Operated in a Manner Similar to an Electric Bell on a Battery Circuit

with platinum. A piece of brass wire, O, is soldered to the diaphragm disk B and the soft-iron armature H, to connect them solidly. The tone of the horn can be adjusted with the screws L and N. The faster the armature vibrates, the higher the tone, and vice versa. The connections are the same as for an electric bell.—Contributed by James P. Lewis, Golden, Colo.

Combination Meat Saw and Knife

A very handy combination knife and meat saw can be made of an old discarded saw blade. The blade is cut on a line parallel with the toothed edge, allowing enough material to make a good-sized blade, then the straight part is ground to a knife edge and a wood handle attached at one end. The handle is made in halves, placed one on each side of the blade, and riveted together, then the projecting metal is ground off to the shape of the handle.—Contributed by A. C. Westby, Porter, Minn.

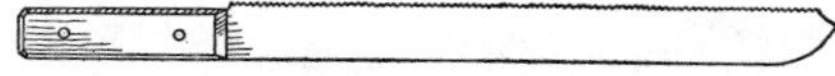
The Blade of the Knife is Cut from the Toothed Side of a Discarded Saw Blade

Clamp Used as a Vise

A carpenter's wood clamp fastened to the edge of a bench, as shown in the sketch, makes a good substitute for

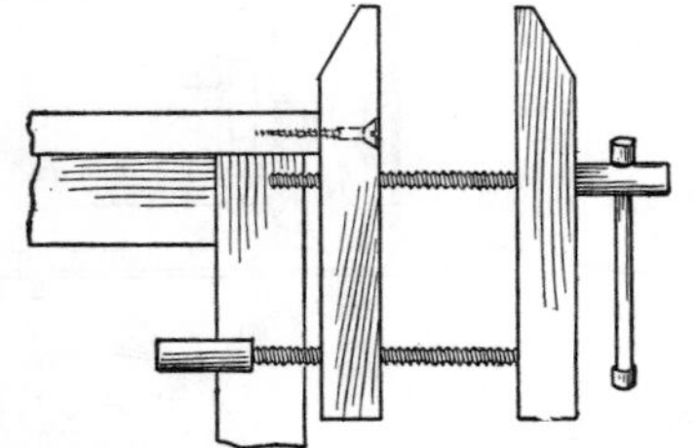

The Clamp Attached to a Bench Top will Serve the Purpose of a Vise in Many Instances

a vise for many kinds of light work. If the clamp is located over or in front of the bench post, holes must be bored in the latter to admit the ends of the clamp screws. A hole is bored through the shoulder screw and a handle attached as shown.—Contributed by H. W. J. Langletz, Harrisburg, Pa.

Wire Expansion Meter

When there is a current of electricity in an electrical conductor a certain amount of heat is generated due to the opposition or resistance of the conductor to the free passage of the electricity through it. The heat thus generated causes a change in the temperature of the conductor and as a result there will be a change in its length, it contracting with a decrease in temperature and expanding with an increase in temperature. The tempera-

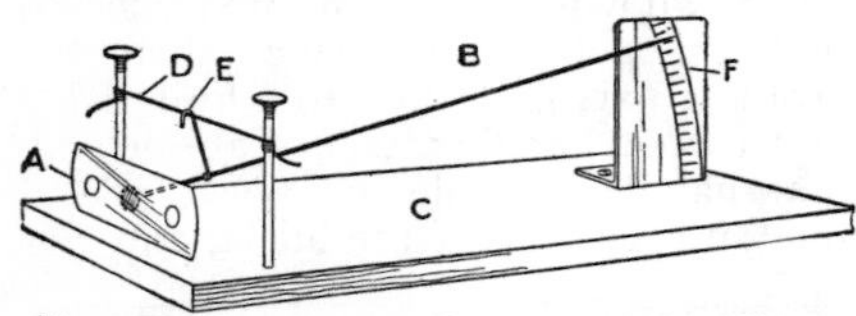

Meter for Measuring the Expansion of Metal Wires Which are Heated by Electricity

ture of the conductor will change when the current in it changes, and hence its length will change, and it will reach a constant temperature or a constant length when the current in it is constant in value and the rate at which it is giving off heat is exactly equal to the rate at which heat is being generated in it.

The fact that there is an actual change in the length of the conductor due to a change in current in it constitutes the fundamental principle of the following simple instrument.

The parts needed in its construction are as follows: An old safety-razor blade; one 8-in. hatpin; two medium-size nails; a short piece of German-silver wire; a small piece of sealing wax; a ½-in. board for the base, approximately 3½ in. by 10 in., and a small piece of thin sheet brass. Remove the head from the hatpin and fasten the blunt end in the center of the safety-razor blade A with a piece of sealing wax so that the pin B is perpendicular to the blade as shown. Now drive the two nails into the board C, so that they are about ¼ in. from the edges and 1½ in. from the end. Fasten the piece of German-silver wire D to these nails as shown. The size of this wire will depend upon the value of the current to be measured. Make a small hook, E, from a short piece of rather stiff wire and fasten it to the hatpin about 1 in. from the razor blade. The length of this hook should be such that the pointed end of the hatpin will be at the top of the scale F when there is no current in the wire, D. The scale F is made by bending the piece of sheet brass so as to form a right angle and fastening it to the base. A piece of thin cardboard can be mounted upon the surface of the vertical portion of the piece of brass and a suitable scale inked upon it. The instrument is now complete with the exception of two binding posts, not shown in the sketch, that may be mounted at convenient points on the base and connected to the ends of the German-silver wire, thus serving as terminals for the instrument.

The completed instrument can be calibrated by connecting it in series with another instrument whose calibration is known and marking the position of the pointer on the scale for different values of current.

How to Make a Fire and Burglar Alarm

A very serviceable fire and burglar alarm may be installed by anyone who can work with carpenters' tools and who has an elementary knowledge of electricity. Fire and burglar alarms are divided into two general types, called "open circuit" and "closed circuit," respectively.

In the open-circuit type of alarm all the windows, doors, and places to be protected are equipped with electrical alarm springs which are in circuit with an ordinary vibrating bell and battery, and these alarm springs are all normally open. When a window or door is disturbed or moved more than a predetermined amount, the bell circuit is closed and the alarm sounded. The arrangement of such an alarm is shown in Fig. 1. A switch, A, is placed in circuit so that the alarm may be disconnected during the day and the opening and closing of doors and windows will not operate the bell. It is best not to place a switch in the fire-alarm circuit as this circuit should be in an operating condition at all times.

The alarm switch controlled by the window consists of a narrow metal plate, B, and a spring, C, mounted in a recess cut in the side of the window frame. The spring C is bent into such a form that its upper end is forced into contact with the plate B, when the window is raised past the outwardly projecting part of the spring C, and the bell circuit is thus closed. The position of the alarm switch can be adjusted so that the window may be opened a sufficient distance to permit the necessary ventilation but not allow a burglar to enter.

The alarm switch controlled by the door is arranged in a different manner. In this case the free end of the spring D is held away from contact with the spring E by the edge of the door, which forces the spring D back into the recess cut in the door jamb. When the door is opened the spring E is permitted to move out and come into contact with the spring or plate E, and the alarm circuit is thus closed. The form of the spring D can be so adjusted that the door may be opened some distance, but not enough to allow a person to enter, before the alarm is sounded.

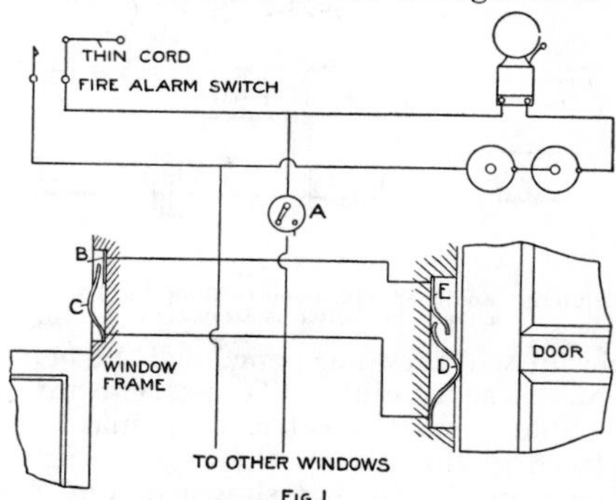

Fig. 1
Connections and Wiring Diagram Showing an Open-Circuit Fire and Burglar Alarm

An alarm switch, identical with that just described for the door, should be mounted in the upper part of the window frame to take care of the upper sash. This alarm switch may be located low enough to permit the window to be lowered for the purpose of ventilation without sounding the alarm.

The wires for these various alarm switches should be run as near completely concealed as possible to prevent them being tampered with by curious parties, who may unintentionally break one of the conductors and thus make some part of the system inoperative. It might be best to test the system occasionally, to make sure all switches are in operating condition.

The fire-alarm switch consists of two springs that are held from contact with each other by means of a thin cord. This switch is placed in the location to be protected, or wherever a fire is most likely to break out, such as over the furnace, in the coal bin, etc. When the cord is destroyed the springs make contact and the alarm is sounded. A metal having a very low melting temperature may be used instead of the cord, and the alarm will be sounded when the temperature exceeds a certain amount and the actual occurrence of a fire thus prevented. In some cases, the fire-alarm switch may be completely destroyed and the alarm

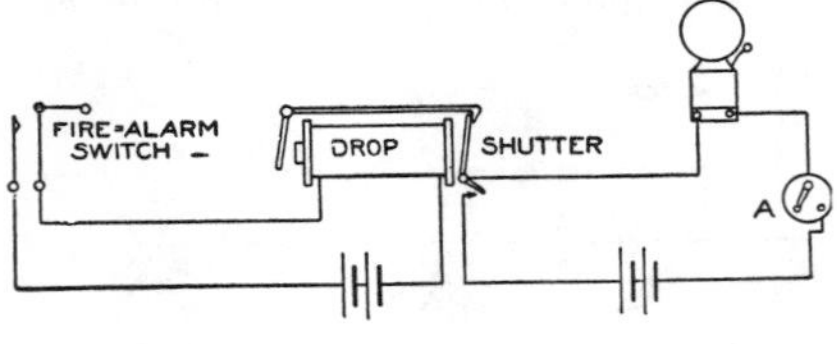

Fig. 2

Circuit Equipped with Drop to Ring the Bell in Case the Switch is Destroyed

circuit will then be opened and the bell will cease ringing. To prevent this trouble a small electric drop may be placed in the circuit, the arrangement being similar to that shown in Fig. 2. When the shutter of the drop falls, due to the closing of the alarm circuit, there is a second circuit closed, and this second circuit remains closed until the shutter is restored to its vertical or normal position, or the switch, A, is thrown to the open point. The addition of the drop in the burglar-alarm circuit may prove to be an advantage, as a burglar cannot stop the alarm, after he has once closed any of the alarm switches and operated the drop, by simply restoring the window or door to its original position.

In the closed-circuit type, the alarm

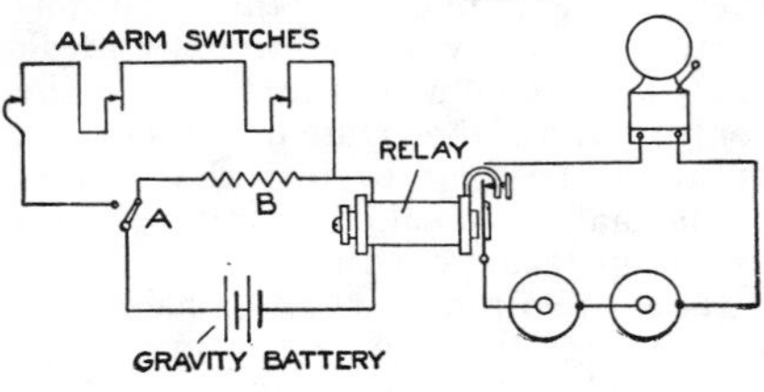

Fig. 3

Wiring Diagram Showing Connections for a Closed-Circuit Burglar and Fire Alarm

switches are all normally closed and the alarm is sounded by opening the circuit at some point. The arrangement of such an alarm is shown in Fig. 3. The alarm switches are all connected in series in this case and in circuit with a closed-circuit battery and relay or drop. The drop or relay controls a local circuit composed of an open-circuit battery and an ordinary vibrating bell.

The operation of a drop on a closed circuit is a little different from its operation on a normally open circuit. The drop for the closed circuit must be so constructed that its latch holds the shutter in a vertical position when there is a current in the drop winding, but allows it to fall as soon as the drop circuit is opened.

An ordinary telegraph relay may be used in connection with the closed-circuit alarm. The connections to the relay are such that the bell circuit is normally open and remains so until the armature of the relay is released, which does not occur until the circuit of which its winding is a part is opened at one of the alarm springs. A special switch, A, and resistance, B, are shown connected in circuit in Fig. 3, the object of which is as follows: When it is desired to disconnect the alarm springs or make them inoperative they must be replaced by another circuit which will permit a sufficient current to pass through the relay winding at all times, to prevent its armature from being released and sounding the alarm. The switch A is so constructed that either the alarm switches or the resistance B is in series with the battery and relay winding at all times, there being no open-circuit position for the switch.

The fire-alarm switch for this type of signal may be made from a narrow piece of tin foil, or some metal having a low melting temperature, mounted between two insulated clips that are connected in the alarm circuit.

Strips of gold or silver foil may be placed on windows and connected in the alarm circuit, which will give a protection from theft by breaking the glass.

Two or three gravity cells will serve very nicely for the closed-circuit battery, while several dry cells will do for the open-circuit or bell battery.

All types of alarm switches can be

purchased at any up-to-date electrical supply house, but their construction and operation is so simple that they may be easily made by almost anyone. A detailed description of the construction of the various parts of the above circuits will not be given here, but such details can be safely left to the ingenuity of the person installing the system.

It is easily seen from the above description that a burglar who might discover that a house was wired for alarm would be greatly perplexed to know what to do, for the very thing that would prevent one kind of alarm from ringing would cause the other to ring.

Removing a Rear Bicycle Sprocket

If a bicycle rider desires to remove the rear sprocket for changing the gear, or for any other reason, and there is no large pipe wrench at hand, a piece of tube or pipe, as shown in the

The Piece of Pipe Gives a Leverage Equal to That of a Large Pipe Wrench

sketch, can be used as a lever. Fasten one end of the chain in one end of the pipe with a wedge and place the other end of the pipe on a sprocket. The chain is then placed over the sprockets and a leverage equal to any pipe wrench is secured.—Contributed by Jno. V. Loeffler, Evansville, Ind.

Hand Propeller-Wheel Attachment for a Rowboat

The rear fork of an old bicycle frame, with the crank hanger attached, and the rear hub constitute the main parts of the propelling device. One of the cranks is cut from the hanger and a bracket attached to the frame, as shown, for making it fast to the stern of the boat. Two propeller blades are bolted to the rear hub. A rudder is fastened to the rear tube of the frame with hooks and eyes so that it can be turned with a handle at the top, or

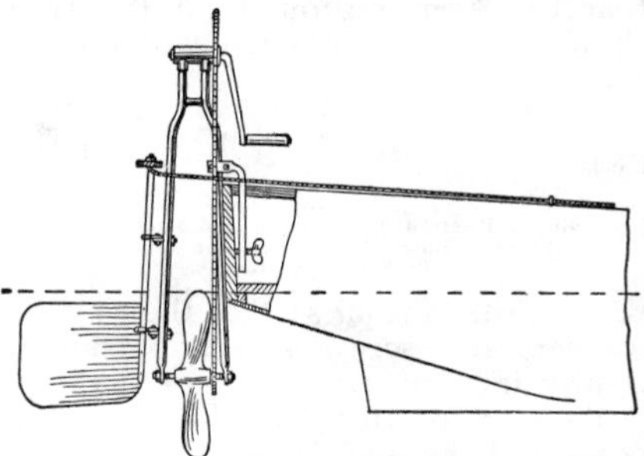

The Rear Fork of a Bicycle with Its Parts Constitutes the Main Propeller Attachment

with ropes run to a wheel. The illustration shows the connection of the device to a boat.—Contributed by Berge Lion, Fresno, Cal.

An Attached Back for a Photographic Printing Frame

In using the ordinary photographic printing frame with a spring-pressure back, the back must be entirely removed from the frame to put in the paper, and as this operation is carried on in a dim light, the back is often mislaid, causing no little inconvenience and delay. To do away with this an-

The Back, being Hinged to the Frame, Prevents It from being Mislaid

noyance, I placed at one end of the frame, as shown in the sketch, a second hinge made of cloth or any pliable material. When the pressure springs are released, the back swings down on this auxiliary hinge, and after changing the papers, it is instantly closed by a slight movement of the hand, making it very rapid and easy to use.—Contributed by Thos. L. Parker, Wibaux, Mont.

Repairing a Worn Stop Cock

The plug of a worn stop cock, or one that has been reground, of the type shown in the illustration will project

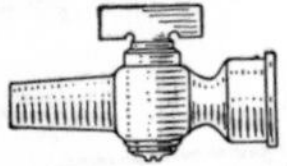
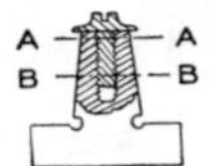

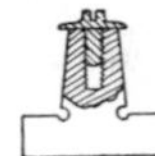

Removing a Portion of the Plug and Shortening the Screw Allows the Parts to be Drawn Tightly Together

beyond the bottom so that the ring, or washer, and screw will not draw it tightly into place.

To remedy this trouble, file off a portion of the plug on the line AA and also file off a sufficient amount of the screw on the line BB. When the plug is replaced and the washer and screw drawn up, the stop cock will be as good as a new one.—Contributed by James M. Kane, Doylestown, Pa.

Tool Holders Made of Brass Clips

Hangers to grip tool handles can be easily formed of sheet metal in any desired material. The clips are shaped as shown at A in the sketch. Any

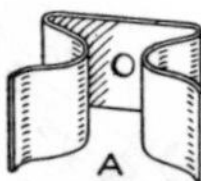

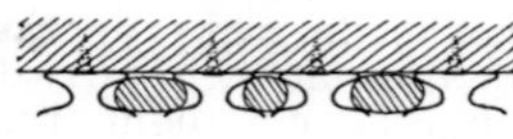

The Clips can be Set So That They will Grip Any Size Tool Handle

number of the clips may be fastened with screws to a wood crosspiece or a wall in such a manner as to make openings into which the handles of the tools are pressed. Before fastening the clips they should be spaced for the widths of the handles.—Contributed by F. H. Tillotson, Sycamore, Ill.

Removing Perspiration Stains from Delicate Cloth

Lay the stain in the cloth over some blotting paper, and sponge the cloth with a grain-alcohol and ether solution, which should be made by mixing equal portions of each. The sponging should be quite vigorous and kept up until the cloth is dry, then the spot should be touched lightly with ammonia water, which can be purchased at any drug store. This will leave a slight blur, which can be removed by rubbing with French chalk on the wrong side. The chalk is cheap and can be procured with the ammonia water. Do not forget the blotting paper, as it keeps the solution from forming a ring around the spot.

Buttonhole Cutter

If the buttonhole scissors are mislaid or there are none at hand, the holes may be cut in the manner shown in the sketch. Place a piece of wood, having a width equal to the length of the buttonhole, on the table and lay the cloth over it in the line where the holes are required, then draw a sharp knife

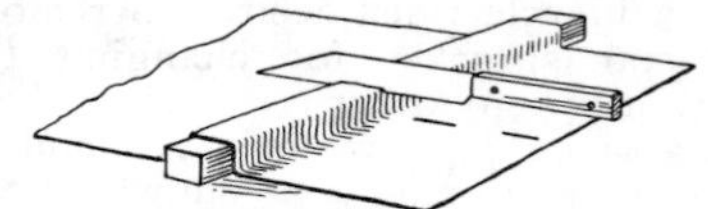

Sharp Knife Drawn across the Cloth Laid over a Piece of Wood Cuts the Holes

across the cloth on the wood where the holes are marked. This will cut the cloth neatly and accurately.—Contributed by A. S. Thomas, Gordon, Can.

Filing Small Rods in a Lathe

Reducing the diameter of a small rod by filing while it is turning in a lathe is a difficult thing to do, as the pressure of the file on one side bends the rod. The filing may be easily accomplished by using two files, as shown in the sketch. In this manner almost any amount of pressure can be applied by

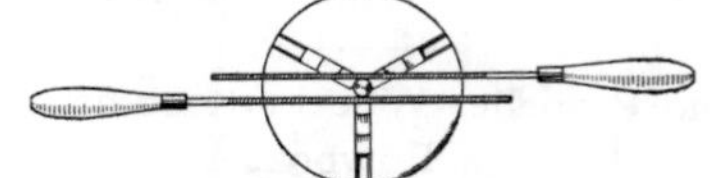

The Pressure of One File Against the Other Prevents the Rod from Bending

squeezing the files together without danger of bending the rod.—Contributed by J. F. Tholl, Detroit, Mich.

¶Young sleepwalkers may be cured if watched and given a good switching until they are wide awake.

A D'Arsonval Galvanometer

A galvanometer in which the moving part of the instrument is a permanent magnet controlled by the action of the earth's magnetic field and the magnetic effect of a current in a coil of wire, that usually surrounds the magnet, has the great disadvantage of having its indications changed, although the current itself may remain constant, due to a change in the strength of the magnetic field in which the instrument operates. The operation of instruments of the above type is satisfactory only in localities where there is a practically constant magnetic field for them to operate in, which it is almost impossible to have, due to the presence of permanent and electric magnets and magnetic materials such as iron and steel.

An instrument constructed as follows will not have the above disadvantage and its operation will be a great deal more satisfactory, as its indications will be practically independent of outside disturbances. In this instrument, the moving part is the coil carrying the current, and it moves in a permanent magnetic field so strong that other disturbing magnetic effects can be neglected. The coil is hung by means of a fine wire and the twist in this wire is the only force acting to bring the coil back to its zero position, after it has been deflected, and maintain it there.

The construction of the magnet and containing case for the instrument will be taken up first. Obtain a piece of Norway iron, ½ in. square and about 9 in. long. Bend this piece into the form shown in Fig. 1, and file off the inner edges until they are parallel and about ⅞ in. apart. Drill four ⅛-in. holes in the ends of this piece, two in each end, as indicated. This piece of iron is first tempered and then magnetized by placing it in contact with a powerful electromagnet. Cut a second piece from some soft iron with dimensions corresponding to those given in Fig. 2. Drill two ⅛-in. holes, A and B, in this piece as shown in the sketch. This second piece is mounted between the poles of the magnet, as

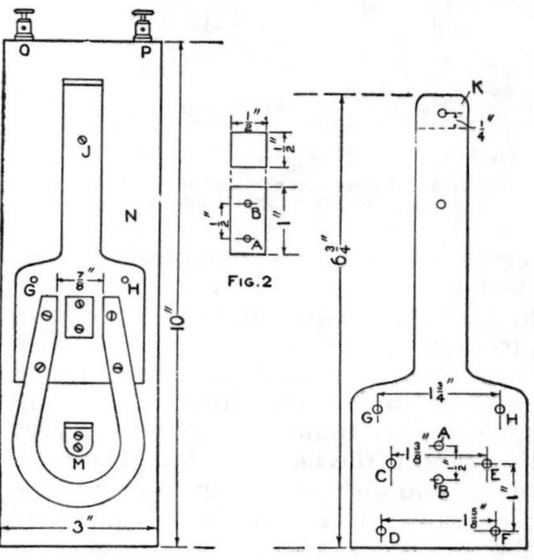

The Permanent Magnet and Its Brass Support, and Their Position on the Base

follows: Cut from some $\frac{1}{32}$-in. sheet brass a piece similar to the one shown in Fig. 3. Drill the holes indicated and thread those designated by A, B, C, D, E, and F to take a ⅛-in. machine screw. Bend the upper end of the piece over at the point indicated by the dotted line until it is perpendicular to the lower part. The center of the hole in the projecting part K, when it is bent over, should be about ¼ in. from the outer surface of the main part of the piece. The small piece of iron is then fastened to the piece of brass with two round-headed screws that pass through the two holes in it and into the holes A and B in the brass piece. The magnet is mounted, also with small brass screws, so that the main part of the magnet and the piece of brass extend in opposite directions, as shown in Fig. 1. The assembled parts are then mounted on a wooden board, whose dimensions are given in Fig. 1, with three brass screws that pass through the holes G, H, and J, as shown.

The moving coil of the galvanometer is constructed as follows: Cut from some 1/8-in. pine a piece 1 1/8 in. long and 5/8 in. wide. Cut two other

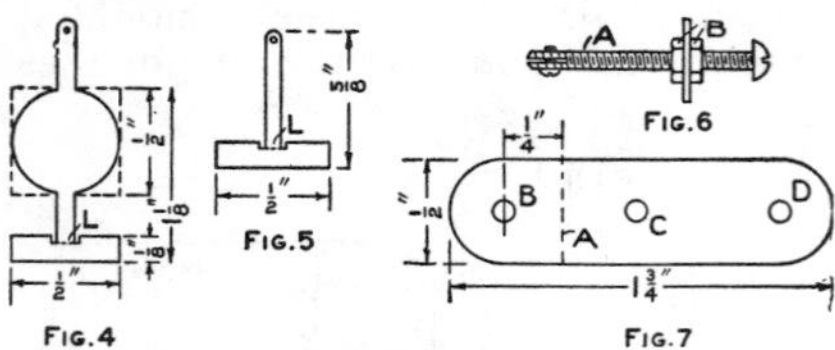

Upper and Lower Connections to the Coil and Supports, and the Supports for Suspension

pieces whose dimensions, except their thickness, are 1/4 in. larger than the first piece. Then fasten these two pieces to the sides of the first, with three or four small screws through each of them, thus forming a small spool. Saw about 16 slots with a very fine saw in the edges of the projecting pieces and a short way into the edge of the center piece. Wind on this spool about 300 turns of No. 38 gauge silk-covered copper wire. Start with the terminal of the wire in the center of one end of the spool, with a few inches of free wire for making connections, and end up with the terminal in the center of the opposite end of the spool. A small thread is then passed through the slots under the coil and tied, thus serving to hold the various turns of wire together when the coil is removed from the form. The coil should be given a coat of shellac as soon as it is removed from the form.

Two pieces must now be attached to the top and bottom of the coil to be used in making electrical connections and suspending the coil. Cut from some very thin sheet brass two pieces whose dimensions correspond to those given in Figs. 4 and 5. Drill a small hole in the center of each of these pieces. Bend the lower part of each piece over at the dotted lines L until it is perpendicular to the main portion of the piece. The bent-over portions of these two pieces are then fastened to the ends of the coil with some fine thread, making sure that they are in the center of the ends before they are fastened. The terminals of the coil are now soldered to these pieces. It would be best to place a sheet or two of thin paper between the brass pieces and the coil, to prevent any part of the coil, except the ends, from coming into contact with the brass pieces. Obtain a small piece of thin mirror and mount it with some glue, as shown by the dotted lines in Fig. 4.

The upper support for the suspension is shown in Fig. 6 and consists of a 1/8-in. threaded screw, A, that passes through the hole in the part K, Fig 3, and is provided with two lock nuts, B. The lower end of this screw should be slotted a short distance, and a small screw put through it, perpendicular to the slot, so that a wire can be easily clamped in the slot by turning up the screw. Next, take a piece of 1/32-in. brass, as shown in Fig. 7, and bend it at the dotted line A until it forms a right angle. The hole B should be threaded to take a 1/8-in. screw. The holes C and D are for mounting the piece on the back of the instrument. Slot the end of a 1/8-in. screw, about 1/2 in. long, and put a screw through the end as for the upper support for the suspension. This piece is mounted below the position the coil is to occupy, as shown by M, Fig. 1.

A case should be made for the galvanometer whose inside dimensions correspond to those of the piece N, Fig. 1, and whose depth is about 3/4 in. more than the thickness of that piece. Four pieces of wood can be fastened in the corners that will allow the case to slip just far enough on the piece N to make the edge of the case and the back surface of the piece N flush. Cut an opening in the front of this case, about 2 in. long and 1 in. wide, in such a place that the center of the opening

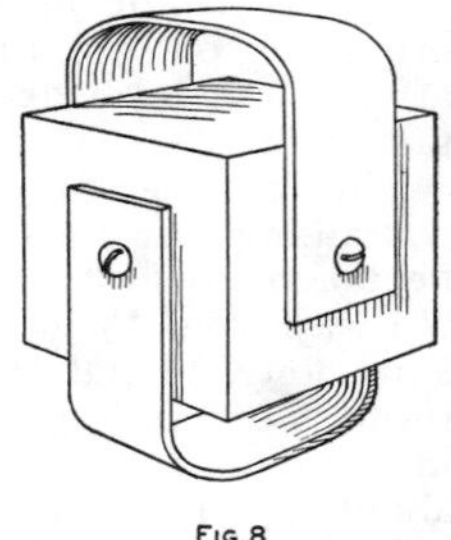

Fig.8

is about level with the ends of the magnet. Fasten, back of this opening, a piece of thin glass with four small screws whose heads rest upon the edge of the glass. The interior of this case and all the parts should be given a coat of lampblack mixed with a little vinegar. Two small binding posts, O and P, are mounted on the upper end of the piece N and connected to the upper and lower supports for the suspension of the coil.

This galvanometer will work best, of course, when it is in an exactly vertical position and the following simple device, when attached to it, will allow it to assume this position independent of the level of the surface its base may rest upon. Cut from some 1/8-in. brass two pieces, 1/2 in. wide and 2 1/2 in. long. Drill a 1/8-in. hole in the center of each end of them, 1/4 in. from the end, and a 1/4-in. hole through the center of each. Bend these pieces to a 3/4-in. radius. Cut from some 1/2-in. hard wood a block, 1 1/4 in. square. Fasten the two pieces of brass to the wooden block with 1/8-in. screws, as shown in Fig. 8. One of these pieces is fastened to the upper end of the piece N, Fig. 1, so that the galvanometer will hang vertically. The other piece is fastened to a bracket from which the galvanometer is suspended. A suitable bracket for this purpose can be easily made. When the galvanometer is hung in this way, two binding posts are mounted on the bracket, and connected to the two on the galvanometer. In this way the galvanometer will not be disturbed when making connections.

The suspension is made as follows: Take a piece of small copper wire and roll it out flat. Solder one end of a piece of this wire in the hole in the piece of brass, with the mirror mounted on it. Fasten a piece of the same wire to the lower brass piece, attached to the coil. The upper piece of wire is then clamped in the end of the screw A, Fig. 6, so that the coil hangs perfectly free about the iron core. The lower piece of wire is bent around a small rod several times and its end fastened in the slot in the lower screw.

The deflection of the instrument is read by causing a beam of light from a lamp or candle to be reflected from the mirror to a scale located in front of the instrument. If the light from the lamp is allowed to shine through a small slit in a piece of dark paper, there will be a streak of light reflected upon the scale, instead of a spot.

To use this instrument in measuring larger currents than it will safely carry, connect it in parallel with another resistance which will carry the larger part of the total current. The galvanometer can be calibrated with this resistance, which is known as a shunt.

How to Make Advertising Lantern Slides

Procure some old discarded photographic films and remove the gelatin coating by soaking them in hot water. When dry, write the desired words on the thin celluloid and place it between two pieces of glass, lantern-slide size, and bind them as in making a lantern slide.

With the use of a carbon paper a very nice slide can be made by writing the words on a typewriter, and it will serve the purpose of an expensive announcement slide.—Contributed by F. P. Dickover, Atkinson, Neb.

Utilizing Old Brush Handles

The handle cut from an old dusting brush, fitted with the brass end of a shotgun shell, makes a first-class tool handle. The handle is cut off at A and the wood cut down to fit tightly into the brass shell.—Contributed by James M. Kane, Doylestown, Pa.

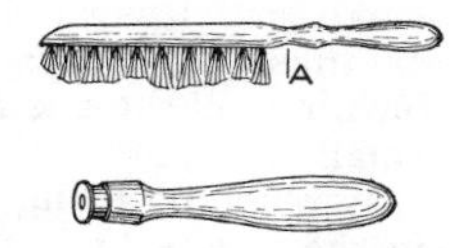

Tincture-of-iodine stains may be removed from clothing or the skin by using strong ammonia water.

Preserving Paints and Pastes

White lead, thick shellac, and pastes that are used occasionally may be preserved by laying a piece of leather over the exposed surface. When these materials are kept in cans, cut a piece of leather from the upper of a heavy boot of such a size that it will drop freely into the container. Form a handle on the leather disk by driving a nail through its center from the under side. Press the disk down smoothly over the surface of the contents and a thin film of oil will soon form over the disk, effectually excluding the air. A loose cover is placed over the container, to keep out dust.—Contributed by Luther McKnight, Colorado City, Col.

A Burner for Soldering Small Work

As it was necessary for me to solder the joints of fine wires on electrical instruments, and other small work, I found myself in need of a blowpipe that gave a small but very hot and easily directed flame, was automatic in its operation and required no blast.

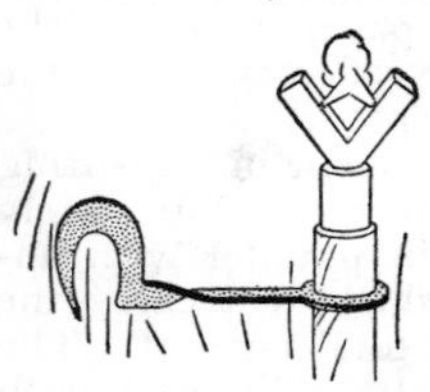

I tried an ordinary acetylene burner on coal or city gas, and found it gave an intensely hot, nonluminous flame, due to the forced draft of air through the small holes. This flame will melt silver, copper and, also, silver solder. Its great advantage lies in the fact that it may be used for sweating together small articles rapidly and with great neatness. I always keep this blowpipe burning, as the gas it consumes is very small, and the burner is kept within easy reach by using a hanger, as shown in the illustration.

A single jet of flame is obtained by stopping up one of the tips, which is very useful in many ways. This flame may contain a small luminous spot on some city gas, but it does not interfere with the heat.—Contributed by Arthur Worischek, New York City.

A Safety-Match-Box Holder

A holder, as well as a tray, for safety matches can be made from any ordinary tobacco can. The metal on one

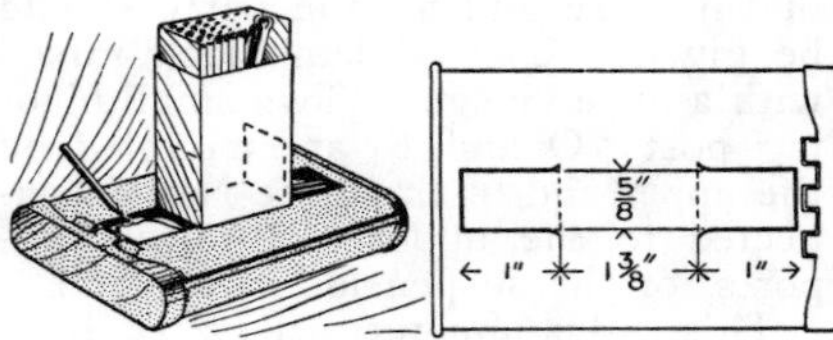

The Match Box is Held Upright between Standards Formed from the Tin of the Tobacco Box

side is cut as shown and the pieces bent up to form standards for holding the match box in an upright position. The openings left where the metal was raised are used for dropping the burned matches into the box. The hinged cover is used for emptying the tray.—Contributed by David B. Lutz, E. St. Louis, Ill.

Removing Ink Stains from Book Leaves

When the leaves of a book are accidentally stained with ink it can be removed quite readily by the following process: After removing as much of the ink as possible with a camel's-hair brush dipped in water, soak the stained parts in a solution of oxalate of potash, or better still, oxalic acid. This will remove all the ink. Treat again with water, as before, so that when it dries out no salt will appear on the paper. This process does not affect printer's ink.—Contributed by S. G. Thompson, Owensboro, Ky.

A Needle-Spray Nozzle

To make a needle-spray nozzle, either insert a 22-caliber cartridge in a small tube, or place a 45-caliber shell over the end of the tube and solder it in place. The end is perforated to make one or more small holes, as desired.

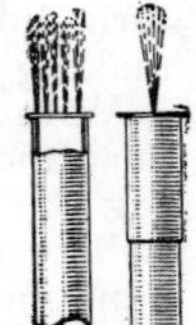

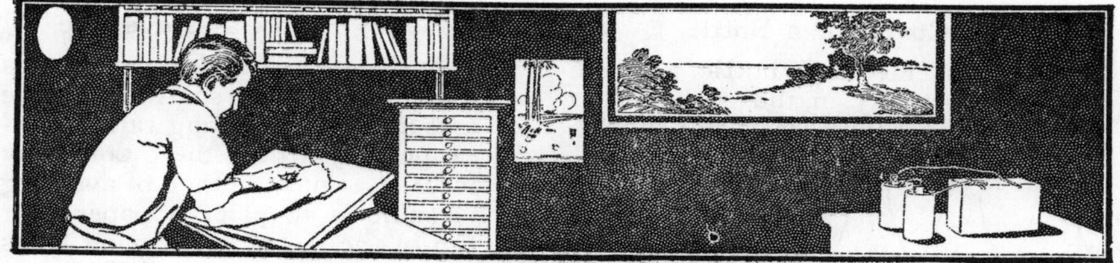

How to Make an Electrotype Stamp

The method described in the following produces a very good metal stamp for any name, initial, drawing, etc.

Procure a smooth and perfectly level sheet of brass about $\frac{1}{16}$ in. thick and about 3 by 4 in. in size. Nickelplate the brass so that the copper deposit will not stick to it. If a small plating outfit is not at hand the piece may be plated at a local plating works for a nominal price. Dip the plate in melted paraffin until the coating is about $\frac{1}{16}$ in. thick and see that no metal is exposed. Drill a hole in one corner and attach a wire.

Draw the letters or sketch desired, using a metal stylus having a sharp point, taking care to make the lines scratched in the wax clean and open to the surface of the metal (Fig. 1).

A large open-mouthed bottle or glass tank will be required for the plating solution, which is made by dissolving copper sulphate in water until the solution is saturated with the sulphate and then adding a few drops of sulphuric acid. Immerse the plate in the solution as shown in Fig. 2 and connect with the zinc pole of the battery. Put a piece of pure copper in on the opposite side of the jar and connect with the carbon pole of the battery, using care in each case to keep the connection of the wire and the upper part of the plate above the surface. One or two dry cells will be sufficient. If the current is right, the deposit on the waxed plate will be a flesh pink; if too strong, it will be a dirty brick color and the plate will have to be washed and the current reduced. When the desired thickness of metal is deposited, remove the plate and pour boiling water on the back. This will remove the thin copper shell and the nickeled plate may be laid away for future use.

Procure a flat pan and after placing the shell in it, face down, sprinkle a little resin or soldering flux on the back. Lay three or four sheets of the lead from tea packages on the back of the shell and heat it over a spirit lamp or on the stove until the lead melts and runs into the crevices on the back of the copper, thus making it solid and suitable for mounting. Mount as shown in Fig. 3 with small brass screws and after polishing the surface to remove dirt, etc., the stamp is ready for use.

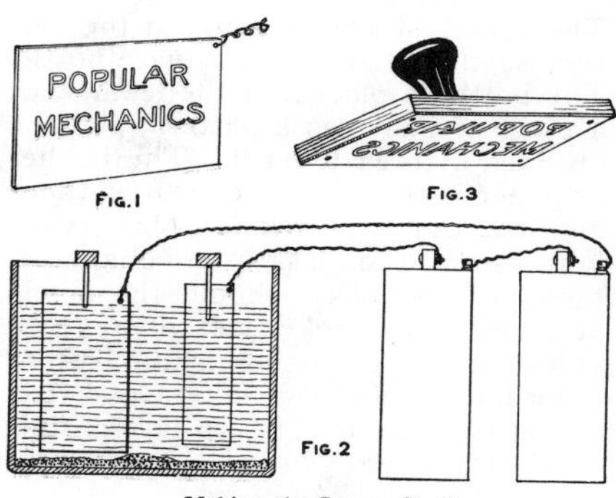

Making the Copper Shell

An ordinary stamp pad will do for inking, but the best ink to use is printer's slightly thinned, as the ordinary rubber stamp ink is not suitable for a metal stamp.—Contributed by S. V. Cooke, Hamilton, Ont.

A Cover for a Bottle

If a glass medicine bottle is to be carried constantly in the pocket, it is best to cover it with leather or rubber.

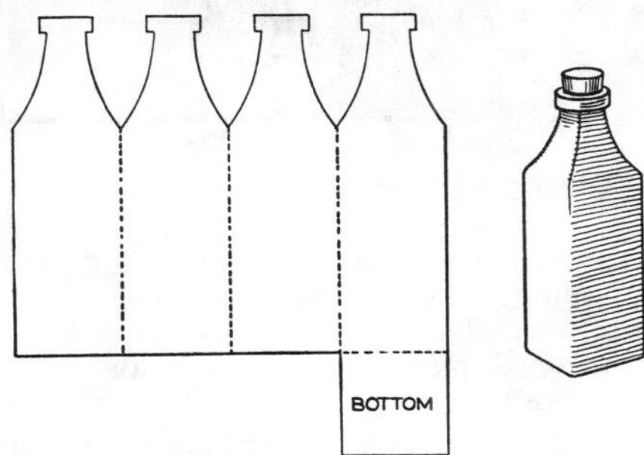

Pattern for Making a Bottle Cover of Leather or Rubber for Bottles Carried in the Pocket

The sketch shows how to cut the pattern so that it will fit a square bottle. The bottle is placed on the leather, or a piece of paper as a pattern, and the outlines marked upon it. The leather or paper is then folded over four times and cut out as shown. This cover will prevent the glass from being scattered in the pocket should the bottle be accidentally broken. It always provides a means of distinguishing it from other bottles of the same type and size.—Contributed by James M. Kane, Doylestown, Pa.

Boring a Long Hole

The usual method of boring a hole through a piece of wood longer than the bit is to bore from each end.

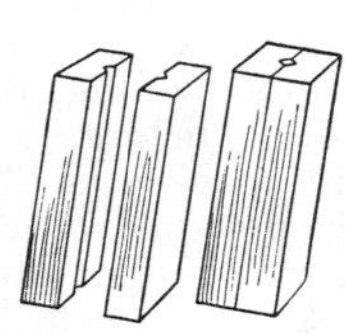

To make the hole straight by this method, split the wood or saw it in halves, then make a knife kerf in both pieces on a center line of the hole and glue the pieces together. The spur of the bit will follow the kerf from either end, and the result will be a meeting of the holes, almost perfectly in the center. — Contributed by Ernest J. Dickert, Niagara Falls, N. Y.

Covering for a Gas-Stove Top

While frying or cooking on a gas stove the grease will spatter over the top and make the cleaning rather difficult, especially where there are many crevices. A simple method of avoiding this trouble is to place a paper over the top of the stove, with round holes cut out for each burner a little larger than the pots and pans used in the cooking. This will keep the stove very clean with a minimum of bother. A paper cut to fit the under pan will keep that part clean.—Contributed by S. F. Warner, East Orange, N. J.

Homemade Skis

Not having a bent board suitable for a pair of skis, I proceeded to make the skis in the following manner: A cheese box was procured and two pieces cut out of the side, each 15 in. long and 3 in. wide. These were used for the upturned ends and two boards,

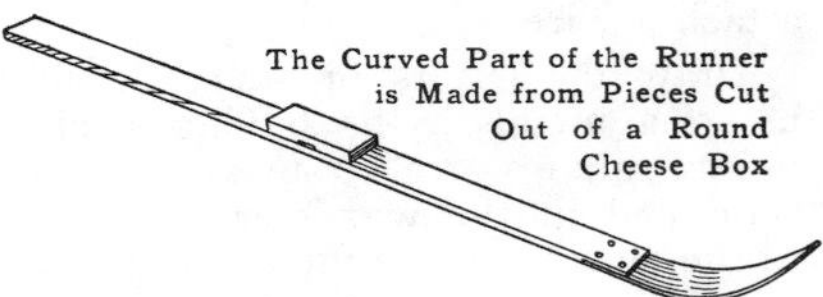

The Curved Part of the Runner is Made from Pieces Cut Out of a Round Cheese Box

6 ft. long and 3 in. wide, served as the runners. A notch, 4 in. long and 1/8 in. deep, was cut in one end of each board to receive one end of the thin curved pieces cut from the cheese box, which were fastened with screws. The upper end of each thin piece was cut to a point.

A piece for the foot, 10 in. long and 3 in. wide, with a notch 1 in. wide and 1/4 in. deep, was fastened in the center of the runner. A strap is run through the notch for holding the ski to the foot.—Contributed by Henry Meuse, Reading, Mass.

¶To remove iron rust or ink stains from cloth, use a warm solution of oxalic acid with a few crystals of citric acid added. Repeat the washings until the stain is removed.

How to Make a Dry Cell

The containing vessel for the cell should be made from sheet zinc. It should be cylindrical in form, approximately 2½ in. in diameter and 6 in. long. This vessel is to form the negative terminal of the cell and a suitable connecting device, similar to the one shown in the sketch, should be provided and securely fastened to the upper edge of the vessel. The vessel should be lined with some heavy blotting paper, both sides and bottom.

Place into a glass jar a small quantity of chloride-of-zinc crystals, and pour over them ½ pt. of distilled water. Allow the crystals to dissolve at least one-half hour. If the crystals all dissolve, add more until some remain in the bottom of the jar, or until the liquid is saturated. Pour off the solution and dilute it by adding an equal part of distilled water. Add to this solution sal ammoniac, in the proportion of 1 lb. of sal ammoniac to every 2 qt. of liquid. Fill the dry-cell vessel with this solution and allow it to remain until the blotting paper is completely saturated.

Obtain a good size electric-light carbon, about ⅝ in. in diameter, and file one end down as shown. Drill a hole through the carbon and mount a terminal.

Make a mixture of equal parts of finely powdered carbon and manganese dioxide of sufficient amount to almost fill the vessel. Add to this mixture some of the solution and thoroughly mix them. Continue adding solution until a thick paste is formed.

Pour the solution out of the vessel and allow the latter to drain for a few minutes in an inverted position. Place the carbon rod in the center of the vessel and pack the paste down around it, being careful not to move the carbon rod from its central position. The vessel should be filled with the paste to within about ⅝ in. of the top. The lower end of the carbon rod should not be nearer the bottom of the vessel than ½ in. Over the top of the paste place a mixture of equal parts sand and fine sawdust and then, over this, a layer of pitch, which acts as a seal for the cell. A layer of blotting paper should

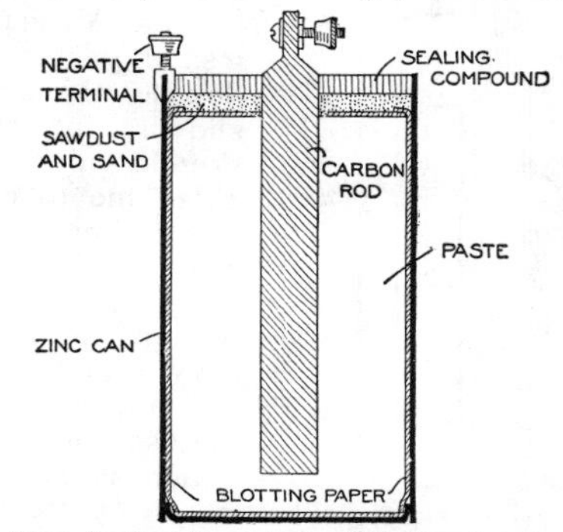

Cross Section through the Cell, Showing the Construction and Location of the Parts

be placed between the sand-sawdust mixture and the carbon-manganese mixture. The side lining of the vessel should be turned in before the sand-sawdust mixture is placed in the top of the cell. The outside of the cell should be covered with some heavy pasteboard, which will serve to insulate the negative terminal from the surface upon which the cell rests.

A Hose-Nozzle Handle

A handle for a garden-hose nozzle is easily made of a piece of wire and the wooden part of a package carrier. The wire is bent to receive the hose at A, and, after the handle is slipped on, the other end is formed to fit tightly over the brass nozzle at B.

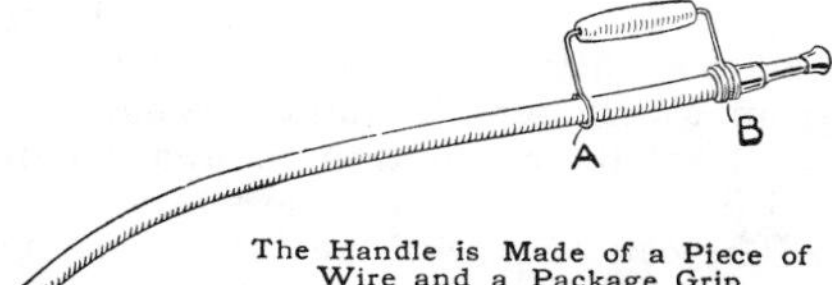

The Handle is Made of a Piece of Wire and a Package Grip

The hose nozzle can be easily carried with the handle, which will keep the hand dry.—Contributed by F. G. Marbach, Cleveland, O.

Guide for Cutting Mortises

After spending considerable time in cutting one mortise in a piece to make the settee described in a recent issue of Popular Mechanics Magazine, I devised the plan shown in the sketch which enabled me to cut all the mortises required in the time that I cut one in the ordinary manner. Two metal plates, one of which is shown in the sketch, having a perfectly straight edge, are clamped on the piece with the straight edge on the line of the mortise. A hacksaw is applied through holes bored at the ends and a cut sawed along against the metal edges.—Contributed by George Gluck, Pittsburgh, Pennsylvania.

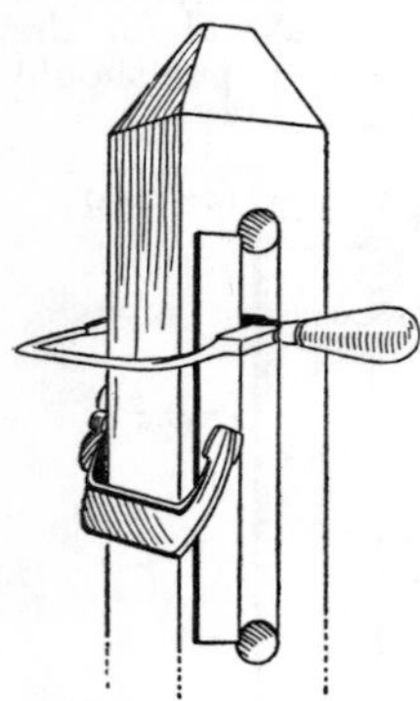

Insect-Proof Poultry Roost

To protect the poultry from mites and other insects while roosting, I constructed a roost hanger, as shown, with oil cups made of empty shoe-polish cans. The cover of the box was nailed to the roost and the bottom, for holding the oil, on top of the roost support. A large nail was driven through the support from the under side and through the center of the can bottom, so that about 1¼ in. projected above the latter.

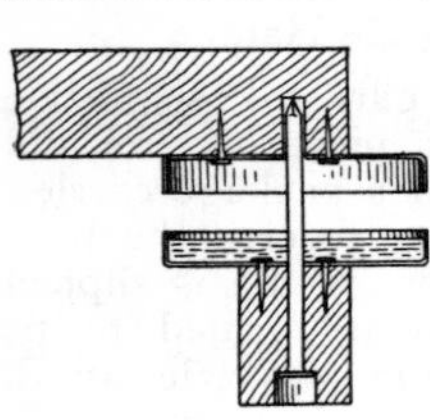

The can cover was perforated in the center and a hole, about ½ in. deep, was drilled in the roost so that the end of the nail would easily slip into it. The bottom of the can was filled with a mixture of kerosene, vaseline and carbolic acid and the roost set in place. Both ends of each roost are fixed in the same way. This makes it impossible for any insects to get on the roost.—Contributed by Rudolph Netzeband, St. Louis, Mo.

To Prevent Shade Rollers from Unwinding

Obtain a stick for the hem on the lower end of the shade that is 2 in. longer than the shade is wide. Place two small wood screws in the window casing below the shade roller in such a position that they will catch the ends of the stick when the shade is raised to the top.—Contributed by Harry E. Kay, Ossining, N. Y.

A Screen and Storm-Door Cushion

A good cushion that will prevent a spring door from slamming can be made out of material cut from an old rubber boot or, better still, from an old hollow rubber ball. Three strips of heavy rubber, 1¼ in. long and ⅜ in. wide, are cut and each fastened with two tacks so that the center will make a hump, as shown in the sketch. One cushion is fastened near the top, one near the bottom, and one in the center, in the rabbet of the door frame.—Contributed by D. Andrew McComb, Toledo, O.

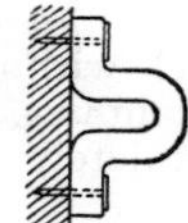

Repairing a Coaster Brake

Anyone having a bicycle coaster brake that is apparently useless because it will not brake, can easily repair it in the following manner: Remove the inner hub by unscrewing the cones and insert a piece of clock spring, about the same width as the brake shell and almost as long as

its inside periphery. Replace the parts and the repair will render the brake quite as efficient as a new one. The spring serves as a braking surface for the expanding steel shoes of the brake.—Contributed by Heber H. Clewett, Pomona, Cal.

Flypaper Holder

The ordinary method of using sticky flypaper is quite annoying, as it cannot be easily removed from anything that may come in contact with its sticky surface. The best way to avoid this trouble is to make a holder for the paper, and one can be constructed of a piece of wire and a metal cover taken from a jelly glass. The wire is threaded at one end on which the cover is

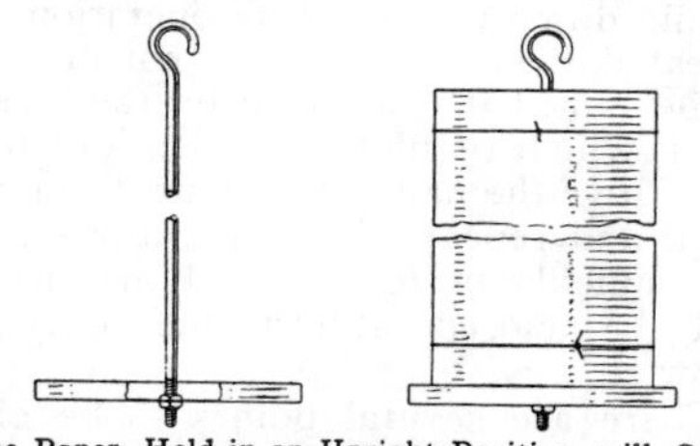

The Paper, Held in an Upright Position, will Catch More Flies Than If Placed Flat

clamped between two nuts. The upper end of the wire is shaped into a hook for hanging it wherever desired. The paper is rolled with the sticky side out and tied with strings, then slipped over the wire and set into the inverted cover. The cover prevents any of the sticky substance from dripping onto the floor and the wire holds it from being blown about the room.—Contributed by Percy de Romtra, Cape May Point, N. J.

A Fish Rake

The fish rake can be made in any size, for minnows or salmon, but it is especially adapted for fish that run in schools, like smelt, herring and minnows. Procure a piece of wood, 7 ft. long, 4 in. wide and 7/8 in. thick, and make a handle 3 ft. long on one end. Dress the other end to an edge, rip off a 1-in. strip and drill holes to receive nails or pieces of wire from the back, through the edge, and projecting about

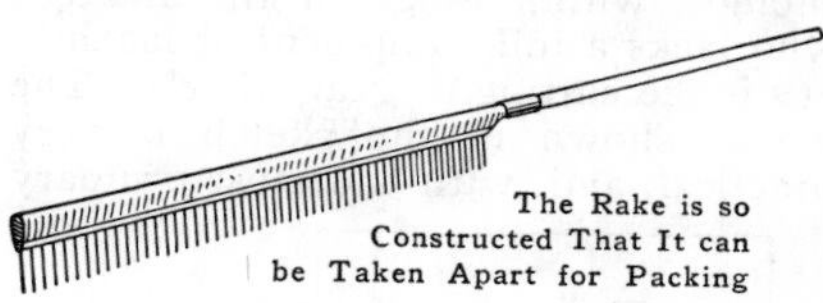

The Rake is so Constructed That It can be Taken Apart for Packing

4 in. The strip is then replaced and fastened with screws. The handle can be cut from the blade and jointed by using tubing. This makes it handy to take apart and pack.—Contributed by L. W. Pedrose, Seattle, Wash.

To Harden Small Blocks of Wood

Small blocks of wood can be hardened so that they will not split so easily when small screws are inserted by boiling them in olive oil for about 10 minutes. The olive oil can be kept for future use. If it is desired to waterproof the blocks after hardening them, they should be placed in melted paraffin and allowed to cool in the solution. This gives the block of wood a good appearance and makes it nonabrasive and waterproof.

Homemade Clothesline Reel

It is much better to make a small reel, like the one shown, for a clothesline than to wind the line on the arm, the usual method of getting it into shape for putting away.

The reel consists of two strips of wood, 16 in. long, 3 in. wide and 7/8 in. thick. These are joined together with two pieces of broom handle, allowing a space of 9 in. between the sides and an extending handle of 5 in. on opposite sides, as shown.—Contributed by Bert Longabaugh, Davenport, Iowa.

Gear-Cutting Machine

Perhaps the last thing that would be thought within range of the amateur who lacks a full equipment of machinery is the cutting of gear wheels. The device shown in the sketch is very practical, and, with the most ordinary

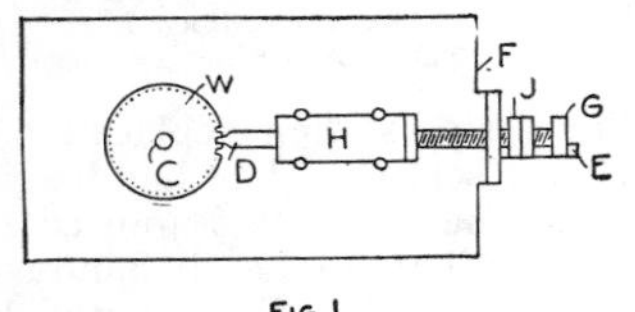

Fig. 1

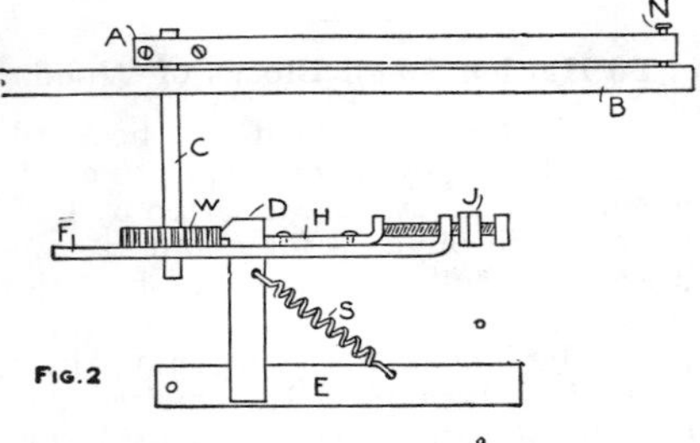

Fig. 2

Details of Gear-Cutting Machine

assortment of iron-working tools, will serve to turn out an accurate gear.

No system of supports is shown, as they are easily supplied. A flat, square board, B, as large as can be obtained—2 ft. on a side being the safest minimum—is used for a dial. A sheet of paper is pasted over the entire board and a large circle drawn on it. This circle is divided into as many parts as there are to be teeth in the gear. A depression is made with a prick punch at each division. A shaft, C, is run through the center, to which an arm, A, is firmly attached. A nail, N, is placed at the end of the arm so that the point can enter each of the punch marks on the periphery or circumference of the circle. A blank wheel, W, is attached to the shaft C, in the position shown, and resting on the iron plate or strap F. A cutting tool, D, works up and down in a slot in F. This cutter is held away from the blank wheel by the spring S, and moved up to it by the screw G, acting through the sliding member H. A stove bolt may be used for G, with the nut firmly fastened to the strap F. The cutter is actuated with a handle E, whose motion is limited by the pegs as shown. In Fig. 2 is shown a top view of the strap E, with a cross section of the cutter and the slot in which it works.

The operation of the mechanism is as follows: With the blank wheel in place set the nail N in one of the punch marks and move the handle E downward. This will make a slight cut on the wheel. Then give the screw G a turn or two, which will make the cutter take a deeper bite, and push the handle down again. This operation is repeated, screwing G constantly deeper, until it is stopped by the locknut J, which regulates the depth of the cut. Move the nail N to the next punch mark and repeat. The operations are very quickly performed and the circle will be closed almost before you know it.

There are several points to be observed. The accuracy depends upon three things. First, the slot through which the cutter passes must be tight-fitting, even at the expense of working hard. Second, the shaft C must fit tightly in the holes made for it through B and F, also the arm A must be firmly attached, the shaft being filed flat at the point of attachment. The blank wheel should be keyed on the shaft or securely fastened with a setscrew. Third, the nail N must enter the punch marks accurately. As the grinding circle is so much larger than the blank, any error here is greatly reduced in the finished wheel. Once in a punch mark the nail must not be allowed to slip until the tooth has been cut.

In practice, it will be found better, after each stroke of the handle, to give a quarter turn outward to the screw G, thus avoiding the scraping of the tool on the up stroke. The cutter can be made of any suitable steel with the cutting point ground to give whatever shape is desired for the tooth. The best shape for any particular purpose can be found by reference to a book on gears.

This cutter is adapted, of course, only to the softer metals. For experimental purposes a blank cast in type metal is excellent and will last as long probably as required. The mechanism here described will cut brass perfectly well and a gear made of this more durable metal will answer for a finished construction. Type-metal blanks commend themselves because they are so easily cast, any flame which will melt solder being sufficient, and the molds, of wood, plaster of Paris or any easily worked material, being quickly constructed.—Contributed by C. W. Nieman, New York City.

A Potato Peeler

The guard is made of a piece of wire about 1 in. shorter than the blade of an ordinary table knife. The ends of the wire are turned into a coil to re-

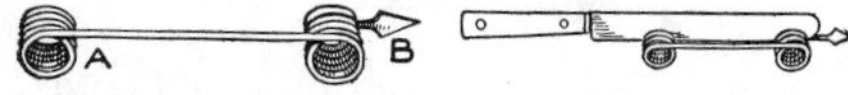

Guard Made of Wire

semble a coil spring with coils close together. Allow enough wire to project on one end to be flattened and pointed for an eye extractor.

When this device is placed on the knife, the contrivance works on the same principle as a spokeshave. The first setting peels the potato without any appreciable waste, the other setting may be as desired for cutting slices.—Contributed by H. W. Ravens, Seattle, Washington.

An Easy Way to Develop Roll Film

This is simply a different motion to the tiresome seesaw one usually employs when films are being developed. In wetting them down previous to immersion in the developer, do not keep them in the water long enough to become limp, but remove them after a few quick dips, says Camera Craft. They will then retain some of their curling tendency, so that by taking one end in one hand and gradually lowering the

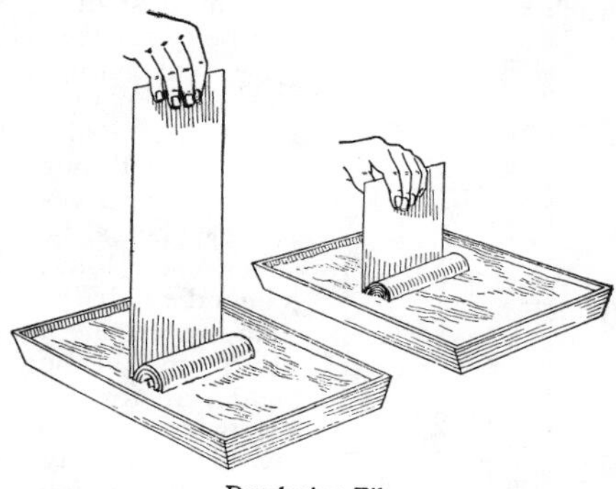

Developing Film

film into the dish of developer and then raising it out of the dish, it will be found that the film will roll and unroll quite readily, much as one would let out or wind in a reel. This method will result in quicker development, because the roll is nearly always immersed in developer. The method necessitates using only one hand, making it possible to develop a second strip at the same time with the other. The illustration shows quite clearly just how the film will behave.

A Shoe Hanger

An inexpensive shoe hanger can be made of a strip of tin, about ½ in. wide and as long as the space will permit. Cut notches along one edge and bend the tin and tack or screw it on a strip

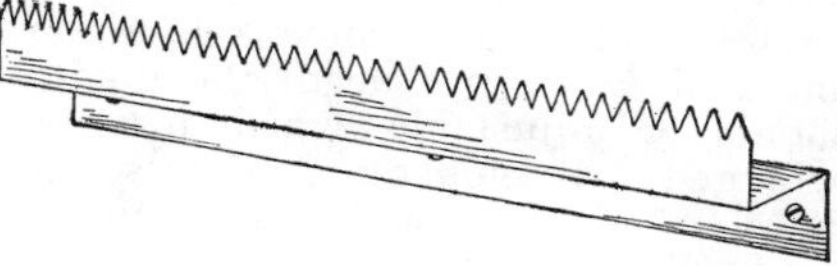

Notched Metal Hanger

of board or to the inside of the closet door. The shoes are hung up by the heels with the toes down.—Contributed by C. R. Poole, Los Angeles, Cal.

How to Make a Small Vertical Drill

A small hand drill with a three-jaw chuck that will take the smallest drill can be purchased very reasonably. For ordinary work these drills do very well, but for comparatively deep holes, or when using long, slender drills, some sort of a stand should be made, if for no other reason, to avoid breaking the drills, which is almost invariably due to the side motion of the hand. There are other reasons, however, for making such a stand, and these lie in the fact that it is impossible to drill by hand at right angles with the surface of the metal, or to hold such a drill sufficiently steady to avoid widening the hole around the top.

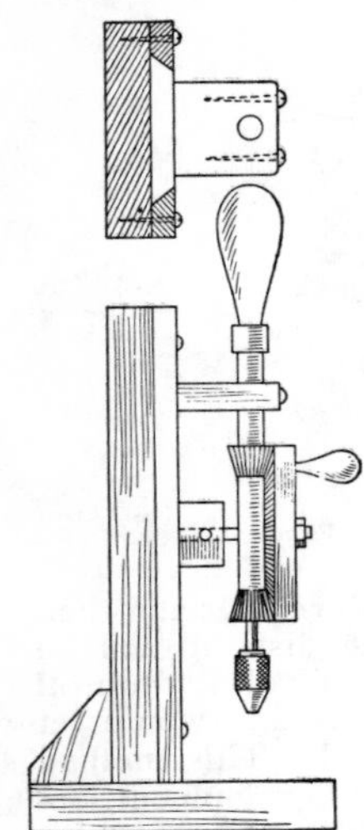

As each make of hand drill will require a somewhat different form of stand, no detailed description need be given of the one illustrated. The principal point is to have the base and standard securely set at right angles to each other, and then provide a smoothly sliding piece to which the hand drill may be clamped. The edges on this slide and the corresponding guides should be planed off to an angle of 45 deg. One of the guides should be adjustable, which may be arranged by elongating the screw holes and placing small washers under the heads of the screws that hold this guide to the main standard.

A neat little hand drill, arranged in this manner and firmly secured to the bench, may also be used for finishing the ends of small shafts, either flat or pointed, for polishing screw heads, etc., to all of which it gives that workmanlike appearance that can only be had when things are polished with a true rotary motion.—Contributed by John D. Adams, Phoenix, Ariz.

Decorating Candles

Candles can be easily decorated by the following method: The designs can be selected from paper prints which are tightly wrapped around the candle with the design in contact with the wax. Strike a match and play the flame over the back of the paper. Allow time enough for the melted wax to harden and then remove the paper. The print will be transferred to the wax.

Select designs that are not larger than the circumference of the candle. A good impression of ink on thin paper works best.—Contributed by J. J. Kolar, Maywood, Ill.

Homemade Hacksaw Frame

A home workshop not having a complete set of tools may be supplied in many ways with tools made by the owner. The hacksaw frame illustrated is one of these. The frame is made of hard wood. The saw end is inserted in a slot sawed in the handle end, and a screw or small bolt holds it in place. The other end is equipped with a bolt having a sheet-metal head, as shown at A. The blade is kept from turning by a projection of the sheet metal which fits in a saw cut made in the frame.—Contributed by W. A. Henry, Galesburg, Ill.

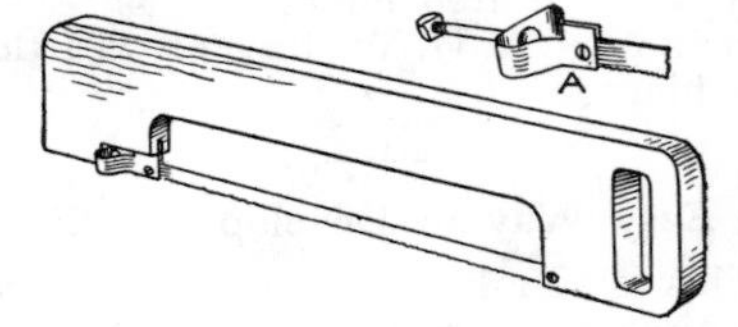

Hacksaw Frame, Cut from Hard Wood, with Fittings Attached to Draw the Blade Taut

Drill Press on an Ordinary Brace

As the greater part of the energy required for drilling metal by hand is used for feeding the drill, I made what I term a drill box in which the brace is held perfectly true and pressure is applied by a weight. The feed can be changed for the different metals and sizes of drills, also for drilling the hard outside of castings and relieving the drill for the softer body. The constant feed will cause the drill to turn out a long chip, and a number of holes may be drilled to a uniform depth by using the same feed and counting the turns of the brace handle.

To build the box, first find the dimensions of the brace, as shown in Fig. 1: the diameter of the head A, the clearance B from the top of the head to 1/4 in. above the top of the handle C, and the over-all length D when the longest drill is in the brace. Make a box having an inside length equal to the dimension D, plus whatever additional height may be necessary for the work. Make the inside width twice the distance C, plus 6 in. for clearance; and the inside depth the length C, plus one-half of the dimension A, plus 3 in. Use material 7/8 in. thick and nail the parts together to form a rectangular frame. Cut a piece of broomstick as long as the dimension B, and two pieces of wood as long as the inside width of the box and as wide as the dimension B. Cut two pieces 1/16 in. longer than the dimension A and as wide as the length B. Nail these latter pieces together as shown in Fig. 2, leaving a square space in the center. This frame is to be nailed inside of the top of the box flush with the front, but before doing so lay it on top of the box to determine where the center of the square space will come, and bore a hole, large enough for the round

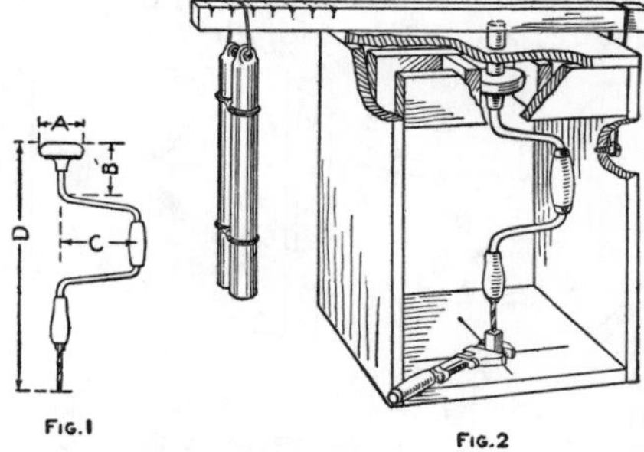

The Weights Apply a Constant Pressure to the Drill, Which can be Easily Turned

stick cut from the broom handle to slip through easily, then nail the frame on the under side of the top piece.

Procure a tough piece of wood, 1 1/2 in. square and long enough to project 2 in. over the right and 10 in. over the left side of the box top, and when in this position, locate the hole bored for the round stick and bore a hole in the square stick, 1/8 in. deep, to coincide with it. Place the head of the brace in the guide and push it up until it touches the top of the box and block it up in this position, then drop the round stick through the hole and rest it on the head of the brace. Place the socket in the lever over the top of the round stick. Make a loop, 8 in. long, of heavy wire and hang it over the right end of the lever and mark the box at the lower end of the loop. Turn in a large screw 1/2 in. below this mark allowing it to project enough to hook the loop under it. Remove the round stick and put a screw at the point the bottom of the loop reaches when the lever is flat on the top of the box. Another screw turned in between these two will be sufficient to hold the lever in position. Different-sized weights, of from 5 to 10 lb., are used on the lever, but for small drills the weight of the brace alone is sufficient.—Contributed by Maurice Coleman, W. Roxbury, Mass.

Homemade Picture-Frame Miter Box

Any person wishing to make a picture frame, or to cut down an old one, requires a miter box for that purpose,

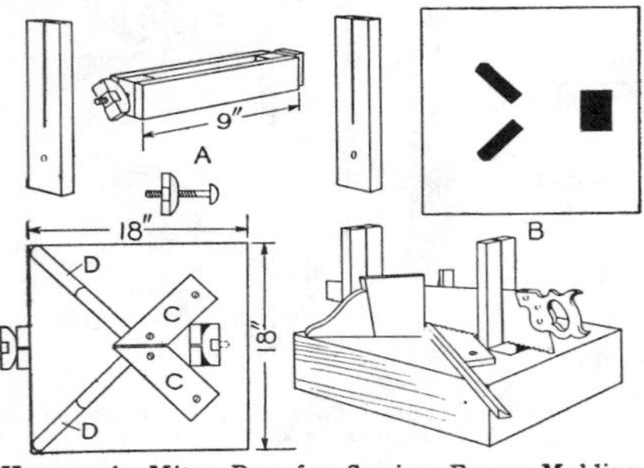

Homemade Miter Box for Sawing Frame Molding and to Hold the Parts for Fastening Together

so that the molding may be properly held while sawing it, and also for nailing the corners together. I made a miter box, as shown, and found it to be just the thing for this purpose. It is built on a base similar to an overturned box, the saw guides being held on the ends of a piece, constructed as shown at A. Holes are cut in the top, as shown at B, for one of the guides and for the two wedges. Two pieces, C, are fastened with their outer edges at perfectly right angles on the top.

The frame parts are clamped against the pieces on top with the wedges driven in between the frame parts and the brackets DD. After cutting the frame parts they are tightly held in place while fastening them, in any manner desired.—Contributed by A. S. Thomas, Amherstburg, Can.

Tank-Development Methods Used in Tray Development

If there are a number of plates to be developed, place a rubber band, about 1/8 in. wide, around the ends of each plate and put them together in a tray. The bands keep the plates apart. The developer is made up as for a tank and poured over the plates, then another tray, or dark covering, is placed over the top. Allow this to stand, rocking the tray from time to time, the same length of time as is required for tank development.—Contributed by Earl R. Hastings, Corinth, Vermont.

A Pushmobile Racer for Ice

The pushmobile shown in the illustration takes the place of the one with rollers that is now so popular with the boys. The materials required, usually found about any home, consist of a foot board, 1 in. thick, 2 1/2 in. wide and 2 ft. long; two pieces of wood, each 3/4 in. thick, 2 1/2 in. wide and 9 in. long; one steering post, 1 in. thick, 1 1/2 in. wide and 30 in. long; one handle, 6 in. long; one small hinge; one carriage bolt, 1/2 in. in diameter and 2 1/2 in. long; two 1/2-in. washers; a few screws, and a pair of discarded ice skates.

One of the 3/4-in. thick pieces is fastened solidly to one end of the foot board with the ends flush. The other piece is swiveled with the bolt at the opposite or front end of the foot board so that at least one-half of the piece projects beyond the end. The steering post is hinged to the projecting end. The skates are fastened to the

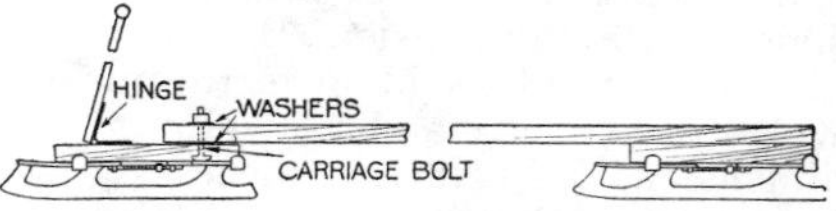

Homemade Pushmobile, Constructed the Same as the Wheeled Kind, with Runners for Snow and Ice

3/4-in. pieces for runners. The manner of propelling the racer is the same as for the pushmobile.—Contributed by W. E. Crane, Cleveland, O.

Homemade Ellipsograph

By CHELSEA CURTIS FRASER

An efficient ellipsograph is the only device that will make true ellipses of various sizes quickly, and such a machine is in demand on some classes of work in a drafting room. Its cost, however, is prohibitive where only few ellipses are to be drawn, but a person handy with tools can make an apparatus that will do the work as well as the most expensive instrument.

The completed ellipsograph, herein described, will appear as shown in Fig. 1. It consists of two main parts, the base and the arm. The former is a hardwood piece, A, Fig. 2, to the side center of which is attached another hardwood piece, B. This latter piece may be dovetailed into A, but an ordinary butt joint will suffice, as a one-piece base, C, also of hard wood, is glued to the bottom surfaces of the pieces A and B, thus securely holding them together. Before gluing, however, care must be taken to see that the piece B is exactly at right angles with the piece A. This can be done with a try-square. Dimensions are given in Fig 2. The same letters are used throughout for the same parts.

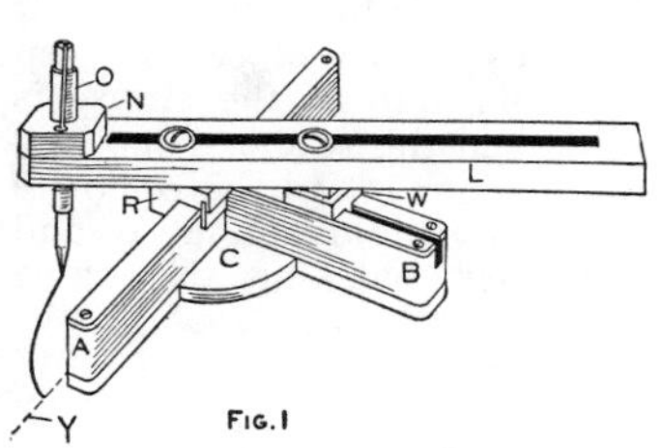

Practically Any Size or Proportion of Ellipse, from 1½ to 16 In. Maximum Diameter, can be Drawn with an Instrument of This Size, and Larger Instruments will Work Equally Well

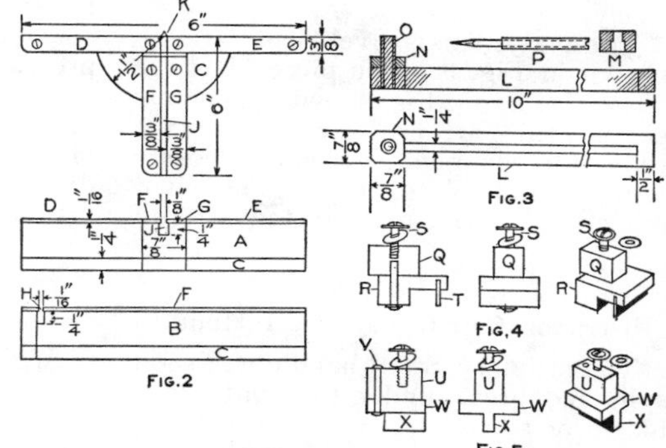

A $\frac{1}{16}$-in. groove, H, is cut out at the juncture of A and B, to admit the flange of the minor-axis swivel head. Another groove, J, is made along the longitudinal center of the piece B, to receive the spine of the major-axis swivel head. Sheet brass plates, D and E, are cut from $\frac{1}{16}$-in. stock and attached to the top of the piece A with screws. The plates F and G are of the same material and fastened in a like manner to the upper surface of the piece B. All plates project slightly where they touch the groove borders, as shown. This is to provide a bearing for the projections on the sliding parts against metal instead of wood. A piece of thin celluloid or brass plate, K, is inserted in the bottom side of the base C so that the point will be exactly in line with the center groove J, and extend outward ⅛ in. This point indicates the center of all ellipses to be drawn. In the bottom of the base C, at each end, drive an ordinary pin and cut it off so that a part of it will project beyond the surface of the wood. These extending ends are pointed with a file, and serve to keep the instrument from slipping when in use.

The arm L is shown in Fig. 3. It is made of either maple or birch. Follow the dimensions given, cutting a slot through it longitudinally, as shown at M, narrower on the upper side than on the lower, the upper being ¼ in. wide. An octagon-shaped piece of wood, N, ½ in. thick, is glued to the end, to give a good seating for the sleeve O, which is a piece of ½-in. solid-brass rod, 2 in. long, drilled to receive closely the pencil sheath. The latter, P, can be made from a section of brass tubing such as is used in a bicycle-pump valve. The upper end is notched to receive a rubber band, and an ordinary pencil can be cut down to fit closely into the other end. The piece O fits tightly in a hole bored through N and L.

The detail of the minor-axis swivel head is shown in Fig. 4. This swivel head consists of two pieces of brass, one, marked Q, being ⅜ in. square by ¾ in. long and the other, R, ⅞ in. square by ½ in. long, with a notch cut out as shown. These parts, as well as the somewhat similar ones for the major-axis swivel head, can be cast cheaply, or block brass may be cut with a hacksaw and filed to the right shape. A shortened dry-cell screw, S, with washer, to fit a tapped hole drilled in the piece Q, serves to bind the head where desired on the arm. The flange T is a piece of $\frac{1}{16}$-in. brass driven into a slot cut in the piece R. The piece R is pivoted to the piece Q, as shown, by means of a piece of wire nail which engages Q, by friction, the lower end being fitted with a washer and riveted loosely so that the parts will turn freely.

The major-axis swivel-head detail is shown in Fig. 5. The piece U is the same size as Q, Fig. 4, with its screw set a little farther forward to make room for the pivot V, which loosely joins U and W together. The pivot is made of a wire nail, riveted on both ends. The piece W is of brass, ½ in. thick, ¾ in. wide and ⅞ in. long. The spine X is made just thick enough to pass freely in the groove J, Fig. 2. A screw taken from a discarded dry-battery cell is used to bind the head to the arm.

To operate the ellipsograph, draw a line, Y, Fig. 1, on the paper, which is to mark the major axis of the ellipse. About midway of its length make a point to represent the center. On the latter set the point K, Fig. 2, and adjust the bottom forward edge of the base C parallel with the line Y. Set the minor-axis swivel head at such a point on the arm L that, when the latter is directly on top of the piece B, the pencil will touch the paper at a distance from the center, marked by K, equal to half the minor axis of the proposed ellipse. To secure the major axis swing the arm until it is parallel with the piece A, leaving the major-axis swivel head unset, and set it when the pencil point has been adjusted to the proper major radius.

Grasp the arm with the right hand between the swivel heads and bearing down, swing the pencil end from right to left. The rubber band will keep it constantly on the paper with even pressure. When half of the ellipse is completed detach the rubber band and reverse the instrument to the opposite side of the longitudinal line Y and draw the other half in the same manner.

Protector Cap for a Chisel Handle

The ordinary chisel handle will soon split and break under the continuous blows of a mallet. A very good and inexpensive method of preventing this is to procure an ordinary patent bottle cap and place it on the end of the handle. It is advisable to shape the end of the handle like a bottle top in order to firmly hold the cap in place.—Contributed by Bert Verne, San Diego, Cal.

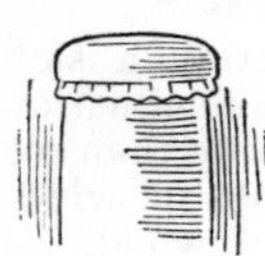

Sweeping Compound

A good sweeping compound may be made as follows: Mix ½ pt. of warm paraffin oil with 2 oz. of melted paraffin wax and add 2 oz. of artificial oil of sassafras. Then pour the mixture into 10 lb. of sawdust and work the whole thoroughly together. Add to this mixture 4 lb. of clean sand and ½ lb. of coarse salt. Each article mentioned is comparatively cheap, and the compound can be kept in an open container.—Contributed by Loren Ward, Des Moines, Iowa.

Freezing a Basin to a Chair

Fill a basin or pot half full of snow, and secretly put a handful of table salt in it and place the vessel on a chair or table, wetting the space where it is to be set. After holding the basin in place for about two minutes, continually stirring the contents, it will freeze to the chair so solidly that when the basin is lifted the chair will come along with it.

This experiment is quite interesting to an audience and can be performed at any assemblage with success. If the instructions are carried out closely, the trick will always succeed and the audience will consider it magic. Even if performed in a warm room, the combination of snow and salt will reduce the temperature below the freezing point where the bottom of the vessel comes in contact with the chair seat.—Contributed by Harry Slosower, Pittsburgh, Pa.

An Envelope and Stamp Moistener

A moistener for postage stamps or envelopes can be easily made from a screw-top jar. A strip of felt cut as wide as the jar is deep and made into a roll large enough to fit the neck of the jar serves as a wick. The metal top is perforated, and, after filling the jar with water, it is screwed into place. This makes a very inexpensive moistener for the library desk.

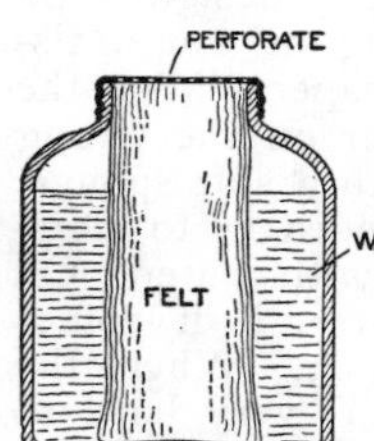

A Homemade Drill Press

An ordinary breast drill is used in the construction of this drill press, it being rigidly secured to a piece of oak, A, 2 in. square and 18 in. long, which

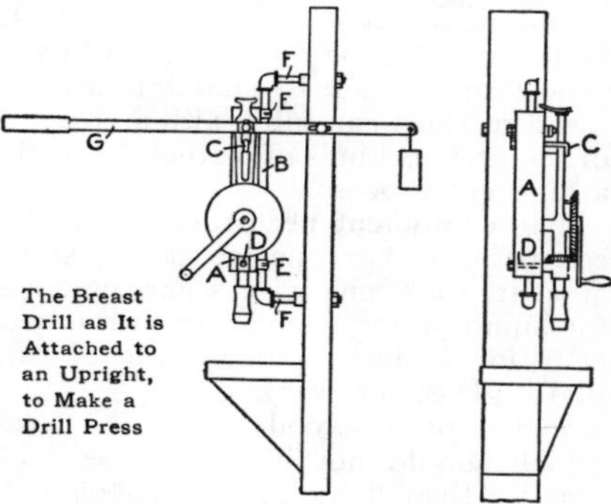

The Breast Drill as It is Attached to an Upright, to Make a Drill Press

is a sliding member on the pipe B. In attaching the breast drill to the wood, a bolt, having a hook on the head end, was used at the top, at C, and a stud at the bottom D. Pipe clips, EE, were attached on one side of the block to fit loosely over the pipe B. The vertical part of the pipe is supported by two horizontal pieces, FF, which are fastened to a post. A feed lever, G, is pivoted at the top of the vertical piece of oak A and fulcrumed on the post with a bolt through a slot, the extending end carrying a weight as a counterbalance. The illustration clearly shows the construction of this very useful drill press.—Contributed by W. A. Ready, Boston, Mass.

¶A pair of bicycle trousers guards makes excellent sleeve bands when the cuffs are turned back and rolled above the elbows.

Arts-Crafts Leather Work

By MARY C. SCOVEL

PART I

Coin Purse—Back

Leather work is one of the most interesting of the crafts, first, because the material is so pliable that any-one can work it, and secondly, because any ordinary article can be made by simply following the directions carefully, although each of the various kinds of leather demands a different process.

The equipment necessary is simple, consisting of two special tools costing 50 cents each, one with a narrow edge for lining patterns, and one with broad ends for tooling; and a piece of tin, plate glass, or very smooth hard wood, which should not be smaller than 9 by 12 in. A soft sponge, a triangle, a rule, tracing paper and a hard pencil are also needed.

A Mat

The first attempt should be made on a piece of Russian calf-skin. This may be purchased at any leather store or craft shop and costs about 50 cents a square foot, if cut to measure. Whole skins contain from 8 to 12 sq. ft. and cost about 35 cents a square foot. Calfskin may be had in almost any color.

The coin purse will be the first article described. The size, pattern and design must first be determined. It consists of three parts, the front, back and flap, as shown in the sketch. This purse will require a piece of leather 4 by 8 in., in order to allow an extra ¼ in. outside of the pattern to pin the leather on the board while transferring the design. The upper flap C folds over the front of the purse D. The design must be divided, the part belonging to C placed on the flap, and the part belonging to the front D, on the lower part of the front.

Coin Purse—Front

Take a piece of paper and fold it in accordance with the desired proportions of the purse, taking care that the design for the front D is on the same side of the paper as that of the flap C. The space F under the flap is without any design. The design for the front D is on the lower part of the upper division of the pattern. Fold the part F behind H, and then the part C behind H and F. Turn the pattern over for the proper position of the purse. Draw the entire design on tracing or tough tissue paper. Wet the leather on the wrong or unfinished side with a soft sponge. Pat the leather and endeavor to moisten, but not soak it, with water. On some leather the water, if it comes through, leaves a stain. When the leather is too wet it is very hard to tool, as the tool sticks and makes an uneven background.

Pin the design firmly down against the leather and fasten the leather with thumb tacks on the outer margin.

With a hard pencil go over every line of the design with a firm, even pressure. If the leather is properly moistened, this will leave a clear outline of the design when the tracing paper is removed. Then with a lining tool—the tool with the narrow edge—go over the lines on the leather with a strong, firm stroke. Should a line design only be desired, this operation finishes the decoration.

Two other methods may be used: tooling or stamping. The design shown does not go to the edge of the pattern. A margin of at least ⅛ in. between the edge of the pattern and design must be left for tooling and stamping. For tooling, after lining the pattern, use the broad end of the tool and make even, long strokes to press down the background. If the background is not easily pressed down, the leather is too dry. Take it off the board and moisten the back again, move the tool back and forth and around until the background is comparatively smooth. Keep the edges very sharp between parts pressed down and those that remain raised. The depth of pressing down the background is a matter of taste, but it should be tooled down enough to make the design stand out plainly. Fold the parts together and line with silk to match the leather and then stitch up the front and back parts of the purse close to the edge. This can be done on any sewing machine, or by a shoemaker. The circle M in the pattern is the catch or button which can be furnished and put on by a shoemaker, or at a trunk store.

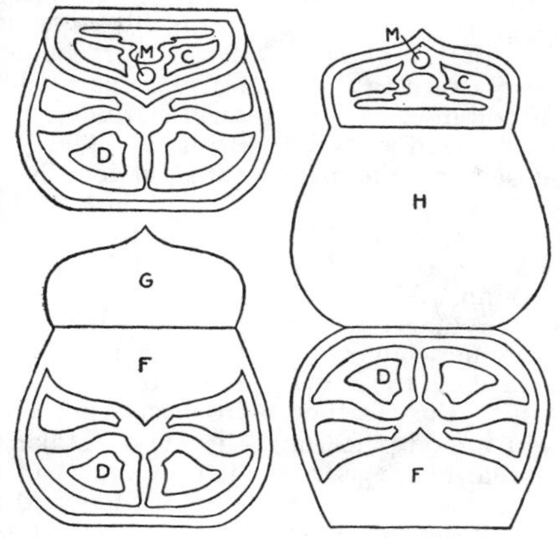

Pattern for Purse

Any ordinary article of leather can be stitched on a sewing machine in the home. To do this successfully the stitch must be long and the needle of a large rather than a small size. Try the stitch on a scrap of leather before sewing the article. If the foot or feed of the machine mars the leather, place tissue paper or a plain piece of paper over the leather and stitch through both. After making the stitch the paper can be pulled away. Use as heavy a silk as the needle will take. The card case, coin purse, stamp case and bags can all be stitched on an ordinary machine, if the above directions are followed. In stitching any soft leather, such as ooze cow or ooze calf, if paper is not put between the leather and the machine, the stitching will stretch the leather. In making bags, instead of stitching on a machine one can punch holes close together with a small punch, and then with strips of leather sew the sides together over and over, or in any manner desired. If no machine is at hand, nor a shoemaker's shop nearby, a large pin or awl may be used to prick holes in the leather, and then the parts sewed together with needle and silk. Use a

Stamp-Case Pattern

running or over-and-over stitch. An over-and-over stitch from one end of the seam to the other and back to the beginning of the seam, makes an X-shaped stitch which gives a very good finish.

The second method after tooling is stamping. Line the pattern as described. Purchase a common carpenter's nail set, with the head not too large. The smaller sets fit the patterns better and make smaller circles. Moisten the leather as described. Use a wooden mallet to strike the tool in stamping the background. This may be done either along circular lines or in a more irregular manner, but avoid striking the tool too hard, as too much pressure cuts through the leather. Other stamping tools of good patterns may be purchased at hardware stores or crafts shops.

A needle book or stamp case is another handy article to make in leather. The sketch shows the design. A piece of Russian calf, 6¼ by 3¾ in., is necessary. This allows ¼ in. on each side and end for pinning down the pattern. Fold a piece of paper into three parts as A, B and C, the front being A; the back, B, which is folded underneath the part A. The flap C folds up with B and then over A toward the front. When the pattern is open, the design for all parts must be on the same side of the paper. The design for the back B is put on the leather upside down. When the pattern is folded this makes the design upright. The parts A, B and C are equal in length and width. The part C may be cut in any shape desired, but keep the tongue D long and narrow. Make two horizontal cuts in the front A about $\frac{3}{16}$ in. apart.

These cuts must be at the same distance from the bottom of the front as the narrowest part of the tongue is from the end. The tongue will then fit the cuts. Make the horizontal cuts a little wider than the tongue. The design is put on the leather in the same manner. It can be worked out in line, tooling or stamping. The parts A and B are sewed together.

The mat illustrated is another useful article and easy to make. Any size may be used, and the method of lining or tooling the design, or both, gives a very beautiful effect.

How to Make a Wood Lathe

A strong, substantial lathe in which wood and light metal articles may be turned can be made by carefully following the description below and the detailed drawings of the parts.

The bed is made of two pieces of straight-grained, smooth, 2 by 4-in. hard wood, 5 ft. long. They are held apart at each end by blocks of wood 2 in. wide. The bed can, of course, be made longer or shorter if desired, but the above dimensions are very satisfactory. The frame of the headstock, Figs. 1 and 2, is made of hard wood. The two end pieces have the dimensions and shape shown. These are fastened with screws to the base.

The base has a slider, a strip of wood 1 in. thick and 10 in. long, wide enough to slide smoothly between the bed pieces, nailed to its bottom, 2 in. from the rear end. Two ½-in. holes are bored through the baseboard and slide. Two ½-in. bolts are run through these holes and through another slide and board which runs on the under side of the bed.

When the nuts on these bolts are tightened, the headstock is firmly clamped to the bed. A half-round, wedge-shaped piece is fastened with screws in the frame against the front end, to serve as a brace against any strain, and will also add to its appearance. The spindle is of tool steel or steel tubing, ¾ in. in diameter and 14 in. long. Threads are cut on one end.

A hardened steel collar, ¼ by 1½ in., is riveted on the spindle so it may turn against another collar of the same size on the headstock. Another collar is fastened with screws to the rear end

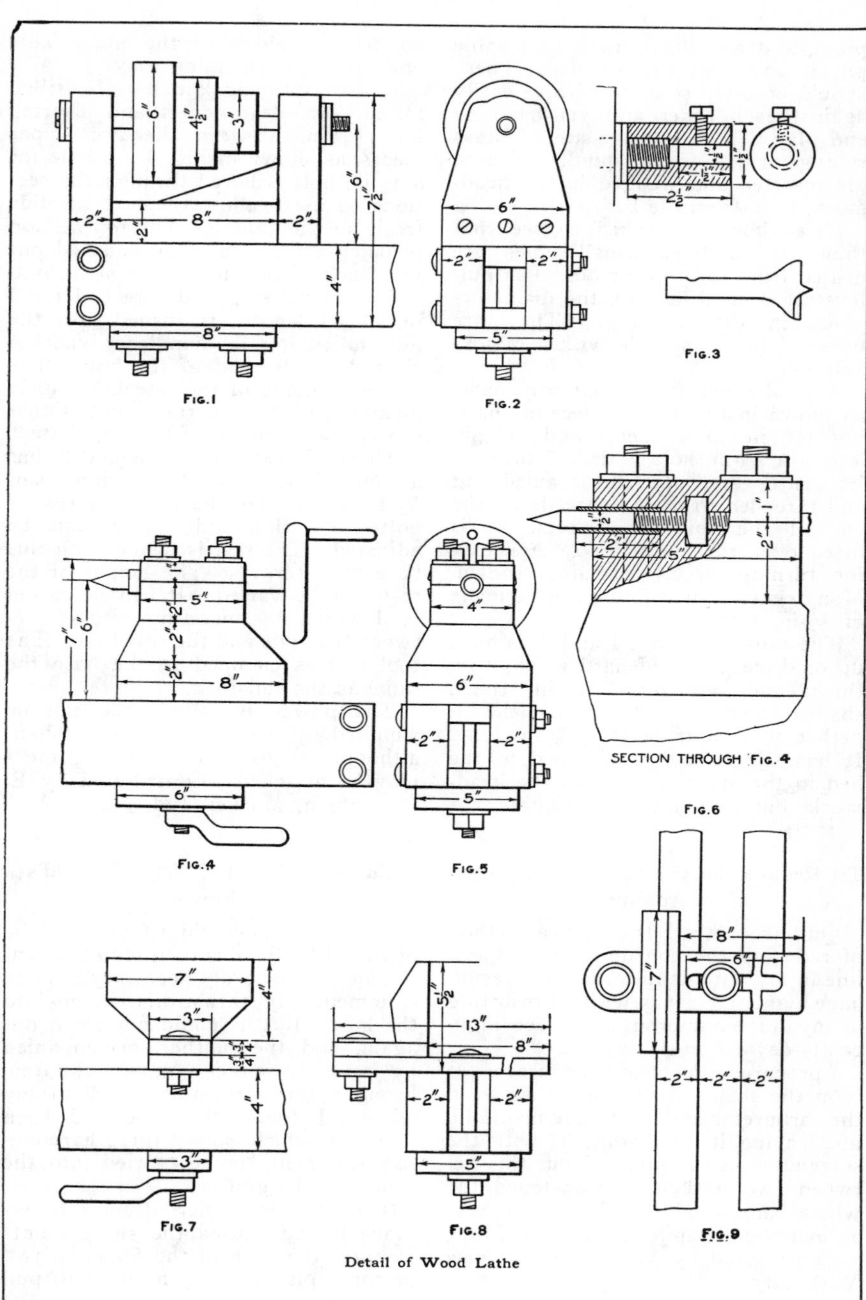

Detail of Wood Lathe

piece, and a collar with a removable pin is fixed on the spindle. These should be fitted so as to revolve easily against each other and yet have no end play. The bearings are of brass tubing drilled for a spindle. These are inserted and wedged in the headstock, 6 in. from the bed.

Care should be taken to see that they are in line. Small holes are drilled from the top for oil. The pulleys are 2 in. wide with the diameters given in the drawing. They are fastened to the spindle with a removable pin.

A good chuck for this lathe is made, as shown in Fig. 3, of a piece of shafting 1½ in. in diameter and 2½ in. long. A ½-in. hole is drilled through its center and one end reamed out and threaded to fit the threads on the end of the spindle. A setscrew is fitted over the ½-in. hole. A center for turning wood is also shown. Many centers, drills, etc., can be made of ½-in. tool steel.

The tailstock, Figs. 4 and 5, is built up of three pieces of hard wood, 2 in. thick, and one piece, 1 in. thick, shaped as shown. These are held together with four bolts, 7½ in. long. It has sliders and is clamped to the bed in the same manner as the headstock, but only one bolt is used. A handle is welded to the nut. This will make the clamping easy.

A piece of tubing, 2 in. long, is drilled for a ½-in. dead center and inserted for 1½ in. between the two upper pieces, as shown in Fig. 6. A hole for a ½-in. bolt is bored through the sections so as to allow the bolt to slide freely in the tubing. The top section is taken off and a place chiseled out just back of the tube for a ½-in. nut. A bolt, 7 in. long and threaded for 2 in. of its length, is turned into the nut and tubing. A handle or wheel is riveted on the end of the bolt. The center is made of tool steel, ½ in. in diameter, with a tapering point. Other centers can be made of ½-in. tool steel.

The tool rest, Figs. 7, 8 and 9, has a slide, ¾ by 3 by 13 in., with a slot ½ by 6 in. The base of the rest is bolted on this slide so it can be adjusted. The rest is fastened on this base with screws. The height of the rest can be varied. It can be raised or lowered by inserting wedges between the slide and the rest base. The tool rest is clamped to the base the same as the tailstock.

The power for this lathe can be supplied by means of a countershaft, although a foot-power arrangement may be attached.—Contributed by E. E. Hulgan, Marion, Ind.

To Reduce the Gasoline Consumption of an Automobile

Quite recently I tried out a method of reducing the consumption of gasoline in my automobile, and, as a result, have higher efficiency without resorting to any of the numerous and exceedingly costly devices on the market.

I procured a piece of wire screen, cut it in the shape of the gasket between the carburetor and the intake manifold, but leaving it blind, that is, with the screen across the inlet. I put this between two gaskets and fastened the whole back in place. The result was an increase of 3 miles per gallon of fuel. —Contributed by W. J. Weber, New York City.

Cutting a Tin Ball from a Child's Finger

A three-year-old child found a globe of tin with a hole cut through the center, and—it is hardly necessary to state —immediately thrust his finger into the hole. But he could not get it out again, and the mother, accompanied by several other small children, brought the screaming child to my office. I found the hole had been punched, which caused three harpoon-like fragments to be carried into the center of the globe.

The mother in her attempt to remove it had caused the sharp points to enter the flesh of the finger in two or three places. Any attempt to pull the ball off, drove the points of the harpoons deeper into the finger, and it was therefore a question of cutting the tin or the finger. But what kind of an instrument could I use on this tin globe?

I had nothing in my case that would cut it. My 35 years of medical experience gave me no help. The tin was as hard and smooth as a glass marble. Yet, it would have been ridiculous to be thus conquered by a tin whistle, so after some meditation I called to mind that I had a pair of heavy tinner's snips in the basement. By using the utmost care I succeeded in cutting a small incision in the round ball, and then with the points of the shears I cut the metal away from the finger.

Such an accident may come under the observation of any parent, and if so, he can use the same method to relieve the child where medical assistance is not near at hand.—Contributed by R. W. Battles, M. D., Erie, Pa.

Child's Seat for Theaters

As children must hold tickets for theaters the same as adults, but the ordinary chair is too low to permit a child to see the performance, an auxiliary seat such as shown in the sketch

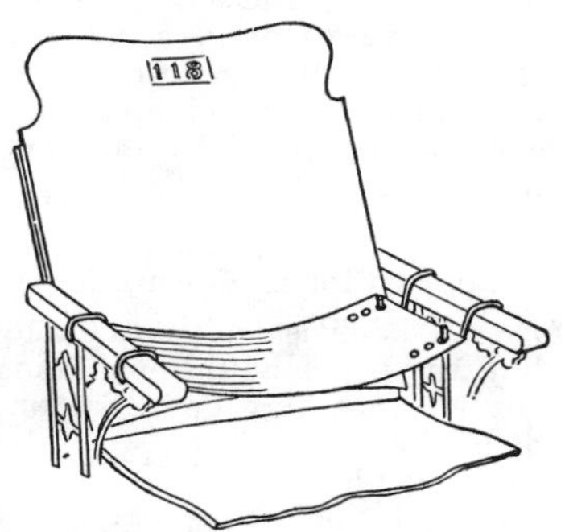

Seat in a Theater Chair

would sometimes be desirable as it elevates the child so its head will be on a level with those of other spectators. The seat is made of a strip of canvas with eyelets for wire hooks that fit over the arms of the ordinary theater chair. It is necessary to have extra eyelets at one end of the canvas to adjust it to varying widths of seats.—Contributed by W. A. Jaquythe, Richmond, Cal.

Holding Spoon on a Hot Dish

After repeatedly burning my fingers in the attempt to prevent the spoon from sliding into the hot dish, I de-

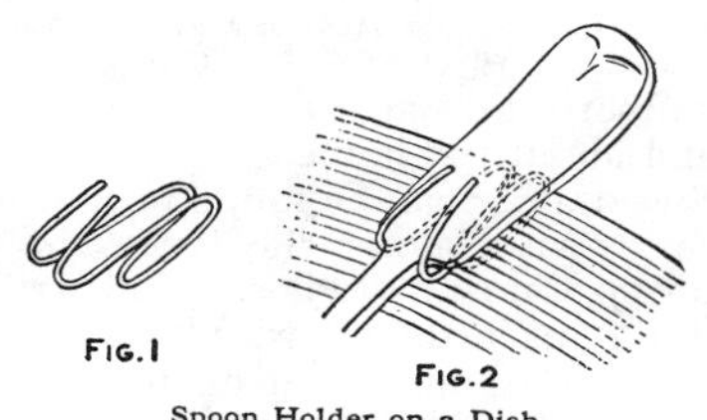

Spoon Holder on a Dish

cided to do a little inventing on my own hook. Taking a clean, straight hairpin I bent it to the shape shown in Fig. 1, and after hooking it over the edge of the dish, I placed the spoon in it as shown in Fig. 2, and my troubles were at an end.—Contributed by Miss Genevieve Warner, Kalamazoo, Mich.

Locating Gas and Electric Fixtures in the Dark

A gas or electric fixture in the center of a room is quite hard to locate in the dark; more so if it is a single-light pendant. The location may be easily found if the fixture is marked as follows: Coat small pieces of cardboard on both sides with phosphorus and suspend them from the fixtures with small wires. No matter how dark the room may be, the phosphorus on the cardboard can be readily seen. The phosphorus is the same as used on matches and can be obtained from any druggist. The phosphorus, being poisonous, should be handled as little as possible, and, after using, should be returned to the water-filled jar in which it was received when bought. If left in the open, it may cause fire.—Contributed by Katharine D. Morse, Syracuse, N. Y.

A Pea-Shooting Gun

The gun consists of only two parts. The barrel may be either a piece of bamboo fishing pole or a section of sweet alder. The spring is a piece of corset steel, such as can be usually found about the home.

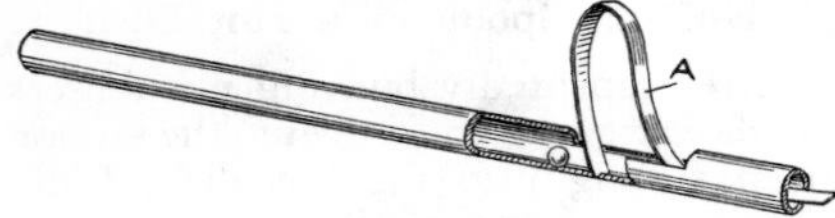

A Pea-Shooting Gun Made of a Piece of Alder and a Corset String

Sweet alder can be found in the summer growing along the fences in the country almost anywhere. Find a stalk, about 1 in. in diameter, which is good and straight, and cut it off to a length of 6 or 7 in. Make a ram rod of wood and use it to punch out the pith of the alder, rendering the bore as smooth as possible. An old bamboo pole of like dimensions may be used instead.

Cut out a section of the wood, 2½ in. long, beginning 1½ in. from one end of the tube. The depth of this cut should be almost halfway through the piece. The corset steel is then inserted into the short end of the tube and bent over so that its other end will touch the bottom of the open part of the bore. A nick is made with a knife across the bottom of the bore at this point, to let the spring catch a little. The ammunition is placed before the caught end of the spring, as shown, and discharged by hooking the forefinger over the spring at the point A and pulling backward as when pulling the trigger of a gun.

It is necessary to keep the muzzle elevated a little after the ammunition is placed in position, otherwise the pea will roll out before the spring has a chance to strike it.

Coloring Electric-Light Globes

Often it is desired to produce certain effects in lighting which demand a different-colored light than that given by the modern tungsten lamp. As an example, a soft, mellow light is sometimes desired similar to that given by the old carbon-filament lamp. In such cases it is a great mistake to install the carbon lamps on account of their exceedingly poor efficiency.

The ordinary tungsten lamp has an average efficiency of about 1.2 watts per candlepower, while the carbon-filament lamp requires about 3 watts per candlepower. Therefore, it is much more economical to color the globe of the tungsten lamp so as to produce the required color than to use the carbon lamp. Of course, both lamps must be colored when any color other than a soft, yellow light is desired.

A cheap coloring solution may be made as follows: Soak a small amount of gelatin in cold water for several hours, then boil it and strain it through a piece of fine cloth. While the solution is still hot, add a small quantity of aniline dye of the desired color that has been previously mixed in a small quantity of cold water. The lamps are dipped in the solution and then allowed to cool in a vertical position so that the coating will be more uniform.

A more satisfactory coloring solution may be made from celluloid. Obtain quite a number of old photographic films and remove all the gelatin by washing them in hot water. Then dissolve them in a solution of equal parts of ether and alcohol. Add the coloring solution and dip the lamps. The coating produced by this method is impervious to water.

Support for an Open Book

When a book is laid on a table for reading the pages at the beginning or end, it will not stay open flat on account of the difference in the thickness of the open parts. One person, doing a great deal of reading, uses a small card, with the corner cut out, which is placed under the side of the book having the smallest number of leaves, as shown.

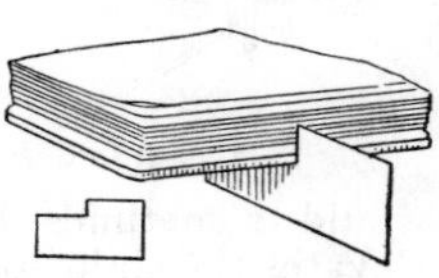

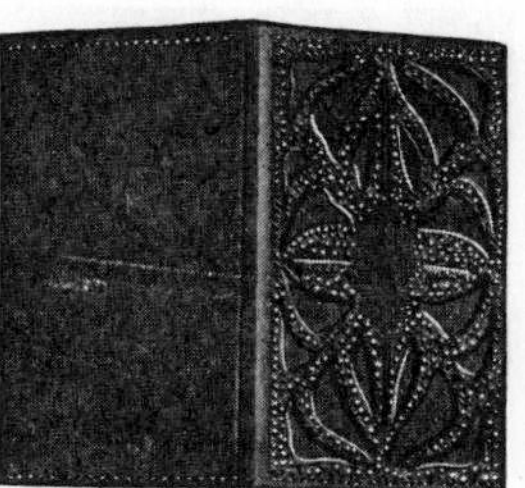

[Some Conventional Designs for Cardcases

Arts-Crafts Leather Work

By MARY C. SCOVEL

Part II

When laying out designs for leather work, avoid making them too small and intricate. Bold, simple designs are the best. The relation between the shapes of the background and of the design should be well balanced. The design should not be so small that the large background shapes overbalance it. One good way is to let the design partly follow or repeat the contour of the object. If the article be rectangular in shape, let some of the lines of the design follow rectangular lines; and if circular, follow the curves of the circle.

The first piece of leather work considered, will be an artistic cardcase. The foundation of a cardcase is a rectangle. Take a piece of paper 10 by 4¾ in. and fold it in the middle, making each side 5 in., then fold in 2 in. on each outside edge toward the center. This last fold makes the pocket of the case. If a deeper pocket is desired, a longer piece of paper must be used, and the fold more than 2 in. Cut out the leather according to the paper pattern and allow at least ¼ in. for the margin. This gives enough extra material for fastening the leather on a board outside of the pattern. Moisten the leather on the rough or unfinished side. Remember that, as previously stated, Russian calfskin is the best for tooling. Place the folded paper on the right side of the leather, then with a ruler, triangle and lining tool draw the vertical lines where the paper is folded. If the leather is moistened enough, the tool will make a deep line. Make these lines where the leather is to be folded in the center, and for each pocket. Line all around the pattern on four sides to indicate the outside border of the pattern. Note that there are four vertical panels or rectangles, two wide ones and two narrow ones, as the leather lies flat on the board. Select either of the wider rectangles for the front of the cardcase. Transfer the design onto this side. Place the paper on the moistened leather and go over all the lines of the design with a hard pencil. When this is done, take the paper away and deepen the lines of the design with the lining tool. If tooling is desired, use the broad-end tool and

Stampcase

Back of Magazine Cover

Silk Lining of Magazine Cover

press down the background with firm even strokes. Keep the background and edges of the design sharp. If stamping is desired, make rows of small circles, regular or irregular, by using the nail set and a wood mallet. The inside or lining is made of skiver leather or silk. The two center rectangles are the only parts lined. Cut out the piece of silk or leather about $\frac{1}{16}$ in. less at the top and bottom of the rectangles and 1/4 in. wider on each side. If leather is used, apply library paste on its back, then place carefully on the inside, smooth it down firmly and put it under a heavy weight to dry. If silk is used, apply the paste around the edges for a width of about 1/4 in., and put it under the weight. The case is then folded and sewed at top and bottom. Cut off the surplus leather about 1/8 in. from the stitches.

The next article is the useful magazine cover, which anyone should delight in making. It requires a piece of leather 11 by 15 in. Allow enough margin to fasten it to the board. Fold the narrow edges together. The design can be placed on either side. A border design bounded by rectangular lines is very suitable. The margin allowed around the design shown in the illustration is 1 in. from the front edge, 1 1/2 in. from the top edge, and 2 1/4 in. from the bottom edge. The design is 5 1/4 in. wide. It is placed on the moistened leather and lined, tooled or stamped as described for the cardcase. The inside of this cover is lined with heavy silk. Allow a 1/4-in. margin to turn in on all four sides. Two strips made of the lining material, 2 1/2 in. wide and 11 in. long, are placed 1 1/2 in. from each side, over the lining on the inside. The lining, strips and the leather are stitched together about 1/8 in. from the edge on all four sides. The strips are to hold the magazine in place as the cover of the book is slipped between the cover and the strip.

Other kinds of leather, such as ooze cow and ooze calf, may be used, but these only allow the method of cutting out the design, as shown in the

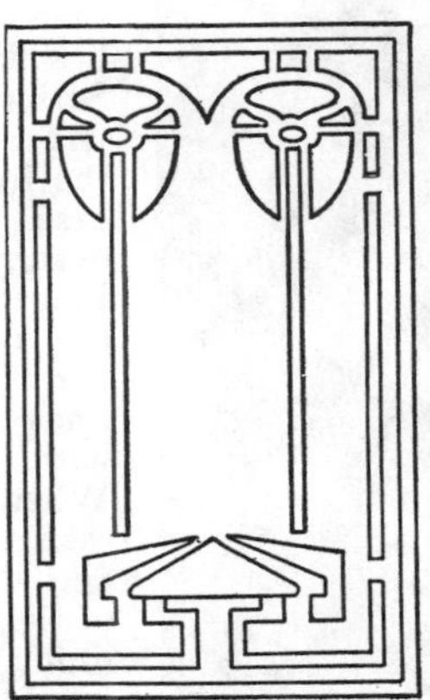

Cover Designs for Cardcases

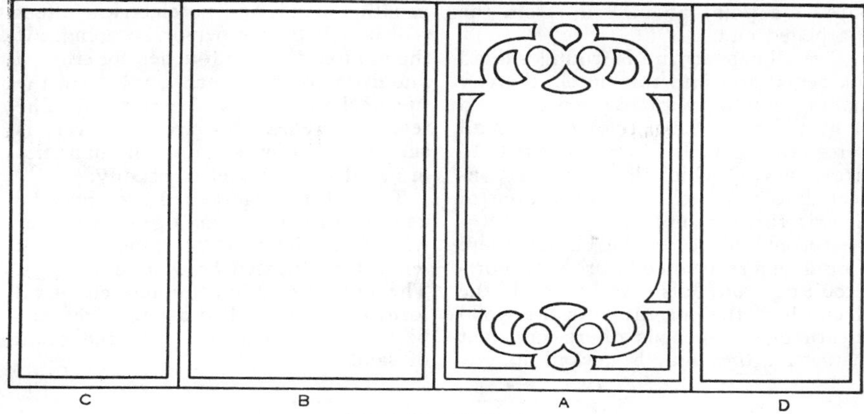

Pattern for a Cardcase

bag and stampcase. The design is traced on the wrong or smooth side of the leather. Do not moisten the ooze leather. Fasten the leather firmly on the board and cut out the design with a sharp knife. A soft silk is best for the lining. Apply the paste on the leather near the edge of the design and after laying the silk in place, put it under a weight to dry.

Handbags

The stampcase and handbags are laid out, and the designs made in the same manner as for the cardcase and magazine cover, but instead of stitching the edges on the handbags, they are joined with thongs run through holes cut in the edges of the leather. The stampcase edges are sewed together. Bear in mind that Russian calf is used for tooling and stamping, and ooze cow or calf for perforated designs.

Furnace Electrodes of Lead Pencils

Furnace electrodes frequently consist of carbon rods, and if there is a short gap between them, forming a

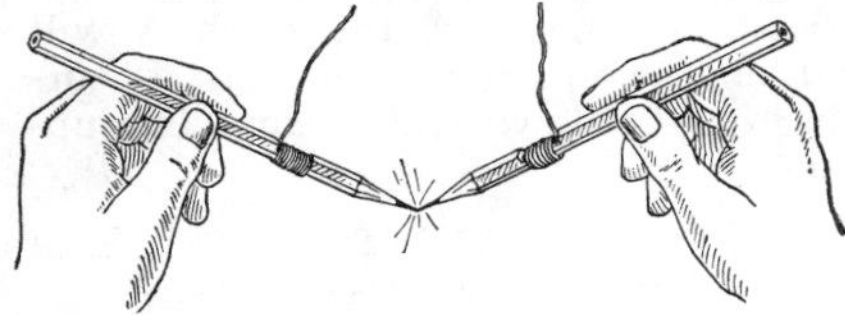
Pencil Electrodes Which Furnish Intense Heat

break in the circuit, the current jumps across that gap, forming an "arc." The intense heat of the arc is used in fusing and melting metals. As large electrodes are necessary for use in furnaces where great masses of metal are melted, so small electrodes are adapted to finer or more delicate work, says Popular Electricity.

As the lead or graphite in a lead pencil is a form of carbon, it will make an excellent electrode for small work. Two ordinary lead pencils, costing only one cent each, may be used. They are first sharpened as if they were to be used for the usual purpose of writing. Then a small notch is cut in one side of each pencil, laying the lead bare at a point about 2 in. from the sharpened end.

A small copper wire is wound around the pencil and into this notch, thereby making contact with the exposed lead or graphite. By means of these small wires the pencils are connected to larger wires, which in turn are connected to a switchboard or source of electric-current supply.

At some place in the circuit there should be a resistance to prevent short-circuiting and also to control the strength of the current. As the wood sheath on the pencils offers sufficient insulation, they may be picked up, one in either hand, and no electrical effect will be felt by the person so doing. If the pointed tips are touched together, a fine little arc, not much larger than the tips of the pencils, will be formed. The temperature of this arc, however, is such that fine wires or small quantities of metal may be melted readily.

These little lead-pencil arcs may be used to fuse very small gold or silver wires, or platinum thermometers, or wires for tungsten or tantalum lamps. The bead or globule of molten metal formed on the end of a fine wire need be no longer than a small-sized grain of sand.

Coat and Trousers Hangers

The hanger is simple in construction and can be easily made by following

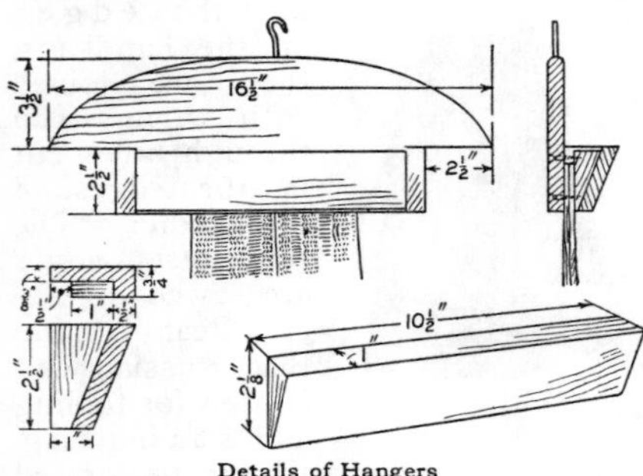

Details of Hangers

the dimensions given in the drawing, and the directions given below.

The back is first marked off on a soft-pine board and cut out. The curved edge should be rounded off so as to prevent injury to the coat. The two end pieces are then made, and fastened to the back with screws as shown. The wedge is ripped diagonally from stock and the smaller edge made slightly round. The wedge slides in between the two end pieces, and after the trousers have been put in place, is pushed down until it holds them securely. The hanger is a screw hook turned into the wood, or it may be made of a piece of heavy wire run through a hole in the back and bent over on the bottom edge. The wood may be stained any desired color and then given two coats of shellac.—Contributed by Olaf Tronnes, Wilmette, Illinois.

Mending Broken Fountain-Pen Barrels

Broken fountain-pen barrels may be mended by the use of melted shellac. This can be done by heating some dry shellac and applying it to the fracture. Do not scrape off the surplus shellac, but shape it with a heated iron. A pen with such a repair has been in use for two years.—Contributed by G. D. Whitney, Pittsburg, Pa.

Jig-Saw Blades

The ordinary form of jig-saw blade has a tendency to pull the fiber of the wood in one direction, thereby producing a jagged cut. To overcome this I made several blades with teeth as shown in the sketch. After the downstroke is completed, the teeth A will cut on the upstroke, the teeth B cutting on the downstroke, etc. The up-

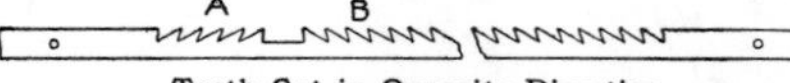

Teeth Cut in Opposite Direction

stroke teeth should be a trifle longer than the others and from 4 to 6 in number.—Contributed by Phillip Caflish, Buffalo, N. Y.

Leaded-Glass Panels for Furniture

Certain kinds of furniture may be greatly improved in appearance by the use of simple glazed panels in the door frames. It would be inappropriate to have anything elaborate in a small cabinet for the reception of china as it distracts the attention from the contents, but a simple leaded diapering or pattern of small design, such as shown in Figs. 1 and 2, would be quite in place and have a good effect. For other purposes more elaborate effects can be worked out in deep shades, says Work, London.

A hanging cabinet with leaded panels is shown in Fig. 3. These panels for the doors are in the design shown in Fig. 2. Panels of this design can be used either for furniture or for small windows. The process of making these panels is not difficult and the ordinary workman can form them, the only difficult part being the soldering of the joints.

The beginner should confine himself to plain glazing, the design being formed by piecing together glass of different shades. The method of procedure is to first make a small sketch in color to a scale of about 1 in. to the foot, carefully arranging the parts and colors. A full-sized panel can be drawn from this sketch. The effect of plain glazing depends entirely on the arrangement of the lead lines and the art glass. In the full-sized drawing

A Small Hanging Cabinet with Doors Having the Leaded-Glass Design Shown in Fig. 2

the shapes are arranged so that they may be easily cut, all long forms being either avoided in the design, or divided by a cross-lead to guard against breakage in the cutting.

Two simple forms of glazing are shown in Figs. 1 and 2. The one shown in Fig 4 is somewhat different, the top of the panel being decorated with simple curves. This general design is considerably elaborated in Figs. 5, 6 and 7. It is desirable to decorate only a part of a window so that the maximum of light may gain access.

Two simple treatments of a sailing craft are shown in Figs. 8 and 9. The effect of the introduction of this design in one of the panels of a small cabinet is shown in Fig. 1.

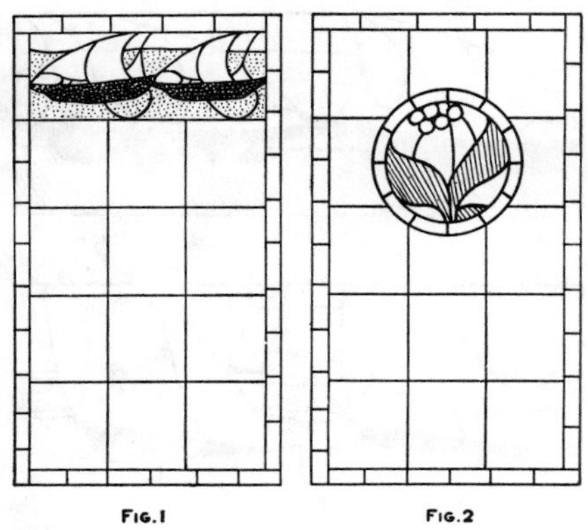

Simple Leaded Diapering of Small Design for a Small China Closet or Cabinet

An example of plain glazing is shown in Fig. 10. This is a piece of simple leading and yet very effective, involving no difficulty of construction.

For this lead glazing a quantity of strip lead, the section of which is shown in Fig. 11, will be required. This can be purchased from dealers in art-glass supplies. The lead is sold on spools and it must be straightened before it can be worked. This is most easily done by fastening one end and pulling on the other. The glass for this work must be reasonably thin as no advantage is gained by the use of thick material, and it is difficult to cut. A piece of art glass has a right and a wrong side, the side on which the spots and streaks appear is the right side, and it is cut on this side. The tools required are a glass cutter, a heavy knife and soldering appliances.

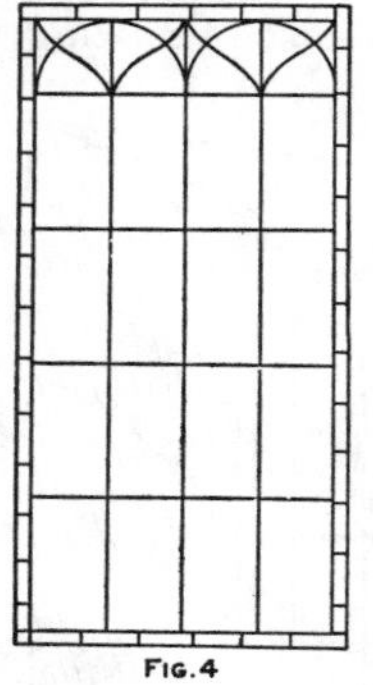
Fig. 4

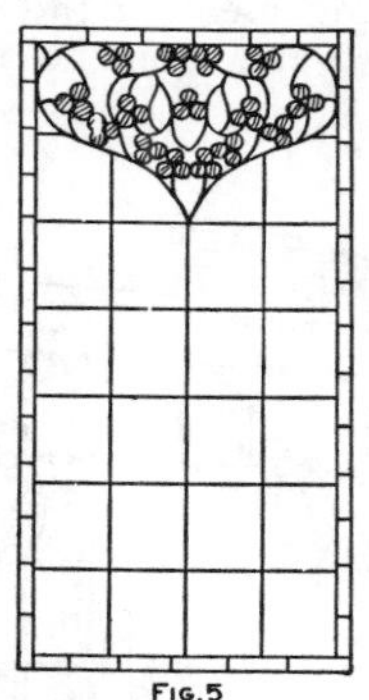
Fig. 5

Fig. 6

Only a Part of the Top of Each Window is Highly Decorated so That the Maximum Light may Gain Access

Fig. 7

Two Windows Placed Together May Have Their Tops Leaded to Produce a Combined Effect

Sketch out the lines of the design full size on paper, drawing in only one side of a symmetrical pattern and tracing the other. After the design has been prepared, the next step is to make a cutting pattern. To do this, take a piece of tracing cloth and lay it on the drawing. Trace the lines and go over them with a brush dipped in black, making the lines exactly the same thickness as the core of the lead, or the thickness of the distance the glasses are separated from one another, as shown in Fig. 11. Each division is marked for the color it is to be and the paper is then cut into sections on each side of the broad line. These pieces form the patterns for cutting similar shapes from heavy cardboard which serve as templates for cutting the glass.

Proceed to cut the glass by laying a pattern on the right side and scoring around with the cutter guided by the pattern. Little difficulty will be experienced in this work if the general design does not have very irregular shapes.

When the various pieces of glass

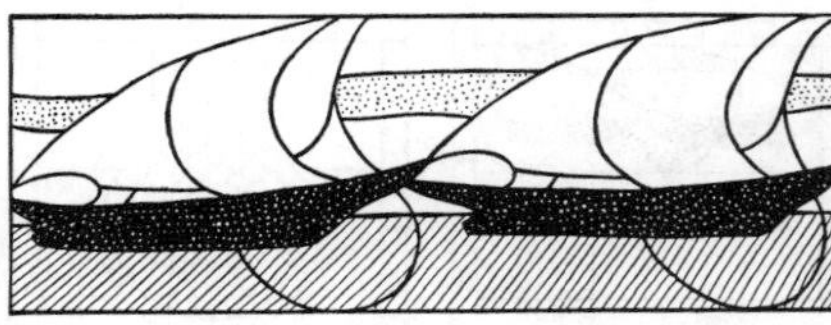
Fig. 8

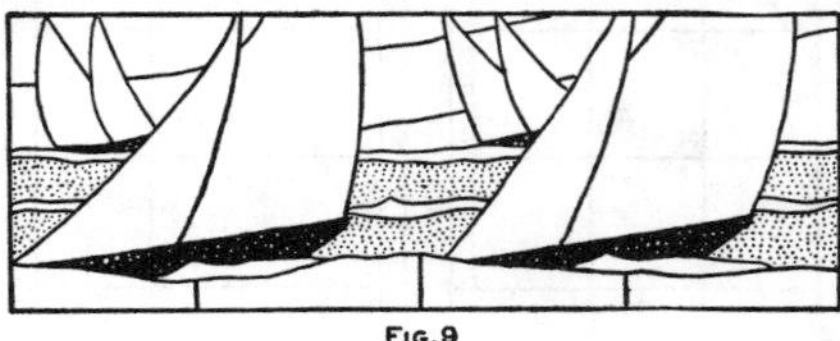
Fig. 9

Two Designs for the Tops of Windows, Showing Treatments of Sailing Craft

have been successfully cut and are ready for leading up, arrange them in position on the preliminary sketch, and then measure the outside leads and cut one piece for each side, the lead being cut to fit against the core of the other at the joint, as shown in Figs. 12 and 13. Proceed to cut the lead for the long curves obtaining the length by bending the strips along the lines of the design. As each is cut it will be found convenient to tack it in position on the working table by means of small brads, so as to simplify the measuring and cutting of the other parts. Continue until the panel is complete, when, after truing up, it is

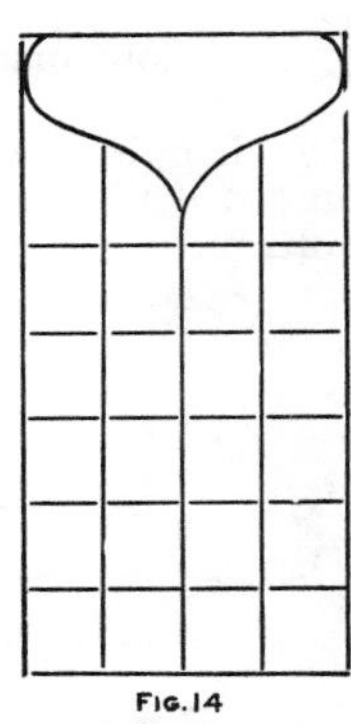

The Lead Frame is First Made, the Long Lines are Put in and Then the Short, Horizontal Ones

ready for soldering. This is done in the usual way but requires extraordinary care to avoid the possibility of melting the lead. The overlapping parts of the leads are pressed well against the glass in each division to keep it from rattling.

In making up the squares and rectangles such as appear in Figs. 2, 4, 5, 6 and 7, lead the long lines first, adding the shorter, horizontal pieces last. The sketch, Fig. 14, will clearly illustrate this part of the work. The sketch shows the starting of the panel, Fig. 5.

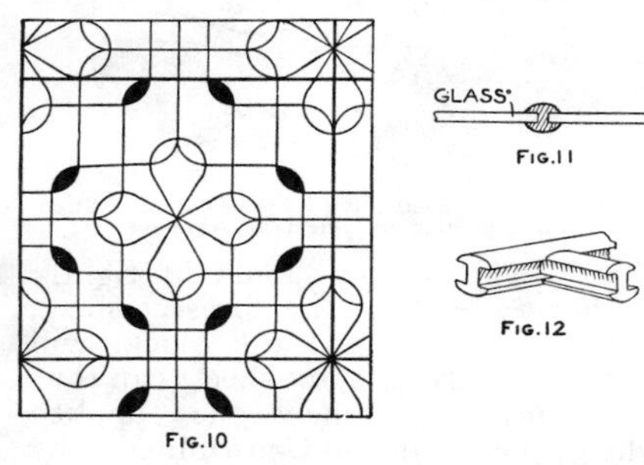

Example of Plain Glazing with Cross Section of Glass and Lead Strip, also Showing Joint

Raising Cucumbers on a Trellis

A novelty in cucumber culture, tried recently with great success, is as follows: As soon as the vines are about 18 in. long, stretch wire mesh 24 in. wide on poles alongside the row of plants and train the vines on the wire. The cucumbers will grow larger and the plants will require less care than when they are on the ground.

A Barrel Boat

A boat that any handy boy can easily make is constructed of a barrel which is kept with the opening cut in one side up by two 4 by 6-in. timbers and two tie pieces, 2 by 4 in. The lengths of these pieces will depend on the size of the barrel.

A good watertight barrel should be selected and an opening cut in the center between the hoops, of such a size as to allow the body of the occupant room for handling an oar. The timbers are attached to the barrel with iron straps—pieces of old hoops will do. The two tie pieces are put across the timbers at the ends of the barrel and spiked in place.

The boat is to be propelled with a single, double-end paddle. There is no danger of the boat capsizing or the water splashing into the barrel.

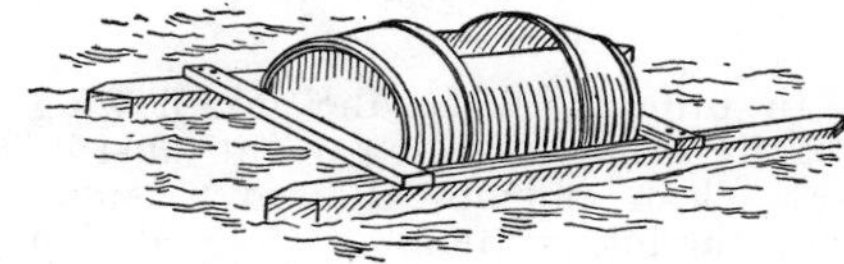

Boat Made of a Barrel Which is Kept from Capsizing by Timbers Attached

Homemade Wing Nuts

A handle taken from a worn-out faucet, drilled out and threaded for a bolt, makes a good wing nut. A dis-

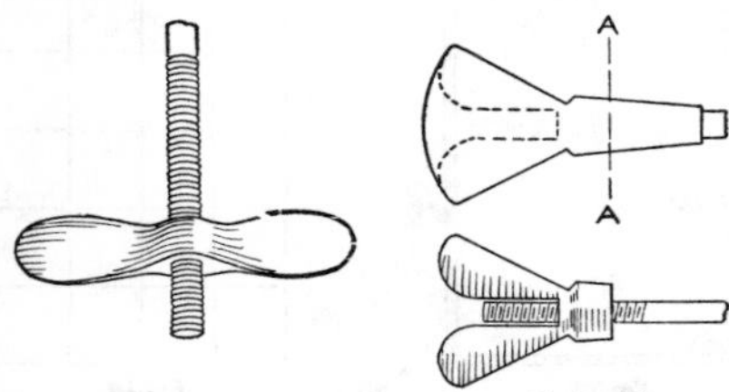

Wing Nuts Made of Discarded Parts Taken from a Faucet or a Gas Bracket

carded gas-bracket key, cut off on the line AA and with the part within the dotted lines filed out, then drilled and threaded, also makes a good wing nut.

A Spool-and-Ball Puzzle

Procure an empty basting-thread spool and make a hole in its side, at A, just large enough to receive a 1/4-in. steel ball. A piece of celluloid, B, is wrapped around the flanges, as shown, and fastened with small brads. An old

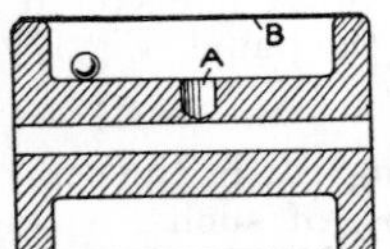

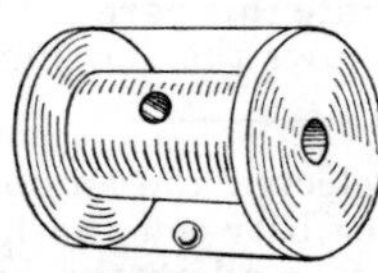

The Steel Ball is Not So Easily Run Into the Hole as It Appears

negative film, well cleaned, is suitable for the celluloid. Be sure to put the steel ball in before fastening the celluloid in place.

The difficulty of the puzzle is to get the ball into the hole.—Contributed by R. C. Knox, Waycross, Ga.

To Start the Ink Flowing from a Drawing Pen

In order to keep the ink flowing readily from a drawing pen it must be kept clean and not allowed to stand with the ink in the nibs. A good plan is to have a small piece of velvet fastened to the drawing board or upon a small block, conveniently located where the pen may be drawn across it as in making a line. The tuft of the velvet will clean out the partly dried ink between the nibs.—Contributed by H. L. Woodward, Washington, D. C.

A Pencil-Sharpener Stick

Do not discard the sandpaper stick or pencil sharpener used by a draftsman just because all the abrasive sheets have been removed. Make use of it indefinitely by fitting a wedge in one edge, as shown in the illustration, to hold fresh sheets of sand or emery

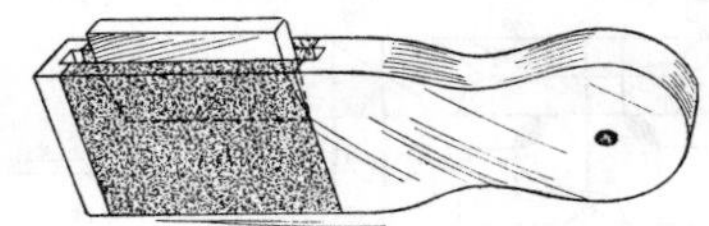

A Wedge Attachment for a Pencil-Sharpener Stick for Changing the Sheets of Abrasive

paper. The wedge should fit tightly so that the ends of the abrasive sheet, when wound around the block, will be held tightly. Worn sheets can thus be removed and new ones applied when necessary.—Contributed by Chas. J. La Prelle, Flushing, L. I.

Splice for Round Belts

Sash cords or round belts are easily spliced with a coil spring, and for belts this joint will run smooth and noiseless. The coil should be a close fit on the belt, and after turning one end halfway into the spring, the belt itself is twisted in the reverse direction as many times as there are coils remain-

A Coil Spring Used for Splicing Sash Cords or Small Round Belts

ing in the spring, before the other end is turned into it to meet the first.—Contributed by F. S. Cummings, Detroit, Michigan.

¶When painting wireless instruments use black asphaltum, as it has high insulating qualities.

Amateur Mechanic's Combination Lathe

By JOE V. ROMIG

The thing most desired by a young mechanic is a lathe, but the cost of these machines is usually too high to be considered by the average boy, and consequently he is hampered in executing more difficult work. The combination lathe shown in the illustration comes as near filling the wants of most boy mechanics as could be wished, the attachments making it more than a lathe so that various kinds of work other than turning may be accomplished. The materials necessary are few, and, outside of a few parts, it can be constructed by the average boy at home with ordinary tools.

The material used for the construction of the frame consists of either well seasoned oak or maple, 2¾ in. wide and 1½ in. thick. These timbers can be purchased surfaced on all sides, and they must be straight and true to size. The lengths to cut the pieces are given on the general drawing. The end standard at the headstock is cut to the full length so that the upper end is used as a bearing for the headstock spindle. A vise jaw, about 2½ ft. long and of the same kind and dimension material as the frame, is attached with screws made of bolts on the standard, at the tailstock end of the lathe. The feet are made of two boards for each standard, and are of the same material as the frame and ⅞ in. thick. After cutting the pieces to the right length, making sure that the ends are square, and boring the holes to receive the bolts snugly, they are put together, the horizontal pieces for the ways and feet at perfect right angles to the uprights. This will insure the parts running freely in the finished machine. All bolts should be supplied with a washer under both head and nut, and the nuts drawn up tightly.

The Main Ambition of a Boy Mechanic is to Own a Lathe

The headstock extends 7 in. above the upper surface of the ways, thus making a swing of 12 in. One of the standards of the headstock is the extension of the lathe standard, as previously mentioned; the other standard being cut 9¾ in. long and attached with bolts between the ways in the same manner as the lathe standards are fastened. A block, 3 in. long, is fastened between these standards to aid in holding them rigid. The bearings for the spindle, which is a piece of steel, ¾ in. in diameter and about 9 in. long, are made in the upper ends of the standards in the following manner:

A 1¼-in. square is laid out on the upper end of each standard, with its center exactly over the center for the shaft, and the wood is cut out to make a square hole, which should be slightly tapering one way or the other toward the center of the standard, to hold the babbitt metal used for the bearing. A ⅜-in. hole is bored, vertically down from the upper end of each standard and in the center, to meet the square hole. This is used as a gate for pouring the melted metal in and later to make an oil hole. Prepare 8 pieces of cardboard to hold the melted metal standard. A split or solid pulley may be used, as desired, on the shaft between the standards. If a solid pulley is used, it must be slipped on the shaft as the latter is run into the bearings.

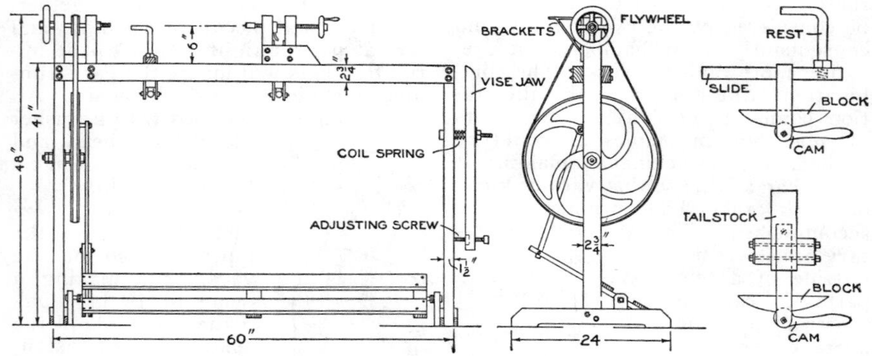

Detail of the Plain Lathe, Showing the Construction of the Clamp Devices for the Tailstock and Rest Slide, and the Manner of Attaching a Vise Jaw on the End of the Lathe Bed

in the square holes while it cools, by cutting them about 2 in. square and making a hole in the center of each, ¾ in. in diameter. Two of these pieces are held between the two standards while the shaft is run through them and the square holes. Paint the parts of the shaft used in the bearing with thick white lead, or wrap it with one thickness of writing paper, then line it up perfectly parallel with the ways in both directions and tack the cardboard pieces to the standards. Place the remaining two cardboard disks on the ends of the shaft and tack them to the standards also. Place putty over all the edges and pour melted babbitt metal into the hole at the top. When the metal is cool, remove the cardboard disks and turn the shaft, first in one direction and then in the other, until it can be taken from the bearings. A ⅛-in. hole is then drilled through the metal in the top for an oil hole. The ends of the shaft should be threaded by a machinist, and nuts fitted to it and faced up true. The threads should be cut just long enough to allow the back of each nut to turn freely against a washer placed on the shaft against the The pulley is fastened to the shaft with a pin run through a hole drilled in them. If a small flywheel is attached to the outer end of the spindle it will aid in keeping a steady motion.

The same procedure is carried out in the construction of the tailstock bearings. The standards for this part are about 8 in. long and are bolted at right angles to and between two pieces that rest on top of the ways. The shaft is threaded full length, which should be done in a lathe by a machinist to get a true thread, and the melted metal run on it to make an internal thread in the bearing. A nut is run on the threads of the shaft between the standards, and provided with a small handle for use in locking the shaft when it is set on work between centers. A small handwheel is attached to the back end of the shaft, into the rim of which a handle is set to make the turning easy.

The faceplate consists of a disk of metal, 6 in. in diameter and ¼ in. thick, attached with $\frac{3}{16}$-in. machine screws to a ¾-in. nut. The disk is drilled in various places to receive ordinary wood screws. The faceplate should be made by a machinist so that the sur-

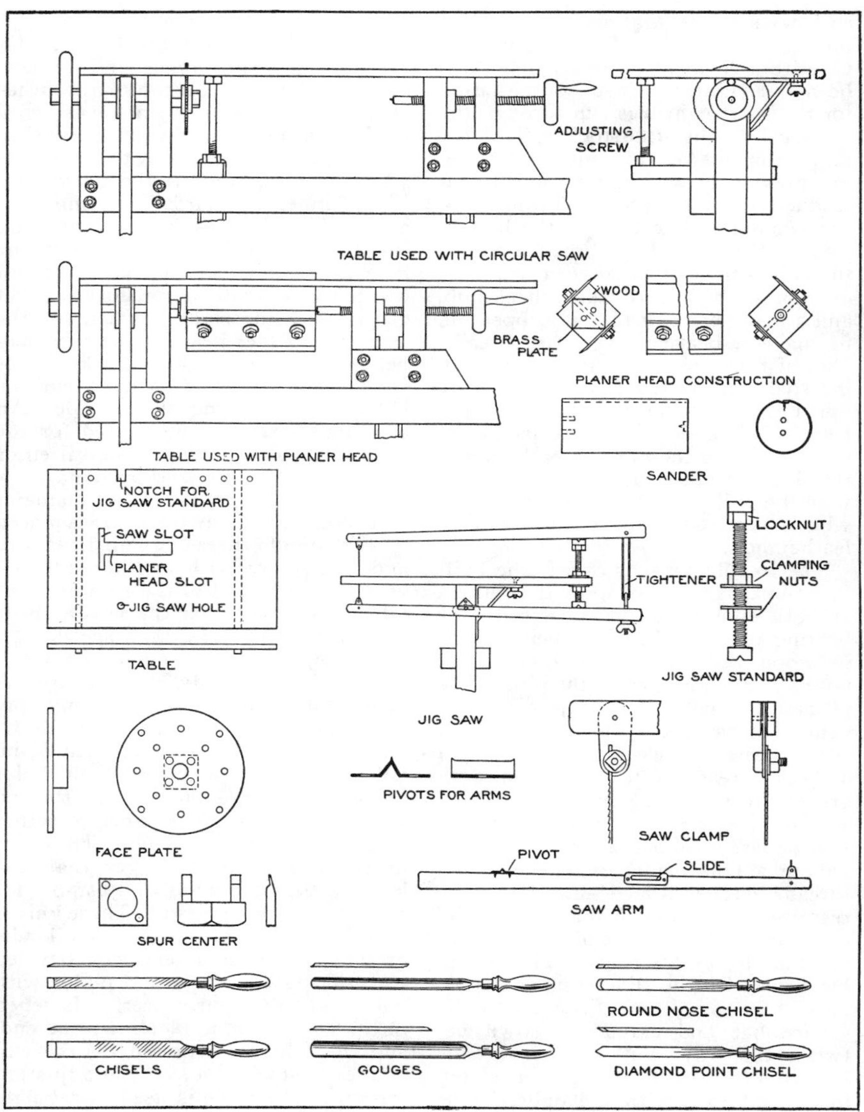

Detail of the Various Attachments for Use in Connection with the Lathe for Sawing, Planing and Sanding, and the Shape of the Tools Used in Turning, Together with the Faceplate and Spur Construction

face of the face can be turned true. The spur center is made of a ¾-in. nut, drilled in opposite corners for ¼-in. pins, 1¼ in. long.

The drive wheel for this lathe was taken from an old discarded washing machine. Such a wheel is a very common part of various kinds of machinery and usually one that will answer the purpose can be found in a junk pile. One from 20 to 24 in. in diameter will be about right. A ½-in. bolt is used for the shaft, which is run through the standard at the headstock end of the lathe from the outside, the threads being previously cut long enough to introduce a nut between the wheel and the standard for clamping the bolt in place. The extending threaded end of the bolt is then supplied with two nuts, one on each side of the wheel hub, and a short piece of pipe is slipped on, to make a bearing over the threads. One of the spokes is drilled and a pin inserted and fastened to receive the upper end of the pitman from the treadle. The wheel is adjusted on the shaft with the nuts on each side of the hub so that its face runs true with the pulley on the headstock. The wheels are connected with a 1-in. leather belt.

The treadle consists of a frame built up of boards and swung in the centers at both ends on ⅜-in. steel rods, for bearing pins, the bearings being made of wood standards with ⅜-in. holes bored in them to receive the pins. The pitman is made of wood, its length being determined by measurement of the distance between the crank pin and the treadle-arm end when both are at their lowest point.

The slide for the rest consists of a 1-in. square steel bar, about 10 in. long, having a hole drilled in one end and threads cut with a ½-in. tap. The rest used in this hole is made of a ½-in. rod, threaded on one end and bent at right angles on the other. The clamping device for the slide is made of two bars, 1 in. by $\frac{3}{16}$ in., fastened to the square bar and extending down between the ways with sufficient ends beneath to attach a wooden clamp block and cam with a handle. This construction is clearly shown in the drawing. If only a lathe is required, the machine would be complete as now described, but the other attachments illustrated will greatly add to its usefulness and the owner will be well repaid by making them.

Attachments

One table is used for the circular saw, planer head, sander, and jig saw, and it is attached on top of the headstock and tailstock standards with bolts, run through the back edge of the board and the ends of two brackets which are screwed to the back edge of the inner standards. Thumb nuts are used on the bolts to aid in making the change quickly. More than one hole is provided in the back edge of the board, so that the tailstock bracket can occupy the right position for the sander or planer head, as the case may be. The holes in the bracket ends should be somewhat larger than the bolt, to allow tilting of the table. An adjusting screw is substituted for the rest, so that the table can be raised or lowered to suit the work in hand.

The circular saw is 5 in. in diameter and should have fine teeth. It is placed on the spindle threads against the nut, and held there with another nut and washer on the end of the spindle. The table is attached over the saw, and the spindle is driven at a high speed.

The planer head is made of a wood block, 9 in. long and 2¾ in. square. A ⅜-in. hole is bored through one way near each end, as shown in the drawing, and two steel knives, with ½-in. holes coinciding with the ⅜-in. holes in the wood, are made and attached with their edges opposite or projecting diagonally from the corners. The holes in the knives being larger than the bolts, makes the knives adjustable for setting the cutting edges. These knives may be made from an old saw blade, ground to size and one edge beveled and sharpened. A brass plate, with holes to fit the spur center, is fastened in the center of the block, on one end, and the other is centered for the cup of the tailstock screw. The adjusting screw for the table is used to regulate the cut.

The sander is constructed of a wood piece, 9 in. long and 3⅜ in. in diameter. A groove is cut in one side of the rounding surface to admit the ends of the abrasive which may be fastened there with tacks.

An emery wheel can be used on the spindle in the same manner as the circular saw. Procure a wheel, 5 in. in diameter with a 1/2-in. face and having a lead center. The hole should be bored out and tapped to fit the threads on the lathe spindle, and to have the grinding surface run true, this work should be done in a lathe by a machinist.

The drawings show the construction of the jig-saw attachment. The standard on which the arms are pivoted is made of a 1/2-in. bolt, threaded for its entire length and with a groove cut in the head and nut to receive the arm pivots. A locknut is used beneath the notched nut to hold the adjustment. Two nuts and washers are used near the center of the bolt for clamping the attachment to the table. The pivots are made of sheet metal, bent and drilled as shown. The small projection at each end of the edge is raised slightly by hammering the corner of the metal. These projections prevent the arms from sliding sideways. The clamps for holding the ends of the saw blades are easily made of thin sheet steel, or brass, with a 3/16-in. bolt and washer at the end for the clamp. The tension of the blade is secured by a piece of wire, an eyebolt and a thumb nut, connecting the rear ends of the arms as shown. The frame is driven by the spur center. The pins are removed from the center and a 1/4-in. pin is inserted in one of the holes so that it will project 5/8 in. The pin runs in a slot cut in a brass plate that is attached to the lower arm.

Very serviceable tools can be made of discarded files by grinding them to shape on the emery wheel. Always use a fine whetstone to finish the edge on a woodworking tool.

Hanging a Clothesline Taut

The line is equipped with rings, one at each end, used for convenience in quickly hanging the line, which is then drawn taut with a lever. A screwhook is fastened in one end post and at the other end a screwhook is attached to a lever which is pivoted to the post. The lever should be about 3 ft. long, 1 in. thick, 3 in. wide at one end, and

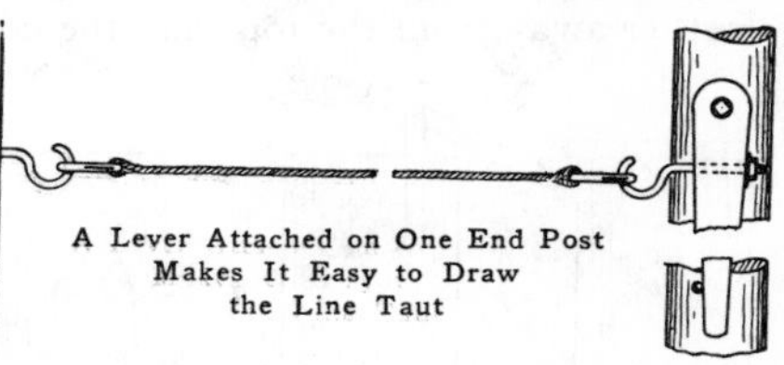

A Lever Attached on One End Post Makes It Easy to Draw the Line Taut

1 1/2 in. wide at the other, or handle, end. A large wood screw is used to attach it to the post. A pin is placed in the post to hold the lever when the line is drawn taut.—Contributed by Warren E. Crane, Cleveland, Ohio.

A Double Latch for a Door

This latch is suitable for outbuildings, small shops and sheds, as it can be opened from both sides of the door and is easily applied. It consists of a rod of suitable size which is bent in the shape shown in the sketch after the rod is inserted through a hole bored near the edge of the door. The spring of the metal will hold the catch in place.

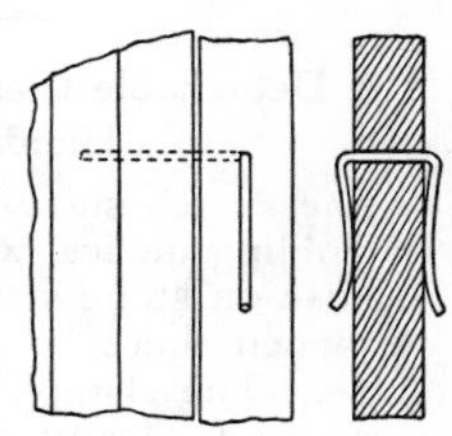

Maulstick Used as a Ruler

Procure a cork having the same diameter as the knob on the maulstick and make a hole in the center so that it will slide on the stick. This is very handy for using the stick as a ruler, as it forms a sliding rest.

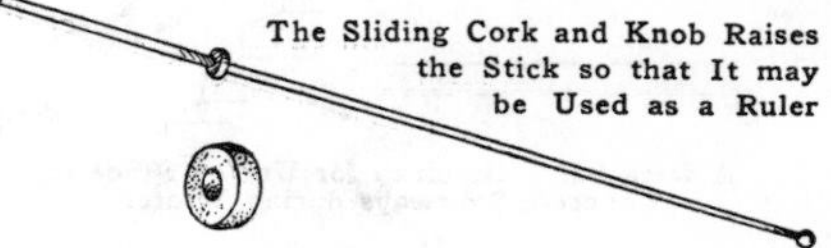

The Sliding Cork and Knob Raises the Stick so that It may be Used as a Ruler

Hinge with a Wide Swing

In constructing a box I needed a hinge that would carry the cover farther away from the top than the or-

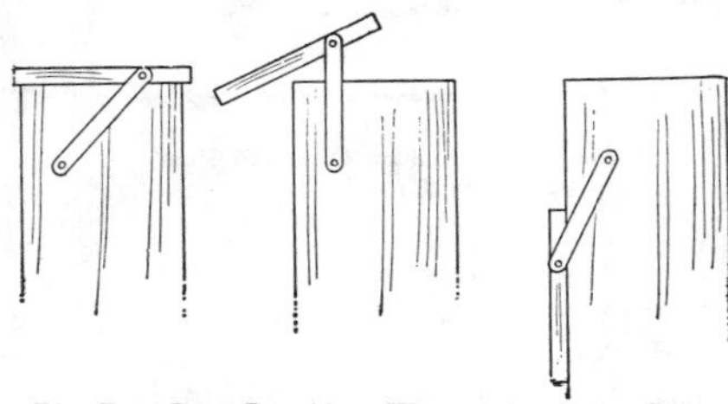

The Two Bars Provide a Way to Carry the Cover Away from the Box

dinary double-leaf hinge. I found that two pieces of 1/4 by 5/8-in. wrought iron, attached in the manner shown, answered the purpose. By using roundhead screws it was unnecessary to countersink the metal.—Contributed by James M. Kane, Doylestown, Pa.

A Detachable Clamp for Stairway Handrails

The sketch shows a handrail clamp, or holding device, which is detachable, for use on stone stairways in the winter when there is ice or snow on the steps. The clamps are made of $\frac{3}{16}$-in. strap iron, of any desired width, conforming to the shape of the balustrade and provided with a hook at either end. To the inside end of the band an upright is riveted and to this upright is riveted an ordinary handrail holder to take the handrail. A heavy thumb screw allows the clamp to be fastened firmly to the balustrade at the outside.

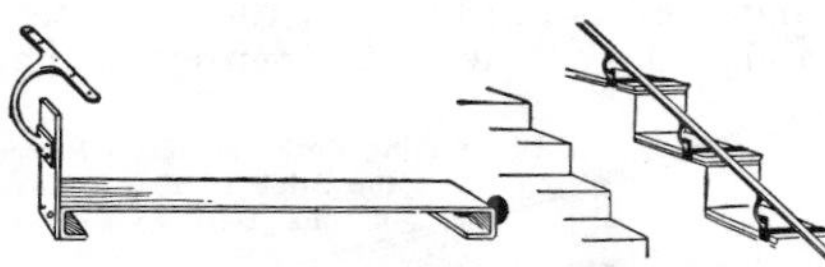

A Detachable Handrail for Use on Stone or Concrete Stairways during Winter

This is a simple and inexpensive device which affords protection against falls.—Contributed by John De La Mater, Chicago, Ill.

A Homemade Leather Punch

An empty bottle-neck rifle cartridge can be easily made into a leather punch by grinding the edge of the opening sharp and cutting a hole near the top in one side. The hole is for removing the leather slugs and should be just a little larger in diameter than the inside diameter of the shell. The cartridges can be had in various sizes and almost any size of punch can be made.—Contributed by Merhyle F. Spotts, Shelby, Ohio.

A Wood-Scraper Handle

In using a plain scraper on the surface of wood the task grew exceedingly tiresome and I lightened the tedious work to some extent by making a handle for the scraper. The handle consisted of a piece of wood, 1 in. thick, 3 in. wide, and 6 in. long. A cut was made in the edge of the wood the width of the scraper blade and about 3 in. deep, and a bolt run through a hole bored centrally in the side, about

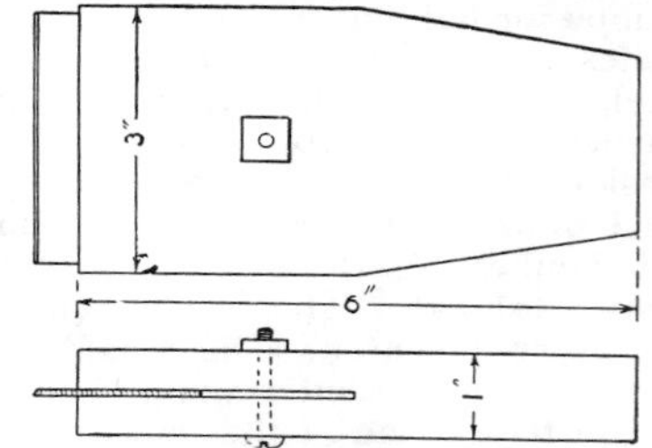

A Handle Attached to a Plain Scraper Blade Makes the Work Much Easier

2 1/2 in. from the lower edge. The blade was clamped in place with the bolt.—Contributed by J. D. Keiley, Yonkers, New York.

Polishing Gunstocks

The fine polish applied to gunstocks and wood parts of tools will not wear well, and if one cares for a fine finish, a much better and more durable polish can be applied as follows: Soak the wood in linseed oil for a week and then rub the surface with an oil-soaked cloth for a short time every day, for a couple of weeks.

A Prick-Punch Center Gauge

A simple instrument for finding and marking the center of shafting, etc., can be easily made of three pieces of sheet brass and a small prick punch.

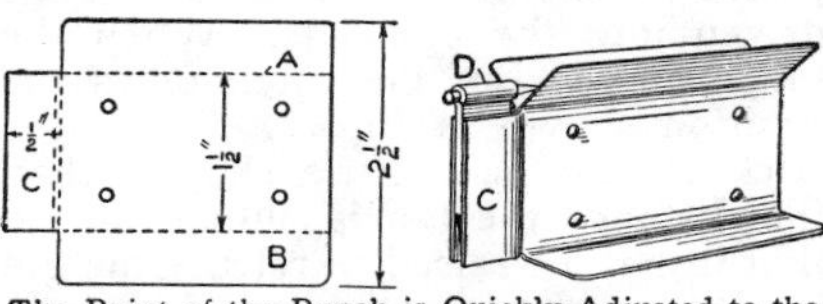

The Point of the Punch is Quickly Adjusted to the Center of the Work

Take two pieces of stiff sheet brass, 2½ by 3 in. in size, and cut two corners, ½ in. square, out at one end of each piece as shown in the sketch. Bend the metal on the dotted line A, until it stands at an angle of 45 deg. The part B should be bent up in the same direction, but at right angles to the plate, while the part C should be bent out only slightly. A hole should be drilled near each corner for rivets. Be sure that the two plates are bent in opposite directions, then rivet them firmly together.

Roll one end of a strip of sheet brass, $\frac{7}{16}$ in. wide and 2¾ in. long, into a tube large enough to firmly hold a small steel prick punch. Place the opposite end of the brass strip in between the two ends C. These ends should spring together slightly in order to hold the punch D at any height it may be placed. If accurately made, the point of the punch will be exactly in the center of the V-shaped trough.

In use, to find and mark the center of a round bar, it is placed in the trough with the end just touching the point of the punch. The brass holding the punch is raised between the parts C until the point of the punch is brought as near to the center of the shaft as can be judged. Press the point of the punch against the end of the shaft and turn the latter in the trough. If the punch marks a circle the center has not been found. This is corrected by slowly moving the punch up or down until the point ceases to make a circle, then the punch is tapped with a hammer to mark the exact center.

A Whirligig Clapper

A good noise maker for Halloween or any other occasion, can be made by carefully following the directions here given. The box is the first thing to make. It is constructed of wood pieces, ½ in. thick, and consists of two ends and two sides. The ends are each 1½ in. square and the sides 1½ in. wide and 6 in. long. These parts are nailed together with the ends lapping the sides.

The ratchet wheel A is a disk of hard wood, 1½ in. in diameter. Its rim is divided into eight equal parts, and notched with a knife as shown. It is placed in the forward end of the box on a wood axle of ⅜-in. diameter to which it is glued. One end of this axle is squared and projects 1 in. beyond the side of the box. The squared end passes through a square hole in the end of the crank C, which is a piece of wood ¾ in. thick, 1 in. wide and 4 in. long, and is fastened with brads and glue. At the other end of the crank, a similar hole connects with a handle whittled to the shape shown at B.

A flat piece of steel spring, ½ in. wide and long enough to reach from the rear end of the box to the teeth of the ratchet wheel, is shaped as shown at D. The spring may be made from a stiff piece of corset steel or bicycle trousers guard. The spring is fastened with a nail through the end and box sides and a second nail passes through the sides over the spring, about 2 in. forward from the first nail. This is to give the spring tension on the teeth.

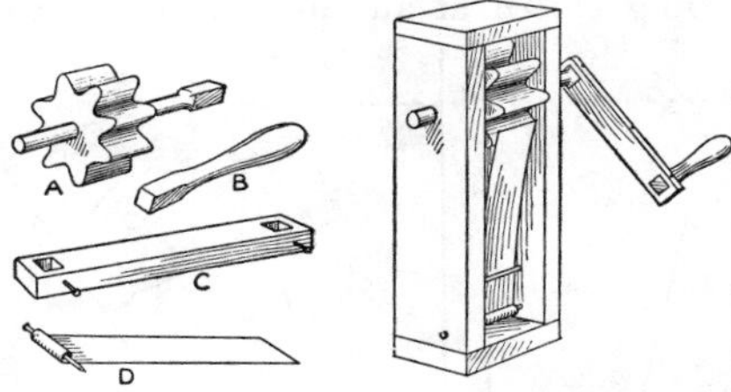

Detail of the Parts and How They are Assembled to Make the Clapper

To operate the clapper, it is allowed

to hang straight down, while the right hand grasps the handle and whirls the box in a circle around to the left.—Contributed by C. C. Fraser.

Box Partitions

As I needed a box with a number of narrow partitions and it was impossi-

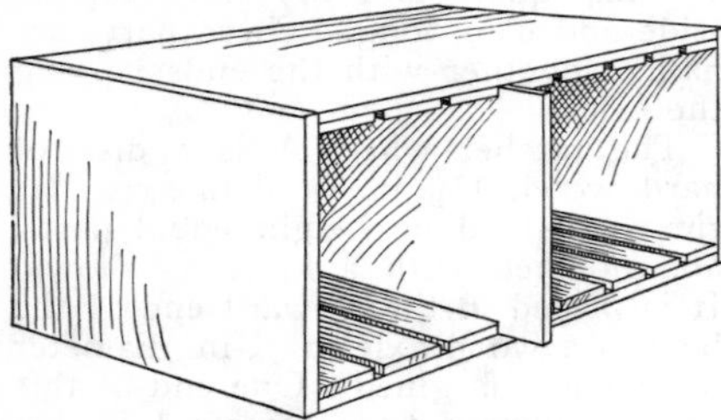

Grooves for the Partitions Made with the Use of Small, Thin Strips of Wood

ble to cut grooves for the sections without removing the bottom, I spaced off the places for the partitions with pieces of thin wood and fastened these in place with small nails clinched on the outside of the box. This method was much more rapid and satisfactory than sawing the grooves and cutting them out with a wood chisel.—Contributed by James M. Kane.

Safety Catch for a Flour Bin

A flour bin, counterbalanced to swing closed at all times, is liable to

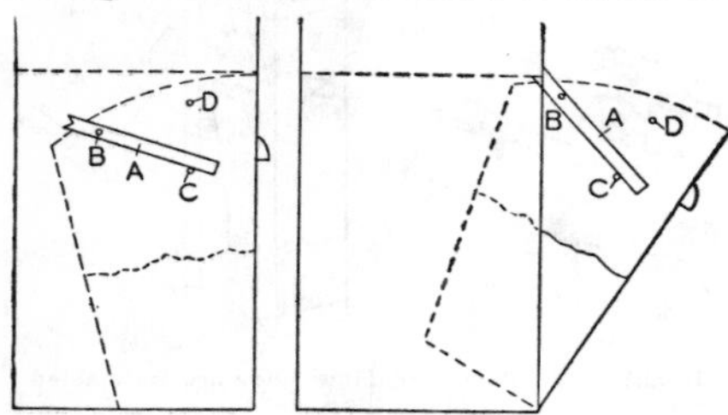

Automatically Operated Catch to Hold a Flour Bin Out While Taking Flour from It

catch the arm of the one taking out flour. To make it safe, I applied the device shown in the sketch. The bin, at rest, is shown in Fig. 1. The safety catch consists of a stick of wood, A, notched at one end, and is pivoted at B on a small bolt. Two stops, C and D, are located on the side of the box to prevent the catch from being thrown out of position when the bin is quickly pulled out. These stops are nails driven into the box side. When the bin is pulled out the catch takes the position shown in Fig. 2. The catch stick should be a little shorter than the distance the bin is pulled out, so that it may be raised to release the bin for its return.—Contributed by O. F. Fouche, Erie, Pa.

A Homemade Whistle

Procure two empty No. 30 gauge brass cartridge shells. Cut one shell 3/8 in. shorter than the other, then flatten and bend them as shown in the sketch. The mouthpiece should be at an angle of 60 deg. File a slot, 3/16 in. in width, about 1/2 in. from the end. File off the flange on the shorter shell so that it will fit snugly against the

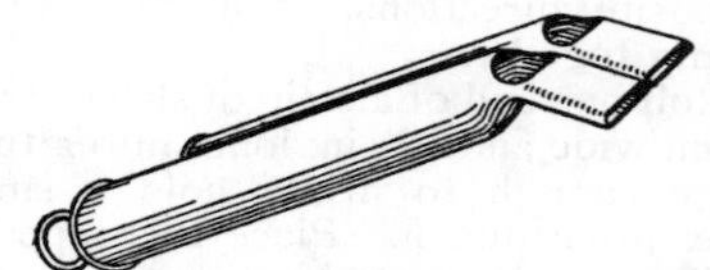

The Tapering End of a Cartridge Shell is Flattened and Bent to Make a Whistle

side of the other and solder them together. A ring may be soldered on the end of the long shell to fasten it on a chain or string. To give the whistle a shrill sound place a large shot in each shell before flattening them.—Contributed by Peter Veneman, Paterson, New Jersey.

How to Emboss Stationery

A person's monogram or any special lettering embossed on stationery is quite expensive. The engraving of the dies by experts commanding high salaries, and the subsequent presswork necessary to give relief to the design upon the paper cause an expense which the economical person hesitates to accept, much as the refinement and individuality of the embossed work may be admired. But there is a way by which almost anyone may emboss stationery at home with one's own design at no expense whatever. The work is easy and the results pleasing, and monograms or lettering thus done will compare very favorably with the printer's work, especially if there is a good design to follow and the work is done with care. A little artistic ability will, of course, aid one in preparing a design, but is not essential, for the letters required may be cut from printed matter and used as a guide for tracing. There is no limit to the varieties of work possible by this process. Single letters, monograms, words or designs are suitable for reproduction in raised characters.

All the materials required for embossing the stationery are the envelope or paper on which the design is to appear, a stylus and a blotter. The paper should be of fair quality. If it is too thin the stylus point is likely to push through it. The linen-finished papers of medium weight and tough texture give excellent results, although almost any grade of good writing paper can be used successfully. As embossing by this process can be done well only through one thickness of paper, in working on envelopes it is best to put the design on the central portion of the flap, or turn it up and make the design in the left-hand corner of the envelope.

The stylus may be any kind of a pencil-like instrument, easy to grip between the fingers, with a hard, smooth point, rounded slightly so that it will not cut the paper. The ordinary bone stiletto, used in embroidering, makes an ideal tool for this purpose. If this is not to be had, a substitute is easily whittled from a piece of hard wood. Even a wire nail, with its point smoothed with a file, may be used, the upper portion being wound with string to afford a better grip.

The blotter should be white, perfectly clean, and of good weight. A thin, hard blotter will not produce a good raised letter as a softer one will. When the surface of a blotter has become covered with creases from repeated use, it should be discarded and a new one substituted.

As it is best to adopt a distinctive form of monogram or design for stationery and to use it without deviation, it should be selected or worked up with care until something is outlined that will suit. With the design settled upon and drawn on a piece of paper, go over

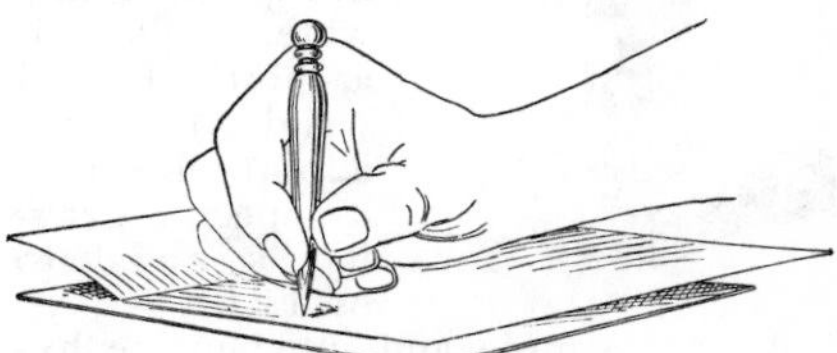

Manner of Holding the Stylus When Tracing the Design on the Back Side of the Paper

it with a soft pencil to deposit sufficient graphite for an impression. Lay the pattern, face down, upon the back of the paper to be embossed, and directly opposite the spot on the other side where the raised characters are to appear. With the handle of a knife or scissors rub over the back of the pattern till the graphite has left the tracing of the design reversed on the writing paper.

The pattern is now laid aside until required for transferring the design to another sheet of writing paper. Lay the blotter on some smooth, hard surface, such as a desk leaf or table top and lay the writing paper on the blotter, reversed design uppermost. Hold the stylus firmly at an angle as shown in the illustration and keep the blotter and paper from moving with the other hand. Carefully trace the design, using considerable pressure to insure a good relief upon the opposite side of the paper. A soft eraser should be used to remove the guide marks on the back of the sheet when the relief is finished.

After a little practice with a certain design, if it is not too intricate, the operator will find that it can be reproduced quite faithfully freehand, without the use of the pattern, but, of course, the use of the pattern will be the only guarantee of exact duplicates.

A Homemade Hydrometer

The hydrometer is an instrument used in determining the specific gravity of a liquid, such as acids, etc. The specific gravity of any material is the ratio of the weights of equal volumes of the material and water. Thus if a pint of acid weighs 1.2 times a pint of water, its specific gravity is said to be 1.2.

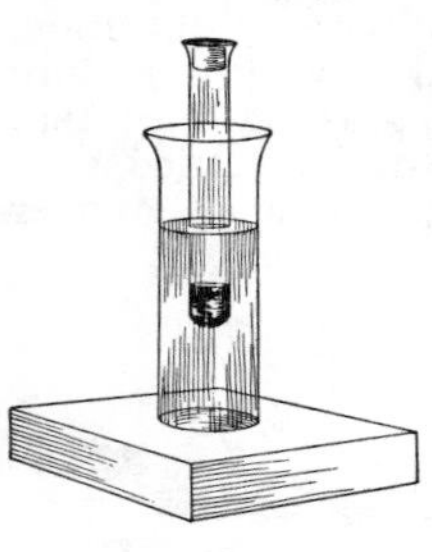

A very simple and inexpensive hydrometer, similar to the one shown in the sketch, may be easily constructed, and will give quite satisfactory results, if the scale on the instrument is carefully marked when it is calibrated.

Purchase from the local druggist or doctor two test tubes, one large enough to contain the other, as shown. The smaller tube is to form the hydrometer proper, while the larger one is to serve as a containing vessel in which the liquid to be tested is placed. The large tube should be mounted in a vertical position, by placing it in a hole bored in a small block of wood, or a suitable metal or wooden frame may be made that will accommodate one or more tubes.

The small tube is loaded at the lower end with a quantity of shot, or other heavy metal, in such a way that it will stand in a vertical position when it is placed in a vessel of water. The amount of the loading will depend upon whether the hydrometer is to be used in determining the specific gravity of liquids heavier or lighter than water. If the liquids are heavier than water, the loading should be such that the tube is almost entirely immersed when placed in water; if lighter, only sufficient loading should be used to make the tube stand upright in water. After the amount of loading has been determined it should be fastened in place by means of a small quantity of calcined plaster. A small cork should now be placed in the open end of the tube, and the tube sealed by coating the end with shellac, or melting a small quantity of resin or sealing wax over the top of the cork with a hot soldering iron.

Now place in the large tube a quantity of as pure water as can be obtained—fresh rain water will answer very well and distilled water still better. Immerse the small tube in the water in the large tube and allow it to come to rest. Make a small mark on the small tube with a file, level with the surface of the water in the large tube. If the hydrometer is placed in a liquid lighter than water and allowed to float, the mark made on the tube will always be below the surface of the liquid in which the instrument is placed, and the mark will be above the surface of the liquid when the liquid is heavier than water.

The hydrometer may be calibrated by making use of a hydrometer borrowed from the druggist or doctor. The two hydrometers should be immersed in the same liquid and the tube of the newly made instrument marked to correspond with the markings on the borrowed instrument. If the liquid is heavier than water to start with, its specific gravity can be reduced by adding water, and as the water is added the hydrometers will both rise.

A Stirring Stick

The stirring, or mixing, stick shown in the sketch deserves its name, as it will stir evenly all the way around. It consists of two flat sticks, one two-thirds the width of the other, which

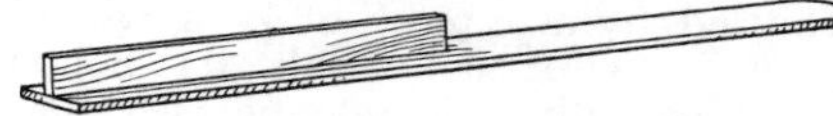

A Flat Surface Strikes the Liquid No Matter Which Way the Stick is Moved

are nailed together as shown. The narrow one is only long enough to enter the depth of the liquid.—Contributed by Frank J. Rempe, Oakland, California.

A Telescoping Support for a Hinged Shelf

The supporting arm of the hinged shelf is constructed of a piece of gas pipe and a length of iron rod which

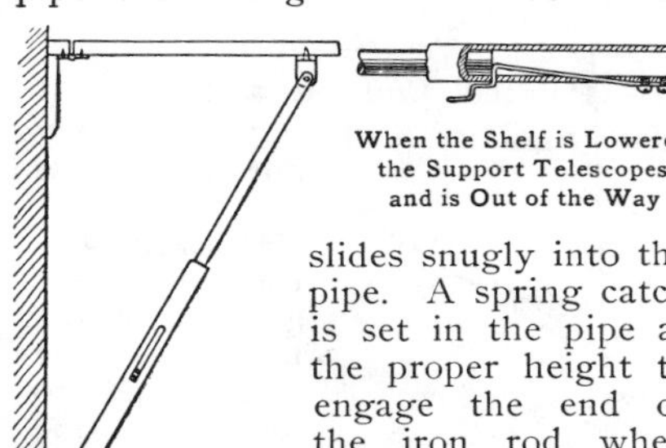

When the Shelf is Lowered the Support Telescopes and is Out of the Way

slides snugly into the pipe. A spring catch is set in the pipe at the proper height to engage the end of the iron rod when the shelf is up. This spring must be of good size, as it holds the entire weight of the shelf. A large clock spring is suitable. One end of the spring is bent outward and upward to form a releasing handle. The other end is drilled for the two machine screws which hold it to the pipe. The spring works in a rectangular slot, cut lengthwise of the pipe. The pipe must extend 8 or 10 in. beyond the spring. The ends of the rod and of the pipe are pivoted with screws or rivets on angle pieces screwed to the shelf and wall.—Contributed by Donald A. Price, Wilmington, Del.

A Bug Powder

To secure a nonpoisonous roach and bug powder mix dry 3 lb. plaster of Paris with 2 lb. of sugar, then add 1 oz. of pulverized aniseed. The addition of a little corn meal will help to draw the pests.—Contributed by Loren Ward, Des Moines, Iowa.

How the Capacity of an Incubator may be Doubled

About 10 days after setting the incubator one may easily start another hatch by placing more eggs on top of the incubator in the following manner: Make a pad about 1 in. thick of any cotton material and place it on top of the incubator. Cut four pieces of boards, 1 by 4 in., and fit them around the top of the incubator. Nail them together as in making the sides and ends of a box. Pad the inside of this frame about 1 in. thick and tack it on top of the incubator, being careful that none of the material comes too close to the lamp. Place the eggs inside of this tray and cover them with a pad about 3 in. thick. Turn the eggs the same as those on the inside. When the first hatch comes out, place the eggs kept on top in the incubator after having cleaned it with a solution of carbolic acid.—Contributed by Hattie J. Day.

Homemade Rivet Set

Desiring to rivet some pieces of leather together and having no rivet set, I hastily made one from a strip of heavy sheet tin, ¾ in. wide. This was rolled at one end, as shown in the sketch, and the other end notched to fit over the rivet end. The rolled

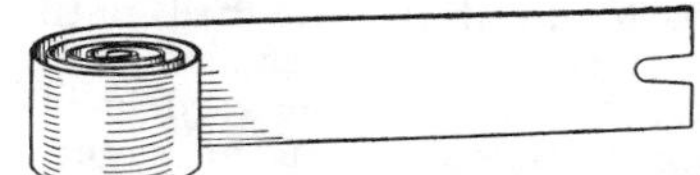

A Strip of Tin Shaped to Take the Place of a Rivet Set

end formed the part for setting the washer and the slotted end held the washer down while the first blows of the hammer were struck.

Wash Bottle for Laboratory Use

A large-mouth bottle neck is provided with a stopper, having three brass or glass tubes as shown, the tube A being fitted with a thick piece of rubber tubing, B, stoppered at its lower end. A slit is cut at C, and allows the air blown in through the tube A to pass into the bottle, but will close automatically and hold the pressure within the bottle.

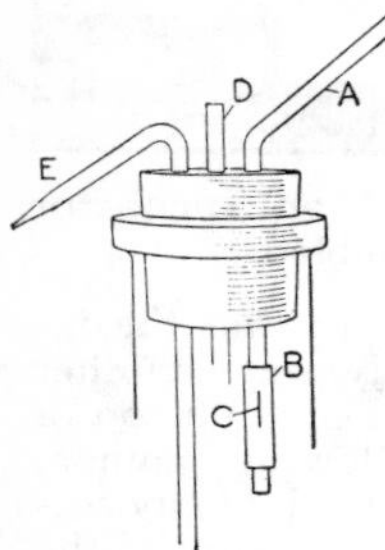

If the relief tube D is closed with the thumb the water is forced out in a steady stream through the nozzle E. The water will continue to run for some time after the lips are removed from the air tube, but the removal of the thumb from the tube D will stop the flow of water instantly.—Contributed by W. Schilling, San Francisco, Cal.

Typewriting on Card Stock

Anyone having tried to typewrite on cards or heavy stock has doubtless experienced much trouble in getting the card to feed properly. If at all heavy, it will resist the curving so strongly that it will not be carried around the platen, and the edge of the card is very apt to catch on the pressure rolls and cause the platen to slip.

The remedy is very simple and consists in running a sheet of paper through ahead of the card until an edge of about ½ in. remains, then inserting the edge of the card inside of the projecting edge of the paper and turning the platen. The paper overlapping the card prevents the edge of the latter from catching on the pressure rolls and keeps it in close contact with the platen so that it will pass through without trouble.—Contributed by Thos. L. Parker, St. Paul, Minn.

A Furniture Polish

A homemade furniture polish that will compare with any known polish, is composed of the following chemicals and oils. Mix 3 oz. of turpentine very gradually with 6 oz. of linseed oil, then add 3 oz. of grain alcohol, 3 oz. of 5-per-cent acetic acid, and ½ oz. of butter of antimony. Apply with a cloth and use a good friction. As the substance might prove harmful to children if taken internally, see that it is kept out of their reach.—Contributed by Loren Ward, Des Moines, Iowa.

Pointed End on a Hoe

The rounding end on the ordinary hoe is useless in many instances for getting under growing plants, to cut out the weeds and to loosen up the earth. I find that shaping the hoe ends as shown in the sketch is very effective in getting up close to a plant and under spreading vines.—Contributed by R. F. Pohle, E Lynn, Mass.

Starting a Siphon

Roll up a soft rubber hose tightly so that it will be flattened to force out all the air and drop one end into the liquid, then let the coil unwind as it falls down on the outside. The uncoiling causes a slight vacuum in the hose and the liquid follows it up and starts the flow instantly.—Contributed by L. J. Monahan, Oshkosh, Wis.

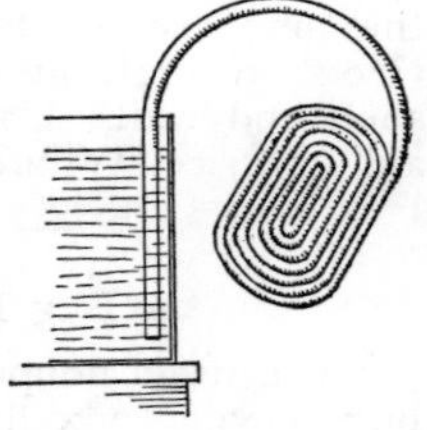

¶Paint spots on window glass can be readily removed with a penny.

A Homemade Blowtorch

The torch shown in the sketch requires no air pump. Instead of forcing a small stream of gasoline into a heated burner it converts the gasoline into gas in the chamber and blows a small jet of it through a very small hole into the combustion chamber.

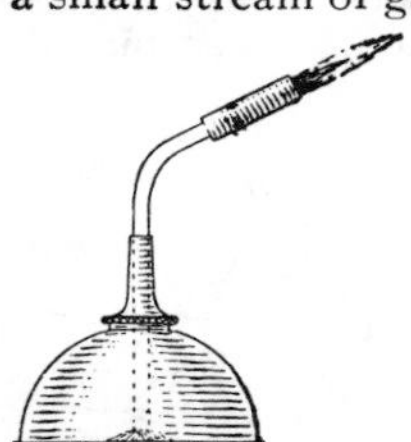

A medium-sized and strong oilcan is used for the reservoir, the spout being cut off close to the screw part and a steel or brass tube, about $\frac{5}{16}$ in. in diameter, soldered to the stub end. The tube is bent as shown. A piece of wicking is drawn into the tube so that the upper end is within 1/4 in. of the tube end. The end of the tube is then fitted with a piece of brass rod with a very small hole in the center. The hole is made in the following manner: Before the piece is cut from the rod, it is held in a vise and the sharp end of a scriber is carefully driven into the center. A little oil placed on the scriber point will keep it from sticking in the metal. Measure the depth of the hole and cut the rod off just above the point. File the end of the piece cut off with a fine file until the point of the hole is reached. This hole must be so small that light can be barely seen through it.

The combustion chamber is made of a piece of brass tubing driven over the end of the smaller tube on the spout. About 1/2 in. from the back end of the larger tube four or more holes are drilled to admit air to the gas.

Fill the can about three-fourths full of gasoline and allow time for the wick to become saturated to the upper end. Hold a lighted match to the rear of the burner, and the heat will convert the gasoline into gas which will then burn with a nice white flame about 1 in. long. The success of the torch depends altogether on the fineness of the hole in the end of the tube and the tight soldering of all the joints.

A Rule Gauge

The method of using the thumb as a gauge on a rule in scribing long boards is not always satisfactory, especially if the board has a rough edge. It is always best to have a regular gauge, but in the absence of one, an attachment for an ordinary carpenter's rule can be quickly made from a piece of tin, although one made of sheet brass is better, in appearance as well as for service. Cut out the metal, as shown by the dimensions, and roll the two sides up, stopping at the dotted lines. The ends A and B are turned out slightly so that they will slide easily along the edge of the board. The gauge will snap on a rule easily and

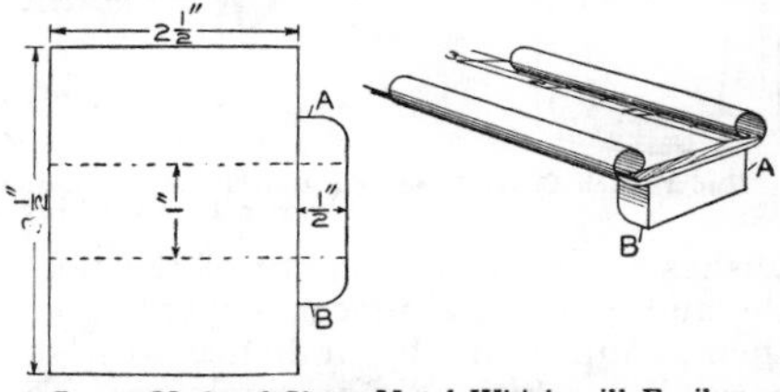

Gauge Made of Sheet Metal Which will Easily Snap on a Carpenter's Rule

will stay where it is placed.—Contributed by H. J. Blacklidge, San Rafael, Cal.

A Match Holder

The holder consists of a small box, the same size as a match box, with a sloping spring bottom and spring wires covering the lower part of the front side. One end of the match box is removed and the contents dumped into the holder. The matches fall to the lower sloping edge, where one match at a time can be easily removed. —Contributed by Bert Verne, San Diego, Cal.

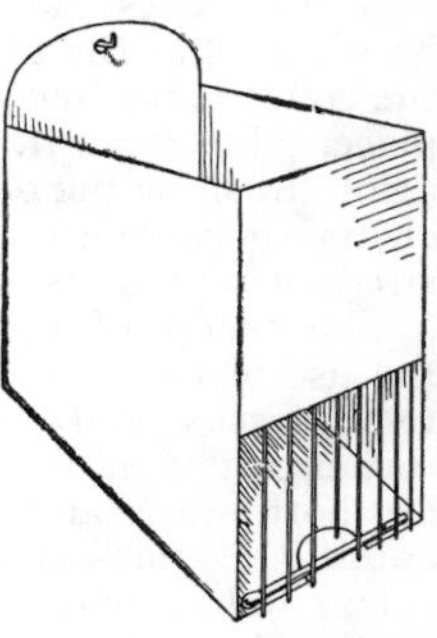

Trick Bottles and Glasses

By GEORGE W. CATLIN

The performer presents to his audience two pasteboard covers, one bottle and one glass. Saying that he wishes to secure the safety of the bottle and glass, he places covers over them, cautioning the audience to note carefully which cover incloses the glass and which the bottle. Then he says that, to prevent any misunderstanding as to their positions, it is desired the audience designate which cover holds the glass. The response will be unanimous, "the left" or "the right" as the case may be, but on raising that cover the bottle is exposed. Covering the bottle again, and asking the audience if they were quite sure that their eyes did not deceive them, he states that the glass is really under the cover just lifted and returned to its place. To prove it, the cover is lifted again, to show the glass this time. The changing can' be done as often as desired, or will amuse the crowd.

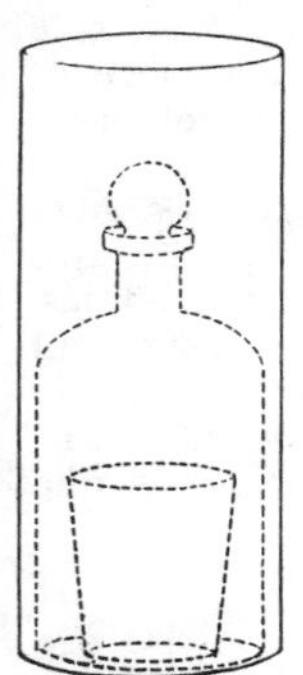

Under Each Cover Used Is a Bottle and Glass, and by Pinching the Cover the Bottle is Made to Rise with It, Thus Leaving the Glass in View

The secret of the trick consists in the use of two covers, two bottles and two glasses, and the manner of performing it is as follows: The bottles are bottomless and of such size as to admit the glass without sticking. A round hole is cut in one side of each bottle, about 2½ in. above the bottom. This can be accomplished in a drill press by using a round copper tube, with fine emery applied to its end, as a drill. The hole should be so placed that a finger will strike the top of the glass when both bottle and glass are set on the same surface. If dark-colored bottles are used, a false bottom can be made and fitted in each bottle above the upper edge of the glass. This bottom can be cemented in place and made liquid-tight, so that some wine may be placed in the bottle and poured into the opposite glass to show that it holds liquid. In doing this part of the trick, make no more changes with the wine in one glass.

Under each cover is a bottle and tumbler, and by pinching the cover, the bottle is made to rise with it, thus leaving the tumbler in view. When it is necessary to show the bottle, just raise the cover, and the bottle covers the glass. When the bottle is lifted from the table, the thumb is inserted in the hole to press the tumbler against the opposite side, where it is held and raised with the bottle. Be sure to keep the side of the bottles with the hole back and away from the audience.

It will be seen that it matters not which cover is mentioned; the performer can show just the article he desires.

CONTENTS